'First edition, *Islāmic Counselling: An Introduction to Theory and Practice* has finally received its long awaited second edition: *Islāmic Counselling and Psychotherapy*. This edition builds on the comprehensive concepts and theories shared in the original and will no doubt be as valuable an asset to the world of Islāmic Counselling and Psychotherapy in terms of practice and education. It is an essential resource for psychotherapy students, academics and practitioners as well as an interesting read for those who have a curiosity for the subject matter.'

Khalida Haque, *SNCPS (Accredited), psychotherapist, UK*

'The revised edition of this essential book, *Islāmic Counselling and Psychotherapy* 2nd edition written by Professor Dr. G. Hussein Rassool, skilfully navigates the intricate joining of spirituality and psychotherapy. The inclusion of postmodern therapeutic approaches, such as narrative and hope therapy, adds a contemporary layer to the discourse, ensuring that readers are equipped with the latest insights in the field. This edition offers a reflective exploration of the expanding role of Islāmic psychotherapists, highlighting their evolving responsibilities and contributions within the broader context of mental health. The in-depth examination of the integration of Qur'ânic teachings and hādīth into the therapeutic process enriches the reader's understanding of the profound connections between faith and mental well-being. Additionally, the book introduces an Islāmic perspective on dream interpretation, unlocking new dimensions in the exploration of spiritual and psychological realms. Addressing ethical challenges specific to Islāmic psychotherapy, Professor Rassool provides valuable guidance for practitioners navigating complex issues, ensuring a culturally sensitive and ethically sound practice. This work is not only a crucial resource for Muslims navigating mental health but also an invaluable read for anyone interested in the harmonious integration of spirituality into the therapeutic process.'

Razia Bhatti-Ali, *PhD, consultant clinical psychologist (Connect Health Ltd/Bupa), UK*

'At this point in the history of our Ummah, it is essential that scholars of experience and courage, each in their own field, envision a re-construction of the current disciplines and propose robust new ways of dealing with contemporary phenomena. Current systems, including in the discipline of psychology and in the variety of phenomena related to it, are proving ineffective in improving the human condition. That is why I was happy to see this extensive new study done by Professor G. Hussein Rassool, critiquing the current paradigm and proposing new ways of analysis and counselling on Islāmic foundations. May Allaah reward Professor Rassool and widen the circles of benefit of his work to Muslims and humanity writ large.'

Jasser Auda, *PhD, President of Maqasid Institute Global at the International Peace University, South Africa*

'*Islāmic Counselling and Psychotherapy* is a groundbreaking work that seamlessly weaves Islāmic teachings into the fabric of modern psychotherapy. A vital resource for practitioners and scholars alike, this book offers a comprehensive guide, harmonising the Islāmic principles with contemporary therapeutic techniques. Its depth and relevance make it an indispensable tool, fostering a holistic understanding of counselling within the Islāmic framework.'

Zuleyha Keskin, *PhD, Associate Head of School at the Centre for Islāmic Studies and Civilisation, Charles Sturt University, Australia*

'*Islāmic Counselling and Psychotherapy* by Professor Dr. G. Hussein Rassool is an indispensable resource that bridges the gap between mainstream counselling and the specific needs of Muslim clients. This second edition represents a significant milestone, offering a comprehensive exploration of the intricate interplay between Islāmic principles and psychotherapeutic practices.

The book covers a wide array of topics, from the foundational understanding of Islāmic therapy to ethical considerations and the scope of Islāmic psychotherapy. It critically examines various psychotherapeutic approaches through an Islāmic lens, providing insights into their compatibility with Islāmic principles. Professor Dr. G. Hussein Rassool delves into practical intervention strategies within Islāmic psychotherapy, addressing the integration of Qur'anic verses, dream interpretation, halāl-harām considerations, and presenting the Siraat Al-Islāmic Psychotherapy Practice Model. What makes this edition particularly valuable is its updated content, exploring postmodern psychotherapy approaches like narrative and hope therapy. The author sheds light on the evolving role of Islāmic psychotherapists and addresses ethical challenges specific to this field. The inclusion of an Islāmic perspective on dream interpretation adds a unique dimension to the exploration of spiritual and psychological realms and tools. Furthermore, Professor Rassool emphasizes the importance of therapists integrating spirituality, religion, psychology, and cultural awareness when working with Muslim clients. The book serves as a primer in Islāmic psychotherapy, offering professionals, novice therapists, and students the tools and knowledge to enhance the effectiveness and culturally sensitive nature of therapeutic interventions.

As someone deeply invested in the field of counselling and psychotherapy at a clinical set up like that of a hospital, I highly recommend *Islāmic Counselling and Psychotherapy* to practitioners, educators, and anyone seeking a profound understanding of how Islāmic principles can be integrated into the therapeutic process. Professor Rassool's meticulous research, practical guidance, and commitment to cultural sensitivity make this book an invaluable contribution to the field.'

Zulekha Shakoor Rajani, *counselling and spiritual psychologist at Mind and Brain Hospital, India*

'Alhamdulillahirabbil 'alamiin. All praise is to Allāh, the Lord of the world. It is with much pleasure that I should write an endorsement of another of Professor G. Hussein Rassool books, titled *Islāmic Counselling and Psychotherapy*. As the readers of *Islāmic Psychology* have already known, he is the most productive author in the world today in the science of Islāmic psychology. Now another mark of his prolificacy will soon be published. The title that he has decided to cover, become an answer for the long-awaited guidelines in the area of Islāmic counselling and psychotherapy. The book covers the important elements of understanding counselling and psychotherapy from an Islāmic perspective: From the conceptual understanding, ethics, explanation of different approaches applied in the conventional psychotherapy seen critically from Islāmic perspective, as well as current practices based on Islāmic approaches – including family therapy. This book is a must read for those who teach, learn and practice counselling and psychotherapy. The teachers, students and practitioners who feel the need to better understand and support their Muslim clients with their unique worldview.'

Emi Zulaifah, *PhD, Vice Dean of religious, students, alumni and partnership affairs, Universitas Islam Indonesia, Indonesia*

ISLĀMIC COUNSELLING AND PSYCHOTHERAPY

Islāmic Counselling and Psychotherapy: An Introduction to Theory and Practice provides foundation-level knowledge of and perspective on the fundamental principles and practices of counselling and psychotherapy from an Islāmic perspective.

This groundbreaking practical framework incorporates Islāmic spirituality, religion, and cultural contexts into the therapeutic process. It makes the case that authentic Islāmic spirituality, based on submission to God, forms the cornerstone of good mental health. The book's foundation focuses on the therapist's role and ethical considerations specific to Islāmic psychotherapy. It explores the integration of Qur'ânic teachings and hadīths and delves into dream interpretation and the clinical applications of the Siraat Al-Islāmic psychotherapy practice model. This thoroughly revised new edition also highlights advances and developments in scholarship and evidence-based practices and introduces postmodern psychotherapy approaches like narrative and hope therapy. This text provides a clear understanding of the nature, scope, and process of Islāmic psychotherapy for Islāmic practitioners or clinicians working with Muslim clients.

G. Hussein Rassool, PhD, is Professor of Islāmic Psychology, Centre for Islāmic Studies & Civilisations, Charles Sturt University, Australia. He is a fellow of the International Association of Islāmic Psychology and the Royal Society of Public Health.

ISLĀMIC COUNSELLING AND PSYCHOTHERAPY

An Introduction to Theory and Practice

Second Edition

G. Hussein Rassool

LONDON AND NEW YORK

Designed cover image: tunart/© Getty Images

Second edition published 2025
by Routledge
4 Park Square, Milton Park, Abingdon, Oxon, OX14 4RN

and by Routledge
605 Third Avenue, New York, NY 10158

Routledge is an imprint of the Taylor & Francis Group, an informa business

© 2025 G. Hussein Rassool

The right of G. Hussein Rassool to be identified as author of this work has been asserted in accordance with sections 77 and 78 of the Copyright, Designs and Patents Act 1988.

All rights reserved. No part of this book may be reprinted or reproduced or utilised in any form or by any electronic, mechanical, or other means, now known or hereafter invented, including photocopying and recording, or in any information storage or retrieval system, without permission in writing from the publishers.

Trademark notice: Product or corporate names may be trademarks or registered trademarks and are used only for identification and explanation without intent to infringe.

First edition published by Routledge 2016

British Library Cataloguing-in-Publication Data
A catalogue record for this book is available from the British Library

ISBN: 978-1-032-59191-9 (hbk)
ISBN: 978-1-032-58634-2 (pbk)
ISBN: 978-1-003-45341-3 (ebk)

DOI: 10.4324/9781003453413

Typeset in Times New Roman
by Apex CoVantage, LLC

Dedicated to Idrees Khattab ibn Adam Ibn Hussein Ibn Hassim Ibn Sahaduth Ibn Rosool Ibn Olee Al Mauritiusy, Isra Oya, Asiyah Maryam, Idrees Khattab, Adam Ali Hussein, Reshad Hassan, Yasmin Soraya, BeeBee Mariam, Bibi Safian & Hassim, Dr Najmul Hussein, and Mohammed Ali.

CONTENTS

List of figures — xiv
List of tables — xv
Preface to the second edition — xvi
Preface — xviii
Acknowledgements — xx

PART I
The essence of Islāmic therapy: context and background illuminated — 1

1 The foundation of Islāmic psychotherapy — 3

2 Islāmic counselling and psychotherapy: from faith to psychology — 20

3 Unveiling the role of the Islāmic psychotherapist: exploring the nature and scope of psychotherapy — 35

4 Ethical framework in Islāmic psychotherapy — 51

5 Navigating ethical challenges in Islāmic psychotherapy — 65

PART II
The intersection of Islām and psychotherapy: understanding congruent and non-congruent psychotherapeutic approaches   75

6   Illuminating the psyche: an introduction to psychoanalytic therapy   77

7   Harmony and dissonance: Jungian therapy and Islāmic psychotherapy   93

8   Humanistic therapy re-envisioned through an Islāmic perspective   110

9   Islāmic insights into cognitive–behaviour therapy: path to healing mind, soul, and behaviour   128

10 Uniting faith and therapy: the Islāmic perspective on solution-focused brief therapy   150

11 Narrative therapy through an Islāmic lens   171

12 Hope therapy: finding strength in faith   186

13 Before the *Nikah*: Islāmic perspectives on pre-marital preparation   200

14 Sacred bonds and marital challenges: Islāmic-oriented marital therapy   215

PART III
The healing path: practical intervention strategies in Islāmic psychotherapy   233

15 Healing hearts and minds: Integrating Qur'ân and *hādīths* in Islāmic psychotherapy   235

16 Journey through the night: An Islāmic approach to dream interpretation   246

17 Challenging boundaries: *halāl/harām* considerations in complementary therapies   264

18	The Siraat Al-Islāmic psychotherapy practice model	286
19	Psychotherapy and harm reduction in addiction: an Islāmic perspective	305
20	Clinical applications of the Siraat Al-Islāmic psychotherapy practice model	325
21	Beyond the couch: Islāmic approaches to research in psychotherapy	336
22	Islāmic psychotherapy: tackling challenges, employing strategies, cultivating competence	359

Index   *368*

FIGURES

1.1	The *tawhīdic* paradigm.	5
1.2	The role of *fitrah* in Islāmic psychotherapy.	8
2.1	Key components and principles of Islāmic psychotherapy.	30
3.1	The therapeutic modalities in Islāmic psychotherapy.	36
3.2	Directive, non-directive, and integrated approaches to Islāmic psychotherapy.	40
5.1	The ethical dilemma decision-making model.	70
8.1	Rogers's seven stages of change.	116
9.1	The five-step sequence of *maraatib al-qasd*.	131
12.1	Snyder's assumptions of hope theory.	187
12.2	The cyclical relationship between pathways and agency thinking.	188
18.1	Principles of the Siraat Al-Islāmic psychotherapy practice model.	287
18.2	The consultation stages of the SIPPM.	291
21.1	The integrated research methodology in Islāmic psychotherapy.	347
21.2	The five stages of the *maqasid* methodology.	349
21.3	Cycles of reflections.	351
21.4	The seven elements of the *maqasid* framework.	353

TABLES

2.1	Contributions of some classical scholars to mental health and psychology	25
2.2	Differences between mainstream and Islāmic psychotherapy	29
3.1	Some key aspects of the generic roles of an Islāmic psychotherapist	44
4.1	Some examples of Islāmic ethics in the Qur'ân	55
4.2	Comparison of values between mainstream and Islāmic psychotherapy	61
6.1	Classical psychoanalysis and psychodynamics approaches	80
7.1	Some of the key Jungian archetypes	99
7.2	Comparison between Jungian psychology and Islāmic traditions	106
9.1	The CBT therapist's role and function	135
10.1	Key steps in solution building and problem solving in SFBT	154
10.2	Questions in Islām-inspired SFBT for Muslims	167
11.1	Principles of narrative therapy	172
11.2	Tools used as part of narrative therapy	178
13.1	Educational contents in pre-marital counselling	211
14.1	Key considerations in incorporating an Islāmic perspective in marital therapy	221
16.1	What you should do when you experience dreams	254
16.2	Methodologies of dream interpretation	260
18.1	Key components of a relapse prevention programme	301
19.1	A decisional balance matrix: pros/cons of current behaviour and pros/cons of change	312
20.1	Stages of the SIPPM	332
21.1	Differences between secular and Muslim researchers	342
21.2	The seven elements of the *maqasid* framework	354

PREFACE TO THE SECOND EDITION

This book, published over eight years ago, offers readers a robust foundation and insight into counselling from an Islāmic perspective. Its widespread popularity is evident in its translations into numerous languages including Basa Indonesian, Russian, Turkish, and Arabic. The book has resonated with audiences in various countries, reflecting its broad appeal and influence in the field of Islāmic counselling. For Muslim individuals, their faith plays a central role in shaping their worldview, values, and coping mechanisms. It is within this context that Islāmic counselling and psychotherapy emerges as a distinct discipline, integrating Islāmic principles with established counselling and psychotherapy theories and techniques.

This new edition represents a milestone in the development of Islāmic counselling and psychotherapy, embarking on an exploration of the intricate interplay between Islāmic principles and psychotherapeutic practices. Beginning with a foundational understanding in the opening chapters, the book establishes the ethical considerations and scopes of Islāmic psychotherapy. It illuminates the unique role of the Islāmic psychotherapist and addresses the ethical challenges inherent in this specialised field. The second part, "The Intersection of Islām and Psychotherapy," critically examines various psychotherapeutic approaches through an Islāmic lens. The chapters explore the compatibility or incongruence of psychoanalytic therapy, Jungian therapy, humanistic therapy, cognitive behaviour therapy, and solution-focused brief therapy with Islāmic principles. Additionally, there is an examination of the Islāmic perspectives on pre-marital preparation, marital therapy, narrative therapy, and hope therapy. Advancing to the third part, "The Healing Path," the focus shifts to practical intervention strategies within Islāmic psychotherapy. Chapters delve into the integration of Qur'ânic verses and *hādīths*, an Islāmic approach to dream interpretation, considerations of *halāl/harām* boundaries in complementary therapies, and the introduction of the Siraat Al-Islāmic psychotherapy practice model. Further exploration encompasses addiction and harm reduction, clinical applications of the practice model, Islāmic research approaches in psychotherapy, and strategies for overcoming challenges and cultivating competence. The central thesis of the book revolves around advocating for therapists to integrate spirituality, religion, psychology, and cultural awareness when dealing with Muslim clients. However, a crucial emphasis is placed on ensuring that these therapeutic and spiritual interventions remain aligned with Islāmic beliefs and practices. The book highlights the idea that therapists working with Muslim clients can leverage a holistic approach that incorporates various dimensions of spirituality, religion, and cultural context but that this must be done in a manner that aligns with Islāmic principles and values.

The revised edition of this book brings forth a wealth of new content, delving into postmodern psychotherapy and counselling approaches such as narrative and hope therapy. Furthermore, the updated edition explores the expanding role of Islāmic psychotherapists, shedding light on their evolving responsibilities and contributions within the field. It pays special attention to ethical challenges specific to Islāmic psychotherapy, offering insights into navigating these complex issues. One significant enhancement in the new edition involves a deeper examination of the integration of Qur'ânic teachings and *hādīths* within the therapeutic process of Islāmic counselling and psychotherapy. This new edition also introduces an Islāmic perspective on dream interpretation, adding another layer to the exploration of spiritual and psychological dimensions. Addressing contemporary considerations, the book examines the *halāl/harām* considerations in complementary therapies, recognising the importance of aligning therapeutic interventions with Islāmic ethical guidelines. The clinical applications of the Siraat Al-Islāmic psychotherapy practice model are also discussed, offering practitioners practical insights into applying this model in their therapeutic work. Lastly, the book expands its scope to include Islāmic approaches to research in the field of psychotherapy. This addition acknowledges the growing importance of research in informing and advancing Islāmic psychotherapy practices.

This book is a primer in Islāmic psychotherapy and sets out to provide a clear framework on the nature, scope, and processes of Islāmic counselling and psychotherapy. The book's purpose is to provide professionals, novice therapists, and students with the tools and knowledge to bridge the gap between mainstream counselling and psychotherapy approaches and the specific needs of Muslim clients. By offering practical guidance and theoretical foundations, it aims to enhance the effectiveness and culturally sensitive nature of therapeutic interventions with Muslim clients. The book also offers much practical wisdom not only to Muslims but to readers interested in integrating spirituality in the therapeutic process.

Professor Dr G. Hussein Rassool
27 February 2024

PREFACE

The need to develop culturally appropriate counselling intervention strategies in working with Muslim clients, and to understand and accept the legitimacy of alternative worldviews, is beyond dispute. Given the rapidly growing populations of Muslims in Western societies, it is imperative to develop a better understanding of their psychosocial and spiritual needs and concerns. The Muslim community is experiencing Islāmophobia, microaggressions, prejudices, hate crimes, and social exclusion related to their cultural and religious identity. In addition, as a consequence of these interrelated factors, there are indicators of the corresponding rise of Muslims in need of psychological and counselling services. More counsellors are coming into contact with Muslim clients, and it is not unusual to find that counselling professionals find themselves at a loss to intervene effectively with these clients. For the clients, this situation is commonly experienced as an inability of counsellors to fully understand their religio-cultural needs. Muslim clients are being offered counselling primarily with a Eurocentric worldview that is rooted in the Judaeo-Christian tradition and reflects the dominant values of the larger society.

This book provides a basic understanding of Islāmic counselling and fulfils an emerging need in the understanding of counselling approaches congruent with Islāmic beliefs and practices. Islāmic counselling is a contemporary response that has much in common with other therapeutic modalities but is based on an Islāmic understanding of the nature of human beings. The approaches and strategies of Islāmic counselling challenge the existing mainstream models of counselling and suggest that counsellors must accept the notion of "culture-specific" strategies in delivering appropriate and effective counselling interventions with Muslim clients.

Islāmic counselling is a form of counselling that incorporates spirituality into the therapeutic process. The goal of this type of integrative counselling is to address a variety of underlying psychological needs from a faith-based perspective. Given that the principles and practice of Islāmic counselling are not yet in a form where its actual implementation can be monitored, it first requires guidelines that can be integrated into a theoretical framework, a purpose towards which this book is directed. Designed as an introduction for counsellors, its goal is to inform the reader about how the seemingly diverse roles of the Islāmic counsellor fit together in a comprehensive manner. The book is seen as a preliminary mapping exercise and as agenda setting to provide a stimulus and encourage further examination and development of the nature, approaches, and processes of Islāmic counselling. Muslims scholars and clinicians should share in this development with non-Muslim counsellors and academics.

ACKNOWLEDGEMENTS

All Praise is due to Allāh and may the peace and blessings of Allāh be upon our Prophet Muhammad (ﷺ) his family and his companions.

I extend my heartfelt thanks to Grace McDonnell, publisher at Routledge, for her invaluable suggestions and guidance throughout the development of the proposal of the second edition of the book. Her constructive feedback has been instrumental in shaping the content and direction of this book. I would also like to express my gratitude to Sara Hafeez, editorial assistant at Routledge, for her unwavering support and assistance throughout this endeavour. I would like to acknowledge the support and encouragement of my colleagues at the Centre for Islāmic Studies & Civilisations, Charles Sturt University, Australia. In particular, I extend my sincere appreciation to Dr Zuleyha Keskin, Associate Head of School at the Centre for Islāmic Studies and Civilizations, for her support. I express my gratitude to the past and current students of Islāmic Counselling and Psychology (Level 2); Addiction Counselling and Islāmic Psychology; Islāmic Marriage Counselling; and Mental Health, *Jinn* Possession and Islāmic Psychology at Al-Balagh Academy for the invaluable lessons and insights they have provided me throughout my journey in this field. Their dedication and commitment to learning and exploring the anatomy of Islāmic psychotherapy and counselling have been instrumental in shaping my knowledge and skills in this domain.

I am incredibly grateful to my beloved parents, who instilled in me the importance of education. Their unwavering love and guidance have been instrumental in shaping who I am today, and I am truly grateful for their wisdom and encouragement. I am humbled and deeply grateful for the unwavering love and support of Mariam, Idrees Khattab Ibn Adam Ali Hussein Ibn Hussein Ibn Hassim Ibn Sahaduth Ibn Rosool Al Mauritiusy, Adam Ali Hussein, Reshad Hasan, Yasmin Soraya, Isra Oya, Asiyah Maryam, Nabila Akhrif, Nusaybah Burke, Musa Burke, Fatima Zahra,

Dr Najmul Hussein, and Mohammed Ali. Their presence in my life is a blessing, and I am forever indebted to them for their love, support, and inspiration.

I am grateful to acknowledge the invaluable contributions of my teachers, who have played a crucial role in enabling me to deepen my understanding of authentic Islām. Through their guidance and teachings, I have been able to embark on the right path, following the Creed of *Ahlus-Sunnah wa'l-Jamaa'ah*. I sincerely pray to Allāh that He forgives me and accepts my humble effort in writing this book. May He make it a source of benefit and fruitfulness for all those who find it useful and informative. May this book serve as a means of guidance and understanding for those who seek knowledge and insight. Finally, whatever benefits and correctness you find within this book are out of the Grace of Allāh, Alone, and whatever mistakes you find are mine alone. I pray to Allāh to forgive me for any unintentional shortcomings regarding the contents of this book and to make this humble effort helpful and fruitful to any interested parties.

مَّآ أَصَابَكَ مِنْ حَسَنَةٍ فَمِنَ ٱللَّهِ ۖ وَمَآ أَصَابَكَ مِن سَيِّئَةٍ فَمِن نَّفْسِكَ ۚ

- *Whatever of good befalls you, it is from Allāh; and whatever of ill befalls you, it is from yourself.* (An-Nisā' 4:79, interpretation of the meaning)

The author and publishers would like to thank Mohamed Omar Salem, Mohamad Medhat Ali, and the Islāmic Medical Association of North America for permission to reproduce the Islāmic version of the twelve steps of Alcoholics Anonymous, originally published in Salem, M.O. & Ali, M.M. (2008). 'Psycho-spiritual strategies in treating addiction patients: experience at Al-Amal Hospital, Saudi Arabia.' *Journal of the Islāmic Medical Association of North America*, 40 (4), 161–165. In addition, we are also grateful to Dr Jasser Auda for permission to reproduce Chart 2, p. 100, and Chart 3, p. 102 from Auda, J. (2021). *Re-envisioning Islāmic Scholarship: Maqasid Methodology as a New Approach.* Swansea, UK: Claritas Books.

Praise be to Allāh, we seek His help and His forgiveness. We seek refuge with Allāh from the evil of our own souls and from our bad deeds. Whomsoever Allāh guides will never be led astray, and whomsoever Allāh leaves astray, no one can guide. I bear witness that there is no god but Allāh, and I bear witness that Muhammad is His slave and Messenger (*Sunan al-Nasa'i: Kitaab al-Jumu'ah, Baab kayfiyyah al-khutbah*).

- *Fear Allāh as He should be feared and die not except in a state of Islām (as Muslims) with complete submission to Allāh* (Ali-'Imran 3:102).[1]
- *O mankind! Be dutiful to your Lord, Who created you from a single person, and from him He created his wife, and from them both He created many men and women, and fear Allāh through Whom you demand your mutual (rights), and (do not cut the relations of) the wombs (kinship) Surely, Allāh is Ever an All-Watcher over you)* (Al-Nisā' 4:1).
- *O you who believe! Keep your duty to Allāh and fear Him and speak (always) the truth)* (Al-Aĥzāb 33:70).
- *What comes to you of good is from Allāh, but what comes to you of evil, [O man], is from yourself* (An-Nisā 4:79).

The essence of this book is based on the following notions:

- The foundation of Islām as a religion is based on the Oneness of God.
- The source of knowledge is based on the Qur'ān and *hādīths* (*Ahl as-Sunnah wa'l-Jamā'ah*).
- Empirical knowledge from sense perception is also a source of knowledge through the work of classical and contemporary Islāmic scholars and research.

- Islām takes a holistic approach to health: physical, psychological, social, emotional, and spiritual health cannot be separated.
- Muslims have an Islāmic or Qur'ânic worldview that is different from the Western-oriented worldview.
- It is a sign of respect for Muslims to utter or repeat the words "Peace and Blessing Be Upon Him" after hearing (or writing) the name of Prophet Muhammad (ﷺ).

Note

1 The translations of the meanings of the verses of the Qur'ān in this book have been taken, from Saheeh International, *The Qur'ān: Arabic Text* with corresponding English meanings.

PART I
The essence of Islāmic therapy
Context and background illuminated

1
THE FOUNDATION OF ISLĀMIC PSYCHOTHERAPY

Introduction

In the below verse of the Qur'ân, Allāh commands His believing servants to help one another perform righteous, good deeds and to avoid sins.

وَتَعَاوَنُواْ عَلَى ٱلْبِرِّ وَٱلتَّقْوَىٰ ۖ وَلَا تَعَاوَنُواْ عَلَى ٱلْإِثْمِ وَٱلْعُدْوَٰنِ ۚ

- *Help you one another in virtue, righteousness, and piety; but do not help one another in sin and transgression.*

(Al-Mā'idah 5:2, interpretation of the meaning)

This passage emphasises the importance of mutual support and cooperation in matters of virtue, righteousness, and piety, while also cautioning against assisting one another in sinful or transgressive behaviour. So, helping and doing good to others is part of the process. Abu Hurayrah (may Allāh be pleased with him) reported Allāh's Messenger (ﷺ) as saying,

> Verily, Allāh, the Exalted and Glorious, would say on the Day of Resurrection, "O son of Adam, I was sick but you did not visit Me." He would say, "O my Lord; how could I visit Thee whereas Thou art the Lord of the worlds?" Thereupon He would say, "Didn't you know that such and such servant of Mine was sick, but you did not visit him, and were you not aware of this that if you had visited him, you would have found Me by him? O son of Adam, I asked food from you but you did not feed Me." He would say, "My Lord, how could I feed Thee whereas Thou art the Lord of the worlds?" He said, "Didn't you know that such and such servant of Mine asked food from you, but you did not feed

him, and were you not aware that if you had fed him you would have found him by My side?" The Lord would again say, "O son of Adam, I asked drink from you but you did not provide Me." He would say, "My Lord, how could I provide Thee whereas Thou art the Lord of the worlds?" Thereupon He would say, "Such and such of servant of Mine asked you for a drink but you did not provide him, and had you provided him drink you would have found him near Me."

(Muslim)

This *hadīth* (a saying, action, or approval attributed to the Islāmic Prophet Muhammad (ﷺ)) highlights the core principle of compassion and social responsibility in Islām. It emphasises that acts of kindness and care towards others are not only virtuous deeds but also seen as acts of worship. By demonstrating empathy, visiting the sick, feeding the hungry, and helping those in need, individuals alleviate the suffering of others, fulfil their spiritual obligations, and draw closer to Allāh. It serves as a poignant reminder of the vital role that compassion and benevolent actions play in both the social and psychological dimensions, as well as in one's spiritual journey. The verse, from Chapter Al-Mā'idah (5:2), highlights the ethical foundation of Islāmic psychotherapy, guiding therapists to align therapeutic goals with Islāmic principles. It emphasises building a strong therapeutic alliance based on ethical conduct, fostering virtuous character traits, and strengthening clients' spiritual connection with Allāh. Therapists must maintain strict adherence to Islāmic values, avoiding any collaboration in or support for sinful behaviours.

Islāmic psychotherapy is a distinctive approach to psychospiritual interventions that integrates Islāmic principles into the therapeutic process. It is rooted in the interplay of epistemology, ontology, and axiology within the Islāmic tradition. Foundational aspects include Islāmic monotheism, integration of faith and psychology, the Islāmic worldview, spirituality, culture, the role of the Qur'ân, and Sunnah, understanding human nature, and an overarching paradigm that shapes therapy. These elements contribute to a holistic understanding, facilitating healing and growth within the Islāmic framework.

Islāmic monotheism as the foundation of Islāmic psychotherapy

The concept of *tawhīd* is of utmost importance in Islām, as it underpins the meaning and significance of all acts of worship and rituals, both inward and outward. *Tawhīd*, or monotheism, is a core concept in Islāmic psychology and psychotherapy, emphasising the belief in the oneness of Allāh and His exclusive right to be worshipped. *Tawhīd* originates from the Arabic verb *"Wahad,"* meaning "making one" or "asserting oneness" (Wehr & Cowan, 2020). In the context of therapy, *tawhīd* underlines the interconnectedness between human well-being and the recognition of the divine. It stresses the singularity of Allāh's existence and His significance in the therapeutic process.

Foundation of Islāmic psychotherapy **5**

Tawhīd comprises three main themes: *tawhīd ar-Ruboobeeyah*, emphasising Allāh's sovereignty as the sole Creator and controller of the universe; *tawhīd al-'Ibādah*, stressing the exclusive worship of Allāh without intermediaries; and *tawhīd al-Asma wa'l-Sifat*, the Oneness of the Divine Names and Attributes. The first theme highlights Allāh's complete control over creation, while the second emphasises the principle of directing all forms of worship solely to Allāh. The third theme's *tawhīd* means affirming the names and attributes of Allāh and believing that there is none like unto Allāh in His names and attributes. For a comprehensive explanation of *tawhīd*, see Philips (2005). Together, these themes form the core of Islāmic theology, guiding the beliefs and practices of Muslims.

The *tawhīdic* paradigm

The *tawhīdic* paradigm in Islāmic psychotherapy integrates monotheistic principles into the therapeutic process, serving as a foundational framework, as depicted in Figure 1.1. It emphasises spiritual alignment by recognising Allāh as the ultimate source of guidance and surrendering to His will. Individuals are encouraged to align their actions with the intention of seeking Allāh's pleasure and adhering to His commandments. Spiritual alignment involves integrating faith into all aspects of life; striving to embody Islāmic values and virtues; and engaging in acts of worship, prayer, Qur'ânic reflection, and supplication to deepen one's spiritual connection with Allāh.

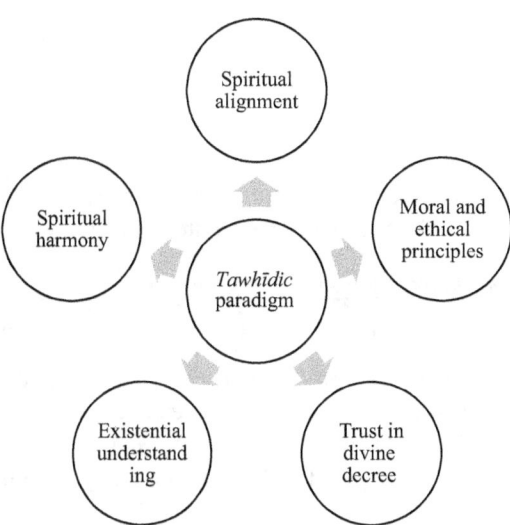

FIGURE 1.1 The *tawhīdic* paradigm.

Islāmic psychotherapy prioritises the spiritual dimension, encouraging individuals to find solace, guidance, and support in their faith. The *tawhīdic* paradigm promotes adherence to moral and ethical values rooted in Islāmic teachings. These values, including righteousness, justice, compassion, and honesty, are integrated into the therapeutic process. Islāmic psychotherapy guides individuals to make choices aligned with these principles, promoting psychological well-being and fostering a sense of integrity and accountability.

The *tawhīdic* paradigm in Islāmic psychotherapy emphasises belief in Allāh's divine wisdom and decree. This therapeutic approach helps individuals trust in Allāh's plan, accept life's challenges with patience and prayer, and find comfort in divine decree (*qadr*). Trusting in Allāh's plan can alleviate anxiety and facilitate emotional healing. The therapeutic framework encourages clients to rely solely on Allāh (*tawakkul*) for their recovery, strengthening their faith and resilience. Additionally, *tawhīd* helps individuals explore existential aspects of life, find purpose and meaning in their relationships with Allāh, and align their goals and actions with Islāmic teachings for inner peace and fulfilment.

The concept of *tawhīd* is closely intertwined with the concept of *fitrah* in Islāmic thought, particularly in terms of its metaphysical implications. *Fitrah* is often described as the innate, natural disposition or primordial nature that every human being is born with. *Fitra* or *fitrah* (Arabic: فطرة) is an important concept in Islāmic psychotherapy because it is embedded in the human soul, and it is an essential facet of human behaviour:

> The Qur'ān makes it clear that we are all born with an innate sense of the truth and belief of God's existence, and we possess a certain intuitive knowledge of the moral good. The essence of the *fitrah* is the natural spiritual nature of man and having a predisposition to submit to the One God.
> *(Rassool, 2023, p. 98)*

Fitrah embodies the notion that human beings are not endowed with a blank moral slate (*tabula rasa*) but are hardwired with an innate sense of morality and truth. The Qur'ān uses the concept of *fitrah* in the following way:

فَأَقِمْ وَجْهَكَ لِلدِّينِ حَنِيفًا ۚ فِطْرَتَ ٱللَّهِ ٱلَّتِى فَطَرَ ٱلنَّاسَ عَلَيْهَا ۚ لَا تَبْدِيلَ لِخَلْقِ ٱللَّهِ ۚ ذَٰلِكَ ٱلدِّينُ ٱلْقَيِّمُ وَلَٰكِنَّ أَكْثَرَ ٱلنَّاسِ لَا يَعْلَمُونَ

- *So, direct your face towards the religion, inclining to truth. [Adhere to] the Fitrah of Allāh upon which He has created [all] people. No change should there be in the creation of Allāh. That is the correct religion, but most of the people do not know.*
  (Ar-Rum 30:30, interpretation of the meaning)

According to Ibn Kathir's exegesis (2000), the verse referenced emphasises the importance of adhering to *tawhīd*, the Islāmic concept of monotheism. Islāmic teachings encourage believers to dedicate themselves to the worship of Allāh alone and follow the religion of Ibrahim (Abraham). This religion, guided by Allāh with utmost perfection, aligns with the inherent inclination and *fitrah* (natural disposition) of mankind. Allāh created human beings with the capacity to recognise and acknowledge His oneness and *tawhīd*, emphasising that there is no deity worthy of worship except Him. It is believed that every human being is born with an innate inclination towards recognising the truth and seeking a connection with the divine, which is part of their *fitrah*.

The meaning of *fitrah* is found in the following *hādīth* narrated by Abu Hurayrah (may Allāh be pleased with him): Allāh's Messenger (ﷺ) said, "Every child is born with a true faith of Islām (i.e. to worship none but Allāh Alone) but his parents convert him to Judaism, Christianity, or Magainism, as an animal delivers a perfect baby animal. Do you find it mutilated?" (Bukhârî (a)). Allāh's Messenger (ﷺ) informed us that every child is born with *fitrah*; this means that the child submits to the laws of Allāh as his Lord and Creator, and his soul adheres to the correct beliefs and truth. His parents and the socialisation process make him follow the religion of the parent or significant others.

Tawhīd, rooted in the metaphysical implications of *fitrah*, reflects the innate inclination of individuals towards monotheism and the acknowledgment of Allāh's oneness from birth. *Fitrah* serves as the metaphysical basis for *tawhīd*, suggesting that belief in *tawhīd* is deeply ingrained in human nature. In Islāmic psychotherapy, spiritual growth involves reestablishing one's innate *fitrah* and belief in *tawhīd*. This is achieved through acts of worship, self-reflection, and continuous efforts to align one's life with the oneness of Allāh.

The metaphysical implications of *fitrah* extend to recognising *tawhīd* within the broader context of creation, according to Islāmic theology. *Fitrah* teaches that everything in the universe reflects Allāh's oneness, encouraging individuals to reflect on these signs to strengthen their belief in *tawhīd*. This concept transcends specific ethnicities, cultures, and times, affirming that *tawhīd* is a fundamental truth inherent in all human beings. Psychospiritual problems are seen as a symptom of misalignment with the *fitrah*, and the goal in Islāmic spirituality and psychotherapy is to return to this state by purifying one's beliefs and actions (Figure 1.2).

Epistemology, ontology, and axiology in Islāmic psychotherapy

Islāmic psychotherapy is grounded in the core principles of epistemology, ontology, and axiology deeply embedded in the Islāmic tradition. These foundational elements serve as the underpinning theoretical and philosophical constructs that define this therapeutic approach. Together, they establish a distinctive framework through which psychospiritual distress is grasped and treated, offering a unique perspective in the field of mental health.

Epistemology, a branch of philosophy concerned with the study of knowledge and how it is acquired, forms a fundamental component of Islāmic psychotherapy. The term is derived from the Greek *epistēmē* ("knowledge") and *logos*

8 The essence of Islāmic therapy

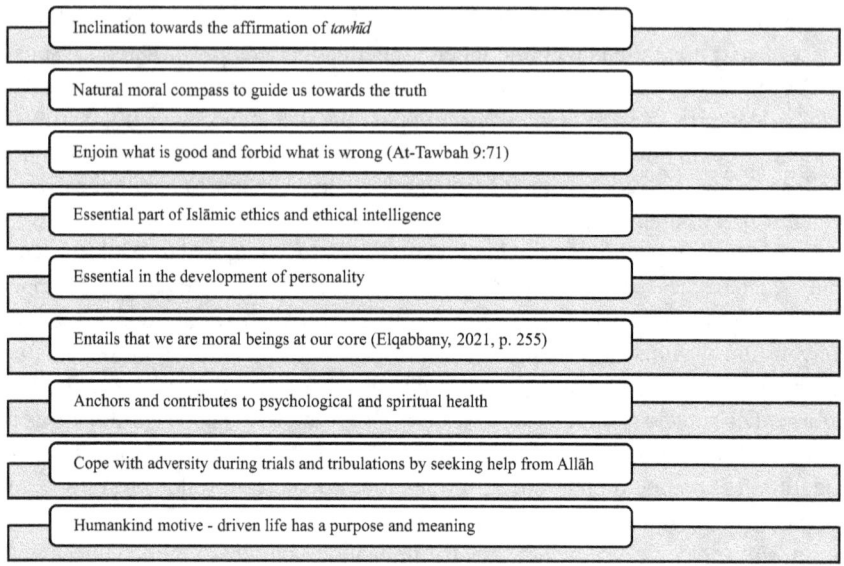

FIGURE 1.2 The role of *fitrah* in Islāmic psychotherapy.

("reason"), and accordingly, the field is sometimes referred to as the theory of knowledge (Stroll & Martinich, 2023). In Islāmic scholarship, it is acknowledged that true knowledge comes from multiple sources, including divine revelation, intuition, empirical observation, and rational inquiry. The Qur'ān and *hādīths* (*'Ilm naqli*) play a central role in the epistemology of Islāmic psychology and psychotherapy.

In addition, in Islāmic epistemology, the sources of knowledge are from rational knowledge based on human intellect (*'aql*), observation, and empirical evidence (*'ilm 'aqli*): "This systematic integration of the sources and means of knowledge into a synthesised approach is known as epistemological [relating to theory of knowledge] integration (*al-takamul al-ma'arifi*)" (Rassool, 2023, p. 5). The foundation of knowledge is the Qur'ān, which is viewed as the springhead of all knowledge and all sciences, not because it contains the knowledge itself but rather because it inspires the Muslim to develop a distinctive vision of the unity among the various spheres of knowledge. The notion of this unity arises out of an awareness of the unity of the divine and its applications to the various spheres of human knowledge (Malkawi, 2014, p. 20).

Malkawi (2014) emphasises that the Qur'ān is viewed as the springhead of all knowledge and sciences, inspiring holistic and interconnected dimensions, by recognising the unity of the divine in all spheres of human knowledge. By recognising the unity of the divine and its relevance to various fields, the Qur'ān encourages individuals to integrate their understanding of the world, society, and other disciplines, fostering a comprehensive and interconnected approach to knowledge acquisition and application. In addition to the sources of knowledge from the Qurʾān, there are also the *ḥadīths* (actions, statements, or tacit approvals of Prophet Muhammad (ﷺ). From the *ḥadīths*, we learn about the *Sunnah*, which are the practices of the Messenger of Allāh (ﷺ). It is divine revelation from Allāh and the *Sunnah* of Prophet Muhammad (ﷺ) that become the primary and most fundamental sources of knowledge.

In addition to divine revelation, knowledge can also be acquired through sense perception and rationalism, which should not be overlooked. While giving priority to revelation does not diminish the value of scientific knowledge gained through empiricism, intuition, and reason, it suggests that scientific evidence should be evaluated based on the criteria of divine revelation. Rassool (2021) suggested that Muslim psychologists should prioritise Islāmic ethical considerations over rationality and empirical evidence and that these should become secondary to the primary sources. Enquiring or probing is permissible in Islām so as to arrive at the truth (Leaman, 2006, p. 571). Epistemology within the context of Islāmic psychotherapy is intricately connected to both scholarly consensus (*ijma*) and reasoning, all operating within the confines of Islāmic doctrines. While divine knowledge remains predominant, Islāmic psychotherapy places a significant emphasis on the importance of individual reasoning and interpretation (*ijtihad*) that aligns with the principles of Islām.

The notion that knowledge should be interconnected, complementary, and organically linked to the knowledge of God is an important concept within classical Islāmic scholarship. Classical Muslim scholars, despite belonging to different schools of thought, shared the belief that all branches of knowledge should ultimately lead to a deeper understanding of Allāh and His creation. Malkawi (2014) suggested that the classical Muslim scholars, despite their different school of thought, agreed that

> knowledge should be interconnected, complementary, and organically linked to the knowledge of God. In the view of these scholars, the fact that all sciences originate from a single divine source is the foundation for the ultimate integration and unity of knowledge.
>
> *(p. 12)*

Malkawi (2014) argues for the interconnectedness of knowledge, asserting that both religious and secular knowledge can coexist with the knowledge of God. He maintains that there is no fundamental contradiction between divine knowledge from Islāmic sources and rational, empirical knowledge. According to Malkawi, all knowledge ultimately stems from a single divine source, encouraging a holistic integration and unity of knowledge. He emphasises the Islāmic principle of divine oneness, *tawḥīd*, as the foundation for both the unity of knowledge and epistemological integration.

This perspective aims to bridge the perceived gap between secular and religious knowledge, highlighting their inherent interconnectedness within Islāmic scholarship. This constitutes a frame of reference and foundation for a monotheistic

Islāmic psychotherapy, the incorporation of the Qur'ân and the traditions of the Prophet (*Sunnah*) into the epistemological foundation of Islāmic psychotherapy. These sacred sources serve as the core upon which therapeutic interventions and techniques are constructed, all aligning congruently with Islāmic principles. Thus, these principles underline the therapist's commitment to offering clients guidance and support deeply rooted in Islāmic values.

Ontology is "the philosophical study of being in general, or of what applies neutrally to everything that is real" (Simons, 2015). Islāmic psychotherapy draws from ontological principles that explore questions of existence and reality. It recognises the dualistic nature of human beings, encompassing both physical and metaphysical aspects such as *nafs* (self), *'aql* (intellect), *rûh* (soul), *ihsas* (emotion), and *qalb* (heart). This holistic viewpoint emphasises the interconnectedness among these elements, highlighting that achieving psychological well-being requires more than addressing physical and psychosocial factors.

Islāmic psychotherapy acknowledges the complexity of human life and advocates for a thorough examination of physical, social, psychological, and spiritual aspects in alignment with Islāmic principles. It offers a comprehensive framework that considers the holistic dimensions of individuals – their mind, body, and spirit – in the pursuit of psychospiritual health. Ontologically, in Islāmic psychotherapy, the concept of *fitrah* holds a significant role in understanding human nature and spirituality. Therapists focus on reconnecting individuals with their *fitrah*, facilitating spiritual healing and self-exploration. The aim is to help clients recognise their intrinsic spirituality and connection with God, leading to a deeper understanding of life's purpose and the pursuit of meaning. Through self-reflection and introspection, clients rediscover their innate longing for the divine, fostering holistic psychological and spiritual development.

Axiology, which is the study of values, holds great significance in Islāmic psychotherapy. Islāmic psychotherapy integrates Islāmic teachings and principles as a comprehensive framework for understanding moral values and ethical conduct. Therapists emphasise the importance of ethical behaviour and moral conduct for psychological well-being. They highlight aligning actions with Islāmic ethical values such as justice, kindness, gratitude, integrity, and honesty. By incorporating these values into therapy, individuals are encouraged to live in accordance with their spirituality and religious beliefs, fostering personal growth, emotional healing, and spiritual development known as *tazkiyah an-nafs*. Integrating Islāmic values within therapy enhances psychological and spiritual well-being, providing individuals with fulfilment and purpose.

Islāmic worldview

Islāmic psychotherapy is rooted in an Islāmic worldview (*tasawur or ru'yah al-Islām li al-wujud*), which draws from the Qur'ân, *Sunnah*. and Islāmic civilisation. This worldview offers a holistic understanding of reality, human existence, and life's purpose, guided by Islāmic teachings and principles. A worldview, as defined by Akhmetova (2021), encompasses various elements such as positions, attitudes, values, stories, and expectations that shape perspectives and behaviours. Within the Islāmic or Qur'ânic worldview, Muslims interpret and engage with the world, understanding life's purpose, human nature, ethics, relationships, and broader existence. This worldview guides decision-making processes and influences actions and interactions with others, providing a framework for navigating life's complexities. The Islāmic worldview encompasses both visible and hidden aspects of existence and is fundamentally ethical and monotheistic, grounded in the belief in a singular God. According to Al-Attas, the Islāmic worldview, or *ru'yat al-Islam lil-wujud*, emphasises the Islāmic perspective on existence and contrasts with secular or atheist worldviews by focusing on the belief in the existence and oneness of God. Relationships within this worldview must align with the Islāmic understanding of God, as highlighted by Hassan (1994).

The Islāmic worldview, rooted in the *tawhīdic* paradigm, encompasses all aspects of life for its followers. It is founded on three fundamental principles: *tawhīd* (theism), *khilâfah* (vicegerency), and *'adâlah* (justice). These principles not only frame the Islāmic worldview, they also constitute the fountainhead of the objectives (*maqasid*) and the strategy of Man's life in this world (Abdullah & Nadvi, 2011, p. 271). The Islāmic worldview extends beyond the concept of *tawhīd* to encompass a comprehensive ethical aspect known as *akhlāq* or morality. This dimension emphasises fundamental principles including profound respect for humanity, pursuit of social justice, promotion of equality, fostering inclusive relationships, moral courage, acceptance of diversity with tolerance, practice of restraint and forgiveness, disciplined living, commitment to charitable acts, sanctity of human life, application of reason in decision-making, acknowledgment of accountability, and the paramount importance of justice for individuals and society (Alwee, 2005). This ethical aspect of the Islāmic worldview is vividly reflected in various teachings, as exemplified by the following Qur'ânic verse. Allāh says,

لَّيْسَ ٱلْبِرَّ أَن تُوَلُّوا۟ وُجُوهَكُمْ قِبَلَ ٱلْمَشْرِقِ وَٱلْمَغْرِبِ وَلَٰكِنَّ ٱلْبِرَّ مَنْ ءَامَنَ بِٱللَّهِ وَٱلْيَوْمِ ٱلْءَاخِرِ وَٱلْمَلَٰٓئِكَةِ وَٱلْكِتَٰبِ وَٱلنَّبِيِّۦنَ وَءَاتَى ٱلْمَالَ عَلَىٰ حُبِّهِۦ ذَوِى ٱلْقُرْبَىٰ وَٱلْيَتَٰمَىٰ وَٱلْمَسَٰكِينَ وَٱبْنَ ٱلسَّبِيلِ وَٱلسَّآئِلِينَ وَفِى ٱلرِّقَابِ وَأَقَامَ ٱلصَّلَوٰةَ وَءَاتَى ٱلزَّكَوٰةَ وَٱلْمُوفُونَ بِعَهْدِهِمْ إِذَا عَٰهَدُوا۟ۖ وَٱلصَّٰبِرِينَ فِى ٱلْبَأْسَآءِ وَٱلضَّرَّآءِ وَحِينَ ٱلْبَأْسِۗ أُو۟لَٰٓئِكَ ٱلَّذِينَ صَدَقُوا۟ۖ وَأُو۟لَٰٓئِكَ هُمُ ٱلْمُتَّقُونَ

- *Righteousness is not in turning your faces towards the east or the west. Rather, the righteous are those who believe in Allāh, the Last Day, the angels, the Books, and the prophets; who give charity out of their cherished wealth to relatives, orphans, the poor, "needy" travellers, beggars, and for freeing captives; who establish prayer, pay alms-tax, and keep the pledges they make; and who are patient in times of suffering, adversity, and in "the heat of" battle. It is they who are true "in faith," and it is they who are mindful "of Allāh."*

(Al-Baqarah 2:177, interpretation of the meaning)

The Islāmic worldview is characterised by its ethical and moral values, which serve as foundational principles guiding Muslims' behaviour and providing coherence to their lives. Beyond just an epistemological system, Islām offers a methodology for understanding and engaging with all aspects of life. These values provide Muslims with a framework for interpreting the world, making decisions, and finding meaning in their experiences. They also shape interactions with others and guide the pursuit of a righteous and purposeful life. By embracing the comprehensive Islāmic worldview, Muslims navigate the complexities of the world while staying firmly grounded in their faith and values. The Islāmic worldview significantly influences Islāmic psychotherapy's perspectives on human suffering, resilience, and well-being. Core concepts like *tawhīd*, *qadr* (divine decree), and *akhirah* (belief in the afterlife) are integral to this worldview. These elements shape therapists' understanding of clients' mental health issues through a distinct lens rooted in Islāmic beliefs. By incorporating the Islāmic worldview into their practice, therapists can offer clients a culturally sensitive and faith-based approach that aligns with their religious beliefs and values.

Human nature: the inner world

Islāmic psychotherapy, deeply rooted in Islāmic philosophy and theology, offering a unique perspective on human behaviour and the inner psyche. It recognises several metaphysical elements within the inner world of humans, including the self (*nafs*), the soul (*rûh*), the heart (*qalb*), and the intellect (*'aql*).

These elements, part of the inner realm (*alam-e-batin*), are interconnected and influence an individual's thoughts, actions, and character. According to Islāmic belief, developing and purifying these inner faculties are essential for spiritual growth and closeness to Allāh. Imam Ghazâlî (1982) emphasised the interconnections and interdependence of the *nafs*, *rûh*, *'aql*, and *qalb*. *Nafs* represents the inner self, *rûh* refers to the spiritual essence that connects humans with the divine, *'aql* represents reason and intellect, and *qalb* symbolises the centre of emotion and spiritual perception. These elements work harmoniously to shape the nature of a person's soul within the Islāmic framework. It is essential to understand these concepts within the broader context of Islām's theological framework. For a comprehensive account of the inner world of a human being, see Rassool (2023). Here is a brief overview of these elements.

In Islāmic psychology, *nafs* represents the lower self, characterised by base desires and instincts. It undergoes three stages of development: *nafs al-ammāra bissu'* (inclined towards fulfilling desires) (Yusuf 12:53), *nafs al-lawwāma* (recognising faults and seeking self-improvement) (Al-Qiyamah 75:2), and *nafs al-muṭma'innah* (content and at peace following Allah's guidance) (Fajr 89:27–28). These stages depict the progression towards spiritual growth and alignment with divine values. In Islāmic psychotherapy, the concept of *nafs* is a fundamental framework for holistic self-exploration and healing. It emphasises the understanding of one's inner self and its interplay with desires, emotions, and thought patterns while acknowledging the intricate interplay between *nafs* and external influences.

The *rûh*, or soul, is the spiritual essence within every human being, serving as the connection between individuals and the divine in Islāmic belief. It is mentioned in the Qur'ān in various contexts, representing metaphysical entities like angels, revelation, or divine inspiration. According to Islāmic teachings, Allāh bestows the *rûh* to each human being at the moment of creation, infusing the physical body with life and consciousness. The *rûh* is eternal, transcending the confines of the physical realm, maintaining its unique identity and consciousness. In the afterlife, individuals are held accountable for the choices, actions, and deeds undertaken during their earthly existence.

According to scholars of *Ahlus-Sunnah wal Jamma'ah* like Ibn Taymîyyah and Ibn Qayyim of Jawziyyah, the terms *nafs* and *rûh* are interchangeable. They argue that the three states of the *nafs* mentioned in the Qur'ān can also apply to the *rûh*. However, there are other scholars who assert that *nafs* and *rûh* are distinct entities. They suggest that the *nafs* refers to the soul while it is within the body, while the *rûh* denotes the soul when separated from the body. (Sharfuddin, 2021). For a critical examination and overview of different perspectives on the interchangeability of *nafs* and *rûh*, see Rassool (2023, pp. 134–137).

In Islāmic psychology, *'aql* is referred to as the rational faculty of the soul or mind. It can also be understood as "dialectical reasoning" (Esposito, 2004, p. 22). The root meaning of the word *'aql* is associated with shackles, suggesting that "*'aql* acts as a faculty that restrains or controls the impulses of the *hawā* [the animal self]" (Skinner, 2019, p. 23). The *'aql* is a divine gift from Allāh bestowed upon humans, serving as a tool for maintaining moral goodness and fostering ethical intelligence. It enables individuals to engage in reasoned thinking, make sound judgments, and navigate morally and ethically complex situations. In the Qur'ān, verses highlight the importance of intellect and reasoning, stressing the failure to use it for guidance (Al-Anfal 8:22; Al-Mulk 67:10; Al-Haj 22:46). Imam Al-Ghazālī (2010) outlines five functions of *'aql*, including cognitive operations and knowledge of the heart (*qalb*). In Islāmic psychotherapy, *'aql* is important for promoting psychological well-being by challenging distorted thoughts and guiding moral and ethical development. Islāmic scholars hold divergent opinions on the anatomical seat of intellect, with some attributing it to the brain and others to the heart. A brief overview of scholars and their positions is examined in Rassool (2023, pp. 150–152).

In Islāmic tradition, the term "heart" (قلب) (*qalb*) carries profound spiritual significance, representing the innermost essence of an individual. Al-Ghazālī (1995) described the heart as having a dual nature. Firstly, he acknowledges the physical heart, the organ responsible for circulating blood, which is linked to the presence of the spiritual essence or *rûh*. Secondly, Al-Ghazālī emphasises the spiritual heart, divine and intricately connected to its physical counterpart. He regards the spiritual heart as the core and essence of a person, endowed with the capacity to perceive, know, and discern spiritual and divine realities. Al-Ghazālī attributes to the spiritual heart a fundamental role in spiritual perception and connectivity with the divine, describing it as the locus of intuition, inner knowing, and spiritual awareness (p. 234). He goes on to maintain that the spiritual heart is the essence of a man. In man, it is what

> perceives, knows, is aware, is spoken to, and is responsible for its actions. It has connection with the physical heart and the minds of most men have been baffled in trying to grasp the mode of the connection. . . . It [the heart] is like king and the soldiers are like servants and helpers.
>
> *(Al-Ghazālī, 1980/1982, p. 3)*

Al-Ghazālī portrays the essence of a person as a complex and multifaceted entity, encompassing faculties such as perception, knowledge, awareness, and moral responsibility. This essence is closely linked to the physical heart, indicating a profound integration of the physical and spiritual aspects of human existence. Al-Ghazālī's metaphor of the heart as a king with soldiers as servants and helpers underscores the heart's crucial role in guiding and governing one's actions and moral choices. This passage indicates the intricate relationship between the spiritual and physical realms within the human experience and highlights the challenge that many individuals face in comprehending the exact nature of this connection. Ibn al-Qayyim Al-Jawziyyah (n.d.) classified the *qalb* into three types due to its functional aspects of life and death:

> the first type of heart is the living, humble, soft, attentive and heedful heart. The second type is the brittle, dry and dead heart. The third type is the diseased heart, either it is closer to securing itself or it is closer to its devastation.
>
> *(p. 141)*

Ibn al-Qayyim Al-Jawziyyah's classification of the human heart into three distinct types provides valuable insights into the spiritual and moral dimensions of individuals. The first type, the living and humble heart, signifies a state of vitality, humility, attentiveness, and mindfulness. Referred to as "the truthful and sound (*salīm*) heart" (Ibn al-Qayyim, p. 136), it represents security and truthfulness. This heart is open to growth, receptive to moral and spiritual development, and responsive to positive influences. It remains secure from committing any form of idolatry or polytheism (*shirk*) due to its soundness. Free from carnal desires, it adheres to the order and prohibitions of Allāh.

According to Ibn al-Qayyim (n.d.), the spiritually dead heart represents a state in which it lacks true spiritual life and divine connection. Characterised by ignorance of Allāh's knowledge and commands, it submits to worldly temptations, fantasies, desires, and materialistic pleasures. In this state, the heart directs its emotions and actions towards things other than Allāh, driven solely by base desires rather than seeking divine pleasure. Ibn al-Qayyim's classification underscores the significant influence of the heart's spiritual state on individual beliefs, attitudes, and behaviours.

Shaykhul-Islām Ibn Taymiyyah (n.d.) identifies three types of hearts: the spiritually dead heart, the sound or healthy heart, and the diseased heart. The spiritually dead heart is characterised by prioritising base desires over the true purpose of existence, devoid of genuine love for Allāh and His commands. In contrast, the sound heart seeks closeness to Allāh and prioritises His pleasure. The diseased heart presents a more diluted situation, potentially on the path to recovery or moral decay. It highlights the dynamic nature of the human heart, influenced by competing calls towards Allāh and worldly matters and responding to the prevailing influence at any given time. Shafi (2011) emphasises that the human heart is continuously subjected to the influence of two callers: one beckoning towards Allāh, His Messenger, and the Hereafter and the other towards worldly, temporal matters. The heart's response is dictated by the one that is closest and most predominant at that time.

The spiritually dead heart, driven by base desires, is susceptible to alternating between moral good and deviant behaviours. It lacks the commitment to righteousness and readily succumbs to the temptations of the material world. Its attachment to worldly pleasures causes it to be swayed by its desires, resulting in inconsistent moral choices and actions. While it may occasionally align with ethical values, the spiritually dead heart often turns to deviant behaviours when its base desires dominate. In a *hādīth* narrated by An-Nu'man bin Bashir, Allāh's Messenger (ﷺ) says, "Beware! There is a piece of flesh in the body if it becomes good (reformed), the whole body becomes good, but if it gets spoilt, the whole body gets spoilt and that is the heart" (Bukhârî (b)). According to Shaykhul-Islām Ibn Taymiyyah (n.d.),

> The trials that are presented to the hearts are the causes of its disease. They are the trials of carnal desires and doubts, the trials of aimless wandering and misguidance, the trials of sins and innovations and the trials of oppression and ignorance. The first type [i.e. carnal desires] leads to the corruption of desire and intent and the second type [i.e. doubts] leads to the corruption of knowledge and belief.
>
> *(p. 145)*

The trials presented to the heart, including carnal desires, doubts, aimless wandering, sins and innovations, oppression, and ignorance, have the potential to corrupt and weaken the heart. Carnal desires distort intentions, doubts erode knowledge and beliefs, aimless wandering leads to spiritual disorientation, and sins hinder growth. Oppression and ignorance further exacerbate the heart's vulnerability. Despite these negative elements, the heart also serves as a conduit for divine guidance to reach individuals through the *fitrah*. This is the polished mirror.

It is important to note that according to Islāmic belief, only Allāh the Almighty has complete knowledge of the inner world of a person. This knowledge extends to the minutest details of an individual's essence, including their thoughts and intentions and the state of their inner faculties. This belief stresses the idea of divine knowledge and emphasises the importance of sincerity and humility in one's spiritual journey, as Allāh alone truly knows the depths of the human soul.

Spirituality, culture, and psychotherapy

Islāmic psychotherapy recognises the profound significance of spirituality within the scope of human existence and acknowledges that cultural factors play a vital role in shaping individuals' experiences and their psychosocial and psychospiritual health. Particularly among ethnic minorities, where religion and culture are deeply intertwined, the importance of cultural traditions and identities is emphasised (Worland & Vaddhanaphuti, 2013). Islāmic psychotherapy places a strong emphasis on acknowledging and respecting this interplay within the therapeutic context. It recognises that cultural diversity within the Muslim community greatly shapes how individuals perceive and address their mental health challenges. The approach values the rich cultural diversity present and understands that culture profoundly influences individuals' experiences and coping mechanisms. Intercultural therapy, as outlined by Kareem (1999), is a specialised form of psychotherapy designed to address the needs of culturally diverse groups. It emphasises the importance of factors such as race, culture, beliefs, values, attitudes, religion, and language in clients' lives.

Islāmic psychotherapists display sensitivity and awareness towards the unique cultural contexts of their clients, acknowledging that certain subjects or diagnoses may carry social stigma within specific cultural settings and within Muslim communities. They approach sensitive matters with tact and cultural competence, integrating cultural values, beliefs, and practices into therapy. This may include incorporating religious teachings, rituals, and practices as therapeutic tools, aligning therapy with clients' cultural backgrounds. Islāmic psychotherapy recognises the central role of spirituality and culture in individuals' identities, taking a holistic approach to mental health by exploring the interplay between spirituality, culture, and psychological well-being. Islāmic psychotherapy requires therapists to deeply comprehend Islāmic teachings and the diverse cultural expressions within the Muslim community. This in-depth understanding equips therapists with the tools necessary to negotiate the complex interplay of spirituality, culture, and mental health.

Paradigm of Islāmic psychotherapy

Islāmic psychotherapy is a therapeutic approach that integrates Islāmic principles, values, and beliefs, considering spirituality and cultural context to promote mental health outcomes. The paradigm of Islāmic psychotherapy emphasises the interconnectedness of the physical, social, psychological, environmental and spiritual dimensions of human existence. While there is no single, universally accepted paradigm of Islāmic psychotherapy, it generally includes the following key elements:

- Belief in monotheism or *tawhīd*
- Belief in divine revelation as a source of knowledge about Allāh; the hidden world; and the nature, meaning, and purpose of life
- Belief in connecting the religious characteristics with belief in the supernatural and invisible world
- Adoption of Prophet Muhammad (ﷺ) as a role model with an outstanding character (*khuluqyl 'adhiym*) and following his *Sunnah*
- Belief in the metaphysical components of the self: *qalb* (heart), *rûh* (soul), *nafs* (desire-nature or behavioural inclination), and *'aql* (intellect, reason), each term signifying a spiritual entity
- Belief in the fundamentals of Islāmic anthropology and the concept of *fitrah*
- Belief in Islāmic ethical and moral values
- Belief in Qur'ânic and prophetic guidance
- Belief in the integration of faith and psychology
- Belief in knowledge integration and integrated research (*maqasid*) as a methodology in Islāmic psychology
- Belief in cultural competence and sensitivity
- Belief in the holistic dimension of Islāmic psychotherapy: biological, social, psychological, and spiritual

The paradigm of Islāmic psychotherapy encompasses the integration of Islāmic principles, values, and spiritual practices with evidence-based therapeutic modalities. It blends Islāmic teachings with psychological theories for culturally sensitive and scientifically validated therapy. Unlike traditional approaches, it considers both empirical observation and supernatural phenomena rooted in divine revelation for a broader understanding of human behaviours and experiences. The paradigm acknowledges the interaction between the visible and invisible worlds, recognising that belief systems encompass metaphysical components of the self, including the heart (*qalb*), soul (*rûh*), desire-nature or behavioural inclination (*nafs*), and intellect or reason (*'aql*). These components are viewed as spiritual entities and form the foundation for understanding and studying Islāmic psychology. This paradigm offers a comprehensive approach to mental health that is rooted in Islāmic values and tailored to the needs of Muslim individuals.

Conclusion

Islāmic psychotherapy integrates spiritual dimensions and divine guidance, surpassing secular psychological theories by acknowledging the influence of spirituality on human behaviour and experiences. It embraces a multifaceted approach integrating knowledge, spirituality, culture, and ethics, grounded in a robust epistemological framework. Built upon the *tawhīdic* paradigm, it combines faith and psychology to understand human nature comprehensively. Recognising individuals as multidimensional beings, it emphasises addressing spiritual, psychological, and cultural components in therapy. Islāmic psychotherapy offers a holistic approach rooted in the Islāmic worldview, providing profound opportunities for healing and personal development in mental health.

References

Abdullah, M., & Nadvi, M. J. (2011). Understanding the principles of Islāmic worldview. *The Dialogue*, *4*(3), 268–289.

Akhmetova, E. (2021). *ITKI 6001 Methodology of scientific research and concept formation*. Institute of Knowledge Integration Academy (IKI-IIIT).

Al-Ghazālī, A. H. (1995). *Disciplining the soul, refining the character, and curing the sicknesses of the heart*. Islāmic Texts Society.

Al-Ghazālī, A. H. (2010). *The marvels of the heart: Science of the spirit* [Book 21, in *Iḥyā' 'ulūm al-dīn (The revival of the religious sciences*, W. J. Skellie, Trans.)]. Fons Vitae.

Alwee, A. I. (2005). *Ethical dimension of Islām*. Paper presented at Young AMP's Focus Group Discussion Series No. 1, National University of Singapore. Retrieved September 13, 2023, from http://thereadinggroup.sg/Articles/Ethical%20Dimension%20of%20Islam.pdf.

Bukhârî (a). *Sahih al-Bukhârî 1385* [In-book reference: Book 23, Hadīth 137. USC-MSA web (English) reference: Vol. 2, Book 23, Hadīth 467].

Bukhârî (b). *Sahih al-Bukhârî 52* [In-book reference: Book 2, Hadīth 45. USCMSA web (English) reference: Vol. 1, Book 2, Hadīth 50].

Hassan, K. M. (1994). The Islāmic worldview. In A. M. Yaacob & A. F. A. Rahman (Eds.), *Towards a positive Islāmic world-view: Malaysian and American perceptions* (pp. 11–33). Institute of Islāmic Understanding Malaysia.

Ibn al-Qayyim Al-Jawziyyah. (n.d.). *Ighathatu'l-Lahfan fi Masayid al-Shaytan* (Vol. 1, pp. 11/11–191). Cited in Ibn al-Qayyim. *Diseases of the hearts & their cures* (A. Rumaysah, Trans., pp. 33–42). Daar Us-Sunnah Publishers.

Ibn Kathir. (2000). *Tafsir ibn Kathir* (J. Abualrub, N. Khitab, H. Khitab, A. Walker, M. Al-Jibali, & S. Ayoub, Trans.). Darussalam Publishers and Distributors.

Iman Ghazâlî. (1982). *'Ihya' 'Ulum al-Din* (M. F. Karim, Trans., Vol. 3, pp. 2–3). Kitab Bhavan.

Kareem, J. (1999). *Intercultural therapy: Themes, interpretations and practice*. Blackwell Science Ltd.

Leaman, O. (Ed.) (2006). *The Qur'ân: An encyclopaedia*. Routledge.

Malkawi, F. H. (2014). *Epistemological integration: Essentials of an Islāmic methodology*. The International Institute of Islāmic Thought.

Muslim. *Sahih Muslim 2569* [In-book reference: Book 45, Hadīth 54. USC-MSA web (English) reference: Book 32, Hadīth 6232].

Philips, A. A. B. (2005). *The fundamentals of Tawheed* (Islāmic Monotheism). International Islāmic Publishing House.

Rassool, G. Hussein (2021). *Islāmic psychology: Human behaviour and experience from an Islāmic perspective*. Routledge.

Rassool, G. Hussein (2023). *Islāmic psychology: The basics*. Routledge.

Shafi, S. A. R. R. (2011). *The types of hearts*. Retrieved September 14, 2023, from www.Islam21c.com/spirituality/3333-three-types-of-hearts.

Sharfuddin, S. (2021). *The concept of Rûh in Islām*. Retrieved September 14, 2023, from http://rahbar.co.uk/theconcept-of-rûh-in-Islam.

Shaykhul-Islām Ibn Taymiyyah. (n.d.). *Diseases of the hearts & their cures* (A. Rumaysah, Trans.). Daar Us-Sunnah Publishers.

Simons, P. (2015). Ontology. *Encyclopedia Britannica*. Retrieved September 12, 2023, from www.britannica.com/topic/ontology-metaphysics.

Skinner, R. (2019). A beginner's guide to the concept of Islāmic psychology. *Journal of the British Islāmic Medical Association, 3*(1), 22–26.

Stroll, A., & Martinich, A. P. (2023). Epistemology. *Encyclopedia Britannica*. Retrieved September 12, 2023, from www.britannica.com/topic/epistemology.

Wehr, H., & Cowan, J. M. (2020). *A dictionary of modern written Arabic*. Retrieved from www.bnpublishing.com

Worland, S., & Vaddhanaphuti, C. (2013). Religious expressions of spirituality by displaced Karen from Burma: The need for a spirituality sensitive social work response. *International Social Work, 56*(3), 3840402.

2
ISLĀMIC COUNSELLING AND PSYCHOTHERAPY

From faith to psychology

Introduction

In the 21st century, Islāmic psychology, psychotherapy, and counselling have evolved significantly as academic disciplines and practical fields, largely in response to the Islāmic awakening (*aṣ-ṣaḥwah l-'islāmiyyah*) or Islāmic revival (*tajdīd*). This awakening, which represents a collective response to the historical and post-colonial challenges faced by Muslim communities worldwide, occurred as a reaction to historical, post-colonial challenges, globalisation, socioeconomic disparities, political oppression, and genocide. This awakening has sparked a profound re-envisioning and reimagining of Islāmic thought and scholarship, driving an intellectual and spiritual revolution that seeks to address the unique psychological, emotional, social, and spiritual needs of Muslims within a contemporary framework. Islāmic psychology and counselling have emerged to reconcile psychological well-being with Islāmic teachings, providing essential support to Muslims with mental health challenges. Islāmic psychotherapy and counselling offer structured approaches to integrating faith and psychology, helping individuals align their Islāmic beliefs with their psychological and spiritual wellness.

Islāmic psychotherapy and counselling integrate Islāmic principles, teachings, and ethics with psychological theories and interventions to address psychospiritual disorders and mental health. It emphasises aligning actions, thoughts, and emotions with Islāmic values and traditions, recognising the interconnectedness of body, mind, and soul. Providing a supportive environment, Islāmic counselling allows individuals to explore psychological struggles within an Islāmic framework, utilising spiritual interventions for healing and growth. Key considerations include acknowledging diversity within Muslim communities; cultural influences; and the interplay between religion, society, and individual experiences. This chapter explores the evolution, concepts, foundational principles, therapeutic techniques, and considerations in Islāmic counselling and psychotherapy.

Evolution of Islāmic counselling and psychotherapy

Muslim communities globally are increasingly recognising and addressing mental health issues, leading to a demand for faith-based interventions. Muslims, like other populations, confront challenges such as anxiety, depression, trauma, and stress-related disorders. However, they also face specific stressors including discrimination, prejudice, Islāmophobia, and sociopolitical issues that exacerbate mental health challenges. Additionally, psychosocial issues stemming from intergenerational conflict, refugee status, and radicalism contribute to the complexity of mental health issues within Muslim communities (Rassool, 2019).

In the context of this chapter and the book as a whole, the terms counselling and psychotherapy will be used interchangeably. This choice of terminology reflects a recognition of the overlapping and complementary nature of these two disciplines in the realm of mental health support and therapeutic interventions. The evolution of Islāmic psychotherapy reflects a response to the increasing recognition of mental health concerns within Muslim communities and a departure from historically dominant secular approaches rooted in Eurocentric and Orientalist paradigms. The rise of considerations of Islām in psychological sciences is partly due to dissatisfaction with secular psychology, criticised for its exclusion of spiritual dimensions and labelled "soulless psychology." Although the term "psychology" suggests the study of the soul or spirit, secular approaches frequently neglect spirituality, religious experiences, and ethical behaviours. This alienation of the spiritual or religious dimensions within the paradigm of so-called soulless psychology means that "religious ideas, practice, and organisations lose their influence in the face of scientific and other knowledge" (McLeish, 1995, p. 668). This exclusion can marginalise religious influences, limiting the understanding of human behaviours and experiences.

A criticism often directed at ethnocentric approaches to psychotherapy and counselling is that they stigmatise and marginalise both individuals and entire cultural groups (Charema & Shizha, 2008). The limitations of these Eurocentric and Orientalist approaches to psychotherapy and counselling become especially marked when working with Muslim clients. These individuals possess religious and cultural values, beliefs, and practices that profoundly inform their perceptions of mental health. The secular traditional psychotherapeutic approach can be limiting and fail to capture the full complexity of the holistic nature of human behaviours and experience. Many individuals with strong religious beliefs often encounter a dissonance or lack of resonance between their worldviews and the secular approaches employed in mainstream psychotherapeutic practices. For Muslim clients, this dissonance can create a distinct need for a psychologically informed approach that acknowledges and incorporates Islāmic traditions and principles leading to the revival of *ilm an-nafs* (the psychology of the self).

Theare are significant distinctions between Islāmic psychotherapy and Western-oriented psychotherapeutic approaches. These distinctions encompass the rejection of certain fundamental philosophical principles regarding human nature and personality development, the emphasis on collectivistic values, the cultivation of ethical standards, and the incorporation of Islāmic beliefs and practices. Islāmic counselling and psychotherapy, firmly rooted in Islāmic traditions, recognises the significance of integrating religious teachings, ethics, and spirituality into the therapeutic process. It offers a unique approach that acknowledges the multidimensional nature of human beings and emphasises the interconnectedness between the mind, body, and soul.

By incorporating Islāmic principles and values, Islāmic psychotherapy provides individuals with the opportunity to address their mental health concerns in a manner that resonates with their religious beliefs and aligns with their quest for meaning and purpose. This integration aims to offer a holistic approach to mental health that takes into account the physical, social, psychological, and spiritual dimensions of individuals' lives. The field of Islāmic psychotherapy has witnessed the emergence of models and approaches tailored to offer faith-based interventions, combining Islāmic spirituality with psychological techniques. While some pseudo-models face methodological challenges and lack empirical validation, a few have proven effective and operational within clinical practice. In Western countries, significant progress has been made in establishing therapeutic and counselling centres and support services for Muslim clients, offering tailored therapeutic interventions and resources aligned with Islāmic principles, catering to the specific needs of individuals and families.

The establishment of Islāmic psychology and psychotherapy programmes and institutions marks a significant development in response to the increasing demand for specialised education in this field. While their numbers are relatively limited, academic institutions and universities have begun offering accredited university certificates, advanced diplomas, and PhD programmes in Islāmic psychology and psychotherapy. Additionally, various institutions and clinical services recognise the growing demand and offer courses and institutional certification options in Islāmic psychology and psychotherapy, albeit without formal university accreditation. The proliferation of online resources and outreach initiatives has collectively shaped the landscape of Islāmic psychotherapy programmes.

Meanwhile, research in the field of Islāmic psychotherapy remains limited, although pockets of exemplary practices demonstrate promising approaches aligned with Islāmic principles. However, dissemination of these practices to a broader audience is constrained, highlighting the need for greater outreach and knowledge sharing. Despite these challenges, there has been a surge in books published on Islāmic psychology and psychotherapy, particularly through the Focus Series by Routledge. These books offer authentic, practical, and concise insights based on cutting-edge research and focus on various aspects of Islāmic psychology and psychotherapy, client groups, methodologies, approaches, educational development, Islāmic research scholarship, and critical analyses of theoretical and historical ideas (Rassool, 2023a).

In summary, the evolution of Islāmic psychotherapy in the 21st century is characterised by a growing recognition of mental health issues, the integration of Islāmic values with contemporary psychological approaches, the establishment of academic programmes and research, and the development of specialised services and resources. These developments collectively reflect a concerted effort to address mental health challenges while respecting Islāmic principles and cultural contexts.

Historical context

Islāmic psychotherapy integrates Islāmic principles, values, and teachings into the counselling and therapeutic process. This therapeutic approach is grounded in an understanding of human nature that incorporates spirituality. Rassool (2019) noted that discussions surrounding Islāmic psychotherapy have often been intertwined with Islāmic psychology, reflecting the historical connection between spirituality and healing in Islām. In essence, Islāmic therapy or counselling has roots as old as the inception of spirituality within the Islāmic tradition.

The historical roots of Islāmic counselling and psychotherapy can be traced to the early days of Islām, particularly through the life and teachings of Prophet Muhammad (ﷺ). Prophet Muhammad was not only a spiritual leader but also served as a source of guidance and support for individuals facing various challenges. His interactions with companions demonstrated his compassion, empathy, and ability to provide counselling, advice (*naseehah*) guidance, and solace to those in need. For example, Prophet Muhammad (ﷺ) would offer emotional support to his companions by lending a listening ear, providing advice, and helping them navigate difficult situations.

On the authority of Abu Ruqayyah Tameem ibn Aus ad-Daari (may Allāh be pleased with him), Prophet Muhammad (ﷺ) said, "'Religion is *naseehah*.' The companions asked, 'To whom, O Messenger of Allāh?' He replied, 'To Allāh, His Book, His Messenger, the leaders of the Muslims, and their common folk'" (Muslim (a)). This *hadīth* emphasises the importance of offering sincere advice on various aspects of the Islāmic faith, such as following the teachings of Alláh and the guidance of Prophet Muhammad (ﷺ). In another *hadīth*, Abu Hurayrah (may Allāh be pleased with him), narrated that the Messenger of Allāh (ﷺ) said, "The rights of a believer over a believer are six," among them being "if he asks you for advice, you have to give him advice" (Muslim (b)). Offering *naseehah* to fellow Muslims encompasses providing sincere guidance, directing them towards rectifying actions in both worldly life and the hereafter, shielding from harm, assisting in times of need, facilitating advantages, motivating towards good deeds, gently forbidding what is wrong, and demonstrating compassion in interactions.

Classical Islāmic polymath scholars have made significant contributions to the field of psychotherapy, offering valuable insights and guidance through their extensive writings. This chapter explores specific examples of these contributions, focusing on the works of Al-Kindi, Ibn-Sina, Al-Razi, Al-Ghazâlî, Al-Balkhi, Ibn Taymiyyah al-Ḥarrānī, Ibn Qayyim Al-Jawziyyah, Ibn Hazm, Ar-Rāghib Al-Aṣbahānī, Ibn al-Jawzī, Ibn Rajab al-Ḥanbalī, and Ibn Khaldūn. These scholars provided unique perspectives by integrating Islāmic principles with psychological concepts, addressing topics such as human consciousness; perception; the nature of dreams; social psychology and cultural influences; and the roles of intellect, emotions, and interconnectedness between mental and physical health; they also contributed to therapeutic interventions, addressing both psychological and physical aspects and including music and art therapy. Table 2.1 presents the contributions of some classical scholars in mental health, psychospiritual development and growth, and psychology in general.

This historical context led to the phrase the "Dodo Bird Revival of Islāmic Counseling" (Rassool, 2019), signifying the resurgence of interest in these therapeutic approaches.

Islāmic psychotherapy: concept

The field of Islāmic counselling and psychotherapy lacks a consistent and universally accepted definition. While there is abundant literature discussing Islāmic psychotherapy and counselling, there is a lack of clear operational definitions for these concepts. Many authors tend to discuss Islāmic psychology rather than specifically describing Islāmic counselling (Rassool, 2018). This ambiguity is reflected in an analysis of websites promoting Islāmic counselling and psychotherapy that also fail to provide precise operational definitions. Thus, despite various explanations and attributes assigned to Islāmic psychotherapy and counselling, there remains a need for a clear and universally accepted definition in the field.
Zakaria and Akhir (2016) categorise Islāmic counselling and psychotherapy into three dimensions: traditional, modification, and integrative. In the traditional dimension, counselling is rooted in the psychological advice and wisdom of Prophet Muhammad (ﷺ), deeply grounded in Islāmic theology. The modification dimension closely resembles orthodox counselling but incorporates Islāmic beliefs and practices into its philosophical foundations and intervention strategies. In the integrative dimension, psychotherapy or counselling blends key aspects of conventional therapies with fundamental elements of Islām, including *aqeedah* (faith), *'ibâdah* (worship), and *Shari'ah* (Islāmic law). This approach aims to integrate mainstream counselling and psychotherapy techniques with core Islāmic principles.

Some authors argue that Islāmic counselling resembles Western counselling paradigms, incorporating eclectic or integrated approaches while emphasising the inherent spiritual dimension. Abdullah (2009) suggests that Islāmic counselling is comparable with Western counselling but integrates central Islāmic tenets; the

TABLE 2.1 Contributions of some classical scholars to mental health and psychology

Scholar	Contribution
Al-Kindi: Abu Yusuf Ya'qub ibn Ishaq al-Kindi	Nature of dreams and their significance in the context of human consciousness and perception
Ibn-Sina: Abu Ali al-Husayn ibn Abd Allah ibn Sina	Role of the intellect in human cognition and knowledge acquisition; influence of emotions on human behaviour and well-being; interpretation of dreams and their significance in understanding the human psyche; identified conditions such as depression and anxiety and proposed therapeutic interventions, including the use of music and art as forms of therapy
Al-Razi: Abu Bakr Muhammad ibn Zakariya al-Razi	A wide range of psychological conditions; interconnectedness of mental and physical health; therapeutic interventions consider both the mind and the body; pharmacological treatments for mental health; significance of psychological and environmental factors in the healing process
Imam Al-Ghazâlî: Abu Hamid Muhammad ibn Muhammad Al-Ghazâlî	Self-reflection and self-examination as essential components of personal development and mental well-being; purification of the soul (*tazkiyah al-nafs*); cultivation of virtuous character traits (*akhlaq*) as a means of achieving mental and spiritual health practices such as meditation, prayer, and *tafakkur* (contemplation)
Al-Balkhi: Abu Zayd Al-Balkhi	Classification of various disorders; interplay between psychological and physical well-being; pharmacological treatments; use of therapeutic techniques including cognitive restructuring, behavioural interventions, and relaxation to address psychological distress
Ibn Taymiyyah: Taqī ad-Dīn 'Aḥmad ibn 'Abd al-Ḥalīm ibn 'Abd al-Salām al-Numayrī al-Ḥarrānī	Role of the mind (*aql*) and emotions (*nafs*) in human behaviour and spiritual growth; interconnectedness of the soul (*nafs*), spirituality, and emotional well-being; importance of cultivating virtuous character traits and avoiding sinful behaviour. Self-examination and self-reflection (*muhasabah*) align with contemporary psychological concepts of self-awareness and introspection.
Ibn Qayyim Al-Jawziyyah: Ahmad ibn Abdul-Halim ibn Abdas-Salam ibn Abdullah ibn Abi Qayyim al-Jawziyyah	Psychological well-being and spiritual development; relationship between the soul, the body, and emotional well-being; importance of cultivating positive emotions such as gratitude, patience, and love as key factors for psychological health; importance of positive emotions and their role in psychological health offer a holistic approach

(*Continued*)

TABLE 2.1 (Continued)

Scholar	Contribution
Ibn Hazm: Abu Muhammad Ali ibn Ahmad ibn Sa'id ibn Hazm	Understanding of emotions; psychological well-being; the nature of love and attachment; and the impact of relationships on mental health. Insights into emotional bonds, attachment styles, and the cultivation of healthy relationships have influenced the field of psychotherapy.
Ar-Rāghib Al-Aṣbahānī: Muḥammad ibn Muḥammad ibn Muḥammad ibn Aḥmad Al-Ḥusaynī Al-Aṣbahānī	Self-actualisation; educational psychology; physical and cognitive development; individual differences and personality traits; behavioural treatment through *ibâdah* ("worship"); theory of different emotions
Ibn al-Jawzī: ʿAbd al-Raḥmān ibn ʿAlī ibn Muḥammad Abū al-Farash ibn al-Jawzī	Development psychology; cognitive development; importance of self-awareness, self-reflection, and self-control as vital aspects of spiritual and psychological development; effects of harmful emotions and toxic thoughts on individuals' mental health and well-being; strategies for emotional regulation, purification, and refinement of the soul; honesty, patience, humility, and gratitude as essential elements of one's psychological and spiritual well-being
Ibn Rajab al-Ḥanbalī: Imam Abd Al-Rahman ibn Ahmad ibn Rajab al-Ḥanbalī	Purification of the heart and the importance of cultivating positive character traits; holistic development of the human being (i.e. spiritual, ethical, emotional, physical, and sexual); self-examination and self-reflection; repentance (*tawbah*) as a psychological and spiritual process; importance of contentment (*qana'ah*) and gratitude (*shukr*) as psychological and spiritual virtues; reliance on God, patience (*sabr*), and seeking solace in prayer and supplication; practical guidance on how to overcome negative traits and habits through introspection, repentance, and self-discipline
Ibn Khaldūn: Walī al-Dīn ʿAbd al-Raḥmān ibn Muḥammad ibn Muḥammad ibn Abī Bakr Muḥammad ibn al-Ḥasan Ibn Khaldūn	Exploration of human behaviour and group dynamics; concept of *'asabiyyah,* or group solidarity, and its impacts on social structures and individual behaviour; cultural psychology and role of psychological factors in societal change, including the psychological motivations of rulers and the psychological impacts of societal norms and values on individuals; development of social psychology and the understanding of human behaviour in a sociocultural context. Behaviour, attitudes, and mentalities of rulers, leaders, and societies can influence historical events.

Source: adapted from Rassool and Luqman (2023), Rassool (2023b).

author proposes that Islāmic counselling blends counselling and psychotherapy with Islāmic principles, aiming to help clients achieve positive change. This integration is reflected in descriptions of Islāmic counselling, such as its utilisation of integrative counselling principles with the added dimension of the relationship between the client and their creator (Sakoon.co.uk). Additionally, concepts like Qur'an-centred counselling are rooted in Qur'anic principles of reflection and restoration (Muslim Family Matters, n.d.).

I described Islāmic counselling as "a form of counselling which incorporates spirituality into the therapeutic process and has a faith-based perspective" (Rassool, 2016, p. 193). However, because the starting point of Islāmic psychotherapy and counselling focuses on the *nafs* or self rather than the psyche (mind), Rassool (2018, 2020) has redefined Islāmic psychotherapy and counselling as "an application of interpersonal skills in the development of the self [(*nafs*), intellect (*aql*), body (*jasad*) and heart (*qalb*)] based on Islāmic spirituality." Building upon the earlier definitions, this expanded definition seeks to encompass the overarching framework of Islāmic psychotherapy and counselling. It adopts a holistic approach by acknowledging the all-encompassing nature of the self and recognising the interconnections between the psychological and metaphysical domains. By acknowledging the holistic nature of the self, this definition encapsulates all dimensions of human nature and emphasises the intricate interplay between psychological and metaphysical elements.

Some Islāmic therapists or clinical service providers prefer to use the terms "psychotherapy" and "counselling" interchangeably. Al-Karam (2018) defines Islāmically integrated psychotherapy as a modern therapeutic approach that integrates Islāmic teachings, principles, and interventions with Western therapeutic methods and psychological interventions. On the other hand, Keshavarzi et al. (2021) use the label "traditional Islāmically integrated psychotherapy" instead of "Islāmic psychotherapy" and describe it as an integrative model of mental health care grounded in Islāmic principles and drawing upon empirical truths in psychology. This approach emphasises the integration of spiritual and psychological elements to offer comprehensive support for Muslim clients.

Baqutayan (2011) defines Islāmic counselling as a process of problem solving using the Qur'ân and *Sunnah*, emphasising techniques based on confidentiality, trust, respect, good listening habits, and understanding. The ultimate goal is to connect individuals with Allāh and offer spiritual solutions. Islāmic counselling also emphasises spiritual solutions rooted in love and fear of Allāh, as well as fulfilling responsibilities as servants of Allāh on Earth. Hamjah and Akhir (2013) suggest that aspects of the Islāmic approach to counselling and psychotherapy include *aqeedah* (faith), *'ibâdah* (worship/ultimate devotion and love for God), and *'akhlaq* (moral conduct). Ali et al. (2004) and Johansen (2005) point out that informal counselling and advice can be sought from religious leaders or *imams* rather than psychotherapists or counsellors.

Within the framework of this chapter and the overarching theme of this entire book, Islāmic psychotherapy is defined as a therapeutic approach that integrates Islāmic spirituality and evidence-based psychology to promote holistic well-being encompassing mental, emotional, and spiritual health. Islāmic psychotherapy is deeply rooted in Islāmic principles and values, emphasising the integration of Islāmic ethical behaviours and drawing from the rich spiritual and moral tradition of Islām. Its core aim is to foster a profound connection between individuals and their faith, assisting them in navigating life's challenges while remaining anchored in their religious beliefs. Table 2.2 outlines the differences between mainstream and Islāmic psychotherapy based on religious relationships, sources of knowledge, understandings of illness and mental health maintenance, responses to illness, values, growth, and development in counselling. Additionally, the focus, purpose, process, and intervention strategies of counselling are compared to distinguish between the two approaches.

The literature demonstrates a range of perspectives, with some emphasising the integration of Islāmic principles and practices into counselling and psychotherapy while others focus on similarities with Western counselling paradigms. From a brief review of the literature there are many commonalities can be deduced from the earlier definitions and explanations of Islāmic counselling and psychotherapy (Rassool, 2021). The main elements include the following:

- Based on the Qur'ân and the *Sunnah*
- Incorporates spirituality into the therapeutic process
- Based on two Qur'ânic principles: reflection and restoration
- Integrates Islāmic teachings, principles, philosophies, and/or interventions with Western therapeutic approaches
- Derives from Islāmic sciences of self
- Utilises the major tenets of integrative counselling with the added dimension of the relationship between the client and his/her creator
- Includes good aspects of mainstream counselling and incorporates the Qur'ân, and Sunnah, of Prophet Muhammad (ﷺ)

Islāmic psychotherapy as a contemporary approach shares some commonalities with other therapeutic modalities. One of its fundamental and distinguishing features is the acknowledgment of the profound role of spirituality in individuals' health and wellness. At its core, Islāmic psychotherapy recognises that human beings are not merely physical or psychological entities – they are also spiritual beings. The interconnectedness of the mind, body, and spirit is a foundational principle in this approach. Further development and consensus are needed to establish a more cohesive conceptual and theoretical framework for Islāmic psychotherapy.

TABLE 2.2 Differences between mainstream and Islāmic psychotherapy

	Mainstream psychotherapy	Islāmic psychotherapy
Orientation	Judaeo-Christian	Islāmic
Religious relationship	Oppositional Secular	Integrated
Sources of knowledge	Man-made theories and empirical evidence based on Western scientific paradigm	Divine revelation Qur'ân and *Sunnah* Evidenced-based
What causes illness?	Bio-psychosocial factors	Bio-psychosocial + spiritual factors
Sound mental health	No divine intervention. biological or biopsychosocial factors	Submission to God Integration of material and spiritual life
Values	Materialistic and individualistic. Socio-moral value structure Value-laden and dependent	God consciousness Spiritual–divine will Islāmic values and morality Collectivism
Growth & development	Cognitive and psychosocial development	Spiritual, cognitive, & psychosocial development
Focus	Limited focus on the physical world	Disregard for spiritual aspects of human beings Seen and unseen worlds
Purpose	Promotes personal growth/self-understanding	Promotes the clear purpose and meaning of life
Process	Individual-based and individual-focused	Mutual responsibility Social and community obligation Healthy altruism
Responses to illness	Psychological reactions	Spiritual reactions: patience prayers and supplications
Relationship between mind and body	Mind–body interaction	Mind–body–soul interaction
Personal development	Unlimited freedom	Freedom based on the *Shar'iah*
Therapeutic strategies	Based on humanistic, cognitive–behavioural, and psychoanalytical interventions	Based on humanistic, cognitive–behavioural, and spiritual interventions
Dream technique	Dream analysis (Freudian, Jungian)	Use of prophetic analysis of dreams (unlike psychoanalysis)
Undesired (negative) behaviour	Rationalisation	Therapy of repentance

Source: adapted from Rassool (2016).

30 The essence of Islāmic therapy

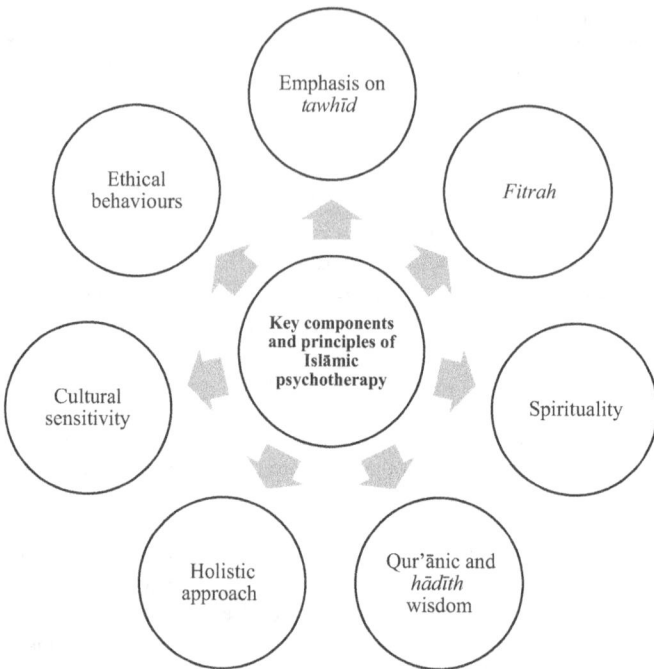

FIGURE 2.1 Key components and principles of Islāmic psychotherapy.

Principles of Islāmic psychotherapy

The principles and key components of Islāmic psychotherapy include spirituality, *tawhīd*, the Qur'ân and *Sunnah*, interconnectedness, a holistic approach, interaction with faith, ethical behaviours, and cultural sensitivity. Figure 2.1 presents the key components and principles of Islāmic psychotherapy emphasises the spiritual dimension, rooted in Islāmic beliefs, as a central tenet of the therapeutic approach. It acknowledges spirituality (*fitrah*) as inherent to human nature and crucial for achieving optimal mental, emotional, and spiritual health. Islāmic psychotherapy recognises that spirituality permeates all aspects of life, including relationships, work, religious practices, rituals, and personal growth. By integrating spirituality into therapy, individuals can experience a holistic approach to healing, addressing existential questions and finding meaning and purpose in their experiences.

In Islāmic psychotherapy, the concept of *tawhīd*, the core principle of Islāmic monotheism, holds significant importance in shaping one's mental and emotional well-being. By connecting with their *fitrah* and deepening their understanding of *tawhīd*, individuals can find solace, draw strength from their faith, and gain a sense of purpose and meaning in their experiences (Rassool, 2023b). Internalising this belief helps individuals develop a deeper understanding of their purpose and significance in the world, finding comfort and strength in their relationships with the divine. The connection between individuals and the divine, provide a moral compass, source of strength, guidance, and direction for making informed decisions. This connection encourages engaging in acts of worship, prayer, Qur'ânic recitation, and reflection and recognising signs of God's presence in one's life. This belief offers comfort and reassurance during challenging times, reminding individuals that they are not alone in their trials and tribulations (Rassool, 2023b).

The Qur'ân contains verses highlighting the significance of spirituality in Islāmic psychotherapy. For instance, it underscores the importance of remembering God and finding tranquillity (*sakinah*) through remembrance (*dhikr*). Allāh says in the Qur'ân:

أَلَا بِذِكْرِ ٱللَّهِ تَطْمَئِنُّ ٱلْقُلُوبُ

- *Unquestionably, by the remembrance of Allāh hearts are assured.*
  (Ar-Ra'd 13:28, interpretation of the meaning)

This verse highlights the therapeutic potential of spirituality in alleviating emotional distress and promoting inner peace. Ibn Qayyim al-Jawziyyah (2020) (may Allāh have mercy on him) said,

> In the heart are disorders that cannot be remedied except by responding to Allāh. In it is a desolate feeling that cannot be removed except by intimacy with Him solitude. In it is sadness which will not leave except by happiness with knowing Him and truthfulness in his dealings. In it is anxiety that is not made tranquil except by gathering for His sake and fleeing to Him from His punishment. In it is a fire of regret which cannot be extinguished except by satisfaction with His commands, prohibitions, and decrees, and embracing patience with that until the time he meets Him. In it is a strong desire that will not cease until He is the only one who is sought. In it is a void that cannot be filled except by His love, turning to Him, always remembering Him, and being sincere to Him. Were a person to be given the entire world and everything in it, that would never fill the void.

In these statements, Ibn al-Qayyim emphasises that the disorders of the heart with various emotional and spiritual afflictions can only be achieved by responding to, and remembering, Allāh. It depicts the heart's ailments, including desolation, sadness, anxiety, and regret, which can only be alleviated through intimacy with Allāh, seeking solace in His commands and embracing patience. Ibn-al-Qayyim stresses that the ultimate remedy for the void within the heart is found in seeking Allāh's love, turning towards Him, and maintaining unwavering sincerity in faith, highlighting that worldly riches can never fill this void as its true fulfilment lies in the divine connection. 'Abdullah bin Busr narrated that a man said, "O Messenger of Allāh (ﷺ), indeed, the legislated acts of Islām have become too much for me, so inform me of a thing that I should stick to." He (ﷺ) said, "Let not your tongue cease to be moist with the remembrance of Allāh" (Tirmidhî).

The concept of remembering Allāh (*dhikr*) holds significant importance in Islāmic teachings, particularly concerning diseases of the heart. In Islāmic belief, the heart is considered the centre of human consciousness and spirituality. Diseases of the heart, such as arrogance, envy, greed, and hatred, are seen as spiritual ailments that disrupt one's connection with Allāh and with fellow beings. The remembrance of Allāh through various forms of *dhikr*, such as prayer, recitation of Qur'ânic verses, and invoking His names and attributes, is believed to cleanse and purify the heart. *Dhikr* serves to remind individuals of their dependence on Allāh, fosters humility, and helps in overcoming negative traits and emotions. By engaging in consistent remembrance of Allāh, individuals strive to attain inner peace, contentment, and spiritual fulfilment.

Islāmic psychotherapy operates on the core principle of recognising the interconnectedness of the mind, body, and spirit within human existence. This approach acknowledges that disturbances in one dimension can affect others, such as emotional issues leading to physical ailments or spiritual disconnection contributing to psychological distress. By addressing these dimensions comprehensively, Islāmic psychotherapy seeks to establish harmony and balance, aiming for enduring healing and growth. Therapists in Islāmic psychotherapy work with clients to address psychological concerns while considering their spiritual and physical aspects. They encourage exploring emotional and spiritual well-being, recognising their close interconnection. By addressing root causes across these dimensions, Islāmic psychotherapy offers a holistic and sustainable approach to healing, emphasising the importance of treating the whole person.

Cultural sensitivity is a fundamental principle in Islāmic psychotherapy, stressing therapists' acknowledgment of and respect for the diverse cultural expressions within Muslim communities. Nolan and West (2015) emphasise the importance of considering spirituality, religion, culture, race, and ethnicity in therapy. Therapists aim to adjust their approaches to accommodate varying cultural manifestations of Islām, ensuring that interventions meet individual clients' unique needs and preferences. For instance, therapists may incorporate culturally relevant examples, metaphors, or storytelling techniques to resonate with clients' cultural backgrounds, facilitating deeper understanding and connection in the therapeutic process. This approach promotes a more empathetic and respectful therapeutic experience for Muslim clients.

The principle of using evidence-based psychology in Islāmic psychotherapy involves integrating scientific research and empirical evidence to inform psychological assessment, diagnosis, and treatment. This approach relies on sense perception, rationalism, observation, and experimentation to inform therapeutic interventions and decision-making processes. Psychologists utilise well-established research findings to ensure that psychological practices are grounded in empirical evidence, leading to more reliable and effective outcomes. Within an Islāmic framework, scientific evidence is evaluated based on criteria provided in divine revelation. Rassool (2023c) suggests that Islāmic ethical considerations should take precedence over rationality and empirical evidence while acknowledging that both approaches stem from the same divine source. Thus, there is no contradiction between transmitted divine knowledge from the Qur'ān and *Sunnah* and rational, empirical knowledge: both originate from God.

Conclusion

Islāmic psychotherapy is a therapeutic approach that recognises the importance of integrating Islāmic principles and spirituality into the processes of healing and personal growth. It encompasses a range of therapeutic models and techniques that are informed by Islāmic teachings, values, and practices. Islāmic psychotherapy places emphasis on the interconnectedness of the mind, body, and spirit, viewing individuals as holistic beings with psychological, emotional, and spiritual dimensions. At its core, Islāmic psychotherapy recognises the central role of spirituality in providing guidance, meaning, and healing. Islāmic psychotherapy interventions may include elements such as prayer, meditation, Qur'ânic recitation, reflection on Islāmic teachings, and seeking forgiveness and guidance from Allāh.

Cultural sensitivity is a vital aspect of Islāmic psychotherapy, as it takes into account the unique cultural backgrounds and experiences of individuals seeking therapy. Additionally, Islāmic psychotherapy integrates evidence-based psychological theories and practices with Islāmic teachings and values. It emphasises the compatibility between psychology and Islām, utilising psychological approaches supported by empirical research while remaining consistent with Islāmic ethical guidelines. This field continues to grow and adapt, highlighting the ongoing importance of combining Islāmic spirituality with psychological principles to support individuals on their journeys towards mental, emotional, and spiritual health.

References

Abdullah, S. (2009). *Islāmic counseling & psychotherapy trends in theory development*. Retrieved September 7, 2023, from www.Islamicity.org/3549/Islamic-counseling-psychotherapy-trends-in-theory-development/.

Ali, S. R., Liu, W. M., & Humedian, M. (2004). Islām 101: Understanding the religion and therapy implications. *Professional Psychology: Research and Practice, 35*(6), 635–642.

Al-Karam, C. Y. (Ed.). (2018). *Islāmically integrated psychotherapy: Uniting faith and professional practice* (Abstract). Templeton Press.

Baqutayan, S. M. S. (2011). An innovative Islāmic counseling. *International Journal of Humanities and Social Science, 1*(21), 178–183.

Charema, J., & Shizha, E. (2008). Counselling indigenous Shona people in Zimbabwe: Traditional practices versus Western Eurocentric perspectives. *AlterNative: An International Journal of Indigenous Peoples, 4*(2), 123–139. https://doi.org/10.1177/117718010800400209.

Hamjah, H. S., & Akhir, M. N. S. (2013). Islāmic approach in counseling. *Journal of Religion and Health, 52*(1), 279–289. https://doi.org/10.1007/s10943-013-9703-4.

Ibn Qayyim al-Jawziyyah. (2020). *Ranks of the divine seekers [Madārij As Salikīn]* (Vol. 3/156). Brill (English).

Johansen, T. M. (2005). Applying individual psychology to work with clients of the Islāmic faith. *Journal of Individual Psychology, 6*(2), 174–184.

Keshavarzi, H., Khan, F., Ali, B., & Awaad, R. (2021). *Applying Islāmic principles to clinical mental health care: Introducing traditional Islāmically integrated psychotherapy.* Routledge.

McLeish, K. (1995). *Key ideas in human thought.* Prima Publishing.

Muslim (a). *Sunnah.com reference: Hadīth 7, 40 Hadīth an-Nawawi.* Retrieved September 5, 2023, from https://sunnah.com/nawawi40:7.

Muslim (b). *Sunnah.com reference: Book 16, Hadīth 1* (English translation: Book 16, Hadīth 1481. Arabic reference: Book 16, Hadīth 1437). Retrieved September 5, 2023.

Muslim Family Matters (n.d.). Islāmic Counselling. http://www.muslimfamilymatters.com/component/zoo/item/islamic-counselling-courses, (accessed 27 June 2024).

Nolan, G., & West, W. (2015). Introduction. In G. Nolan & W. West (Eds.), *Therapy, culture and spirituality.* Palgrave Macmillan.

Rassool, G. Hussein (2016). *Islāmic counselling: An introduction to theory and practice.* Routledge.

Rassool, G. Hussein (2018). Towards the development of a theoretical framework and model of Islāmic psychotherapy and counselling: Challenges and opportunities (Unpublished paper).

Rassool, G. Hussein (2019). Chapter 22: Islāmic counselling: The Dodo Bird revival. In G. Hussein Rassool (Ed.), *Evil eye, Jinn possession and mental health issues from an Islāmic perspective.* Routledge.

Rassool, G. Hussein (2020). *Towards a redefinition of Islāmic psychotherapy and counselling* (Lecture at Al-Balagh Academy. Islāmic Counselling and Psychology-Level 2, July 2020).

Rassool, G. Hussein (2021). Re-examining the anatomy of Islāmic psychotherapy and counselling: Envisioned and enacted practices. *Islāmic Guidance and Counseling Journal, 4*(2). https://doi.org/10.25217/.

Rassool, G. Hussein (2023a). *Advancing Islāmic psychology education: Knowledge integration, model, and application.* Routledge.

Rassool, G. Hussein (2023b). *Islāmic psychology: The basics.* Routledge.

Rassool, G. Hussein (2023c). The Fitrah: The spiritual nature of human behaviour. In G. Hussein Rassool (Ed.), *Islāmic psychology: The basics* (pp. 98–117). Routledge.

Rassool, G. Hussein, & Luqman, M. M. (2023). *Foundations of Islāmic psychology from classical scholars to contemporary thinkers.* Routledge.

Sakoon.co.uk. *What is Islāmic counselling.* Retrieved September 7, 2023, from www.sakoon.co.uk/counselling/what-is-Islamic-counselling/.

Tirmidhî. *Jami'at-Tirmidhî 3375* (In-book reference: Book 48, Hadīth 6. English translation: Vol. 6, Book 45, Hadīth 3375). Hasan (Darussalam). https://sunnah.com/tirmidhi:3375.

Zakaria, N., & Akhir, N. S. M. (2016). Redefining Islāmic counseling according to the perspective of Malaysian Muslim counselors. *Advanced Science Letters, 22*(9), 2215–2219. https://doi.org/10.1166/asl.2016.7570.

3
UNVEILING THE ROLE OF THE ISLĀMIC PSYCHOTHERAPIST

Exploring the nature and scope of psychotherapy

Introduction

Islāmic psychotherapy is a versatile field grounded in Islāmic principles and values, offering support for a wide range of mental health and well-being issues. It addresses challenges such as mental health disorders, emotional struggles, alcohol and substance use disorders, trauma, identity crises, grief, and spiritual turmoil. Islāmic psychotherapy is inclusive and can be applied in various settings, including individual, group, couples, and family therapy sessions. It caters to Muslims seeking therapy aligned with their Islāmic beliefs and individuals from diverse cultural backgrounds interested in integrating spirituality into their therapeutic journey. Therapeutic techniques in Islāmic psychotherapy blend spiritual practices like Qur'ânic and *Sunnah* integration with evidence-based psychological interventions.

Islāmic psychotherapy employs a holistic approach that integrates elements from various therapeutic modalities, including cognitive–behavioural therapy (CBT), acceptance and commitment therapy, solution-focused brief therapy (SFBT), narrative therapy, humanistic therapy, and marital and couples therapy. The goal is to provide culturally sensitive and spiritually integrated support to individuals seeking mental health and emotional well-being while adhering to Islāmic principles. Therapists offer flexibility in therapy styles, including directive, non-directive, integrated, and eclectic approaches, adjusting their techniques to meet the unique needs and preferences of clients. This approach allows Islāmic psychotherapy to provide effective support tailored to individual requirements while respecting Muslims' cultural and spiritual backgrounds. This chapter aims to explore the nature, scope, and key components of Islāmic psychotherapy, including the roles of Islāmic psychotherapists.

36 The essence of Islāmic therapy

Nature and scope of Islāmic psychotherapy

The scope of Islāmic psychotherapy is multifaceted and encompasses a wide range of psychological and spiritual issues within the framework of Islāmic principles and values. Therapists integrate Islāmic principles and psychological techniques to help clients manage and overcome these challenges, emphasising psychospiritual well-being and strengthening the connection with Allāh through practices like prayer (*salah*), Qur'ân recitation, and *dhikr* (remembrance of Allāh). Islāmic psychotherapy provides emotional support and therapy for individuals experiencing distress, relationship problems, and personal crises, focusing on developing resilience and coping strategies rooted in Islāmic teachings. Additionally, it extends its scope to include family and marital therapy, assisting couples in navigating conflicts and fostering healthy relationships based on Islāmic values.

Islāmic psychotherapy is adaptable to various settings, including individual, couples, family, and group therapy, catering to diverse populations. It serves

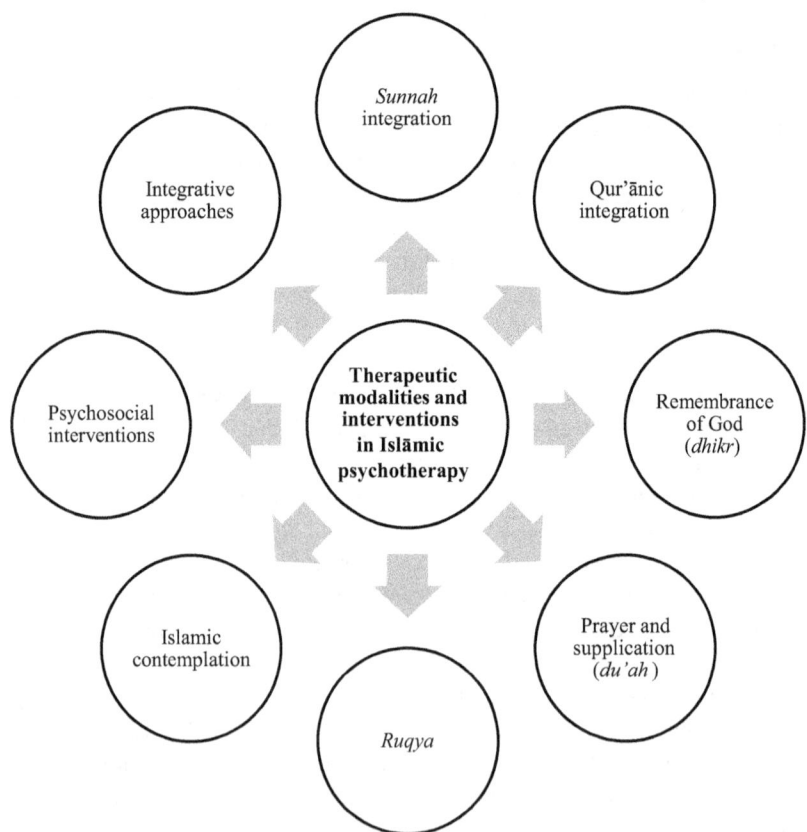

FIGURE 3.1 The therapeutic modalities in Islāmic psychotherapy.

Muslims seeking therapy while honouring their Islāmic beliefs and individuals from different cultural backgrounds interested in integrating spirituality into their therapeutic journeys. It also utilises a diverse array of therapeutic techniques and approaches, including spiritual interventions such as Qur'ānic integration, *Sunnah* integration, remembrance of God (*dhikr*), prayer and supplication (*dua'h*), incantation (*ruqya*), and contemplation. Beyond addressing specific psychological issues, Islāmic psychotherapy tackles challenges related to the Muslim community and culture. Therapists assist clients in navigating cultural expectations, community pressures, and acculturation while preserving their Islāmic identities. They may also offer psycho-educational programmes and workshops to raise awareness about mental health issues, promote early intervention, and provide tools for maintaining psychological and spiritual well-being within the Muslim community.

It is worth emphasising that the scope of Islāmic psychotherapy can differ based on the therapist's training, expertise, and approach. Some therapists may concentrate on the integration of Islāmic principles, while others might combine Islāmic and mainstream psychological theories and methods. Nevertheless, the overarching objective remains consistent: to offer psychospiritual assistance and healing while upholding Islāmic values and teachings. Clients seeking Islāmic psychotherapy can anticipate culturally sensitive and spiritually integrated approaches to addressing their mental health and emotional well-being.

Styles of therapy

Islāmic psychotherapy, akin to traditional psychotherapy, incorporates various therapeutic styles tailored to address diverse client needs. Therapists may employ directive, non-directive, and integrated approaches, each with its unique principles and techniques, adaptable to different therapeutic contexts based on client requirements and therapist expertise. Unlike mainstream therapy, where therapists often prefer one approach, Islāmic psychotherapy stands out by integrating both directive and non-directive elements, providing a more comprehensive and holistic approach to care. Consequently, the field of Islāmic psychotherapy encompasses a range of styles, including directive and non-directive methods.

Directive style in therapy

The directive approach in psychotherapy involves the therapist taking an active and guiding role in the therapeutic process. Therapists provide guidance, advice, and interventions based on Islāmic principles to help clients address their issues and achieve therapeutic goals. This approach is structured and goal oriented, with therapists taking on an expert or authoritative role and offering clear instructions and strategies to clients. Directive approaches such as CBT, gestalt therapy, and SFBT are effective for clients who require clear guidance and have limited problem-solving skills. They offer efficient methods for problem-solving, providing short-term solutions, and they may be necessary when clients struggle to understand the consequences of their behaviour.

In Islāmic psychotherapy, the directive approach involves the therapist actively providing guidance, advice, and specific directives rooted in Islāmic principles, teachings, and ethical guidelines. This may include drawing upon Islāmic literature, Qur'ânic verses, *Sunnah*, and Islāmic jurisprudence (*fiqh*) to offer practical solutions and interventions tailored to the client's needs. For example, therapists may help clients apply Islāmic ethical frameworks in decision-making, teach the importance of gratitude (*shukr*) to overcome depression, offer Islāmic techniques for anger management, or guide clients struggling with anxiety to reflect on Qur'ânic verses that can offer guidance or emphasising Allāh's mercy. This approach is beneficial for clients seeking clear instructions or immediate guidance aligned with their Islāmic values. CBT, a directive approach used in Islāmic psychotherapy, focuses on changing individuals' self-beliefs and often involves tasks or homework between sessions, with the therapist acting as an advisor and educator to facilitate change.

Research suggests that many Muslims prefer directive approaches in psychotherapy to non-directive approaches (Kesharvarzi & Haque, 2013; Mir et al., 2015) as they feel more comfortable with therapists who provide guidance and actively direct the therapeutic process. This preference may stem from cultural and religious backgrounds that emphasise respect for authority and seeking guidance from knowledgeable individuals. Certain aspects of CBT align closely with the preferences and expectations of some Muslims from Arab and South Asian cultures, who appreciate structured learning and guidance (Haque, 2004). In these cultures, the dynamics between Muslim therapists and their clients can resemble those between teachers and learners (Al Issa, 2000), with Muslim clinicians often needing to adopt more directive and assertive approaches than Western therapists. This is because Arab and South Asian cultures value expert advice and self-disclosure, contrasting with the more non-directive approach common in Western cultures. Therapists should adapt their approaches to meet the specific needs and preferences of their Muslim clients, recognising that individual preferences may vary.

Non-directive style in therapy

The non-directive style, also known as client-centred or person-centred therapy, prioritises creating a non-judgmental, empathetic, and supportive therapeutic environment where clients are encouraged to explore their thoughts, feelings, and experiences at their own pace. Therapists refrain from giving advice or direction, instead taking a facilitative role and allowing clients to freely explore their thoughts and emotions; the focus is on creating a safe space for self-expression, self-reflection, and personal growth. Therapists provide unconditional positive regard and empathy, serving as active listeners rather than experts. This approach is less structured and allows clients to lead the conversation, emphasising their perceptions of problems over the problems themselves.

Non-directive therapy, developed by Carl Rogers and his colleagues, is a foundational aspect of person-centred therapy. The goal is to help clients discover their thoughts and emotions to understand their worldviews or frames of reference. Initially termed "non-directive therapy," it evolved into "client-centred" and eventually "person-centred" therapy. Person-centred counselling emphasises client engagement and the quality of the client–therapist relationship, with minimal use of techniques.

Some proponents advocate a non-directive approach to therapy with Muslim clients, suggesting that it can be suitable within Islāmic culture. However, findings from Al-Thani and Moore's (2012) study, although supportive of this approach, cannot be generalised to the entire Muslim population or those with Islāmic cultural backgrounds due to its limited sample size and context specificity within Qatari society. Thus, those authors tend to favour therapies offering a more structured and directive approach.

It is important to acknowledge the diversity within Muslim communities worldwide, as cultural, social, and individual differences can influence how individuals perceive and engage with therapy. Amer and Jalal (2012) argue that while non-directive approaches like Rogerian therapy may suit some Muslims raised in the West, immigrants and those from Arab, Asian, and Central and South American backgrounds may prefer therapists who are more directive. Dwairy (2006) suggests that Muslim Arab clients may feel disappointed and confused with non-directive humanistic approaches, often leading to premature termination of therapy; thus, they tend to favour therapies offering a more structured and directive approach. In an Islāmic cultural context, the non-directive approach may not be suitable for all clients. Some may require more direct guidance or interventions tailored to their specific needs. Islāmic psychotherapists must remain flexible and adaptable, employing a range of therapeutic techniques and approaches to address clients' holistic needs effectively.

Integrated therapy

In essence, the integrated approach to therapy combines elements from both directive and non-directive styles, aiming to foster growth, healing, and well-being while respecting the client's unique needs and spiritual connection. Therapists in integrated therapy follow a specific theoretical framework that guides the integration process, harmoniously blending elements from various theories to create a unified and structured approach. Techniques from CBT, SFBT, and client-centred therapy are integrated with Islāmic principles, teachings, and values. This approach recognises the importance of clients' faith and spirituality, aiming to enhance complementarity between different theories. Integrated therapy also takes a holistic view of the clients, considering their psychological, emotional, social, and spiritual dimensions of health. A summary of directive, non-directive, and integrated therapeutic styles is presented in Figure 3.2.

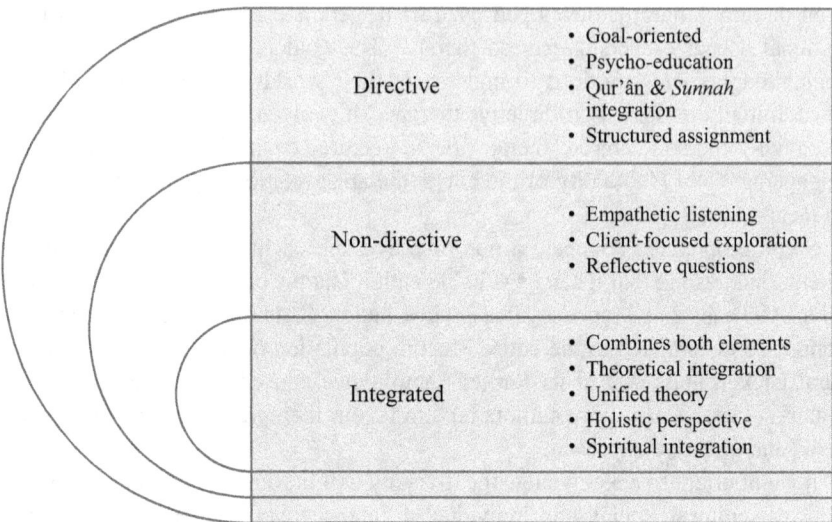

FIGURE 3.2 Directive, non-directive, and integrated approaches to Islāmic psychotherapy.

Integrated styles in Islāmic psychotherapy

Integrated therapy within an Islāmic context involves consciously blending therapeutic theories and approaches with Islāmic traditions and spirituality to create a unified treatment model. Therapists develop frameworks combining various modalities with Islāmic teachings, values, and practices, guided by a clear theoretical foundation. The goal is to provide holistic therapy addressing psychological, spiritual, and cultural dimensions.

Therapists plan and design therapy to ensure the unified integration of concepts and traditions, promoting synergy between psychological interventions and Islāmic spirituality for client benefit, for example integrating the principles of CBT with Islāmic teachings. Therapists work with clients to identify and challenge negative thought patterns and behaviours while incorporating Islāmic concepts like *tawakkul* (trust in Allāh), gratitude (*shukr*), and self-compassion. For example, clients may learn to reframe anxious thoughts by trusting in Allāh's plan and practicing gratitude. In another example, in treating depression, the therapist may incorporate gratitude journaling, which encourages the person to reflect on and express gratitude to Allāh for His blessings. This practice not only aligns with the principles of CBT, such as challenging negative thought patterns, but also incorporates Islāmic teachings on gratitude and reliance on Allāh.

An illustration of the integrated approach can be seen in the utilisation of behavioural exposure techniques combined with Islāmic coping strategies and beliefs to address anxiety or phobias. Therapists work with clients to create exposure hierarchies tailored to their specific fears, gradually exposing them to triggers while incorporating Islāmic coping mechanisms. Clients may practice *dhikr* (remembrance of Allāh) or recite specific supplications or Qur'ânic verses that offer solace and reassurance during exposure exercises. Prayer is also encouraged as a coping mechanism, allowing clients to seek solace and strength from Allāh before, during, and after sessions. This approach not only addresses psychological aspects but also integrates clients' Islāmic faith, enriching therapy with culturally sensitive elements.

In the utilisation of a unified and integrated style, therapists may employ both direct and non-directive approaches in therapeutic encounters. This versatility allows therapists to offer a well-rounded and adaptive form of facilitation and non-facilitation, respecting Islāmic values while addressing clients' mental health concerns. For instance, in the case of a client experiencing anxiety related to personal and spiritual issues, an Islāmic psychotherapist may opt for an integrated approach. Initially, the therapist may take a directive stance, offering guidance on utilising specific Qur'ânic verses or supplications known for their calming effects. This directive step aligns with the therapist's role as a facilitator of Islāmic spiritual practices that aid in managing the client's anxiety.

However, the therapeutic process does not stop there. In the integrated therapeutic approach, the therapist may transition from a directive to a non-directive mode to more deeply explore the underlying causes of the client's anxiety. Initially, the therapist provides guidance on utilising specific Qur'ânic verses. Subsequently, in a non-directive stance, the therapist creates a non-judgmental space for the client to freely express emotions and spiritual concerns, encouraging self-reflection and exploration of anxiety's root causes from an Islāmic perspective. This integrated approach skilfully combines directive elements that incorporate Islāmic teachings with non-directive aspects that prioritise client autonomy and self-exploration.

In an integrated approach, therapists may employ a variety of techniques and strategies based on their training, client needs, and the therapeutic context. This can range from primarily directive or non-directive styles to a combination of modalities tailored to the client's needs. The continuous expansion of knowledge in therapeutic modalities and Islāmic principles is crucial for therapists using this approach to effectively address client needs. While the integrated approach shows promise, empirical research on its effectiveness within Islāmic psychotherapy is limited. Further research is needed to explore and validate the outcomes and benefits of this approach for individuals seeking therapy within an Islāmic framework.

Integrated therapy from an Islāmic perspective

Integrated therapy involves merging techniques from different schools of thought, therapeutic modalities, and theoretical orientations. Unlike eclectic therapy, which also incorporates techniques from different modalities, integrated therapy emphasises a unified approach rather than simply selecting techniques based on pragmatic considerations. This adaptability enables therapists to cater to clients' diverse needs while respecting Islāmic principles. For example, CBT techniques like cognitive restructuring may be combined with Islāmic affirmations to help clients challenge negative thought patterns while incorporating Islāmic values. By integrating Qur'ânic verses and *hadîths*, clients are encouraged to replace negative self-talk with positive Islāmic affirmations. For instance, clients can repeat affirmations that emphasise their value as a creation of Allāh or themselves as examples of the limitless mercy of Allāh. When a client struggles with self-worth, the therapist may encourage them to repeat affirmations such as "I am a valuable creation of Allāh "or "Allāh's mercy is infinite." One verse from the Qur'ân that highlights the infinite mercy of Allāh is the following:

وَرَحْمَتِى وَسِعَتْ كُلَّ شَىْءٍ

- *And My mercy encompasses all things.*
  (Al-A'raf, 7:156, interpretation of the meaning)

This verse serves as a reminder of Allāh's boundless compassion, forgiveness, and love for His creation.

An Islāmically modified CBT can be used in an integrated approach. For instance, when working with a client experiencing anxiety, the therapist first conducts a thorough assessment to understand the client's specific concerns and thought patterns and then introduces the Islāmically modified CBT techniques, which typically involve identifying and challenging negative thought patterns and beliefs. In the context of Islāmic teachings, the therapist can encourage the client to explore relevant Qur'ânic verses and *hadîths* that emphasise trust in Allāh's plan and reliance (*tawakkul*) on Him during times of distress. For example, the therapist may guide the client to reflect on Qur'ânic verses that highlight Allāh's promise to be with those who place their trust in Him (Quran 65:3):

وَمَن يَتَوَكَّلْ عَلَى ٱللَّهِ فَهُوَ حَسْبُهُ

- *And whoever puts their trust in Allāh, then He 'alone' is sufficient for them.*
  (At-Talaq 65:3, interpretation of the meaning)

Other examples include *hadîths* that emphasise the importance of supplication (*du'ah*) in seeking relief from anxiety. These Islāmic teachings can be integrated into cognitive restructuring exercises. The therapist helps the client recognise negative thought patterns related to anxiety and encourages them to replace these thoughts with Qur'ânic verses or supplications that instil a sense of trust in Allāh's predestination (*qadr*) and control.

Through consistent practice, the client can gradually reframe their thought patterns and experience reduced anxiety while drawing strength from their faith. Narrative therapy with Islāmic life story combines narrative therapy techniques with exploration of clients' faith and spiritual journeys within Islām. Therapists help clients examine how their faith provided hope and inner strength during challenges, reframing their life narratives for empowerment. Clients and therapists identify Islāmic values like trust in Allah's plans (*tawakkul*), forgiveness (*maghfirah*), and gratitude (*shukr*), exploring their influence on experiences and relationships. This integrated approach addresses psychological aspects while enriching the therapeutic process with culturally sensitive elements aligned with the client's Islāmic faith. Integrated therapy can be tailored to incorporate Islāmic principles, values, and teachings, making it culturally sensitive and effective for Muslim clients.

Islāmic psychotherapist's competence

The role of an Islāmic psychotherapist is vital in providing guidance and support to individuals who seek assistance through Islāmic psychotherapy. For a comprehensive account of the role, competence, and scope of practice of the Islāmic psychotherapist, see Rassool (2023, Chapter 4). Competence in Islāmic psychology is a fluid process based on a continuum where different components of competency can be expanded.

I developed a model for building the competence of Islāmic psychotherapists based on four specific domains in which any psychotherapist should retain competence during their career development (Rassool, 2023): "The domains of competence include Islāmic ethics, fundamental competencies, functional competencies, and developmental competencies" (p. 84). The first domain is Islāmic ethics ('*akhlaq*), which derive from the Qur'ān and *Sunnah*. The second domain is fundamental competencies; these are the knowledge and values which underlie the function of the Islāmic psychotherapist. The roles are subdivided into specific and enabling roles. The third domain of the proposed model is functional competencies,

> which encompass the professional activities of the Islāmic psychotherapist. The competencies focus on therapeutic skills, assessment, therapeutic interventions, research, clinical supervision, and education and training. The practitioner should have embedded in their clinical and professional practice values, virtues, and morals grounded in the Islāmic tradition.
> *(Rassool, 2023, p. 90)*

The final domain is continuing professional development:

> This set of competencies addresses the requirement to keep up to date on knowledge and address any knowledge gaps after the completion of training as a psychotherapist, because psychology knowledge is constantly growing and changing, which makes area of competency a lifelong goal.
> *(Rassool, 2023, p. 93)*

Roles of an Islāmic psychotherapist

Table 3.1 summarises the roles and responsibilities of Islāmic psychotherapists.

TABLE 3.1 Some key aspects of the generic roles of an Islāmic psychotherapist

Key role	Role
Islāmic knowledge and expertise	Demonstrating sound knowledge of the Qur'ân, the *hadīths*, and Islāmic jurisprudence relevant to mental health and well-being
Assessment and diagnosis	Conducting interviews, evaluations, and assessments to assess the nature and severity of clients' emotional and psychological issues
Care planning	Developing an individualised care plan tailored to the client's specific concerns and goals
Incorporating Islāmic values	Integrating Islāmic principles, ethics, and values into the therapeutic process
Cultural competence	Considering clients' cultural and religious contexts
Therapy & support	Utilising evidence-based therapeutic techniques and interventions to facilitate healing and personal growth
Spiritual guidance	Strengthening clients' connections with their faith and spirituality; engaging in acts of worship or seek forgiveness and repentance
Education and awareness	Reducing the stigma associated with mental health in the Muslim community and promoting awareness of available resources
Collaboration	Working as part of a multidisciplinary team; collaborating with Islāmic scholars, faith leaders, or *imams*
Referral	Referring clients to specialists or scholars when appropriate
Ethics and confidentiality	Prioritising confidentiality to ensure that clients feel comfortable sharing their thoughts, emotions, and concerns during therapy; dealing with ethical dilemmas
Advocacy/Outreach	Empowering individuals; policy and system-level advocacy; collaborating with faith leaders; marshalling community resources and support; community outreach to raise awareness about mental health issues
Continuing education and professional development	Keeping updated on the latest research, therapeutic techniques, and approaches in Islāmic psychotherapy; undertaking regular clinical supervision
Research	Research is vital for Islāmic psychotherapists to develop culturally sensitive interventions and deepen their understanding of mental health within the context of Islāmic beliefs, values, and cultural norms. It helps refine approaches and contributes to advancing knowledge in the field.

In relation to having Islāmic knowledge and expertise, there is the prerequisite that Islāmic psychotherapists should have a formal academic background in psychology and psychotherapy and have knowledge in the fundamentals of Islāmic belief/creed (*aqeedah*), principles of Islāmic law (*usul al-fiqh*), principles of *hādīth* and *hādīth* methodology, *seerah*, *tafsir* (exegesis), and Qur'ānic science. This is in contrast with traditional Islāmic integrated psychotherapy (TIIP), which requires therapists (*Khalil/Rafiq*) to have

> proficiency in Arabic; prerequisite courses in Islāmic studies; basic Islāmic law (*mukhtasạ r al-qudūrī* or its equivalent); basic Islāmic theology (*sharḥ al-ʿaqīdah al-ṭaḥāwiyyah* and *badʾ al-amālī*); *hādīth* studies (*riyāḍ al-sāliḥīn* and *mishkāt al-masʾābīḥ*); and Qurʾān studies (*tarjumat al-Qurʾān* and *tafsīr al-jalālayn/al-nasafī*) (the latter being taught for therapists specifically).
>
> *(Khan et al., 2021, p. 52)*

Rassool (2023) argues that

> an Islāmic therapist may not need to be proficient in Arabic to attain a good comprehension of Islām or Islāmic psychotherapy. However, they should be able to recite the Qur'ān with adequate *tajweed* (rules), which may come into use in the therapeutic process with clients. This could be supplemented by the use of *Tafsir* of the Qur'ān in English language.
>
> *(p. 88)*

The fundamental role of the Islāmic psychotherapist involves assessing clients' emotional and psychological issues through interviews and evaluations. This information guides the development of personalised treatment plans considering clients' concerns, goals, and cultural/religious backgrounds. However, in certain types of psychotherapy, diagnosis may be considered taboo or approached cautiously, especially in therapies that reject traditional diagnostic labels and prioritise a non-pathological or anti-diagnostic stance. These approaches, such as the anti-psychiatry movement (Szasz, 1961), humanistic and existential therapies, narrative therapy, postmodern approaches, and cultural considerations, challenge the traditional use of diagnostic labels and advocate understanding individual experiences, personal growth, and empowerment instead. Proponents argue that diagnostic labels can be stigmatising, disempowering, and limiting to individuals' self-exploration and personal development. However, it is important to recognise that the decision to use or avoid diagnoses varies depending on the therapeutic approach, client preferences, specific contexts of therapy, and statutory requirements.

One distinctive aspect of Islāmic psychotherapy is the integration of Islāmic values, ethics, and teachings into the therapeutic process. This involves using Qur'ânic verses, *hādīths*, and other Islāmic resources to offer guidance and support tailored to the client's specific challenges. Islāmic psychotherapy emphasises cultural competence to understand and respect clients' unique backgrounds; referrals to specialists ensure tailored support. Islāmic psychotherapists play a pivotal role in education, awareness, and advocacy within Muslim communities. They strive to reduce mental health stigma by educating clients and communities about mental health issues and available resources. Collaborating with health care professionals, adhering to confidentiality guidelines, and participating in continuous professional development enhance these therapists' effectiveness. Advocacy efforts include destigmatisation, cultural sensitivity, policy change, and empowering individuals to advocate for their mental health. Through these initiatives, Islāmic psychotherapists promote understanding and create a supportive environment for mental health within the Muslim community.

Enabling roles an Islāmic psychotherapist

The enabling roles of the Islāmic psychotherapist are presented in Figure 3.1. These roles include gaining a deep understanding of their Muslim clients' Islāmic worldview, which involves exploring their interpersonal dynamics and comprehending their individual, social, and community orientations. This understanding encompasses factors such as familial ties, cultural backgrounds, and religious beliefs viewed through an Islāmic lens. Recognising the client's cultural perspectives, as emphasised by Ibrahim (1985), is crucial for establishing rapport and building a trusting therapeutic relationship. When therapists are sensitive to their clients' cultural and religious perspectives, it cultivates a sense of connection and resonance. Additionally, if the therapist and the client share a common Islāmic worldview, it strengthens the client's trust in the therapeutic process. This trust is pivotal for fostering hope and optimism, which are transformative elements in therapy, facilitating solutions (Frank and Frank, 1991).

In contrast to conventional psychotherapy, the enabling role of an Islāmic psychotherapist includes the practice of offering advice, which is traditionally viewed as a therapeutic error in mainstream therapy. However, recent evidence suggests that advice giving in psychotherapy can be context dependent, influenced by cultural and social factors, as well as variables related to both the client and therapist (Duan et al., 2018). In Islāmic psychotherapy, the act of offering advice is considered essential within the Islāmic faith, reflecting a distinct approach to therapy rooted in religious teachings. This divergence in the approach to advice giving in Islāmic psychotherapy can be rooted in religious teachings.

In an Islāmic context, offering advice is considered an essential element of the faith. Prophet Muhammad (ﷺ) emphasised the concept of *naseehah*, which translates to advice and sincerity. According to a *hādīth* narrated by Tameem ibn Aus ad-Daree, the Prophet stated that "The *deen* (religion) is *naseehah* (advice, sincerity)" (Muslim). In Islāmic psychotherapy, the principles of sincerity and advice, as emphasised by Ibn Kathir (2000), highlight the importance of guiding individuals in the Muslim community towards actions and decisions that serve their best interests. This principle aligns with the broader notion of advice giving in Islāmic psychotherapy, where therapists offer guidance considering the spiritual and cultural dimensions of the client's life.

In Islām, sincere advice entails a comprehensive set of principles articulated by scholars like Ibn Rajab (may Allāh have mercy on him). It begins with a genuine love for others, desiring for them what one desires for oneself and actively detesting what one dislikes for oneself. This foundation includes empathy, compassion for well-being, reverence for elders, and sharing in moments of grief and joy. Sincere advice also involves prioritising the collective welfare of the Muslim community over personal gain, making sacrifices for the greater good, and avoiding anything harmful to the community. Ultimately, sincere advice reflects a sincere desire for others' well-being, encompassing genuine love, hope for harmony and unity, and fervent prayers for success and protection. As Ibn Rajab (2018) stated, sincere advice aims for all kinds of good for the recipient, seeking to achieve it sincerely. In a *hadîth*, Abu Hurayrah said, "I heard the Messenger of Allāh (ﷺ) say, 'The rights a Muslim has over another Muslim are six' and then he mentioned that among them is 'When he asks him for advice, he should give him good counsel'" (Al-Adab Al-Mufrad). Rassool (2016) suggested the following:

> Giving *naseehah* involves guiding them towards that which will correct their affairs in both this life and the next. It involves protecting them from harm, helping them in times of need, providing what is beneficial for them, encouraging them to do good, and forbidding them from evil with kindness and sincerity, and showing mercy towards them.
>
> *(Rassool, 2016, p. 18)*

In addition, *naseehah* entails enjoining what is good (*al-ma'roof*) and forbidding what is evil (*al-munkar*) with kindness and sincerity while also demonstrating mercy towards others. According to Rassool (2016), the act of giving advice (*naseehah*) is considered a communal obligation (*fard kifayah*). This means that if a satisfactory number of people fulfil this obligation, then the responsibility is lifted from the community as a whole, and it becomes an individual obligation based on one's ability. Allāh, may He be exalted, says the following in the Qur'ān:

ادْعُ إِلَىٰ سَبِيلِ رَبِّكَ بِٱلْحِكْمَةِ وَٱلْمَوْعِظَةِ ٱلْحَسَنَةِ ۖ وَجَٰدِلْهُم بِٱلَّتِى هِىَ أَحْسَنُ

- *Invite to the way of your Lord with wisdom and good instruction and argue with them in a way that is best.*

  (An-Nahl 16:125, interpretation of the meaning)

Advice should be given based on knowledge and clear proof. As-Saʿdi (may Allāh have mercy on him) said,

> Wisdom dictates that giving advice to others should be done on the basis of knowledge, not ignorance, and that one should start with that which is more important, then that which is less important, and with that which is easy to explain and understand, and that which is more likely to be accepted. The advice should be given in a kind and gentle manner. If the person to whom the advice is given pays heed to this approach, which is based on wisdom, all well and good; otherwise, we should move on to exhorting him with good instruction, which means enjoining what is right and forbidding what is wrong, accompanied by mention of the reward from Allāh for doing good and the punishment for doing wrong.
>
> (As-saʿdi, n.d., p. 452)

One neglected role of an effective therapist is the instillation of hope; instilling hope is an important part of psychotherapy and counselling, especially in existential psychotherapy. Yalom (2005) cites it as the first of eleven "primary factors" in the therapeutic experience. The instillation of hope is also important in Islāmic psychotherapy and counselling. Rassool (2023) explains that

> the instillation of hope offers a path back to a sense of possibility in our lives when almost all seems lost. For believers, it is asking God, the Almighty, to offer forgiveness, true blessings, and hope in trials and tribulations. Allāh informs us in the Qur'ān that with difficulty there is ease, and then He reaffirms this information (by repeating it).
>
> (p. 78)

فَإِنَّ مَعَ ٱلْعُسْرِ يُسْرًا
إِنَّ مَعَ ٱلْعُسْرِ يُسْرًا

- *For indeed, with hardship* [will be] *ease* [i.e. relief]. *Indeed, with hardship* [will be] *ease.*

(Ash-Sharh 94:5–6, interpretation of the meaning)

Hope is an important element within the Islāmic spiritual framework, serving as a beacon for improvement and future ease. In Islāmic psychotherapy, hope therapy (Cheavens & Guter, 2018) integrates narrative, solution-focused, and cognitive–behavioural techniques. Rassool and Khan (2023) suggested that Islāmic hope therapy entails a therapeutic approach that centres on the concept of God's Mercy and the profound meaning and purpose of life. This approach cultivates a potent spiritual motivation within the client, ultimately reducing vulnerability to conditions like depression and anxiety by fortifying individuals' trust and faith. It is recommended that psychotherapists incorporate hope therapy into Islāmic psychotherapy to expedite the process of healing.

Islāmic psychotherapists can contribute to the training and supervision of other staff in the practice of Islāmically modified psychosocial interventions and spiritual healing. They perform their clinical roles according to rigorous ethical principles and codes of conduct. The TIIP practitioner, according to Khan et al. (2021), embodies a unique role that combines elements of a clinician and a *shaykh*, termed Rafiq/Khalil. Unlike a Sufi *shaykh* or a conventional clinician, the TIIP therapist integrates Islāmic and clinical methods within an Islāmic worldview, aligning with Islām's foundational principles of change. This approach draws from Sufi traditions and ideologies, reflecting a holistic understanding of therapy that encompasses spiritual and psychological dimensions.

The proposition of attaining the level of Rafiq/Khalil practitioners as outlined in Khan et al.'s model (2021) integrates modern behavioural research into Islāmic principles. However, the comparison with "The Emperor's New Clothes" raises doubts about the practicality and realism of rapidly training Islāmic psychotherapists in this model. It questions whether clinicians possess the necessary qualities and knowledge to achieve this expertise and whether individuals claiming to be pseudo *shaykhs* can effectively facilitate change in Muslim clients without sufficient evidence to support their efficacy and effectiveness. To excel in Islāmic psychotherapy, practitioners must integrate faith (*iman*), knowledge (*ilm*), good character ('*akhlaq*), and the qualities of a "master" therapist. This synthesis enables practitioners to offer high-quality care, addressing both psychological and spiritual aspects of clients' well-being within Islāmic values.

Conclusion

It is essential for individuals seeking therapy from an Islāmic psychotherapist to ensure that the therapist is qualified and licensed and has the necessary expertise in both mental health and Islāmic studies to provide effective and ethical care. In conclusion, the role of an Islāmic psychotherapist is multifaceted, encompassing expertise in Islāmic knowledge, individualised treatment planning, psychotherapy or counselling, and spiritual support. By integrating Islāmic teachings and principles into therapy, these professionals provide holistic care and guidance, promoting emotional, psychological, and spiritual well-being within the framework of Islām.

References

Al-Adab Al-Mufrad. *Al-Adab Al-Mufrad 991* (In-book reference: Book 42, Hadîth 27. English translation: Book 42, Hadîth 991). Sahih (Al-Albani). https://sunnah.com/adab:991

Al-Issa, I. (2000). *Al-Junun: Mental illness in the Islāmic world.* International Universities Press, Inc.

Al-Thani, A., & Moore, J. (2012). Nondirective counselling in Islāmic culture in the Middle East explored through the work of one Muslim person-centered counselor in the State of Qatar. *Person-Centered & Experiential Psychotherapies, 11*(3), 190–204.

Amer, M., & Jalal, B. (2012). Individual psychotherapy/counseling. In S. Ahmed & M. M. Amer (Eds.), *Counselling Muslims: Handbook of mental health issues and intervention*. Routledge.

As-Saʿdi. (n.d.). Tafseer as-Saʿdi. Cited in Islām Q&A. (2018). *Etiquette of giving advice*. Retrieved September 10, 2023, from https://Islamqa.info/en/answers/225160/etiquette-of-giving-advice.

Cheavens, J. S., & Guter, M. M. (2018). Hope therapy. In M. W. Gallagher & S. J. Lopez (Eds.), *The Oxford handbook of hope* (pp. 133–142). Oxford University Press.

Duan, C., Knox, S., & Hill, C. E. (2018). Advice giving in psychotherapy. In E. L. MacGeorge & L. M. Van Swol (Eds.), *The Oxford handbook of advice* (online). Oxford Handbook Online. http//doi.org/10.1093/oxfordhb/9780190630188.013.11.

Dwairy, M. (2006). *Counseling and psychotherapy with Arabs and Muslims: A culturally sensitive approach*. Teachers College Press.

Frank, J. D., & Frank, J. B. (1991). *Persuasion and healing: A comparative study of psychotherapy*. Johns Hopkins University Press.

Haque, A. (2004). Psychology from Islāmic perspective: Contributions of early Muslim scholars and challenges to contemporary Muslim psychologists. *Journal of Religion and Health, 43*(4), 357–377. https://doi.org/10.1007/s10943-004-4302-z.

Ibn Kathir. (2000). *Tafsir ibn Kathir* (J. Abualrub, N. Khitab, H. Khitab, A. Walker, M. Al-Jibali, & S. Ayoub, Trans.). Darussalam Publishers and Distributors.

Ibn Rajab. (2018). *Jaami ʿal-ʿUloom waʾl-Hukam* (p. 80) [cited in Islām Q&A. (2018). *Etiquette of giving advice*. Retrieved September 10, 2023, from https://Islamqa.info/en/answers/225160/etiquette-of-giving-advice].

Ibrahim, F. A. (1985). Effective cross-cultural counseling and psychotherapy: A frame-work. *The Counseling Psychologist, 13*, 625–638.

Kesharvarzi, H., & Haque, A. (2013). Outlining a psychotherapy model for enhancing Muslim mental health within an Islāmic context. *The International Journal for the Psychology of Religion, 23*(3), 230–249.

Khan, F., Keshavarzi, H., & Rothman, A. (2021). The role of the TIIP, therapist scope of practice and proposed competencies. In H. Keshavarzi, F. Khan, B. Ali, & R. Awaad (Eds.), *Applying Islāmic principles to clinical mental health care: Introducing traditional Islāmic ally integrated psychotherapy* (pp. 38–66). Routledge.

Mir, G., Meer, S., Cottrell, D., Mcmillan, D., House, A., & Kanter, J. W. (2015). Adapted behavioural activation for the treatment of depression in Muslims. *Journal of Affective Disorders, 180*, 190–199. https://doi.org/10.1016/j.jad.2015.03.060

Muslim. Hadîth #7. Zarabozo, J. M. (2008). *Commentary on the forty Hadîth of Al-Nawawi* (Vol. 1, p. 397). Al-Basheer Company for Publications and Translations.

Rassool, G. Hussein (2016). *Islāmic counselling: An introduction to theory and practice*. Routledge.

Rassool, G. Hussein (2023). Role, competence, and scope of practice of the Islāmic psychotherapist. In G. Hussein Rassool (Ed.), *Islāmic psychology: The basics*. Routledge.

Rassool, G. Hussein, & Khan, W. N. A. (2023). Hope in Islāmic psychotherapy. *Journal of Spirituality in Mental Health*. https://doi.org/10.1080/19349637.2023.2207751.

Szasz, T. (1961). *The myth of mental illness*. Harper & Row.

Yalom, I. D. (2005). *The theory and practice of group psychotherapy* (5th ed.). Basic Books.

4
ETHICAL FRAMEWORK IN ISLĀMIC PSYCHOTHERAPY

Introduction

Ethics is a branch of philosophy dealing with moral issues and moral judgements. It is defined as "the moral principles that govern a person's behaviour or the conducting of an activity" (Oxford Dictionaries, 2024). Ethics in psychotherapy and counselling involves moral principles governing professional behaviour and activities. Professional organisations emphasise cultural competence and sensitivity to foster ethical practice, especially in multicultural therapy settings (Sue & Sue, 2012). Ethical codes establish standards and protect clients from harm. Therapists working with Muslim clients must understand Islāmic practices and ethical principles to prevent or minimise ethical dilemmas and value diverse perspectives on ethical decision-making. This chapter aims to explore the perspectives of universal ethics and the ethical framework applicable to Islāmic psychotherapy. It will provide an overview of the sources and guiding principles of Islāmic law and examines the ethical dilemma and considerations faced by practitioners when working with Muslim clients.

Universal ethics and values in psychotherapy

Ethical practice is essential for all psychotherapists and counsellors. The ethical perspectives and decision-making models that prevail are primarily based on Western values, which draw upon Judaeo-Christian tradition (Lovering & Rassool, 2014). In the international milieu, the existence of a set of ethical norms that are applicable to all cultures and religions without exception is a topic of ongoing debate (Winkler, 2022). The discussion on ethical frameworks highlights differing viewpoints regarding universal ethical principles versus cultural relativism. Some advocate for universal ethical standards rooted in shared human values (Anabo et al., 2019), while others emphasise cultural contexts and differing viewpoints (Eshetu, 2017). There is an urgent call for interfaith and intercultural ethics, suggesting that universal ethics can be grounded in natural law, perceived through religious and secular lenses, or based on a supreme principle derived from human nature, particularly human dignity (Winkler, 2022).

The codes of ethics in psychotherapy and counselling are based on universally accepted principles outlined by Beauchamp and Childress (2012):

- Beneficence: psychotherapists are obliged to promote the well-being and benefit of their clients, providing effective interventions.
- Non-maleficence: therapists must avoid causing harm or exploitation to clients and minimise potential negative consequences.
- Fidelity: professionals should fulfil their obligations with integrity, loyalty, and trustworthiness, adhering to ethical standards.
- Autonomy: clients have the right to make independent decisions, and therapists should empower them to do so based on informed choices.
- Justice: fair treatment and equality should be ensured in providing services and access to care, without discrimination or bias.

The foundation of ethical codes in psychotherapy rests on universal values such as beneficence, non-maleficence, fidelity, responsibility, integrity, justice, and respect for people's rights and dignity, as outlined in the American Psychological Association's Ethical Principles of Psychologists and Code of Conduct (APA, 2017). Barnett (2008) adds self-care as a crucial value guiding ethical practice, suggesting that neglecting it can impede the implementation of other ethical values. Principle A of the General Principles of the Ethics Code underscores the significance of self-care in upholding moral standards and promoting the well-being of both professionals and clients. However, Barnett and Teehan (2022) note that while the ethical code mandates that psychotherapists avoid exploitative or harmful behaviours towards clients, it lacks explicit guidance on effectively meeting the individual treatment needs of each client.

Islāmic bioethics and psychoethics

Islāmic bioethics and psychoethics are branches of ethics that analyse moral and ethical dilemmas within the framework of Islāmic principles and values, particularly in the context of medical and psychological practices. Islāmic bioethics, Islāmic guidance on ethical issues related to human life, addresses moral concerns in medical and biological research and applications (Shomali, 2008). Islāmic psychoethics, on the other hand, involves integrating Islāmic beliefs into psychotherapeutic practices in a manner consistent with Islāmic teachings. It offers guidance and standards for therapists to deliver culturally sensitive and morally sound psychological interventions.

Islāmic tradition places great significance on the Qur'ân and *Sunnah* in providing guidance on the complex relationship between medicine and ethics. The development of Prophetic medicine (*tibb al-nabawi*) by scholars such as Ibn al-Qayyim and Al-Dhahabi has significantly influenced discussions on medical care and ethical considerations within the Islāmic tradition. In Islām, there is a theological belief that God is the ultimate healer, capable of both causing and curing illnesses. Therefore, while relying on God for healing is preferred, seeking medical intervention is also encouraged as an expression of trust in God (*tawakkul*).

The study of moral values and medicine in Islāmic tradition has been integrated across various academic fields, including law, theology, Sufism, philosophy, and etiquette (*adab*). Classical scholars like Ibn Rushd, renowned for authoritative works on Islāmic law (*fiqh*); Ibn al-Nafis, known for philosophical contributions and as a Muslim jurist in the Shafi'i school of law; and Abu Abd Allah al-Mazari, a prominent Maliki jurist, have significantly contributed to the development of ethical and moral values within Islāmic thought.

In contemporary times, the study of ethics within the Islāmic tradition has evolved towards interdisciplinary approaches, bridging biomedical sciences with religious scholarship. Unlike classical scholars, contemporary scholars recognise the importance of integrating bioethics and medical ethics within Islāmic discourse. The Islāmic tradition, while not initially delineating bioethics as a distinct field, offers rich insights into the ethical considerations of medicine scattered across various disciplines. Ghaly (2023) emphasises the significance of this interdisciplinary approach in modern Islāmic bioethics, highlighting institutions like the Islāmic Organization for Medical Sciences in Kuwait.

Throughout history, ethical principles within the Islāmic tradition have been applied that reflect a commitment to ethical values in medical practice and research. From the early days of the Islāmic state to contemporary times, scholars have contributed to understanding and implementing ethical considerations within the framework of Islāmic teachings, fostering a dynamic dialogue between medicine, ethics, and religious principles. Ethical guidelines and controls were established for medicine to govern the behaviour of physicians (WHO, 2005), even during the lifetime of Prophet Muhammad (ﷺ).

In the Islāmic Caliphate, measures like inspection and control (*hisbah*) were put in place to ensure the proper conduct of physicians and to hold them accountable for their practices. It was emphasised by Islāmic scholars in the field of law that individuals practicing in a particular field must possess proficiency in their respective areas. These efforts aimed to regulate the field of medicine and uphold its ethical standards within the Islāmic society. The Messenger of Allāh (ﷺ) is narrated to have said, "Anyone who practises medicine when he is not known as a practitioner will be held responsible" (Abū Dāwūd). This statement underlines the importance of accountability in the field of medicine.

In Islāmic ethics, individuals practicing medicine or psychotherapy must hold proper credentials and recognition as health care practitioners, ensuring the welfare and safety of clients. This principle emphasises that Islāmic psychotherapists need specialised knowledge, skills, and training to provide competent care, aligning with broader Islāmic ethical principles of responsibility and accountability. Upholding professional competence is essential, reflecting the Islāmic ethos of fulfilling duties with excellence (*ihsan*) across personal, professional, and social domains. This commitment ensures that clients receive effective therapeutic interventions from qualified professionals who adhere to ethical standards, thereby safeguarding their well-being and upholding Islāmic values.

Islāmic ethics based on the Qur'ân and the *Sunnah*

Islāmic ethics draws from the Qur'ân and the *Sunnah* as its primary sources, forming the foundation of Islāmic law and guiding personal and social conduct. These sources stress universal values such as justice, honesty, compassion, forgiveness, humility, and integrity, applicable to all individuals regardless of background. Respect for others' rights is fundamental within Islāmic ethics.

The concept of *ijtihad* in Islāmic law allows for deductive reasoning and independent legal interpretation, incorporating the consensus and opinions of knowledgeable individuals, scholars, and jurists. This process enables flexibility and adaptability to address societal changes (Doi, 1997), contributing to the evolution of the legal system. The ultimate purpose of ethics in Islām is directed towards the individual, as stated by Al-Attas (2013).

In Islām, individuals perform actions they believe to be good because they are instructed by God and His Messenger. Trusting that their actions will please God, Muslims strive to align their conduct with Islāmic principles and teachings. What Al-Attas (2013) is suggesting is the centrality of God's guidance and approval in shaping the moral behaviour of individuals. In Islām, ethical behaviour is deeply rooted in divine guidance, which motivates Muslims to live moral lives in an effort to obtain God's favour. This state of affairs is not merely a matter of personal preference or societal norms. Some examples of Islāmic ethics in the Qur'ân are presented in Table 4.1.

The following *hadīths* are some of the examples that reflect the comprehensive ethical framework of Islām, encompassing personal conduct, family, society, and the environment. In relation to modesty and decency (*hayaa'*). It is narrated that the Prophet (ﷺ) remarked, "Modesty is part of *Iman* (faith)" (Muslim (a)). For humility (*tawadu*), the Messenger of Allāh (ﷺ) said, "Verily, Allāh has revealed to me that you should adopt humility. So that no one may wrong another and no one may be disdainful and haughty towards another" (Muslim (b)). There is also a *hadīth* that relates to fair treatment (*ihsan*) towards women. According to Abu Hurayrah (may Allāh be pleased with him), the Messenger of Allāh (ﷺ) said, "The believers who show the most perfect Faith are those who have the best behaviour, and the best of you are those who are the best to their wives" (Tirmidhî).

TABLE 4.1 Some examples of Islāmic ethics in the Qur'ân

Ethics	Source	Verses
Compassion and kindness (*rahma*)	Qur'an (16:90)	Indeed, Allāh orders justice and good conduct and giving to relatives and forbids immorality and bad conduct and oppression. He admonishes you that perhaps you will be reminded.
Charity and generosity (*sadaqah*)	Qur'an (2:267)	O you who have believed, spend from the good things which you have earned and from that which We have produced for you from the earth. And do not aim towards the defective therefrom, spending [from that] while you would not take it [yourself] except with closed eyes. And know that Allāh is Free of need and Praiseworthy.
Forgiveness (*maghfirah*)	Qur'an (3:134)	Who spend [in the cause of Allāh] during ease and hardship and who restrain anger and who pardon the people – and Allāh loves the doers of good.
Justice (*adl*)	Qur'an (4:58)	Indeed, Allāh commands you to render trusts to whom they are due and when you judge between people to judge with justice.
Gratitude (*shukr*)	Qur'an (14:7)	And [remember] when your Lord proclaimed, "If you are grateful, I will surely increase you [in favour]; but if you deny, indeed, My punishment is severe."
Honesty and integrity (*amanah*)	Qur'an (4:135)	O you who have believed, be persistently standing firm in justice, witnesses for Allāh, even if it be against yourselves or parents and relatives.
Honouring parents (*birr al-walidayn*)	Qur'an (17:23)	And your Lord has decreed that you do not worship except Him, and to parents, good treatment. Whether one or both of them reach old age [while] with you, say not to them [so much as], 'uff,' and do not repel them but speak to them a noble word.
Patience and perseverance (*sabr*)	Qur'an (2:155–157)	And We will surely test you with something of fear and hunger and a loss of wealth and lives and fruits, but give good tidings to the patient, who, when disaster strikes them, say, "Indeed we belong to Allāh, and indeed to Him we will return."
Truthfulness (*sidq*)	Qur'an (33:70)	You who have believed, fear Allāh and speak words of appropriate justice.

In relation to environmental stewardship (*himaayah*), Prophet Muhammad (ﷺ) passed by Sa'd while he was performing ablution. The Prophet said, "What is this extravagance?" Sa'd said, "Is there extravagance with water in ablution?" The Prophet said, "Yes, even if you were on the banks of a flowing river" (Ahmad). With reference to honesty in trade and business ('*adl* and *amanah* in trade), the Prophet (ﷺ) said,

> The buyer and the seller have the option of cancelling or confirming the bargain unless they separate, and if they spoke the truth and made clear the defects of the

goods, them they would be blessed in their bargain, and if they told lies and hid some facts, their bargain would be deprived of Allāh's blessings.

(Bukhârî)

Finally, a *hadīth* related to compassion to animals (*rahma*), Prophet Muhammad (ﷺ) said, "A woman was punished in Hell because of a cat which she had confined until it died. She did not give it to eat or to drink when it was confined, nor did she free it so that it might eat the vermin of the earth."

(Bukhârî & Muslim)

Principles of Islāmic ethics

Islāmic law, encompassing the principles of Islāmic ethics, extends to various areas including medicine and health care practices. It upholds the values necessary for professionalism and effective service to individuals, families, and communities (El-Hazmi, 2002). Islāmic ethics prioritises the dignity of humanity, considering individuals honoured beings in the eyes of God and ensuring the preservation of fundamental rights such as life, freedom, property, health, and sufficiency throughout one's lifetime (WHO, 2005). Adhering to Islāmic ethical values and principles, individuals use the Islāmic framework to address moral and ethical dilemmas.

Shar'iah, Islāmic jurisprudence, governs all aspects of behaviour and life, effectively addressing moral issues within medicine from a legal standpoint. Kasule (2008) suggests that *Shar'iah*, rooted in a moral system, offers comprehensive guidance. Unlike a conventional legal system, *Shar'iah* encompasses a broader scope and purpose, serving as a moral system that addresses various moral issues in medicine from a legal perspective, as described by Coulson (1964). *Fiqh*, jurisprudence, regulates ritual practices, medical hygiene, social etiquette, and serves as a composite science of law and morality, with its exponents (*fuqaha*-sing; *faqih*) acting as guardians of the Islāmic conscience (Coulson, 1964).

Al-Shatibi (d. 1388), a prominent Islāmic scholar, made significant contributions to Islāmic jurisprudence, particularly in the field of *maqasid al-Shar'iah*, which focuses on the higher objectives or purposes of Islāmic law. He argued that Islāmic legal rulings aim to promote the welfare and well-being of individuals and societies (Al-Raysuni, 2018). *Maqasid al-Shar'iah* is based on the concept that Islāmic law aims to preserve and fulfil five primary objectives, also known as the "five essentials" or "higher goals":

- Preservation of religion (*hifz al-din*): this objective involves protecting and preserving the principles, teachings, and practices of the Islāmic faith, including monotheism, devotion to Allāh, and religious rituals.
- Preservation of life (*hifz al-nafs*): Islāmic law places significant importance on preserving human life, prohibiting actions that cause harm, violence, or endangerment.

- Preservation of intellect (*hifz al-'aql*): *Shar'iah* recognises and encourages the importance of rationality, intellect, and knowledge, promoting intellectual development and critical thinking.
- Preservation of lineage/progeny (*hifz al-nasl*): Islāmic law aims to preserve and strengthen family and societal structures, promoting marriage, protecting family rights, and ensuring the continuity of lineage and future generations.
- Preservation of property (*hifz al-mal*): *Shar'iah* ensures the protection of property rights, advocating for economic justice and equitable distribution of wealth within society while prohibiting theft, fraud, and exploitation.

These objectives highlight the holistic approach of Islāmic law towards promoting individual and societal well-being, emphasising principles of justice, compassion, and human dignity.

Islāmic law's principle of justice intends to ensure that everyone receives what they are due by having a fair distribution of benefits (Al-Swailem, 2006, 2007). This principle extends to the domains of medicine and health care, as Islāmic law encompasses all the facets of professionalism necessary to provide appropriate services to individuals, families, and communities (El-Hazmi, 2002). The *Qawa'id al-Fiqhiyyah* (or *'ilm al-qawa'id al-fiqhiyyah*) (Al-Hisni, 1997; Elgariani, 2012) known as the legal maxims, act as a guiding framework to address complex legal matters and adapt Islāmic law regarding present-day circumstances. These principles provide a basis for understanding the objectives of Islāmic law and make it easier to apply it to a variety of situations. Examples of these legal maxims comprise the following: "acts are evaluated based on the intentions behind them," acknowledging that the motive behind an action has significance in legal considerations; "certainty takes precedence over doubt," meaning that when there is a clear certainty in a circumstance, it should not be discounted because of doubts; "hardship leads to ease," indicating that during challenging circumstances, there may be allowances or facilitations provided to alleviate difficulties; and "harm must be eliminated", emphasising the importance of preventing or removing any harmful consequences to individuals or society. Lastly, "custom serves as the basis for judgment" recognised the role of established customs and societal practices in shaping legal decisions. The legal maxims discussed constitute crucial principles in the domain of Islāmic jurisprudence. The legal maxims of Islāmic law provide reliable tools for navigating its intricacies, aiding in determining legal rulings and resolving moral and ethical dilemmas. When combined with the higher objectives of Islāmic law, they uphold its principles and purposes, offering practical guidance for legal and ethical decision-making in various contexts.

There are a number of principles of Islāmic ethics, and the foremost highlights "the inherent honour and dignity of all human beings" (WHO, 2005, p. 1). Within Islāmic teachings, there is a strong emphasis on the belief that every person, irrespective of their race, gender, or social status, is endowed with intrinsic worth bestowed by Allāh. Alláh says in the Qur'ân,

وَلَقَدْ كَرَّمْنَا بَنِىٓ

- *And indeed, We have honoured the Children of Adam.*

(Al-'Isrā' 17:70, (interpretation of the meaning)

Allāh tells us how He has honoured the sons of Adam and made them noble by creating them in the best and most perfect of forms. It is stated that honouring an individual includes ensuring their full health and well-being, respecting their personality, privacy, and secrets. It acknowledges their right to receive all relevant medical information and to be the sole decision-maker regarding their health within the framework of these values (Ibn Kathir, 2000). The principle of honouring every individual in Islāmic ethics entails protecting and advancing their health and well-being while respecting their personality, privacy, and confidentiality. It affirms their right to receive comprehensive information about medical procedures and to make autonomous decisions within Islāmic ethical boundaries. This principle highlights patient-centred care, prioritising dignity, autonomy, and rights are upheld as service consumers.

The second principle is that every human being has the right to live and to the maintenance of life. Allāh says in the Qur'ân,

وَمَنْ أَحْيَاهَا فَكَأَنَّمَآ أَحْيَا ٱلنَّاسَ

- *And whoever saves one – it is as if he had saved mankind entirely.*

(Al-Mā'idah 5:32, interpretation of the meaning)

In Islām, the concept of life-saving encompasses more than physical preservation; it includes psychological, spiritual, and social aspects (WHO, 2005). Islāmic teachings stress the interconnectedness of the mind, body, and spirit, emphasising the importance of holistic well-being. Additionally, Islām promotes the establishment of a just society that respects human dignity and enhances individuals' overall quality of life.

The third principle is based on equity. Muslims consider justice in its general context to be one of the most obligatory and necessary obligations, since Allāh commanded it in His sayings (Al-Jaza'iry, 2001):

إِنَّ ٱللَّهَ يَأْمُرُ بِٱلْعَدْلِ وَٱلْإِحْسَٰنِ وَإِيتَآئِ ذِى ٱلْقُرْبَىٰ وَيَنْهَىٰ عَنِ ٱلْفَحْشَآءِ وَٱلْمُنكَرِ وَٱلْبَغْىِ

- *Indeed, Allāh orders justice and good conduct and giving to relatives and forbids immorality and bad conduct and oppression.*

(An-Naĥl 16:90, interpretation of the meaning)

إِنَّ ٱللَّهَ يُحِبُّ ٱلْمُقْسِطِينَ

- *Indeed, Allāh loves those who act justly.*
  (Al-Hujurāt 49:9, interpretation of the meaning)

قُلْ أَمَرَ رَبِّى بِٱلْقِسْطِ

- *Say* [O Muhammad], *"My Lord has ordered justice."*
  (Al-'A'rāf 7:29, interpretation of the meaning)

God's teachings on Islām emphasise the principle of equity, urging individuals to practice fairness and justice in all aspects of life. Through the Qur'ân, God gives a general command to uphold equity, whether it is in providing truthful testimony, making just judgments, seeking reconciliation, or fulfilling the rights of the oppressed. Verses such as *"And when you testify, be just"* (Qur'ân 6:152, interpretation of the meaning); *"when you judge between people to judge with justice"* (Qur'ân 4:58, interpretation of the meaning); *"then make a settlement between them in justice and act justly"* (Qur'ân 49:9, interpretation of the meaning); and *"and concerning the oppressed among children and that you maintain for orphans* [their rights] *in justice"* (Qur'ân 4:127, interpretation of the meaning) serve as reminders of the importance of practicing fairness and justice in all aspects of life.

In Islām, the concept of equity is embedded various aspects of life, including health care and psychotherapy. Justice with Allāh entails monotheistic worship, while justice in judgments between people mandates fair treatment and rightful dues. Within family relations, justice involves equal treatment of wives and children. Justice in speech necessitates truthful testimony and avoiding falsehood. Lastly, justice in beliefs requires adherence to truth and scepticism towards unrealistic claims (Al-Jaza'iry, 2001). In the contexts of health care and psychotherapy, the Islāmic principle of equity stresses the need for the most extensive equality in distributing health resources and offering preventive and therapeutic care. This principle prohibits any form of discrimination based on gender, race, belief, political affiliation, social or judicial factors, or any other consideration. This aligns with the World Health Organization's motto, "Health for all," emphasising the importance of inclusive and non-discriminatory health care practices (WHO, 2005, p. 2)

The fourth principle features the aspiration to achieve excellence and consistently perform at a high level in all endeavours. This commitment to high quality is esteemed and sought after in every aspect of life. It is one of the fundamental values enjoined by God: "God enjoins equity and doing well" (Qur'ân 16:90, interpretation of the meaning). It was narrated from Shaddad bin Aws that the Messenger of Allāh (ﷺ) said, "Allāh has prescribed *al-ihsan* (proficiency) in all things (Ibn Majah). The principle of *ihsan* is a fundamental aspect of Islām, embodying the concept of doing things with excellence. It not only encompasses performing tasks in the best possible manner but also extends to acts of charity and kindness towards those who are vulnerable, needy, and less fortunate in society. This principle emphasises the importance of generosity, compassion, and service to the disadvantaged members of the community.

The fifth principle is causing no harm. It is narrated by Ibn 'Abbas (may Allāh be pleased with him) that Allāh's Messenger (ﷺ) said, "There should neither be harming (of others without cause), nor reciprocating harm (between two parties)" (Ahmad & Ibn Majah). From an Islāmic perspective, causing harm to others or engaging in unjust retribution is strictly prohibited. Scholars classify harm into two categories: actions that solely harm others and those that may bring personal benefit but harm society. Islām emphasises avoiding both categories, prioritising the well-being and collective welfare of individuals and communities. The combination of Islāmic law's higher objectives, legal maxims, and ethical principles provides practical guidelines for legal and ethical decision-making. Together, they form a comprehensive framework for moral and legal judgments that uphold justice, safeguard rights, and foster the welfare of individuals and society in line with Islāmic principles.

In addition to the universal ethical principles mentioned (beneficence, non-maleficence, justice, fidelity, and autonomy), Islāmic psychoethics include distinctive principles such as *tawhīd* (monotheism); *niyyah* (intention); *taqwa* (consciousness of God); *akhlaq* (virtue, morality, good manners and character); and *ihsan* (pursuit of excellence). These principles provide a comprehensive framework for ethical decision-making in Islāmic psychotherapy. Both Islāmic psychotherapy and conventional psychotherapy share universal ethical principles like autonomy, beneficence, non-maleficence, and confidentiality while also having differences shaped by Islāmic values and beliefs (Table 4.2).

In Islāmic psychotherapy ethics, beneficence (*ihsan*) emphasises doing good and showing compassion, while non-maleficence aligns with preventing harm and promoting well-being. Though the concept of justice is shared by conventional and Islāmic psychotherapy, there are some differences in how they are applied because of the latter's unique religious context. For example, in Islāmic psychotherapy, therapists may consider the notion of *hisbah*, which involves addressing any unjust behaviours or wrongdoings within the individual or the community. This may include promoting moral accountability and encouraging individuals to rectify their actions in line with Islāmic teachings.

Fidelity in Islāmic ethics encompasses loyalty, trustworthiness, and fulfilling promises. Autonomy and personal responsibility are acknowledged in both conventional and Islāmic psychotherapy. However, the value of autonomy is acknowledged and respected in Islāmic psychotherapy to a certain extent, balancing individual needs with communal and spiritual obligations (*fard kifaya*) as well as broader societal contexts. The ethical framework considers the relationships between individual autonomy and communal/spiritual values inherent in Islāmic culture.

TABLE 4.2 Comparison of values between mainstream and Islāmic psychotherapy

Values and themes	Mainstream psychotherapy	Islāmic psychotherapy
Ethical framework & values	Secular	Integration of faith: Islāmic values and principles (*tawhīd*)
Ethical codes	Universal	and or Islāmic Universal
Autonomy	Yes	Within Islāmic parameters (*tadbir*)
Beneficence	Yes	Yes (*ihsan*)
Non-maleficence	Yes	Islāmic principle of avoiding harm and promoting well-being *(la darar wa la dirar)*
Equality and Justice	Yes	Yes, promoting fairness and equal treatment or justice ('*adl*)
Fidelity	Yes	Yes, ethically sound and effective treatment
Informed consent/ Confidentiality	Yes	Yes (*ijazah*) Yes (*sitr al-aurah*)
Boundaries/Dual relationship	Clear boundaries	Dual relationship; no clear boundaries
Accountability	Professional	Before Allāh; professional
Trust in and reliance on God	No	Yes, acknowledging that ultimate control lies with Him (*tawakkul*)
Forgiveness. Repentance	No	Recognising the importance of forgiveness for personal healing and interpersonal reconciliation (*tawbah*)
Rituals and practices	No	Incorporation of religious practices such as prayer, remembrance of God, and supplication to support inner healing and emotional well-being
Personal development and purification	Continuing professional development	Continuing professional development; purification of the soul (*tazkiyah an-nafs*)
Social justice	Specific to liberation psychology	Addressing inequality, discrimination, or oppression

Islāmic psychotherapy emphasises addressing social justice issues within the Muslim community, including inequalities, discrimination, and oppression experienced by marginalised groups. Islām promotes fairness, equity, and the elimination of social injustices. Islāmic psychotherapy recognises the interconnectedness of mental health with social, cultural, and environmental contexts. In line with the principle of preventing unnecessary or ineffective interventions (*takhalli al-tadawi bi al-tada'iyat*) and creating iatrogenic disorder (Tao & Clements, 2022), Islāmic psychotherapy upholds the moral obligation to provide clients with valuable therapeutic care that avoids unintended harmful effects on their well-being.

Conclusion

Islāmic psychotherapy distinguishes itself from mainstream psychotherapy by acknowledging and prioritising the spiritual dimension inherent in individuals. It recognises that justice extends beyond interpersonal interactions and encourages clients to align their actions with the teachings of Islām. Ethical principles rooted in Islām, such as striving for God-consciousness (*taqwa*), following divine guidance, and promoting righteousness, are integral to Islāmic psychotherapy. Clients are guided to integrate these principles into their therapeutic journeys. Islāmic jurisprudence (*fiqh*) may be referenced to address moral and ethical issues, respecting the rulings and teachings of Islāmic scholars and promoting justice, equity, and fairness. Therapists assist clients in reflecting on their moral responsibilities and taking steps to rectify their actions in accordance with Islāmic teachings.

The principle of *hisbah* encourages individuals to uphold ethical standards and foster virtuous behaviour within their communities. Islāmic psychotherapy emphasises complete reliance on God *(tawakkul)* for all aspects of life and well-being, underlining the importance of trusting in God's guidance throughout the therapeutic process. Perhaps as Islāmic psychotherapists we need to take the Islāmic oath adapted from "The Oath of A Muslim Physician (Islāmic Medical Association of North America, 1977 cited in The Federation of Islāmic Medical Associations, 2018).

- Allāh, grant me the strength, patience, and dedication to adhere to this Oath at all times.
- Allāh, we praise You as the Teacher, the Unique, the Majestic, and the Glorious. You are the Eternal Being who created the universe and all its creatures. We worship and serve only You, recognising idolatry as a grave injustice.
- Grant us the strength, patience, dedication, and integrity to uphold the values of truthfulness, honesty, modesty, mercy, and objectivity. Help us acknowledge our mistakes, learn from them, and forgive the wrongs of others.
- Bestow upon us the wisdom to bring comfort and counsel, leading others towards peace and harmony. Help us understand that our profession is sacred, entrusted with the precious gifts of life and intellect.
- Enable us to be worthy of this privileged position, approaching it with honour, dignity, and righteousness. May we devote our lives to serving all of humanity, regardless of their wealth, knowledge, faith, or ethnicity. Grant us the patience, tolerance, virtue, and reverence to fulfil this duty with your love in our hearts and compassion for all your servants.
- In taking this oath, we solemnly swear in Your name, the Creator of the heavens and the earth, and we commit to following the guidance You have revealed to Prophet Muhammad (ﷺ). We keep in mind the verse from Al-Ma'idah (5:32), *And whoever saves one – it is as if he had saved mankind entirely.*

- Allāh, we entrust our oath and endeavours to Your guidance and mercy. May our actions as Islāmic psychotherapist be a reflection of our devotion and service to You. Amen.

References

Ahmad. *Musnad Aḥmad 7065*. Sahih (authentic) according to Ahmad Shakir. Al-Albani in his *Silsilah As-Sahihah* (#3292) and graded it Hasan. https://sunnah.com.

Ahmad, & Ibn Majah. *Sunnah.com reference: Book 7, Hādīth 171* (English translation: Book 7, Hādīth 924. Arabic reference: Book 7, Hādīth 918). https://sunnah.com.

Al-Attas, M. N. (2013). *Islam: The concept of religion and the foundation of ethics and morality*. IBFIM.

Al-Hisni, & Taqi al-Din. (1997). *Kitab al-Qawa'id*. Maktabat al-Rushd.

Al-Jaza'iry, A. B. J. (2001). Justice and equity. In *Minhaj al Muslim*. Darussalam. Retrieved September 16, 2023, from www.islaam.net/main/display.php?id=1280&category=76.

Al-Raysuni, A. (2018). *Imam Al-Shatibi's theory of higher objectives and intents of Islāmic law*. Kube Publishing Ltd.

Al-Swailem, A. (2006). *Bio-ethics from the Islāmic point of view*. Bio-ethics and Regulatory Aspects of Bio-medical Workshop.

Al-Swailem, A. (2007). *Nursing and nurses' ethical issues from Islāmic perspectives*. Building Bridges to the Future, 2nd International Nursing Conference.

American Psychological Association. (2017). *Ethical principles of psychologists and code of conduct* (2002, amended effective June 1, 2010, and January 1, 2017). www.apa.org/ethics/code.

Anabo, I. F., Elexpuru-Albizuri, I., & Villardón-Gallego, L. (2019). Revisiting the Belmont Report's ethical principles in internet-mediated research: Perspectives from disciplinary associations in the social sciences. *Ethics Information Technology, 21*, 137–149.

Barnett, J. E. (2008). Impaired professionals: Distress, professional impairment, self-care, and psychological wellness. In M. Herson & A. M. Gross (Eds.), *Handbook of clinical psychology* (Vol. 1, pp. 857–884). John Wiley & sons.

Barnett, J. E., & Teehan, D. (2022). Ethics and values in psychotherapy. *Psychotherapy Bulletin, 57*(2), 11–16.

Beauchamp, T. L., & Childress, J. F. (2012). *Principles of biomedical ethics* (7th ed.). Oxford University Press.

Bukhârî. *Sahih al-Bukhârî 2110* [In-book reference: Book 34, Hādīth 63. USC-MSA web (English) reference: Vol. 3, Book 34, Hādīth 323]. https://sunnah.com.

Bukhârî, & Muslim. *Riyad as-Salihin 1600* (In-book reference: Book 17, Hādīth 90). https://sunnah.com.

Coulson, N. (1964). *A history of Islāmic law*. Edinburgh University Press.

Doi, A. R. (1997). *Shariah: The Islāmic law*. Ta-Ha.

Elgariani, F. S. (2012). *Al-Qaw'id al-Fiqhiyyah (Islāmic legal maxims): Concept, functions, history, classifications and application to contemporary medical issues* [Submitted to the University of Exeter as a thesis for the degree of Doctor of Philosophy in Arab and Islāmic Studies. Retrieved September 17, 2023, from https://ore.exeter.ac.uk/repository/bitstream/handle/10036/4001/ElgarianiF.pdf].

El-Hazmi, M. A. F. (Ed.). (2002). *Ethics of genetic counseling in Islāmic communities*. Al-Obeikan Bookstore (Arabic).

Eshetu, Y. (2017). Understanding cultural relativism: A critical appraisal of the theory. *International Journal of Multicultural and Multireligious Understanding, 4*(6), 24–30.

Ghaly, M. (2023). *Module 1: Classical Islāmic bioethics, scholarly disciplines: Theology*. Hamad Bin Khalifa University. Retrieved September 14, 2023, from www.edx.org/learn/ethics/hamad-bin-khalifa-university-Islamic-bioethics.

Ibn Kathir. (2000). *Tafsir ibn Kathir* (J. Abualrub, N. Khitab, H. Khitab, A. Walker, M. Al-Jibali, & S. Ayoub, Trans.). Darussalam Publishers and Distributors.

Ibn Majah. *Sunan Ibn Majah 3170* (In-book reference: Book 27, Hādīth 9. English translation: Vol. 4, Book 27, Hādīth 3170). Sahih (Darussalam). https://sunnah.com.

Kasule, O. H. (2008). *Medical ethics from Maqasid Al Shari'a*. Retrieved September 17, 2023, from http://Islamthought.wordpress.com/2008/12/14/medical-ethics-from-maqasid-al-shari%E2%80%99a/.

Lovering, S., & Rassool, G. Hussein (2014). Ethical dimensions in caring. In G. Hussein Rassool (Ed.), *Cultural competence in caring for Muslim patients*. Palgrave Macmillan.

Muslim (a). *Sahih Muslim 36a* [In-book reference: Book 1, Hādīth 61. USC-MSA web (English) reference: Book 1, Hādīth 57]. https://sunnah.com.

Muslim (b). *Riyad as-Salihin 1589* (In-book reference: Book 17, Hādīth 79). https://sunnah.com.

Oxford Dictionaries. (2024). *Ethics*. Retrieved June 3, 2024, from https://www.oxfordreference.com/search?q=Ethics&searchBtn=Search&isQuickSearch=true

Shomali, M. A. (2008). Islāmic bioethics: A general scheme. *Journal of Medical Ethics and History of Medicine*, *1*(1).

Sue, D. W., & Sue, D. (2012). *Counseling the culturally different: Theory and practice* (6th ed.). Wiley.

Tao, Z., & Clements, N. K. (2022). Iatrogenesis and health inequity. *AMA Journal of Ethics*, *24*(8), E717–E719.

The Federation of Islāmic Medical Associations (FIMA). (2018). *The oath of a Muslim physician*. Retrieved September 20, 2023, from https://fimaweb.net/the-oath-of-a-muslim-physician/#:~:text=We%20serve%20no%20other%20god%20besides%20Thee%20and,comfort%20and%20counsel%20all%20towards%20peace%20and%20harmony.

Tirmidhî. *Riyad as-Salihin 278* (In-book reference: Introduction, Hādīth 278) (Hadīth Hasan Sahih). https://sunnah.com.

Winkler, E. A. (2022). Are universal ethics necessary? And possible? A systematic theory of universal ethics and a code for global moral education. *SN Social Science*, *2*, 66. https://doi.org/10.1007/s43545-022-00350-7.

World Health Organization (WHO). (2005). *Islāmic code of medical and health ethics* (EM/RC52/7). WHO Regional Committee for the Eastern Mediterranean. Retrieved September 16, 2023, from http://applications.emro.who.int/docs/EM_RC52_7_en.pdf.

5
NAVIGATING ETHICAL CHALLENGES IN ISLĀMIC PSYCHOTHERAPY

Introduction

Ethical dilemmas are common in the practice of therapy, and managing these dilemmas requires careful consideration and adherence to a robust ethical framework. Cultural, spiritual, and ethical factors significantly influence responses to ethical challenges in mental health practice. In Islāmic psychotherapy, practitioners must navigate ethical dilemmas at the intersection of faith, culture, and psychology. This chapter explores these complexities and introduces the ethical dilemma decision-making model, which integrates Islāmic ethics into the decision-making process. The model offers therapists a structured approach to addressing ethical dilemmas in line with Islāmic principles and values, emphasising the importance of seeking guidance and consulting Islāmic teachings to ensure ethical practice.

Professional ethical code of practice

The professional ethical code of practice in psychotherapy is a set of guidelines and standards that govern the conduct and behaviour of psychotherapists. Professional ethical codes in psychotherapy delineate therapists' responsibilities, principles, and values to safeguard their clients' well-being and integrity. Although variations exist among accrediting bodies and professional associations, common principles underlie these codes (ACA, 2014; APA, 2017; BACP, 2013), forming a foundation centred on client welfare and ethical conduct. Professional ethical codes in psychotherapy provide guidelines for therapists' conduct, emphasising client welfare, confidentiality, informed consent, competence, ethical behaviour, multicultural competence, professional relationships, and supervision. These principles ensure effective and ethical care, respect for client autonomy and diversity, and ongoing professional development. These codes ensure that clients receive high-quality care while their rights, well-being, and confidentiality are maintained in culturally sensitive and ethical therapeutic environments.

Adhering to professional ethical codes of practice is essential, but it may not suffice to ensure ethical practice. Barnett (2019) highlights that ethical codes cannot cover all the intricacies and complexities of ethical dilemmas that therapists face. Professionals must use their own judgment to apply ethics codes effectively. The author suggests that changes in societal standards and expectations may require periodic updates to ethics codes to address evolving ethical challenges. Barnett underlines that while some standards in ethics codes offer clear guidance, many are considered overly broad and difficult to apply to the diverse and complex decisions therapists face. He emphasises that ethics codes lack guidance on prioritising principles in conflicts or determining whose needs take precedence when serving multiple individuals.

Ethical dilemmas in Islāmic psychotherapy

Islāmic psychotherapy, like any other form of therapy, encounters various ethical dilemmas that can arise during the therapeutic process. According to Hegde (2019), an ethical dilemma in psychotherapy is a conflict between alternatives where any decision compromises one or more ethical principles. This conflict arises from conflicting moral values within a decision-making situation, making it challenging to determine the morally superior option. Knapp et al. (2017) highlight that ethical dilemmas can be stressful for psychologists who seek to do the right thing but find no clear-cut answers in the APA ethics code.

Islāmic psychotherapy encounters ethical dilemmas categorised into two main groups, as identified by Lindsay and Colley (1995). The first category comprises dilemmas aligned with traditional ethical codes, like maintaining client confidentiality, which involve conflicts between ethical principles and the therapist's duty to protect client privacy. The second category includes tensions arising between the psychologist's preferred practice and constraints imposed by their organisation or setting, covering dilemmas related to treatment approaches, resource allocation, and professional autonomy. Some dilemmas can arise when there are conflicting ethical principles, such as the need to promote a patient's well-being (beneficence) and avoid harm (non-maleficence) while also respecting the patient's autonomy (Knapp et al., 2015). The most common ethical dilemmas therapists face include confidentiality, dual relationships, conduct of colleagues, sexual issues, competence (Lindsay & Clarkson, 1999), privacy, blurriness of boundaries, and multiple or conflicting relationships (Hendrix, 1991; Herlihy & Corey, 2006; Lindsay & Clarkson, 1999; Pope & Vasquez, 2007).

Islāmic psychotherapists may encounter ethical dilemmas regarding the balance between maintaining client confidentiality and obligations based on Islāmic teachings. For instance, a therapist faces a dilemma about disclosing confidential mental health information to a client's designated *imam* or faith leader. This situation presents a conflict between maintaining client confidentiality, a fundamental aspect of therapy, and ensuring that the client receives appropriate support and guidance from their religious leader.

In another example, an ethical dilemma arises when a therapist working with a Muslim client who has disclosed experiencing depression and thoughts of self-harm must balance maintaining confidentiality with addressing potential harm. The client is concerned about stigma within her community if this information is shared outside therapy. The therapist faces the dilemma of protecting confidentiality while ensuring the client's safety. Options include reporting to the multidisciplinary team or outside agencies or involving a trusted religious leader to offer guidance while maintaining confidentiality.

In Islāmic psychotherapy, potential conflicts may arise from dual relationships, where therapists have multiple roles or relationships with clients outside the therapeutic context. For instance, a therapist receives a request from a family member to provide therapy to a distant cousin, highlighting the potential for a dual relationship and conflict of interest. The therapist must maintain professional boundaries and avoid potential biases or conflicts stemming from the familial connection.

Gender preference is an important consideration for both clients and therapists due to religious obligations, cultural norms, and modesty considerations. Some clients may prefer a therapist of the same gender for comfort in discussing sensitive matters. For instance, a male therapist is referred a female client from a conservative Muslim background who requests a same-gender therapist due to discomfort. The therapist respects the client's preference and refers her to a female therapist to ensure her comfort and meet her needs effectively. This demonstrates a commitment to professional boundaries and client care by respecting the client's preferences.

Another ethical dilemma in Islāmic psychotherapy is when the therapist's need to balance the principle of individual autonomy conflicts with respecting collective and culturally specific values within the Muslim community. For instance, a young Muslim woman seeks therapy to discuss her desire to marry someone from a different cultural background, which her family strongly opposes. The therapist must help her make an autonomous decision while considering family dynamics and cultural expectations. To navigate this dilemma, the therapist can employ strategies that involve understanding religious and cultural perspectives, assessing potential harm or risks, and supporting the client in making informed decisions while respecting family dynamics and cultural norms.

In Islāmic psychotherapy, therapists must maintain cultural sensitivity and competence, avoiding assumptions about clients' religious or cultural beliefs and practices. For instance, a therapist is working with a Muslim client who practices a different Islāmic sect than the therapist. This highlights the importance of recognising the diversity within Muslim communities and refraining from making assumptions or judgments about religious differences. Culturally sensitive therapists create safe, inclusive environments that promote understanding, respect, and effective therapeutic outcomes for Muslim clients.

Islāmic psychotherapists, like professionals in any field, may encounter ethical dilemmas when personal values conflict with professional standards. For instance, a therapist who believes certain behaviours contradict Islāmic principles, such as pre-marital relationships or alcohol consumption, may struggle when a client seeks therapy for such issues. The ethical challenge lies in balancing personal beliefs with the professional obligation to provide non-judgmental, client-centred care.

Therapists must navigate these dilemmas with sensitivity, respecting clients' autonomy and cultural backgrounds while upholding ethical principles of objectivity and professional conduct. The therapists should prioritise the client's well-being and autonomy. In the scenario where a client identifies as LGBTQ+ and seeks affirmative therapy, therapists may face an ethical challenge due to a conflict between their personal beliefs and the obligation to provide affirming and supportive therapy. Affirmative therapy validates and advocates for the needs of sexual and gender minority clients, demonstrating an affirming stance towards LGBTQ+ individuals (Hinrichs & Donaldson, 2017). The therapist must prioritise the client's well-being and autonomy, putting aside personal convictions to offer culturally sensitive care that supports the client's identity and mental health needs. From an Islāmic perspective, Qadhi (2022) suggests that

> the current *fatwa* is not about preaching hatred of any individual or group; furthermore, Islāmic law explicitly condemns any acts of vigilante justice. We treat all people as humans and give them the respect and dignity they deserve, regardless of their lifestyles and choices. Furthermore, we welcome anyone intent on living an Islāmic lifestyle to our *masjids* [mosques] and communities, regardless of their personal temptations and desires, and we encourage all Muslims to provide others any spiritual help and support they need and to accommodate all people of all backgrounds as reasonably as possible and within the parameters of the *Shar'iah*.

In Islāmic psychotherapy, obtaining informed consent is important, yet ethical dilemmas may arise due to cultural dynamics. For instance, a therapist working with a Muslim client from a culture where decision-making often rests with the family or religious leader faces challenges in obtaining informed consent. The client may defer decision-making to their family or seek guidance from their religious community, complicating the consent process. The therapist must navigate this dilemma by respecting cultural values, promoting client autonomy, and upholding professional ethics to ensure a balanced approach to informed consent.

Ethical decision model

When psychotherapists encounter ethical dilemmas, it is crucial for them to carefully consider their actions. According to Welfel (2006), relying solely on intuition can present ethical problems, posing risks to the public. Ethical decision-making models serve as valuable resources to assist therapists in fulfilling their ethical obligations in complex situations. These models enable ethical decision-making (Cottone & Tarvydas, 2016; Knapp et al., 2017), address dilemmas related to spirituality and religion in psychotherapy (Barnett & Johnson, 2011), and provide guidance for decisions about boundaries and multiple relationships (Younggren & Gottlieb, 2004). "No single framework can suit every client, nor cover every possible ethical conflict" (Corey et al., 2011, p. 22). One model for dealing with ethical dilemmas is based on a six-step process (adapted from Bond, 2010, p. 228):

- Elicit a description of the dilemma.
- Decide who is facing the dilemma (client, therapist/counsellor, or both).
- Consult a professional code of conduct or ethics.
- Identify courses of action.
- Choose the course of action.
- Implement the decision/evaluation of the outcome.

Barnett and Teehan (2022) made some recommendations in dealing with all ethical dilemmas, focusing on prevention. Here are a summary of the key guidelines (Barnett & Teehan, 2022) to consider when navigating ethical dilemmas in the field of psychotherapy:

- Familiarise yourself with your profession's ethics code, relevant laws in your country or state, and the policies of your institution or organisation. This provides a foundation for understanding the ethical standards that apply to your practice.
- Understand that just because a law or policy allows a certain action, it does not mean that you *must act* in that way.
- Take the time to clarify your own values and be transparent about potential conflicts that may arise. Consult with trusted colleagues who have expertise in ethics when uncertain about how to navigate value conflicts appropriately.
- Maintain open and transparent communication with the public and your clients about the nature of the professional services you provide. This includes clearly articulating any specific religious beliefs or values that may inform your practice, such as faith-based psychotherapy like Islāmic psychotherapy. Inform and publicise this faith-based service on your website and during the informed consent process.

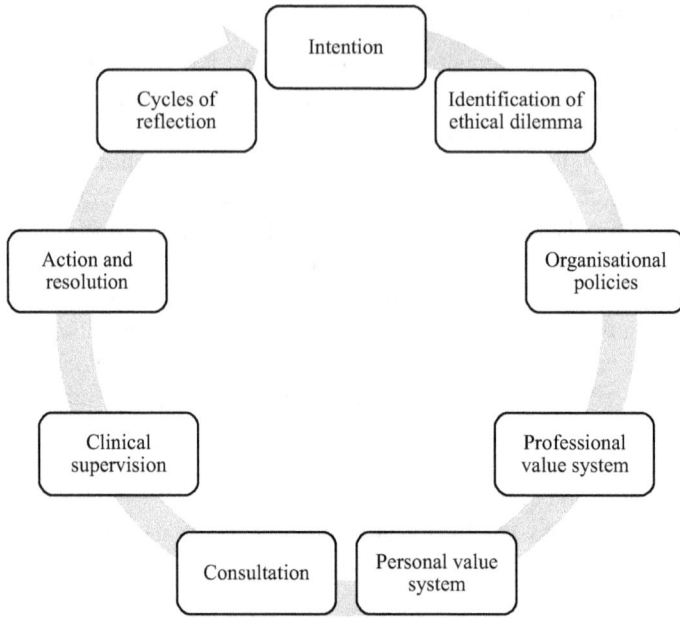

FIGURE 5.1 The ethical dilemma decision-making model.

Ethical dilemma decision-making model

A model has been designed specifically for addressing ethical dilemmas in Islāmic psychotherapy (Figure 5.1). The model emphasises the importance of *niyyah* (intention) as the foundational element. *Niyyah* guides therapists to make ethical choices aligned with Islāmic values and principles. It serves as a moral and ethical compass, enabling therapists to navigate complex dilemmas and prioritise client welfare while upholding Islāmic values. When faced with ethical dilemmas, therapists recognise their intention to act in accordance with Islāmic principles, ensuring sincerity and purity in their decisions.

Identifying the ethical problem is the first step in the ethical dilemma decision-making process for Islāmic psychotherapists. In this initial stage, therapists need to keenly assess the situation to recognise any ethical dilemmas that may be present in their practice. One common ethical problem therapists may face is the conflict between a client's requests or beliefs and Islāmic values or ethical guidelines. Organisational policies are vital within the ethical dilemma decision-making model of Islāmic psychotherapy. These policies encompass various aspects including confidentiality, informed consent, client rights, boundaries, and professional conduct.

When therapists encounter ethical dilemmas, they rely on and adhere to these established policies that govern their practice. This helps ensure professionalism, protect client welfare, and uphold ethical standards. By consulting organisational policies, therapists can maintain consistency in their decision-making processes and ensure adherence to the high standards of their profession. These policies provide clear guidance regarding acceptable practices and boundaries, allowing therapists to make informed decisions that prioritise client well-being. Organisational policies provide explicit guidance on navigating ethical dilemmas like dual relationships and client gifting in Islāmic psychotherapy. For instance, they may prohibit certain relationships or clarify acceptable boundaries. By referencing these policies, therapists can prioritise client well-being and uphold crucial professional boundaries essential for ethical practice. These policies ensure therapists make informed decisions aligned with ethical standards while maintaining the integrity of the therapeutic relationship.

The integration of professional value systems into the ethical dilemma decision-making model is crucial in psychotherapy. It serves as the foundation for ethical decision-making, anchoring therapists to established ethical standards and principles. This inclusion provides clear guidance for therapists and reinforces their commitment to maintaining client well-being and rights. However, professional codes of ethics may not address every possible ethical dilemma a therapist may encounter in their career. Therapists must exercise judgment and rely on their professional values to navigate complex ethical challenges. **The** American Psychological Association Ethics Code (APA, 2017) makes clear that it is intended to provide guidance and that psychologists must consider other available sources of guidance and information. This is reflected by Barnett (2019)**:**

> Further, the use of the words reasonably, appropriate, and potentially are included throughout the Ethics Code to allow psychologists to consider and utilise their own professional judgment when considering how to apply the ethics code, to enable the Ethics Code to be applied broadly to a wide range of circumstances and situations.
>
> *(p. 432)*

The personal value system of a therapist influences how they navigate dilemmas within the ethical decision-making model. This system encompasses the therapist's beliefs, principles, and ethical foundations. Therapists must reflect on their personal values and potential biases when facing ethical dilemmas. In Islāmic psychotherapy, therapists with a well-defined personal value system can assess their beliefs and evaluate their impacts on decision-making. The personal value system serves as a reference point for therapists to assess their responses and identify conflicts between personal values and professional ethics.

Therapists must engage in introspection and ongoing reflection to maintain ethical integrity and prioritise the best interests of the client. Understanding Islāmic rulings and values is essential in addressing ethical dilemmas from an Islāmic perspective. Islāmic rulings, derived from jurisprudence, offer specific guidance on ethical conduct and moral obligations. They provide insight into applying Islāmic principles to contemporary dilemmas. Therapists with a deep understanding of Islāmic rulings can analyse dilemmas, consider relevant principles, and make decisions aligned with Islāmic values. This approach enables them to evaluate ethical dilemmas through an Islāmic lens and uphold ethical standards within the context of Islāmic principles.

Consultation is vital in the ethical dilemma decision-making model, especially in Islāmic psychotherapy. It allows therapists to seek external guidance and mitigate potential gaps in understanding complex dilemmas. Therapists engage in consultations with colleagues, supervisors, faith leaders, or Islāmic scholars to gain diverse perspectives and assess situations comprehensively. In Islāmic psychotherapy, seeking guidance from Islāmic scholars knowledgeable about Islāmic principles is of paramount importance. Their insights and interpretations offer valuable guidance to therapists navigating ethical dilemmas within Islāmic contexts. Clinical supervision is a promising avenue for addressing ethical dilemmas in clinical practice. It involves regular meetings between a supervisor and a therapist, during which the therapist's cases, ethical concerns, and professional development are discussed. By involving others in the decision-making process, therapists can ensure that ethical dilemmas are approached with utmost care and adherence to Islāmic principles.

In the ethical dilemma decision-making model, the action and resolution stages are crucial, signifying the therapist's commitment to addressing ethical issues effectively. During this stage, therapists implement courses of action based on decisions made in the ethical decision-making process. For instance, if a breach of confidentiality is identified, appropriate action may involve addressing the breach with the client, ensuring future privacy protection, and mitigating potential harm. Actions should align with the therapist's ethical values, professional standards, and organisational policies and guidelines.

The resolution stage signifies the conclusion of the ethical dilemma, where therapists assess the outcomes of the action taken and determine if the issue has been appropriately addressed. For instance, following a breach of confidentiality, therapists evaluate whether the steps taken effectively safeguarded client confidentiality and restored trust. Ongoing monitoring and evaluation are crucial to ensure that the chosen action upholds ethical standards. If issues persist or new challenges arise, therapists may need to reassess their approach, seek additional consultation, or adjust therapeutic interventions to better address ethical concerns.

Thorough documentation is essential following the resolution of an ethical dilemma. It serves as a record of the therapist's ethical considerations, decision-making processes, and actions taken to address the dilemma. Documentation fulfils legal requirements, ensures continuity of care, and promotes a learning culture within the therapeutic setting. Additionally, it enables future reference to or review of the ethical dilemma with integrity, clarity, and transparency.

The cycles of reflection stage is integral to the ethical dilemma decision-making model in Islāmic psychotherapy. It signifies the therapists' commitment to continuous learning and ethical development. Through reflection, therapists assess the ethical dilemmas they faced, their decisions, and the outcomes. This process enables them to understand their ethical stances, recognise personal biases, and enhance their decision-making processes. By reflecting on past ethical dilemmas and their resolutions, therapists can identify areas for improvement and refine their ethical competence. They examine the interplay between various ethical principles and Islāmic values, seeking a deeper understanding of their applications within the therapeutic context. This process of reflection enables therapists to develop strategies to address similar challenges more effectively in the future, promoting continual growth in ethical practice. Ultimately, the cycles of reflection stage embodies the ethical responsibility inherent in Islāmic psychotherapy.

The ethical dilemma decision-making model in Islāmic psychotherapy offers a culturally sensitive and holistic approach to addressing ethical challenges. Integrating Islāmic ethics, cultural awareness, and familial considerations, this model provides a comprehensive framework for navigating ethical dilemmas. It reflects a commitment to ethical and culturally competent practice in Islāmic psychotherapy. Following this process-driven model, therapists can effectively manage and address the complexity of real-world ethical dilemmas.

Therapists can enhance the effectiveness of the ethical dilemma decision-making model by evaluating its limitations and supplementing it with continuous self-reflection, consultation with colleagues, and ongoing education. This comprehensive approach allows therapists to better understand ethical dilemmas within diverse cultural contexts and improve their decision-making skills. By integrating additional practices, therapists can ensure that they provide the most effective and culturally sensitive care to their clients.

Conclusion

Ethical dilemmas in Islāmic psychotherapy are complex and multifaceted challenges that require careful consideration and adherence to ethical principles deeply rooted in Islāmic beliefs and practices. Islāmic psychotherapists employ a unique ethical decision-making model that integrates Islāmic ethics, cultural awareness, and the dynamics of the client–family unit. The ethical dilemma decision-making model provides a structured approach to addressing ethical challenges not only in Islāmic psychotherapy but also in various professional fields. It emphasises consistency, transparency, and accountability in decision-making. However, it is critical to acknowledge that ethical dilemmas can be complex and may lack definitive solutions, requiring therapists to exercise sound judgment and consider specific circumstances. While the model promotes consistency and transparency, therapists must recognise the intricacies of ethical dilemmas and apply a faith-centred and culturally sensitive approach. When used within the context of Islāmic values and cultural awareness, the ethical dilemma decision-making model serves as a robust framework to guide therapists in making informed, ethical, and culturally relevant decisions in practice.

References

American Counseling Association (ACA). (2014). *Code of ethics*. ACA. Retrieved September 20, 2023, from www.counseling.org/knowledge-center/ethics.

American Psychological Association. (2017). *Ethical principles of psychologists and code of conduct* (2002, amended effective June 1, 2010, and January 1, 2017). www.apa.org/ethics/code.

Barnett, J. E., & Johnson, W. B. (2011). Integrating spirituality and religion into psychotherapy: Persistent dilemmas, ethical issues, and a proposed decision-making process. *Ethics and Behavior*, 21(2), 147–164. http://dx.doi.org/10.1080/10508422.2011.551471.

Barnett, J. E., & Teehan, D. (2022). Ethics and values in psychotherapy. *Psychotherapy Bulletin*, 57(2), 11–16.

Barnett, J. H. (2019). The ethical practice of psychotherapy: Clearly within our reach. *Psychotherapy*, 56(4), 431–440.

Bond, T. (2010). *Standards & ethics for counselling in action*. Sage Publications.

British Association for Counselling & Psychotherapy (BACP). (2013). *Ethical framework for good practice in counselling and psychotherapy*. BACP.

Corey, G., Corey, M. S., & Callanan, P. (2011). *Issues and ethics in the helping professions*. Cengage Learning.

Cottone, R. R., & Tarvydas, V. (2016). *Ethics and decision making in counseling and psychotherapy*. Springer Publishing Company, LLC.

Hegde, S. (2019). *What is an ethical dilemma?* Retrieved September 18, 2023, from www.scienceabc.com/social-science/what-is-an-ethical-dilemma-definition-examples-real-life.html.

Hendrix, D. H. (1991). Ethics and intra-family confidentiality in counseling with children. *Journal of Mental Health Counselling*, 13(3), 323–333.

Herlihy, B., & Corey, G. (2006). *ACA ethical standards casebook*. American Counseling Association.

Hinrichs, K. L. M., & Donaldson, W. (2017). Recommendations for use of affirmative psychotherapy with LGBT older adults. *Journal of Clinical Psychology*, 73(8), 945–953. https://doi.org/10.1002/jclp.22505.

Knapp, S. J., Gottlieb, M. C., & Handelsman, M. M. (2015). *Ethical dilemmas in psychotherapy: Positive approaches to decision making*. American Psychological Association. https://doi.org/10.1037/14670-000.

Knapp, S. J., VandeCreek, L. D., & Fingerhut, R. (2017). *Practical ethics for psychologists: A positive approach* (3rd ed.). American Psychological Association. http://dx.doi.org/10.1037/0000036-000.

Lindsay, G., & Clarkson, P. (1999). Ethical dilemmas of psychotherapists. *The Psychologist*, 12(4), 182–185.

Lindsay, G., & Colley, A. (1995). Ethical dilemmas of members of the Society. *The Psychologist*, 8(10), 448–451.

Pope, K. S., & Vasquez, M. J. T. (2007). *Ethics in psychotherapy and counseling: A practical guide* (3rd ed.). Jossey-Bass.

Qadhi, Y. (2022). *Fatwa regarding transgenderism*. Fiqh Council of North America. Retrieved September 18, 2023, from https://fiqhcouncil.org/fatwa-regarding-transgenderism/.

Welfel, E. R. (2006). *Ethics in counseling and psychotherapy: Standards, research, and emerging issues* (3rd ed.). Thomson Brooks/Cole Publishing Co.

Younggren, J. N., & Gottlieb, M. C. (2004). Managing risk when contemplating multiple relationships. *Professional Psychology: Research and Practice*, 35(3), 255–260. http://dx.doi.org/10.1037/0735-7028.35.3.255.

PART II
The intersection of Islām and psychotherapy

Understanding congruent and non-congruent psychotherapeutic approaches

6
ILLUMINATING THE PSYCHE
An introduction to psychoanalytic therapy

Introduction

The psychoanalytic approach, pioneered by Sigmund Freud, has profoundly influenced the field of psychotherapy since the late 19th century. Psychoanalytic approaches significantly influenced the field of psychology and continue to have a profound influence to this day. Several therapeutic approaches have either expanded upon the psychoanalytic model, adjusted its concepts and methods, or emerged in response to it (Corey, 2009). Although the roots of psychodynamic therapy and counselling are embedded predominantly in Freud's psychoanalytical approach, other practitioners including Carl Jung, Alfred Adler, Otto Rank, Eric Fromm, Karen Horney, Anna Freud, and Melanie Klein are all widely recognised for further developing the concept and application of psychodynamics. This chapter, "Illuminating the Psyche," focuses on human nature from a psychanalytical perspective. It examines the core principles and the therapeutic process and its relationship between religion, spirituality and psychoanalysis. Finally, the chapter examines psychoanalytical therapy and counselling and their congruence with Islāmic beliefs and practices.

Freud and human nature

Freudian theories profoundly influenced our comprehension of human nature by positing that unconscious processes shape human behaviour and experience. Central to Freud's perspective are the unconscious mind, instincts, personality structure, and childhood development. Freud delineated three levels of the mind: conscious, preconscious, and unconscious, asserting that the latter exerts a profound influence on thoughts, emotions, and actions (Freud, 1901, 1961, 1997). He proposed

DOI: 10.4324/9781003453413-8

two fundamental instincts, *eros* (life instinct) and *thanatos* (death instinct), which drive human behaviour, often conflicting with each other. Freud emphasised the deterministic nature of human behaviour, shaped by irrational forces, unconscious motivations, and biological drives, particularly during psychosexual stages of development in early childhood (Corey, 2009). Both sexual and aggressive drives, Freud argued, significantly influence individual behaviour.

Freud (1961) proposed a personality model comprising the id, ego, and superego, each serving distinct functions in human behaviour. The id operates on the pleasure principle, seeking immediate gratification, while the ego navigates reality by mediating between the id and external demands. The superego represents internalised cultural and moral standards. Freud underscored the significance of early childhood experiences, particularly in psychosexual development stages, including oral, anal, phallic, latency, and genital. Interactions and conflicts during these stages can shape personality formation and lead to unresolved issues or fixations that influence adult behaviour. Unresolved conflicts from early psychosexual stages, such as the oral, anal, and phallic stages, can lead to fixation, where individuals remain stuck in developmental patterns. For instance, someone fixated at the oral stage might exhibit habits like smoking, overeating, or nail-biting. The anal stage, characterised by issues with recognising and expressing anger, may result in a lack of autonomy or obsession with cleanliness and control (Corey, 2009). Fixation at the phallic stage could manifest as immaturity, narcissism, or overt sexualisation, potentially leading to behaviours like serial marriage or polygamy (Ellis et al., 2009). The latency stage marks a period of no further psychosexual development.

Sigmund Freud outlined various defence mechanisms that the ego employs to mitigate anxiety and emotional distress in psychoanalysis. These mechanisms, such as repression, denial, projection, regression, conversion, and displacement, operate unconsciously to reduce anxiety and maintain psychological safety. While they help maintain emotional balance, overuse or misapplication can impede self-awareness and personal growth. Understanding these mechanisms allows individuals to gain insight into their behaviours and emotional responses, empowering them to make more informed coping choices in the face of life's challenges.

Core principles and therapeutic process

Psychodynamic therapy and counselling, forms of talk therapy, aid individuals, couples, families, and groups by uncovering repressed emotions and experiences to make unconscious motives conscious. The therapy aims to explore feelings, thoughts, early-life experiences, and beliefs to gain insights into current problems and behavioural patterns. Similar to peeling back layers of an onion, it reveals hidden emotions, fostering self-understanding and informed choices for improved well-being. Clients examine avoidance of distress and defence mechanisms, identifying recurring patterns to enact change (www.goodtherapy.org, 2018). Freud's psychosexual development stages offer a framework for understanding key developmental tasks across life stages, aiding therapists in assessment and intervention. The core principles of psychoanalytic approach to therapy include the following:

- Early childhood experiences and unconscious events shape individuals' self-perceptions and worldviews.
- Internal experiences are understood in relation to interpersonal relationships.
- Key processes and techniques include identifying recurring themes, discussing past experiences, focusing on emotions, and exploring the therapeutic relationship and fantasy life (Shedler, 2010).
- Core concepts involve transference, resistance, the dynamic unconscious, developmental lenses, countertransference, and psychic determinism (Gabbard, 2005).
- Both client and therapist past experiences influence the therapeutic relationship (Kay, 2006).
- Therapy emphasises recognising and addressing defence mechanisms.
- Free association is a primary method, along with other techniques, of exploring internal conflicts.
- Insight is crucial for positive therapy outcomes.

In both psychoanalysis and psychodynamic therapy, the therapeutic interaction serves as the cornerstone for therapeutic progress. The therapist assumes a supportive and empathetic role, fostering an environment where clients feel accepted, understood, and encouraged to explore their unconscious thoughts, emotions, and experiences. This relationship is characterised by the therapist's neutral stance, avoiding personal disclosure and maintaining a "blank screen" approach. Through this dynamic, clients project their feelings, desires, and conflicts onto the therapist through transference. These shared elements create a safe and conducive space for clients to engage in self-exploration and growth, regardless of whether they are undergoing traditional psychoanalysis or psychodynamic therapy.

Exploring transference dynamics in therapy provides therapists with valuable insights into clients' unconscious processes, facilitating a deeper understanding of their psychological challenges. In psychoanalysis, the therapeutic interaction fosters a strong sense of trust and confidentiality, enabling clients to express themselves openly without fear of judgment or criticism. This trust creates a safe space for the examination of sensitive and complex topics that may be challenging to discuss in other relationships or settings.

Psychoanalytical and psychodynamic approach

Both classical psychoanalysis and psychodynamic therapy are based on Freud's beliefs and concepts, but there are some fundamental differences between these two therapeutic approaches. Some of the features of psychodynamic therapy or counselling as compared with traditional psychoanalysis (Corey, 2009) are that the therapy is geared more to limited objectives than to restructuring one's personality; the therapist is less likely to use the couch; there are fewer sessions each week; there is more frequent use of supportive interventions, such as reassurance, expressions of empathy and support, suggestions, and more self-disclosure by the therapist; and the focus is more on pressing practical concerns than on working with fantasy material. The working alliance or therapeutic relationship is central to psychodynamic therapy and counselling in bringing about change in the client's behaviour. However, it is argued that in psychodynamic therapy, the establishment of the therapeutic alliance is inherently more difficult "because the analyst must scrupulously avoid revealing any aspects of his personality" (Ellis et al., 2009, p. 118).

Contemporary psychodynamic therapy emphasises emotional communication between therapists and clients for information and connection (Luborsky et al., 2008). The therapeutic journey, according to Ellis et al. (2009), includes phases such as analysing resistance, analysing transference, and interpretation (late phase). Psychodynamic therapists commonly employ techniques like maintaining the analytic framework, free association, interpretation, dream analysis, and analysis of resistance and transference (Corey, 2009). Table 6.1 highlights commonalities and differences between classical psychoanalysis and psychodynamic approaches.

TABLE 6.1 Classical psychoanalysis and psychodynamics approaches

	Classical psychoanalysis	*Psychodynamic therapy*
Structure	Multiple sessions per week Lasting for years	Less intensive: One session per week May last for a shorter duration
Time and cost	Significant time commitment and can be costly	Frequent and shorter sessions May be more time and cost effective
Goal	Achieve lasting personality change	Addressing present-day issues and symptoms
	Profound insight into the workings of the unconscious mind	Increasing self-awareness, improving interpersonal relationships, and facilitating personal growth
Focus	Deep exploration of the unconscious Addressing unresolved conflicts	Exploring unconscious dynamics Addressing current issues and symptom relief
Techniques	Free association, dream analysis, and interpretation	Utilises additional interventions such as exploration of the therapeutic relationship, clarification, reflection, and supportive techniques
Therapeutic relationship	Significance of the therapeutic relationship	Significance of the therapeutic relationship
	Neutral and non-disclosing stance to minimise personal influence on the client's transference and free associations	Collaborative relationship Active role of the therapist in guiding the therapy and providing support and guidance

Effectiveness and limitations of Freudian psychoanalytical approach

Psychoanalytic and psychodynamic therapies have undergone extensive research, revealing both strengths and limitations. Critics highlight limitations in the Freudian psychoanalytical approach, such as the use of a narrow sample of neurotic middle-class Viennese women, which raises concerns about generalisability. Additionally, the difficulty in empirically supporting Freudian constructs like the id, ego, and superego, along with an emphasis on sexuality over social factors in personality development, poses challenges to the approach's validity (Fisher & Greenberg, 1985, 1996; Luborsky et al., 2008; Scaturo, 2001; Strupp, 1992; Shedler, 2010). Despite these criticisms, research indicates the effectiveness of psychoanalytic therapy in treating various mental health conditions (Fonagy, 2015). Studies demonstrate its efficacy in addressing depression, anxiety, personality disorders, and specific phobias. Naturalistic and systematic reviews highlight significant improvements in symptomatology, interpersonal problems, quality of life, and overall well-being following psychoanalytic therapy (Leichsenring et al., 2005; Jakobsen et al., 2007; de Maat et al., 2009). Moreover, recent research suggests that psychoanalytic and psychodynamic therapies show promise in reducing suicidal behaviour and self-harm, leading to improved psychosocial well-being (Briggs et al., 2019).

Briggs et al. (2019) cautioned against drawing definitive conclusions from existing research on psychoanalytic and psychodynamic therapies due to limitations such as a small number of trials and low-quality evidence. They emphasised the need for additional high-quality trials to validate findings and ascertain the effectiveness of individual components within these therapies. Equally, Huber et al. (2013) conducted a study aiming to evaluate the effectiveness of long-term psychoanalytic and psychodynamic psychotherapies. Their findings revealed significant outcome differences between treatments at the three-year follow-up, with psychoanalytic therapy demonstrating greater effectiveness. Specific outcomes included improvements in depressive and global psychiatric symptoms, enhanced personality functioning, and better social relations. These results suggest promising benefits of long-term psychoanalytic therapy in addressing various psychological concerns.

However, recent research on the effectiveness of psychoanalytic therapy has yielded mixed results, with both supportive and critical findings. For instance, a meta-study by Leichsenring and Rabung (2011) suggested that long-term psychodynamic psychotherapy was superior to less intensive forms of psychotherapy for complex mental disorders. However, this conclusion was challenged on methodological grounds by Kliem et al. (2012), highlighting the complexities and debates within the field.

The effectiveness of psychoanalytic therapy remains a topic of contention among scholars and practitioners. While some studies offer support for its efficacy in addressing various psychiatric problems, critics argue that psychoanalytic treatment lacks the same level of empirical backing as other therapeutic modalities like cognitive–behavioural therapy. Critics emphasise the need for more robust scientific evidence to establish the efficacy of psychoanalytic therapy and address its complexities comprehensively.

Spirituality, psychoanalysis, and Islām

Religion, spirituality, and psychoanalysis intersect within a complex and multifaceted domain of study and practice. Historical tensions have arisen between religious beliefs and psychoanalytic perspectives, largely due to Freud's critical and sceptical stance towards religion. This scepticism contributed to conflicts and debates regarding the compatibility of religious faith and psychoanalytic theory within both academic and clinical contexts. In his seminal work "The Future of an Illusion," (Freud, 1933/1990), Freud famously characterised religion as a form of wishful thinking or neurosis, reflecting his belief that religious beliefs stemmed from human desires and fears rather than objective truths. He argued that religion provides solace by catering to human instinctual desires and needs, such as the longing for protection, comfort, and relief from existential anxieties.

Freud contended that religious beliefs operate as illusions, drawing strength from these innate desires. He further posited that religion could be viewed as a communal neurosis, mirroring individual neurotic tendencies. According to Freud, religious ideas and rituals serve as coping mechanisms for psychological conflicts and anxieties prevalent in both individuals and societies. For instance, religious rituals like confession may alleviate guilt, a common source of neurosis identified by Freud. Additionally, Freud associated his concept of the Oedipus complex, which involves a child's emotional attachment to the opposite-sex parent and rivalry with the same-sex parent, with his critique of religion. He proposed that religious obedience and worship of a paternal deity are symptomatic of the Oedipal relationship, further illuminating his interpretation of religious phenomena through psychoanalytic theory.

Freud, an atheist of Jewish descent, believed in the non-existence of God and viewed religious belief as a defence mechanism against life's challenges, notably human mortality. Throughout his work, Freud questioned the rationality of religious doctrines and arguments for God's existence, often critiquing religious morality, especially concerning sexual ethics. He posited that religious prohibitions on sexual behaviour and the repression of desires could result in psychological distress and guilt, likening religion to childhood neurosis and distress. While Freud characterised religion as a form of wishful thinking and a defence mechanism, Jones (1991) challenged Freud's perspective, suggesting that religious experiences and doctrines reflect internalised interpersonal patterns shaping our sense of self. It's crucial to recognise that Freud's criticisms of religion were reflective of his personal beliefs, and they were not universally embraced by all psychoanalysts or psychologists.

The relationship between Freudian psychoanalysis and religious thought has historically been marked by hostility, particularly within the Islāmic context. This suspicion stems from the perception that psychoanalysis promotes secularism or atheism, largely due to Freud's writings on religion and the animosity of theologians towards psychoanalysis. Akhtar (2009) noted that psychoanalytic thinking often accepted Freud's atheism at face value, leading to the view that psychoanalysis and religion, including mysticism and spirituality, are inherently antagonistic. Moreover, Freud's denial of the existence of God, the soul, the afterlife, and human free will directly contradicts religious teachings (Badri, as cited in Mura, 2014). Freud proposed that God is essentially an idealised father figure from whom believers seek protection and salvation (Benslama, 2006). These perspectives illustrate the enduring tensions and perceptions of conflict between psychoanalysis and religious belief, particularly in Islāmic contexts. However, from an Islāmic perspective, the Qur'ân contradicts Freud's thesis and states that "God was not born and God did not give birth to" (Al-Ikhlas 112):

ٱللَّهُ ٱلصَّمَدُ
لَمْ يَلِدْ وَلَمْ يُولَدْ

- *Allāh is the Eternal Refuge.*
- *He neither begets nor is born.*

(Al-Ikhlas 112:2–3, interpretation of the meaning)

According to the exegesis of Ibn Kathir (2000), relating to the second and third verses,

(*As-Samad*) is One Who does not give birth, nor was He born, because there is nothing that is born except that it will die, and there is nothing that dies except that it leaves behind inheritance, and indeed Allāh does not die and He does not leave behind any inheritance.

Thus, the notion that God is assumed to have a paternal function is refuted.

Scholars have explored the intersection between psychoanalysis and Sufism (Nurbakhsh, 1978a, b), an Islāmic mystical tradition, to comprehend the psychological and spiritual aspects of human experience. Despite initial rejection by Islām due to psychoanalysis's Jewish origins, atheism, and equating God to an idealised father figure (Keller, 2006), there has been a shift towards reconciling spirituality with the psychodynamic approach to therapy (Arden, 1998; Beit-Hallāhmi, 1996; Black, 2012; Coltart, 1993; Field, 2005; Jones, 1991; Marcus, 2003; Meissner, 1984; Safran, 2012; Tan, 1996). This change reflects a growing recognition of the complementary aspects between psychoanalysis and Islāmic thought and practices (Ad-Dab'bagh, 2001; Akhtar, 2008; Akhtar & Parens, 2001; Benslama, 2009; Etezady, 2001; Fayek, 2004).

The conciliation between Islām and psychoanalysis may be possible on the basis of the enhancement in quality of the therapeutic relationship rather than any psychoanalytic analysis and interpretation (Ad-Dab'bagh, 2001). Etezady (2008) suggests that Muslim clients could benefit intra-psychically by overcoming obstacles to accessing their personal truths and ultimate judgment. Fayek (2004) acknowledges tensions between Islām and psychoanalysis but sees potential for complementarity. Despite his lack of religious affiliation, Fayek believes psychoanalysis can address issues within Islām. He suggests that religion, as an active ethnic identity, could be viewed as part of character defences, as ethnic religious identity is not a matter of choice (Fayek, 2004).

Etezady (2008) suggests that while Islām and psychoanalysis emerge from distinct domains, spiritual and psychological, they share fundamental themes related to self-discovery, moral ideals, and the quest for personal significance. Islām encourages self-knowledge, values, morality, and transcendence while also emphasising the primacy of meaning. Similarly, psychoanalysis seeks to deepen self-awareness through introspection, exploring personal values, and uncovering the significance of individual experiences. This perspective implies that individuals can utilise both Islāmic teachings and psychoanalytic insights to enhance their understanding of themselves and their lives, recognising the value inherent in each tradition's perspectives on human existence.

According to Etezady (2008), faith is viewed as a transformative force central to a believing Muslim's integrity and sense of self. In the context of psychoanalytic therapy, change involves conflict resolution, the removal of fixation points, and the repair of deficits in self-regulation. While scholars have explored the relationships between Islām, Muslims, and psychoanalysis, some analyses may be grounded in secular thinking, leading to distortions about Islām, an overemphasis on Sufism, and perpetuation of negative stereotypes. The incongruence between psychoanalysis and Islām stems from differences in goals, domains, methodologies, and worldviews, highlighting the complexities inherent in integrating these two traditions.

Psychoanalytic therapy and counselling: congruence with Islāmic beliefs

In Islāmic communities, psychoanalytic approaches are not widely accepted as a form of therapy and counselling (Al-Abdul-Jabbar & Al-Issa, 2000; Azhar & Varma, 2000; Rassool, 2016; Sabry & Vohra, 2013) because some of the conceptual frameworks and modalities of the psychoanalytical school have a degree of incongruence with Islāmic values and practices. Although it is reported that some aspects of Freudian psychoanalytic treatment mirror Islāmic concepts, in general, psychoanalytic therapy may not be widely embraced as they do not align with many Muslim clients' religious beliefs. Cognitive-based therapies are often seen as more congruent with the religious perspectives of Muslim clients than psychoanalysis (Amer & Jalal, 2012). The Freudian tradition's historical disregard for religion has led to a lack of integration of religiosity in treatment within the psychodynamic tradition, making it incompatible with Islāmic culture (Badri, 1979).

Freudian psychoanalysis, along with behaviourist and humanistic psychology, is founded on a secular understanding of human nature. Freud's theory posits that human nature is inherently conflicted and driven by unconscious sexual and aggressive instincts influenced by the id, ego, and superego. This secular perspective tends to overlook moral and spiritual dimensions within individuals, leaving religious practice to the discretion of the individual (Haque, 2004). Moreover, psychoanalytic doctrines are predominantly shaped by rationalist theories of human nature, which are in turn rooted in forms of mind–body dualism stemming from Judaeo-Christian religious teachings (Webster, 2005).

The Islāmic perspective on human existence contrasts sharply with the solely materialistic, secular, or immediate-needs-oriented viewpoints prevalent in many psychological frameworks. According to Abdul Razak and Hisham (2012), Islāmic understanding comprehensively acknowledges humans' true nature, their pre-Earthly origin, their mission and role in life, and their eventual return after completing earthly existence. This perspective offers a holistic view of human existence, encompassing physical, psychological, spiritual, and sociocultural dimensions, in contrast to reducing humans to a "here and now" status. The Islāmic viewpoint emphasises a deeper understanding of human existence beyond the material realm, highlighting the significance of spirituality and theological perspectives in shaping individuals' lives and purpose.

Islām teaches that God created humans differently from non-humans because everything is created for humans, as mentioned in the Qur'ân:

هُوَ ٱلَّذِى خَلَقَ لَكُم مَّا فِى ٱلْأَرْضِ جَمِيعًا

- *It is He who created for you all of that which is on the earth.*
  (Al-Baqarah 2:29, interpretation of the meaning)

لَقَدْ خَلَقْنَا ٱلْإِنسَٰنَ فِى أَحْسَنِ تَقْوِيمٍ ۝ ثُمَّ رَدَدْنَٰهُ أَسْفَلَ سَٰفِلِينَ ۝ إِلَّا ٱلَّذِينَ ءَامَنُوا۟ وَعَمِلُوا۟ ٱلصَّٰلِحَٰتِ فَلَهُمْ أَجْرٌ غَيْرُ مَمْنُونٍ

- *We have certainly created man in the best of stature, then We return him to the lowest of the low, except for those who believe and do righteous deeds, for they will have a reward uninterrupted.*
  (At-Tīn 95:4–6, interpretation of the meaning)

Allāh tells us that He has created humans in perfected order, and thus, He has perfected everything in man:

مَّا تَرَىٰ فِى خَلْقِ ٱلرَّحْمَٰنِ مِن تَفَٰوُتٍ

- *You do not see in the creation of the Most Merciful any inconsistency.*
  (Al-Mulk 67:3, interpretation of the meaning)

The purpose of human creation is explained in the Qur'ān:

وَمَا خَلَقْتُ ٱلْجِنَّ وَٱلْإِنسَ إِلَّا لِيَعْبُدُونِ

- *And I did not create the Jinn and mankind except to worship Me.*
  (Adh-Dhāriyāt 51:56, interpretation of the meaning)

This means, "So that they worship Me, willingly or unwillingly" (Ibn Kathir, 2000). Allāh says in the Qur'ān,

فَأَقِمْ وَجْهَكَ لِلدِّينِ حَنِيفًا ۚ فِطْرَتَ ٱللَّهِ ٱلَّتِى فَطَرَ ٱلنَّاسَ عَلَيْهَا ۚ

- *[Adhere to] the fitrah of Allāh upon which He has created [all] people.*
  (Ar-Rūm 30:30, interpretation of the meaning)

This verse means that all humans have been created on *fitrah*, that is, the innate instinct that acknowledges the truth of Allāh's existence.

Freud completely denied free will, believing instead that our thought processes and behaviours are the result of our minds or psyche. This concept is contrary to the Islāmic theory of human nature, where there is substantial room for free will. From an Islāmic perspective, humans have been given free will to make choices regarding their beliefs and deeds. As mentioned in the Qur'ān,

ٱلْحَقُّ مِن رَّبِّكُمْ ۖ فَمَن شَاءَ فَلْيُؤْمِن وَمَن شَاءَ فَلْيَكْفُرْ ۚ

- *The truth is from your Lord, so whoever wills – let him believe; and whoever wills – let him disbelieve.*
  (Al-Kahf 18:29, interpretation of the meaning)

But this free will is not absolute; it has limits. The will of a human being is connected to the will of Allāh, and nothing happens by the will of the individual alone:

وَمَا تَشَاءُونَ إِلَّا أَن يَشَاءَ ٱللَّهُ ۚ

- *And you do not will except that Allāh wills.*
  (Al-'Insān 76:30, interpretation of the meaning)

This does not mean that humans are forced to do anything, but it means "that humans are free to make choices, but the outcome of the choice depends upon the will of Allāh. Else the concept of accountability will lose its purpose" (Ashraf, 2013).

Freud's psychosexual development theory posits that children progress through distinct phases – oral, anal, and phallic – during which their sexual drives are central. Neurosis or perversion may arise from fixation in or regression to these phases.

In contrast, Islām emphasises the inherent goodness of humans, attributing any deviance to upbringing and social influences. According to Islāmic perspective, newborns enter the world in a state of *fitrah*, characterised by a primordial nature devoid of sin and evil. Conversely, Freud's theory suggests that newborns are primarily driven by the id until the development of the ego and superego (Abdul Razak, 2011). Abu Hurayrah reported Allāh's Messenger (ﷺ) as saying, "No child is born but upon *fitrah*. He then said, 'Recite "The nature made by Allāh in which He created man, there is no altering of Allāh's nature; that is the right religion"'" (Muslim). In another *hadīth*, it is narrated by Abu Hurayrah that Prophet Muhammad (ﷺ) said, "Every child is born with a true faith of Islām (i.e. to worship none but Allāh Alone) and his parents convert him to Judaism or Christianity or Magianism" (Bukhârî).

Unlike Christianity, Islām rejects the notion that everyone is born into a state of original sin. The concept of original sin in Christianity is based on the premise that all humans inherit the sin of Adam and Eve, the first humans; this idea holds that humans are born with a load of sin that separates them from God. In this framework, salvation is frequently viewed as a means of cleansing persons from this inherent sin. In contrast, in the Islāmic context, individuals are born in a state of purity and moral neutrality known as *fitrah*. They are not burdened with the origin sins of their ancestors; instead, everyone is responsible for their own acts, and salvation in Islām is attained via faith, good seeds, and requesting God's pardon. Thus, Islām's view on human nature is more optimistic and believes humans have continuous potential for growth and self-development (Samsudin, 2009).

In Islām, the significance of childhood experiences cannot be overstated, as they profoundly shape an individual's personality and moral development. During childhood, a parent's consistent emotional attachment plays a pivotal role in shaping the child's experiences. A stable, strong, and loving family environment, where parents prioritise developing the child's sense of self-worth and dignity, influences childhood experiences and religious orientation. In such an environment, the child develops trust, self-confidence, and a deep-rooted appreciation for parental and divine authority. The Noble Qur'ân highlights the importance of healthy parent–child relationships and emphasises parents' responsibility in nurturing and upbringing their children. Dover (2014) suggested that one of the ways parents can shape their child's behaviour while still maintaining a positive and true view of God is to associate doing good with God. For example, "Allāh loves those who are good to their parents" or "Allāh is most pleased with you when you are doing your homework so you can learn because Allāh loves his creation to gain knowledge through education." In this way, Dover (2014) suggested that "a child's brain can be nurtured with love, good thoughts, and the cultivation of good and righteous behaviour manifest."

In Islām, human sexuality is acknowledged as a natural aspect of human existence, and individuals may experience sexual desires and development at different stages of life. However, modesty and sexual ethics hold significant importance in

Islām, and discussions about sexuality are typically framed within a moral and theological context. Islāmīc teachings emphasise modesty and chastity across various aspects of life, and the role of sexuality and sexual relations is examined within the framework of lawful marriage. From an Islāmic perspective, personality development is influenced by a multitude of factors, including early experiences, attachment, socialisation, role modelling, imitation, and educational development. These variables collectively shape an individual's personality and moral outlook within the context of Islāmic principles and teachings. Samsudin (2009) argues that the remarkable transformation in the personalities of the companions of Prophet Muhammad (ﷺ), including Umar al-Khattab and Abu Dhar al-Ghifari in particular – who changed from being the greatest of bullies during the pre-Islāmic period to among the most pious Muslims upon conversion to Islām – is an outstanding example of how radical personality changes and improvements can occur even during adulthood. It is important to note that while Islām recognises the influence of childhood experiences and human sexuality on personality development, it also emphasises personal accountability and the capacity for individuals to make choices and be responsible for their actions.

The fundamental incongruence between the psychoanalytic approach and Islāmic beliefs lies in the notion of determinism. Freud's theory suggests that human behaviour is determined by unconscious forces and early life experiences that can overpower conscious goals. In contrast, Islāmic teachings emphasise free will, personal responsibility, and moral choice. Individuals are held accountable for their actions according to Islāmic beliefs. Regarding the self, Freud's model provides a structural examination focusing on the interplay of instinctual drives (id), rational decision-making (ego), and moral conscience (superego).

In the literature on Islāmic psychology, despite the theoretical incongruence between psychoanalytic principles and Islāmic teachings, there is a common misinterpretation that equates the concept of *nafs* in Islām with Freud's psychosexual development theory of the id, ego, and superego. Freud's trilogy has been matched with the *nafs al-ammāra bissu* [Yusuf 12:53], *nafs al-mutma'innah* Al-Qiyamah 75:2], and *nafs al-lawwāmah* [Fajr 89:27–28] (Aydin, 2010). Keshavarzi and Ali (2021) proposed that "it is possible to liken the *nafs* in this sense to Freud's conceptualisation of the id" (p. 28). This notion has been rejected by contemporary Islāmic psychology scholars and thinkers because of its Orientalist approach (Rassool, 2023, p. 119). Badri (2021) stated,

> A good and widely held example at the time was their proposition that the Freudian seminal theory of the three structures of personality -namely the id, ego, and superego -are the same as the three spiritual ego states of the soul that are mentioned in the Qur'ān. They claimed that the commanding soul *Nafs al-Ammāra* stands for the id, the soul nafs is exemplified by the ego, and the tranquil soul *Nafs al-muṭma'innah* stands for the superego. This undermined the richer and

metaphysical nature of these Qur'ānic concepts. In the late 1950s, I personally witnessed many Muslim psychologists strongly defend this false belief as if Freud were a spiritually motivated scholar.

(p. xxi)

Rassool (2023) offers a word of caution, stating that, "Students of Islāmic psychology should be mindful of . . . the literature on Islāmic psychology, both print and web-based, from contemporary thinkers who equate Freud's psychoanalytic theory of personality with the states of the *nafs* as stated in the Qur'ān" (p. 120). In Islāmic psychology, the metaphysical elements and the inner psyche that influence human behaviours are the self (*nafs*), the soul (*rûh*), the heart (*qalb*), and the intellect (*'aql*). For a comprehensive account of the *nafs*, see Rassool (2023, Chapter 6). The concept of the self in Islām is rooted in the notion of *fitrah*, representing a spiritually oriented perspective on human nature. *Fitrah* is believed to be a primordial inclination inherent in all human beings, transcending ethnic or religious backgrounds. Muslims strive to nurture and align with the *fitrah*, embracing monotheism and living according to moral virtues. This understanding acknowledges the inherent spiritual dimension of the self and guides individuals towards spiritual alignment and moral living.

Conclusion

While psychoanalysis pioneered the concept of talking therapy, it is widely recognised that the psychoanalytical and psychodynamic approaches to therapy, advocated by figures like Freud, are not congruent with Islāmic principles. Operating from a psychoanalytic perspective may not present Islām in a positive light due to the frameworks and conceptions of psychoanalysis, which may conflict with the theological and spiritual aspects of Islām. Additionally, psychoanalysis primarily focuses on the individual and their unconscious motivations, potentially overlooking the holistic nature of Islāmic ideas and practices. Scholars have suggested that beginning with a model of psychology rooted in secular presuppositions may hinder the ability to view religious belief or practice in a healthy light (Priester et al., 2008).

Muslim clients often perceive psychotherapy as unnecessary and ineffective, preferring spiritual healing, support from friends and family, or medical advice. There are perceived conflicts between psychotherapy and Islām (Smith, 2011) that reflect a diverse range of viewpoints. However, within the psychodynamic model of therapy and counselling, there exist points of congruence that can foster successful client–therapist alliances (Amer & Jalal, 2012). Fisher and Greenberg (1985) suggest that psychoanalytic theory should not be accepted or rejected as a whole but rather evaluated for its individual elements. Further investigation is needed to determine the value and effectiveness of psychoanalytical or psychodynamic therapy techniques with Muslim clients.

References

Abdul Razak, M. A. (2011). *Contribution of Iqbal's dynamic personality theory to Islāmic psychology: A contrastive analysis with Freud and selected mainstream Western psychology* [Doctoral dissertation, International Islāmic University]. Retrieved November 1, 2023, from http://iedf.wikispaces.com/file/view/Thesis+2011.pdf.

Abdul Razak, M. A., & Hisham, N. A. (2012). Islāmic psychology and the call for Islāmization of modern psychology. *Journal of Islām in Asia, 9*(1), 156–183.

Ad-Dab'bagh, Y. (2001). The median: Islāmic faith and mental health. In S. Akhtar & H. Parens (Eds.), *Does God help? Developmental and clinical aspects of religious belief*. Jason Aronson.

Akhtar, S. (2008). *The crescent and the couch: Cross-currents Between Islām and psychoanalysis*. Jason Aronson.

Akhtar, S. (2009). *Comprehensive dictionary of psychoanalysis*. Karnac Books.

Akhtar, S., & Parens, H. (2001). *Developmental and clinical aspects of religious belief*. Jason Aronson.

Al-Abdul-Jabbar, J., & Al-Issa, I. (2000). Psychotherapy in Islāmic society. In I. Al-Issa (Ed.), *Al-Junn: Mental illness in the Islāmic world* (pp. 277–293). International Universities Press.

Amer, M. M., & Jalal, B. (2012). Individual psychotherapy/counseling: Psychodynamic, cognitive-behavioral, and humanistic-experiential models. In S. Ahmed & M. M. Amer (Eds.), *Counseling Muslims: Handbook of mental health issues and interventions*. Routledge.

Arden, M. (1998). *Midwifery of the soul: A holistic perspective on psychoanalysis*. Free Association Books.

Ashraf, M. H. (2013). *Human nature in Islāmic perspective: History of ideas*. Retrieved November 1, 2023, from www.academia.edu/5117884/Human_Nature_in_Islamic_Perspective.

Aydin, H. (2010). Concepts of the self in Islāmic tradition and Western psychology: A comparative analysis. *Studies in Islām and the Middle East Journal, 7*(1), 1–30.

Azhar, M. Z., & Varma, S. L. (2000). Mental illness and its treatment in Malaysia. In I. Al-Issa (Ed.), *Al-Junūn: Mental illness in the Islāmic world* (pp. 163–185). International Universities Press.

Badri, M. B. (1979). *The dilemma of Muslim psychologists*. MWH London Publishers.

Badri, M. B. (2021). Preface. In H. Keshavarzi, F. Khan, B. Ali, & R. Awaad (Eds.), *Applying Islāmic principles to clinical mental health Care: Introducing traditional Islāmically integrated psychotherapy* (pp. 21–23). Routledge.

Beit-Hallāhmi, B. (1996). *Psychoanalytic studies of religion: A critical assessment and annotated bibliography*. Greenwood Press.

Benslama, F. (2006). Islām and psychoanalysis: A tale of mutual ignorance. *Qantare.de*. Retrieved October 31, 2023, from https://qantara.de/en/article/Islam-and-psychoanalysis-tale-mutual-ignorance.

Benslama, F. (2009). *Psychoanalysis and the challenge of Islām*. R. Bononno (Trans.). University of Minnesota Press.

Black, D. M. (2012). *Psychoanalysis and religion in the 21st century: Competitors or collaborators?* Routledge.

Briggs, S., Netuveli, G., Gould, N., Gkaravella, A., Gluckman, N., Kangogyere, P., Farr, R., Goldblatt, M. J., & Lindner, R. (2019). The effectiveness of psychoanalytic/psychodynamic psychotherapy for reducing suicide attempts and self-harm: Systematic review and meta-analysis. *The British Journal of Psychiatry, 214*(6), 320–328. https://doi.org/10.1192/bjp.2019.33.

Bukhârî. *Sahih al-Bukhârî 1385* [In-book reference: Book 23, Hadith 137. USC-MSA web (English) reference: Vol. 2, Book 23, Hadith 467]. https://sunnah.com/bukhari:1385.

Coltart, N. (1993). Psychoanalysis and Buddhism: Does the ego exist? In I. Ward (Ed.), *Is psychoanalysis another religion? Contemporary essays on spirit, faith and morality in psychoanalysis*. Freud Museum.

Corey, G. (2009). *Theory and practice of counseling and psychotherapy*. Thomson Brooks/Cole.

de Maat, S., de Jonghe, F., Schoevers, R., & Dekker, J. (2009). The effectiveness of long-term psychoanalytic therapy: A systematic review of empirical studies. *Harvard Review of Psychiatry, 17*(1), 10–23. https://doi.org/10.1080/10673220902742476.

Dover, H. (2014). Nurturing the love of Allāh into our children. *British Islāmic Nursery*. Retrieved October 30, 2023, from www.britishIslamicnursery.com/nurturing-the-love-of-Allah-into-our-children/.

Ellis, A., Abrams, M., Abrams, L. D., Nussbaum, A., & Frey, R. J. (2009). Psychoanalysis in theory and practice. In *Personality theories: Critical perspectives* (pp. 111–141). Sage Publications.

Etezady, M. H. (2008). Faith and the couch: A psychoanalytic perspective on transformation. *Psychoanalytic Inquiry, 28*(5), 560–569.

Fayek, A. (2004). Islām and its effect on my practice of psychoanalysis. *Psychoanalytic Psychology, 21*(3), 452–457.

Field, N. (2005). *Ten lectures on psychotherapy and spirituality*. Karnac.

Fisher, S., & Greenberg, R. P. (1985). *The scientific credibility of Freud's theories and therapy* (revised ed.). Columbia University Press.

Fisher, S., & Greenberg, R. P. (1996). *Freud scientifically reappraised: Testing the theories and therapy*. John Wiley.

Fonagy, P. (2015). The effectiveness of psychodynamic psychotherapies: An update. *World Psychiatry, 14*(2), 137–150. https://doi.org/10.1002/wps.20235/.

Freud, S. (1901). *The psychopathology of everyday life* (A. Tyson, Trans.). W. W. Norton & Company.

Freud, S. (1961). *Beyond the pleasure principle* (J. Strachey, Ed.). W.W. Norton & Company.

Freud, S. (1990). *New introductory lectures on psychoanalysis*. W.W. Norton & Company (Original work published 1933).

Freud, S. (1997). *The interpretation of dreams* (A. A. Brill, Trans.). Wordsworth Editions Limited.

Gabbard, G. O. (2005). Major modalities: Psychoanalytic/psychodynamic. In G. O. Gabbard, J. S. Beck, & J. Holmes (Eds.), *Oxford textbook of psychotherapy* (pp. 3–13). Oxford University Press.

Haque, A. (2004). Psychology from Islāmic perspective: Contributions of early Muslim scholars and challenges to contemporary Muslim psychologists. *Journal of Religion and Health, 43*(4), 357–377.

Huber, D., Henrich, G., Clarkin, J., & Klug, G. (2013). Psychoanalytic versus psychodynamic therapy for depression: A three-year follow-up study. *Psychiatry, 76*(2), 132–149. https://doi.org/10.1521/psyc.2013.76.2.132.

Ibn Kathir. (2000). *Tafsir ibn Kathir* (J. Abualrub, N. Khitab, H. Khitab, A. Walker, M. Al-Jibali, & S. Ayoub, Trans.). Darussalam Publishers and Distributors.

Jakobsen, T., Rudolf, G., Brockmann, J., Eckert, J., Huber, D., Klug, G., Grande, T., Keller, W., Staats, H., & Leichsenring, F. (2007). Results of psychoanalytic long-term therapy in specific diagnostic groups: Improvement in symptoms and interpersonal relationships. *Zeitschrift fur Psychosomatische Medizin und Psychotherapie, 53*(2), 87–110. https://doi.org/10.13109/zptm.2007.53.2.87.

Jones, J. W. (1991). *Contemporary psychoanalysis and religion: Transference and transcendence*. Yale University Press.

Kay, J. (2006). The essentials of psychodynamic psychotherapy. *FOCUS, 4*(2), 167–172.

Keller, G. (2006). Islām and psychoanalysis: A tale of mutual ignorance, an interview with Fethi Benslama. *Qantara.de*. Retrieved October 31, 2023, from http://en.qantara.de/content/Islam-and-psychoanalysis-a-tale-of-mutual-ignorance.

Keshavarzi, H., & Ali, B. (2021). Foundations of traditional islamically integrated psychotherapy. In H. Keshavarzi, F. Khan, B. Ali., & R. Awaad (Eds.), *Applying islamic principles to clinical mental health care: Introducing traditional islamically integrated psychotherapy*. Routledge.

Kliem, S., Beller, J., & Kroege, C. (2012). Methodological discrepancies in the update of a meta-analysis. *British Journal of Psychiatry, 200*(5), 429; Author reply 429–430.

Leichsenring, F., Biskup, J., Kreische, R., & Staats, H. (2005). The Guttingen study of psychoanalytic therapy: First results. *The International Journal of Psychoanalysis, 86*(2), 433–455.

Leichsenring, F., & Rabung, S. (2011). Long-term psychodynamic psychotherapy in complex mental disorders: Update of a meta-analysis. *British Journal of Psychiatry, 199*(1), 15–22. https://doi.org/10.1192/bjp.bp.110.082776.

Luborsky, E. B., O'Reilly-Landry, M., & Arlow, J. A. (2008). Psychoanalysis. In R. J. Corsini & D. Wedding (Eds.), *Current psychotherapies* (pp. 15–60). Thomson.

Marcus, P. (2003). *Ancient religious wisdom, spirituality, and psychoanalysis*. Greenwood Publishing Group.

Meissner, W. W. (1984). *Psychoanalysis and religious experience*. Yale University Press.

Mura, A. (2014). Islāmism revisited: A Lacanian discourse critique. *European Journal of Psychoanalysis, 1*(Winter), 107–126.

Muslim. *Sahih Muslim 2658d* [In-book reference: Book 46, Hadith 36. USC-MSA web (English) reference: Book 33, Hadith 6425]. https://sunnah.com.

Nurbakhsh, D. (1978a). Sufism and psychoanalysis. Part one: What is Sufism? *International Journal of Social Psychiatry, 24*(3), 204–212. https://doi.org/10.1177/002076407802400309.

Nurbakhsh, D. (1978b). Sufism and psychoanalysis. Part two: A comparison between sufism and psychoanalysis. *International Journal of Social Psychiatry, 24*(3), 213–219. https://doi.org/10.1177/002076407802400031.

Priester, P. E., Khalili, S., & Eluvathingal, E. L. (2008). Putting the soul back into psychology: Integrating religion in psychotherapy. In S. Eshun & R. Gurung (Eds.), *Sociocultural influences on mental health* (pp. 91–114). Blackwell.

Rassool, G. Hussein (2016). *Islāmic counselling: From theory to practice*. Routledge.

Rassool, G. Hussein (2023). *Islāmic psychology: The basics*. Routledge.

Sabry, W. M., & Vohra, A. (2013). Role of Islām in the management of psychiatric disorders. *Indian Journal of Psychiatry, 55*(Suppl. 2), S205–S214. https://doi.org/10.4103/0019-5545.105534.

Safran, J. D. (2012). *Psychoanalysis and Buddhism: An unfolding dialogue*. Wisdom Publications.

Samsudin, Z. (2009). Freudian personality psychology. In *Personality psychology from an Islāmic perspective* (Unpublished paper, 2007). Retrieved October 30, 2023, from http://zakisamsudin.blogspot.com/2009/03/freudian-personality-psychology.html.

Scaturo, D. J. (2001). The evolution of psychotherapy and the concept of manualization: An integrative perspective. *Professional Psychology: Research and Practice, 32*(5), 522–530. https://doi.org/10.1037//0735–7028.32.5.522.

Shedler, J. (2010). The efficacy of psychodynamic psychotherapy. *American Psychologist, 65*(2), 98–109. https://doi.org/10.1037/a0018378.

Smith, J. (2011). *Removing barriers to therapy with Muslim-Arab-American clients* [Psy. D. thesis, Antioch University New England]. Retrieved October 30, 2023, from http://rave.ohiolink.edu/etdc/view?acc_num=antioch1319727578.

Strupp, H. H. (1992). The future of psychodynamic psychotherapy. *Psychotherapy, 29*(1), 21–27.

Tan, S. (1996). Religion in clinical practice: Implicit and explicit integration. In E. P. Shafranske (Ed.), *Religion and the clinical practice of psychology* (pp. 365–390). American Psychological Association.

Webster, R. (2005). *Why Freud was wrong: Sin, science and psychoanalysis*. Orwell Press.

www.goodtherapy.org. (2018). *Psychodynamic therapy*. Retrieved October 19, 2023, from www.goodtherapy.org/learn-about-therapy/types/psychodynamic.

7
HARMONY AND DISSONANCE
Jungian therapy and Islāmic psychotherapy

Introduction

Jungian therapy, developed by Swiss psychiatrist Carl Gustav Jung, offers a psychological approach distinct from traditional Freudian psychoanalysis. Jung's work expanded the understanding of the unconscious mind and its relationship to human growth and development, contrasting with Freud's focus on personal history and early experiences. Jungian psychology emphasises the exploration of the unconscious, archetypes, and the individuation process. Unlike Freudian psychoanalysis, which centres on the individual's personal history, Jungian therapy delves into deeper layers of the unconscious and the collective unconscious, offering a broader framework for understanding human behaviour and development.

The collective unconscious is a fundamental aspect shared by all humans, containing archetypes, symbols, and themes that shape behaviours, emotions, and experiences. Jung's work explores concepts like complexes, introversion and extraversion, persona, and shadow, contributing to our understanding of conscious potential and the self (ego). This chapter aims to examine the theoretical framework of Jungian therapy, Jung's perspective on human nature, and the therapeutic approach, including core principles and processes. Additionally, it will explore the alignment of Jungian therapy with Islāmic beliefs.

Spirituality, Sufism, and analytical therapy

Religion and spirituality have played significant roles in the lives of individuals and communities and often intersect with psychology and therapeutic practices. Roesler and Reefschläger (2022) contend that Jungian psychotherapy represents a prototype of spiritually integrated psychotherapy due to Jung's emphasis on spirituality. They argue that Jung's psychology laid the groundwork for spiritually inspired psychotherapy approaches in the 20th century. Jungian therapy explores deeper dimensions of the psyche, including the collective unconscious, archetypes, and spiritual aspects of human experience. Jung recognised the influence of spirituality and the sacred on psychological well-being and personal growth. The focus on individuation as a spiritual journey, along with respect for personal spiritual beliefs, makes Jungian therapy a deeply holistic and spiritually attuned approach to psychotherapy.

Jungian therapy acknowledges the significance of spiritual experiences in the human psyche but does not promote or adhere to any specific religious doctrine or belief system. While it welcomes spirituality in clients' lives, it does not engage in religious practice within the therapeutic process. Trosclair and Bass III (2020) note that Jung recognised that mainstream religions may not provide stability or inspiration for everyone. Jungian therapy is not religiously oriented but rather a psychospiritual approach that explores the unconscious mind, archetypes, and individuation. It offers a psychological framework for understanding and embracing the spiritual dimensions of an individual's life without prescribing any specific religious belief.

Jung (1970) acknowledged that individuals often experienced feelings of insignificance, inadequacy, and hopelessness, which he attributed to spiritual crises. He observed that these crises emerged as the influence of traditional religions, especially Christianity, waned in Western societies over the past few centuries. Jung recognised the existential void created by the diminishing role of organised religion and identified the search for spiritual meaning as a fundamental aspect of human experience. Jung (1933) stated that,

> To me the crux of the spiritual problem today is to be found in the fascination which the psyche holds for modern man . . . if we are optimistically inclined, we shall see in it the promise of a far-reaching spiritual change in the Western world. At all events, it is a significant phenomenon . . . important because it touches those irrational and, as history shows, incalculable psychic forces which transform the life of peoples and civilizations in ways that are unforeseen and unforeseeable. These are the forces, still invisible to many persons today, which are at the bottom of the present "psychological" interest.
>
> *(Academy of Ideas, 2017)*

Jung notes a widespread fascination with the human psyche in contemporary society, indicating a notable change in the spiritual aspect of Western cultures. He emphasises the need to acknowledge the deep influence of unconscious psychological forces on both individuals and entire civilisations, even if these forces are not readily apparent to everyone. Jung suggests that the growing interest in psychology today might foreshadow unexpected and transformative shifts, offering the possibility of a more profound exploration of spiritual aspects in modern existence.

Jung's fascination with Sufism originated from a deep appreciation of its meaningful symbols and thoughtful practices. When he looked into Sufi ideas, Jung noticed some striking similarities with his own thoughts about individuation; for instance, "individuation" is like the journey to becoming psychologically complete or whole. For Jung, there were also parallels between Sufi concepts like *fana* (dissolution of the ego) and his own ideas on individuation. This connection prompted Jung to regard Sufism as a fountain of wisdom regarding the quest for psychological integration.

In Sufism, *fana* denotes the ego's termination of its desires and attachments, facilitating a connection with the divine or spiritual realm. Similarly, Jung perceived individuation as a process wherein individuals confront and dismantle their ego's expanded beliefs and limitations, revealing a more authentic self. Both Sufis and Jung discussed the importance of relinquishing selfish desires to achieve a deeper understanding of oneself and connect with higher truths. While Jung maintained his psychological framework, he admired Sufism's practical methods, including music, poetry, and whirling dervishes, for promoting self-awareness and spiritual development. Jung particularly appreciated how these practices accessed deeper layers of the psyche (Jung, 1969c, paras. 196, 201). For an in-depth exploration of Sufism, Islām, and Jungian psychology, refer to Spiegelman et al. (1991).

Jung and the story of Moses and Khidr

In his writings, Jung (1969c) expresses deep respect and admiration for Islām as a monotheistic religion characterised by its unwavering commitment to the oneness of God. Jung acknowledges the Qur'ân as a profound religious masterpiece and praises Islām for its focus on the individual's relationship with God and the spiritual dimension of human existence. Jung also highlights the spiritual and psychological benefits of Islām, noting its capacity to help individuals connect with their spiritual selves and find meaning in life through practices like prayer and fasting. Overall, Jung's writings reflect his deep appreciation for the richness and depth of Islāmic spirituality and its profound impact on individuals and societies.

Jung (1969b) examined the Qur'ân, particularly the story of Moses and Khidr, Chapter 18 (Al-Kahf 18:9–26), analysing it as a metaphor for the individuation process, the journey towards wholeness that integrates both conscious and unconscious aspects of the psyche (paras. 154–171). In brief, this is the story of the Companions of the Cave (Al-Kahf 18:9–26), a number of young men who were driven out of their homes because they believed in the unicity of Allāh (*tawhīd*). They slept in a cave for many years (309 lunar years, which is 300 solar years). When they woke up, they felt they had slept for a day or half a day. One of them went to the town to get some food, and the town dwellers were amazed at his appearance and the old coins he was using. The story shows us how Allāh protects the righteous who believe in Him no matter how hard their situation is and that Allāh has the power to resurrect anyone He wills even after a long sleep of death, as He did in case of the Companions of the Cave.

In the context of the story of Moses and Khidr, Ubai bin Ka'b narrated that the Prophet (ﷺ) said, "Once the Prophet (ﷺ) Moses stood up and addressed Bani Israel. He was asked, 'Who is the most learned man amongst the people?' He said, 'I am the most learned.'" Allāh admonished Moses as he did not attribute absolute knowledge to Him (Allāh). So Allāh inspired him with, "At the junction of the two seas, there is a slave amongst my slaves who is more learned than you [Khidr]." Moses said, "O my Lord! How can I meet him?" (Bukhârî). Regarding the narrative found in Surah Al-Kahf (18:60–82), it describes the voyage that Moses and his youthful aide take till they come across Khidr. Moses requests permission from Khidr to follow in order to benefit from Khidr's wisdom. Khidr, though, cautions Moses that he would not be able to tolerate him. Moses's initial perception of Khidr's deeds and their underlying wisdom is actually exceeded as the story progresses.

In his analysis, Jung describes Moses as the "representative of consciousness, with its emphasis on clarity, differentiation, and law" (para. 155) and "representing an established order, a formulated, conscious morality" (para. 163). He contrasts Moses' reliance on "rational knowledge" with Khidr's embodiment of "an irrational wisdom" (para. 167). Jung characterises Moses as in contrast representing an established moral order and conscious morality, suggesting a contrast between structured consciousness and intuitive insight.

Jung stresses the necessity for Moses to relinquish his preconceived notions and conscious directives in order to embrace the profound wisdom offered by Khidr (para. 171). Moses symbolises clear thinking, judgment, and adherence to moral codes, a conscious and structured approach according to Jung. In contrast, Khidr represents a wisdom that defies clear-cut rules and may appear irrational to Moses. Jung stresses that for Moses to understand Khidr's profound wisdom, he must release fixed ideas and conscious control. Jung underlines the discrepancy between Khidr's enigmatic, deeper wisdom and Moses' rule-bound thought process. Jung suggested that,

> Khidr may well represent the Self. His qualities symbolise him as such: he is said to have been from born in a cave, so in darkness. He is the "Long-lived One," who continually renews himself, like *Elijah*. Like Osiris, he is dismembered at the end of time, by the Antichrist, but is able to restore himself to life. He is analogous to the second Adam . . . he is a counsellor, paraclete. . . . Khidr represents not only the higher wisdom but also a corresponding way of acting which is beyond human reason.
>
> *(Jung, 1968a, p. 247)*

Jung proposed that Khidr could symbolise the self, as evidenced by his characteristics such as being born in a cave and associated with darkness-symbols often connected to the self. Referred to as the "Long-lived One," Khidr signifies continuous renewal, facing challenges yet rejuvenating himself. He assumes a role akin to a guiding and comforting presence, offering wisdom and support beyond ordinary human reasoning. Jung (1969d) utilised Khidr as a representative set of symbols illustrating the process of transformation. His interpretation of Khidr stems from the belief that religious experiences are psychological expressions originating from a single psychic function inherent in the collective unconscious that influences various world religions (Purrington, 2021).

From a Jungian perspective, certain archetypal motifs in Al-Kahf (18:60–82) – such as the cave, the youth, and the sleepers – might be explored for their deeper psychological significance and examined for potential messages about personal growth and transformation. Accordingly, the story of the sleepers in the cave suggests that individuals who confront the darkness of the unconscious undergo a transformative process that can result in significant changes in personality that may be perceived positively or negatively. Such changes are often symbolised as a form of spiritual growth or immortality, reflecting the profound impact of delving into the depths of one's psyche (cited in Purrington, 2020). From an Islāmic perspective, the story of Khidr and Moses teaches believers to trust in Allāh's wisdom even when events seem perplexing or challenging. It emphasises the notion that Allāh's plan is ultimately for the best, even if it is not immediately clear to us. The narrative encourages believers to maintain faith in Allāh's greater purpose and to accept that seemingly negative situations may lead to positive outcomes in the long run.

Jung and Qur'ânic interpretation

Jung's interpretations of Qur'ânic stories and Sufi concepts have been subjected to criticism. Critics argue that Jung, being a Western psychologist, may not fully grasp the cultural and religious nuances embedded within Islāmic scriptures and Sufi traditions. Islāmic scholars have raised concerns about how Jung's understanding may not fully align with the perspectives embedded in Islāmic scholarship, which takes into account the specific linguistic, historical, and cultural contexts that shape the exegesis (*tafsir*) of the Qur'ân. The critiques suggest that a respectful engagement with Islāmic texts requires a thorough appreciation of the linguistic and cultural nuances that define the Qur'anic context. They contend that his interpretations might reflect Western biases and lack a deep understanding of the intricate theological and spiritual dimensions of Islām. While both Sufism and Jungian psychology emphasise inner reflection and the journey towards psychological wholeness, each technique takes a slightly different route to psychological unification (Abidi, 2021). Contrary to the idea by Jung that individuation occur spontaneously, it has been suggested that "individuation does not occur spontaneously and means true path in the Qur'ân, that it takes place in sleep, that it has dreams of transformation related to individuation, that it has some stages" (Malak-Akgün, 2021, p. 43).

Jungian's view on the development of human nature

Jung's perspective on human nature and personality development is multifaceted, highlighting the inherent potential within each individual. He believed that personality and its potential are innate, existing as a blueprint awaiting development from birth (Hopwood, 2023; Jung, 1968b). Jung emphasised that individuals are born with a pre-existing form of the world within them, similar to a virtual image. For Jung (1971), human development is a lifelong process characterised by the integration of various aspects of the psyche. Jung posited that, "By psyche I understand the totality of all psychic processes, conscious as well as unconscious" (CW6 para. 797). Jung's understanding of human nature and personality development is rooted in the interplay between the conscious and unconscious mind, universal archetypes, the process of individuation, and psychological types.

In Jungian psychology, the ego represents the conscious part of our mind, encompassing our thoughts, memories, and emotions of which we are aware. Beyond the ego lies the unconscious mind, where repressed memories, instincts, desires, and archetypal patterns reside. Jung referred to the totality of repressed contents as the "personal unconscious," parallel to Freud's concept. Jung (1933, 1971) emphasised the importance of the unconscious in relation to the development of human nature, claiming that each individual possesses innate potential for growth, self-awareness, and self-realisation throughout their life. This potential is not constrained by age or life circumstances but remains a continuous force within the individual. Through exploration and integration of various aspects of the psyche, individuals can access their inherent capacity for growth, creativity, and personal development.

In Jungian psychology, the central concept is individuation, a process through which individuals achieve psychological fulfilment and wholeness. Unlike other theories that emphasise specific developmental stages, Jungian psychology focuses on individuation as the journey towards integration and completeness. Individuation involves becoming increasingly aware of one's unique psychological reality, strengths, and limitations while also gaining deeper insight into humanity as a whole (Sharp, 2013). This process is shaped by both conscious and unconscious aspects of the self. According to Jung, the path to individuation is highly personalised and involves facing challenges and undergoing transformations throughout one's ongoing journey of personal growth and development. It is a dynamic process that continues throughout life, leading individuals towards a greater sense of self-awareness and fulfilment.

Another key aspect of the development of human nature is the archetypes and collective unconscious. In Jungian psychology (1977), archetypes are universal patterns or themes that influence human thoughts, feelings, and experiences, shaping our worldview. They are ingrained ways of behaviour that are not inherited ideas but rather inherent aspects of human nature, similar to how animals instinctively hatch from eggs or build nests. Jung (1947) believed that archetypes are derived from our collective unconscious, a shared pool of primitive images and symbols inherited from our ancestors. This collective unconscious explains why symbols from different cultures often resemble each other. Examples of Jungian archetypes include the self, mother, wise old person, hero, trickster, shadow, and anima/animus. These archetypes play a significant role in influencing human behaviour and are evident in various aspects of human culture, including dreams, myths, and cultural symbols (Jung, 1947). Table 7.1 presents some of the key Jungian's archetypes.

TABLE 7.1 Some of the key Jungian archetypes

Archetype	Explanation
The Self	The unity of the conscious and unconscious mind representing wholeness, integration, and the realisation of one's potential. Jung called this search for wholeness the process of individuation. This is when your mind feels complete, everything coming together just right. It's like finding and being your true self.
The Persona	Represents the social mask or role we present to the outside world. It reflects how we want others to perceive us and can sometimes conceal our true selves. The persona has been called "the packaging of the ego."
The Shadow	Embodies the darker, repressed aspects of our personality, including our fears, desires, and instincts that are typically considered socially unacceptable or morally wrong. The shadow is like the hidden part of us that holds our fears and desires we might think are not okay. It is a big part of what makes us who we are.
The Anima/Animus	The anima represents the feminine aspects within the male psyche, while the animus represents the masculine aspects within the female psyche. "Masculine" aspects of the psyche such as autonomy, separateness, and aggression were not superior to the "feminine" aspects such as nurturance, relatedness, and empathy. Rather, they form two halves of a whole and play a crucial role in the process of individuation and inner balance.
The Hero	Symbolise the quest for self-discovery, bravery, and the ability to overcome challenges and inner struggles. The hero is a reflection of the individual's inner quest for meaning and purpose. It represents our journey to understand ourselves, face challenges, and grow. It's about finding meaning and purpose inside us.
The Mother	Embodies nurturing, unconditional love, and protection associated with the concept of the Great Mother. Not limited to biological mothers but encompasses any figure or symbol that embodies these nurturing qualities. This is all about love and protection.
The Wise Old Man/Woman	Represents wisdom, guidance, and spiritual insight. Often portrayed as elderly figures who possess deep insights and are sources of wisdom and guidance. They play a significant role in the individuation process. These figures help us figure things out and guide us on our journey to being the best version of ourselves.
The Trickster	Embodies mischief, unpredictability, and a tendency to challenge and disrupt established norms. It serves an important role in breaking down rigid structures and encouraging growth and transformation. They like to shake things up and challenge the way things are.

Sources: Adapted from Jung (1953, 1957, 1959, 1964, 1968a, 1968b).

Jung's idea about how people develop involves both personal and collective dimensions. He focuses on how an individual's inner journey, like personal experiences, connects with the broader collective unconscious and cultural surroundings. Jung stressed that people aren't alone; they are greatly influenced by the culture they're part of including education, socialisation, upbringing, social norms, and cultural values that shape our beliefs, behaviours, and perceptions of the world (worldview). He also highlighted the importance of relationships in shaping our personality, especially early on. Jung believed that relationships are crucial for self-awareness, healing, and growth, giving us chances to explore ourselves and find meaning in life.

In "Modern Man in Search of a Soul" (1933), Jung highlights the challenges posed by modern society and emphasises the importance of genuine connections among a culture that prioritises individualism. He introduces the concept of individuation as the primary aim of human development, leading to a deeper understanding of one's identity, purpose, and place in the world. By harmonising conscious and unconscious elements of the psyche, individuals can unlock their full potential and attain psychological wholeness. Jung contends that psychological wholeness fosters resilience and authenticity, empowering individuals to confront life's challenges with depth and fulfilment. Ultimately, Jung advocates for a journey of self-discovery and integration as a path towards a more meaningful and purposeful existence.

Jung's view of human nature also encompasses spiritual dimensions. He believed that spirituality is a natural and essential aspect of human experience and plays a significant role in the individuation process. This can be explored through encounters with the supernatural, symbolic experiences, and transcendent moments. It is the integration of the transcendent function (the process of unifying and harmonising the conscious and unconscious aspects of the psyche) that facilitates the individual's connection to deeper and more spiritual insights and dimensions of their being. Jung recognised that individuals often undergo spiritual crises as part of their personal development. Crises and conflicts are necessary for growth, and these can lead to profound transformation and a deepening of spiritual awareness. By exploring and integrating the spiritual aspects of their psyche, individuals can navigate these crises and emerge with a stronger sense of purpose and meaning of life. Jung developed the concept of psychological types, distinguishing between introversion and extraversion as well as four cognitive functions: thinking, feeling, sensation, and intuition. Understanding one's psychological type can aid in self-awareness and understanding interpersonal dynamics.

Core therapeutic relationship and techniques of Jungian therapy

In Jungian therapy, the therapeutic relationship is important and defined by trust, active exploration, empathy, and a non-directive approach. The therapist, acting as a compassionate guide, helps clients explore their unconscious for self-awareness, healing, and personal growth. This relationship creates a safe and transformative space, allowing clients to explore their psyches and attain their more authentic selves. Trust and rapport-building are foundational, enabling clients to openly explore their inner worlds. The therapist's empathy and compassion validate the client's experiences, contributing to a supportive therapeutic environment.

In Jungian therapy, the therapist guides clients to interpret and understand their inner thoughts, supporting their healing journeys in a non-directive manner. This approach encourages clients to discover their own solutions without imposing interpretations. Jungian therapy is holistic, incorporating a transpersonal perspective for spiritual growth, emphasising experiential and emotional engagement with the psyche's symbolic aspects. The therapeutic relationship, observed through transference and countertransference, allows the therapist to explore the client's unconscious dynamics. Jungian therapy recognises that genuine transformation extends beyond intellectual understanding. The therapist assists clients in navigating challenges and breakthroughs as they explore the depths of the unconscious.

Techniques in Jungian therapy

Jungian therapy is a comprehensive and multifaceted approach rooted in analytical psychology. It involves a collaborative, long-term, and depth-oriented process between the therapist and the client. Therapists may integrate various techniques and perspectives within the Jungian framework to facilitate exploration and understanding of the unconscious. Some of the techniques used in Jungian therapy include active imagination, dream analysis, amplification, the use of transference and countertransference, word association, and art therapy. Key techniques used in Jungian therapy include the following:

- Active imagination: encourages clients to engage in spontaneous imagery and dialogue to access unconscious material and explore inner conflicts and desires.
- Dream analysis: involves exploring the symbols and themes in dreams to gain insight into the unconscious and its messages.
- Amplification: involves expanding on symbols and images found in dreams or other unconscious material to uncover deeper meanings and associations.
- Transference and countertransference: the therapeutic relationship is explored as a means of understanding unconscious dynamics and projections between the client and therapist.
- Word association: clients respond to words or images with spontaneous associations to reveal unconscious thoughts and emotions.
- Art therapy: utilises creative expression through art media to access and process unconscious material and emotions.

In Jungian therapy, active imagination serves as a fundamental technique where clients consciously engage with their unconscious through creative processes like art, writing, or visualisation. Dream analysis is emphasised to interpret the personal significance of dream symbols and access deeper insights into one's emotions and conflicts. Amplification expands on symbolic material through cultural references to provide a broader context. Transference and countertransference dynamics uncover unconscious patterns, while word association reveals symbolic connections and facilitates deeper exploration. In Jungian therapy, art serves as a crucial tool for expression, exploration, and understanding of the unconscious mind. Through art, clients can access emotions and unconscious material that may be challenging to articulate verbally, providing valuable insights into their inner processes and conflicts. Therapists employ amplification to explore the client's artwork, facilitating the exploration and integration of different aspects of the self.

Evidence of effectiveness of Jungian therapy

Jungian analysis centres on exploring the individual's psyche, delving into unconscious processes, symbols, and archetypes, which are subjective and challenging to measure objectively. While empirical evidence for the effectiveness of Jungian therapy is limited, proponents argue its efficacy through qualitative evidence such as case studies, clinical observations, and client and therapist experiences. Studies in Germany and Switzerland since the 1990s have shown improvements in symptoms, interpersonal problems, personality structure, and everyday life conduct through Jungian therapy (Roesler, 2013). Reviews indicate that Jungian therapy can reduce severe symptoms to psychologically healthy levels (Roesler, 2013), yet further research is necessary to bolster the evidence base and understand its comparative benefits. Therapeutic success in Jungian therapy hinges on factors like therapist–client compatibility, shared worldview, therapist skill, and client motivation.

Jungian therapy: congruent or incongruent with Islāmic beliefs and practices?

The literature explores the Sufi path to spirituality through a Jungian approach, highlighting common themes and concepts in Jungian therapy and Sufism (Spiegelman et al., 1991). Both emphasise self-awareness, inner transformation, and the integration of various aspects of the psyche. Nouriani (2017) examines the parallels between analytical psychology and Islām, advocating for the relevance of Jungian analysis in clinical work with Muslim clients. Similarly, Abidi (2021) discusses incorporating Islāmic principles into Jungian therapy for Muslim clients, noting "the inverse relationship of the Sufi notion of the soul's descent (*tanzih*) and ascent (*tashbih*) to Jung's model of the individuation process" (p. 399). Abidi (2021) finds that integrating Sufi self-knowledge concepts with Jungian individuation processes bridges Islāmic teachings and Western traditions, offering potential therapeutic insights.

There are several potential points of divergence between Jungian therapy and Islāmic beliefs and practices. However, within the broader Islāmic tradition of the Creed of *Ahl al-Sunnah wa'l-Jamaa'ah*, the consensus of the Muslim scholars is opposition or scepticism towards certain Sufi practices and beliefs:

> Usually those that are called Sufis nowadays follow *bid'ahs* (innovations) that constitute *shirk*, as well as other kinds of *bid'ah*, such as when some of them say "*Madad ya sayyid* (Help, O Master)" and call upon the *qutubs* ["holy men"] and recite *dhikr* [remembrance of Allāh] in unison using names which Allāh has not called Himself, like saying "*Huw, Huw* [He, He]" and "*Ah, Ah*" [a contraction of Allāh]. Whoever reads their books will be aware of many of their innovations that constitute *shirk*, and other evils.
> *(Fatawa of Permanent Committee, cited in Islām Q&A, 2003)*

While there are intersections between Jungian therapy and Islāmic beliefs and practices, it is essential to recognise their distinct philosophical, cultural, and religious origins. Jungian psychology emerged within Western culture, shaped by Judaeo-Christian traditions and European philosophical influences, yet distinct from them. Rooted in in-depth psychology and influenced by psychoanalysis, Jung's theories stem from his clinical work, study of mythology, anthropology, and personal experiences. Jungian psychology, as a secular framework, examines the human psyche and spirituality through a psychological lens. While there may be points of convergence, Jungian therapy and Islāmic beliefs arise from separate traditions and contexts.

Jung approaches the concept of God from a human and symbolic perspective, exploring it as a subjective symbol within the human psyche without making theological claims about divine existence. In contrast, Islām is a monotheistic religion with specific theological beliefs and practices centred around the worship of Allāh. Islāmic beliefs assert the existence of God as a foundational tenet, grounded in divine revelation, scriptural teachings, and theological discussions. Islāmic teachings encompass principles, values, and a worldview guiding the beliefs, practices, and ethical conduct of Muslims, rooted in a holistic understanding of life that includes faith, morality, spirituality, and social justice. Jungian psychology relies on various sources, including the exploration of the unconscious, dreams, and personal symbolism, that form the foundation for understanding the human psyche, personal development, and therapy in Jungian psychology. In contrast, Islāmic teachings consider the Qur'ân, the *Sunnah*, and the scholarly interpretation of Islāmic texts as primary sources of guidance for Muslims. Islāmic teachings encourage seeking knowledge and guidance from these sources and following Islāmic principles in personal, social, and professional life.

The divergence between Jungian psychology and Islāmic concepts extends to the notion of self. In Jungian psychology, individuation emphasises integrating all facets of the self, including the shadow, for personal growth. This contrasts with the Islāmic principle of *tawhīd*, underlining absolute submission to Allāh, which may appear conflicting with the pursuit of individuation. While Jungian therapy encourages self-discovery and the integration of the shadow, Islāmic teachings prioritise surrender to Allāh, potentially conflicting with notions of individualism and self-worth.

The exploration and integration of the shadow in Jungian therapy may also clash with Islām's emphasis on suppressing negative desires and avoiding temptations, and Jung's emphasis on the personal and collective unconscious can differ from the Islāmic perspective on the *nafs* (self) and its relationship with divine guidance. Jungian psychology explores the depths of the unconscious mind, while Islāmic teachings stress the purification of the soul (*tazkiyah an-nafs*) with God's divine will. In Jungian psychology, the unconscious is a reservoir of archetypes and symbols, whereas Islām emphasises aligning the self with God's guidance through spiritual purification, conscious choices, and adherence to moral principles. In effect, the Jungian psychological framework lacks a specific moral or ethical system comparable with religious or philosophical approaches.

Ethical considerations in Jungian psychology focus on aspects of the therapeutic relationship, individual respect, non-judgmental exploration, responsibility, confidentiality, and awareness of countertransference. In contrast, Islām provides a comprehensive moral and ethical framework rooted in the Qur'ân and the *Sunnah*, guiding beliefs, behaviours, and interactions with principles promoting righteousness, justice, compassion, and a strong sense of community (*ummah*). Islāmic ethics encompass personal conduct, family life, professional actions, social interactions, and societal matters, emphasising devotion to God, compassion, justice, and righteousness, along with beliefs in the afterlife. In contrast, Jungian therapy emphasises ethical considerations within the therapeutic context focusing primarily on psychological growth and integration within the individual.

Dream interpretation is highly valued in Islām. Prophet Muhammad (ﷺ) himself and his companions engaged in interpreting their own and others' dreams. The ability to interpret dreams was seen as a gift from Allāh and an expression of divine wisdom. Islāmic scholars provide criteria to distinguish between true dreams (*ru'ya*), which are believed to be from Allāh; bad dreams (*hulum*), which are believed to be from *Shaitan* (the devil); and ordinary dreams. It was narrated from Abu Hurayrah (may Allāh be pleased with him) that the Prophet (ﷺ) said,

> Dreams are of three types: glad tidings from Allāh, what is on a person's mind, and frightening dreams from Satan. If any of you sees a dream that he likes, let him tell others of it if he wishes, but if he sees something that he dislikes, he should not tell anyone about it, and he should get up and perform prayer.
>
> *(Ibn Majah)*

In Jungian dream analysis, the emphasis lies on uncovering the individual unconscious by exploring personal symbols and archetypes that provide insights into psychological conflicts, desires, and motivations. Dreams are regarded as gateways into the profound depths of the psyche, with their significance rooted in psychological exploration rather than conveying religious or prophetic messages. On the contrary, within Islāmic traditions, dream interpretation places a substantial focus on deciphering potential Prophetic messages or warnings from Allāh. Interpretations draw upon religious texts and established symbols within Islāmic scholarship, viewing dreams as a mode of divine communication that may contain guidance. The emphasis here is on the spiritual and religious significance of dreams, aligning them with the potential for divine revelation and communication within the Islāmic framework. In summary, Jungian dream analysis and Islāmic dream analysis differ in their origins, frameworks, purposes, and sources of interpretation. While both recognise the significance of dreams, they approach dream interpretation from distinct psychological and spiritual perspectives.

Islāmic beliefs and practices may not be congruent with Jungian psychology and therapy due to several fundamental differences between these two frameworks. The fundamental differences between these frameworks are rooted in distinct psychological, psychospiritual, and theological perspectives. This divergence in focus can result in incongruities in the understanding of concepts such as God, spirituality, and the unconscious, potentially giving rise to conflicts or challenges when attempting to integrate these two perspectives. A summary of a comparison between Jungian therapy and Islāmic psychotherapy is presented in Table 7.2.

Rapprochement between Islāmic psychotherapy and Jungian therapy

Islāmic psychotherapy and Jungian therapy, while distinct, share notable similarities in their approaches to psychological healing. Jungian therapy, as explained by Williams (2019), adopts a holistic stance, addressing the individual's psychological, spiritual, emotional, and social well-being. Similarly, Islāmic psychotherapy embraces a holistic approach to enhance wellness across the entire personality. Both recognise the interconnectedness of an individual's problems and advocate for comprehensive solutions. They highlight the importance of self-exploration and self-awareness as pathways to personal growth, inner development, and healing.

In Islām, the concept of *tazkiyah an nafs*, or spiritual purification, entails introspection, self-reflection (*muhasabah*), and self-awareness to foster a closer relationship with God. Islāmic psychotherapy encourages clients to reflect on their actions, intentions, and character traits. Likewise, Jungian therapy encourages clients to explore their inner world to gain insight into their behaviours and emotional responses.

Both Islāmic psychotherapy and Jungian therapy highlight the significance of spirituality in the healing process. Islāmic psychotherapy integrates principles,

TABLE 7.2 Comparison between Jungian psychology and Islāmic traditions

	Jungian psychology	Islāmic beliefs and practices
Origin and nature	Based on his experiences, observations, studies of psychology, anthropology, mythology, and religious traditions	Based on the religion of Islām, from divine revelation later compiled into the Qur'ān and the *Sunnah*
Cultural and philosophical background	Emerged in the context of Western culture and philosophy	Based on underlying principles, values, and worldviews and are rooted in a holistic understanding of life that encompasses faith, morality, spirituality, and social justice
Religious context	Secular psychological framework	Monotheistic religion. Based with specific theological beliefs and practices for the worship of Allāh
Purpose	Self-discovery and individuation as a means to psychological growth	Devotion to God and moral conduct
Divine focus	Examines the psychological aspects of spirituality, religious symbols, and experiences without asserting theological claims	Submission to a personal and transcendent God
Concept of God	Approach is psychological	Approach is spiritual/religious
Sources of guidance	Individual's unconscious, dreams, and personal symbolism	Qur'ān, *Sunnah*, and scholarly interpretation of Islāmic texts
Moral and ethical framework	Exploration of the individual's psyche and the integration of unconscious aspects	Comprehensive moral and ethical framework based on the Qur'ān and *Sunnah*
Belief in the afterlife	Does not specifically address or emphasise beliefs regarding the afterlife	Concepts such as heaven, hell, and the Day of Judgment
Archetypal Interpretation	Explore archetypes in a more generalised psychological context	Interpreted within the religious framework of Islām
Rituals and Practices	Dialogue and introspection in a psychological approach	Rituals and prayers emphasising submission to God; structured religious practices integral to Islāmic spiritual development
Dream interpretation	Searching for personal symbols and archetypes that offer insight into psychological conflicts, desires, and motivations	Specific interpretations are based on religious texts and established symbols within Islāmic scholarship

values, and teachings from the Qur'ân and *Sunnah* as sources of guidance and solace. Conversely, Jungian therapy acknowledges the spiritual dimension of human experience without confining it to any specific theology. Jung emphasised understanding and integrating individual spiritual experiences and beliefs into overall psychological well-being. Both approaches value the use of symbolism, metaphor, and imagery to access and comprehend the unconscious and conscious mind. Islāmic psychotherapy may incorporate Qur'ânic verses, Prophetic traditions, and symbolic stories to help clients explore inner struggles. Similarly, Jungian therapy employs archetypal symbols and dream imagery to unveil unconscious conflicts and patterns. Both traditions recognise the transformative potential of symbolism and metaphor in facilitating psychological exploration and healing.

There are attempts by several authors to draw parallels between Jungian psychology and elements of Islāmic terminology. Abu-Raiya (2014) compared the Qur'ānic theory of personality with the Jungian theory of the collective unconscious: "noteworthy resemblances were detected also between the Jungian concepts collective unconscious, archetypes, self and individuation and the Qur'ānic constructs *rûh* (spirit), *al-asmaa'* (the names), *qalb* (heart), and *al-nafs al-mutma'innah* (the serene psyche), respectively" (p. 326).

There is rapprochement between Jungian and humanistic psychology. Both Fritz Perls and Jung propose that all elements in a dream reflect aspects of the dreamer's personality or psyche. Similarly, Maslow's hierarchy of needs and Jung's concept of individuation share similarities in highlighting the importance of self-realisation and personal growth (Williams, 2015). In exploring connections between Jungian psychology and Islāmic theology, it's essential to acknowledge their distinct cultural, historical, and philosophical origins. Attempting to equate terms and concepts from these diverse frameworks may oversimplify or misinterpret their intended meanings. Claims of resemblances could be susceptible to semantic explanations and confirmation bias, potentially emphasising similarities while neglecting differences or contradictions. Moreover, when asserting similarities between psychological concepts and religious constructs, such as those found in the Qur'ân, it is critical to consider the historical context and intended meanings of these ideas.

Conclusion

In summary, the exploration of congruence and incongruence between Jungian therapy and Islāmic beliefs highlights shared emphases on self-awareness, introspection, and personal growth, yet reveals fundamental incongruences. Jungian therapy operates within a secular and psychological framework, contrasting with the deeply rooted religious and spiritual context of Islāmic beliefs. Incongruence arises from differing views on healing sources, the role of the divine, and the purpose of psychological and spiritual well-being. Integration of Jungian techniques into an Islāmic framework demands careful attention to avoid diluting religious beliefs. Aligning Jungian therapy with its secular origins may raise compatibility concerns with Islāmic beliefs and practices, highlighting the necessity for thoughtful consideration in psychospiritual interventions for Muslim clients.

References

Abidi, M. H. (2021). Sufism and Jungian psychology: Ways of knowing and being. In N. Pasha-Zaidi (Ed.), *Toward a positive psychology of Islām and Muslims. Cross-cultural advancements in positive psychology* (Vol. 15). Springer.

Abu-Raiya, H. (2014). Western psychology and Muslim psychology in dialogue: Comparisons between a Qur'ānic theory of personality and Freud's and Jung's ideas. *Journal of Religion and Health, 53*, 326–338. https://doi.org/10.1007/s10943-012-9630-9.

Academy of Ideas. (2017). *Carl Jung and the spiritual problem of the modern individual.* Retrieved August 5, 2023, from https://academyofideas.com/2017/06/carl-jung-spiritual-problem-modern-individual/#:~:text=Those%20suffering%20from%20a%20spiritual%20problem%2C%20due%20to,the%20form%20of%20a%20strong%20hunger%20for%20power.

Bukhârî. *Sahih al-Bukhârî 122* [In-book reference: Book 3, Hadith 64. USC-MSA web (English) reference: Vol. 1, Book 3, Hadith 123]. https://sunnah.com/bukhari:122.

Hopwood, A. (2023). Jung's model of the psyche. *Society of Analytical Psychology.* Retrieved August 5, 2023, from www.thesap.org.uk/articles-on-jungian-psychology-2/carl-gustav-jung/jungs-model-psyche/.

Ibn Majah. *Sunan Ibn Majah 3906* (In-book reference: Book 35, Hadith 14. English translation: Vol. 5, Book 35, Hadith 3906). Sahih (Darussalam). https://sunnah.com.

Islām Q&A. (2003). *What is Sufism?* Retrieved August 8, 2023, from https://Islamqa.info/en/answers/47431/what-is-sufism.

Jung, C. G. (1933). *Modern man in search of a soul.* Harcourt Brace.

Jung, C. G. (1947). *On the nature of the psyche.* Ark Paperbacks.

Jung, C. G. (1953). *Two essays on analytical psychology* (Vol. 7 of The collected works of C. G. Jung). Princeton University Press.

Jung, C. G. (1957). *The collected works of C. G. Jung. Vol. 9 (Part 2): Aion: Researches into the phenomenology of the self.* Princeton University Press.

Jung, C. G. (1959). *The archetypes and the collective unconscious* (2nd ed., Vol. 9, Part 1 of The collected works of C. G. Jung). Princeton University Press.

Jung, C. G. (1964). *The archetypes and the collective unconscious* (2nd ed., Vol. 9, Part 1 of The collected works of C. G. Jung). Princeton University Press.

Jung, C. G. (1968a). *The archetypes and the collective unconscious* (2nd ed., Vol. 9, Part 1 of The collected works of C. G. Jung). Princeton University Press.

Jung, C. G. (1968b). *Psychology and alchemy* (Vol. 12 of The collected works of C. G. Jung). Princeton University Press.

Jung, C. G. (1969b). Psychology and religion: The autonomy of the unconscious. In C. Jung (Ed.), *The collected works of C. G. Jung* (2nd ed., Vol. 11, pp. 3–33). Princeton University Press.

Jung, C. G. (1969c). *Psychology and religion: West and east* (Vol. 11 of The collected works of C. G. Jung). Princeton University Press.

Jung, C. G. (1969d). Concerning rebirth. In G. Adler & R. F. C. Hull (Eds.), *Collected works of C. G. Jung. Vol. 9 (Part 1): Archetypes and the collective unconscious* (pp. 111–148). Princeton University Press.

Jung, C. G. (1970). *Civilization in transition* (Vol. 10 of The collected works of C. G. Jung). Princeton University Press.

Jung, C. G. (1971). *Psychological types* (Vol. 6 of The collected works of C. G. Jung). Princeton University Press.

Jung, C. G. (1977). *The symbolic life* (Vol. 18 of The collected works of C. G. Jung). Princeton University Press.
Malak-Akgün, B. (2021). Answers to Carl Gustav Jung in the perspective of the Quran: The process of individuation. *Spiritual Psychology and Counseling, 6*(2), 43–61. https://dx.doi.org/10.37898/spc.2021.6.2.135.
Nouriani, D. S. (2017). Islāmic cultures and Jungian analysis. *Jung Journal, 11*(3), 9–25. https://doi.org/10.1080/19342039.2017.1331695.
Purrington, M. (2020). *Carl Jung and Islām*. Retrieved August 8, 2023, from https://carljungdepthpsychologysite.blog/2020/02/22/carl-jung-and-Islam/.
Purrington, M. (2021). *In 1940, Jung analysed Sura 18 of the Koran, Moses encounters Khidr, whom he looks for his instruction*. Retrieved December 30, 2023, from https://carljungdepthpsychologysite.blog/2021/11/17/in-1940-jung-analyzed-sura-18-of-the-koran-moses-encounters-khidr-whom-he-looks-to-for-instruction/.
Roesler, C. (2013). Evidence for the effectiveness of Jungian psychotherapy: A review of empirical studies. *Behavioural Science* (Basel), *3*(4), 562–575.
Roesler, C., & Reefschläger, G. I. (2022). Jungian psychotherapy, spirituality, and synchronicity: Theory, applications, and evidence base. *Psychotherapy, 59*(3), 339–350. https://doi.org/10.1037/pst0000402.
Sharp, D. (2013). *Jung Lexicon: A primer of terms & concepts*. Inner City Books (Print). Retrieved August 3, 2023, from https://jungpage.org/learn/jung-lexicon#individuation.
Spiegelman, J. M., Khan, I., Fernandez, T., & Spiegelman, J. M. (1991). *Sufism, Islām and Jungian psychology*. New Falcon Publication.
Trosclair, G., & Bass III, P. (2020). *Jungian therapy: How it works & what to expect*. Retrieved August 3, 2023, from www.choosingtherapy.com/jungian-therapy/.
Williams, R. (2015). Jungian analysis and humanistic psychotherapy: Critical connections – Past, present and future. *Self & Society, 43*(3), 197–199. https://doi.org/10.1080/03060497.2015.1092322.
Williams, R. (2019). *C. G. Jung: The basics*. Routledge.

8
HUMANISTIC THERAPY RE-ENVISIONED THROUGH AN ISLĀMIC PERSPECTIVE

Introduction

The humanistic approach in Western psychology, emerging in the mid-20th century, prioritises client-centred methods and focuses on self-growth, autonomy, self-actualisation, and the premise that each person has the potential for self-improvement and self-fulfilment. Contrasting with prevailing psychological theories like behaviourism and psychoanalysis, which often concentrated on pathology and unconscious processes, humanistic psychology, associated with figures like Abraham Maslow and Carl Rogers, focuses on the premise that each person has the potential for self-improvement and self-fulfilment. Valuing subjective experiences and unique identities, humanistic therapy aims to foster psychological growth by recognising and addressing personal needs and ambitions.

Humanistic therapy is a multifaceted approach that embraces a diverse collection of practical approaches: existential, constructivist, and transpersonal. Existential therapy emphasises freedom, experiential reflection, and responsibility, while the constructivist approach focuses on personal and social constructs of psychological growth. The transpersonal perspective highlights spiritual and transcendent dimensions of psychological wellness. Despite their diverse viewpoints, these philosophies within humanistic psychology explore what it means to be fully human and how that understanding contributes to a vital or fulfilled life (Schneider & Leitner, 2002). Humanistic psychology stresses deep personal inquiry into life's meaning and purpose. This chapter aims to examine the central principles of humanistic therapy and its congruence with Islāmic traditions. It also explores re-envisioning humanistic therapy through an Islāmic perspective, identifying areas of alignment with Islāmic traditions and worldview.

DOI: 10.4324/9781003453413-10

The humanistic psychology view of human nature

The humanistic view of human nature is a positive psychological paradigm that emphasises the inherent goodness and potential for progress in each individual. It highlights the importance of self-concept, self-discovery, and congruence, along with positive interpersonal relationships and values like empathy and compassion for personal growth. Central to this perspective is the alignment of beliefs, ideals, and behaviours to achieve wholeness and integration, fostering self-acceptance and meaning in life through conscious awareness and self-reflection. Humanistic therapy provides a supportive environment for self-exploration, empowerment, and overall personal growth, emphasising personal choice, autonomy, and responsibility in human behaviour and development, contrary to deterministic views. This perspective acknowledges humans as active participants in their own growth, capable of pursuing paths towards fulfilment and well-being.

Humanistic therapy adopts a holistic perspective on human nature, focusing on self-development, growth, and personal responsibilities. It views human nature as inherently good, emphasising individuals' ability to maintain healthy relationships and make choices for their well-being and others'. According to Rogers (1987), individuals are trustworthy, resourceful, and capable of self-understanding and self-direction, paving the way for effective and productive lives. Humanistic theory considers human nature as shaped by genetic factors, early development, environmental influences, and an innate drive for growth throughout life. Realising human potential for positive development hinges on fostering a climate of respect and trust (Corey, 2022). In this framework, the self is seen as an organised set of characteristics unique to each individual, shaped by relationships and influenced by conditions of worth. It comprises the real self and the ideal self, with congruence between the two, representing alignment. A widening gap between the real and ideal selves can lead to psychological issues (Rogers, 1987).

According to Rogers (1987), a fully functioning person is open to both positive and negative experiences, capable of interpreting emotions and trusting their instincts. They embrace change without distorting or denying experiences, are receptive to feedback, and demonstrate creativity, leading to fulfilled lives. Characterised by congruence and integration, fully functioning individuals live fully in the present moment with inner freedom, experiencing the richness and challenges of existential living (Freeth, 2007). Some of the essential characteristics of humanistic therapy (CSAT, 1999) are

- Empathic understanding of the client's frame of reference and subjective experience
- Respect for the client's cultural values and freedom to exercise choice
- Exploration of problems through an authentic and collaborative approach to helping the client develop insight, courage, and responsibility

- Exploration of goals and expectations, including articulation of what the client wants to accomplish and hopes to gain from treatment
- Clarification of the helping role by defining the therapist's role but respecting the self-determination of the client
- Assessment and enhancement of client motivation both collaboratively and authentically
- Negotiation of a contract by formally or informally asking, "Where do we go from here?"
- Demonstration of authenticity by setting a tone of genuine, authentic encounter

The humanistic perspective, prominent in counselling and psychotherapy, particularly in Rogers' client-centred therapy, emphasises a supportive and empathetic therapeutic approach. This method encourages clients to explore their feelings and thoughts in a non-judgmental setting. In contrast to deterministic and pessimistic viewpoints, humanistic psychology highlights the innate potential for growth, self-discovery, and positive change within individuals. It emphasises individuality, personal responsibility, and the significance of subjective experiences in promoting psychological well-being.

The Rogerian approach to therapy

The Rogerian approach, known as non-directive therapy, emphasises client autonomy by fostering an empathetic, non-judgmental, and supportive therapeutic environment. Aligned with humanist principles, it prioritises experiential processes over exploring the early childhood origins of clients' issues, as seen in psychoanalysis. This approach shifts the role of the expert from the therapist to the client, empowering them to find their own solutions (McLeod, 2013; Nelson-Jones, 2014). Rogers' therapy and counselling are characterised by three core conditions essential for a healthy therapeutic relationship: (1) congruence between the therapist and the client; (2) unconditional positive regard towards the client; and (3) empathy with the client. Mearns and Thorne (2007) define the role of each core condition: empathy as a process; unconditional positive regard as an attitude; and congruence as a "state of being" in the therapeutic relationship with the client (p. 81).

The first element of the therapeutic relationship in Rogers' client-centred therapy (1980) can be described as genuineness, realness, or congruence. It emphasises the importance of the therapist being authentic and transparent in the therapeutic relationship, not putting up a professional front or personal facade. This transparency allows the client to see through the therapist and experience a genuine connection. The therapist openly expresses their feelings and attitudes without holding back, creating a close match between their inner experiences, awareness, and communication with the client (Rogers, 1957, pp. 115–116).

Congruence, also known as genuineness, is a core principle in therapy that fosters a genuine and empathetic therapeutic relationship. When therapists embody congruence, clients feel safe to explore their thoughts and emotions, facilitating personal growth and self-discovery. This authenticity forms the foundation of the Rogerian approach to therapy, empowering clients to develop genuine communication skills. In client-centred therapy, self-disclosure involves therapists sharing personal facts or experiences with clients (Rogers, 1957), although congruence does not necessitate unrestricted self-disclosure by the therapist. Rather, self-disclosure should be purposeful, serving specific therapeutic objectives while respecting professional boundaries and the client's comfort level. Therapists cautiously employ self-disclosure to enhance the client's self-exploration and understanding, ensuring relevance to the client's needs and therapeutic goals. Overall, self-disclosure in client-centred therapy is utilised strategically to foster the therapeutic relationship and promote client insight.

Unconditional positive regard in client-centred therapy indicates the therapist's unconditional acceptance and non-judgmental support for the client, irrespective of their thoughts, feelings, or behaviours. It involves the therapist's genuine warmth, respect, and acceptance towards the client, creating a safe and trusting therapeutic environment where clients can explore their experiences openly. Rogers (1980) highlights that when therapists maintain a positive and accepting attitude towards the client's emotions, therapeutic progress is more likely. This approach values the client unconditionally irrespective of their current emotional state, fostering a deep sense of acceptance and validation within the therapeutic relationship.

Rogers (1980) posited that conditional support contributes to psychological issues by fostering denial of unacceptable aspects of oneself, distorting the self-concept, and promoting unhealthy behaviours. In client-centred therapy, establishing an atmosphere of unconditional positive regard is crucial. This acceptance permits clients to express emotions freely without fear of rejection, although it does not condone dysfunctional behaviour. Unconditional positive regard encompasses genuine warmth, empathy, acceptance without judgment, encouragement of self-expression, open communication, and support for self-acceptance and growth.

The third facilitative aspect of the relationship in the person-centred therapy is empathic understanding. This involves the therapist's capacity to grasp the client's emotions, thoughts, and experiences from their perspective. Rogers (1980) emphasised the rarity of genuine empathic listening in daily life and its transformative power in therapy. Through active listening and sensitive reflection, therapists serve as mirrors, enabling clients to explore their inner world and foster self-understanding. This reflective stance creates a safe space for clients to express themselves authentically and pursue personal growth and well-being. That is, the therapist's role is to act as a mirror, reflecting the client's internal world back to them in a way that facilitates their self-exploration and understanding. By maintaining this reflective stance, therapists can provide a safe environment for clients to freely express themselves and work towards their own growth and well-being.

Full empathy, as described by Watson (2002), involves a deep understanding of the client's experiences, encompassing both their cognitive and emotional aspects.

This comprehensive form of empathy, operating on interpersonal, cognitive, and affective levels, is identified as the most potent factor driving client progress in therapy. Therapists should develop adaptive responsiveness to their clients, enabling them to empathise deeply and comprehend their profound experiences. According to Rogers, if therapists communicate these attitudes, their clients are able to grow psychologically, become less defensive and more self-aware, and change their behaviour in a positive way. The basic drive to fulfilment implies that people will move towards health if the way seems open for them to do so (Corey, 2022).

Person-centred therapy diverges from psychoanalytical or cognitive behaviourist approaches by prioritising client empowerment, self-exploration, and holistic integration. Rogers (1977) outlines its objective as not solely problem solving but facilitating clients' personal growth to better navigate present and future challenges. The therapy centres on the individual, aiming to foster openness to experiences, bolster self-esteem, align idealised and actual selves, enhance self-understanding, and cultivate healthier emotional expression and relationships (www.minddisorders.com, 2023).

Self-actualising tendency

The self-actualising tendency, a key concept in humanistic psychology emphasised by Maslow and Rogers, signifies an innate drive within individuals towards personal growth and fulfilment. It reflects the inherent human capacity to pursue life goals and realise one's maximum potential, driven by a universal desire for growth, autonomy, and freedom from external influences (Schunk, 2022). Rogers (1951) describes this tendency as fundamental to human nature, representing the organism's innate striving to enhance its own experiences and achieve self-actualisation.

Maslow's (1943, 1954) hierarchy of needs categorises human needs into five levels, starting with physiological needs at the base and progressing through safety, belongingness, and self-esteem, culminating in self-actualisation. According to Maslow, individuals must satisfy lower-level needs before advancing to higher ones, with self-actualisation representing alignment between one's ideal self and actual behaviour. Rogers (1963) describes a self-actualised individual as fully functioning and deeply in tune with their emotions and aspirations. Unconditional positive regard, as emphasised by Proctor et al. (2016), is identified as crucial for the development of a fully functioning individual.

The client-centred approach posits that three specific conditions are sufficient for individuals to tap into their own resources, gain self-understanding, and develop into fully functioning persons (McLeod, 2013). The therapist, by embodying certain attitudinal qualities, plays a pivotal role in nurturing the client's actualising tendency (Bozarth, 1998). This inherent drive stimulates growth, enhances capacities, fosters autonomy, and serves as a constructive force present in all organisms. While it can be suppressed or corrupted, the actualising tendency persists as long as the organism is alive. It effectively addresses issues such as guilt, stress, and the regulation of needs, drives, pleasure-seeking, and creativity.

Rogers's seven stages of change

Rogers (1961) introduced his theory of the seven stages of change in individuals through therapy, explaining what clients might experience during the transformative process. These stages are crucial for comprehending human development and evolution, illustrating how individuals can grow and adapt in response to life experiences. They provide a framework for facilitating change in others by fostering self-awareness, exploration, choice, and integration within a supportive and empathetic environment. Rogers emphasised that individuals transition not merely from one state of stability to another but rather from rigidity to fluidity, from stasis to process, highlighting the dynamic nature of personal growth and transformation. Rogers stressed humans' preference to transition from states of stability to adaptability and change, highlighting the inherent inclination towards growth and development. He emphasised the need for flexibility and openness to new experiences rather than adhering to rigid structures. Rogers also noted that the progression between stages is not necessarily linear, with individuals often exhibiting characteristics of multiple stages simultaneously or even regressing at times, as observed in the stages of change model by Prochaska and DiClemente (1992). Feltham and Dryden (2004) consider Rogers' seven stages of process as one model of stages of change, depicting the dynamic nature of personal transformation. Figure 8.1 presents Rogers's seven stages of change.

The seven stages of client process outlined by Rogers (1961) mirror the progression individuals may experience throughout therapy, parallel to the stages depicted in the stages of change model by Prochaska and DiClemente (1992):

- Stage One: clients are closed off and defensive, similar to the pre-contemplation phase. They may not voluntarily seek counselling or therapy.
- Stage Two: clients become slightly less rigid and may discuss external events or others, indicating pre-contemplation.
- Stage Three: clients consider accepting self-responsibility but may focus on themselves as objects rather than expressing present feelings, similar to entering therapy.
- Stage Four: clients start to be critical of themselves and discuss present feelings, similar to the contemplation phase.
- Stage Five: clients express present emotions and rely more on their decision-making abilities, indicative of the action/decision-making phase.
- Stage Six: clients show rapid growth towards congruence and develop unconditional positive regard for others, signalling closure of formal therapy.
- Stage Seven: clients become fully functioning, open to life's changes, and self-actualising individuals, parallel to the maintenance phase.

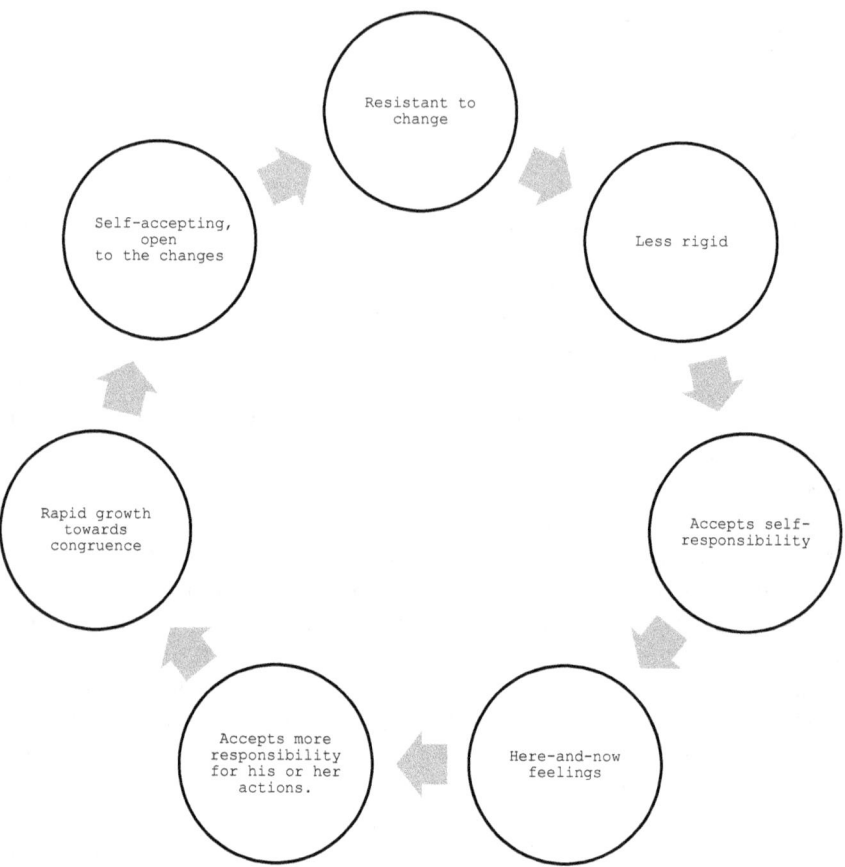

FIGURE 8.1 Rogers's seven stages of change.

The seven stages of the therapeutic process represent a natural progression towards self-awareness, responsibility, and positive regard, culminating in personal growth and self-actualisation. However, they are not meant to be a framework for pushing clients forward. According to Merry (2014), interventions should not be aimed at accelerating the client's progress from one stage to the next, as this may be counterproductive. Instead, therapists should respect the client's natural rate of growth and development. Creating a supportive, empathetic, and non-judgmental environment fosters a solid therapeutic relationship, allowing clients the freedom to explore their thoughts and emotions at their own pace.

The role of the therapist

In person-centred therapy, the therapist's primary focus is on cultivating a therapeutic environment that fosters the client's continuous growth (Patterson, 2000). Unlike other therapeutic approaches that rely heavily on techniques or strategies, the essence of person-centred therapy lies in the therapist's behaviours and attitudes (Rogers, 1961). Research suggests that personality change in clients is more influenced by the therapist's attitude than their specific knowledge or techniques (Bozarth et al., 2002). This therapeutic approach prioritises building relationships over employing specific techniques. The therapist maintains a non-directive stance, refraining from steering the conversation and allowing the client complete freedom to choose what to discuss. The therapist's role is to understand the client's worldview and offer support for them to discover their own solutions (Corey, 2022).

Person-centred therapy emphasises the therapist's genuineness, acceptance, and empathy as catalysts for change (Corey, 2022). Therapists avoid traditional practices like taking a history, asking leading questions, making interpretations, or evaluating client ideas, maintaining a non-directive approach (Broadley, 1997). Rogers acknowledged the potential utility of interpretation but gave it less emphasis compared to psychoanalysis. He believed clients are experts on their experiences, and therapists should create a secure environment for self-exploration. In person-centred therapy, the focus is on the client's self-discovery and self-acceptance within a non-directive and empathetic therapeutic relationship.

Limitations of client-centred therapy

Critics argue that Carl Rogers' humanistic approach lacks scientific rigour and empirical evidence compared to other established theories. Humanistic psychology, focusing on individual autonomy and self-determination, may conflict with Islāmic teachings that emphasise obedience to Allāh's will and seeking guidance from religious authorities. However, Islāmic teachings also encourage independent decision-making guided by a moral and ethical framework. Critics posit that client-centred therapy is subject to criticism lacks empirical evidence supporting its effectiveness (Client-centered therapy, 2006), and internal dimensions emphasised in humanistic psychology may be viewed as narcissistic (Robbins, 2008; Taylor, 2001). The field faces challenges in evaluation and has been criticised for its perceived lack of empirical rigour (DeRobertis, 2022; DeRobertis & Bland, 2021). Additionally, client-centred therapy has faced criticism for claims of inadequate training, as Carl Rogers did not advocate specific training (Client-centered therapy, 2006).

Divergence and alignment: Islāmic spirituality and client-centred therapy

The applicability of the client-centred therapy approach to non-Western clients or in the Islāmic context underwent ongoing deliberation (AbdAllāh, 2011; Al-Thani, 2012; Badri, 2014; Mohamad et al., 2011; Nassar-McMillan & Hakim-Larson, 2003; Poyrazli, 2003; Rassool, 2016). Although Islāmic psychotherapy and counselling exhibits Islāmic spirituality and religiosity as a way of life (Lubis, 2011), the framework of client-centred therapy in its purest form is not fully congruent with Islāmic principles and practice.

Somehow, spirituality is not formally addressed or recognised in person-centred theory (Barrineau, 1990), but it is not unfamiliar with it. Rogers (1980) acknowledged its importance in several of his writings. He described moments of transcendence and connection with the unknown within oneself and others, suggesting that these experiences contribute to healing and a sense of interconnectedness. Rogers emphasised the significance of spiritual dimensions in human experiences even though they may not be formally integrated into the theory itself (Barrineau, 1990; Rogers, 1980). However, he seems to indicate that a deep and transformative experience where the individual is in touch with the unknown aspects within themselves. This spiritual essence is conveyed by Al-Thani (2012):

> Both Islāmic society and the Person-Centred Approach (PCA) are interested in applying 'spirituality' to helping and supporting clients psychologically. Irrelevant as to how the term is applied, both approaches seek to provide a safe atmosphere where people feel accepted and loved.
>
> *(p. 18)*

Both Islāmic society and the person-centred approach share a commitment to integrating spirituality into psychological support by prioritising the establishment of a safe and inclusive environment. According to Al-Thani (2012), they both aim to provide psychological support that acknowledges and respects the spiritual dimension of individuals, fostering holistic well-being.

The concept of spirituality encompasses diverse meanings depending on the context in which it is discussed. In secular societies, spirituality is recognised as extending beyond religious beliefs and is often associated with the pursuit of self-awareness and self-actualisation (Rassool, 2000). While secular perspectives view spirituality in broader terms, there is still a connection between religiosity and spirituality in counselling, as both offer solutions to human struggles (Corey, 2022). In the Islāmic context, spirituality is closely intertwined with religious beliefs and practices, with Islām serving as the spiritual path for salvation and a way of life (Rassool, 2014, 2016). This highlights the multifaceted nature of spirituality, acknowledging its various interpretations across different contexts while emphasising its integral connection to religious dimensions in the Islāmic framework.

Al-Thani (2012) highlights significant positive similarities between the patient-centred approach and the Islāmic perspective in various aspects such as the nature of human beings, spirituality, self-responsibility, the fully functioning person, and the core conditions. Both Islām and the patient-centred approach highly value human beings and emphasise individual responsibility for personal actions and inner changes. They both encourage clients to become fully functioning individuals with positive attitudes towards self and others, taking responsibility for their actions and choices (Al-Thani, 2012). Moreover, both Islām and the patient-centred approach emphasise the importance of self-awareness in facilitating individual change. The patient-centred approach aligns closely with Islāmic psychotherapy and counselling as it prioritises the therapeutic relationship and encourages clients to be active and accountable for their behaviours (Al-Shenawi, 1998).

Humanistic psychology highlights the significance of positive psychology and overall well-being, including factors like happiness, fulfilment, and life satisfaction. In a similar vein, Islāmic teachings advocate for the pursuit of happiness, contentment, and serenity (*sakina*) as natural outcomes of a balanced and virtuous life aligned with God consciousness *(taqwâ)*. However, client-centred therapy, rooted in humanistic principles, tends to focus on personal growth and self-actualisation, often without explicitly incorporating the spiritual and religious dimension in the pursuit of happiness and wellness. Humanistic psychology and Islāmic teachings converge in their emphasis on the inherent potential for growth within individuals and the importance of personal development. Both promote self-actualisation or self-purification (*tazkiyah an-nafs*), highlighting autonomy, personal responsibility, and the exercise of free will in decision-making processes. Islāmic principles encourage moral decisions based on ethical intelligence, echoing the humanistic value of individual autonomy and personal responsibility.

Within therapeutic relationships, humanistic psychology lays a major emphasis on building qualities like empathy, active listening, and compassion. These characteristics are consistent with Islāmic teachings that emphasise the importance of compassion, mercy (*rahma*), and empathy for others. In Islāmic tradition, Prophet Muhammad (ﷺ) is regarded as an example of empathy and compassion, acting as a model for believers to follow in their dealings with their fellow humans. He showed genuine concern and sympathy for those around him, regardless of their origin, social rank, or religious beliefs. Both humanistic psychology and Islāmic teachings emphasise the importance of genuine empathy and compassionate care in interpersonal relationships. Humanistic psychology asserts that morality, ethical values, and good intentions serve as the primary motivators of human behaviour. It suggests that adverse social or psychological experiences often stem from deviations from these innate tendencies towards goodness and ethical behaviour (GoodTherapy, 2018). Islāmic traditions provide a well-defined moral and ethical framework, emphasising personal responsibility, accountability, and the pursuit of righteousness.

While there are areas of congruence between humanistic psychology and Islāmic traditions, it is essential to acknowledge existing incongruences due to divergent perspectives and values. The application of client-centred therapy to Muslim clients faces challenges stemming from inherent differences in values and cultural orientations. Western-oriented societies highly value assertiveness, open expression of emotion, individual decision-making, and personal freedom (Sue & Sue, 1999), which can clash with Islāmic principles opposing approaches based on individualism, relativism, and humanism (AbdAllāh, 2011; Badri, 1996). In the Islāmic context, traditional and authoritarian values such as privacy in family matters, respect for authorities, limited expression of emotion, and group decision-making are prevalent (Nassar-McMillan & Hakim-Larson, 2003; Poyrazli, 2003). These differences underline the importance of considering the cultural context when applying therapeutic approaches.

From an Islāmic perspective, a fundamental concern with the client-centred approach lies in its non-directive, egalitarian therapist-client relationship style that relies on the therapist's personal qualities for facilitating the client's personal growth (Mohamad et al., 2011). The non-directive and non-judgmental nature of client-centred therapy may be deemed confusing, particularly in the early stages of therapy (Dwairy, 2006). A more active and structured therapeutic approach is considered effective within this cultural context (Basit & Hamid, 2010). The discrepancy in cultural expectations emphasises the importance of adapting therapeutic approaches to align with the values and preferences of Muslim clients. Critics argue that maintaining genuine, non-judgmental relationships in client-centred therapy is unrealistic due to the inherent judgments in social interactions (Badri, 2014). The artificial nature of the therapy setting may enable therapists to appear genuinely accepting (Masson, 1994). There are concerns that therapists, in striving to be non-judgmental and supportive, may compromise congruence and genuineness in their therapeutic responses (Yusoff, 2011).

In multicultural counselling contexts, the commitment to unconditional positive regard may face challenges, especially in societies where moral and religious teachings, such as in Islāmic communities, are highly valued (MacDougall, 2002). This critique emphasises the potential cultural incongruence of the concept of unconditional positive regard within the Islāmic faith (Badri, 2014). There are certain facets of human behaviour that are not acceptable within the realm of Islām. Allāh says in the Qur'ân,

قُلُوبُهُم مُّنكِرَةٌ وَهُم مُّسْتَكْبِرُونَ
لَا جَرَمَ أَنَّ ٱللَّهَ يَعْلَمُ مَا يُسِرُّونَ وَمَا يُعْلِنُونَ ۚ إِنَّهُ لَا يُحِبُّ ٱلْمُسْتَكْبِرِينَ

- *Their hearts are disapproving, and they are arrogant . . . Assuredly, Allāh knows what they conceal and what they declare. Indeed, He does not like the arrogant.* (An-Naĥl 16:22–23, interpretation of the meaning)

It is narrated on the authority of Abdullah that the Messenger of Allāh (ﷺ) observed that "He who has in his heart the weight of a mustard seed of pride shall not enter Paradise" (Muslim). The Qur'ân contains a number of verses related to unacceptable behaviours including mischief (Qur'ân 2:11–13); corruption (Qur'ân 2:205; 16:88; 30:41); transgression (Qur'ân 4:14); lying (Qur'ân 6:21); evil (Qur'ân 17:11; 30:10); and adultery or fornication (Qur'ân 24:2–3). 'Abdullah bin 'Amr bin Al-'As (may Allāh be pleased with him) narrated:

The Prophet (ﷺ) said, "Whosoever possesses these four characteristics, is a sheer hypocrite; and anyone who possesses one of them, possesses a characteristic of hypocrisy till he gives it up. When he is entrusted with something, he proves dishonest; when he talks, he tells a lie; when he makes a covenant, he acts treacherously; and when he quarrels, he utters foul language.

(Bukhārī & Muslim)

Humanistic psychology places a strong emphasis on the individualistic notions of self-actualisation and self-realisation. However, it is important to note that Islāmic teachings offer a more comprehensive perspective on the self that transcends individualistic ideals. The Islāmic understanding of the self underscores communal responsibilities (*ummah*) and emphasises a balance between individual well-being and collective harmony, diverging from the individualistic approach of humanistic psychology. In Islāmic terms, the concept of self-actualisation aligns with the *fitrah*, described as guiding humanity "to the true faith of Allāh and the complete fulfilment of their potential" (Utz, 2011, p. 47).

According to Tahir (2011), every individual is born with *fitrah*, which represents a state of inherent self-actualisation. However, upbringing and maturity may alter one's perception of reality, leading to the need to rediscover or refresh this reality. Seeking divine guidance and revealed steps allows individuals to attain self-gratification and align with their innate potential. However, in Ozsoy's perspective (2010), achieving one's full potential, termed self-actualisation, requires a comprehensive understanding of oneself, encompassing elements like self-esteem, self-concept, and self-confidence. These components form the foundation for realising one's capabilities and aspirations, emphasising the significance of a balanced perception of the self.

The client-centred therapy approach emphasises self-actualisation as the key to personal growth, with therapists refraining from direct influence on clients' processes. This concept aligns with Islāmic teachings, which also prioritise self-transformation and human potential (Amer & Jalal, 2012). In Islāmic teachings, individuals are viewed as vicegerents on earth, representing God, and are encouraged to fulfil this role by actualising their full potential across various dimensions of existence, as described in the Qur'an (2:30). For Muslims, the route of self-actualisation is only possible through the path laid down by Allāh and the guidance of the last Messenger of God (ﷺ). Allāh says in the Qur'ân,

إِلَّا مَن تَابَ وَءَامَنَ وَعَمِلَ عَمَلًا صَٰلِحًا فَأُو۟لَٰٓئِكَ يُبَدِّلُ ٱللَّهُ سَيِّـَٔاتِهِمْ حَسَنَٰتٍۢ ۗ وَكَانَ ٱللَّهُ غَفُورًۭا رَّحِيمًۭا

- *Except for those who repent, believe and do righteous work. For them, Allāh will replace their evil deeds with good. And ever is Allāh Forgiving and Merciful.*

(Al-Furqān 25:70, interpretation of the meaning)

That is, "those who repent in this world to Allāh for all of those deeds, for then Allāh will accept their repentance ... and will replace the evil deeds with good merits" (Ibn Kathīr, 2000). Other verses in the Qur'ân reinforced this:

وَمَن يَعْمَلْ سُوءًا أَوْ يَظْلِمْ نَفْسَهُ ثُمَّ يَسْتَغْفِرِ ٱللَّهَ يَجِدِ ٱللَّهَ غَفُورًا رَّحِيمًا

- *And whoever does a wrong or wrongs himself, but then seeks forgiveness of Allāh will find Allāh Forgiving and Merciful.*

(An-Nisā' 4:110, interpretation of the meaning)

أَلَمْ يَعْلَمُوٓا۟ أَنَّ ٱللَّهَ هُوَ يَقْبَلُ ٱلتَّوْبَةَ عَنْ عِبَادِهِۦ

- *Know they not that Allāh accepts repentance from His servants.*

(At-Tawbah 29:104, interpretation of the meaning)

قُلْ يَٰعِبَادِىَ ٱلَّذِينَ أَسْرَفُوا۟ عَلَىٰٓ أَنفُسِهِمْ لَا تَقْنَطُوا۟ مِن رَّحْمَةِ ٱللَّهِ ۚ إِنَّ ٱللَّهَ يَغْفِرُ ٱلذُّنُوبَ جَمِيعًا ۚ إِنَّهُۥ هُوَ ٱلْغَفُورُ ٱلرَّحِيمُ

- *Say, "O My servants who have transgressed against themselves [by sinning], do not despair of the mercy of Allāh. Indeed, Allāh forgives all sins. Indeed, it is He who is the Forgiving, the Merciful.*

(Az-Zumar 39:53, interpretation of the meaning)

Amer and Jalal (2012) suggested that this aspect shows how Islāmic beliefs do not promote the idea of dwelling in the past but promote self-actualisation.

The promotion of self-actualisation in psychotherapy and counselling with Muslim clients has faced criticism, particularly within Islāmic collective societies. Al-Bahadel (2004) argues that self-actualisation is not culturally acceptable, as it may be perceived as selfishness that disrupts social harmony. The maintenance of the collective structure by means of community obligation (*fard kifaya*) is more important than the autonomy of the self, that is, some sort of community self-actualisation rather than individual actualisation. In Qatari society, self-actualisation can lead to social rejection and sanctions (Al-Thani, 2012), while Dwairy (2009) warns that it may create conflicts within families and broader social circles. An alternative perspective suggests that self-actualisation and social reform can be achieved through religious practices like fasting and prayer, especially during Ramadan (Choudhury, 2010).

Finally, client-centred therapy adopts a non-directive approach, prioritising empathic listening and refraining from imposing guidance or views on the client. In contrast, Islāmic psychotherapy often assumes a directive role, offering interpretations, recommendations, and guidance rooted in Islāmic teachings and values. This directive approach integrates religious, ethical, and moral guidance, addressing faith, ethical dilemmas, spiritual practices, and religious ceremonies. The distinction highlights the differing therapeutic styles between client-centred therapy and Islāmic psychotherapy, with the latter adopting a more active and directive role aligned with Islāmic principles.

Client-centred therapy: applying the core conditions in an Islāmic context

In the context of Islāmic traditions, the value of client-centred therapy lies in therapists' thoughtful adaptations and modifications that respect the client's perspectives and integrate Islāmic concepts and values into the therapeutic process. This involves discussing the client's relationship with Allāh, exploring religious experiences, and addressing how beliefs impact well-being using Islāmic terminology. These adjustments aim to enhance rapport and empathy with Muslim clients, fostering a more effective therapeutic relationship that acknowledges their cultural and religious background.

The core conditions of client-centred therapy, as outlined by Rogers, are considered essential for therapeutic change, emphasising psychological contact, congruence, unconditional positive regard, and empathic understanding (Rogers, 1957, 2004). In an Islāmic context, spiritual solutions rooted in love and fear of Allāh, along with fulfilling responsibilities as servants of Allāh (Hallen, 2002, cited in Sandarwati, 2013). Al-Thani (2012) notes alignment between the person-centred approach's core conditions and Islāmic principles, such as striving for perfection (*ihsan*), trust, acceptance, understanding, genuineness, respect, humility, and cultivating beneficial habits, including love for what is beneficial for oneself and others.

The instillation of Islāmic values, such as moral behaviour, is based on the Qur'ān and *Sunnah*. A Muslim needs to try to emulate the behaviour and the morality of Prophet Muhammad (ﷺ). Allāh confirms that in the following verse:

لَّقَدْ كَانَ لَكُمْ فِى رَسُولِ ٱللَّهِ أُسْوَةٌ حَسَنَةٌ لِّمَن كَانَ يَرْجُوا۟ ٱللَّهَ وَٱلْيَوْمَ ٱلْءَاخِرَ وَذَكَرَ ٱللَّهَ كَثِيرًا

- *There has certainly been for you in the Messenger of Allāh an excellent pattern (model) for anyone whose hope is in Allāh and the Last Day and [who] remembers Allāh often.*

(Al-'Ahzāb 33:21, interpretation of the meaning)

Allāh describes Prophet Muhammad's (ﷺ) patience in listening to others:

ٱلنَّبِىَّ وَيَقُولُونَ هُوَ أُذُنٌ ۚ قُلْ أُذُنُ خَيْرٍ لَّكُمْ يُؤْمِنُ بِٱللَّهِ وَيُؤْمِنُ لِلْمُؤْمِنِينَ وَرَحْمَةٌ لِّلَّذِينَ ءَامَنُوا۟ مِنكُمْ ۚ وَٱلَّذِينَ يُؤْذُونَ رَسُولَ ٱللَّهِ لَهُمْ عَذَابٌ أَلِيمٌ

- *And say, "He is an ear." Say, "[It is] an ear of goodness for you that believes in Allāh and believes the believers and [is] a mercy to those who believe among you."*

(At-Tawbah 9:61, interpretation of the meaning)

Prophet Muhammad (ﷺ) is our role model and example in showing compassion about others' concerns. The following verse describes the character of the Prophet (ﷺ) in dealing with his followers:

فَبِمَا رَحْمَةٍ مِنَ ٱللَّهِ لِنتَ لَهُمْ ۖ وَلَوْ كُنتَ فَظًّا غَلِيظَ ٱلْقَلْبِ لَٱنفَضُّوا۟ مِنْ حَوْلِكَ ۖ فَٱعْفُ عَنْهُمْ وَٱسْتَغْفِرْ لَهُمْ وَشَاوِرْهُمْ فِى ٱلْأَمْرِ ۖ فَإِذَا عَزَمْتَ فَتَوَكَّلْ عَلَى ٱللَّهِ ۚ إِنَّ ٱللَّهَ يُحِبُّ ٱلْمُتَوَكِّلِينَ

- *So, by mercy from Allāh, [O Muhammad], you were lenient with them. And if you had been rude [in speech] and harsh in heart, they would have disbanded from about you. So, pardon them and ask forgiveness for them and consult them in the matter. And when you have decided, then rely upon Allāh. Indeed, Allāh loves those who rely [upon Him].*

('Ali 'Imrān 3:159, interpretation of the meaning)

According to Al-Qarnee (2002), gentleness and goodness are essential in making relationships with the self and others healthy and effective, as the Prophet (ﷺ) stated, "Whenever gentleness is present in something, that thing is beautified; when gentleness is removed from something, that thing becomes spoiled" (p. 437). The following is a summary of client-centred therapy from an Islāmic perspective:

- Therapist should be well-versed in Islāmic teachings and be open to discussing and integrating them into the therapeutic process when appropriate.
- The therapist needs to have a deep understanding of the religious (and cultural) background of the Muslim client but to be aware that different clients have different levels of religious understanding. Having trust in Allāh (*tawakkul*) is one of the Islāmic core conditions.
- The therapist needs to understand the Islāmic worldview of the Muslim client.
- Structuring is necessary whenever a client does not know what is involved in the therapeutic relationship – how the therapist will function and what is expected of the client – or holds misconceptions about the process (Patterson, 1996).
- The discussed similarities, especially self-actualisation, can be modified when counselling a Muslim client to accommodate Islāmic values, the Qur'ân, and Prophetic teachings (Al-Thani, 2012, p. 309).
- Islāmic psychotherapists and counsellors should use a balance between directive and non-directive approaches (psychological and spiritual direction; guiding and advising; making suggestions; disclosing thoughts and feelings).
- Interpersonal communications styles should be adapted because of cultural and sociopolitical factors (Wehrly, 1995).
- The therapist should encourage the client to work from within and build a healthy relationship with the self (Al-Thani, 2012, p. 309).
- Using spiritual interventions and incorporating humanistic techniques, such as journaling and contemplation, with Islāmic spiritual practices to promote self-awareness and personal growth.

- The therapist sensitively encourages the Muslim client to follow the Qur'ân and the teachings of Prophet Mohammad (ﷺ).
- Family and other significant relationships need to be considered as part of the therapeutic process.
- Gratitude should be shown to Allāh when there is improvement in the client's state or circumstances (core condition, if appropriate).

References

AbdAllāh, S. S. (2011). *Islāmic theological and spiritual foundations of resilience: Implications for counseling and psychotherapy with Muslims*. Paper presented at the International Conference on the Psychology of Resilience.

Al-Bahadel, D. (2004). *The feasibility of introducing counseling for woman and family therapy into society within Saudi Arabia* [Unpublished PhD thesis, University of East Anglia].

Al-Qarnee, A. A. (2002). *Do not be sad*. International Islāmic Publishing House.

Al-Shenawi, M. M. (1998). *Theories of counseling and psychotherapy*. Ghareeb House for Printing, Publishing and Distribution.

Al-Thani, A. S. (2012). An Islāmic modification of the person-centred counselling approach. *QScience.com*. Retrieved November 5, 2023, from www.qscience.com/page/books/impcca.

Amer, M. A., & Jalal, B. (2012). Individual psychotherapy/counselling. In S. Ahmed & M. M. Amer (Eds.), *Counseling Muslims: Handbook of mental health issues and interventions*. Routledge.

Badri, M. B. (1996). Counseling and psychotherapy from an Islāmic perspective. *Al-Shajarah*, *1*(1–2), 25–28.

Badri, M. B. (2014). Can the psychotherapy of Muslim patients be of real help to them without being Islāmised? *Islāmic-World.net*. Retrieved November 5, 2023, from http://Islamic187.rssing.com/browser.php?indx=7717208&item=27.

Barrineau, P. (1990). Chicago revisited: An interview with Elizabeth Sheerer. *Person-Centered Review*, *5*(4), 416–424.

Basit, A., & Hamid, M. (2010). Mental health issues of Muslim Americans. *Journal of the Islāmic Medical Association of North America*, *42*(3), 106–110. https://doi.org/10.5915/42-3-5507.

Bozarth, J. D. (1998). *Person-centered therapy: A revolutionary paradigm*. PCCS Books.

Bozarth, J. D., Zimring, F. F., & Tausch, R. (2002). Client-centered therapy: The evolution of a revolution. In D. J. Cain & J. Seeman (Eds.), *Humanistic psychotherapies: Handbook of research and practice* (pp. 147–188). American Psychological Association.

Broadley, B. T. (1997). The nondirective attitude in client-centered therapy. *The Person-Centered Journal*, *4*(1), 18–30.

Bukhârî, & Muslim. *Riyad as-Salihin 1543* (In-book reference: Book 17, Hadith 33). https://sunnah.com/riyadussalihin:1543.

Center for Substance Abuse Treatment (CSAT). (1999). Chapter 6: Brief humanistic and existential therapies. In *Brief interventions and brief therapies for substance abuse* [SAMHSA/CSAT Treatment Improvement Protocol (TIP) Series, No. 35]. SAMHSA. Retrieved November 2, 2023, from www.ncbi.nlm.nih.gov/books/NBK64939/.

Choudhury, M. A. (2010). Self-actualization: Experience of Ramadan. *Horizon*, *197*, 4. Retrieved November 5, 2023, from www.squ.edu.om/Portals/33/almasar/Horizon%20197%20.pdf.

Client-centered therapy. (2006). *The Harvard Mental Health Letter*, *22*(7), 1–3.

Corey, G. (2022). *Theory and practice of group counseling*. Cengage Learning.

DeRobertis, E. M. (2022). Epistemological foundations of humanistic psychology's approach to the empirical. *Journal of Theoretical and Philosophical Psychology*, *42*(2), 61–77. https://doi.org/10.1037/teo0000181.

DeRobertis, E. M., & Bland, A. M. (2021). Humanistic and positive psychologies: The continuing narrative after two decades. *Journal of Humanistic Psychology*, 1–33. https://doi.org/10.1177/0022167821100835.

Dwairy, M. (2006). *Counseling and psychotherapy with Arabs and Muslims: A culturally sensitive approach*. Columbia University Teachers' College.

Dwairy, M. (2009). Culture analysis and metaphor psychotherapy with Arab-Muslim clients. *Journal of Clinical Psychology: In Session*, *65*(2), 199–209. https://doi.org/10.1002/jclp.20568.

Feltham, C., & Dryden, W. (2004). *Dictionary of counselling*. Wiley.

Freeth, R. (2007). *Humanizing psychiatry and mental health care: The challenge of the person-centered approach*. Radcliffe Publishing.

GoodTherapy. (2018). *Humanistic psychology (humanism)*. Retrieved November 5, 2023, from www.goodtherapy.org/learn-about-therapy/types/humanistic-psychology.

Ibn Kathir. (2000). *Tafsir ibn Kathir* (J. Abualrub, N. Khitab, H. Khitab, A. Walker, M. Al-Jibali, & S. Ayoub, Trans.). Darussalam Publishers and Distributors.

Lubis, S. A. (2011). Islāmic counselling: The services of mental health and education for people. *Religious Education*, *106*(5), 494–503. https://doi.org/10/1080/00344087.2011.613347.

MacDougall, C. (2002). Rogers's person-centered approach: Consideration for use in multicultural counseling. *Journal of Humanistic Psychology*, *42*(2), 48–55. https://doi.org/10.1177/0022167802422005.

Maslow, A. H. (1943). A theory of human motivation. *Psychological Review*, *50*(4), 370–396.

Maslow, A. H. (1954). *Motivation and personality*. Harper and Row.

Masson, J. M. (1994). *Against therapy*. Common Courage Press.

McLeod, J. (2013). *An introduction to counselling* (5th ed.). Open University Press.

Mearns, D., & Thorne, B. (2007). *Person-centered counseling in action* (3rd ed.). Sage Publications.

Merry, T. (2014). *Learning and being in person-centred counselling*. PCCS Books.

Mohamad, M., Mokhtar, H. H., & Abu Sama, A. (2011). Person-centered counseling with Malay clients: Spirituality as an indicator of personal growth. *Procedia – Social and Behavioral Sciences*, *30*, 2117–2123. https://doi.org/10.1016/j.sbspro.2011.10.411.

Muslim. *Sahih Muslim 91c* [In-book reference: Book 1, Hadith 173. USC-MSA web (English) reference: Book 1, Hadith 166]. https://sunnah.com/muslim:91c.

Nassar-McMillan, S. C., & Hakim-Larson, J. (2003). Counseling considerations among Arab Americans. *Journal of Counseling and Development*, *81*(2), 150–159.

Nelson-Jones, R. (2014). *Nelson-Jones' theory and practice of counselling and psychotherapy* (6th ed.). Sage Publications.

Ozsoy, Z. (2010). A true understanding of self for self-actualization. *The Fountain Magazine*. Retrieved November 5, 2023, from www.fountainmagazine.com/Issue/detail/A-True-Understanding-of-Self-for-Self-Actualization.

Patterson, C. H. (1996). Multicultural counselling: From diversity to universality. *Journal of Counseling and Development*, *74*(3), 227–231.

Patterson, C. H. (2000). *Understanding psychotherapy: 50 years of client centered theory and practice*. PCCS Books.

Poyrazli, S. (2003). Validity of Rogerian therapy in Turkish culture: A cross-cultural perspective. *Journal of Humanistic Counseling, Education and Development*, *42*(1), 107–115.

Prochaska, J. O., & DiClemente, C. C. (1992). Stages of change in the modification of problem behaviors. *Programme Behaviour Modification*, *28*, 183–218.

Proctor, C., Tweed, R., & Morris, D. (2016). The Rogerian fully functioning person: A positive psychology perspective. *Journal of Humanist Psychology*, *56*(5), 503–529.

Rassool, G. Hussein (2000). The crescent and Islām: Healing, nursing and the spiritual dimension: Some considerations towards an understanding of the Islāmic perspectives on caring. *Journal of Advanced Nursing*, *32*(6), 1476–1484.

Rassool, G. Hussein (2014). *Cultural competence in caring for Muslim patients*. Palgrave Macmillan.
Rassool, G. Hussein (2016). *Islāmic counselling: An introduction to theory and practice*. Routledge.
Robbins, B. D. (2008). What is the good life? Positive psychology and the renaissance of humanistic psychology. *The Humanistic Psychologist, 36*(2), 96–112.
Rogers, C. R. (1951). *Client-centered therapy: Its current practice, implications and theory*. Constable.
Rogers, C. R. (1957). The necessary and sufficient conditions of therapeutic personality change. *Journal of Consulting Psychology, 21*(2), 95–103. Reprinted (1992) in *Journal of Consulting and Clinical Psychology, 60*(6), 827–832.
Rogers, C. R. (1961). *On becoming a person*. Houghton Mifflin.
Rogers, C. R. (1963). The concept of the fully functioning person. *Psychology and Psychotherapy, 1*(1), 17–26. https://doi.org/10.1037/h0088567.
Rogers, C. R. (1977). *Carl Rogers on personal power: Inner strength and its revolutionary impact*. Delacorte Press.
Rogers, C. R. (1980). *A way of being*. Houghton Mifflin Company.
Rogers, C. R. (1987). Rogers, Kohut, and Erickson: A personal perspective on some similarities and differences. In J. K. Zeig (Ed.), *The evolution of psychotherapy* (pp. 179–187). Brunner/Mazel.
Rogers, C. R. (2004). *On becoming a person*. Constable.
Sandarwati, E. M. (2013). Theoretical framework. In *The implementation of Islāmic guidance and counseling model* [Thesis, State Institute for Islāmic Studies]. Retrieved November 5, 2023, from http://eprints.walisongo.ac.id/207/3/091111072_Bab2.pdf.
Schneider, K. J., & Leitner, L. M. (2002). Humanistic psychotherapy. In M. Hersen & W. H. Sledge (Eds.), *The encyclopedia of psychotherapy* (Vol. I, pp. 949–957). Elsevier Science/Academic Press.
Schunk, D. H. (2022). *Learning theories: An educational perspective* (8th ed.). Pearson, Inc.
Sue, D. W., & Sue, D. (1999). *Counseling the culturally different: Theory and practice* (3rd ed.). John Wiley.
Tahir, M. A. (2011). Ibrahim's hierarchy of needs. *Islām & Psychology*. Retrieved November 5, 2023, from http://Islamandpsychology.blogspot.com/2011/05/ibrahims-hierarchy-of-needs.html.
Taylor, E. (2001). Positive psychology and humanistic psychology: A reply to Seligman. *Journal of Humanistic Psychology, 41*(1), 13–29.
Utz, A. (2011). *Psychology from an Islāmic perspective*. International Islāmic Publishing House.
Watson, J. C. (2002). Re-visioning empathy. In D. J. Cain & J. Seeman (Eds.), *Humanistic psychotherapies: Handbook of research and practice* (pp. 445–471). American Psychological Association.
Wehrly, B. (1995). *Pathways to multicultural counseling competence: A developmental journey*. Brooks/Cole.
www.minddisorders.com. (2023). *Person-centered therapy*. Retrieved November 2, 2023, from www.minddisorders.com/Ob-Ps/Person-centered-therapy.html.
Yusoff, Y. B. Md. (2011). *Counselling and religious and spiritual values: A Malaysian study* [PhD thesis, The University of Waikato]. Retrieved November 6, 2023, from http://researchcommons.waikato.ac.nz/bitstream/handle/10289/5834/thesis.pdf?sequence=5.

9
ISLĀMIC INSIGHTS INTO COGNITIVE–BEHAVIOUR THERAPY

Path to healing mind, soul, and behaviour

Introduction

Cognitive–behavioural therapy (CBT) is a widely employed and effective method in mental health, emphasising the intricate relationship between thoughts, feelings, and behaviours. It acknowledges that negative thought patterns contribute to various psychological issues and focuses on modifying these patterns to promote positive emotional and behavioural outcomes (Beck, 1976; Ellis, 1962). CBT recognises the role of cognitive, emotional, physiological, and behavioural factors in maintaining psychological problems. By employing a range of techniques, including cognitive restructuring, problem-solving, behavioural activation, and emotion regulation, CBT aims to replace maladaptive cognitions with more constructive ones. This approach empowers individuals to understand how their thoughts influence their emotions and behaviours, facilitating positive changes in their lives.

CBT has proven effective for various psychological conditions, including anxiety, stress, depression, eating disorders, panic disorder, and phobias (Butler et al., 2006; Hofmann et al., 2012; Leahy & Holland, 2000). The diverse strategies and techniques within CBT share a common underlying philosophy (Hamdan, 2008). Modern CBT includes variations such as meta-cognitive therapy, mindfulness-based therapy, mindfulness-based cognitive therapy, dialectical behaviour therapy, acceptance and commitment therapy, internet-based CBT, and the use of mobile devices to augment CBT (Beck & Haigh, 2014; Bee et al., 2008; Hofmann, 2011; Hofmann & Asmundson, 2008; Hofmann et al., 2013; Khoury et al., 2013; Linehan, 2000; Mundy & Hofmann, 2014; Sauer-Zavala et al., 2012; Segal et al., 2013; Swain et al., 2013).

Key features of CBT include its action-oriented and problem-solving approaches, aiming for symptom reduction, improved functioning, and remission of the disorder

Islāmic insights into cognitive–behaviour therapy 129

(Hofmann et al., 2012). CBT is a structured and evidence-based therapy typically consisting of 6 to 20 sessions, aimed at helping individuals gain insight, challenge negative thought patterns, and develop coping mechanisms. Integrating Islāmic principles into CBT can enhance its relevance and effectiveness for Muslim clients. This involves aligning therapeutic techniques with Islāmic values, spirituality, and cultural nuances, exploring the cognitive theory of human nature and the therapist's role from an Islāmic perspective. This chapter examines the cognitive theory of human nature, the therapist's role, and the effective philosophy underlying the use of CBT for Muslim clients. It explores the integration of CBT from an Islāmic perspective, highlighting the significance of aligning therapeutic techniques with Islāmic values and spirituality.

Key pioneers in the development of CBT

Several key figures have significantly contributed to the development and advancement of CBT, shaping its theoretical foundations and practical applications. These pioneers have played a crucial role in establishing CBT as a widely practiced and influential therapeutic approach in the field of psychology and mental health. Here are a few notable pioneers in the field.

Abu Zayd Ahmed ibn Sahl Balkhi, a Persian Muslim polymath from the ninth century, is regarded as the pioneer father of cognitive therapy. His ideas, discussed in "Sustenance for Body and Soul" (Badri, 2013), laid the groundwork for some aspects of modern cognitive–behavioural principles. He introduced therapeutic interventions involving gradual exposure to anxiety-inducing situations to desensitise individuals and help them overcome negative emotions. Al-Balkhi's concept of reciprocal inhibition, or healing through opposites, predicted modern cognitive–behavioural techniques like exposure therapy. Joseph Wolpe reintroduced this approach over a thousand years later in 1969 (Badri, 2013). Exposure therapy, a cornerstone of modern CBT, operates on similar principles, gradually exposing individuals to feared stimuli to alleviate anxiety or fear.

Al-Balkhi's concept of reciprocal inhibition, resembling exposure therapy, aims to gradually desensitise individuals to anxiety-inducing stimuli, reducing their emotional impact. While Al-Balkhi's writings may not directly address cognitive processes, exposure therapy in contemporary cognitive–behavioural approaches often involves cognitive restructuring, modifying maladaptive thoughts linked to anxiety. References to scholars like Al Kindi and At-Tabari using cognitive strategies suggest an extensive Islāmic tradition of addressing mental health through cognitive interventions, challenging the notion that cognitive therapy solely originated in the West (Haque, 2004a).

Aaron Beck's contributions to cognitive behavioural interventions in the mid-20th century are significant, challenging traditional psychoanalytic theory and laying the foundation for modern cognitive therapy (Beck & Fleming, 2021). While Beck's work is crucial, other pioneers such as Other contributors in the development of cognitive therapy and its variations include Albert Ellis (rational emotive behaviour therapy); Donald Meichenbaum (cognitive restructuring); Maxie Clarence Maultsby (rational behaviour therapy); Judith Beck (highlighting CBT in its application in treating mood and anxiety disorder and training therapists in CBT); and Marsha Linehan (dialectical behaviour therapy, designed for individuals with borderline personality disorder), all contributing to the comprehensive and evidence-based approach widely practiced today. Beck's work, alongside that of these pioneers, has been instrumental in the evolution of cognitive-behavioural therapy.

Cognition, motivation, and spirituality

The CBT perspective on human nature emphasises individuals as active agents shaping their thoughts, emotions, and behaviours. It rejects the notion of individuals as passive victims, highlighting their capacity to influence mental well-being. CBT recognises the dynamic interplay of thoughts, emotions, and behaviours, attributing significant influence to cognitive processes. It stresses individuals' agency in shaping their mental and emotional experiences and subsequent actions.

'Aql, translated as "cognition," is a central concept in Islāmic psychology, theology, and philosophy and is also referred to as dialectical reasoning (Esposito, 2004). It is considered a fundamental aspect of human nature and is seen as a gift from God that distinguishes humans from other creatures. It encompasses mental faculties like perception, knowledge acquisition, understanding, and reasoning, emphasising intellect within the Islāmic framework.

'Aql is nurtured to deepen faith, gain knowledge, and make informed decisions. Scholars like Al-Jawzi and Al-Ghazālī provide different perspectives, with Al-Jawzi (2004) highlighting sensory-cognitive processing, self-evident truths, experiential knowledge, and ethical intelligence, while Al-Ghazālī (2010) adds a fifth function related to the knowledge of the heart (*qalb*). In essence, *'aql* can be seen as a subset of cognitive processes focused on reasoning, understanding, and moral judgement. The detailed anatomical seat and relationships with *qalb* and *nafs* can be explored further in "Islāmic Psychology: The Basics" (Rassool, 2023a).

Maraatib al-qasd in Islāmic tradition refers to the "degrees of motivation" or "levels of intention" (Abdul-Rahman, 2023). This concept addresses the various levels of intentionality and motivation underlying an individual's actions, particularly those related to worship and religious acts. The framework encompasses thoughts, motivation, and actions, emphasising the importance of the purity of intention in Islām. Abdul-Rahman (2023) presents a five-step sequence in Figure 9.1, illustrating the holistic nature of this conceptual framework for human behaviour.

The concepts described represent different aspects of the mental processes within Islāmic psychology:

- *Al-haajis*: signifies fleeting and transient thoughts that come and go swiftly, often reflecting the natural flow of mental processes without much significance

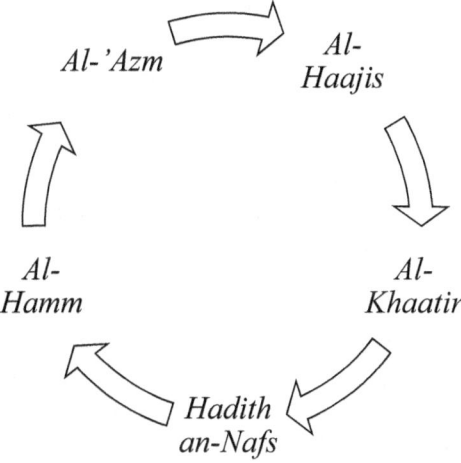

FIGURE 9.1 The five-step sequence of *maraatib al-qasd*.

- *Al-khaatir*: involves thoughts that enter the mind and are consciously chosen or engaged with by the individual, suggesting a level of control and awareness over the thoughts one entertains
- *Hadīth an-nafs*: refers to an internal dialogue where thoughts are carefully analysed, indicating a thoughtful and contemplative approach to mental processes
- *Al-hamm*: denotes the motivation to act influenced by mental processes that affect one's emotional state, acknowledging the interplay between thoughts and emotions in driving behaviour
- *Al-'azm*: represents a resolute determination to carry out a specific action, implying a firm commitment without room for reconsideration, indicating a high level of dedication and determination in pursuing a chosen course of action

Islāmic teachings often emphasise the significance of being aware of one's thoughts, intentions, and actions, seeking to align them with principles of sincerity, virtue, and obedience to God. These concepts provide a framework for self-reflection and personal development in the context of Islāmic spirituality.

Ibn al-Qayyim emphasised the significance of monitoring one's thoughts, which he termed *khawaatir*, due to their potential to influence both spiritual and psychological well-being. *Khawaatir* collectively refers to the thoughts that flood our minds throughout our waking hours: "anything a person does begins as an inner thought, a concealed speech or an internal dialogue" (Ibn al-Qayyim, 1981, p. 173). By being mindful of *khawaatir*, or intrusive thoughts and inner whispers, individuals can enhance spiritual progress, attain inner peace, and improve moral conduct. This concept resonates with principles of CBT, which emphasising the impact of beliefs on emotions and behaviours.

Badri (2000) noted parallels between *khawaatir* and "automatic thoughts," which the cognitive therapist Aaron Beck (1976) claims to have discovered in the

1970s! (p. 22). In his teachings, Ibn al-Qayyim (1981) highlighted the importance of enhancing spiritual progress, inner serenity, and moral conduct by cultivating awareness of *khawaatir*. Ibn Qayyim also developed the notion that transitory thoughts become real actions and established attitudes:

> The *khawaatir* lead to conscious thinking. Nest thinking will be transferred to or stored in the memory and the memory will transform it into a volition and a motive which will be acted out in real life as an action.
>
> *(p. 173)*

From an Islāmic perspective, Ibn al-Qayyim's teachings on *khawaatir* emphasise the recognition and management of the multitude of thoughts that occupy our minds. He acknowledges the impossibility of completely eliminating *khawaatir* but underlines the importance of individuals with faith choosing to embrace positive thoughts while avoiding harmful ones. Ibn al-Qayyim emphasises that genuine and virtuous actions are rooted in a deep connection with God, highlighting the internal and reflective dimensions of deeds. In essence, his concept of *khawaatir* encourages Muslims to understand, monitor, and guide their thoughts for the betterment of their spiritual, mental, and emotional well-being.

Abdul-Rahman (2023) conceptualises *khawaatir* as a complex interplay of internal and external forces. Internally, our unconscious mind conceals conflicting thoughts and desires, while externally, influences stem from spiritual or moral entities like God, angels, or negative forces such as temptations associated with Satan (p. 8). This perspective implies that our thoughts, feelings, and actions are shaped by a dynamic amalgamation of internal and external influences. In contemporary Islāmic understanding, *khawaatir* represents the convergence of competing forces from our unconscious, which may manifest internally within us (our unconscious mind), or externally such as spiritual or moral forces as distinct agents (divine, angelic, or satanic). Internally, our unconscious mind contains various thoughts and desires that might be in conflict with each other. Externally, there are influences from things like our beliefs about God, angels (positive spiritual influences), or negative influences (like temptations or harmful thoughts associated with Satan).

Al-Ghazālī's (2011) approach revolves around the integration of the intellect (*'aql*) and its impact on human behaviour (*al-akhlāk*). He describes the mind as *al-nāsih al-masyīr*, acting as an advisor and regulator of human behaviour, intricately connected to the heart (*qalb*), the central command centre for human actions. Al-Ghazālī emphasises the interplay of various mental faculties, including the imaginative faculty (*quwā al-khayal*), contemplative faculty (*al-tafakkur*), memory faculty (*al-hifz*), remembering faculty (*al-tadzakkur*), and delusional faculty (*al-wahm*). Imbalance or weakness in these faculties, especially when they deviate from religious principles, detrimentally affects human well-being in both worldly life and the hereafter. Al-Ghazālī posits that the key to happiness lies in achieving mental well-being (*al-sihhah al-nafsiyyah*). Arroisi and Rahmadi (2022) suggest that human cognitive psychology, as conceptualised by Al-Ghazālī and Ibn Qayyim, revolves around the idea of a holistic mind, combining *'aql, nafs, qalb*, and rûh, facilitating a meaningful life in both worldly life and the hereafter (p. 18). For a more in-depth exploration of conscious thought emergence and its significance, Abdul-Rahman (2023) provides comprehensive insights.

In contemporary times, CBT is widely regarded as a secular and evidence-based intervention approach. Ellis (1980) criticised theology and religious practices, arguing that they often impose rigid norms, leading to self-criticism and detrimental psychological effects when individuals fall short of these expectations. Ellis, like Rogers (1951), highlighted the potential for religious doctrines to contribute to feelings of guilt, shame, or inadequacy, particularly fostering irrational beliefs and emotional distress. Ellis specifically critiqued aspects of religious thinking that encourage absolutistic and perfectionist ideals, rooted in his philosophical stance on reason and irrationality.

However, within the broader field of CBT, some practitioners may integrate religious and spiritual principles into their therapeutic methods, acknowledging their significance in mental health. CBT's theory sees psychological and behavioural problems as originating from an individual's belief system and internal dialogue. Faulty or irrational thoughts, developed in childhood, lead to dysfunctional attitudes and beliefs that manifest in behaviour. CBT emphasises personal responsibility in creating emotional problems and empowers individuals to recognise and change their irrational cognitions.

Cognitive behavioural therapy: an overview

The epistemological foundations of CBT encompass empiricism, constructivism, and collaborative empiricism (Beshai et al., 2012a; Wright, 2006). Rooted in rationalism, CBT prioritises empirical evidence, emphasising objective observation and grounding interventions in scientific research. From a constructivist standpoint, CBT acknowledges the subjective nature of human perception and understanding, recognising that individual experiences and cognitive processes shape interpretation. The influence of cognitive biases and schemas on event interpretation is also acknowledged within the framework of CBT.

Collaborative empiricism, as described by Wright (2006), serves as the cornerstone of a collaborative therapeutic relationship in CBT. Therapists and patients work together to identify maladaptive cognitions and behaviours, validate their accuracy, and enact necessary adjustments. The primary objective is to help patients define problems and acquire skills to manage them effectively. Within CBT, there exists an epistemological tension between empirical and constructivist approaches, with variations even in the terminology used to describe each method. While contemporary CBT methods often lean towards the constructivist perspective (Winter, 2008), the overall epistemology of CBT integrates elements of empiricism, constructivism, collaborative empiricism, and pragmatism.

CBT is a psychotherapeutic approach centred on the notion that our thoughts (cognitions) significantly influence our feelings and behaviours, rather than external factors like people, situations, or events. Beck (1976) introduced the concept that individuals can develop consistent patterns of negative or irrational thoughts that contribute to susceptibility to emotional problems. CBT operates on the principle that an individual's activity encompasses three modalities: behaviour, emotion, and cognition. Dobson and Dozois (2010) provide a comprehensive definition of cognitive–behavioural theory with three key propositions:

- Thinking and cognitions have an impact on behaviour.
- Cognitive activity is accessible and can be modified.
- Desired behavioural changes may result from alterations in thinking.

CBT operates on three shared assumptions. First, cognitive activity affects behaviour, suggesting that an individual's evaluation of events influences their responses (Dobson & Dozois, 2010; Steiman & Dobson, 2004). Second, cognitive activity is accessible, monitorable, and alterable. The third assumption is that desired behaviour change can be achieved through cognitive change, implying that modifying thinking patterns leads to behavioural changes. A key concept in CBT is the idea of schemas, described as "cognitive structures that organise and process incoming information" (Dobson & Dozois, 2010, p. 14). Schemas represent systems of information that shape how individuals think and interpret the world, often synonymous with terms like core and irrational beliefs (DeRubeis et al., 2010). Developed through developmental influences and life experiences, schemas play a crucial role in regulating self-worth and behavioural coping strategies. Well-adjusted individuals possess schemas allowing realistic appraisals of life events, while maladjusted individuals may experience distorted perceptions, faulty problem-solving, and psychological disorders (Beck, 1976; Dozois & Beck, 2008). CBT interventions often target schemas to address and modify maladaptive thought patterns.

The role and function of the therapist

A CBT therapist's role is multifaceted, involving a variety of responsibilities to facilitate the therapeutic process and create positive change in clients. Table 9.1 presents key components of a CBT therapist's role and function.

The primary role of a CBT therapist is to help clients identify and modify their thinking patterns using evidence and rationality. CBT practitioners typically structure treatment sequentially, beginning with addressing maladaptive automatic thoughts (Beshai et al., 2012a). Therapeutic progress unfolds by resolving maladaptive automatic thinking, challenging illogical ideas, and replacing rigid "shoulds," "oughts," and "musts" with preferences. Subsequent stages involve demonstrating how illogical thinking maintains emotional disturbances, minimising irrational

TABLE 9.1 The CBT therapist's role and function

Key component	Explanation
Collaborative relationship	The therapist develops a collaborative and empathic relationship with the client, thus providing a safe and supportive environment.
Assessment and conceptualisation	The therapist conducts an in-depth assessment to understand about the client's concerns, challenges, and objectives. They collaborate with the client to construct a conceptualisation of the problems they are experiencing, recognising unhelpful thought patterns, harmful behaviours, and emotional difficulties.
Goal setting	The therapist establishes clear, measurable, attainable, relevant, and time-bound (SMART) goals with the client that address the client's issues. These objectives set a defined course for therapy and serve as a road map for the client's improvement.
Psychoeducation	The therapist teaches clients about the key principles of CBT; the interconnection between thoughts, emotions, and behaviours; and how these interactions might contribute to psychological problems. This education empowers clients to develop insights into their mental processes.
Cognitive restructuring	The therapist helps clients recognise and challenge negative or irrational thought patterns. They assist clients in examining the evidence for and against their beliefs, exploring alternate viewpoints, and developing more balanced and realistic thinking.
Behavioural techniques	The therapist introduces and implements approaches for the modification of maladaptive behaviours. These may include exposure treatment, behavioural trials, psychoeducation, or skill training to address specific issues.
Skill building and homework assignments	Therapists teach clients coping skills such as problem-solving approaches, interpersonal skills, communication skills, stress management strategies, and emotion regulation techniques. To encourage therapeutic success, therapists may prescribe homework activities that allow clients to practise and apply these skills between sessions.
Relapse prevention	The therapist assists clients in developing strategies and methods for maintaining improvement and avoiding lapse and full-blown relapse. This may entail identifying possible triggers, developing coping methods, and developing plans to effectively manage future challenges.
Monitoring Progress	The therapist keeps track of the client's progress and development and provides feedback on their accomplishments on a regular basis, regularly reviewing and adapting interventions based on the client's response and feedback.

thoughts, promoting a reasonable life philosophy, and exploring and modifying dysfunctional fundamental beliefs and schemas.

Therapists aim to help clients establish more adaptive and reasonable thought patterns, challenging irrational beliefs and encouraging the adoption of preferences over rigid musts (Corey, 2015). Further phases focus on modifying thinking patterns, minimising irrational ideas, and developing a rational philosophy of life. In later stages, therapists explore clients' core beliefs with the goal of changing dysfunctional core schemas (Persons & Davidson, 2001). In the process of CBT, therapists employ various cognitive and behavioural techniques. They use open-ended questions to help clients recognise rigid patterns of dysfunctional thinking and explore new perspectives, incorporating "Socratic" questioning and guided discovery methods (Wright, 2006). CBT distinguishes itself through the use of homework and outside-of-session techniques, the therapist's active direction of session activities, a psychoeducational approach, and a focus on the current and future functioning of the client. Additionally, CBT emphasises providing clients with information about their disorders, allocating significant time to evaluate, challenge, and modify clients' cognitions (Beshai et al., 2012a; Dobson & Dozois, 2010). Overall, the therapist's role in CBT is to provide guidance, support, and evidence-based therapies to clients in their journey towards enhanced mental health, providing knowledge and resources while acknowledging and respecting the client's unique experiences, values, and goals.

Harmony and discord: exploring the alignment of cognitive–behavioural therapy with Islāmic principles for Muslim clients

The examination of the philosophical and theoretical foundations of CBT by Dozois et al. (2019) and Beshai et al. (2012a) reveals potential philosophical dissonance between CBT and the Islāmic tradition. However, Beshai et al. (2012a) highlight potential areas of conflict between CBT and Islāmic traditions, despite underlying principles that may seem divergent. These areas of conflict include differing views on the nature of reality (empiricism/science), the sources of individual misfortune, behavioural or emotional change, self-control, and individual rights. Conflict may arise from philosophical differences, beliefs regarding predestination and control, changes in behaviour and emotion, moral and ethical behaviours, and the balance between autonomy and reliance on God. These potential sources of conflict require careful consideration and exploration to reconcile the principles of CBT with those of the Islāmic tradition.

The potential conflicts between Islāmic principles and CBT are identified in terms of rationalism versus constructivism. Islāmic principles align more closely with rationalism, which emphasises the existence of an absolute, objective reality accessible through the senses. The Islāmic tradition places significant value on reasoning (*'aql*), with the Qur'ân encouraging believers to study, reflect, and use their intellect to comprehend God's signals in nature. Classical Islāmic scholars, such as Ibn Al-Haytham, Ibn Ḥayyān, Ibn Sina, Al-Biruni, and Ibn Khaldun, contributed to laying the foundations for an empirical, experimental, and quantitative approach to scientific inquiry (Rassool, 2023b). These scholars utilised specific methodologies depending on the nature of the investigation in their quest for knowledge. It is worth noting that rationalism, reason, and revelation are not antagonistic but rather complementary.

Another point of potential conflict arises from Islāmic beliefs attributing both positive and negative events to divine determination and Allāh's will. Islāmic theology emphasises the concept of *qadr* or divine decree, as the sixth pillar of faith (*iman*). This belief acknowledges that Allāh is the architect of everything, predestining both moments of ease and moments of hardship. Muslim clients, therefore, may not necessarily view themselves as the sole architects of their challenges and instead attribute life circumstances to Allāh's divine plan. This is clearly reflected in the Qur'ân. Allāh says,

إِنَّا كُلَّ شَيْءٍ خَلَقْنَاهُ بِقَدَرٍ

- *Indeed, all things We created with predestination.*
  (Al-Qamar 54:49 interpretation of the meaning)

قُل لَّن يُصِيبَنَا إِلَّا مَا كَتَبَ ٱللَّهُ لَنَا هُوَ مَوْلَىٰنَا ۚ وَعَلَى ٱللَّهِ فَلْيَتَوَكَّلِ ٱلْمُؤْمِنُونَ

- *Say, "Never will we be struck except by what Allāh has decreed for us; He is our protector." And upon Allāh let the believers rely.*
  (At-Tawbah 9:51, interpretation of the meaning)

قُل لَّا أَمْلِكُ لِنَفْسِي ضَرًّا وَلَا نَفْعًا إِلَّا مَا شَاءَ ٱللَّهُ ۗ لِكُلِّ أُمَّةٍ أَجَلٌ ۚ إِذَا جَاءَ أَجَلُهُمْ فَلَا يَسْتَأْخِرُونَ سَاعَةً ۖ وَلَا يَسْتَقْدِمُونَ

- *Say, "I possess not for myself any harm or benefit except what Allāh should will. For every nation is a [specified] term. When their time has come, then they will not remain behind an hour, nor will they precede [it]."*
  (Yūnus 10:49, interpretation of the meaning)

So good, evil, and whatever happens in this world happens by Allah's will.

وَإِن تُصِبْهُمْ حَسَنَةٌ يَقُولُوا هَـٰذِهِ مِنْ عِندِ ٱللَّهِ ۖ وَإِن تُصِبْهُمْ سَيِّئَةٌ يَقُولُوا هَـٰذِهِ مِنْ عِندِكَ ۚ قُلْ كُلٌّ مِّنْ عِندِ ٱللَّهِ ۖ فَمَالِ هَـٰؤُلَاءِ ٱلْقَوْمِ لَا يَكَادُونَ يَفْقَهُونَ حَدِيثًا

- *But if good comes to them, they say, "This is from Allāh"; and if evil befalls them, they say, "This is from you." Say, "All [things] are from Allāh." So, what is [the matter] with those people that they can hardly understand any statement?*
  (An-Nisā' 4:78 interpretation of the meaning)

This is explained by Sheikh Muhammad Ibn al-'Uthaymin:

> They may be reconciled by noting that the first verse refers to the decree of Allāh, for example, it is from Allāh; He is the one who decrees it. The second verse refers to the cause for example, i.e. whatever of evil befalls you, you are the cause, and the One Who decrees evil and decrees the punishment for it is Allāh.
>
> *(Islām Q&A, 2009)*

In cognitive theory, individuals are free and thus capable of controlling their thoughts, assumptions and core beliefs. In contrast, Islāmic principles view that individuals' actions are not entirely free. Metaphysical entities act upon, and to some extent control, human behaviour (Beshai et al., 2012a). It is important to understand that the concepts of predestination and free will do not negate one another: both are considered equally true. Bynum (2006) stated,

> everything that occurs in the reality of the material world we live in is a direct result of Allāh's will. Human will is but an instrument of the will of Allāh and therefore does not have an independent existence in the overall trend of Islāmic thought. Even though the concept of "testing" is present, Allāh's will is never subservient to human will.

The potential challenge arises when reconciling CBT, which emphasises that individuals have the ability to make changes in their own lives, with Islāmic beliefs that stress ultimate divine control. In Islām, faith in God and acceptance of His will are paramount, while CBT promotes change through self-reliance, self-efficacy, and human action. Muslims may find CBT's emphasis on self-dependence incompatible with Islām's focus on reliance on God.

From an Islāmic perspective, desirable changes in behaviours and emotions are contingent upon God's will, as "everything that takes place in creation happens according to God's will" (Philips, 2007, p. 146). This highlights a potential philosophical tension between CBT's emphasis on individual empowerment and Islām's emphasis on divine will (Beshai et al., 2012a). It seems that whatever action takes place is by His own wish. In the Qur'ān, Allāh says,

إِنْ هُوَ إِلَّا ذِكْرٌ لِّلْعَٰلَمِينَ
لِمَن شَاءَ مِنكُمْ أَن يَسْتَقِيمَ
وَمَا تَشَاءُونَ إِلَّا أَن يَشَاءَ ٱللَّهُ رَبُّ ٱلْعَٰلَمِينَ

- *It is not except a reminder to the worlds. For whoever wills among you to take a right course. And you do not will except that Allāh wills – Lord of the worlds.*
  (At-Takwīr 81:27–29, interpretation of the meaning)

This is clear evidence indicating that the actions of Allāh's creatures are according to Allāh's will. If Allāh did not wish them to act, the action would not have occurred (Philips, 2007, p. 147).

CBT seeks to change behavioural patterns in order to reduce discomfort and increase well-being. Certain CBT-targeted behaviours may be considered morally unacceptable in an Islāmic context; Muslim clients seeking treatment while keeping to Islāmic beliefs and principles may experience stress or conflict as a result of this. When dealing with such difficulties, CBT therapists must approach treatment with cultural competence and respect for the client's religious beliefs. Understanding how certain behaviours are perceived within an Islāmic ethical framework that may be relevant to the desired behaviours is critical, as is the development of therapeutic goals that are compatible with those values.

Psychological disorders in the Islāmic perspective are often seen as originating from or permitted by God, and they may be viewed as tests or punishments. Muslim clients might perceive these challenges as opportunities for spiritual growth, purification, and tests of their faith, patience, or resilience. This perspective is influenced by theological and cultural beliefs, shaping how Muslims from various cultures perceive and cope with mental health issues. Some may find solace in enduring the trials of a disorder, believing it can lead to spiritual blessings and purification of sins (Abu-Ras et al., 2008; Beshai et al., 2012a; Haque, 2004b; Padela et al., 2012; Rassool, 2000). In a *hadīth* narrated by A'isha (may Allāh be pleased with her), Allāh's Messenger (ﷺ) says, "There is nothing (in the form of trouble) that comes to a believer even if it is the pricking of a thorn that there is decreed for him by Allah good or his sins are obliterated" (Muslim). Others may interpret their psychospiritual afflictions as a call to self-reflection, repentance, and seeking God's pardon. In effect, trials and tribulations in life teach us that we must adhere to Allāh's natural and moral laws.

In CBT, the conceptualisation of the self often aligns with an individualistic approach, emphasising self-awareness, autonomy, and the protection of individual rights. Conversely, Islāmic principles assert that the self is inseparable from others, prioritising the collective's rights and interests over those of the individual. This alternative perspective highlights individuals' connectivity and reliance within a broader social context, where individual rights may be sacrificed for community interests. The Islāmic framework emphasises collective good, guiding decision-making and actions to prioritise the larger community and maintain harmony. Despite Islām's emphasis on individual free will and accountability, collectivistic values play a central role in the Muslim *ummah*. Qur'ânic principles and *hadīths* stress the importance of working for the collective good, caring for others, preserving unity in the face of opposition, and striving towards common goals (Beshai et al., 2012a). This difference in the conceptualisation of the self poses a potential clash between CBT's individualistic focus and Islāmic principles that highlight the importance of common goals. Collectively on a community level, according to Imam Dr Mufti Abduljalil Sajid (2012),

> a Muslim's obligation is to establish what is right and eradicating what is wrong; Strive for an Islāmic identity supporting, promoting and protecting a Muslim way of family life; Dealing with health and educational issues and for the creation of a condition wherein perseverance of mutual compassion and well-being prevail for the benefit of the individual.

The Qur'ān sees no contradiction between unity and commanding good and forbidding wrong. Allāh says,

وَٱلْمُؤْمِنُونَ وَٱلْمُؤْمِنَٰتُ بَعْضُهُمْ أَوْلِيَآءُ بَعْضٍ ۚ يَأْمُرُونَ بِٱلْمَعْرُوفِ وَيَنْهَوْنَ عَنِ ٱلْمُنكَرِ وَيُقِيمُونَ ٱلصَّلَوٰةَ وَيُؤْتُونَ ٱلزَّكَوٰةَ وَيُطِيعُونَ ٱللَّهَ وَرَسُولَهُۥٓ ۚ أُو۟لَٰٓئِكَ سَيَرْحَمُهُمُ ٱللَّهُ ۗ إِنَّ ٱللَّهَ عَزِيزٌ حَكِيمٌ

- *The believing men and believing women are allies of one another. They enjoin what is right and forbid what is wrong and establish prayer and give zakat and obey Allāh and His Messenger. Those – Allāh will have mercy upon them. Indeed, Allāh is Exalted in Might and Wise.*

(At-Tawbah 9:71, interpretation of the meaning)

By commanding what is right and forbidding what is wrong, collectivism provides a mechanism whereby the Muslim *ummah* can fight off various social, moral and spiritual ills and maintain a healthy and dynamic life (Shafaat, 1987). It was narrated from Anas bin Malik (may Allāh be pleased with him) that the Messenger of Allah (ﷺ) said, "None of you truly believes until he loves for his brother" and "for his neighbour, what he loves for himself" (Ibn Majah). The importance of this *hadīth* is to show how people are supposed to relate to each other. It also negates the base emotions such as envy and establishes the vision of a society built upon love and compassion, where every member works for the good of all members (Zarabozo, 1999). In summary, Islāmic collectivism is clearly visible within Muslim families and the *ummah*. Brotherhood, equality, and compassion are key Islāmic beliefs that shape social interactions and relationships and constitute the foundation of the Muslim social system.

The main areas of dissonance between CBT and Islāmic ideology involve the client's religious dedication, the nature of the presenting problem, the modification of standard CBT for Muslim clients, the targeted level of cognitive change in treatment, and the language used in therapy sessions (Beshai et al., 2012a; Thomas & Ashraf, 2009). These disparities highlight the need to address the client's religious zeal, adapt therapeutic methods to align with Islāmic values, reconsider the extent of cognitive change in treatment, and be mindful of language use. Therapists must recognise and adapt to the unique components of Islāmic faith and practice, ensuring cultural sensitivity and respect for Muslim clients' religio-cultural identities when integrating CBT principles with Islāmic beliefs (Beshai et al., 2012a; Rassool, 2023b).

CBT: an Islāmic perspective

Throughout history, humans have sought answers to psychological and spiritual problems through faith and religious beliefs. In the time of Prophet Muhammad (ﷺ), the gradual prohibition of alcohol in Islām bears similarities to modern behaviour therapy, particularly systematic desensitisation. Al-Balkhi's introduction of reciprocal inhibition and rational cognitive therapy represents a significant historical contribution to psychology, focusing on changing inner thinking and irrational beliefs to eliminate emotional disorders.

Al-Balkhi employed therapeutic techniques such as relaxation, reciprocal inhibition, rational cognitive therapy, and a psychospiritual religious cognitive approach. Cognitive restructuring, a commonly used cognitive-behavioural technique, aligns with the Islāmic thinking style advocated by early Muslim scholars like Ibn al-Qayyim (Yusaf, 2019). These historical perspectives demonstrate the profound psychological understanding of early Islāmic scholars and how their ideas resonate with cognitive therapy principles, emphasising the role of rational thinking in influencing emotions and behaviours (Badri, 1976, 2013; Haque, 2004a; Yusaf, 2019).

There are unique facets and several techniques in the Islāmic cognitive therapy approach that have been developed by Muslim academics and clinicians. The significant cognitions from the Islāmic faith that can be incorporated into the therapeutic process with Muslim clients include the understanding of the reality of this world and its temporality (Qur'ân, 28:60; 29:64); the focus on the Hereafter (Qur'ân 3:15); recalling the purpose and effects of distress and afflictions (Qur'ân 2:155–6); trusting and relying on Allāh (*tawakkul*) (Qur'ân 3:159); understanding that after hardship there will be ease (Qur'ân 94:5–6); focusing on the blessings of Allāh, remembering Allāh and reading the Qur'ân (13:28); and supplication (*du'ahs*) (Qur'ân 2:186). When applied to spiritually motivated Muslims, Islāmically adjusted CBT can lead to four positive outcomes: quicker recovery, improved treatment adherence, lower recurrence rates, and reduced treatment inequities (Husain & Hodge, 2016). Examples of spiritually modified cognitive interventions include focusing on self-control, self-worth in Allāh, high frustration tolerance, acceptance of others, achievement, needing approval and love, accepting responsibility, accepting self-direction, and self-acceptance (Hodge & Nadir, 2008).

In the cognitive restructuring model suggested by Hamdan (2008), clients are taught to identify and evaluate automatic thoughts and dysfunctional core beliefs leading to problem behaviours. They examine and discuss their most distressing problems, modify automatic thoughts, and then work on modifying core beliefs and assumptions by examining evidence and seeking alternative explanations. For Muslim clients, cognitions from Islāmic faith can be used as alternative explanations for dysfunctional thoughts, tailored to the specific needs of each client. However, it is important to note that cognitive restructuring may be inappropriate when addressing fundamental Islāmic principles, such as *tawhīd* (belief in the Oneness of God), various Islāmic religious practices and obligations, or obedience to parental wishes. In such cases, CBT therapists may focus on fostering healthy communication skills, creating boundaries, and integrating Islāmic principles with individual autonomy and personal growth rather than challenging core Islāmic beliefs (Walpole et al., 2013). For example, it is neither acceptable nor beneficial for cognitive restructuring to dispute or modify the notion of *tawhīd*, dealing with a variety of Islāmic religious practices and obligations, or obedience to parental wishes.

Opposite therapy, proposed by Al-Ghazālī, is a strategy that encourages individuals to overcome spiritual deficiencies by focusing on the opposing attributes of their negative tendencies. This imaginative technique involves acting as if the opposite quality is present (Rosila & Yaacob, 2013). For instance, if someone is struggling with ignorance, Al-Ghazālī advises using imagination to actively seek knowledge. Similarly, if a person is experiencing feelings of hatred, the treatment involves redirecting attention towards cultivating love. The approach suggests that intentionally practicing positive traits that counteract and replace negative aspects can foster personal and spiritual growth. Clients can gain knowledge by engaging with knowledgeable Muslims and, if experiencing hatred, can imagine and practice love to replace negative feelings (Al-Ghazālī, 1998; Badri, 2000; Rizvi, 1989; Rosila & Yaacob, 2013). Essentially, it is about intentionally selecting and practicing positive traits that counteract and replace bad aspects, encouraging personal and spiritual growth. This concept expresses the idea that consciously developing virtuous characteristics can assist individuals in overcoming spiritual obstacles.

In Islāmic cognitive therapy, contemplation or deep thought is a technique emphasised in the Qur'ân and *Sunnah*. The focus on meditating on the creation and bounties of Allāh is believed to enhance faith, leading to improved deeds and behaviour. Contemplation is considered the beginning and key to all good and is viewed as the best function of the heart. Verses in the Qur'ân, such as Al-Imran 3:190–1, Al-Mulk 67:3–4, and Al-Mu'minun 23:62, highlight the fundamentals of contemplation, including its application to life in the Hereafter, the ultimate aim for individuals (Badri, 2000; Ibn al-Qayyim al-Jawziyyah, n.d.; Rosila & Yaacob, 2013). Other techniques compatible with CBT in an Islāmic context include the use of supplications, prayers, the power of suggestion, and remembered wellness. CBT's more directive approach, focus on current and future functioning, and emphasis on homework align well with Islāmic values and may be effective with Muslim clients. The incorporation of practical and outside-of-session assignments, a characteristic of CBT, echoes with Islāmic traditions and may be particularly appealing to Muslim clients (Benson, 1996; Carter & Rashidi, 2004; Hamdan, 2008; Rosila & Yaacob, 2013; Abudabbeh & Hays, 2006; Husain & Hodge, 2016).

In Islām-modified CBT, guiding Muslim clients to reflect on relevant Qur'ānic verses addressing their specific challenges is highly valuable. This involves reading verses related to patience, gratitude, or seeking forgiveness and discussing their application to the client's situation. Developing personalised positive affirmations based on Islāmic teachings is encouraged, reinforcing good thoughts and countering negative self-talk on a daily basis.

The practice of self-reflection and *tawbah* (repentance) is vital in fostering personal development and resilience, involving an ongoing process of challenging thoughts and behaviours contrary to Islāmic law. Clients engage in honest self-reflection, admit mistakes without judgment, and accept responsibility for their actions, aligning with Islāmic beliefs on seeking God's forgiveness and emphasising divine kindness for constructive development. Gratitude journaling, incorporating the Islāmic concept of gratitude (*shukr*), involves keeping a diary to express gratitude for blessings, experiences, and people. This practice aligns with Islāmic beliefs, strengthens the connection to Allāh's bounties, and enhances overall well-being and contentment.

These techniques aim to address psychological challenges while respecting and integrating Islāmic beliefs, values, and practices into the therapeutic process (Rassool, 2021). It is essential to note that the application of these techniques may vary based on individual needs and the therapist's expertise in providing Islām-modified CBT. In light of the limited research on CBT modified to incorporate beliefs and practices drawn from clients' spiritual narratives, it is difficult to draw definitive conclusions (Tan, 2013). A tentative conclusion from the limited evidence suggests that research on CBT modified with Islāmic tenets may improve a variety of psychospiritual outcomes.

CBT: what works for Muslim clients?

Religion-adapted cognitive-behavioural therapy has demonstrated effectiveness in systematic reviews, with common adaptations involving the integration of religious content into cognitive restructuring, psychoeducation, and motivation. Additionally, religious activities such as behavioural activation, meditation, and prayer are utilised to aid cognitive restructuring, along with the incorporation of religious values and coping strategies. The review highlights the efficacy of CBT, particularly when culturally adapted for Muslim clients (de Abreu Costa & Moreira-Almeida, 2022).

A comprehensive review of CBT comprising 269 meta-analytic studies and 106 meta-analyses explored its efficacy across various psychological problems. The review encompassed substance use disorder, schizophrenia, depression, bipolar disorder, anxiety disorders, somatoform disorders, eating disorders, insomnia, personality disorders, anger and aggression, criminal behaviours, general stress, distress related to medical conditions, chronic pain, fatigue, and distress related to pregnancy complications and hormonal conditions. Strong evidence was found supporting the effectiveness of CBT for anxiety disorders, somatoform disorders, bulimia, anger-control problems, and general stress (Hofmann et al., 2012). Similar findings were reported in the treatment of these conditions (Butler et al., 2006).

A systematic review by Naeem (2019) emphasised the importance of considering cultural factors when utilising CBT for social anxiety across diverse cultures. Practical suggestions are provided to enhance cultural competence, acknowledging the significance of addressing cultural nuances in CBT and proposing directions for future research. In a study by Mir et al. (2019), the examination of culturally adapted behavioural activation for Muslim clients with depression demonstrated its effectiveness, particularly using "positive religious coping" as a health resource. Another study applying acceptance and commitment therapy with a Turkish population in London reported reductions in depression, anxiety, and emotional distress (Perry et al., 2019). Additionally, a case report on family-based CBT for obsessive-compulsive disorder in Saudi Arabia highlighted the potential applicability of CBT in the region when thoughtfully implemented (Alatiq & Alrshoud, 2018).

Several studies have indicated the effectiveness of religious or spiritual therapy for Muslim clients experiencing anxiety, depression, and bereavement (Azhar & Varma, 1995a, b; Azhar et al., 1994; Hook et al., 2010; Razali et al., 1998). Notably, when addressing depression, the therapy's efficacy tends to be more pronounced when combined with medication. Hamdan (2008) proposed a form of religious psychotherapy where unproductive beliefs are identified and replaced with beliefs rooted in Islām. This approach represents a variation of cognitive therapy that incorporates religious themes. Hook et al. (2010) reviewed studies on religious therapy for depression among Muslim clients and concluded that it's challenging to ascertain whether the improvement observed in participants undergoing religious therapy is solely due to the religious aspect or if it's a result of receiving more therapy sessions per week. Consequently, there is limited evidence supporting the specificity of Muslim psychotherapy for depression.

Limited evidence suggests the specificity of Muslim psychotherapy for anxiety (Hook et al., 2010). Regarding clients' religiosity, some studies indicate that religious therapy may enhance outcomes for highly religious clients but not for those less religious (Razali et al., 2002). Wahass and Kent (1997) suggest potential benefits of Muslim-accommodative CBT for schizophrenia when combined with medication, although there is insufficient evidence to fully support its efficacy. In a randomised clinical trial, Ebrahimi et al. (2013) found that for patients with dysthymic disorder, spiritually augmented psychotherapy is more effective than medication and CBT in modifying dysfunctional attitudes, though it shows no significant difference from CBT in reducing depressive symptom severity. These findings support the effectiveness of psychotherapy enriched with cultural dimensions and religious teachings.

The effectiveness of CBT among Muslim populations raises concerns, as most studies on CBT efficacy have focused on individuals from Western, Judaeo-Christian backgrounds (Beshai et al., 2012b; Hodge, 2004). While research suggests the efficacy of cognitive interventions based on Islāmic principles, methodological issues and the need for high-quality research remain significant concerns. More robust studies are essential for providing definitive insights into the empirical soundness of modified CBT with Islāmic spiritual interventions.

Conclusion

There is a consensus among Islāmic scholars that the principles of cognitive therapy align with Islāmic values. However, dissonance arises from the operationalisation of cognitive therapy in Western psychotherapy paradigms. To enhance congruence with Islāmic values, therapists are encouraged to use a spiritually modified cognitive therapy model. The brief, time-limited, collaborative, directive, evidence-based, and cost-effective nature of cognitive–behavioural therapy makes it an ideal therapeutic tool for Muslim clients. Islāmic discourse values reason, logical conversation, psychoeducation, and consultation, all of which correlate well with CBT approaches. While current models of Islām-modified CBT may need further development and refinement through evidence-based research, religious-oriented Muslim clients stand to benefit significantly from cognitive therapy modified with Islāmic tenets.

References

Abdul-Rahman, Z. (2023). The lost art of contemplation. *Yaqeen Institute*. Retrieved November 17, 2023, from https://yaqeeninstitute.org/read/paper/the-lost-art-of-contemplation.

Abudabbeh, N., & Hays, P. A. (2006). Cognitive-behavioral therapy with people of Arab heritage. In P. A. Hays & G. Y. Iwamasa (Eds.), *Culturally responsive cognitive-behavioral therapy: Assessment, practice, and supervision* (pp. 141–159). American Psychological Association.

Abu-Ras, W., Gheith, A., & Cournos, F. (2008). The Imam's role in mental health promotion: A study at 22 mosques in New York City's Muslim community. *Journal of Muslim Mental Health*, 3(2), 155–176. http://dx.doi.org/10.1080/15564900802487576.

Alatiq, Y., & Alrshoud, H. (2018). Family-based cognitive behavioural therapy for obsessive-compulsive disorder with family accommodation: Case report from Saudi Arabia. *The Cognitive Behaviour Therapist*, 11. https://doi.org/10.1017/S1754470X1800017X.

Al-Ghazālī, A. H. (1998). *Iḥyā' 'ulūm al-Dīn [The revival of the religious sciences]* (Vol. 2). Dar al-Kutub al-Ilmiah.

Al-Ghazālī, A. H. (2010). *The marvels of the heart: Science of the spirit* [Book 21, in *Iḥyā' 'ulūm al-dīn (The revival of the religious sciences*, W. J. Skellie, Trans.)]. Fons Vitae.

Al-Ghazālī, A. H. (2011). *Iḥyā' 'ulūm al-Dīn [The revival of the religious sciences]*. Dār al-Minhaj.

Al-Jawzi, A. A. (2004). *Akhbar al-Azkiya*. Dar Ibn Hazm.

Arroisi, J., & Rahmadi, M. A. (2022). Theory of mind in Ghazali and Ibn Qayyim Al Jauzi perspective: Analysis model on Islāmic psychology. *International Journal of Islāmic Psychology*, 5(1), 8–28.

Azhar, M. Z., & Varma, S. L. (1995a). Religious psychotherapy in depressive patients. *Psychotherapy and Psychosomatics*, 63(3–4), 165–168.

Azhar, M. Z., & Varma, S. L. (1995b). Religious psychotherapy as management of bereavement. *Acta Psychiatrica Scandinavica, 91*(4), 233–235.

Azhar, M. Z., Varma, S. L., & Dharap, A. S. (1994). Religious psychotherapy in anxiety disorder patients. *Acta Psychiatrica Scandinavica, 90*(1), 1–3.

Badri, M. (1976). *Islām and alcoholism*. American Trust Publications.

Badri, M. (2000). *Contemplation: An Islāmic psychospiritual study* (p. 22). International Institute of Islāmic Thought.

Badri, M. (2013). *Abu Zayd al-Balkhi's sustenance of the soul: The cognitive behavior therapy of a ninth century physician*. International Institute of Islāmic Thought (IIIT).

Beck, A. T. (1976). *Cognitive therapy and the emotional disorders*. International Universities Press.

Beck, A. T., & Haigh, E. A. (2014). Advances in cognitive theory and therapy: The generic cognitive model. *Annual Review of Clinical Psychology, 10*, 1–24. https://doi.org/10.1146/annurev-clinpsy-032813-153734.

Beck, J. S., & Fleming, S. (2021). A brief history of Aaron T. Beck, MD, and cognitive behavior therapy. *Clinical Psychology in Europe, 3*(2), e6701. https://doi.org/10.32872/cpe.6701.

Bee, P. E., Bower, P., Lovell, K., Gilbody, S., Richards, D., Gask, L., & Roach, P. (2008). Psychotherapy mediated by remote communication technologies: A meta-analytic review. *BMC Psychiatry, 8*, 60.

Benson, H. (1996). *Timeless healing: The power and biology of belief*. Simon & Schuster.

Beshai, S., Clark, C. M., & Dobson, K. S. (2012a). Conceptual and pragmatic considerations in the use of cognitive-behavioral therapy with Muslim clients. *Cognitive Therapy and Research, 37*(1), 197–206. https://doi.org/10.1007/s10608-012-9450-y.

Beshai, S., Dobson, K. S., & Adel, A. (2012b). Cognition and dysphoria in Egypt and Canada: An examination of the cognitive triad. *Canadian Journal of Behavioural Science, 44*(1), 29–39.

Butler, A. C., Chapman, J. E., Forman, E. M., & Beck, A. T. (2006). The empirical status of cognitive-behavioral therapy: A review of meta-analyses. *Clinical Psychology Review, 26*(1), 17–31.

Bynum, R. (2006). Islām, predestination and free will. *New English Review*. Retrieved November 19, 2023, from www.newenglishreview.org/Rebecca_Bynum/Islam,_Predestination_and_Free_Will/

Carter, D. J., & Rashidi, A. (2004). East meets West: Integrating psychotherapy approaches for Muslim women. *Holistic Nursing Practice, 18*(3), 152–159.

Corey, G. (2015). *Theory and practice of group counseling*. Cengage Learning.

de Abreu Costa, M., & Moreira-Almeida, A. (2022). Religion-adapted cognitive behavioral therapy: A review and description of techniques. *Journal of Religion and Health, 61*(1), 443–466. https://doi.org/10.1007/s10943-021-01345-z.

DeRubeis, R. J., Webb, C. A., Tang, T. Z., & Beck, A. T. (2010). Cognitive therapy. In K. S. Dobson (Ed.), *Handbook of cognitive-behavioral therapies* (3rd ed., pp. 277–317). The Guilford Press.

Dobson, K. S., & Dozois, D. J. (2010). Philosophical and theoretical bases for the cognitive-behavioral therapies. In K. S. Dobson (Ed.), *Handbook of cognitive-behavioral therapies* (3rd ed., pp. 3–38). The Guilford Press.

Dozois, D. J. A., & Beck, A. T. (2008). Cognitive schemas, beliefs and assumptions. In K. S. Dobson & D. J. A. Dozois (Eds.), *Risk factors in depression* (pp. 121–143). Elsevier/Academic Press.

Dozois, D. J. A., Dobson, K. S., & Rnic, K. (2019). Historical and philosophical bases of the cognitive-behavioral therapies. In K. S. Dobson & D. J. A. Dozois (Eds.), *Handbook of cognitive-behavioral therapies* (pp. 3–31). The Guilford Press.

Ebrahimi, A., Neshatdoost, H. T., Mousavi, S. G., Asadollahi, G. A., & Nasiri, H. (2013). Controlled randomized clinical trial of spirituality integrated psychotherapy, cognitive-behavioral therapy and medication intervention on depressive symptoms and dysfunctional attitudes in patients with dysthymic disorder. *Advanced Biomedical Research, 2*, 53. https://doi.org/10.4103/2277-9175.114201.

Ellis, A. (1962). *Reason and emotion in psychotherapy.* Lyle Stuart.

Ellis, A. (1980). *The case against religion.* American Atheist Press.

Esposito, J. (2004). *The Oxford dictionary of Islām.* Oxford University Press.

Hamdan, A. (2008). Cognitive restructuring: An Islāmic perspective. *Journal of Muslim Mental Health, 3*(1), 99–116.

Haque, A. (2004a). Psychology from Islāmic perspective: Contributions of early Muslim scholars and challenges to contemporary Muslim psychologists. *Journal of Religion and Health, 43*(4), 357–377. https://doi.org/10.1007/s10943–004–4302-z.

Haque, A. (2004b). Religion and mental health: The case of American Muslims. *Journal of Religion and Health, 43*(1), 45–58.

Hodge, D. R. (2004). Working with Hindu clients in a spiritually sensitive manner. *Social Work, 49*(1), 27–38.

Hodge, D. R., & Nadir, A. (2008). Moving toward culturally competent practice with Muslims: Modifying cognitive therapy with Islāmic tenets. *Social Work, 53*(1), 31–41.

Hofmann, S. G. (2011). *An introduction to modern CBT: Psychological solutions to mental health problems.* Wiley-Blackwell.

Hofmann, S. G., & Asmundson, G. J. (2008). Acceptance and mindfulness-based therapy: New wave or old hat? *Clinical Psychology Review, 28*(1), 1–16.

Hofmann, S. G., Asmundson, G. J., & Beck, A. T. (2013). The science of cognitive therapy. *Behavior Therapy, 44*(2), 199–212.

Hofmann, S. G., Asnaani, A., Vonk, I. J. J., Sawyer, A. T., & Fang, A. (2012). The efficacy of cognitive behavioral therapy: A review of meta-analyses. *Cognitive Therapy and Research, 36*(5), 427–440. https://doi.org/10.1007/s10608-012-9476-1.

Hook, J. N., Worthington, E. L., Jr., Davis, D. E., Jennings, D. J., II, & Gartner, A. L. (2010). Empirically supported religious and spiritual therapies. *Journal of Clinical Psychology, 66*(1), 46–72.

Husain, A., & Hodge, D. R. (2016). Islāmically modified cognitive behavioral therapy: Enhancing outcomes by increasing the cultural congruence of cognitive behavioral therapy self-statements. *International Social Work, 59*(3), 393–405.

Ibn al-Qayyim. (1981). *Al-Fawa'id [The spiritual benefits]*. Dār al-Nafā'is.

Ibn al-Qayyim al-Jawziyyah. (n.d.). *The key to the house of bliss [Miftah Dar al-Sa'adah]*. Ri'asat al-Ifta.

Ibn Majah. *Sunan Ibn Majah 66* [In-book reference: Introduction, Hadith 66. English translation: Vol. 1, Book 1, Hadith 66]. Sahih (Darussalam). https://sunnah.com.

Islām Q&A. (2009). *124504: Evil is part of the creation of Allāh and not attributing it to Allāh is part of proper verbal etiquette.* Retrieved November 19, 2023, from http://Islamqa.info/en/124504.

Khoury, B., Lecomte, T., Fortin, G., Masse, M., Therien, P., Bouchard, V., Chapleau, M. A., Paquin, K., & Hofmann, S. G. (2013). Mindfulness-based therapy: A comprehensive meta-analysis. *Clinical Psychology Review, 33*(6), 763–771.

Leahy, R. L., & Holland, S. J. (2000). *Treatment plans and interventions for depression and anxiety disorders.* Guilford Press.

Linehan, M. M. (2000). The empirical basis of dialectical behavior therapy: Development of new treatments versus evaluation of existing treatments. *Clinical Psychology: Science and Practice, 7*(1), 113–119. https://doi.org/10.1093/clipsy.7.1.113.

Mir, G., Ghani, R., Meer, S., & Hussain, G. (2019). Delivering a culturally adapted therapy for Muslim clients with depression. *The Cognitive Behaviour Therapist, 12*, 1–14. Article E26. https://doi.org/10.1017/S1754470X19000059.

Mundy, E. A., & Hofmann, S. G. (2014). Cognitive-behavioral therapy: Next generation of treatments. *FOCUS, 12*(3), 267–274. https://doi.org/10.1176/appi.focus.12.3.267.

Muslim. *Sahih Muslim 2572* [In-book reference: Book 45, Hadith 65. USC-MSA web (English) reference: Book 32, Hadith 6241]. https://sunnah.com.

Naeem, F. (2019). Cultural adaptations of CBT: A summary and discussion of the Special Issue on Cultural Adaptation of CBT. *The Cognitive Behaviour Therapist, 12.* Article E40. https://doi.org/10.1017/S1754470X19000278.

Padela, A. I., Killawi, A., Forman, J., DeMonner, S., & Heisler, M. (2012). American Muslim perceptions of healing key agents in healing, and their roles. *Qualitative Health Research, 22*(6), 846–858.

Perry, A., Gardener, C., Oliver, J. E., Taş, Ç., & Özenç, C. (2019). Exploring the cultural flexibility of the ACT model as an effective therapeutic group intervention for Turkish speaking communities in East London. *The Cognitive Behaviour Therapist, 12.* https://doi.org/10.1017/S1754470X18000041.

Persons, J. P., & Davidson, J. (2001). Cognitive-behavioral case formulation. In K. S. Dobson (Ed.), *Handbook of cognitive behavioral therapies* (pp. 86–110). The Guilford Press.

Philips, A. A. B. (2007). *The clash of Islāmic civilizations: An Islāmic view.* Al-Hidaayah Publishing & Distribution.

Rassool, G. Hussein (2000). The crescent and Islām: Healing, nursing, and the spiritual dimension: Some considerations towards an understanding of the Islāmic perspectives on caring. *Journal of Advanced Nursing, 32*(6), 1476–1484.

Rassool, G. Hussein (2021). Sins, Tawbah and the process of change. *International Journal of Islāmic Psychology, 4*(1), 26–33.

Rassool, G. Hussein (2023a). *Islāmic psychology: The basics.* Routledge.

Rassool, G. Hussein (2023b). *Integrated research methodologies in Islāmic psychology.* Focus Series. Routledge.

Razali, S. M., Aminah, K., & Khan, U. A. (2002). Religious-cultural psychotherapy in the management of anxiety patients. *Transcultural Psychiatry, 39*(1), 130–136.

Razali, S. M., Hasanah, C. I., Aminah, K., & Subramaniam, M. (1998). Religious sociocultural psychotherapy in patients with anxiety and depression. *Australian & New Zealand Journal of Psychiatry, 32*(6), 867–872.

Rizvi, S. A. A. (1989). *Muslim tradition in psychotherapy and modern trends.* Seraj Munir.

Rogers, C. R. (1951). *Client-centered therapy: Its current practice, implications, and theory.* Houghton Mifflin.

Rosila, N., & Yaacob, N. (2013). Cognitive therapy approach from Islāmic psycho-spiritual conception. *Procedia-Social and Behavioral Sciences, 97*(6), 182–187.

Sajid, M. A. (2012). Common moral grounds for the common good: An Islāmic perspective. *Universal Peace Federation.* Retrieved November 20, 2023, from www.uk.upf.org/index.php?option=com_content&view=article&id=494:common-moral-grounds-for-the-common-good-an-Islamic-perspective&catid=73:elc&Itemid=195.

Sauer-Zavala, S., Boswell, J. F., Gallagher, M. W., Bentley, K. H., Ametaj, A., & Barlow, D. H. (2012). The role of negative affectivity and negative reactivity to emotions in predicting outcomes in the unified protocol for the transdiagnostic treatment of emotional disorders. *Behaviour Research and Therapy, 50*(9), 551–557. https://doi.org/10.1016/j.brat.2012.05.005.

Segal, Z. V., Williams, J. M. G., & Teasdale, J. D. (2013). *Mindfulness-based cognitive therapy for depression* (2nd ed.). Guilford Press.

Shafaat, A. (1987). Commanding good and forbidding evil. *Islāmic Perspectives.* Retrieved November 19, 2023, from www.Islamicperspectives.com/CommandingGood.htm.

Steiman, M., & Dobson, K. S. (2004). Psychotherapy with adults. In F. W. Kaslow & T. Patterson (Eds.), *Comprehensive handbook of psychotherapy. Vol. 2: Cognitive-behavioral approaches.* John Wiley & Sons.

Swain, J., Hancock, K., Hainsworth, C., & Bowman, J. (2013). Acceptance and commitment therapy in the treatment of anxiety: A systematic review. *Clinical Psychology Review, 33*(8), 965–978. https://doi.org/10.1016/j.cpr.2013.07.002.

Tan, S.-Y. (2013). Addressing religion and spirituality from a cognitive-behavioral perspective. In K. I. Pargament (Ed.), *APA handbook of psychology, religion, and spirituality, Vol. 2: An applied psychology religion and spirituality* (pp. 169–187). American Psychological Association.

Thomas, J., & Ashraf, S. (2009). Exploring the Islāmic tradition for resonance and dissonance for cognitive therapy for depression. *Mental Health, Religion and Culture, 14*(2), 183–190.

Wahass, S., & Kent, G. (1997). Coping with auditory hallucinations: A cross-cultural comparison between western (British) and non-western (Saudi Arabian) patients. *The Journal of Nervous and Mental Disease, 185*(11), 664–668.

Walpole, S. C., McMillan, D., House, A., Cottrell, D., & Mir, G. (2013). Interventions for treating depression in Muslim patients: A systematic review. *Journal of Affective Disorders, 145*(1), 11–20.

Winter, D. A. (2008). Cognitive behaviour therapy: From rationalism to constructivism? In R. House & D. Loewenthal (Eds.), *Against and for CBT: Towards a constructive dialogue?* (pp. 137–145). PCCS Books.

Wright, J. H. (2006). Cognitive behavior therapy: Basic principles and recent advances. *FOCUS, 4*, 173–178. https://focus.psychiatryonline.org/doi/full/10.1176/foc.4.2.173.

Yusaf, S. (2019). *Spirituality in clinical practice: An Islāmic perspective* (PowerPoint). Retrieved November 20, 2023, from www.slideserve.com/callie-flores/spirituality-in-clinical-practice-an-Islamic-perspective-powerpoint-ppt-presentation.

Zarabozo, J. M. (1999). *Commentary on the forty Hadith of Al-Nawawi* (3 vols.). Al-Basheer Company for Publications & Translation.

10
UNITING FAITH AND THERAPY
The Islāmic perspective on solution-focused brief therapy

Introduction

Solution-focused brief therapy (SFBT) was developed by Steve de Shazer and Insoo Kim Berg in the 1980s as a postmodern psychotherapy approach focused on problem-solving rather than problem analysis. It operates on the principle that clients are the authorities in their own lives, and therapists assist in identifying and amplifying their existing strengths and resources to achieve their goals (O'Connell, 2001). SFBT is known for its brevity, goal-oriented nature, and emphasis on helping clients establish clear, concise, and realistic goals and solutions. The approach aims to facilitate clients in achieving their preferred outcomes by eliciting and co-constructing solutions to their problems.

SFBT emphasises leveraging clients' strengths, resources, and abilities to empower them to enact positive changes. Therapists view clients as experts in their own lives, and therapy is oriented towards fostering growth rather than addressing pathology (De Shazer et al., 1986; O'Connell, 2001). Research has demonstrated the effectiveness of SFBT across various problem presentations and populations, including psychosocial issues, mental health problems, parenting difficulties, school challenges, addictions, and domestic violence. This chapter provides an overview of solution-focused brief therapy, discussing its orientation, theoretical foundations, alignment with Islāmic principles, therapeutic techniques, and implications for practice.

Theoretical framework

SFBT is grounded in social constructivism and integrates various therapeutic approaches into a distinctive method (Cepeda & Davenport, 2006). It operates on foundational assumptions categorised around service users, problems, change, and practice (Wheeler & Vinnicombe, 2011). SFBT assumes that each client is unique,

DOI: 10.4324/9781003453413-12

possesses internal and external resources, and can identify solutions to contextual problems. The approach adopts a client-centred, collaborative stance, recognising clients as experts in their lives. Clients have the potential for self-change, and therapists are not viewed as the sole experts.

SFBT emphasises that clients are not the problem themselves and that complex issues may not always require complex solutions. Change is seen as dynamic, with small changes having a significant impact. Even minor shifts can be instrumental in resolving clients' issues, and small increments of change can lead to larger ones. The approach encourages clients to increase the frequency of current useful behaviours and recognises that solution behaviours already exist for clients (Corey, 2017; Trepper et al., 2012). The basic tenets that inform SFBT should be to encourage clients to increase the frequency of current useful behaviours (Trepper et al., 2012). Walter and Peller (1992, 2000) and Corey (2017) proposed the following principles of SFBT:

- Solution-focused therapists nudge clients to view different perspectives of solutions to the problem.
- The solution may or may not be directly related to the problems or issues.
- Each solution is unique to the individual based on her or his specific needs and problems.
- Clients have the readiness to change.
- Clients are experts in their problems and solutions.
- Incremental changes lead to bigger changes.
- If something works, be pragmatic and continue to use the approach(es).
- Focus is on the strengths of the individual and not on his or her weaknesses.
- The potential to change is sometimes blocked by negative cognitions.
- For every problem, there are exceptions.
- Solution-focused therapists facilitate clients to view their problems from different perspectives.

SFBT is a client-centred therapy designed to help individuals envision a future where their problems are solved by exploring exceptions, strengths, and resources. The therapy aims to collaboratively construct a pathway towards realising this vision while fostering hope, optimism, and positive expectations about change. Unlike traditional psychotherapies, SFBT is evidence based and solution driven, minimising therapist self-disclosure to empower clients in decision-making. It is a short-term, positively oriented approach focused on achieving favourable outcomes (Bakker et al., 2010; Trepper et al., 2010).

SBFT: the evidence

SFBT is an evidence-based approach known for its efficiency and effectiveness in addressing various behavioural and psychological issues. SFBT stands out for its evidence-based status, shorter duration, cost-effectiveness, and compassionate approach, making it a preferred therapeutic option for various psychological, behavioural, and family problems (Bond et al., 2013; Gingerich & Peterson, 2013; Kim, 2008; Kim et al., 2018; Lovelock et al., 2011; Schmit et al., 2016). Research supports the efficacy of SFBT in addressing a variety of issues. Studies have shown its success in reducing depression, anxiety, and mood-related disorders in adults (Maljanen et al., 2012); treating addiction and decreasing severity and trauma symptoms (Kim et al., 2018); and managing child behavioural problems (Bond et al., 2013). Additionally, SFBT has been found effective in addressing emotional, behavioural, and interpersonal issues (Kim et al., 2018).

SFBT, while offering efficiency and effectiveness, may present challenges for individuals with serious issues or difficulties building trust due to its brief duration. Its emphasis on the present and future may be less suitable for clients needing time to explore complex traumas. The client-led nature of SFBT could lead to misalignment of goals, as clients may want to explore past traumas, potentially hindering the solution-focused approach. Clients' autonomy in determining therapy conclusion may lead to early termination despite ongoing therapeutic benefits. Nonetheless, SFBT remains valuable for short-term, goal-oriented therapy. SFBT aligns with an Islāmic model of psychotherapy, and further exploration will delve into its orientation, theoretical framework, and congruence with Islāmic beliefs and practices, as well as therapeutic interventions and implications (Johnson, 2011).

The therapeutic relationship and process

In SFBT, the therapeutic relationship is pivotal for facilitating positive outcomes. The quality of the client–counsellor alliance is a reliable predictor of positive clinical outcomes (Ardito & Rabellino, 2011). Unlike traditional approaches, therapists in SFBT adopt a less directive stance, serving as facilitators in the client's treatment journey. Clients are regarded as the experts in the process, defining meaningful goals and solutions (Corey, 2017). Therapists empower clients to envision a future without problems and guide them towards change without imposing specific solutions. The collaborative process involves joint exploration of therapy goals, avoiding the imposition of personal goals or shape goals from their own worldview by the therapist (Rassool, 2016).

The main therapeutic task consists of helping clients imagine how life would be different without the problems and issues and what it will take to bring about these changes (Gingerich & Eisengart, 2000). This collaborative approach and client-centred focus characterise the SFBT process, emphasising the clients' expertise in defining their goals and driving the change process (Corey, 2017; Walter & Peller, 1992). Walter and Peller (1992) describe four areas of exploration that characterise the process of SFBT:

- Find out what the client is hoping to achieve from the collaboration. SFBT is about finding out what clients want rather than searching for what they do not want.

- Do not look for pathology, and do not attempt to reduce clients by giving them a diagnostic label. Instead, look for what clients are doing that is already working and encourage them to continue in that direction.
- If what clients are doing is not working, encourage them to experiment with doing something different.
- Keep therapy brief by approaching each session as if it was the last and only session.

In SFBT, the therapeutic process involves collaboratively constructing a picture of the desired "solution" while identifying internal strengths and external resources to achieve it. Therapists listen attentively and respond according to the client's worldview, fostering a collaborative and client-centred environment. Trepper et al. (2012) emphasise that therapists and clients together co-construct new and altered meanings through the process of listening, absorbing, connecting, and client responding, contributing to meaningful change. Regardless of the presenting problem, SFBT operates consistently to establish common ground between therapist and client. Questions strategically posed during therapy initiate conversations that lead towards co-constructing new and altered meanings, facilitating meaningful change (Bavelas et al., 2000a).

In SFBT, the therapeutic process entails collaborative language construction, goal setting, and solution-building techniques between the therapist and client (Bavelas et al., 2000a, 2000b; McGee et al., 2005). Through this process, the therapist and client work together to create a vision of the desired solution and identify the resources necessary to achieve it. During assessment interviews, practitioners listen to and absorb clients' words and meanings, using them to formulate and ask the next question (Trepper et al., 2010).

The therapeutic process in SFBT remains consistent across various client presentations. In the initial session, SFBT therapists aim to establish a contract around the client's best hopes, cultivate a collaborative relationship, foster a climate for change, clarify the client's goals, highlight their resources, and negotiate tasks (O'Connell, 2017). The steps involved in solution building and problem-solving are outlined by De Jong and Berg (2012). Refer to Table 10.1 for a depiction of these key points in the SFBT process.

Role of therapist and therapeutic goals

In SFBT, the therapist assumes a collaborative and guiding role, contrasting with psychoanalytical and humanistic approaches (Raskin & Rogers, 2005). Rather than being seen as an expert, the therapist serves as a facilitator, helping clients recognise and amplify their existing strengths and resources. The therapeutic environment focuses on positive language to promote solution-focused thinking, engaging clients in a collaborative process valuing their competence (Guterman, 2015). While therapists offer expertise in the process of change, clients are regarded as

TABLE 10.1 Key steps in solution building and problem solving in SFBT

Solution	Therapist on interventions
Presentation of problems by the clients	How can I be useful to you?
	Listens respectfully and carefully as clients answer the question.
Collaboration in developing well-formed goals	What will be different in your life when your problems are solved?
Facilitating clients in exploring these exceptions	When did you observe about those times when your problems were not present or when the problems were less severe?
Facilitating clients in exploring these exceptions	What did you do to make these events happen?
Communication, solution-building	Summary feedback, encouragement
	What would you notice or what would need to be done before the next session to further solve your problems?
Evaluation	Evaluate the progress in reaching satisfactory solutions (rating scale)
	What do you need to do before you see the problems as being solved?
	What next steps will you need to take in solving the problems?

Source: Adapted from De Jong and Berg (2012).

experts on what they want to change. The therapist's responsibilities include asking solution-focused questions, employing specialised SFBT techniques, and offering feedback to guide the therapeutic process (Gingerich & Eisengart, 2000). Central to this approach is helping clients envision desired changes and identifying the steps needed to achieve them. Therapists mirror clients' language, utilise goal-directed and future-oriented questions, and maintain a focus on what is working and right throughout the therapy process (Bubenzer & West, 1993).

In SFBT, therapists are urged to engage clients in identifying and discussing therapy goals early in the therapeutic relationship, ideally during the initial session. This practice echoes the belief that individuals are capable of defining meaningful personal goals and have the necessary resources to address their challenges (Corey, 2017). Through a collaborative process, therapy goals are established aiming to facilitate positive change and enhance the client's overall well-being. The goals of SFBT include

- Goal identification: therapists collaborate with clients to articulate clear and defined therapy goals, emphasising the client's intended future outcomes.
- Variety of goals: goals may involve changing perspectives, improving performance in problematic situations, and enhancing client strengths and resources.

- Positive and client-centred goal setting: goals should be stated positively in the client's language, process-oriented (Walter & Peller, 1992), achievable in the present, specific, measurable, attainable, relevant, and time-bound (SMART).
- Variety of goals: there is a variety of goals, such as changing the view of a situation or a frame of reference, changing the performance of the problematic situation, and enhancing client strengths and resources (O'Hanlon & Weiner-Davis, 2003).
- Solution building: SFBT capitalises on the client's strengths, resources, and exceptions to explore novel alternatives and co-create meaningful change strategies.
- Problem-solving: therapists assist clients in breaking free from the confines of their problems by developing and implementing solutions to alleviate or resolve concerns.
- Skill development: SFBT promotes the development of new skills and adaptive behaviours aligned with the client's desired outcomes, with therapists providing support and celebrating successes.

In SFBT, therapeutic goal setting is a collaborative process that respects each client's uniqueness. Therapists refrain from imposing their own goals or shaping them based on their worldview (Walter & Peller, 1992). SFBT goals aim to empower clients, leverage their strengths, and create practical solutions leading to meaningful change and improved well-being. The therapeutic process in SFBT is geared towards generating significant and lasting solutions that foster positive behavioural changes.

Techniques used in solution-focused brief therapy

Solution-focused therapists have a range of intervention strategies when assisting clients in discovering solutions and creating a more satisfying life. Both de Shazer (1988) and Walter and Peller (1992) offer useful mapping of therapeutic interventions of SFBT, helping therapists facilitate the construction of solutions. However, the techniques describe briefly below must be implemented from the foundation of a collaborative working relationship.

Pre-therapy change

In the initial stages of SFBT, therapists employ open-ended questioning to facilitate constructive and exploratory dialogues with clients. During the pre-therapy change phase, typically in the first session, therapists may pose questions like, "What have you done since you made the appointment that has made a difference in your problem?" (de Shazer, 1985, 1988). This question and others in a similar vein aim to elicit reflections from the client on any positive actions or changes they might have initiated since scheduling the therapy session. Other questions that may be asked include

- What changes have you noticed that have happened or started to happen since you made the appointment for this session?
- What have you noticed since you made the call to come in?
- What needs to happen today so that when you leave you'll think this was a good session?

In the first therapy session, by asking about such changes, the therapist can elicit, evoke, and amplify what clients have already done by way of making positive change (Corey, 2017, p. 384).

Exception questions

In SFBT, therapists assume that certain periods in the client's life were devoid of the identified problem or the problem had minimal impact. Exploring these problem-free or less challenging periods is a valuable strategy for uncovering solutions. By asking questions about what was different during these times, therapists aim to uncover clues that can contribute to finding solutions (Guterman, 2015). This approach empowers clients by identifying coping strategies they used during those exceptions, providing valuable insights for the therapeutic process. Examples of exception questions include

- Tell me about times when you do not get angry.
- Tell me about the times you felt better about yourself.
- When was the last time that you feel you had a better day? What was it about that day that made it a better day?
- Was there ever a time when you felt happy in your relationship?
- Was there ever a time when you felt happy in your life?
- Can you imagine a time when the problem was not present in your life?

Miracle question

This is a core technique in SFBT enabling the client to think outside the box. The miracle question is a goal-oriented question that is useful when a client has a negative or pessimistic view of future life. This kind of question also would enable to reflect and examine new possibilities and outcomes for the future. The therapist asks,

> If a miracle happened and the problem you have was solved overnight, what would be different in your life? . . . Now, I want to ask you a strange question.

Suppose that while you are sleeping tonight and the entire house is quiet, a miracle happens. The miracle is that the problem which brought you here is solved. However, because you are sleeping, you do not know that the miracle has happened. So, when you wake up tomorrow morning, what will be different that will tell you that a miracle has happened and the problem which brought you here is solved?

(de Shazer, 1988, p. 5)

Coping questions

This type of questioning is to gain insights into how the client has manage to cope and the coping strategies used. Examples of coping questions include

- How did you manage to overcome these problems after everything you have been through?
- What it is exactly that has helped you through this so far?
- How do you keep going when you feel anxious or depressed?
- What holds you back from hurting yourself when you feel sad?
- What keeps you hopeful when things do not seem right?

De Shazer et al. (1986) suggested that these questions enable the client to identify the internal and external resources that have helped them so far, which they might not have been consciously aware of before.

Scaling questions

Solution-focused therapists use scaling questions to help clients assess their feelings, track progress, or monitor incremental change, especially in areas where changes may not be easily observed, such as feelings or moods (de Shazer & Berg, 1988). Scaling questions involve rating the severity of a problem on a scale from 1 to 10, allowing both the therapist and the client to visualise the current state of the problem. For example, when addressing anxiety, a therapist might ask, "If 10 is the most anxious and 1 is the most relaxed, how would you rate your anxiety right now?" This technique can be applied to various conditions including panic attacks, motivation to change, hopefulness, depression, self-esteem, and confidence (de Shazer & Berg, 1988). Scaling questions serve as valuable tools for assessing and discussing the status of identified problems or issues.

Compliments

Compliments "provide(d) an effective 'anesthetic' for the task assignment that followed" (de Shazer, 1988, p. 471). This type of response overlaps with the other techniques, involves the therapist offering encouragement, and values the strengths that the client does have. This is a form of positive reinforcement, and "its purpose is to support the orientation toward solution" (de Shazer et al., 1986, pp. 216–217). The therapist will use both direct compliments (in reaction to what the client has said) and indirect compliments to encourage the client to notice and compliment themselves, for example using paraverbal communication to highlight the positive strengths of the client (e.g. "You seemed to have had a lot of strengths to manage that situation").

Consultation break

A common technique in SFBT is to split one session with a break. This allows the client to reflect on what was already said and think about potential solutions to their problems. After the break, the therapist offers an encouraging and therapeutic message about the client's ability to seek solutions to their problems.

Formulate first-session tasks

In SFBT, therapists typically conclude the first session by prompting clients to reflect on what they want to continue happening in their lives, emphasising strengths and initiating the solution-generating process. Subsequent experiments or assignments are derived from aspects that clients are already doing or experiencing, such as exceptions, thoughts, or feelings that align with the direction of their goals (de Shazer et al., 2007). This approach harnesses clients' existing positive elements to bolster progress towards their desired outcomes. The therapist might say,

> Between now and the next time we meet, I would like you to observe, so that you can describe to me next time, what happens in your (family, life, marriage, relationship) that you want to continue to have happened.
> *(de Shazer, 1985, p. 137)*

Homework in SFBT is personalised to clients' goals and solutions, offering suggestions for them to try rather than assigning tasks. This approach, rooted in client collaboration, enhances optimism and hope regarding their situation (de Shazer, 1985).

Therapist feedback to clients

In SFBT, therapists often take a 5- to 10-minute break towards the end of each session to provide clients with summary feedback. This feedback, as highlighted by Walter and Peller (1992), acknowledges partial goal attainment or offers reassurance, especially when progress has been reasonable but limited. The approach normalises setbacks, recognising that success in therapy is not always linear and that lapses and relapses are integral parts of the treatment journey. The goal is to help clients develop realistic expectations, build resilience, and understand that setbacks are a normal aspect of progress (Walter & Peller, 1992).

The termination phase of SFBT

Guterman (2015) suggests that the primary objective of SFBT is to bring about its conclusion. The termination phase, albeit challenging, typically begins with discussions early in treatment about whether it is appropriate to end therapy. Termination occurs when clients have either constructed a satisfactory solution or no longer derive benefit from therapy. Scaling questions assist therapists in evaluating progress and determining whether therapy should continue. Prior to concluding therapy, therapists assist clients in identifying strategies to maintain the changes achieved. During termination, therapists help clients anticipate challenges, cope with stressors, and devise solutions to sustain positive changes. Given the succinct and present-focused nature of solution-focused therapy, clients may address additional concerns in the future (Corey, 2017; De Jong & Berg, 2012).

SFBT: congruence with Islāmic principles

The SFBT model of therapy generally aligns with Islāmic beliefs, although some adaptations are necessary for cultural sensitivity (Chaudhry & Li, 2011). Rassool (2016) highlighted several aspects of SFBT that resonate with Islāmic principles, including minimal self-disclosure, empowerment, positive orientation, pre-session change, goal setting, competence seeking, and the miracle question. From an Islāmic perspective, SFBT reinforces the concept of individual responsibility and accountability for actions. However, when working with Muslim clients, it's crucial for SFBT to integrate Islāmic values, ethics, and codes of behaviour into the therapeutic process (Chaudhry & Li, 2011; Rassool, 2016). Valiante (2003) identified Qur'ânic concepts that align with aspects of SFBT, emphasising action, free will, the ability to make choices, personal responsibility, individual responsibility, kinship, and the capacity for self and societal change (*jihad*). According to Valiante, the Qur'ân serves to guide humanity in finding holistic solutions for the entire person, body, mind, and soul. Islām, in this context, is seen as a practical guide for applying solutions through actions in our daily lives. Allāh says in the Qur'ân,

ذَٰلِكُمْ يُوعَظُ بِهِۦ مَن كَانَ يُؤْمِنُ بِٱللَّهِ وَٱلْيَوْمِ ٱلْءَاخِرِ ۚ وَمَن يَتَّقِ ٱللَّهَ يَجْعَل لَّهُۥ مَخْرَجًا وَيَرْزُقْهُ مِنْ حَيْثُ لَا يَحْتَسِبُ

- *That is instructed to whoever should believe in Allāh and the Last day. And whoever fears Allāh – He will make for him a way out. And will provide for him from where he does not expect.*

(Aṭ-Talāq 65:2–3, interpretation of the meaning)

Similar to the tenets of SFBT, Islāmic principles also focus on individual behaviour and strengths and place stronger emphasis on action than on retrospective insight. The successes in this "life and in the Hereafter are measured not solely in terms of personal inter-psychic growth, but in terms of personal growth as shown in relationship to others and to God" (Valiante, 2003). This is endorsed in the Qur'ân:

إِنَّ ٱللَّهَ لَا يُغَيِّرُ مَا بِقَوْمٍ حَتَّىٰ يُغَيِّرُوا۟ مَا بِأَنفُسِهِمْ

- *Indeed, Allāh will not change the condition of a people until they change what is in themselves.*

(Ar-Ra'd 13:11, interpretation of the meaning)

The Qur'ânic principle highlighted in the verse emphasises the importance of individuals' initiating meaningful change within themselves. It stresses the notion that even minor positive actions or modifications can lead to significant improvements, aligning with the concept of incremental progress. Bidwell (1999) further suggests that change provides an opportunity to enhance life and that problems are temporary and exist only because of the power attributed to them. Thus, the verse encourages understanding the power of small, meaningful changes in bringing about positive transformations in one's life.

Further congruence between SFBT and Islāmic principles includes the notions of individuality, free will, and accountability. There is no difference between the genders in relation to individuality based on faith, deeds, and actions (An-Naĥl 16:97). There is also prominence given to goal setting in SFBT, which reflects the Qur'ānic worldview that there is no divorce between thought and action (Valiante, 2003). This is parallel with this Qur'ānic statement:

وَأَن لَّيْسَ لِلْإِنسَٰنِ إِلَّا مَا سَعَىٰ

- *And that there is not for man except that [good] for which he strives.*

(An-Najm 53:39, interpretation of the meaning)

Valiante (2003) also claimed that "SFBT's emphasis on individual behaviour for the locus of change, rather than race and culture, is parallel to the Qur'ânic concept of 'vicegerency,' or being representatives of God." This is reflected on the verse of the Qur'ân, and Allāh says,

إِنِّى جَاعِلٌ فِى ٱلْأَرْضِ خَلِيفَةً

- *Indeed, I will make upon the earth a successive authority.*

(Al-Baqarah 2:30, interpretation of the meaning)

Hope and possibilities, central to the theory of SFBT, resonate with Islāmic beliefs, according to Rassool (2016). In Islām, believers face trials with hope and patience, reflecting their faith in Allāh. Muslims place their trust in Allāh and find solace in their religious practices, maintaining hope even in challenging times. Those who demonstrate patience in adversity are promised rewards in both the present life and the Hereafter. This aligns with the emphasis on hope and resilience in SFBT, highlighting the compatibility between SFBT principles and Islāmic teachings (Rassool, 2016).

Both SFBT and Islāmic beliefs underscore the inherent capacity of individuals to overcome challenges and effect positive transformations in their lives. SFBT emphasises exploiting individuals' existing strengths and resources while steering clear of negative aspects, fostering optimism and a vision of a brighter future. Similarly, Islāmic teachings encourage hope, optimism, and trust in God's mercy, suggesting that challenges can be overcome through patience, perseverance, and positive actions. Both SFBT and Islāmic beliefs advocate maintaining a positive outlook and embracing the potential for positive change, aligning closely in their emphasis on hope and optimism. In relation to hope and optimism, Allāh says in the Qur'ân,

فَإِنَّ مَعَ ٱلْعُسْرِ يُسْرًا
إِنَّ مَعَ ٱلْعُسْرِ يُسْرًا

- *For indeed, with hardship* [will be] *ease* [i.e. relief]
- *Indeed, with hardship* [will be] *ease*

(Inshirah 94: 5–6, interpretation of the meaning)

وَلَا تَهِنُوا۟ وَلَا تَحْزَنُوا۟ وَأَنتُمُ ٱلْأَعْلَوْنَ إِن كُنتُم مُّؤْمِنِينَ

- *So do not weaken or do not grieve, and you will be superior if you are* [true] *believers.*

(Ali-'Imran 3:139, interpretation of the meaning)

In a *hadīth*, it was narrated from Anas (may Allāh be pleased with him) that the Prophet (ﷺ) entered upon a young man who was dying and said, "How do you feel?" He responded, "I have hope in Allāh, O Messenger of Allāh, but I fear my sins." The Messenger of Allāh (ﷺ) said, "These two things [hope and fear] do not coexist in the heart of a person in a situation like this, but Allah will give him that which he hopes for and keep him safe from that which he fears" (Ibn Majah).

Rassool and Khan (2023) highlight that among the fast-paced nature of contemporary life, individuals may grapple with feelings of despair and pessimism. They propose that maintaining hope rooted in faith, trust in God's mercy, and the belief in divine ease amid challenges serves as a vital antidote. Lala (2023) suggests that the Qur'ān uniquely influences feelings of hope and fear, reflecting diverse psychological aspects of these emotions. The Qur'ān guides believers to express hope and fear in ways that lead to positive behaviours, emphasising the transformation of emotions into ethical actions. Ultimately, it promotes lasting hope and aids in managing fear, nurturing a positive outlook among believers.

Both SFBT and Islāmic principles underline individual empowerment and accountability. SFBT empowers clients to identify and implement their solutions, recognising their capacity for positive change; similarly, Islāmic values encourage accountability, self-improvement, and ethical decision-making. Both emphasise agency, urging individuals to actively shape their lives and contribute to their well-being and others'. This alignment centres on the compatibility between SFBT and certain Islāmic traditions.

SFBT and Islāmic values on collaboration and consultation also have some parallels. Collaboration between the therapist and the client is an important part of the therapeutic process in SFBT. Similarly, the notion of *shura* in Islāmic teachings emphasises consultation and group decision-making. This Islāmic principle stresses the importance of seeking guidance and collaborating with others to make sound decisions. Allāh says in the Qur'ān,

وَشَاوِرْهُمْ فِى ٱلْأَمْرِ

- *And consult with them in the matter.*
(Āli Imrān, 3:159, interpretation of the meaning)

وَأَمْرُهُمْ شُورَىٰ بَيْنَهُمْ

- *And whose affair is determined by consultation among themselves.*
(Ash-Shura 42:38, interpretation of the meaning)

Consultation with others, or *mashwara*, was a practice of the Messenger of Allāh (ﷺ), and he taught Muslims how to apply it in their daily life. Al-Hasan said, "People never seek advice without being guided to the best possibility available to them . . . and manage their affairs by mutual consultation" (Al-Adab Al-Mufrad). Both SFBT and Islāmic values prioritise collaboration, whether in therapy or decision-making processes. This mutual emphasis reflects a recognition of the benefits of combining perspectives for positive outcomes. However, while there are similarities, it is essential to acknowledge that SFBT is a psychological approach that may not align perfectly with all aspects of Islāmic principles and practices.

The Islāmic perspective, rooted in the belief of the oneness of Allah, heavily influences the views and behaviours of Muslims. Islāmic principles, drawn from the Qur'ān and Prophet Muhammad's (ﷺ) teachings, provide comprehensive guidance for various aspects of life including morality and personal conduct. In contrast, SFBT operates within a secular framework, emphasising practical and solution-oriented approaches without explicit religious or spiritual themes. Individuals with a monotheistic perspective may feel a disconnect with SFBT due to its secular nature. For those seeking therapy within the context of Islāmic teachings, approaches like Islāmic psychotherapy, which incorporate religious or spiritual components, may better align with their worldview, addressing moral dilemmas and providing spiritual meaning to their challenges.

The difference in problem orientation between SFBT and Islāmic principles is evident in their temporal emphases. SFBT is future-oriented, prioritising the identification and pursuit of desired outcomes and solutions, while Islāmic principles focus on addressing and resolving current difficulties within religious teachings and moral norms, encouraging progress. In family conflicts, SFBT envisions an improved future with enhanced family relations, focusing on strengths and solutions. Equally, an Islāmic approach involves addressing current disputes through concepts like repentance, seeking forgiveness, patience, and communication rooted in Islāmic values.

The fundamental difference between Islāmic beliefs and SFBT lies in the concept of divine intervention. Islāmic teachings emphasise *tawakkul*, surrendering to God's will and trusting in divine guidance, while SFBT focuses on the client's potential for change without explicitly addressing divine direction. For Muslim clients, incorporating prayer and trust in divine intervention is significant, especially during significant life challenges. While SFBT empowers clients to achieve practical changes, it may not explicitly acknowledge the spiritual dimension or divine guidance sought by Muslim clients. This contrast highlights the importance for Muslim clients of seeking therapeutic approaches that align with both their practical and spiritual needs.

There is also dissonance between Islāmic principles and SFBT particularly regarding techniques like the miracle question, the concept of sin and evil, and the understanding of social hierarchy in Islāmic society. While the miracle question is a useful tool for Muslim clients seeking swift resolutions to their problems, it may not fully align with Islāmic beliefs. Solution-focused therapists commonly employ the miracle question to help clients envision a future without their problems and set concrete therapeutic goals. Valiante (2003) suggested that the miracle question has a dual connotation: clinical (set specific and concrete goals) as well as religious (a belief in change beyond the control of the individual), which parallels the concept of the unicity of God (*tawhīd*). While the miracle question links actions to change, it also emphasises God's role as the ultimate controller in easing life's trials and tribulations. Chaudhry and Li (2011) suggested that "For Muslim clients who are looking for a swift resolution of their problems, the miracle question is a useful way to start" (p. 112).

According to Muhammad (2012), the miracle question "links actions to change which further establishes the Islāmic view of . . . God as the ultimate controller to ease trials and tribulations of life through miracles" (p. 35). However, Allah answers the prayers of those who call upon Him:

لَا تَقْنَطُوا مِن رَّحْمَةِ ٱللَّهِ ۚ إِنَّ ٱللَّهَ يَغْفِرُ ٱلذُّنُوبَ جَمِيعًا ۚ إِنَّهُ هُوَ ٱلْغَفُورُ ٱلرَّحِيمُ

- *Do not despair of the mercy of Allah. Indeed, Allah forgives all sins. Indeed, it is He who is the Forgiving, the Merciful.*

(Az-Zumar 39:53, interpretation of the meaning)

It is stated that, "Everyone who offers supplication receives a response, but the response may vary. Sometimes he will get exactly what he asked for, and sometimes he will be compensated (with something equivalent)" (Al-Haafiz Ibn Hajar, cited in Islām Q&A, 2012). The Messenger of Allāh (ﷺ) said,

> There is no Muslim who offers supplication in which there is no sin or severing of ties of kinship, but Allāh will give him one of three things in return for it: either what he asked for will be hastened for him, or (reward) will be stored up for him in the Hereafter or an equivalent evil will be diverted from him.
>
> (Ahmad, cited in Islām Q&A, 2012)

However, Muslim clients may not feel comfortable with the idea and/or the language of a miracle. Rassool (2016) argued that "For Muslims, miracles are only the work of Allāh who the Creator and Upholder of the universe is and has the ultimate power to change human conditions and situations." Rassool suggests alternatives to the miracle question that reflect cultural and religious beliefs, for example, "If God accept your prayer, how would you be different from what you are now?" (p. 160). An alternative to miracle questions is questions that reflect cultural/religious beliefs in phrasing outcome questions. That is, therapists should use future-oriented outcome questions for achieving the same therapeutic purpose (Lee & Mjelde-Mossey, 2004). Examples include questions like, "If God accepts your prayer, how would you be different from what you are now?" These alternative questions maintain a future-oriented focus and align more closely with the religious and cultural perspectives of Muslim clients.

SFBT's theoretical flaw involves the assumption that human intentions are always good and the failure to recognise sin and evil in individuals and social systems. This perspective contrasts with Islāmic beliefs, which reject the notion of inherent human evil and assert the concept of *fitrah*, signifying a neutral state inclined towards good. Islam emphasises human free will and personal responsibility for choices, allowing individuals to choose between good and evil (Bidwell, 1999; Rassool, 2016). Bidwell (1999) raises concerns regarding the potential content of preferred solutions in SFBT, questioning whether these solutions might conflict with Islāmic principles or inadvertently substitute one undesirable behaviour for another. Muslim clients may reject solutions that are incompatible with their beliefs. Moreover, the issue of self-disclosure in therapy presents challenges for some Muslim clients due to cultural and religious norms, leading to reluctance to share personal or family information outside the family context. Chaudhry and Li (2011) underline the importance of trust and confidence in therapy, suggesting that longer-term approaches may be necessary for effective change in individuals or family systems.

In summary, the incongruence between Islāmic beliefs and SFBT arises from differences in theological perspectives, problem orientation, challenges with the miracle question, considerations of sins and evils, and the acknowledgment of divine intervention. Clients seeking therapy within an Islāmic framework may find a mismatch between the secular, future-oriented nature of SFBT and the holistic, present-focused, and spiritually grounded approach often preferred by Muslims. Therapists operating in diverse cultural and religious contexts should be mindful of these differences and, when suitable, explore integrating elements of their clients' religious beliefs into the therapeutic process.

Islām-inspired SFBT

Islām-inspired SFBT (IiSFBT) integrates principles from Islāmic teachings into the therapeutic approach, aligning it more closely with the values and beliefs of individuals who follow Islāmic principles. To accommodate cultural, religious, and societal aspects, alternative models such as "culture-infused counselling" (Arthur & Collins, 2005) and "religious/spiritual-infused counselling" have been proposed. According to Lambert (2008), this model involves determining the most salient points of the complaint to generate solutions from within the family, extended family, religion, and culture for support while also locating intermediaries for advocacy.

Islāmic monotheism should be the foundation of IiSFBT; *tawhīd* emphasises seeking unity and coherence in all aspects of life. By incorporating *tawhīd*, the therapist helps clients establish a connection between their faith and the therapeutic process. The focus is on seeking solutions and empowering individuals to trust in God's guidance. While SFBT is inherently future-oriented, an Islām-inspired approach might place additional emphasis on addressing present challenges in accordance with Islāmic teachings. An IiSFBT therapist will facilitate the Muslim client in identifying present-focused problem resolution within an Islāmic ethical framework. For instance, the therapist might help clients explore how their actions align with Islāmic values and guide them in making choices consistent with their faith.

The integration of *tawakkul* (reliance on God) in goal setting is a key component of IiSFBT. Therapists encourage clients to trust in God's guidance while actively working towards their goals, aligning their aspirations with Islāmic principles. This approach emphasises the importance of recognising God's role in guiding the therapeutic journey while taking personal responsibility for actions. For instance, clients may develop goals consistent with Islāmic teachings, seeking God's guidance through prayer and depending on patience as taught in Islām. By promoting trust, inner peace, and reliance on God, IiSFBT enhances clients' perseverance, resilience, and overall well-being as they pursue their goals.

Within the solution-focused framework, the therapist may apply Islāmic coping strategies. For example, assisting clients in identifying how their spiritual practices can be effective resources in overcoming obstacles and maintaining mental well-being. The spiritual resources and interventions include prayer (*salah*); reflection and contemplation (*tafakkur*); seeking refuge in God (*tawakkul*); reciting the Qur'ân; remembrance of God (*dhikr*); patience (*sabr*); gratitude (*shukr*); and acts of charity (*sadaqah*).

The use of Qur'ānic narratives with clients to derive insights and inspiration for addressing their challenges can be utilised in IiSFBT. Therapists can collaborate with the client to explore solutions that are of relevance to the client. This approach involves drawing parallels between a client's situation and the experiences of individuals in Qur'ānic narrative. These lessons can serve as sources of inspiration and practical guidance for the client's current challenges.

For example, if a client is grappling with forgiveness, the therapist might explore the story of Prophet Joseph (Yusuf) (Qur'ān 12), who forgave his brothers despite the hardships they inflicted upon him. The therapist and client discuss the underlying themes of forgiveness, mercy, and resilience in the story and apply those principles to the client's own situation. The therapist facilitates the client's exploration of how they can embody these teachings, cultivating forgiveness and healing in their own lives. In the case of a Muslim client struggling with resilience, the therapist might draw parallels with the story of Prophet Jacob (Ya'qūb) and his perseverance and endurance through hardship. There are other verses in the Qur'ān that the therapist and client could extract lessons, principles, and guidance embedded in the narratives from.

In relation to techniques, the miracle question has been examined from an Islāmic perspective in the previous section. An alternative set of questions can be used in Islāmic-inspired SFBT to generate solutions from significant others, the extended family, and religion. Table 10.2 provides a list of questions that can be used. Some of the questions have been adapted from Lambert (2008) to accommodate Muslim clients.

In an IiSFBT approach, the therapist serves as a facilitator, aiding the client in connecting with their faith and drawing inspiration and guidance from Qur'ânic stories. This collaborative process involves an examination of these timeless narratives to extract insights applicable to contemporary issues. The therapist integrates Islāmic values, beliefs, practices, and the Islāmic worldview into the SFBT framework, creating a more spiritually compatible and personally meaningful therapeutic experience for the client.

Conclusion

SFBT is a non-confrontational talk therapy that explore clients' existing strengths and support networks. Its simplicity aligns well with the preference for face-saving techniques in cultures like those of East Asia and among many

TABLE 10.2 Questions in Islām-inspired SFBT for Muslims

- Are there specific family members who have faced similar challenges and successfully navigated them?
- How did they solve the challenges?
- What does your significant others or the family think about the problem?
- Can you think of a time when someone close to you provided valuable support or a solution to a problem?
- Who in your life, such as family members or friends, might have insights into your current situation or could offer support?
- What do others normally do in this situation?
- Reflect on a time when your family or religious community worked together effectively. How can you apply those strengths now?
- Imagine your ideal scenario where your significant others, extended family, and religious values are all contributing positively. What would that look like?
- Are there teachings or principles from your Qur'ân or *Sunnah* that could guide you in approaching this challenge?
- How has your faith supported you in overcoming difficulties in the past, and how can it be a resource now?
- What Islāmic practices might bring comfort or clarity as you work towards a solution?
- What does the *imam* or religious scholar say you should do about this?
- Would that work in this situation? Why or why not?
- Who could help with the barriers you have identified?
- What strategy could help make this change?
- What (or who) make you feel better when this happens?

Muslim clients. However, clients seeking more in-depth therapy may overlook SFBT's potential if the therapeutic alliance is not sufficiently established, highlighting the crucial role of the alliance particularly in the early stages of treatment (Boghosian, 2011). An Islām-inspired approach to SFBT can be effective for Islāmic psychotherapists working with Muslim clients provided that there is alignment between Islāmic principles and the underlying assumptions of SFBT. It is essential for Islāmic psychotherapists to grasp the philosophical assumptions and techniques of SFBT, allowing them to integrate religious or spiritual considerations and sanctify the discipline in accordance with Islāmic beliefs (Hankle, 2016). By applying basic modifications and considering religious or spiritual aspects, SFBT can become a suitable psychological intervention for Muslim clients within an Islām-inspired framework.

References

Al-Adab Al-Mufrad. *Al-Adab Al-Mufrad 258* (In-book reference: Book 13, Hadith 3. English translation: Book 13, Hadith 258). Sahih (Al-Albani).

Ardito, R. B., & Rabellino, D. (2011). Therapeutic alliance and outcome of psychotherapy: Historical excursus, measurements, and prospects for research. *Frontiers in Psychology*, 2(270), 1–11.

Arthur, N., & Collins, S. (2005). Introduction to culture-infused counselling. In N. Arthur & S. Collins (Eds.), *Culture-infused counselling: Celebrating the Canadian Mosaic* (pp. 3–40). Counselling Concepts.

Bakker, J., Bannink, F., & Macdonald, A. (2010). Solution-focused psychiatry. *The Psychiatrist, 34*(7), 297–300. https://doi.org/10.1192/pb.bp.109.025957.

Bavelas, J. B., Coates, L., & Johnson, T. (2000b). Listeners as co-narrators. *Journal of Personality and Social Psychology, 79*(6), 941–952.

Bavelas, J. B., McGee, D., Phillips, B., & Routledge, R. (2000a). Microanalysis of communication in psychotherapy. *Human Systems, 11*, 3–22.

Bidwell, D. R. (1999). Hope and possibility: The theology of culture inherent to solution-focused brief therapy. *American Journal of Pastoral Counseling, 3*(1), 3–21.

Boghosian, S. (2011). *Counseling and psychotherapy with clients of Middle Eastern descent: A qualitative inquiry* [PhD thesis, Utah State University]. Retrieved September 7, 2014, from http://digitalcommons.usu.edu/etd/898.

Bond, C., Woods, K., Humphrey, N., Symes, W., & Green, L. (2013). The effectiveness of solution focused brief therapy with children and families: A systematic and critical evaluation of the literature from 1990–2010. *Journal of Child Psychology and Psychiatry, 54*(7), 707–723.

Bubenzer, D. L., & West, J. D. (1993). William Hudson O'Hanlon: On seeking possibilities and solutions in therapy. *The Family Journal, 1*(4), 365–379. https://doi.org/10.1177/1066480793014016.

Cepeda, L. M., & Davenport, D. S. (2006). Person-centered therapy and solution-focused brief therapy: An integration of present and future awareness. *Psychotherapy: Theory, Research, Practice, Training, 43*(1), 1–12.

Chaudhry, S., & Li, C. (2011). Is solution-focused brief therapy culturally appropriate for Muslim American counselees? *Journal of Contemporary Psychotherapy, 41*(2), 109–113.

Corey, G. (2017). *Theory and practice of counseling and psychotherapy*. Cengage Learning.

De Jong, P., & Berg, I. K. (2012). *Interviewing for solutions* (4th ed.). Cengage Learning.

de Shazer, S. (1985). *Keys to solution in brief therapy*. W. W. Norton & Company.

de Shazer, S. (1988). *Clues: Investigating solutions in brief therapy*. W. W. Norton & Company.

de Shazer, S., & Berg, I. K. (1988). Constructing solutions. *Family Therapy Networker, 12*, 42–43.

de Shazer, S., Berg, I. K., Lipchik, E., Nunnally, E., Molnar, A., Gingerich, W., & Weiner-Davis, M. (1986). Brief therapy: Focused solution development. *Family Process, 25*(2), 207–221.

de Shazer, S., Dolan, Y. M., Korman, H., Trepper, T., McCullom, E., & Berg, I. K. (2007). *More than miracles: The state of the art of solution-focused brief therapy*. Haworth Press.

Gingerich, W. J., & Eisengart, S. (2000). Solution-focused brief therapy: A review of the outcome research. *Family Process, 39*(4), 477–498.

Gingerich, W. J., & Peterson, L. T. (2013). Effectiveness of solution-focused brief therapy: A systematic qualitative review of controlled outcome studies. *Research on Social Work Practice, 23*(3), 266–283. https://doi.org/10.1177/1049731512470859.

Guterman, J. T. (2015). *Mastering the art of solution-focused counseling*. Wiley, Online ebook. https://doi.org/10.1002/9781119221562.

Hankle, D. (2016). Christian worldview and the use of narrative therapy in the Christian counseling setting. *Journal of Christian Healing, 32*(1), 5–14.

Ibn Majah. *Sunan Ibn Majah 4261* (In-book reference: Book 37, Hadith 162. English translation: Vol. 5, Book 37, Hadith 4261). Hasan (Darussalam). https://sunnah.com/ibnmajah:4261.

Islām Q&A. (2012). *Fatwa 177561. Does the fact that Allah answers the prayers of the disbelievers indicate that what they believe is true?* Retrieved November 23, 2023, from http://Islamqa.info/en/177561.

Johnson, D. (2011). *A solution-focused approach to group dynamics in counseling: Or, Sister Hazel explains it all for you*. University of San Diego, School of Leadership and Education Sciences, COUN 525 Group Dynamics in Counseling. Retrieved November 21, 2023, from https://daviddeanjohnson.blogspot.com/2013/04/a-solution-focused-approach-to-group.html.

Kim, J. S. (2008). Examining the effectiveness of solution-focused brief therapy: A meta-analysis. *Research on Social Work Practice, 18*(2), 107–116.

Kim, J. S., Brook, J., & Akin, B. A. (2018). Solution-focused brief therapy with substance-using individuals: A randomized controlled trial study. *Research on Social Work Practice, 28*(4), 452–462.

Lala, I. (2023). The Qur'an and emotional well-being: Hope and fear in the Qur'an. *Pastoral Psychology, 72*, 245–275. https://doi.org/10.1007/s11089-023-01060-4.

Lambert, L. (2008). A counselling model for young women in the United Arab Emirates: Cultural considerations. *Canadian Journal of Counselling (Revue Canadienne de Counseling), 42*(2), 101–116.

Lee, M. Y., & Mjelde-Mossey, L. A. (2004). Cultural dissonance among generations: A solution-focused approach with East Asian elders and their families. *Journal of Marital and Family Therapy, 30*(4), 497–513.

Lovelock, H., Matthews, R., & Murphy, K. (2011). *Evidence-based psychological interventions in the treatment of mental disorders: A literature review* (3rd ed.). Australian Psychological Society.

Maljanen, T., Paltta, P., Härkänen, T., Virtala, E., Lindfors, O., Laaksonen, M. A., Knekt, P., & Helsinki Psychotherapy Study Group. (2012). The cost-effectiveness of short-term psychodynamic psychotherapy and solution-focused therapy in the treatment of depressive and anxiety disorder during a one-year follow-up. *Journal of Mental Health Policy and Economics, 15*(1), 13–23.

McGee, D., Del Vento, A., & Bavelas, J. B. (2005). An interactional model of questions as therapeutic interventions. *Journal of Marital and Family Therapy, 31*(4), 371–384.

Muhammad, H. (2012). *Muslim mental health: Considerations for psychotherapy and counseling: A literature review*, in partial fulfilment of the requirements for the Degree of Master of Arts in Adlerian Counseling and Psychotherapy, Adler Graduate School. Retrieved November 23, 2023, from www.alfredadler.edu/sites/default/files/Hadiyah%20Muhammad%20MP%202012.pdf.

O'Connell, B. (2001). *Solution-focused stress counseling*. Continuum [as cited in O'Connell, B., & Palmer, S. (2003). *Handbook of solution-focused therapy* (pp. 1–6). Sage Publications].

O'Connell, B. (2017). The first session. In *Solution-focused therapy* (3rd ed., pp. 39–76). Sage Publications.

O'Hanlon, W. H., & Weiner-Davis, M. (2003). *In search of solutions: A new direction in psychotherapy* (Revised ed.). W. W. Norton & Company.

Raskin, N. J., & Rogers, C. R. (2005). Person-centered therapy. In R. J. Corsini & D. Wedding (Eds.), *Current psychotherapies* (pp. 130–165). Thomson Brooks/Cole.

Rassool, G. Hussein (2016). *Islāmic counselling. An introduction to theory and practice*. Routledge.

Rassool, G. Hussein, & Khan, W. N. (2023). Hope in Islāmic psychotherapy. *Journal of Spirituality in Mental Health*. https://doi.org/10.1080/19349637.2023.2207751.

Schmit, E. L., Schmit, M. K., & Lenz, A. S. (2016). Meta-analysis of solution-focused brief therapy for treating symptoms of internalizing disorders. *Counseling Outcome Research and Evaluation, 7*(1), 21–39. https://doi.org/10.1177/2150137815623836.

Trepper, T. S., McCollum, E. E., De Jong, P., Korman, H., Gingerich, W., & Franklin, C. (2010). *Solution focused therapy. Treatment manual for working with individuals*. Research Committee of the Solution Focused Brief Therapy Association. Retrieved November 21, 2023, from www.solutionfocused.net/f/SFBT_Treatment_Manual.doc.

Trepper, T. S., McCollum, E. E., De Jong, P., Korman, H., Gingerich, W., & Franklin, C. (2012). Solution focused therapy treatment manual. In C. Franklin, T. S. Trepper, W. J. Gingerich, & E. E. McCollum (Eds.), *Solution-focused brief therapy: A handbook of evidence-based practice* (pp. 20–38). Oxford University Press.

Valiante, W. C. (2003). Family therapy and Muslim families: A solution focused approach. *WIAMH – Newsletter*, *2*(4), 16. Retrieved November 21, 2023, from www.canadianIslamiccongress.com/docs/family.php.

Walter, J. L., & Peller, J. E. (1992). *Becoming solution-focused in brief therapy*. Routledge.

Walter, J. L., & Peller, J. E. (2000). *Recreating brief therapy: Preferences and possibilities*. W. W. Norton & Company.

Wheeler, J., & Vinnicombe, G. (2011). Some assumptions of solution-focused practice. *Context*, 40–42. Retrieved November 21, 2023, from www.sfontour.com/wp-content/uploads/2019/08/Some-assumptions-of-solution-focused-practice.pdf.

11
NARRATIVE THERAPY THROUGH AN ISLĀMIC LENS

Introduction

Narrative therapy is a psychotherapeutic approach that focuses on clients' stories and experiences to facilitate positive change in their psychological well-being. Developed by Michael White and David Epston in the 1980s, narrative therapy centres on using narratives and metaphors, aligning with Islāmic perspectives that often draw on stories and teachings from the Qur'ân and *hadīths*. This therapeutic method is applicable to individuals, couples, or families.

White and Epston (2009) define narrative approaches as centring people as experts in their own lives and viewing problems as separate entities. According to this definition, narrative approaches assume that individuals possess various skills, competencies, beliefs, values, commitments, and abilities that can assist them in reducing the influence of problems in their lives (cited in Wallis et al., 2011). Narrative therapy aims to enhance psychological health by providing alternative emotional expressions and bolstering resilience and coping skills. The approach empowers individuals to become narrators, transforming problematic narratives into positive and productive ones. This involves changing self-defeating stories and replacing them with strengths-based narratives (White & Epston, 1990; Harms, 2007; Wallis et al., 2011). Harms (2007) suggests that the goal of narrative therapy is to change clouded or self-defeating stories, restoring them with strengths-based narratives. My aims with the chapter are to examine the theoretical framework of narrative therapy, the therapeutic relationship and process, and techniques used and to explore the divergence and congruence of narrative therapy with Islāmic beliefs and practices.

DOI: 10.4324/9781003453413-13

Theoretical framework

Narrative therapy, rooted in postmodern social constructionist theories, challenges the notion of an objective reality by emphasising that reality is socially constructed through interactions. White and Epston (1990) highlight major narrative assumptions, including respecting each client's viewpoint, maintaining a separation between the client and the problem, avoiding victim blaming, and recognising clients as experts in their own lives with the potential to address problems. Parry and Doan (1994) further emphasise the absence of absolute truth, with meaning being constructed in social, cultural, and political contexts. Additionally, people create meaning through narratives within their dominant culture, and the problem is separated from the person, identified as the "problem story." One key principle is the avoidance of diagnostic labelling. Table 11.1 presents some of the principles of narrative therapy.

TABLE 11.1 Principles of narrative therapy

Principles	*Key components*	*Explanation*
Intentionality	Reasons and purposes	• There is aways an intention and purpose for one's actions and behaviours (Stillman, 2016).
Narrative metaphor	Stories: meaning and interpretation	• Stories can influence people's emotions, behaviours, and relationships in making sense of the world. • People are active creators of meaning, values, and identity, and there are multiple ways of interpreting and narrating the same events.
Externalisation	External problem People vs problem	• People separate themselves from their problems and perceive them as external entities that can be named, examined, and changed (Stillman, 2016).
Personal agency	Control: actions and destiny	• A person "is encouraged to find his/her own voice and to make choices about how he/she wants to live" (Shapiro & Ross, 2002, p. 99). • In a sense, it means having an internal locus of control and being able to control one's own actions and destiny.
Identity proclamation	Preferred identity: Ideal self	• People declare their preferred identity to themselves and others through actions, words, and relationships (Stillman, 2016). • It is a way of affirming and expressing the ideal self and how one wants to live.
Sub-story development	Exploration and expansion of subplots	• This involves exploring and expanding the stories that are secondary or alternative to the dominant or problem-saturated ones (Duvall & Young, 2017).

Narrative therapy: the evidence

Narrative therapy has demonstrated therapeutic efficacy across various conditions and settings, proving beneficial for individuals, families, and communities (Kelley, 2011). It particularly stands out in helping clients overwhelmed by negative experiences, thoughts, or emotions, showing positive outcomes in addressing consequences of adverse childhood experiences, domestic violence, attachment issues, and bullying (Lonne, 2015). Researchers have investigated its effectiveness in improving school behaviour in attention deficit hyperactivity disorder (Looyeh et al., 2012), addressing psychological distress and emotional symptoms (Cashin et al., 2013), treating social phobia in children (Looyeh et al., 2014) and post-traumatic stress disorder (Erbes et al., 2014); enhancing empathy, decision-making, and social skills in children (Beaudoin et al., 2016); treating depression and anxiety (Shakeri et al., 2020); improving marital satisfaction (Ghavibazou et al., 2020); rediscovering life wisdom (Chow & Fung, 2021); enhancing couple relationships and preventing conflicts (Chimpén-López et al., 2021); and addressing attention deficit hyperactivity disorder (Fatahi et al., 2021).

While narrative therapy is widely used, critics question its long-term efficacy compared with established approaches, citing concerns about oversimplification of issues and neglect of multifaceted factors. Challenges such as role reversal for clients, cultural barriers, and limited cognitive skills may hinder effectiveness. The subjective nature of personal narratives and clients' tendency to present stories in a positive light pose additional obstacles. Moreover, the lack of an agenda for clients and the absence of absolute truths in life could limit the suitability of narrative therapy for all individuals.

The therapeutic relationship and process

In narrative therapy, the therapist acts as a facilitator, allowing the client to lead the therapeutic process. The therapist adopts a stance of curiosity and humility, similar to a cultural anthropologist, encouraging clients to reflect on the stories that shape their lives. Clients are empowered to construct their narratives through their cultural lens, externalise their problems, and deconstruct dominant and problematic stories. The therapist enables clients to explore more productive and preferred narratives that serve as resources for growth and development.

In narrative therapy, the therapeutic relationship is characterised by the therapist's attitudes and competence, fostering rapport, respect, and collaboration with the client. The approach prioritises non-judgmental, victim-blaming-free interactions that emphasise caring, curiosity, openness, and empathy in communication. The goal is to enhance the client's internal perspective and external worldview, empowering them as the expert and author of their narratives or stories.

Through a collaborative relationship, both client and therapist work towards improving the outcomes of the narratives. Diagnosis is avoided, as the problem and the client are seen as separate entities. The therapist's role is to explore the client's strengths and positive aspects through their narratives, enabling the creation of new narratives and positive perspectives on experiences to achieve desired outcomes. This dynamic process involves the client actively re-authoring their own narrative and life events with the therapist's support. The role of the narrative therapist include the following (adapted from "The Social Work Graduate"):

- Analyse problematic stories that disempower people.
- Externalise people's problems, discussing them as separate from the individual.
- Deconstruct negative or problem-based stories to reveal alternative views that reinforce strengths.
- Use these alternative views to reconstruct positive stories that empower.
- Encourage the client to share these positive stories with others as they live out these new narratives.

In narrative therapy, language serves as a tool for facilitating change, with therapists often asking questions from a position of not knowing the answers (Goolishian & Anderson, 1992). The approach involves exploring the effects of problems on individuals' lives, distinguishing the meaning a problem has acquired from the individual themselves (Laube, 1998). Assessment in narrative therapy differs significantly from traditional methods, focusing more on discovering and externalising the problem (Parry & Doan, 1994). Clients learn to separate themselves from the problem through this process. Initial sessions often involve storytelling, followed by questioning to identify the nature of the problem. Narrative therapists employ various skills such as empathic listening, open and closed questioning, clarification, paraphrasing, probing, and summarising to facilitate the therapeutic process (Laube, 1998; Parry & Doan, 1994).

Techniques used in narrative therapy

There are a variety of techniques and exercises used in narrative therapy, including putting together your narrative; externalisation; deconstruction; unique outcomes; use of metaphor; and existentialism. These techniques are integral to narrative therapy's emphasis on developing a therapeutic relationship, deconstructing problem stories, integrating preferred narratives of identity, and embracing and living out these narratives. The approach also respects diverse cultural understandings of healing and well-being, acknowledging the importance of community and collective healing practices (Vromans & Schweitzer, 2015).

Putting together your narrative

In narrative therapy, therapists assist clients in constructing and examining their narratives, aiding them in identifying dominant and problematic stories in their lives. This process, often termed "re-authoring" or "re-storying," allows clients to explore various meanings and interpretations of their experiences (Vinney, 2019). Therapists pay close attention to "problem-saturated descriptions," which represent the client's current events or dominant life stories causing distress.

Effective listening skills enable therapists to probe and question, gaining insight into the client's thoughts, beliefs, and social context surrounding these events (Payne, 2006). Using the client's language is paramount in this process, as it facilitates clarity and understanding. As the narrative unfolds, a cycle of reflection develops with the therapist's guidance, leading to the identification of key issues or challenges within the narrative. This collaborative exploration helps clients gain new insights and perspectives on their experiences.

Externalisation

In narrative therapy, therapists facilitate the process of externalisation, which involves creating distance between the individual and their problems. This approach allows clients to view their problems or behaviours as external things rather than intrinsic aspects of themselves (Bennet, 2018). By personifying the problem and referring to it as "it" or "the," clients can separate themselves from the issue at hand. For instance, instead of saying "I am stressed or worried," clients might express, "I am currently living with stress or anxiety."

This externalisation technique empowers clients to focus on changing unwanted or negative behaviours by shifting the perspective from personalising the problem to viewing it as a separate entity. Open-ended questions such as "When did you become aware of the stress?" facilitate this process of externalisation, encouraging clients to explore their experiences and responses to the problem. The Dulwich Centre (2022) proposes an initial discussion framework consisting of four areas to facilitate the externalisation of the problem in narrative therapy:

- Characterising the problem in an experience-near way: therapists listen as clients discuss the problem, allowing them to express their experiences and perspectives.
- Connecting the problem to its antecedents, effects, and links with others: this step involves exploring the origins and consequences of the problem, as well as its connections to other aspects of the client's life.
- Having the client describe their experience of and position on the effects of the problem: clients are encouraged to articulate how the problem impacts them personally and to reflect on their stance regarding its effects.
- Locating this experience and position within the client's wider values: therapists help clients situate their experiences and perspectives within their broader values and beliefs.

Through repeated practice and exploration of these areas, the externalisation of the problem empowers clients to shift their focus towards changing negative and unwanted behaviours, fostering personal growth and development.

In narrative therapy, narrative metaphors serve as therapeutic tools to assist clients in reframing their experiences. A metaphor is "a figure of speech in which a word or phrase literally denoting one kind of object or idea is used in place of another to suggest a likeness or analogy between them" (www.merriam-webster.com). This suggests a likeness or analogy between different objects or ideas used to understand the client's worldview and the stories that have shaped their lives and identities. Narrative metaphor emphasises that individuals actively create their own stories and meaning, enabling them to construct more empowering narratives about themselves and their lives.

Deconstruction

Deconstruction is another phase of narrative therapy from enables the client gain clarity in their stories. A client may get clouded in their stories, which might need more exploration and clarification. A narrative therapist would collaborate with the client to break down their story into smaller parts, clarifying the problem and making it more coherent (Wallis et al., 2011). For example, questions that aim to deconstruct the problem include

- What is going on when the anxiety is present?
- What emotions do you tend to experience when you are experiencing stress?
- Tell me about a time that you managed to cope with the stress. How was that situation handled differently?
- Have there been recent times when you managed your life despite still having stress?
- How did it feel when you put up with the problem?

After deconstructing the stories and achieving clarity, the narrative therapy process moves to the phase of reconstruction. Complex problems can sometimes lead to generalisation, making them overwhelming and seemingly unsolvable. To facilitate narrative reconstruction, O'Connor et al. (2008) suggest the following steps:

- Uncover the narratives: identify dominant, devalued, and key player narratives
- Identify narrative functions: understand the roles of different narratives in the client's life
- Validate narratives: acknowledge the significance of the identified narratives
- Build alternative narratives (re-authoring): construct new narratives that empower the client
- Retell the story in a new way (re-storying): narrate the client's story in an empowering manner
- Create further social validation: establish an audience that supports the new narratives

This process allows clients to explore the depth of their problems, identify specific threats, and consider the impact of religious, sociocultural, and political contexts on their issues (O'Connor et al., 2008). In this way, the client is able to explore the depth of the problem and identify the specific threat posed by the problem.

Unique outcomes

Unique outcomes in narrative therapy involve identifying exceptions to prevailing negative stories, offering contrasts that challenge existing narratives (Gonçalves et al., 2009). Clients often become rooted in negative narratives, and the therapist's role is to assist them in considering alternative, more positive stories. This technique is applied when a client's narrative is dominated by problems and negative events. The therapist identifies exceptional positive outcomes and guides the client to view the narrative from a new perspective, fostering the development of more positive stories (Bishop, 2011). It is a process of reimagining the problem, empowering the client with positive outcomes that can help overcome challenges (AIPC, 2010). The underlying principle emphasises the client's agency in actively re-authoring their own lives. Questions during exploration might include inquiries such as, "When does the problem or stress not affect your life or your relationship?"

Existentialism

Existential therapy offers a philosophical approach to understanding human challenges and perspectives on the world. Some existential therapists refrain from using technical interventions, aiming to preserve the integrity and honesty of the therapeutic relationship (Ackerman, 2017). Phenomenological therapy, a common practice in existential work, involves systematically describing conscious awareness to grasp essences and understand universal meanings (van Deurzen, 2015). This approach encourages individuals to set aside assumptions and biases, allowing them to explore their conscious awareness and create their own meaning and purpose in life. It is about understanding the human experience and clarifying the life one wishes to lead (Iacovou & Weixel-Dixon, 2015).

Existential therapy employs various techniques to explore clients' ability to live authentically (van Deurzen, 2012). While many existential therapists draw from psychoanalysis, CBT, SFBT, person-centred therapy, and gestalt therapy, they maintain a distinct philosophical approach (Adams, 2013; Deurzen & Adams, 2016). Narrative therapy utilises several tools, summarised in Table 11.2, to facilitate the therapeutic process.

Divergence and congruence of narrative therapy with Islāmic beliefs and practices

Narrative therapy, a postmodern therapeutic approach, is not inherently aligned with Islāmic traditions due to its secular nature. The postmodern notions of pluralism and moral relativism may cause dissonance in the Islāmic worldview of

TABLE 11.2 Tools used as part of narrative therapy

Tool	Examples
Therapeutic documents	Written documents: declarations, certificates, handbooks, letters, notes from a session, film, lists, photos, etc. that summarise the person's discoveries and describe the person's own perceived progress
Remembering	Draws on memories of significant people, e.g. strangers who have made an important positive contribution to their life or famous people who have indirectly contributed to the person's life by examples of courage and integrity
Rituals and celebrations	These mark significant steps of a journey and are often included at the conclusion of therapy.
Outsider-witnesses	An outsider-witness is an invited audience to a therapy conversation. Outsider-witnesses may be family, friends, professionals, or just people who have previously experienced similar difficulties. The presence of an outsider-witness means it is much more likely that steps a person makes in the therapy room can be translated into action in their daily lives (Carey & Russell, 2003).
The tree of life	The tree of life is an exercise based on the idea of using the tree as a metaphor to tell stories about one's life. Participants are invited to think of a tree, its roots, trunk, branches, leaves, etc., and imagine that each part of the tree represents something about their life (Dulwich Centre, 2009).

Source: Adapted from "The Social Work Graduate."

Muslim clients, leading to a disconnect between postmodernism and spirituality. This disconnect can result in a "spiritual groundlessness and yearning for connection" (Moules, 2000, p. 233). However, its flexible framework allows for modification and integration with Islāmic beliefs, values, and cultural context. The congruence between narrative therapy and Islāmic teachings depends on how its principles and techniques are adapted. Nonetheless, certain assumptions and practices within narrative therapy may not align with Islāmic beliefs and practices. In Islām, there are sacred narratives based on six core beliefs that unite most Muslims and shape their interpretation of experiences and understanding of reality: (1) the reality of one God (*tawhīd*); (2) beliefs in the existence of angels (*malaikah*); (3) belief in holy books *(kutub)*; (4) belief in the prophets (*nubuwwah*); (5) belief in the Day of Judgement and the afterlife (*akhirah*); and (6) beliefs in predestination (*qadr*). These core beliefs is what unite most Muslims.

Narrative therapy and Islāmic doctrine diverge notably in their epistemological views. Narrative therapy asserts that knowledge is socially constructed, influenced by cultural and social factors (White & Epston, 1990), while Islāmic beliefs emphasise objective knowledge derived from divine revelation, independent of social constructions. While recognising societal influences on knowledge, Islām maintains a strong belief in absolute truth grounded in divine guidance through the Qur'ān and the *Sunnah*, asserting that objective knowledge is inherently linked to divine revelation. Islāmic epistemology maintains that objective knowledge is not solely constructed by society but is inherently linked to divine guidance. Islāmic beliefs serve as a framework for interpreting knowledge within specific social and cultural contexts, with the Qur'ān considered the ultimate truth and guide for humanity. Muslims are obligated to align their beliefs and actions with these objective truths to maintain connection with Allāh In narrative therapy, Muslim clients would adhere to Islāmic virtues, morality, and good character, aligning with Qur'ānic teachings. Therapists, both Islāmic and non-Islāmic, must consider the emphasis on objective truth in Islām, ensuring alignment with the Qur'ān and the *Sunnah* in therapy to address the profound impact of Islāmic principles on individuals' worldview and well-being.

The misalignment between the philosophical assumptions of narrative therapy and the Islāmic worldview is an important consideration, particularly for Muslim clients and therapists. The individual's experiential worldview, integral to narrative therapy's framing system, represents a "story within a story". This highlights the significance of recognising the client's unique lens shaped by religious, social, cultural, political, and historical contexts, particularly for Muslim clients and therapists. Al-Attas (2001) emphasises that from an Islāmic perspective, worldview constitutes a vision of reality and truth (*ru'yat al-Islām li al-wujud*), encompassing both this life and the hereafter, resulting in a duality of worldviews. Effective therapy requires a shared worldview between client and therapist, enhancing interventions' success (Blow et al., 2012, p. 13). Therapists demonstrating self-awareness of their own and their clients' worldviews can better empathise with Muslim clients' experiences and address their issues and goals.

Understanding clients through their universal, group, and individual identities, facilitated by worldview, is crucial in psychotherapy and counselling (Sue & Sue, 2012). Research suggests ethnic minority clients prefer ethnically similar therapists (Coleman et al., 1995). For Muslim clients, narrative therapy based on an Islāmic worldview can be effective with cultural sensitivity, avoiding imposition of conflicting values or Eurocentric values. Therapists should respect the Islāmic worldview, understand religious practices based on the Qur'ān and *Sunnah*, employ models like cultural empathy (Ibrahim, 1991), and actively support clients' beliefs, which can be challenging for non-Muslim therapists.

A notable divergence between narrative therapy and Islāmic principles is evident in their contrasting views on individual autonomy and the role of divine will. Narrative therapy emphasises individual autonomy, viewing clients as authors of their own stories with personal agency to create change. On the contrary, Islāmic principles acknowledge individual free will and responsibility for choices and actions but emphasise the limits of human agency, subjecting autonomy to the divine will and decree (*al-qadaa' wa'l-qadr*). This conflict highlights the disparity between narrative therapy's emphasis on individual autonomy and Islām's belief in the decisive influence of divine will on human actions. Allāh says in the Qur'ân,

قُل لَّن يُصِيبَنَآ إِلَّا مَا كَتَبَ ٱللَّهُ لَنَا هُوَ مَوْلَىٰنَا ۚ وَعَلَى ٱللَّهِ فَلْيَتَوَكَّلِ ٱلْمُؤْمِنُونَ

- *Say, "Never will we be struck except by what God has decreed for us; He is our protector." And upon God let the believers rely.*
(interpretation of the meaning, At-Tawbah 9:51)

In Islāmic psychotherapy, the concept of individual autonomy and divine will and decree can coexist by integrating Islāmic principles into the therapeutic process. Islāmic therapists strive to strike a balance between recognising individual control over actions and surrendering to Allāh's plan. This involves understanding the connection between personal choices and the broader plan set by Allāh, emphasising the importance of seeking guidance and having complete trust (*tawakkul*) in Allāh.

A criticism of narrative therapy is that it encourages clients to focus on individual exploration of personal experiences, beliefs, and values without adequate consideration of their interconnectedness with God, family, and community. This self-focused approach can lead to family conflicts, especially when the client neglects familial impact. For Muslim clients, this limited family involvement contradicts Islāmic traditions valuing family.

This criticism is echoed in Hayward's statement (2019) that narrative therapy, like systemic therapies, does not prioritise family relationships. Instead, the approach places emphasis on individual psychology, as noted by Minuchin (1998). In Islāmic therapy, the family holds significant importance and serves as a sacred and continuous source of support for individuals. Families in Islām often exhibit strong bonds and involvement, contributing to individual well-being (Sabry & Vohra, 2013). Incorporating family into therapy is crucial for Islāmic therapists, ranging from gathering collateral information to active participation in therapy sessions. Islāmic therapists strike a balance between client self-focus and family involvement, aligning with therapeutic goals. This approach allows for exploring dominant narratives and co-constructing alternative narratives with support from both individual and familial relationships.

A significant disparity between narrative therapy and Islāmic principles lies in their treatment of spirituality and religious practices. Narrative therapy, rooted in Western culture, typically does not explicitly address spirituality or religion unless it is individually significant for the client, often emphasising individual spirituality and diverse beliefs. In contrast, Islāmic traditions closely integrate spirituality and religion, viewing them as complementary aspects of a Muslim's life. The terms "spirituality" and "religiosity" may not align neatly with Islāmic perspectives, as spirituality in Western culture emphasises individual beliefs, while Islām encompasses specific doctrines, practices, and rituals.

Islāmic psychotherapists recognise the interconnectedness of spirituality and religion in the lives of Muslim clients, a distinction crucial for therapy. Narrative therapists, despite striving for sensitivity to diverse beliefs, may inadvertently introduce cultural biases or generalisations due to their Eurocentric approach. They often lack the knowledge to explore how Islāmic beliefs and practices shape clients' narratives, values, and identities, and their worldviews may not align with those of Muslim clients. In contrast, Islāmic psychotherapists integrate spiritual approaches and interventions as integral to therapy, recognising the inseparable connection between spirituality and religion in the lives of Muslim individuals.

Narrative therapy and Islāmic traditions converge in their use of storytelling as a potent tool for shaping self-understanding and worldview. In narrative therapy, clients share their stories, reflect on experiences, and construct new narratives. Similarly, Islām deeply values storytelling, particularly through narratives in the Qur'ân and *Sunnah*, which offer moral lessons, a way of lifestyle and behaviours and spiritual principles. For Islāmic therapists using a narrative approach, the focus is on aligning personal narratives with Islāmic tradition, reflecting on life within the framework guided by the Qur'ân and the *Sunnah*. Metaphors serve as a point of congruence between narrative therapy and Islāmic traditions.

In narrative therapy, metaphors serve as creative tools to explore, challenge, and reshape narratives, helping clients construct more empowering stories about themselves. Sue et al. (2022) highlight the use of metaphoric statements and stories, enabling clients to develop personal images that imply therapeutic plans of action. Witztum et al. (1988) suggest that therapists use metaphoric statements and stories to allow clients to develop their own private and idiosyncratic images, implicitly conveying therapeutic plans of action, which can resolve clients' problems. In Islāmic traditions, metaphors are prevalent in the Qur'ân, conveying profound spiritual and moral concepts. Metaphors in the Qur'ân serve to capture complex ideas, make them more accessible, and stimulate deeper contemplation (*tafakkur and tadabbur*). Armstrong and Munro (2018) suggest that adherent Muslims possess a naturally metaphorical way of thinking that aligns with postmodern therapeutic skills and draws on past Qur'ânic solutions for contemporary problems. Islāmic psychotherapists can utilise the techniques of "metaphor therapy" (Ahammed, 2010) to address life's larger questions, serving as a persuasive device to strengthen Muslims' faith in God and convince disbelievers to believe in God.

Metaphors from the Qur'ân offer significant potential in Islāmic psychotherapy by fostering reflective cycles, contemplation, and insight, inspiring hope and resilience, facilitating emotional expression, and conveying profound spiritual truths. They bridge the gap between therapist and client, enhancing communication and understanding, while providing a symbolic framework for conceptualising clients' experiences and challenges. Suhadi (2011) emphasises that Islāmic psychotherapists using a narrative approach should be grounded in the study of the Qur'ân and its exegeses (*tafsir*), operating within their competence and scope of practice.

A contemplative-based approach to narrative therapy, as suggested by Blanton (2007), incorporates contemplative skills, metaphors, modified interventions, and broader views of reality and self, aligning well with Islāmic beliefs and practices. Badri (2018) addresses the neglect of the spiritual dimension in Western psychology and highlights Islāmic contemplation (*tafakkur*) as a potent tool connecting the mind, heart, and soul, defined as "a cognitive spiritual activity in which the rational mind, emotion, and spirit are combined" (Henzell-Thomas, 2018, p. xi). Islāmic healing through contemplation, as outlined by Badri (2018), involves reflecting on God, seeking solace, and healing psychological disorders seen as "sickness of the soul" (p. viii). This is a kind of Islāmic healing through an inner vision of God, the contemplation of visible signs of the Creator, and a focus on the understanding and acceptance of our mission in this life. Adapted tools for Muslims in narrative therapy include skills, values, and stories cards for young Muslims; the Life Certificate to honour lost loved ones (Dulwich Centre, 2022); and written prayers like the collect (Rundio & Wong, 2021). Attachment-focused narrative interventions are also available for Muslim religious couples (Karris & Katarena, 2019)

Conclusions

Narrative therapy can be an effective tool for the Islāmic psychotherapist working with Muslim clients when there is congruence between an Islāmic worldview and the underlying philosophical assumptions of the approach. In this context, the Qur'ān and *Sunnah* become integral components of the therapeutic process, aiding Muslim clients in deriving meaning and purpose in their lives. From a narrative therapy perspective, addressing behaviours conflicting with Islāmic jurisprudence (*Shar'iah*) requires the rewriting of narratives in alignment with Islāmic sacred teachings. While a dissonance exists between narrative therapy and the Islāmic worldview, particularly in the social construction of knowledge, Islāmic psychotherapists can still effectively utilise narrative therapy by understanding its underlying philosophical assumptions as these would enable them to "sanctify" the discipline, making it more reflective of how God continues to "be the healing force in all healing arts" (Hankle, 2016, p. 13). Hankle's (2016) observation is applicable to the Islāmic worldview. This understanding allows them to integrate the approach in a way that aligns with the Islāmic worldview, emphasising the role of God as the ultimate healing force.

References

Ackerman, C. E. (2017). *9 best narrative therapy techniques & worksheets* [+*PDF*]. Retrieved January 4, 2024, from https://positivepsychology.com/narrative-therapy/.
Adams, M. (2013). *A concise introduction to existential counselling*. Sage Publications.
Ahammed, S. (2010). Applying Qur'ânic metaphors in counseling. *International Journal of Advanced Counselling, 32*, 248–255. https://doi.org/10.1007/s10447-010-9104-2.

AIPC. (2010). *Narrative therapy*. Retrieved January 4, 2024, from www.aipc.net.au/articles/narrative-therapy/#:~:text=The%20most%20important%20aspect%20of%20 Narrative%20Therapy%20is,the%20therapeutic%20relationship%2C%20in%20 particular%20the%20therapist%E2%80%99s%20attitudes.

Al-Attas, M. N. (2001). *Prolegomena to the metaphysics of Islām: An exposition of the fundamental elements of the worldview of Islām* (pp. 252–256). ISTAC.

Armstrong, A. M., & Munro, l. (2018). Insider/outsider: A Muslim woman's adventure practicing 'alongside' narrative therapy. *Australian and New Zealand Journal of Family Therapy, 39*(2), 174–185.

Badri, M. (2018). *Contemplation: An Islāmic psychospiritual study*. The International Institute of Islāmic Thought.

Beaudoin, M., Moersch, M., & Evare, B. S. (2016). The effectiveness of narrative therapy with children's social and emotional skill development: An empirical study of 813 problem-solving stories. *Journal of Systemic Therapies, 35*(3), 42–59.

Bennet, T. (2018). *Externalization narrative therapy: Separate yourself from your problems*. Retrieved January 4, 2024, from https://thriveworks.com/blog/externalizing-problem-counseling-technique-narrative-therapy/.

Bishop, W. H. (2011). *Narrative therapy summary*. Retrieved January 4, 2024, from www.thoughtsfromatherapist.com/2011/05/16/narrative-therapy-summary/.

Blanton, G. P. (2007). Adding silence to stories: Narrative therapy and contemplation. *Contemporary Family Therapy, 29*, 211–221.

Blow, A. J., Davis, S. D., & Sprenkle, D. H. (2012). Therapist-worldview matching: Not as important as matching to clients. *Journal of Marital and Family Therapy, 38*(1s), 13–17.

Carey, M., & Russell, S. (2003). Outsider-witness practices: Some answers to commonly asked questions. *The International Journal of Narrative Therapy and Community Work, 2003*, 3.

Cashin, A., Browne, G., Bradbury, J., & Mulder, A. (2013). The effectiveness of narrative therapy with young people with autism. *Journal of Child and Adolescent Psychiatric Nursing, 26*(1), 32–41.

Chimpén-López, C. A., Pacheco, M., Pretel-Luque, T., Bastón, R., & Chimpén-Sagrado, D. (2021). The couple's tree of life: Promoting and protecting relational identity. *Family Process*, 1–14. https://doi.org/10.1111/famp.12727.

Chow, E. O. W., & Fung, S. F. (2021). Narrative group intervention to rediscover life wisdom among Hong Kong Chinese older adults: A single-blind randomized waitlist-controlled trial. *Innovation in Aging, 5*(3), igab027. https://doi.org/10.1093/geroni/igab027

Coleman, H., Wampold, B. E., & Casali, S. L. (1995). Ethnic minorities' ratings of ethnically similar and European American counselors: A meta-analysis. *Journal of Counseling Psychology, 42*(1), 55–64. https://doi.org/10.1037/0022-0167.42.1.55.

van Deurzen, E. V. (2012). *Existential counselling and psychotherapy in practice* (Revised 3rd ed.). Sage Publications.

van Deurzen, E. (2015). Phenomenological therapy. In E. Neukrug (Ed.), *The SAGE encyclopedia of theory in counseling and psychotherapy* (Vol. 2, pp. 772–776). Sage Publication.

van Deurzen, E., & Adams, M. (2016). *Skills in existential counselling & psychotherapy*. Sage Publications.

Dulwich Centre. (2009). The "tree of life" in a community context. *CONTEXT, 105*, 50–54. Retrieved January 4, 2024, from https://dulwichcentre.com.au/wp-content/uploads/2014/01/tree-of-life-community-context.pdf.

Dulwich Centre. (2022). *Muslim contributions to narrative therapy and community work*. Retrieved January 4, 2024, from https://dulwichcentre.com.au/muslim-contributions-to-narrative-therapy-and-community-work/.

Duvall, J., & Young, K. (2017). Narrative family therapy. In J. Lebow, A. Chambers, & D. Breunlin (Eds.), *Encyclopedia of couple and family therapy*. Springer.

Erbes, C. R., Stillman, J. R., Wieling, E., Bera, W., & Leskela, J. (2014). A pilot examination of the use of narrative therapy with individuals diagnosed with PTSD. *Journal of Traumatic Stress*, *27*(6), 730–733. https://doi.org/10.1002/jts.21966.

Fatahi, N., Bardideh, M., Talebi Bahman Biglou, R., Gholami, Z., Akbarinejad, M., & Hoshyar, N. (2021). The effectiveness of narrative therapy on reducing behavior problems and improving self-perception in students. *Quarterly Journal of Child Mental Health*, *7*(4), 297–312. http://dx.doi.org/10.52547/jcmh.7.4.19.

Ghavibazou, E., Hosseinian, S., & Abdollahi, A. (2020). Effectiveness of narrative therapy on communication patterns for women experiencing low marital satisfaction. *Australian & New Zealand Journal of Family Therapy*, *41*(2), 195–207.

Gonçalves, M. M., Matos, M., & Santos, A. (2009). Narrative therapy and the nature of "innovative moments" in the construction of change. *Journal of Constructivist Psychology*, *22*(1), 1–23.

Goolishian, H. A., & Anderson, H. (1992). Strategy and intervention versus nonintervention. *Journal of Marital and Family Therapy*, *18(1)*, *5–15*.

Hankle, D. D. (2016). Christian worldview and the use of narrative therapy in the Christian counseling setting. *Journal of Christian Healing*, *32*(1), 5–24.

Harms, L. (2007). *Working with people: Communication skills for reflective practice*. Oxford University Press.

Hayward, M. (2019). *Critiques of narrative therapy: A personal response*. Retrieved January 4, 2024, from https://theint.co.uk/wp-content/uploads/2019/02/critiques-of-narrative-therapy-a-personal-response.pdf.

Henzell-Thomas, J. (2018). Introduction. Cited in Badri, M. (2000). *Contemplation: An Islāmic Psychospiritual Study*. The International Institute of Islāmic Thought.

Iacovou, S., & Weixel-Dixon, K. (2015). *Existential therapy: 100 Key points and techniques*. Routledge.

Ibrahim, F. A. (1991). Contribution of cultural worldview to generic counseling and development. *Journal of Counselling and Development*, *70*(1), 13–19.

Karris, M., & Katarena, A. (2019). Religious couples re-storying after infidelity: Using narrative therapy interventions with a focus on attachment. *Counseling and Family Therapy Scholarship Review*, *2*(1), 5.

Kelley, P. (2011). Narrative theory and social work treatment. In F. Turner (Ed.), *Social work treatment: Interlocking theoretical approaches* (5th ed., pp. 315–326). Oxford University Press.

Laube, J. J. (1998). Therapist role in narrative group psychotherapy. *Group*, *22*(4), 227–243.

Lonne, B. (2015). *Narrative therapy practice*. Slides from lecture at University of New England, Armidale, Australia in the unit HSSW410 – Social Work Interventions – Models and Skills. Cited in The Social Work Graduate. *Resources for social work graduates. Various social work practice approaches*. Retrieved January 4, 2024, from www.thesocialworkgraduate.com/post/narrative-therapy.

Looyeh, M. Y., Kamali, K., Ghasemi, A., & Tonawanik, P. (2014). Treating social phobia in children through group narrative therapy. *The Arts in Psychotherapy*, *41*(1), 16–20.

Looyeh, M. Y., Kamali, K., & Shafieian, R. (2012). An exploratory study of the effectiveness of group narrative therapy on the school behavior of girls with attention-deficit/hyperactivity symptoms. *Archives of Psychiatric Nursing*, *26*(5), 404–410.

Minuchin, S. (1998). Where is the family in narrative family therapy? *Journal of Marital and Family Therapy*, *24*(4), 397–403.

Moules, N. (2000). Postmodernism and the sacred: Reclaiming connection in our greater-than-human worlds. *Journal of Marital and Family Therapy*, *26*(2), 229–240. https://doi.org/10.1111/j.1752-0606.2000.tb00292.x.

O'Connor, I., Wilson, J., Setterlund, D., & Hughes, M. (2008). *Social work and human service practice* (5th ed.). Pearson Education.

Parry, A., & Doan, R. E. (1994). *Story re-visions: Narrative therapy in the postmodern world.* Guilford Press.

Payne, M. (2006). *Narrative therapy: An introduction for counsellors* (2nd ed.). Sage Publications.

Rundio, M. A., & Wong, A. G. (2021). Writing and praying collects as an intervention in narrative therapy. *Contemporary Family Therapy, 44*, 312–317. https://doi.org/10.1007/s10591-021-09586-6.

Sabry, W. M., & Vohra, A. (2013). Role of Islām in the management of psychiatric disorders. *Indian Journal of Psychiatry, 55*(Suppl 2), S205–S214.

Shakeri, J., Ahmadi, S. M., Maleki, F., Hesami, M. R., Parsa Moghadam, A., Ahmadzade, A., Shirzadi, M.; & Elahi, A. (2020). Effectiveness of group narrative therapy on depression, quality of life, and anxiety in people with amphetamine addiction: A randomized clinical trial. *Iran Journal of Medical Science, 45*(2), 91–99.

Shapiro, J., & Ross, V. (2002). Applications of narrative theory and therapy to the practice of family medicine. *Family Medicine, 34*(2), 96–100.

Stillman, J. R. (2016). How narrative therapy principles inform practice for therapists and helping professionals: Illustrated with vignettes. In V. Dickerson (Ed.), *Poststructural and narrative thinking in family therapy* (AFTA SpringerBriefs in Family Therapy). Springer. https://doi.org/10.1007/978-3-319-31490-7_6.

Sue, D. W., & Sue, D. (2012). *Counseling the culturally diverse: Theory and practice*. John Wiley & Sons.

Sue, D. W., Sue, D., Neville, H. A., & Smith, L. (2022). C*ounseling the culturally diverse: Theory and practice*. John Wiley & Sons.

Suhadi, J. (2011). Metaphor as a stylistic device of Islāmic teaching. *MIQOT: Jurnal Ilmu-ilmu KeIslāman, 35*(1), 187–202.

The Social Work Graduate. *Resources for social work graduates. Various social work practice approaches*. Retrieved January 4, 2024, from www.thesocialworkgraduate.com/post/narrative-therapy.

Vinney, C. (2019). *What is narrative therapy? Definition and techniques*. Retrieved January 4, 2024, from www.thoughtco.com/narrative-therapy-4769048.

Vromans, L., & Schweitzer, R. D. (2015). *Narrative therapy. Encyclopedia of clinical psychology*. John Wiley & Sons. Retrieved January 4, 2024, from https://doi.org/10.1002/9781118625392.wbecp215.

Wallis, J., Burns, J., & Capdevila, R. (2011). What is narrative therapy and what is it not?: The usefulness of Q methodology to explore accounts of White and Epston's (1990) approach to narrative therapy. *Clinical Psychology & Psychotherapy, 18*(6), 486–497.

White, M., & Epston, D. (1990). *Narrative means to therapeutic ends*. W. W. Norton & Company.

Witztum, E., van der Hart, O., & Friedman, B. (1988). The use of metaphors in psychotherapy. *Journal of Contemporary Psychotherapy, 18*, 270–290.

www.merriam-webster.com. Metaphor: Definition & Meaning. *Merriam-Webster*. Retrieved January 4, 2024, from www.merriam-webster.com/dictionary/metaphor.

12
HOPE THERAPY
Finding strength in faith

Introduction

In Islāmic psychotherapy, hope plays a fundamental role as a guiding force for healing and recovery, providing individuals with strength during trials and encouraging them to pursue achievable goals. Drawing from positive psychology, hope is characterised by an optimistic mindset, guiding individuals towards challenging yet attainable objectives. The hope theory asserts that much of human behaviour is goal directed (Rand & Cheavens, 2009). Integrating solution-focused, narrative, and cognitive-behavioural interventions, hope therapy utilises multiple intervention strategies (Lopez et al., 2000, p. 123). Evaluations spanning three decades have affirmed the correlation between hope and successful outcomes (Cheavens & Whitted, 2023). This chapter explores Snyder's assumptions, principles, techniques, and benefits of hope therapy, examining it from an Islāmic perspective and its application in Islāmic psychotherapy.

Hope and hope therapy

Hope is understood as a combination of beliefs, feelings, and actions occurring under specific circumstances, as described by Bruininks (2012). Snyder (2000, p. 8) defines hope as a positive motivational state derived from a sense of successful agency (goal-directed energy) and pathways (planning to meet goals), highlighting the interaction between goal-directed activities and clear strategies. Cheavens and Stigen (2012) further elaborate on hope's components: goals, pathways thinking (ability to identify and develop routes to goals), and agency thinking (belief in one's ability to successfully use pathways to reach goals).

Snyder's theory of hope, prominent in positive psychology, emphasises internal sources, experiences, and effects of hope (Snyder, 2000, p. 8). It highlights a

DOI: 10.4324/9781003453413-14

positive response to uncertainty as important factors in hope development, comprising both cognitive and affective components. While it emphasises actions and prior experiences, it neglects social factors, hope, and psychological processes beyond desires (Snyder, 2002). He asserts that there are at least three aspects of hope to which people can relate, namely: having clear thinking; having strategies to attain the goals; and to actually achieve these goals you need to have the readiness or motivation to attain the goals. Snyder (2002) presented several key assumptions and principles that underpin hope therapy. He suggested that therapists typically "hold the following assumptions about hope, human nature, and the change process" (Snyder, 2002, p. 225), and these assumptions lay the groundwork for understanding how hope can be challenged and applied in a therapeutic setting (Figure 12.1).

- Hope is not merely an emotion but also a cognitive process based on one's ability to achieve specific goals.
- Hope consists of two components, pathways thinking (routes or strategies to achieve a goal) and agency thinking (driving motivation to reach those goals).
- Hope is goal-directed. This means that hope is focused on achieving specific goals or desired outcomes by having a target or a destination in mind.
- Hope can be actively nurtured and enhanced to strengthen and develop positive thinking and cognitive set.

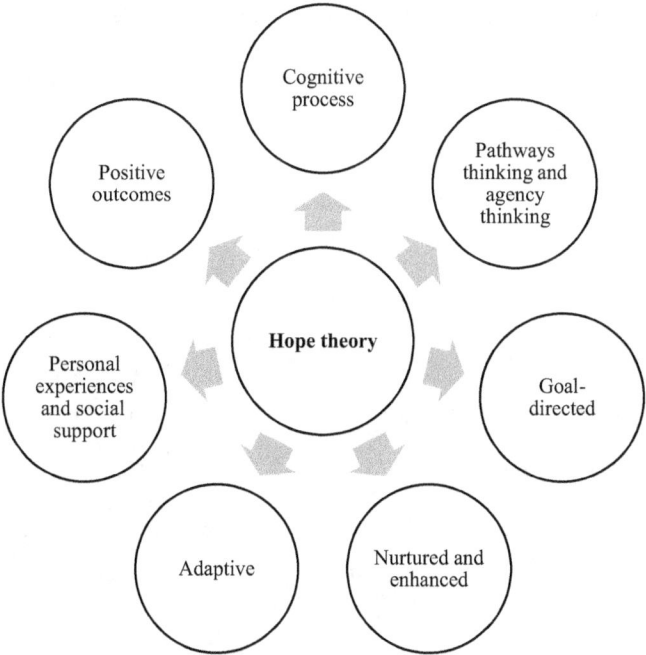

FIGURE 12.1 Snyder's assumptions of hope theory.

188 The intersection of Islām and psychotherapy

- Hope is an adaptive trait that enable individuals to cope with challenges, setbacks, trials, and tribulations to maintain a sense of purpose and resilience.
- Hope is influenced by experiences and social support. Both personal life experiences such as success and failure and social support can have impacts on a person's level of hope.
- Hope is associated with various positive outcomes. It is positively related to life satisfaction and acts as a buffer against negative life events (Valle et al., 2006); contributes to better health, well-being, and lower psychological distress (Greiner et al., 2005; Kylma, 2005); improves physical and mental health outcomes (Scheier & Carver, 1985). Cognitive and emotional hope are strongly related to subjective well-being.

(Pleeging et al., 2021)

Snyder's hope theory emphasises two essential elements for goal progress: pathways thinking and agency thinking. Pathways thinking involves having a clear plan or strategy to achieve goals, serving as a roadmap to overcome challenges and identify paths towards objectives. Agency thinking focuses on self-belief, confidence, and skills to positively influence life, akin to an external locus of control empowering individuals to make informed decisions for positive outcomes. The theory underlines the cyclical relationship between agency and pathways thinking, with the development of more routes leading to positive emotions (Snyder, 2000, 2002) (see Figure 12.2).

Questions to ask in dealing with pathways thinking include

- What is happening in your life right now that you would like to change or improve?

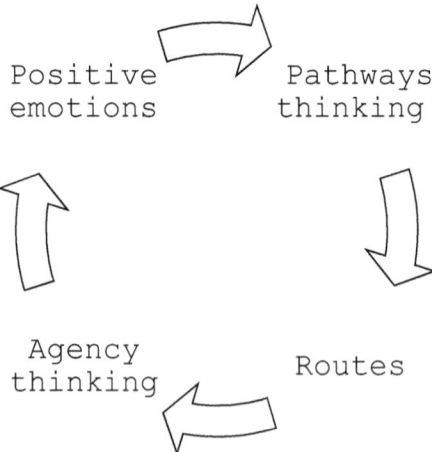

FIGURE 12.2 The cyclical relationship between pathways and agency thinking.

- What specific aims or goals do you have?
- Are there any external factors or circumstances that are creating challenges or barriers in your pathway towards your goals?

There are also specific questions to ask in dealing with agency thinking:

- What specific strengths, skills, or qualities do you possess that can support you in achieving your goals?
- What resources do you have or support networks that have access to assist you in accomplishing your goals?
- What specific actions have you taken in the past that resulted in positive outcomes in similar situations?

Snyder's groundbreaking contributions to hope theory and hope therapy have greatly deepened our understanding of hope as a cognitive process and its capacity to enhance individual well-being and resilience. The key assumptions outlined by Snyder offer therapists and researchers a valuable framework for integrating hope-based interventions into their practices, aiming to cultivate optimistic and positive outcomes (Snyder et al., 1991). Additionally, Snyder et al. (1991) introduced the Adult Dispositional Hope Scale, designed for assessing hope in individuals aged 15 and above.

Basic principles and process of hope therapy

Hope therapy, as conceptualised by Charles Snyder and outlined by Kirmani et al. (2016), is founded on several key principles. It considers the individual's disposition, current emotional state, and situational context, emphasising empathy, rapport building, and trust between therapist and client. The therapy is a sudden, semi-structured intervention focusing on cognitive, behavioural, and emotional changes, highlighting clients' goals, possibilities, and past successes rather than dwelling on issues or failures. The therapist plays an active, directive role, guiding the client to develop a new framework for change while recognising the client as the expert in their situation. Hope therapy is psychoeducational, empowering clients to navigate challenges in pursuing their goals independently. Hope therapy employs a collaborative approach where client and therapist set realistic goals and explore ways to cultivate motivation. It involves developing new strategies to overcome challenges, focusing initially on altering cognitive patterns to foster more hopeful thoughts. This approach integrates techniques from various therapy models, including solution-focused, narrative, and cognitive–behavioural methods.

The process of hope therapy involves two components of instilling hope and the two components of enhancing hope (Lopez et al., 2000); instilling hope incorporates hope finding and hope bonding, and enhancing hope entails hope enhancing and hope reminding. Hope finding involves helping the client to identify and explore sources of hope through storytelling or narratives. The aim is to help the client in identifying current sources of hope that can act as a resource for their challenges. For example, the therapist invites the patient to discuss their own life experiences, emphasising any instances of resilience, success, or personal development. The client can identify occasions when hope significantly influenced their past experiences by thinking back on them.

The goal of hope bonding is to build and strengthen supportive relationships. The aim is to develop bonds with others who can provide support and encouragement. These interpersonal connections can significantly enhance one's sense of hope. The therapist enables the individual to identify and strengthen their support network, whether it's through friends, family, or support groups.

The hope-enhancing stage, according to Lopez et al. (2000), is all about "generating goal thoughts, creating effective pathways leading to goal attainment, and maintaining agency thoughts" (p. 137). Basically, the therapist works with the patient to set reasonable goals, develop action plans, and come up with techniques to reach them. To maintain and strengthen hope over time, the therapist may employ a variety of strategies, including visual imagery, affirmations, pathways checklists, and keeping a gratitude journal.

Hope reminding, as described by Kirmani et al. (2016), involves using reminders about desired goals, barriers, and challenges to help clients stay focused and maintain hope. Interventions in this phase include reviewing personal hope stories, finding a "hope buddy" for assistance or reinforcement, reflecting on successful goal pursuits, and completing automatic thought records to confront barrier thoughts (p. 42). In summary, the process of hope therapy involves assisting a client in the discovery of hope within themselves, relationship bonding and trust with others for support, enhancing that hope with goals and plans, and then using reminders to keep the hope alive and developing.

Hope therapy: an Islāmic perspective

In Islāmic literature, the concept of hope *(raja)* is derived from the Qur'ân and *hādīths*, emphasising themes of reliance on God, optimism, and His mercy and guidance (Wahyuna & Fitriana, 2020). Believers are encouraged to trust in Allāh's benevolence and remain positive in adversity, with hope lying in His mercy and forgiveness (Sudirman et al., 2019). Through an Islāmic lens, hope therapy complements psychospiritual interventions by encouraging individuals to integrate spiritual beliefs and practices, fostering absolute trust in Allāh *(tawakkul)* for cultivating hope, resilience, and well-being. Clients seeking this approach are encouraged to work with Islāmic psychotherapists to integrate these principles into therapy.

Muslims derive hope from their belief in Allāh's boundless kindness and compassion, finding solace in His ever-present guidance and trusting in His wisdom during challenges. Contemplating Allāh's attributes of forgiveness and mercy reinforces hope, while sincere supplication (*du'ah*) strengthens hope by seeking divine guidance and assistance. Despite worldly adversities, Muslims find hope in the belief in the eternal Hereafter, understanding that ultimate reward and happiness lie beyond this temporary life. Islām encourages trust in Allāh's benevolence (*tawakkul*), aligning with the principles of hope therapy (references not provided).

Islāmic beliefs emphasise the importance of patience (*sabr*) during challenging times. Hope therapy aligns with this by recognising patience as a crucial element of hope, enabling individuals to persevere through difficulties while maintaining optimism. Islāmic approaches also highlight positive thinking (*husn al-zann*), believing that Allāh's plan is ultimately for their benefit and trusting in His wisdom. This positive mindset, parallel to hope therapy, directs attention to the positive aspects of life rather than dwelling on negativity. Compassion and forgiveness are integral in Islāmic teachings, promoting kindness towards oneself and others, along with the forgiveness of those who have caused harm. These principles resonate with hope therapy, emphasising self-compassion and letting go of past grievances to foster hope, resilience, and positive relationships. These shared aspects form the Islāmic understanding of hope, contributing to optimism, spiritual strength, and resilience in the face of challenges.

Hope in the Qur'ân

Muslims always remember that we were sent to this world to be tested with trials and tribulations, also known as tests and hardships. This is a recurring theme in the Qur'ân and presents opportunities for individuals to demonstrate patience, faith, and trust in Allāh (God). Allāh says in the Qur'ân,

وَلَنَبْلُوَنَّكُم بِشَىْءٍ مِّنَ ٱلْخَوْفِ وَٱلْجُوعِ وَنَقْصٍ مِّنَ ٱلْأَمْوَٰلِ وَٱلْأَنفُسِ وَٱلثَّمَرَٰتِ ۗ وَبَشِّرِ ٱلصَّـٰبِرِينَ

- *And We will surely test you with something of fear and hunger and a loss of wealth and lives and fruits but give good tidings to the patient.*
(Al-Baqarah 2:155, interpretation of the meaning)

According to the exegesis of Ibn Kathir (2000), Allāh informs us that He tests and tries His servants, sometimes with bounty and sometimes with affliction (fear and hunger; losing loved ones to death, etc.). This verse acknowledges that trials and hardships are a part of Muslims' lives and encourages believers to remain patient during difficult times. Those who endure trials with patience and faith receive blessings and mercy from Allāh.

This is also reflected in Ibn al-Qayyim's statement that, "When Allāh tests you, it is never to destroy you. When He removes something in your possession, it is only in order to empty your hands for an even greater gift" (Ibn Qayyim Al-Jawziyah, 2017). This means that when Allāh tests you with trials and tribulations or takes something away from you, it is not to harm you or make your life worse; rather, it is like preparing you for a bigger and more wonderful gift in the future by removing something smaller or less important from your life. However, it is important to note that Allāh does not impose trials and hardships beyond anyone's capacity to endure. It reflects the concept of divine wisdom in testing individuals and serves as a source of comfort during challenging times. Allāh says in the Qur'ân,

رَبَّنَا وَلَا تُحَمِّلْنَا مَا لَا طَاقَةَ لَنَا بِهِ

- *Allāh does not burden a soul beyond that it can bear.*
(Al-Baqarah 2:286, interpretation of the meaning)

The Qur'ân contains numerous verses that offer guidance, encouragement, and reflections on hope. In contemporary times, hope frequently gives way to despair:

> Not because we do not have reason to hope, but because we are so engrossed and occupied in worldly affairs that we do not allow hope to bloom. We become the victim of despair and hopelessness when we find ourselves unable to move along with the fast pace of this world's affairs.
>
> *(Rassool & Khan, 2023, p. 8)*

However, in such a situation, it is those who have hope in God's mercy and a firm belief in God's promise that during difficult times, Allāh will provide relief and comfort. In other words, along with the challenges, there is always something positive that comes along either by purifying their sins or increasing their rewards in the afterlife. Allāh says in the Qur'ân,

فَإِنَّ مَعَ ٱلْعُسْرِ يُسْرًا
إِنَّ مَعَ ٱلْعُسْرِ يُسْرًا

- *Indeed, with hardship [will be] ease.*
- *Indeed, with hardship [will be] ease.*
(Ash-Sharh 94:5–6, interpretation of the meaning)

These two verses reassure us that with every difficulty, relief is guaranteed. This repetition further emphasises the message that hardship is always followed by relief and that every hardship serves a purpose. Calamity may either, with Allāh blessing and mercy, wipe away a person's sins or elevate their status in paradise. Understanding the two verses can provide solace and hope to individuals who are going through challenges or experiencing difficulties in life. This assurance from Allāh the Almighty helps individuals find strength and motivation to overcome their struggles.

The Qur'ān has many other verses that that reflects the Islāmic view about hope (Sumer, 2021). These verses are intended to give hope to believers who may be lost or undergoing hardships:

- *And whosoever fears Allāh . . . He will make for him a way out. Allāh will provide for him from where he does not expect.*

  (Al-Talaq 65:2–3)

- *Allāh will bring about, after hardship, ease [i.e. relief].*

  (Al-Talaq 65:7)

- *Say, O My servants, you who have transgressed against themselves [by sinning], do not despair of the mercy of Allāh. Indeed, Allāh forgives all sins. Indeed, it is He who is the Forgiving, the Most Merciful.*

  (Az-Zumar 39:53)

- *My sons, go and find out about Joseph and his brother and despair not of relief from Allāh. Indeed, no one despairs of relief from Allāh except the disbelieving people.*

  (Yusuf 12:87)

- *Or do you think that you will enter paradise without such [trials] has not yet come to you as came to those who passed on before you? They were touched by poverty and hardship and were shaken until [even their] messenger and those who believed with hm said, "When is the help from Allāh?" Unquestionably, the help of Allāh is near.*

  (Al-Baqarah 2:214)

- *There has certainly been for you in the Messenger of Allāh an excellent pattern for anyone whose hope in Allāh and the last day and [who] remembers Allāh often.*

  (Al-Azab 33:21)

- *So be not of the despairing.*

  (Al-Hijr 15:55)

- *Wealth and children are [but] adornment of the worldly life. But the enduring good deeds are better to your Lord for reward and better for [one's] hope.*

  (Al-Kahf 18:46)

- *Allāh is with you and will never deprive you of [the reward of] your deeds.*

  (Muhammad 47:35)

- *So do no weaken and do not grieve, and you will be superior if you are true believers.*

  (Ali-'Imran 3:139)

- *And involve Him in fear and aspiration* [hope]. *Indeed, the mercy of Allāh is near to the doers of good.*

  (Al-A'rāf 7:56)

- *So, whoever would hope for the meeting with his Lord – let him do righteous work and not associate in the worship of his Lord anyone.*

  (Al-Kahf 18:110)

- *Indeed, I am near.*

  (Al-Baqarah 2:186)

These highlighted Qur'ânic verses emphasise the virtue of hope in Islām. They highlight the importance of maintaining faith in Allāh's mercy and forgiveness, even in the face of sins. Even if we have committed several sins, Allāh forgives all sins save those involving the association of partners with Him (*shrik*). The verses stress that losing hope in Allāh's kindness is akin to rejecting Him. Despite life's challenges, believers are encouraged to persevere, as Allāh, the Merciful, believes in their potential to overcome difficulties. The trials on the path to paradise are seen as tests, reinforcing the significance of unwavering belief in God's plan, patience in adversity, and reliance on Allāh's mercy and guidance.

Hadīths on hope

Hope is a concept that is encouraged and reflected in various *hadīths* in Islāmic tradition. Here are some selected *hadīths* that emphasise the importance of hope. It was narrated from Anas (may Allāh be pleased with him) that the Prophet (ﷺ) entered upon a young man who was dying and said, "How do you feel?" He said, "I have hope in Allāh, O Messenger of Allāh, but I fear my sins." The Messenger of Allāh (ﷺ) said, "These two things (hope and fear) do not coexist in the heart of a person in a situation like this, but Allāh will give him that which he hopes for and keep him safe from that which he fears" (Ibn Majah (a)). As narrated by Abu Hurayrah (may Allāh be pleased with him), "I heard Allāh's Messenger (ﷺ) saying, 'The heart of an old man remains young in two respects, i.e. his love for the world (its wealth, amusements and luxuries) and his incessant hope'" (Bukhârî (a)). Anas bin Malik narrated the Messenger of Allāh (ﷺ) as saying, "'This is the son of Adam, and this is his life span at his neck,' then He spread His hand in front of him and said, 'And there is his hope'" (Ibn Majah (b)).

In another *hadīth*, Anas reported God's Messenger (ﷺ) as saying, "Seek the time in which hope is placed on Friday from after the afternoon prayer till sunset" (Tirmidhi (a)). Abu Hurayrah (may Allāh be pleased with him) reported the Messenger of Allāh (ﷺ) as saying, "if a thorn pricks a Muslim in this world and he hopes for the reward against it, then Allāh forgives him his sins on the day of Resurrection" (Al-Adab Al-Mufrad). On the authority of Anas (may Allāh be pleased with him),

> I [Anas] heard the Messenger of Allāh (ﷺ) say, "Allāh the Almighty has said, 'O Son of Adam, as long as you invoke Me and ask of Me, I shall forgive you for what you have done, and I shall not mind. O Son of Adam, were your sins to reach the clouds of the sky and you then asked forgiveness from Me, I would forgive you. O Son of Adam, were you to come to Me with sins nearly as great as the Earth, and were you then to face Me, ascribing no partner to Me, I would bring you forgiveness nearly as great as it [too].'"
>
> *(Tirmidhi (b))*

Abu Dharr (may Allāh be pleased with him) reported, The Messenger of Allāh (ﷺ) said to me, "Do not belittle any good deed, even your meeting with your brother with a cheerful face" (Muslim (a)). Suhaib reported that Allāh's Messenger (ﷺ) said,

> Strange are the ways of a believer for there is good in every affair of his, and this is not the case with anyone else except in the case of a believer for if he has an occasion to feel delight, he thanks (God). Thus there is a good for him in it, and if he gets into trouble and shows resignation (and endures it patiently), there is a good for him in it.
>
> *(Muslim (b))*

These *hadīths* highlight the importance of hope, trust in Allāh, and positive attitudes in the life of a believer, offering guidance for maintaining optimism and resilience amid life's challenges. They instil hope by highlighting Allāh's immense mercy and power, encouraging trust (*tawakkul*) in Him (Hussain, 2011). *Hadīths* also emphasise the power of sincere prayers and repentance, reassuring believers of Allāh's readiness to forgive and the value of their good efforts. These *hadīths* highlight the importance of having a positive and optimistic outlook in life, and stress that looking at things with hope and a positive attitude is significant and valuable. summarise and keep references in text.

Islāmic-based hope therapy

Hope therapy, whether conventional or Islāmic-based, seeks to foster hope and resilience. Conventional hope therapy utilises psychological concepts and evidence-based interventions like positive thinking, goal setting, problem-solving, and social support. In contrast, Islāmic-based hope therapy integrates theological principles to provide individuals with a deeper sense of meaning and purpose through Islāmic teachings. Both approaches offer practical techniques for navigating challenges, cultivating optimism, and recognising the role of psychological variables in nurturing hope.

Islāmic-based therapy uniquely integrates Islāmic beliefs and spirituality into the hope-building process, aligning with Islāmic teachings that promote hope, positive attitudes, and optimism during challenges. Recognised for its potential to provide both spiritual and psychological benefits (Farhoush et al., 2021), this approach points out the significance of spirituality in influencing health outcomes. Hope serves as a buffer against sadness, anxiety, and other mental illnesses (Wahyuna & Fitriana, 2020).

Instilling hope in clients during psychotherapy has proven to be an effective approach for enhancing motivation and willpower towards positive outcomes throughout the therapeutic process (Rassool & Khan, 2023). Islāmic-based hope therapy comprises two core components: spiritual guidance and psychological interventions. The spiritual dimension focuses on deepening one's connection with God, recognising Him as the ultimate source of hope and comfort. Encouraging reliance on Allāh and strengthening faith through prayer, this aspect provides solace during trials. Psychological techniques like cognitive–behavioural approaches, solution-focused brief therapy, narrative therapy, resilience-building activities, and coping strategies are integrated into Islāmic hope therapy. This holistic approach addresses both psychological and spiritual aspects of well-being, offering a comprehensive framework for instilling hope (Farhoush et al., 2021).

Islāmic-based hope therapy involves two components in the process of instilling hope and two components in enhancing hope within the Islāmic context (Lopez et al., 2000). Hope finding in this therapy aims to strengthen individuals' hope through their faith and connection with Allāh, utilising Qur'ān or *hādīths*. The Islāmic therapist assists clients in identifying sources of hope by linking personal experiences to relevant Qur'ān or *hādīth* teachings that promote resilience and trust in Allāh's plan. Regular *salah* (prayer), *tawakkul* (reliance on Allāh), and *dhikr* (remembering Allāh) are emphasised as practices to foster a direct connection with Allāh and enhance hope

Islāmic-based hope therapy recognises the importance of building and strengthening supportive relationships within the Muslim community (*ummah*). Islām places a strong emphasis on brotherhood and sisterhood among believers, encouraging the formation of supportive bonds. These relationships serve as a source of comfort, guidance, and assistance during challenging times, fostering hope and emotional support. The principle of mutual assistance (*ta'awun*) is critical, promoting the idea that believers should share each other's burdens. Building solid relationships within the community encourages reciprocal support, establishing a network or self-help group for individuals to rely on in times of need, grounded in moral and ethical ideals. Within this perspective, in following in the footsteps of Prophet Muhammad (ﷺ), ties with His companions exemplified hope bonding within an Islāmic context.

In hope enhancing, Islāmic-based hope therapy encourages individuals to reflect on the attributes of Allāh, fostering hope through cycles of reflection on His mercy and compassion. Instilling hope is based on the belief that Allāh is a constant guide and support through life's trials. Seeking knowledge from Islāmic sources, particularly the Qur'ân or *hādīths*, helps align perspectives with Allāh's guidance, enhancing hope by understanding life's meaning and purpose. Positive thinking and gratitude are promoted to encourage a hopeful mindset, focusing on blessings and expressing gratitude even in adversity. Coping strategies for hope enhancement include techniques like positive affirmations, problem-solving, and stress reduction through relaxation and Islāmic contemplation.

In Islāmic-based hope therapy, hope reminding involves constant reinforcement of set goals amid challenges faced. This includes reminders such as Qur'ânic verses, *hādīths*, supplications, or reflections on Allāh's guidance, emphasising the importance of faith, patience, and trust in Allāh's plan while pursuing goals. This approach serves as continuous spiritual and mental support, helping individuals maintain hope in the face of life's difficulties.

Conclusion

Islāmic-based hope therapy is a holistic approach to promoting hope and wellness, integrating Islāmic teachings, spirituality, and psychological dimensions. It encourages individuals to establish a profound connection with Allāh, have complete faith in the divine, and view life's challenges as opportunities for spiritual growth. This therapy emphasises Allāh's mercy, forgiveness, and guaranteed assistance as sources of hope. Additionally, it underlines the importance of social support within the Muslim community (*ummah*), providing individuals with a sense of belonging and encouragement. Islāmic-based hope therapy addresses spiritual, emotional, and psychological components, empowering individuals to find hope and thrive on their spiritual paths.

References

Al-Adab Al-Mufrad 507. In-book reference: Book 29, Hādīth 17. English translation: Book 29, Hādīth 507. https://sunnah.com/adab:507.

Bruininks, P. (2012). The unique psychology of hope. In G. Hopps & T. Hart (Eds.), *Art, imagination and Christian hope: Patterns of promise*. Routledge.

Bukhârî (a). *Sahih al-Bukhârî 6420*. In-book reference: Book 81, Hādīth 9. USC-MSA web (English) reference: Vol. 8, Book 76, Hādīth 429. https://sunnah.com/bukhari:6420

Cheavens, J. S., & Stigen, C. L. (2012). Hope theory and hope therapy. In N. M. Seel (Eds.), *Encyclopedia of the sciences of learning*. Springer. https://doi.org/10.1007/978-1-4419-1428-6_959

Cheavens, J. S., & Whitted, W. M. (2023). Hope therapy. *Current Opinion in Psychology*, 49, 101509. https://doi.org/10.1016/j.copsyc.2022.101509

Farhoush, M., Jahangirzade, M., Ahmadi, M., Hafezi, M., & Abianeh Morteza, K. (2021). Development of hope therapy package based on the Islāmic approach in the face of the psychological consequences of coronary heart disease. *Journal of Clinical Psychology, 13*(2), 201–211. https://doi.org/10.22075/jcp.2021.21443.1977

Greiner, K. A., Born, W., Nollen, N., & Ahluwalia, J. S. (2005). Knowledge and perceptions of colorectal cancer screening among urban African Americans. *Journal of General Internal Medicine, 20*, 977–983. https://doi.org/10.1007/s11606-005-0244-8

Hussain, F. A. (2011). *Therapy from the Quran and Ahādīth. A reference guide for character development*. Darussalam.

Ibn Kathir. (2000). *Tafsir ibn Kathir* (J. Abualrub, N. Khitab, H. Khitab, A. Walker, M. Al-Jibali, & S. Ayoub, Trans.). Darussalam Publishers and Distributors.

Ibn Majah (a). *Sunan Ibn Majah 4261*. In-book reference: Book 37, Hādīth 162. English translation: Vol. 5, Book 37, Hādīth 4261. Hasan (Darussalam). https://sunnah.com/ibnmajah:4261

Ibn Majah (b). *Sunan Ibn Majah 4232*. In-book reference: Book 37, Hādīth 133. English translation: Vol. 5, Book 37, Hādīth 4232. Sahih (Darussalam). https://sunnah.com/ibnmajah:4232

Ibn Qayyim Al-Jawziyah, M. (2017). *The sayings of Ibn Qayyim al-Jawziyyah* (I. Hawramani, Trans.). Independently Published. https://hawramani.com/the-sayings-of-ibn-qayyim-al-jawziyyah/

Kirmani, M. N., Sharma, P., & Jahan, F. (2016). Hope therapy in depression: A case report. *International Journal of Public Health Mental Health and Neurosciences, 2*(3), 39–44.

Kylma, J. (2005). Dynamics of hope in adults living with HIV/AIDS: A substantive theory. *Journal of Advanced Nursing, 52*(6), 620–630. https://doi.org/10.1111/j.1365-2648.2005.03633.x

Lopez, S. J., Floyd, R. K., Ulven, J. C., & Snyder, C. (2000). Hope therapy: Helping clients build a house of hope. In C. R. Snyder (Ed.), *Handbook of hope: Theory, measures, and application* (pp. 123–150). Academic Press.

Muslim (a). *Riyad as-Salihin 892*. In-book reference: Book 5, Hādīth 49. https://sunnah.com/riyadussalihin:892

Muslim (b). *Sahih Muslim 2999*. In-book reference: Book 55, Hādīth 82. USC-MSA web (English) reference: Book 42, Hādīth 7138. https://sunnah.com/muslim:2999

Pleeging, E., Burger, M., & van Exel, J. (2021). The relations between hope and subjective well-being: A literature overview and empirical analysis. *Applied Research Quality Life, 16*, 1019–1041. https://doi.org/10.1007/s11482-019-09802-4

Rand, K. L., & Cheavens, J. S. (2009). Hope theory. In S. J. Lopez & C. R. Snyder (Eds.), *Oxford handbook of positive psychology*. Oxford University Press, pp. 323–333.

Rassool, G. Hussein, & Khan, W. N. A. (2023). Hope in Islāmic psychotherapy. *Journal of Spirituality in Mental Health*, 2–15. https://doi.org/10.1080/19349637.2023.2207751

Scheier, M. F., & Carver, C. S. (1985). Optimism, coping, and health: Assessment and implications of generalized outcome expectancies. *Health Psychology, 4*(3), 219–247. https://doi.org/10.1037/0278-6133.4.3.219A

Snyder, C. R. (2000). *Handbook of hope: Theory, measures and applications*. Academic Press.

Snyder, C. R. (2002). Hope theory: Rainbows in the mind. *Psychological Inquiry, 13*(4), 249–275. https://doi.org/10.1207/S15327965PLI1304_01

Snyder, C. R., Harris, C., Anderson, J. R., Holleran, S. A., Irving, L. M., Sigmon, S. T., Yoshinobu, L., Gibb, J., Langelle, C., & Harney, P. (1991). The will and the ways: Development and validation of an individual-differences measure of hope. *Journal of Personality and Social Psychology, 60*, 570–585.

Sudirman, S. A., Suud, F. M., Rouzi, K. S., & Sari, D. P. (2019). Forgiveness and happiness through resilience. *Al-Qalb: Jurnal Psikologi Islām, 10*(2), 113–132. https://doi.org/10.15548/alqalb.v10i2.955

Sumer, S. S. (2021). *The basic values of Islām: Alphabetically listed with Islāmic references* (pp. 68–71). A. S. Noordeen.

Tirmidhi (a). *Mishkat al-Masabih 1360*. In-book reference: Book 4, Hādīth 766. https://sunnah.com/mishkat:1360.
Tirmidhi (b). *Reference: Hādīth 42, 40 Hādīth an-Nawawi*. A hasan Hādīth. https://sunnah.com/nawawi40:42.
Valle, M. F., Huebner, E. S., & Suldo, S. M. (2006). An analysis of hope as a psychological strength. *Journal of School Psychology*, *44*(5), 393–406. https://doi.org/10.1016/j.jsp.2006.03.005
Wahyuna, A. H., & Fitriana, S. (2020). The concept of hope in the western and eastern perspective. *International Journal of Islāmic Educational Psychology*, *1*(1). https://doi.org/10.18196/ijiep.1103

13
BEFORE THE *NIKAH*
Islāmic perspectives on pre-marital preparation

Introduction

In Islām, marriage is seen as a sacred union between a husband and wife based on love, compassion, and respect. between a husband and wife. According to Sheikh Muhammad Ibn al-'Uthaymin, marriage is not only a contractual agreement but also aims to foster a pious family and a sound society (cited in Mahmud, 2012). Islām strongly advocates for marriage, viewing it as beneficial on personal and collective levels; aligned with Islāmic principles; and contributing to emotional, spiritual, and physical well-being. Healthy marriages are emphasised in Islāmic teachings and societal values, promoting spiritual progress and God-consciousness (*taqwâ*) and thereby contributing to the overall well-being of individuals and society (ISPU, 2014).

Marriage holds profound importance in Islām, yet contemporary Muslim couples encounter various challenges stemming from evolving dynamics such as conflicts over gender roles, family expectations, cultural norms, and societal pressures. Escalating rates of marital problems and divorce globally among Muslim communities pose significant threats to families and impact the foundational structures of these communities. Divorce, considered a major life stressor, accentuates the urgency for marital education, family therapy, and related services to improve communication and problem-solving skills among couples. From an Islāmic perspective, it is important for families to minimise the risk of marital breakdown and divorce by adhering to methodologies outlined in the Qur'ân and the *Sunnah*. The chapter also focuses briefly on the challenges faced by Muslim couples in contemporary society and examine marriage preparation and the pre-marital Islāmic therapy approach.

DOI: 10.4324/9781003453413-15

Challenges in contemporary society

Contemporary Muslim couples encounter multifaceted challenges within their marriages due to changing dynamics in the modern world. The intersection of Islāmic ideals with cultural practices, especially in multi-ethnic societies, creates tensions and complications. In Western cultures, young Muslim couples often grapple with reconciling Islāmic principles with prevailing societal norms, resulting in conflicts between traditional cultural practices and Islāmic beliefs. These conflicts manifest in various aspects of marital life, including balancing tradition with modernity, managing interfaith and intercultural marriages, addressing communication barriers, negotiating family expectations and pressure, coping with financial strain, navigating parenting issues, bridging cultural and religious differences, and confronting gender dynamics and expectations. Moreover, broader societal misunderstandings of Islām, compounded by Islāmohobia, discrimination, and marginalisation, further aggravate the challenges faced by Muslim spouses, compelling them to overcome cultural expectations that may contradict their Islāmic values. This balancing act adds complexity to marital relationships, requiring couples to overcome diverse expectations while maintaining their faith.

Modern lifestyle and technological advancements pose barriers to effective communication between spouses. Busy schedules, domestic responsibilities, and other commitments limit the quality time available for meaningful communication. While technology enhances communication ease of access, it also introduces challenges. Reliance on digital tools like text messaging and social media may lead to misunderstandings and a lack of emotional depth. Multitasking during conversations can further diminish communication quality.

For Muslim couples, the absence of face-to -face interaction in the present era inhibits emotional connection and understanding, as physical presence and non-verbal cues are crucial elements often missing in digital exchanges. Traditional gender roles are often entrenched in Muslim cultures, with expectations regarding the roles and responsibilities of husbands and wives within the household. The traditional gender roles in Muslim communities often stem from cultural norms rather than religious commands. Pressure to conform to traditional gender roles can limit individual autonomy and lead to conflicts over decision-making, household duties, and expectations for childcare and domestic responsibilities. Achieving a harmonious balance between traditional gender roles and modern, egalitarian expectations poses a significant challenge for some Muslim women.

However, a new generation of Muslim couples is increasingly adopting equity and justice in partnerships. There is a growing emphasis on mutual respect, cooperation, and shared responsibility, allowing spouses to balance family tasks, decision-making, and financial responsibilities in a more egalitarian manner within the framework of *Shar'iah*. This is reflected in the following Qur'ânic verse:

تَعْتَدُواْ وَتَعَاوَنُواْ عَلَى ٱلْبِرِّ وَٱلتَّقْوَىٰ وَلَا تَعَاوَنُواْ عَلَى ٱلْإِثْمِ وَٱلْعُدْوَٰنِ ۚ

- *And cooperate in righteousness and piety, but do not cooperate in sin and transgression.*

(Al-Mā'idah 5:2, interpretation of the meaning)

This verse highlights the importance of the concept of mutual support (*ta'awun*) and encourage couples to work together harmoniously for the benefit of their family unit: "The *ta'awun* concept also has an equality with the concept of sharing. Sharing practices are practiced in human life" (Mazlan & Khairuldin, 2018).

Expectations and pressure within Muslim families can significantly impact marital relationships due to the strong emphasis on family ties and community cohesion in Islāmic culture. In many cultures, arranged marriages are common and sometimes expected. Family members may pressure individuals to marry someone chosen by their parents or elders, even if they prefer to pursue a love marriage. Arranged marriages in many Muslim cultures serve as a means to ensure compatibility, honour family traditions, and strengthen community bonds. However, the pressure to conform to these marital arrangements can result in a multitude of challenges for the individuals involved.

Many individuals may feel a lack of autonomy and control over one of the most crucial decisions of their lives, leading to feelings of powerlessness and resentment. Mismatched expectations regarding partners, relationship dynamics, and future goals can strain marital relationships, hindering the development of intimacy and mutual understanding. Despite efforts to ensure compatibility, differences in personality, values, and lifestyle choices may emerge, causing conflicts and dissatisfaction within the marriage.

It is important to note here that while arranged marriages are common in some Muslim cultures, they are not universal, and many Muslims, particularly in Western countries, choose love marriages based on mutual consent and compatibility with parental or significant others' approval. Attitudes towards arranged marriages are evolving, with increasing emphasis placed on individual choice, consent, and the importance of building healthy, fulfilling relationships based on mutual respect and understanding.

Muslim families often have specific expectations regarding the timing of marriage, particularly for their children. Pressure to marry at a certain age or stage in life can strain relationships if one or both partners feel rushed or unprepared for marriage. Families may prioritise cultural and religious compatibility when seeking a spouse for their children. However, tensions can arise when one partner exhibits a greater degree of cultural or religious conservatism than the other. Such disparities may spark conflicts over lifestyle choices, religious practices, and adherence to family traditions. Conflicts may arise over matters such as dress code, dietary preferences, social interactions, and participation in religious rituals.

Additionally, Muslim families typically place a strong emphasis on having children and raising them according to Islāmic values, and pressure to conceive and raise children can be overwhelming for couples experiencing fertility issues or those who choose to delay parenthood for personal or professional reasons. Muslim families may also have expectations regarding the career paths and financial stability of their children. Pressure to pursue certain professions or achieve specific career milestones can create stress and strain within the marital relationship, especially if one partner feels constrained or unfulfilled in their chosen career path. In some Muslim communities, there may be pressure to uphold social status and prestige through marriage alliances. Families may prioritise marriages that enhance their social standing or reputation within the community, leading to pressure on couples to meet certain criteria or expectations regarding their partner's background, education, or family lineage.

Interfaith and intercultural marriages pose unique challenges for Muslim couples, involving the negotiation of religious practices, cultural customs, and familial expectations. Partners from various ethnic and cultural backgrounds within the Muslim *ummah* may hold distinct viewpoints on practices and beliefs. Rassool (2019) points to the

> great diversity of cultures in Muslim communities in different parts of the world even though a significant majority share the same religious values and practices. However, the attitudes and behaviours of some Muslims are often shaped by cultural practices which may or may not be in concordance with basic Islāmic religious practices.
>
> *(p. 8)*

The main feature of this version of Islām, according to Philips (2007), "is the blind following of local traditions" (p. 33). In interfaith marriages, partners may come from different ethnic and cultural backgrounds, leading to diverse perspectives on faith practices and beliefs. Couples may need to navigate communication style or language differences, familial factors, and cultural and social norms.

In Muslim families, the societal focus on procreation heightens feelings of inadequacy and stress among couples facing conception difficulties, potentially straining marital bonds and worsening emotional burdens. Moreover, the expectation to adhere to Islāmic values in child-rearing adds further weight to couples' responsibilities as they attempt to ensure a balance between cultural traditions, religious teachings, and individual parenting philosophies. For couples opting to delay parenthood, whether for career advancement or personal fulfilment, the pressure to conform to societal norms of timely reproduction can be equally challenging within Muslim communities. Early marriage and family formation are often prioritised, intensifying the perceived obligation to start a family soon after marriage.

Couples may encounter scrutiny from family members, friends, and wider social circles, enhancing feelings of inadequacy and societal disapproval. Additionally, the decision to postpone parenthood may challenge deep-rooted gender roles and expectations within Muslim communities, prompting discussions on individual autonomy, career aspirations, and familial duties.

Parenting in Muslim families involves the delicate balance of adhering to Islāmic principles while overcoming the influences of mainstream culture and education. This delicate balance requires parents to make decisions regarding schooling, religious education, and disciplinary practices that align with their religious beliefs while also considering the realities of contemporary society. However, these decisions often lead to disagreements and tensions within the family unit, highlighting the complexities of reconciling traditional Islāmic values with the demands of modern life. Choosing the appropriate schooling and managing religious education emerge as significant points of contention for Muslim couples. They must strike a balance between providing a strong Islāmic foundation for their children and ensuring exposure to diverse perspectives and academic excellence. Additionally, implementing disciplinary approaches that reflect Islāmic teachings while effectively addressing behavioural issues poses a considerable challenge.

External pressures such as stereotypes, discrimination, and Islāmophobia significantly impact Muslim couples' relationships, introducing unique challenges that demand extra effort and understanding from both partners. Negative stereotypes and biases against Muslims can foster suspicion and mistrust in various social settings, influencing relationship dynamics. Moreover, the clash between individualistic ideals, influenced by globalisation and Western norms, and the collectivist nature of Muslim societies adds complexity to marital dynamics. Liberated Muslim women advocating for personal fulfilment, gender equality, and autonomy may challenge traditional communal values, potentially affecting marital harmony and the broader social fabric. Economic pressures, including the rising cost of living and job instability, further strain Muslim couples' relationships. Financial uncertainties permeate various aspects of marital life, leading to stress and disagreements over lifestyle choices and income stability. Strategic financial management becomes imperative as couples navigate everyday expenses and significant commitments like education and housing. Job instability exacerbates stress levels, impacting family well-being and exacerbating concerns about financial security. Additionally, the lack of accessible relationship education and pre-marital therapy for Muslim couples deprives them of essential skills needed to effectively handle challenges and foster enduring, fulfilling marriages.

In multicultural societies, Muslim couples face complex challenges related to marriage laws, divorce procedures, and child custody arrangements, influenced by both Islāmic law and secular legal systems. Negotiating these challenges presents difficulties and uncertainties for couples as they navigate the intersection of these two legal frameworks. Marriage laws often require compliance with both Islāmic and secular requirements, meaning couples must follow distinct regulations and procedures to validate their marriage.

Divorce proceedings pose another hurdle as Islāmic principles may conflict with secular legal protocols, complicating the process of dissolution. Additionally, child custody arrangements present challenges as Islāmic principles regarding parental rights may clash with secular considerations for the child's best interests. Balancing Islāmic values with compliance with secular legal requirements requires effective communication, legal guidance, and mediation to help Muslim couples navigate these complexities and reach agreements that align with their religious beliefs while meeting legal standards.

Addressing challenges in Muslim marriages involves a combination of adherence to Islāmic principles, effective communication, and adaptability to contemporary societal dynamics. Seeking guidance from religious leaders, Islāmic psychotherapists, and couples' therapists familiar with both Islāmic and cultural contexts can offer valuable support. This approach fosters mutual respect, contributing to the resilience of Muslim marriages. Structural changes in policy development and societal norms may be necessary to tackle certain challenges. Islāmic psychotherapy and couple therapy play crucial roles in helping couples managing modern issues, reinforce shared values, improve communication, and strengthen marital bonds. Bridging the gap between tradition and modernity, Islāmic psychotherapy provides a framework for addressing conflicts and enhance intimacy while aligning with Islāmic principles. However, developing and implementing relationship education and pre-marital therapy is of the upmost priority.

Pre-marital therapy: approaches and models

Pre-marital therapy, also known as pre-marital counselling or education, is a proactive form of therapy designed to help potential couples invest in their relationship. It refers to "a process designed to enhance and enrich pre-marital relationships leading to more satisfactory and stable marriages with the intended consequence being to prevent divorce" (Stahmann, 2002, p. 105). Its goal is to enhance awareness, understanding, and communication skills, providing couples with insights into marital expectations and responsibilities while addressing potential issues and strengthening interpersonal relationships. Imam Mohamed Magid (2008) outlined two approaches to pre-marital therapy: group education and individual therapy. The educational approach focuses on teaching practical skills through workshops, covering topics such as effective communication, conflict resolution, intimacy, financial management, and shared values. This proactive approach aims to prevent divorce and promote more satisfactory and stable marriages.

Pre-marital therapy is a valuable resource for couples preparing for marriage, aiming to cultivate clear awareness of each other, robust communication skills, and effective tools to navigate potential challenges, thereby fostering a strong foundation for a healthy and successful marriage. This form of therapy can be delivered through individual or group sessions, employing various approaches such as skills-based programs, pre-marital inventories, church-based counselling, and self-directed learning methods. Skill-based programmes that emphasise communication and conflict-resolution skills, have demonstrated strong empirical support (Williams, 2007).

Pre-marital inventories, another popular approach, offer couples tailored feedback on a wide range of topics including communication, conflict resolution, personality match, marital expectations, financial matters, leisure activities, family, friends, sexuality, spirituality, and children (Williams, 2007). Church-based pre-marital counselling, which includes skills-based workshops, pre-marital inventories, and private appointments with a priest, can range from one session to numerous sessions of marriage preparation. The most common topics discovered in a survey of the literature on church-oriented marriage preparation programmes were "communication, conflict resolution, egalitarian roles, sexuality, commitment, finances, and personality issues" (Silliman & Schumm, 1999, p. 25). As part of pre-marital counselling, experienced married couples serve as mentors. Finally, many engaged couples use self-directed learning methods or websites to prepare for marriage.

An alternative approach to pre-marital therapy involves personalised counselling sessions tailored to the specific concerns and issues of the future married couple. This individualised approach is particularly important for couples at risk of relationship or marriage dissolution, where pre-marital counselling is considered a necessity to address and mitigate potential challenges. Undertaking pre-marital counselling enables couples to "slow down" or reflect before rushing into marriage and consider important issues of marital relationships they may need to address. Furthermore, there is evidence to suggest that when couples continue to attend pre-marital counselling sessions after being married, their communication skills, approaches, and conflict resolution strategies improve (Williams, 2007). This ongoing support highlights the importance of sustained guidance and counselling to strengthen marital bonds and address evolving challenges even after the marriage has commenced.

Various pre-marital programmes incorporate comprehensive pre-marital assessment questionnaires for couples. Therapists and educators can choose from three main questionnaires: PREmarital Preparation and Relationship Enhancement (PREPARE: Olson & Olson, 1999), Facilitating Open Couple Communication, Understanding and Study (FOCCUS: Markey et al., 1997), and the RELATionship Evaluation (RELATE: Busby et al., 2001). Larson et al. (2002) conducted an evaluation of these questionnaires and recommended PREPARE for couples seeking structured exercises, FOCCUS for those with financial concerns willing to see a therapist, and RELATE for couples not wanting counselling or having limited financial resources. The authors emphasised the importance of professionals aligning their values and priorities when selecting an assessment instrument (Larson et al., 2002).

The Prepare-Enrich programme (Olson, 2018) serves as a comprehensive assessment tool, skill-building programme, and feedback mechanism designed for both pre-marital and married couples. It evaluates various aspects of relationships, including communication, conflict resolution, partner dynamics, financial management, and family history; its popularity derives from the instrument's validity, reliability, and efficiency in assessing a broad range of interpersonal, personality, couple, and family characteristics (Olson, 2018). The programme comprises an online couple assessment and a semi-structured feedback process tailored to the results, guiding couples through discussions and activities.

Advantages of PREPARE include its brevity, comprehensiveness, ease of administration, and availability in multiple languages, including a version for remarried couples. It serves as a valuable resource for couples seeking to understand and enhance various facets of their relationship, providing them with insights and tools for building a strong and resilient partnership (Olson, 2018). However, Larson et al. (2002) noted limitations such as its failure "to measure three factors that predict marital satisfaction: Parental mental illness, similarity of intelligence, and similarity of absolute status. It is the most expensive of the three instruments reviewed" (p. 236).

FOCCUS is widely utilised by therapists and counsellors in pre-marital counselling due to its structured yet flexible framework, which focuses on essential characteristics of a couple's relationship. It aims to enhance communication, strengthen the couple's bond, and establish a foundation for a happy marriage. FOCCUS is designed for interfaith couples, co-habiting couples, and those where one or both partners are remarrying, embodying sacred marriage qualities like permanency, fidelity, openness to children, forgiveness, shared faith in God, and unconditional love (Williams & Jurich, 1995). FOCCUS can be administered to individual or group couples, with strengths including multiple translations for non-English speakers. However, limitations include not assessing three indicators predicting marriage quality and lacking objective evidence for the validity of favoured responses (Larson et al., 2002).

RELATE is a pre-marital questionnaire available in non-denominational English and Spanish, featuring an internet version. It measures personality characteristics, values, family background, and relationship experiences. A unique aspect of RELATE is not requiring counsellor assistance for result explanation; a counsellor manual is provided. RELATE is simple to apply in large groups, but it does not measure one factor that predicts marital quality: similarity of absolute status (Larson et al., 2002).

Various models of pre-marital counselling, often Christian-oriented, prioritise coaching, counselling, problem-solving, education, and empowerment. According to Alizadeh et al. (2021), pre-marital counselling involves imparting knowledge about marriage goals, understanding the psychology of men and women, identifying correct criteria for marriage, and recognising essential circumstances to enter into marriage. It also involves identifying personal risk factors and characteristics of personal flexibility to help couples prepare for marriage, contributing to building a happier and more secure life. Research highlights the effectiveness of pre-marital education, with couples who receive an average of eight hours of counselling showing a 31% lower chance of divorce after four years (Stanley et al., 2006).

Meta-analysis findings from Carroll and Doherty (2003) and Hawkins et al. (2008) strongly indicate that couples can learn to communicate more positively and less negatively through pre-marital counselling. Pre-marital prevention programmes have demonstrated effectiveness in yielding rapid and short-term improvements in interpersonal skills and overall relationship quality, surpassing non-intervention couples in these areas (Carroll & Doherty, 2003). Meta-analyses also indicate modest evidence that marriage and relationship education, focusing on couples' communication skills, serves as both universal and selective or indicated prevention (Blanchard et al., 2009). This implies that such programmes offer valuable tools universally while also targeting at-risk or troubled couples to address and prevent further issues. Alizadeh et al. (2021) emphasise that pre-marital counselling and education encompass a broad spectrum of knowledge, including marriage goals, understanding men and women's psychology, correct criteria for marriage, and essential circumstances for entering into marriage. These findings emphasise the significance of pre-marital intervention in equipping couples with the skills and knowledge necessary to foster healthy and enduring relationships, enhancing marital satisfaction and reducing the risk of divorce.

Pre-marital Islāmic therapy approach

Pre-marital Islāmic therapy integrates Islāmic principles, values, and teachings into the educational and therapeutic process. It is designed to prepare Muslim individuals and couples for the challenges and responsibilities of marriage while addressing their spiritual, emotional, and practical needs. Contrary to the misconception that pre-marital education or counselling is unnecessary, Islām encourages seeking counsel with *imams*, scholars, or elders before marriage, with no restrictions in the *Shar'iah* on such guidance (Rassool, 2016, p. 173).

There are several instances in the authentic traditions of the Messenger of Allāh (ﷺ) in which companions would come and seek his guidance as to whether to marry a particular person or not. A study by Macfarlane (2012) revealed that divorced individuals in the Muslim community had had minimal formal pre-marital counselling, usually limited to brief meetings with an *imam*. The study participants expressed a desire for more extensive pre-marital counselling and easier access to counselling services when experiencing marital issues. Evidence suggests that couples who undergo pre-marital counselling lead happy and satisfied family lives (Chapman & Cattaneo, 2013).

In contrast, for Catholics, engagement in a marriage course called *Pre-Cana* is mandatory before marrying in the church, serving as a form of pre-marital counselling. The emergence of pre-marital counselling and teaching by *imams* and community leaders in some Islāmic communities is a positive development, indicating an understanding of the importance of educating couples for the challenges of marriage while upholding Islāmic values. The imposition of a pre-marital counselling and education requirement by *imams* and faith leaders during the marriage ceremony (*nikah*) could be a proactive step in reducing marital breakdown and divorce in the Muslim *ummah*.

Islāmic organisations have developed pre-marriage counselling questionnaires (ICNA, 2023; Magid, n.d.). A set of 100 pre-marital questions has been created to guide potential couples in identifying crucial issues, covering categories like marriage, religion, family, self, finance, children, and relatives. While the questions may not be universally relevant, responses can be discussed with an Islāmic counsellor or *imam* for guidance (ICNA, 2023; Magid, n.d.). A variety of printed resources, audio-visual materials, and e-learning courses addressing marriage preparation are available for prospective brides, grooms, family advisers, and counsellors (About Islām, 2016; Al Balagh Academy, 2023; Hartford, 2007; Islāmicity eLearning, 2012; Maqsood, 2000; Webb, 2009). Additionally, the WIFAQ Questionnaire for Muslim Couples and Families was developed by Soliman et al. (2022) as a screening tool for family and marriage counselling of Muslim couples in healthcare settings.

For potential Muslim married couples, it is important to examine spiritual and religious beliefs. Discussing these issues ahead of time will help to prevent any misconceptions in learning to manage different opinions. Research evidence suggests that religious involvement, particularly when shared by both marital partners, generally has significant positive influences on various aspects of marriage and family life, including marital fidelity, marital satisfaction, forgiveness, conflict resolution, physical and mental well-being, self-esteem, life satisfaction, and longevity (Christiano, 2000; Dollahite et al., 2004; Marks, 2005, 2006). Intercultural marriages are becoming a feature among Muslim communities globally and should be seen as a blessing in our communities (Bheekoo-Shah, 2018). Allāh says in the Qur'ān,

وَمِنْ ءَايَٰتِهِۦٓ أَنْ خَلَقَكُم مِّن تُرَابٍ ثُمَّ إِذَآ أَنتُم بَشَرٌ تَنتَشِرُونَ
وَمِنْ ءَايَٰتِهِۦٓ أَنْ خَلَقَ لَكُم مِّنْ أَنفُسِكُمْ أَزْوَٰجًا لِّتَسْكُنُوٓا۟ إِلَيْهَا وَجَعَلَ بَيْنَكُم مَّوَدَّةً وَرَحْمَةً
إِنَّ فِى ذَٰلِكَ لَءَايَٰتٍ لِّقَوْمٍ يَتَفَكَّرُونَ
وَمِنْ ءَايَٰتِهِۦ خَلْقُ ٱلسَّمَٰوَٰتِ وَٱلْأَرْضِ وَٱخْتِلَٰفُ أَلْسِنَتِكُمْ وَأَلْوَٰنِكُمْ ۚ إِنَّ فِى ذَٰلِكَ لَءَايَٰتٍ لِّلْعَٰلِمِينَ

- *And of His signs is that He created you from dust; then, suddenly you are human beings dispersing [throughout the earth]. And of His signs is that He created for you from yourselves mates that you may find tranquillity in them; and He placed between you affection and mercy. Indeed, in that are signs for a people who give thought. And of His signs are the creation of the heavens and the earth and the diversity of your languages and your colours. Indeed, in that are signs for those of knowledge.*

  (Ar-Rūm 30:20–22, interpretation of the meaning)

This verse invites believers to contemplate the signs of Allāh in the complexities of human relationships, the creation of mankind, the diversity of the natural world, and the immensity of the universe. It emphasises the need for conscious reflection and appreciation for the wisdom hidden in humanity's and the universe's creation.

It is worth noting that that intercultural marriages are one of the manifestations of the variety of Allāh's creation from a single source; varied languages and cultures are manifestations for people who reflect. For intercultural marriages, additional efforts are required by the therapist or *imam* to enable the potential couple to plan for raising children and explore religious expectations and other concerns arising from such a relationship. Differences often emerge during wedding planning, and these can involve the expectations of partners' families of origin about the wedding ceremony and other religio-cultural issues. Child-rearing practices and education can also bring religious and/or cultural differences to the surface for the first time as decisions about religious practices and education are confronted.

Pre-marital educational programme

A pre-marital educational programme is a formal initiative aiming to equip couples with the knowledge, skills, and tools necessary for establishing a strong and healthy marital foundation. Typically delivered through classes, workshops, or counselling sessions, these programmes cover various facets of marriage, personal growth, and development. Topics often include communication, interpersonal relationships, conflict resolution, financial management, and spiritual intimacy. Key areas in pre-marital counselling encompass role expectations, spiritual and religious beliefs, family of origin issues, communication, conflict resolution, and personal, couple, and family goals (Kift, 2010). A comprehensive pre-marital counselling programme should adopt an educational and skills-oriented approach, complemented by counselling. Involving a multi-professional and multidisciplinary team, such as an *imam*, therapist or counsellor, marriage therapist, psychologist, financial planner, medical practitioner, and gynaecologist, ensures a holistic perspective. The programme should be interactive, incorporating real-life examples and case studies. The curriculum should cover essential topics, details of which can be found in Table 13.1.

A comprehensive pre-marital education programme based on Islāmic principles is designed to equip couples with the knowledge and skills necessary for a successful and fulfilling marital journey. Covering various topics, this programme explores the Islāmic perspectives on marriage, effective communication, conflict resolution, financial management guided by Islāmic principles, building a spiritual connection, understanding gender roles within Islām, and drawing inspiration from the example of Prophet Muhammad (ﷺ).

By integrating Islāmic teachings, the programme provides couples with a comprehensive understanding of how their faith can positively influence their marriage, fostering a harmonious relationship. Emphasis is placed on practical aspects such

TABLE 13.1 Educational contents in pre-marital counselling

Theme	Contents and goals
Qur'ânic and *hadīth* studies	Explore relevant Qur'ânic verses and *hadīths* regarding marriage and family life
Communication skills	Teach the importance of active listening and effective communication; develop skills to articulate feelings, needs, and concerns respectfully
Relationship dynamics	Learn about the stages of relationships and how to maintain a healthy emotional connection; explore family backgrounds, cultural differences, and expectations of extended family involvement, and how to navigate these aspects as a couple; learn to deal with anger
Sexuality education	Examine Islāmic perspectives on marital intimacy; discuss physical and emotional intimacy, including information about sexual health, expectations within a marriage, and strategies for developing a strong bond
Financial management	Learn about budgeting, joint financial planning, debt management, and the importance of financial compatibility in a marriage
Preparing for challenges	Identify potential challenges that couples may face in their married life, such as stress, life transitions, and raising children, and strategies for coping with these challenges effectively
Conflict resolution	Emphasise the virtues of forgiveness and patience in dealing with marital conflicts; provide guidance on resolving conflicts in a manner consistent with Islāmic teachings; introduce the concept of arbitration in Islām as a means of resolving disputes
Parenting Skills	Provide guidance on Islāmic principles of parenting, emphasising joint responsibility in raising children with moral and spiritual values; encourage couples to develop a unified approach to parenting, ensuring consistency and cooperation
Practical skills	Provide practical tips for managing time effectively to balance marital, work, and personal responsibilities; develop problem-solving skills
Building a shared future	Examine goal setting, creating shared values and aspirations and planning for a life together, including discussions around career goals, family planning, and lifestyle choices; encourage self-reflection
Spiritual growth	Encourage couples to set and pursue shared spiritual goals, fostering deeper connections with Allāh and with each other; discuss the benefits of adhering to Islāmic principles and practices such as praying together as a means of strengthening the spiritual bond in marriage

as communication and conflict resolution rooted in patience, forgiveness, and reconciliation. Islāmic values and ethics, including trust, honesty, and mutual respect, are explored to help couples incorporate these principles into their daily lives and decision-making. Financial topics such as shared responsibility and adherence to Islāmic financial rules are covered. The programme highlights the importance of developing a strong spiritual connection through acts of worship and shared Qur'anic reflection in the relationship. Conversations about family and gender roles emphasise mutual respect and cooperation, using the example of Prophet Muhammad (ﷺ) to guide couples in establishing a harmonious family unit. In essence, the program seeks to empower couples emotionally and spiritually.

In summary, a pre-marital educational programme based on Islāmic principles aims to equip couples with the tools, teachings, and understanding essential for establishing a strong and prosperous marriage. Emphasising companionship, love, mercy, and kindness, the programme addresses critical issues like communication, financial management, spirituality, and family dynamics. By guiding couples to adopt Islāmic teachings, the programme directs them to develop a firm foundation for a lifelong journey together, grounded in their shared religion.

Conclusion

Pre-marital therapy or counselling emerges as a proactive and essential resource for couples embarking on the journey of marriage. This educational and therapeutic approach, enriched with Islāmic values, Qur'ânic teachings, and insights from various professionals, addresses crucial issues vital for establishing a healthy and harmonious marital foundation. By emphasising open communication and offering effective tools for conflict resolution, pre-marital counselling highlights the significance of aligning expectations, resolving disagreements based on Islāmic values, and nurturing a deep spiritual connection between partners. The programme encompasses practical topics such as financial management, family planning, and the rights and responsibilities of couples within an Islāmic framework.

However, the absence of relationship education and pre-marital counselling tailored for Muslim couples can impede the development of skills necessary for managing challenges and sustaining happy marriages. Overcoming this obstacle requires the establishment of resources and support systems offering relationship education and pre-marital counselling from an Islāmic perspective. Within an Islāmic framework, pre-marital counselling programmes can provide invaluable guidance on effective communication, conflict resolution, and essential marital skills.

In essence, community leaders, mosques, and Islāmic organisations hold a pivotal role in facilitating relationship education programs, pre-marital counselling services, and ongoing support for Muslim couples. By acknowledging the importance of this facet within the *ummah*'s activities, stakeholders can provide accessible and comprehensive resources to Muslim couples. This initiative aims to equip them with the essential tools and guidance needed to establish and maintain healthy, fulfilling relationships within an Islāmic framework.

References

About Islām. (2016). *Before you say 'i do': 10-step pre-marriage checklist*. Retrieved November 26, 2023, from https://aboutIslam.net/family-life/laying-foundations/10-step-pre-marriage-checklist/
Al Balagh Academy. (2023). *Islāmic marriage counselling -level 1*. Retrieved November 26, 2023, from www.albalaghacademy.org/course/Islamic-marriage-counselling/
Alizadeh, D., Sheykhangafshe, F. B., Pirabbasi, G., & Sheikhli, N. (2021). *The effectiveness of premarital counseling on couples' intimacy and marital satisfaction: A systematic review study*. The first international conference on counselling, Ardabil. Retrieved November 26, 2023, from www.researchgate.net/publication/358126015_The_Effectiveness_of_Premarital_Counseling_on_Couples'_Intimacy_and_Marital_Satisfaction_A_Systematic_Review_Study
Bheekoo-Shah, F. (2018). *Intercultural marriage: Muslim women narrate their stories*. Retrieved November 26, 2023, from https://aboutIslam.net/family-life/husbands-wives/intercultural-marriage-muslim-women-narrate-stories/
Blanchard, V. L., Hawkins, A. J., Baldwin, S. A., & Fawcett, E. B. (2009). Investigating the effects of marriage and relationship education on couples' communication skills: A meta-analytic study. *Journal of Family Psychology, 23*(2), 203–214. https://doi.org/10.1037/a0015211
Busby, D. M., Holman, T. B., & Taniguchi, N. (2001). RELATE: Relationship evaluation of the individual, family, cultural, and couple contexts. *Family Relations: An Interdisciplinary Journal of Applied Family Studies, 50*(4), 308–316. https://doi.org/10.1111/j.1741-3729.2001.00308.x
Carroll, J. S., & Doherty, W. J. (2003). Evaluating the effectiveness of pre-marital prevention programs: A meta-analytic review of outcome research. *Family Relations, 52*(2), 105–118.
Chapman, A. R., & Cattaneo, L. B. (2013). American Muslim marital quality: A preliminary investigation. *Journal of Muslim Mental Health, 7*(2). http://hdl.handle.net/2027/spo.10381607.0007.201
Christiano, K. (2000). Religion and the family in modern American culture. In S. Houseknecht & J. Pankhurst (Eds.), *Family, religion, and social change in diverse societies*. Oxford University Press.
Dollahite, D. C., Marks, L. D., & Goodman, M. A. (2004). Families and religious beliefs, practices, and communities: Linkages in a diverse and dynamic culture context. In M. J. Coleman & L. H. Ganong (Eds.), *The handbook of contemporary families: Considering the past, contemplating the future* (pp. 411–431). Sage Publications.
Hartford, H. (2007). *Islāmic marriage: Initiating and upholding*. Al Fath.
Hawkins, A. J., Blanchard, V. L., Baldwin, S. A., & Fawcett, E. B. (2008). Does marriage and relationship education work? A meta-analytic study. *Journal of Consulting and Clinical Psychology, 76*(5), 723–734.
Institute for Social Policy and Understanding (ISPU). (2014). *Community brief: Promoting healthy marriages & preventing divorce in the American Muslim community*. ISPU.
IslāmiCity eLearning. (2012). Home page. Retrieved November 26, 2023, from www.classroad.com/elearning/info.asp?FID=PreMarriage&welcome=Islamicity
Islāmic Council of North America (ICNA). (2023). *Pre-marriage counseling questionnaire*. Retrieved November 26, 2023, from www.icna.org/pre-marriage-counseling-questionnaire/
Kift, L. B. (2010). *Getting married? 6 great reasons to get pre-marital counseling*. The FMC Directory. Retrieved November 26, 2023, from https://family-marriage-counseling.com/mentalhealth/getting-married-6-great-reasons-to-get-premarital-counseling.htm

Larson, J. L., Newell, K., & Topham, G. (2002). A review of three comprehensive premarital assessment questionnaires. *Journal of Marital and Family Therapy, 28*(2), 233–239.

Macfarlane, J. (2012). *Understanding trends in American Muslim divorce and marriage: A discussion guide for families and communities*. Institute for Social Policy and Understanding.

Magid, M. (2008). *Counseling couples: Islāmic perspective*. Retrieved November 26, 2023, from http://asertif.blogspot.com/2008/11/counseling-couples-Islamic-perspective.html

Magid, M. (n.d.) *Pre-marital questionnaire*. Retrieved November 26, 2023, from www.rahmaa.org/resources/100-questions-by-imam-magid/

Mahmud, B. (2012). *Nuances of marriage (Nikah) in Islām*. Retrieved November 26, 2023, from http://oppressedpeoplesonlineword.ning.com/profiles/blogs/nuances-of-marriage-nikah-in-Islam

Maqsood, R. W. (2000). *The Muslim marriage guide*. Amana Publications.

Markey, B., Micheletto, M., & Becker, A. (1997). *Facilitating open couple communication, understanding, and study (FOCCUS)*. Family Life Office, Archdiocese of Omaha.

Marks, L. D. (2005). Religion and bio-psycho-social health: A review and conceptual model. *Journal of Religion and Health, 44*(1), 173–186.

Marks, L. D. (2006). Religion and family relational health: An overview and conceptual model. *Journal of Religion and Health, 45*(4), 603–618.

Mazlan, N. S., & Khairuldin, W. M. K. F. W. (2018). The concept of Ta'awun in the scientific writing according to Al-Quran. *International Journal of Academic Research in Business and Social Sciences, 8*(11), 932–940.

Olson, D. H. (2018). PREPARE/ENRICH enrichment program. In J. Lebow, A. Chambers, & D. Breunlin (Eds.), *Encyclopedia of couple and family therapy*. Springer. https://doi.org/10.1007/978-3-319-15877-8_378-1

Olson, D. H., & Olson, A. K. (1999). PREPARE/ENRICH Program: Version 2000. In R. Berger & M. (Eds.), *Handbook of preventative approaches in couple therapy* (pp. 196–216). Brunner/Mazel, Inc.

Philips, A. A. B. (2007). *The clash of civilizations: An Islāmic view*. Al-Hidaayah Publishing and Distributions.

Rassool, G. Hussein (2016). *Islāmic counselling. from theory to practice*. Routledge.

Rassool, G. Hussein (2019). *Evil eye, Jinn possession and mental health issues*. Routledge.

Silliman, B., & Schumm, W. R. (1999). Improving practice in marriage preparation. *Journal of Sex and Marital Therapy, 25*(1), 23–43.

Soliman, A., Abdel-Salam, A. S. G., & Ahmed, M. (2022). A diagnostic tool for family and marriage counseling with Muslim couples. *Humanities and Social Sciences Communications, 9*, 188. https://doi.org/10.1057/s41599-022-01201-9

Stahmann, R. F. (2002). Pre-marital counseling: A focus for family therapy. *Journal of Family Therapy, 22*(1), 104–116.

Stanley, S. M., Amato, P. R., Johnson, C. A., & Markman, H. J. (2006). Premarital education, marital quality, and marital stability: Findings from a large, random household survey. *Journal of Family Psychology, 20*(1), 117–126. https://doi.org/10.1037/0893-3200.20.1.117

Webb, S. (2009). Virtual Mosque. *Successful Marriages: Part I-IV*. Retrieved November 26, 2023, from www.virtualmosque.com/relationships/marriage-family/spouse/successful-marriages-part-i/

Williams, L. (2007). Pre-marital counselling. *Journal of Couple & Relationship Therapy, 6*(1/2), 207–217.

Williams, L., & Jurich, J. (1995). Predicting marital success after five years: Assessing the predictive validity of FOCCUS. *Journal of Marital and Family Therapy, 21*(2), 141–153. https://doi.org/10.1111/j.1752-0606.1995.tb00149.x

14
SACRED BONDS AND MARITAL CHALLENGES: ISLĀMIC-ORIENTED MARITAL THERAPY

Introduction

Marriage holds a significant place in Islām, symbolising a divine covenant impacting individuals' spiritual, emotional, and physical well-being. However, Muslim couples encounter challenges in navigating the complexities of relationships amid diverse cultural, religious, and socioeconomic influences. Divorce poses a serious threat to marital harmony.

Marital therapy emerges as an important resource, providing a supportive environment for addressing issues, enhance communication, and foster understanding and empathy. By focusing on effective communication and conflict resolution, marital therapy empowers couples to invest in their relationship proactively. Sessions, typically conducted weekly and involving one or two therapists, aim to strengthen the marital bond and promote progress towards a satisfying and harmonious union, with the number of sessions varying based on the severity of difficulties encountered.

Marital therapy comprises various approaches, including cognitive–behavioural therapy (CBT), emotionally focused tTherapy (EFT), imago relationship therapy (IRT), the Gottman method, solution-focused brief therapy (SFBT), and integrative or eclectic therapy. These approaches target different relationship aspects such as communication patterns, emotional connection, attachment, conflict resolution, friendship building, envisioning hopeful futures, and behaviour modification. Therapists select strategies based on their training, their theoretical orientation, and the couple's specific needs, often customising therapy to the couple's dynamics and preferences. This chapter provides an overview of divorce in Islām and aims to examine current therapeutic practices in marital therapy. The evaluation assesses the congruence between marital therapy approaches and Islāmic beliefs and practices.

DOI: 10.4324/9781003453413-16

Divorce in Islām

In Islām, divorce is permitted as a last resort if maintaining the marriage becomes untenable. Detailed rules outline the processes involved, and couples must exhaust all options, including trial separation, arbitration, and counselling, before deciding to end the marriage religiously and legally. The separation process in divorce must proceed with mercy and respect for the rights and dignity of both spouses. According to Sheikh Muhammad Ibn al-'Uthaymin, while Allāh dislikes divorce, it is not forbidden to His slaves to ease their burden (Islāmic Q&A, 2008). Divorce in Islām can occur through spoken words, written statements, or gestures that indicate the intention to divorce. Various sources provide guidance on divorce in writing (Islāmic Q&A, 2005); via e-mail (Islāmic Q&A, 2004); and by phone, mobile phone, or text message (Islāmic Q&A, 2011). For further information about *Shar'iah* guidelines restricting the issuing of divorces, see Islāmic Q&A (2023).

Muslims' divorce rates, especially in Western countries, have been on the rise in recent years, and online divorce services have facilitated that even more. *Imams* and mental health specialists have expressed concern about marriage problems and dissolutions in their communities (Chapman & Cattaneo, 2013; Siddiqui, 2009). Online divorce services are part of a larger trend in the digitalisation of legal proceedings, but while it offers ease and efficiency, this ease could be influencing divorce rates. Divorce rates in Muslim communities have been increasing globally, with estimates around 20% (Tschannen, 2021). According to Imam Mohamed Magid, divorce is rising irrespective of race, ethnicity, class, or religious affiliation (Siddiqui, 2009). Various factors contribute to divorces within Muslim communities, including incompatibility, conflicts with in-laws, extramarital relationships, addiction to substances, sexual infidelity, conflicting attitudes towards sex, unrealistic expectations, financial negligence, secular individualism, and abuse in various forms (Ayubi, 2021; Chapman & Cattaneo, 2013; Ghayyur, 2010).

Marital therapy: an overview

Marital therapy, a branch of psychotherapy, is designed to assist couples in navigating and resolving emotional or personal challenges within their intimate relationships. Benson et al. (2012) indicates that successful interventions in marital therapy share five fundamental principles: changing relationship perspectives, modifying dysfunctional behaviour, reducing emotional avoidance, improving communication, and enhancing strengths. The therapeutic process encourages both partners to objectively view the relationship, moving away from the "blame game." Different therapeutic approaches, ranging from behavioural to insight-oriented therapies, have empirical support, emphasising altering the understanding of the relationship to enable couples to perceive each other and their interactions more adaptively (Whitbourne, 2012).

In marital therapy, cognitive–behavioural techniques are utilised to modify partners' behaviours and challenge distorted thinking patterns, aiming to foster healthier relational dynamics (see Chapter 9). Therapists may conduct risk assessments, especially in cases involving domestic violence, abuse, or addictive behaviours, and refer clients to specialist agencies as needed. For less severe cases, implementing "time-out" procedures can prevent conflicts from escalating. Additionally, SFBT, which emphasises solutions over problems, is deemed effective in marital therapy contexts. Addressing emotional avoidance, common among some Muslim clients, is crucial to prevent emotional alienation and marital distance, underscoring the significance of expressing and addressing personal feelings within the therapeutic environment.

EFT is a therapeutic approach applicable to individuals, couples, and families, rooted in experiential treatment and incorporating elements of gestalt, person-centred methods, systemic therapy, and attachment theory (Corey, 2018). In the context of couples, EFT aims to comprehend the dynamics of the couple relationship, expand emotional responses, foster new interactions, and nurture the bonding process (Crawley & Grant, 2005). EFT operates on the premise that human emotions are connected to human needs, and addressing them can aid individuals in changing distressing emotional states and enhancing interpersonal connections (Johnson & Greenberg, 1992). The therapeutic process involves three sequential movements: de-escalation of conflict; re-engagement of the withdrawing partner in the relationship by identifying and owning primary emotional experiences; and softening, where dominant partners express their primary vulnerability (Crawley & Grant, 2005).

EFT typically comprises short-term treatment lasting 8–20 sessions, with empirical support for its effectiveness in addressing various issues including depression, interpersonal problems, avoidant personality disorder, and trauma. Research indicates significant progress and improvements in partner interactions, reduced relationship stress, and increased marital satisfaction through EFT (Johnson & Brubacher, 2016; Greenberg, 2017). EFT has been shown to improve partner interactions, lessen relationship stress, and increase marital satisfaction (Wiebe & Johnson, 2016). According to systematic reviews, EFT is effective in enhancing marital satisfaction (Beasley & Ager, 2019) and improving relationships, reducing negative reactions when partners feel upset or scared (Johnson et al., 1999).

Gottman method couples therapy, as outlined by Gottman and Gottman (2015) and Gottman and Silver (2015), is a structured and scientifically based approach aimed at achieving specific therapeutic goals within couples' relationships. This method employs therapeutic techniques to diminish conflict, enhance intimacy, increase affection, and cultivate empathy and understanding between partners. A central concept introduced in this approach is the "Four Horsemen," which represent detrimental communication behaviours: criticism, contempt, defensiveness, and stonewalling. Unaddressed, these behaviours can hinder effective communication and conflict resolution.

The Gottman method emphasises the recognition and addressing of these behaviours, promoting understanding, empathy, and healthy communication skills to strengthen the relationship. Various therapeutic approaches within the Gottman method include focusing on emotion (affective therapy), changing interaction patterns (behavioural), exploring conflicts within the context of dreams (existentially based), considering how couples think about their relationship (cognitive), exploring partners' stories (narrative), examining interaction patterns as a systemic couple therapy, and analysing the role of primary family and past relationships in the present conflict (psychodynamic).

Narrative marital therapy focuses on the stories and narratives that couples construct about their relationship (see Chapter 11). The primary goal is to help couples confront and reframe negative or unhelpful narratives, fostering more positive and empowering stories. By delving into the meanings, beliefs, and values embedded within their narratives, couples gain deeper insights into their relationship dynamics and the influences shaping their interactions. The therapist facilitates the exploration of alternative narratives that highlight the couple's strengths, resources, and successes. This approach assists couples in transitioning from problem-oriented narratives to more positive and solution-focused ones, enabling them to construct a cohesive and fulfilling narrative for their future together.

IRT is a specialised approach aimed at resolving conflicts within couples by addressing underlying issues rooted in past experiences. The term "imago" refers to an unconscious image of familiar love, indicating that individuals are naturally drawn to partners who reflect unresolved issues from their past (Hendrix & LaKelly Hunt, n.d.). IRT focuses on reintroducing romance and nurturing emotional bonds between partners, emphasising empathy, understanding, and connection. Therapists explore these unresolved issues and their impact on the relationship, encouraging active listening, validation, and mirroring of each other's experiences. Structured exercises and activities are employed to deepen the connection, rebuild trust, and promote a healthier and more satisfying relationship.

Marital therapies: congruent with Islāmic teachings?

In examining CBT, SFBT Islāmic, and narrative therapy, their alignment with Islāmic values has been explored in previous chapters. EFT, Gottman method couples therapy, and IRT resonate with Islāmic values due to their emphasis on empathy, compassion, communication, and mutual respect. Despite originating in secular contexts, these approaches can be adapted to align with the Islāmic worldview by incorporating elements of faith, spirituality, and cultural sensitivity. Seeking guidance from knowledgeable scholars and clinicians can assist therapists and couples in navigating these adaptations while remaining faithful to Islāmic teachings and values.

EFT aligns with Islāmic teachings by promoting the acknowledgment and understanding of emotions, along with compassion and empathy. It offers couples a framework for exploring and validating emotions, fostering deeper emotional connections in line with Islāmic principles. However, Islām emphasises moderation and avoiding extremes in emotions, highlighting the importance of emotional management and self-discipline. In certain cultural contexts, expressing intense emotions publicly may be deemed inappropriate, reflecting the Islāmic principle of managing emotions with restraint.

The Gottman method, focused on nurturing friendship, managing disagreements, and establishing shared meaning in relationships, resonates with certain Islāmic teachings on companionship and dispute resolution in marriage. However, some aspects of the method may require adjustments to align with Islāmic values, particularly regarding discussions on intimacy and personal matters. Despite its evidence-based nature, the Gottman method's Western cultural origin may limit its applicability to diverse Muslim clients, potentially overlooking specific cultural norms and values. The standardised assessments and interventions might not fully address the individualised needs of Muslim couples, potentially leading to misinterpretations and judgment. Moreover, the method's emphasis on negative behaviours and its psychological foundation may overlook the spiritual dimensions valued by Muslim couples, necessitating a more holistic approach encompassing both psychological and psychospiritual aspects.

IRT, rooted in Jungian psychoanalysis, explores how childhood experiences and unresolved issues impact adult relationships. However, its emphasis on past influences may not fully align with Islāmic teachings, which prioritise present actions and accountability over past events for fostering understanding and empathy within relationships. Critics argue that psychoanalytic theories, including Jungian ideas, overemphasise childhood development, limiting their explanatory power in understanding the complexity and diversity of human experiences. While intellectually stimulating, these theories may fall short in comprehensively understanding both universal and individual traits that contribute to what makes each person distinctive (Larsen et al., 2017). According to critics, their focus on early developmental phases may not adequately capture the intricacies of human experiences. Islāmic perspectives may offer alternative approaches to addressing the complexities of human relationships and the factors influencing them.

IRT focuses on restoring love relationships through an emphasis on empathy and communication, with the therapist serving as a facilitator (Hannah et al., 2005). The therapeutic approach appears to be non-directive, involving the therapist as a guide rather than a director. In non-directive therapy, the emphasis is on creating a supportive environment for individuals within the relationship to lead the process of healing and growth. However, this non-directive approach may not align with the preferences of Muslim clients, who tend to prefer a more directive therapeutic approach. In addition, IRT might not be suitable for couples dealing with mental health issues unrelated to their relationship, according to Harryman (2008) and Healthy Minded (2023). IRT focuses on restoring love relationships through empathy and communication, with the therapist facilitating the process (Hannah et al., 2005).

IRT lacks explicit attention to spirituality and religiosity as significant factors in couples' lives. While the therapy emphasises emotional connection and healing, it may not adequately address the spiritual dimensions of relationships, which can be essential for many Muslim couples, including those with strong religious beliefs. Therefore, couples seeking therapy that integrates spirituality and religiosity into the healing process may find IRT lacking in this aspect. To ensure congruence with Islāmic teachings, Muslim couples engaged in IRT should openly communicate their religious needs and boundaries to the therapist. Therapists working with Muslim couples may need to make adaptations to incorporate Islāmic spiritual practices, ensuring that any spiritual reflections, rituals, or exercises adhere to the Islāmic worldview. This careful integration of spirituality can help IRT align more effectively with the spiritual and cultural needs of Muslim individuals and couples.

Marital therapy presents compatibility challenges for Muslim clients, particularly with due to the psychodynamic approaches of some of the marital therapies. However, alternative models like CBT or the Gottman method offer valuable techniques for addressing communication, conflict resolution, and shared values. Regardless of the chosen approach, fostering a safe and supportive environment is essential. This environment allows couples to openly discuss concerns, improve communication skills, and deepen mutual understanding. Therapy's effectiveness depends on tailoring the approach to the couple's dynamics and the therapist's ability to meet their unique needs.

Islāmic-oriented marital therapy

Islāmic-oriented marital therapy is a specialised approach to couples therapy that incorporates Islāmic teachings, values, and principles. This approach aims to offer tailored support and guidance to Muslim couples, assisting them in navigating the complexities of marital challenges while maintaining a connection to their faith. The underlying premise is that Islāmic principles provide a comprehensive framework for addressing marital issues, promoting healing, and enhancing overall well-being. The decision to integrate an Islāmic perspective into marital therapy is grounded in several key considerations. This is summarised in Table 14.1.

Islāmic-oriented marital therapy involves a thorough examination of the couple's understanding of marriage within the Islāmic context. Therapists integrate insights from the Qur'ân and *hadīths* with psychological interventions to provide relevant psychospiritual guidance.

The therapy encompasses multiple dimensions of the couple's relationship, addressing aspects such as religiosity, communication dynamics, conflict resolution strategies, intimacy, and roles and responsibilities within the marital framework. Grounded in the idea of strengthening the couple's connection to Allāh, the approach aims to foster empathy; compassion; and the values of love, mercy, forgiveness, and patience.

TABLE 14.1 Key considerations in incorporating an Islāmic perspective in marital therapy

Key consideration	Explanation
Islāmic monotheism and values as a foundation	Monotheism is the foundation of Islāmic-oriented marital therapy. Marital therapy rooted in Islāmic principles aligns with the overarching goal of promoting righteousness, justice, compassion, and mercy, creating a framework for building healthy relationships.
Compliance with Divine commandments	Marital therapy is grounded in complying with divine commandments related to marriage. The framework addresses maintaining family ties, managing conflicts, fulfilling responsibilities, and adhering to gender roles, all in accordance with Islāmic teachings.
Spiritual connection	The spiritual dimension in healing incorporates practices such as prayer (*salah*), seeking forgiveness and reflecting on Quranic teachings and *hadīths*.
Islāmic worldview	Comprehensive worldview: physical, emotional, psychological, and spiritual well-being; holistic approach: recognising that healing in one aspect of life contributes to overall marital health
Conflict resolution: Islāmic ethics	Islāmic ethics provides a set of ethical guidelines for conflict resolution, emphasising patience (*sabr*), forgiveness, and reconciliation. Marital therapy informed by Islāmic principles guides couples in resolving conflicts with fairness, compassion, and a commitment to mutual understanding.
Family and community integration	Islāmic marital therapy acknowledges the role of the family and community in supporting couples, involving religious leaders, mentors, or community resources.
Marital therapy from an Islāmic perspective	Therapists are trained in marital therapy and Islāmic studies and integrate Islāmic principles into their therapeutic approaches.

Prophet Mohammad (ﷺ) used to provide counselling or advice (*naseehah*) on marital issues on a regular basis to couples. The most famous occurrence was between his daughter Fatima and Ali (cousin and son-in-law). Marital counselling can help couples to identify and address destructive patterns of relating, enables improvement in conflict and communication and enhances interpersonal relationships. It was narrated from Abu Hurayrah (may Allāh be pleased with him) that the Messenger of Allāh (ﷺ) said, "Religion is sincerity, religion is sincerity (*al-naseehah*), religion is sincerity." They said, "To whom, O Messenger of Allāh?" He said, "To Allāh, to His Book, to His Messenger, to the *imams* of the Muslims and to their common folk" (An-Nasa'i).

In the context of Islāmic-oriented marital therapy, therapists integrate mainstream therapeutic methods with Islāmic principles, emphasising the importance of culturally competent and sensitive interventions for the diverse Muslim community. When working with Muslim clients, it is important to provide orientation, addressing potential misconceptions. The therapist clarifies that marital therapy is not an arbitration process or a means of obtaining religious rulings but rather a guidance and support service based on psychological expertise, incorporating Islāmic values into discussions (for example, "In our sessions, we will focus on exploring and addressing the challenges you are facing in your marriage. I am here to provide guidance and help you find strategies to improve your relationship based on psychological principles, and we will incorporate your Islāmic values and teachings into our discussions").

In the therapeutic process of Islāmic-oriented marital therapy, it is essential for the therapist to express openness to the needs and suggestions of Muslim clients, aligning their approaches with their clients' ethical values. Discussions may include the Islāmic perspective on marriage, exploring rights and responsibilities from Islāmic teachings, and integrating spiritual interventions to address specific challenges. Emphasising spiritual well-being aims to create a strong foundation for the couple, enabling them to draw strength from Islāmic teachings as they navigate married life. Islāmic-oriented marital therapy seeks to build a deep and lasting relationship with Allāh, fostering a harmonious and spiritually enriched marriage. Adapted guidelines for marriage therapists when working with Muslim clients are provided by Siddiqui (n.d.)

Assess the religiosity of the couple

For a therapist working with a Muslim couple, it is essential to comprehend the role that Islām holds in both spouses' collective and individual lives. The level of commitment to Islāmic beliefs and practices would determine the nature and approach of the therapeutic process. Evaluating religiosity goes beyond simply checking off a list of religious practices; instead, it becomes apparent in the couple's shared worldview and individual perspectives. This is evident in how they discuss Islām and the topics on which they may have disagreements. Understanding their relationship with Islām in these nuanced ways is essential for tailoring effective therapy that aligns with their unique dynamics and beliefs.

Several religiosity scales have been developed specifically for measuring religiosity among Muslims including the Muslim Attitudes Toward Religion Scale (British Muslims) (Wilde & Joseph, 1997); the Psychological Measure of Islāmic Religiousness (American Muslims) (Abu-Raiya et al., 2008); the Attitudes Toward Islām Scale (British Muslim adolescents) (Sahin & Francis, 2002); the Religiosity of Islām Scale (American Muslims) (Jana-Masri & Priester, 2007); the Islāmic Religiosity Scale (Algerian Muslims) (Tiliouine et al., 2009); the Five Dimensions of Muslim Religiosity Scale (Muslims living in selected German cities) (El-Menouar, 2014); the Muslim Daily Religiosity Assessment Scale (Nigerian Muslim students) Olufadi (2017); the Islāmic Religiosity Scale (Turkish Muslims) (Yilmaz & Zollmann,

2014); and the Muslim Religiosity Scale (Malaysian Muslims) (Mohd Mahudin et al., 2016). Researchers and practitioners should carefully select a religiosity scale that aligns with their research or assessment objectives, cultural context, and target population. Additionally, adaptation of these scales may be necessary to capture the unique aspects of religiosity within diverse Muslim communities.

Understand the importance of the Qur'ān and swearing on the Qur'ān

In some cases, Muslim couples may choose to swear or make an oath on the Qur'ān to assert the truth or sincerity of their statements or commitments. It is important to note that the Qur'ān is the word of Allāh, and His word is one of His attributes, so it is permissible to swear by the Qur'ān. The scholars of the Standing Committee said, "It is permissible to swear by Allāh and His Attributes. The Qur'ān is the word of Allāh, which is one of His attributes, so it is permissible to swear by it" (Islām Q&A, 2012).

Assess the level of acculturation

Understanding the religious beliefs, cultural backgrounds, and worldviews of Muslim clients is crucial in marital therapy. Cultural differences within the Muslim community, influenced by regional origins such as India, Pakistan, Bangladesh, or the Middle East, can significantly shape perspectives on marriage and divorce. For example, Muslims from India, Pakistan, and Bangladesh often perceive divorce as a last resort and may find remarriage after divorce challenging. In contrast, Muslims from certain parts of the Middle East may hold a more accepting attitude towards divorce, viewing remarriage after divorce positively and even encouraging it (Siddiqui, 2009).

It is essential to recognise that cultural variations may not always align with Islāmic values, emphasising the importance of distinguishing between Muslim culture and Islāmic culture. Assessing the level of acculturation is vital. Rassool (2019) suggested that, "The exposure to different set of culture, values and beliefs can be a risk factor for mental health, and acculturative stress which may lead to psychological problems or disorders" (pp. 16–17). Collaborating with Muslim professionals and local organisations can provide valuable insights into cultural expectations and religious considerations unique to specific ethno-cultural groups. Understanding these cultural distinctions is crucial, as certain religious peculiarities may contribute to significant challenges and conflicts within Muslim marriages (Rassool, 2019; Siddiqui, 2009).

Consult with scholars when it comes to matters of Fiqh (Islāmic law)

Various legal issues, both from a civil and an Islāmic legal standpoint, may surface in therapy sessions with couples. In such instances, seeking guidance from a reputable Islāmic scholar or engaging in collaborative care with a scholar or *imam* is recommended. Islāmic jurisprudence matters pertaining to marriage encompass a range of topics, for instance the custody of children (*hadana*); the validity of divorce; a woman's right to seek divorce from her husband in Islāmic law (*khula*); domestic violence concerns; consigning divorce to the wife; revoking the divorce (*raj'a*); mutual swearing for accusations of adultery; denial of lineage (*li'an*); observing the waiting period (*iddah*) in cases of menstruation; and providing expenses or provisions (*nafaqa*) for the divorced wife and relatives. Consulting with knowledgeable Islāmic scholars helps address these intricate legal aspects within the framework of both civil and Islāmic laws.

Pay attention to language

Language barriers in marital therapy, especially when clients are not fluent in English or it is not their native language, can present challenges. Communication involves verbal and non-verbal elements, and cultural backgrounds can significantly influence these aspects. Therapists must navigate linguistic differences with sensitivity, as phrases or expressions in a non-English language may carry diverse cultural meanings that can be misinterpreted if taken literally. Additionally, some cultures emphasise indirect communication, expressing distress or unhappiness through metaphorical language rather than direct statements.

Therapists need to be attuned to these cultural nuances for effective communication. For instance, a statement like "I am drowning in my sorrows" may be an expression of emotional struggle rather than a literal description of the person's state. Non-verbal cues also play a substantial role in communication and can vary widely across cultures. Avoiding direct eye contact in Muslim cultures is often seen as a way of respecting boundaries and maintaining modesty. The concept of *ghadd al-basar* (lowering the gaze) is often emphasised in Islāmic teachings, particularly when it comes to interactions between men and women who are not closely related or married. It is vital for therapists to be aware of and respect these cultural and religious norms when working with Muslim clients. In a therapeutic context, therapists should approach eye contact with sensitivity, taking into consideration the individual preferences and religio-cultural background of the client. This may involve being flexible in the therapist's expectations of eye contact and understanding that different cultural practices and interpretations can influence non-verbal behaviours, such as eye contact, body language, and gestures.

Understand the influence of the couple's families on their relationship

In Muslim communities, marriage creates an extended family, and families may desire high involvement in child-rearing practices. This involvement can strain the couple's bond if there is intrusive interference from in-laws (Ezzeldine, 2013). Therapists may encounter situations where parents or in-laws reach out before or after sessions, seeking advice or updates. For example, it is common for a parent to reach out to a therapist before a session with their child and their spouse, providing advice or seeking a report on the session afterward (Siddiqui, 2009). The optimal response is to acknowledge parents' concerns while firmly upholding confidentiality.

Establishing boundaries with overly intrusive in-laws is a delicate process, particularly when one spouse may not perceive the issue as a problem. Ezzeldine (2013) suggests that defining these boundaries is crucial and can be tailored to the unique needs and circumstances of each couple. Several key areas where boundaries can be set include seeking advice, exchanging money, determining the frequency of visits, managing phone calls, navigating holidays, and addressing decisions related to raising children.

Do not fall into the trap of saying who's right and who's wrong

In therapy, adopting a "no-fault" policy is crucial to avoid falling into blame or resentment. Miller and Rollnick (2002) suggested, "I'm not interested in looking for who's responsible, but rather what's troubling you, and what you might be able to do about it" (p. 70). This approach focuses on understanding the difficulties troubling individuals or couples and finding solutions rather than assigning blame. Establishing a no-fault strategy means creating a non-judgmental and supportive environment where clients feel safe to express their concerns without fear of judgment. Respecting the roles of both spouses, regardless of marriage challenges, upholds the dignity and worth of each individual. This principle acknowledges that both partners contribute to the relationship dynamics, fostering a constructive therapeutic process.

Understand the dynamics of power

In therapy with Muslim couples, conflicts related to authority and dominance, especially with biased power relationships, can create tension. It is important to recognise that in marital therapy with Muslim couples, the wife and the couple's children might hesitate to openly express themselves in the presence of the husband (Siddiqui, 2009). This dynamic becomes more pronounced in families where power relationships are biased, with women and children facing authority from the husband and father. Family members, particularly the wife or children, may be reluctant to participate in joint therapy sessions. Respecting the comfort levels and potential weaknesses of everyone concerned, the therapist should avoid being overly insistent. In such cases, the therapist needs to approach sessions with empathy, understanding power dynamics and respecting everyone's comfort levels.

In therapy with Muslim couples facing power imbalances, a gradual and personalised approach is recommended. The therapist can facilitate individual family members to express their views and concerns discreetly, fostering trust and maintaining confidentiality. Separate sessions for individual family members may be considered to provide a safe space for them to voice their experiences and concerns independently. The overarching goal is to create a therapeutic environment where all family members feel heard, understood, and supported.

Be solution focused

In therapy, it is crucial for individuals to take ownership of their problems and actively engage in seeking solutions. The therapist should foster a collaborative partnership, avoiding the role of a rescuer and allowing clients to develop problem-solving self-reliance. The therapist should foster a collaborative partnership with the clients, where they work together to address the clients' concerns. However, it is fundamental for the therapist to avoid the trap of trying to rescue or take responsibility for the client (Whitfield, 1993) or the outcomes of the therapeutic sessions. Therapists, particularly Islāmic therapists dealing with complex familial and cultural factors, need to navigate these intricacies with caution. This involves offering help while preserving the autonomy of the family unit, respecting boundaries, and being attuned to the influence of extended family members. The therapist must strike a balance between providing assistance and upholding ethical principles in the therapeutic process.

Contact an Islāmic or cultural association

Seeking assistance from local or national Islāmic and cultural associations or welfare services can be valuable for Muslim couples, offering resources, guidance, and support tailored to the cultural and religious context of Muslim communities. These organisations often have professionals, therapists, and scholars knowledgeable about Islāmic teachings and marital therapy. Workshops, seminars, or support groups organised by these entities can address common challenges faced by Muslim couples, helping them navigate issues within the framework of their faith and cultural values.

Muslim couples' mediation, arbitration, and *Shar'iah* councils

Mediation, arbitration, and *Shar'iah* councils are alternative dispute resolution methods that can be employed to address conflicts and disputes within Muslim couples. These processes provide a structured and facilitated approach to resolving issues while adhering to Islāmic principles.

Mediation entails the involvement of a neutral third party, known as the mediator, who facilitates communication, comprehension, and negotiation between couples to achieve a mutually acceptable resolution. When working with Muslim couples, it is essential for mediators to be sensitive to Islāmic teachings and to integrate Islāmic principles into the mediation process. This may entail exploring solutions rooted in Qur'ânic teachings, Islāmic jurisprudence, and cultural norms that resonate with the couple's religious and cultural beliefs. The mediation process commences with both spouses willingly engaging in the process, promoting transparent communication to identify underlying concerns and guide the couple towards solutions that both parties can endorse. The mediator refrains from imposing conclusions but rather encourages active involvement in resolving disputes. Islāmic teachings emphasise reconciliation, compromise, and peaceful conflict resolution. Allāh says in the Qur'ân,

وَإِنِ ٱمْرَأَةٌ خَافَتْ مِنْ بَعْلِهَا نُشُوزًا أَوْ إِعْرَاضًا فَلَا جُنَاحَ عَلَيْهِمَآ أَن يُصْلِحَا بَيْنَهُمَا صُلْحًا ۚ وَٱلصُّلْحُ خَيْرٌ

- *And if a woman fears from her husband contempt or evasion, there is no sin upon them if they make terms of settlement between them; and settlement is best.*

(An-Nisā' 4:128, interpretation of the meaning)

This verse acknowledges the likelihood of disputes between spouses and encourages amicable settlement through compromise, aligning with Qur'ânic teachings. It promotes conversation, understanding, and cooperation while adhering to Islāmic ethical norms. Mediation addresses various issues within Muslim couples, including marital disputes, communication breakdowns, parenting disagreements, financial conflicts, asset division, and inheritance matters. It is particularly valuable during divorce or separation, fostering fair resolutions and positive co-parenting relationships. A mediator well-versed in Islāmic jurisprudence, ethics, and cultural nuances is essential for guiding couples towards resolutions that uphold their religious values.

Arbitration is another intervention strategy that provides an opportunity to give the Muslim couple guidance as well as facilitate problem-solving and reconciliation between them. The process is to appoint an impartial arbitrator or a panel of arbitrators who hear both parties' arguments and make a binding decision to resolve the dispute. Islāmic arbitration adheres to *Shar'iah* principles and can involve scholars or individuals well-versed in Islāmic jurisprudence to ensure decisions are in accordance with Islāmic law. Arbitration can be applied to marital issues, financial disputes, or any matter where an impartial decision is needed. The following verses in the Qur'ân, spoken by Allāh, reflect the theme of arbitration:

وَإِنْ خِفْتُمْ شِقَاقَ بَيْنِهِمَا فَٱبْعَثُوا۟ حَكَمًا مِّنْ أَهْلِهِ وَحَكَمًا مِّنْ أَهْلِهَآ إِن يُرِيدَآ إِصْلَٰحًا يُوَفِّقِ ٱللَّهُ بَيْنَهُمَآ

- *And if you fear dissention between the two, send an arbiter from his people and an arbiter from her people if they desire reconciliation. Allāh will cause it between them.*

(An-Nisā' 4:35, interpretation of the meaning)

وَمَا ٱخْتَلَفْتُمْ فِيهِ مِن شَىْءٍ فَحُكْمُهُ إِلَى ٱللَّهِ ۚ ذَٰلِكُمُ ٱللَّهُ رَبِّى عَلَيْهِ تَوَكَّلْتُ وَإِلَيْهِ أُنِيبُ

- And in anything over which you disagree-its ruling is [to be referred] to Allāh. Say "This is Allāh, my Lord; upon Him I have relied, and to Him I turn back."

(Ash-Shūraá 42:10, interpretation of the meaning)

فَلَا وَرَبِّكَ لَا يُؤْمِنُونَ حَتَّىٰ يُحَكِّمُوكَ فِيمَا شَجَرَ بَيْنَهُمْ ثُمَّ لَا يَجِدُوا۟ فِىٓ أَنفُسِهِمْ حَرَجًا مِّمَّا قَضَيْتَ وَيُسَلِّمُوا۟ تَسْلِيمًا

- But no, by your Lord, they will not [truly] believe until they make you, [O Muhammad] judge concerning that over which they dispute among themselves and then find within themselves no discomfort from what you have judged and submit in [full, willing] submission.

(An-Nisā' 4:65, interpretation of the meaning)

فَإِن تَنَٰزَعْتُمْ فِى شَىْءٍ فَرُدُّوهُ إِلَى ٱللَّهِ وَٱلرَّسُولِ إِن كُنتُمْ تُؤْمِنُونَ بِٱللَّهِ وَٱلْيَوْمِ ٱلْءَاخِرِ

- And if you disagree over anything, refer it to Allāh and the Messenger, if you should believe in Allāh and in the Last Day.

(An-Nisā' 4:59, interpretation of the meaning)

The Muslim Arbitration Tribunal, established in 2007 in England, offers an alternative dispute resolution platform for the Muslim community in accordance with Islāmic sacred law and operates under the Arbitration Act 1996. It provides a non-court option alongside the Islāmic *Shar'iah* council. While the tribunal lacks authority to grant divorces recognised in English and Welsh law, it can issue a *talaq* to acknowledge divorce and has jurisdiction over reconciliation between spouses. Muslim couples may also choose arbitration through *Shar'iah* councils, staffed by qualified scholars or experts in Islāmic law who provide legally recognised decisions based on Islāmic principles and handle a variety of issues, including divorce proceedings, financial matters, and family disputes.

Conclusion

For Muslims, reinforcing their religiosity is essential for instilling a profound reverence for God in their actions and to foster enduring marriages. The tenets of Islām, or *deen*, serve as a powerful source to dispel faulty cognitions and to re-educate about roles and responsibilities within marital relationships. Using religious teachings, particularly the *hadīths* of the of the Messenger of Allāh (ﷺ), becomes critical in reducing rising divorce rates among Muslims. Prophet Muhammad (ﷺ) said,

> A woman is married for four things, i.e. her wealth, her family status, her beauty and her religion. So, you should marry the religious woman (otherwise) you will be a loser.

(Bukhârî).

Prophet Muhammad (ﷺ) emphasised the multifaceted nature of marriage and advised believers to prioritise marrying a religiously committed spouse to avoid being at a loss. This guidance extends to women as well, with the Prophet (ﷺ) urging families to marry their daughters to men of strong religious commitment and character to prevent societal tribulations and corruption:

> If there comes to you to marry (your daughter) one who with whose religious commitment and character you are pleased, then marry (your daughter) to him, for if you do not do that, there will be fitnah (tribulation) in the land and widespread corruption.
>
> *(Tirmidhî)*

In contemporary society, a clash often arises between Islāmic principles and prevailing un-Islāmic traditions. Despite the Qur'ânic injunction to approach marital relationships with "mutual mercy and love" (Ar-Rūm 30:21), many couples find themselves pressured to conform to non-Islāmic norms. Struggling Muslim couples frequently turn to religious teachings advocating mediation from family members during marital conflicts. However, immigrant Muslims may encounter challenges in accessing their extended families or appropriate resources to address their issues. In addressing these challenges, the provision and delivery of psychotherapeutic services must be culturally sensitive and tailored to the specific needs of Muslim communities.

References

Abu-Raiya, H., Pargament, K. I., Mahoney, A., & Stein, C. (2008). A psychological measure of Islāmic religiousness: Development and evidence for reliability and validity. *The International Journal for the Psychology of Religion, 18*(4), 291–315. https://doi.org/10.1080/10508610802229270

An-Nasa'i. *Sunan an-Nasa'i 4199*. In-book reference: Book 39, Hadith 51. English translation: Vol. 5, Book 39, Hadith 4204. Sahih (Darussalam). https://sunnah.com/nasai:4199

Ayubi, Z. (2021). Specific issues in Muslim divorce. In K. Ali (Ed.), *Half of faith: American Muslim marriage and divorce in the twenty-first century* (pp. 76–79). OpenBU. https://hdl.handle.net/2144/42505

Beasley, C. C., & Ager, R. (2019). Emotionally focused couples therapy: A systematic review of its effectiveness over the past 19 years. *Journal Evidence Based Social Work, 16*(2), 144–159. https://doi.org/10.1080/23761407.2018.1563013

Benson, L. A., McGinn, M. M., & Christensen, A. (2012). Common principles of couple therapy. *Behavior Therapy, 43*(1), 25–35. https://doi.org/10.1016/j.Beth.2010.12.009

Bukhârî. *Sahih al-Bukhârî 5090*. In-book reference: Book 67, Hadith 28. USC-MSA web (English) reference: Vol. 7, Book 62, Hadith 27. https://sunnah.com/bukhari:5090

Chapman, A. R., & Cattaneo, L. B. (2013). American Muslim marital quality: A preliminary investigation. *Journal of Muslim Mental Health, 7*(2).

Corey, G. (2018). *The art of integrative counseling* (4th ed.). E-Book. Wiley.

Crawley, J., & Grant, J. (2005). Emotionally focused therapy for couples and attachment theory. *Australian & New Zealand Journal of Family Therapy, 26*(2), 82–89.

El-Menouar, Y. (2014). The five dimensions of Muslim religiosity: Results of an empirical study. *Methods, Data, Analyses, 8*(1), 53–78.

Ezzeldine, M. L. (2013). *Before the wedding: Questions for Muslims to ask before getting married*. Kindle Edition.

Ghayyur, T. (2010). Divorce in the Muslim community: 2010 survey analysis. *Sound Vision*. Retrieved November 27, 2023, from www.soundvision.com/article/divorce-in-the-muslim-community-2010-survey-analysis%20%E2%80%8F

Gottman, J. M., & Gottman, J. S. (2015). Gottman couple therapy. In A. S. Gurman, J. L. Lebow, & D. K. Snyder (Eds.), *Clinical handbook of couple therapy* (pp. 129–157). Guilford Press.

Gottman, J. M., & Silver, N. (2015). *The seven principles for making marriage work*. Harmony.

Greenberg, L. S. (2017). *Emotion-focused therapy* (Revised ed.). American Psychological Association. https://doi.org/10.1037/15971-000

Hannah, M. T., Luquet, W., Hendrix, H., Hunt, H., & Mason, R. C. (2005). *Imago relationship therapy: Perspectives on theory*. Jossey-Bass/A Wiley Imprint.

Harryman, W. (2008). Imago therapy – A critique & a proposal. *Integral Options Cafe*. Retrieved November 27, 2023, from http://integral-options.blogspot.com/2008/03/imago-therapy-critique-proposal.html

Healthy Minded. (2023). *Criticism of Imago therapy: A balanced and comprehensive review*. Retrieved November 27, 2023, from https://healthyminded.co/criticism-of-imago-therapy/#:~:text=It%20may%20not%20be%20suitable%20for%20couples%20with,differ%20from%20those%20of%20their%20partner%20or%20therapist

Hendrix, H., & LaKelly Hunt, H. (n.d.). *What is Imago?* Retrieved November 26, 2023, from https://harvilleandhelen.com/initiatives/what-is-imago/

Islāmic Q&A. (2004). *36761: Ruling on divorce via e-mail*. Retrieved November 25, 2023, from http://Islamicqa.info/en/36761

Islāmic Q&A. (2005). *72291: Divorce in writing*. Retrieved November 25, 2023, from http://Islamicqa.info/en/72291

Islāmic Q&A. (2008). *120761: Status of the Hadeeth: The most hated thing before the rise in Muslim divorce rates, especially in Western countries, have been on the rise in recent years, and 'online divorce' services have facilitated that even more. Imams Allāh is divorce*. Retrieved November 25, 2023, from http://Islamicqa.info/en/120761

Islāmic Q&A. (2011). *148520: Divorce by phone*. Retrieved November 25, 2023, from http://Islamicqa.info/en/148520

Islāmic Q&A (2012). *158723: Ruling on swearing by the life of the Qurʾān*. Retrieved November 28, 2023, from http://Islamicqa.info/en/158723

Islāmic Q&A. (2023). *142223. Numerous sharʿi guidelines restrict the issuing of divorces*. Retrieved November 25, 2023, from https://Islamicqa.info/en/answers/142223/numerous-shari-guidelines-restrict-the-issuing-of-divorces

Jana-Masri, A., & Priester, P. E. (2007). The development and validation of a Qur'an-based instrument to assess Islāmic religiosity: The religiosity of Islām Scale. *Journal of Muslim Mental Health*, 2(2), 177–188.

Johnson, S. M., & Brubacher, L. L. (2016). Emotionally focused couple therapy: Empiricism and art. In T. L. Sexton & J. Lebow (Eds.), *Handbook of family therapy* (pp. 326–348). Routledge/Taylor & Francis Group.

Johnson, S. M., & Greenberg, L. S. (1992). Emotionally focused therapy: Restructuring attachment. In S. H. Budman, M. F. Hoyt, & S. Friedman (Eds.), *The first session in brief therapy* (pp. 204–224). Guilford Press.

Johnson, S. M., Hunsley, J., Greenberg, L., & Schindler, D. (1999). Emotionally focused couples therapy: Status and challenges. *Clinical Psychology: Science and Practice*, 6(1), 67–79. https://doi.org/10.1093/clipsy.6.1.67

Larsen, R., Buss, D., Wismeijer, A., & Song, J. (2017). *Personality psychology: Domains of knowledge about human nature*. McGraw-Hill Education.

Miller, W. R., & Rollnick, S. (2002). *Motivational interviewing: Preparing people for change* (2nd ed.). Guilford Press.

Mohd Mahudin N. D., Mohd Noor, N., Dzulkifli, M. A., & Janon, N. S. (2016). Religiosity among Muslims: A scale development and validation study. *Makara Hubs-Asia, 20*(2), 109–120. https://doi.org/10.7454/mssh.v20i2.3492

Olufadi, Y. (2017). Muslim Daily Religiosity Assessment Scale (MUDRAS): A new instrument for Muslim religiosity research and practice. *Psychology of Religion and Spirituality, 9*(2), 165–179. https://doi.org/10.1037/rel0000074

Rassool, G. Hussein (2019). *Evil eye, Jinn possession, and mental health issues: The Islāmic perspective*. Routledge.

Sahin, A., & Francis, L. J. (2002). Assessing attitude toward Islām among Muslim adolescents: The psychometric properties of the Sahin-Francis Scale. *Muslim Education Quarterly, 19*, 35–47.

Siddiqui, S. (2009). *Divorce among American Muslims: Statistics, challenges & solutions*. Retrieved November 25, 2023, from www.soundvision.com/article/divorce-among-american-muslims-statistics-challenges-solutions

Siddiqui, S. (n.d.). *15 guidelines for marriage counselors when dealing with Muslim clients*. Retrieved from https://www.soundvision.com/article/15-guidelines-for-marriage-counselors-when-dealing-with-muslim-clients

Tiliouine, H., Cummins, R. A., & Davern, M. (2009). Islāmic religiosity, subjective well-being, and health. *Mental Health, Religion & Culture, 12*(1), 55–74.

Tirmidhî. *Tirmidhî, 1084*. Classed as Hasan by al-Albani in Sahih al-Tirmidhî, 866.

Tschannen, R. A. (2021). *Divorce rate by country: The world's 10 most and least divorced nations*. Retrieved November 25, 2023, from https://themuslimtimes.info/2021/12/09/divorce-rate-by-country-the-worlds-10-most-and-least-divorced-nations/

Whitbourne, S. K. (2012). 5 principles of effective couples therapy. *Psychology Today*. Retrieved November 27, 2023, from www.psychologytoday.com/blog/fulfillment-any-age/201203/5-principles-effective-couples-therapy

Whitfield, C. L. (1993). *Boundaries and relationships: Knowing, protecting, and enjoying the self*. Health Communications.

Wiebe, S. A., & Johnson, S. M. (2016). A review of the research in emotionally focused therapy for couples. *Family Process, 55*(3), 390–407. https://doi.org/10.1111/famp.12229

Wilde, A., & Joseph, S. (1997). Religiosity and personality in a Moslem context. *Personality and Individual Differences, 23*(5), 899–900.

Yilmaz, O., & Zollmann, F. (2014). Development of an Islāmic Religiosity Scale (IRIS) in a Turkish context. *Archive for the Psychology of Religion, 36*(1), 69–85.

PART III
The healing path
Practical intervention strategies in Islāmic psychotherapy

15
HEALING HEARTS AND MINDS

Integrating Qur'ân and *hādīths* in Islāmic psychotherapy

Introduction

In the contemporary world, individuals encounter complex psychospiritual challenges that go beyond traditional psychological issues, encompassing a wide range of concerns at the intersection of psychology and spirituality. The term "psychospiritual" encompasses various perspectives that bridge psychology and spirituality, acknowledging the vital role of spirituality in human well-being and holistic development (Gleig, 2010). Psychospiritual challenges often involve internal conflicts stemming from deeply held sacred beliefs, known as religious or spiritual struggles (Exline, 2013; Pargament et al., 2005). These struggles can connect with psychological and emotional issues, leading to psychospiritual problems. Examples include conflicts between personal beliefs and religious teachings, cognitive dissonance, and existential questioning. Moral dilemmas, concerns about life's meaning, and responses to trauma, grief, or loss may also contribute to distress, prompting individuals to reassess their religious or spiritual beliefs and seek new sources of meaning and support.

Psychospiritual problems are prevalent across various demographics, including individuals with mood disorders, college students, Muslim war refugees, and those facing challenges during the COVID-19 pandemic (Ai et al., 2005; Upenieks, 2022). These struggles are not limited to specific demographic groups, as individuals of diverse ages, genders, ethnicities, religious affiliations, and socioeconomic status have reported experiencing them (Abu Raiya et al., 2015). Religious or spiritual struggles encompass three main categories: supernatural struggles involving perceptions of deities or evil forces, intrapsychic struggles related to tensions about beliefs and ultimate meaning, and interpersonal struggles involving conflicts with others about religious/spiritual issues (Pargament & Exline, 2020).

DOI: 10.4324/9781003453413-18

The absence of spirituality has been associated with feelings of hopelessness, meaninglessness, and depression, contributing to existential crises, identity conflicts, moral dilemmas, grief, and loneliness (Westgate, 1996). Even atheists acknowledge some form of religious or spiritual struggles, albeit at lower levels compared to theists, particularly in areas such as demonic, doubt, divine, and moral struggles (Sedlar et al., 2018). Atheists demonstrate comparable levels to those of theists in interpersonal and ultimate meaning struggles. Therapists adopting a psychospiritual approach incorporate both psychological principles and spiritual therapeutic interventions.

Alongside evidence-based psychological techniques, therapists draw upon Islāmic teachings, such as recitation of the Qur'ân, reflection on Islāmic concepts and stories, *dhikr* (remembrance of Allāh), and seeking guidance from *hādīths*. Owens et al. (2023) explore interventions that utilise the Qur'ân as a factor in promoting mental health. The identified interventions included *salah* (prayer) and supplicant praying, as well as activities such as recitation, reading, memorising, and listening to the Qur'ân. These interventions aim to reduce anxiety, depression, and stress while enhancing quality of life and coping mechanisms. Owens et al. concluded that the Qur'ân could be effectively utilised for Muslim patients by integrating it into routine health care interventions and delivery platforms, thereby closely aligning with Islāmic lifestyles. The aims of this chapter are to examine the power of faith in Islāmic psychotherapy and the integration of the Qur'ân and *hādīths* in Islāmic psychotherapy.

The power of faith in Islāmic psychotherapy

Islāmic psychotherapy emphasises the significant role of faith (*iman*) in enhancing mental and emotional well-being. Faith, as outlined in the Qur'ân, offers strength, resilience, and hope for individuals navigating psychological challenges. Belief in a compassionate and merciful God forms a cornerstone for mental resilience. The "pillars of *iman*" are belief in Allāh (*tawhīd*); angels (*mala'ika*), divine books (*kutub*), prophets and messengers (*nubuwwah*), the Day of Judgment (*qiyamah*), and divine decree (*qadr*). These pillars establish the foundation of a Muslim's belief system, providing insight into the nature of God, the universe, and human existence. Faith (*iman*) instils a sense of meaning and purpose in life, fostering a profound connection and devotion to Allāh. *Taqwa* (God consciousness) further strengthens the individual's relationship with God. Islāmic teachings emphasise God's mercy, forgiveness, and the belief in predestination (*qadr*), offering a positive outlook on life and instilling hope and optimism, especially during trials and tribulations.

Faith teaches that God's presence provides individuals with strength, resilience, and hope to cope with difficult challenges and overcome setbacks. Trusting in God's wisdom, seeking guidance through prayer, and finding inspiration in the Qur'ân and *hādīths* help believers cope with adversity. Faith instils a renewed sense of purpose and resilience, enabling individuals to confront hardships with determination. Knowing that God is ever present offers solace and hope. Faith also plays a crucial role in cultivating a positive self-image and self-worth. Embracing divine creation, God's love and mercy, seeking forgiveness, nurturing spiritual connections, practicing gratitude, and relying on God's strength contribute to enhanced self-esteem. Trusting in God (*tawakkul*) empowers individuals to surmount challenges, fostering a positive self-perception. The continual process of self-purification (*tazkiyah an-nafs*) through faith facilitates profound transformation, nurturing a healthy self-image and profound self-worth.

Qur'ānic wisdom in Islāmic psychotherapy

The Qur'ān is replete with verses that touch upon the complexities of human nature, emotions, and suffering. It includes guidance on patience (*sabr*); gratitude (*shukr*); forgiveness (*maghfirah*); trust in and reliance or dependence on Allāh (*tawakkul*); hope (*amal*); happiness (*sa'id*); resilience (*al-muruna*); empowerment (*tamkeen*); steadfastness (*ath-thabat*); inner strength (*al-qawwah ad-dakhiliyah*); divine support (*an-nasr min Allāh*); guidance (*al-huda*); humility (*tawadhu*); reassurance (*ta'tmeen*); and healing (*shifa'*), all of which are essential elements in the healing process. Regarding the healing process, Allāh says in the Qur'ān,

وَنُنَزِّلُ مِنَ ٱلْقُرْءَانِ مَا هُوَ شِفَآءٌ وَرَحْمَةٌ لِّلْمُؤْمِنِينَ

- *And We send down in the Qur'ān that which is a healing and a mercy for the believers.*

(Al-Isra 17:82, interpretation of the meaning)

This verse highlights the therapeutic potential of the Qur'ān and emphasises its role in healing and providing solace. It emphasises that the Qur'ān is not merely a book of guidance but also a source of healing and mercy. It signifies that the words and teachings of the Qur'ān have the power to bring healing and comfort to those who believe and follow its guidance. Believers are reassured by verses such as Surah Al-Baqarah (2:286), which reminds them that God does not burden a soul beyond its capacity, offering comfort and reassurance to those navigating life's challenges:

لَا يُكَلِّفُ ٱللَّهُ نَفْسًا إِلَّا وُسْعَهَا

- *Allāh does not charge a soul except [with that within] its capacity.*

(Al-Baqarah 2: 286, interpretation of the meaning)

The exegesis of Ibn Kathir (2000) interprets the verse "Allāh burdens not a person beyond his scope" as a demonstration of Allāh's kindness, compassion, and generosity towards His creation. This verse serves as a reminder that Allāh, in His infinite wisdom, does not impose burdens on individuals beyond their capacity to handle. Allāh is aware of our strengths, weaknesses, and limitations, assuring humanity of His justice and mercy while considering individual circumstances and capabilities. During psychospiritual challenges, this verse instils hope, comfort, and encouragement, prompting believers to have faith in Allāh 's knowledge and decree. It reminds individuals that even during difficult periods, they possess inner strength and resources to face adversity.

Other verses in the Qur'ân provide reassurance to believers that no matter how tough their circumstances may be, relief is guaranteed. They encourage believers to endure with patience, rely on Allāh's help, and trust in His ultimate wisdom. Allāh says in the Qur'ân,

$$\text{فَإِنَّ مَعَ ٱلْعُسْرِ يُسْرًا}$$
$$\text{إِنَّ مَعَ ٱلْعُسْرِ يُسْرًا}$$

- *For indeed, with hardship* [will be] *ease* [i.e. relief].
- *Indeed, with hardship* [will be] *ease.*

(Ash-Sharh (94:5–6, interpretation of the meaning)

This profound verse offers a message of hope and reassurance to those facing difficulties and hardships in their lives. All these verses are poignant reminders to believers that no matter how challenging or overwhelming a situation may seem, difficulties in life are temporary, and relief and ease will eventually come.

Hadīths as therapeutic narratives

The *hadīths*, which comprise the sayings and actions of Prophet Muhammad (ﷺ), offer valuable therapeutic narratives. The Prophet's exemplary character, compassion, and empathetic interactions with people offer a model for therapeutic practice. His emphases on active listening, understanding, and providing solace aligns remarkably with modern psychotherapy principles. These *hadīths* encourage practitioners to approach their clients with a similar spirit of compassion and understanding. In the context of psychotherapy, incorporating *hadīths* that emphasise gratitude, contemplation, and compassionate communication can greatly benefit Muslim clients.

Gratitude-focused *hadīths* can be integrated into therapeutic exercises such as contemplation or journaling, encouraging clients to cultivate mindsets of thankfulness and foster optimism in their lives. By reflecting on these teachings, clients can gain deeper appreciation for the blessings in their lives, shifting their focus towards positivity and enhancing their overall well-being. Contemplation techniques inspired by *hadīths*, such as *dhikr* (remembrance of Allāh), can be utilised to help clients stay present and manage stress. By integrating these *hadīths* into therapy sessions, clients can develop practical tools for effective communication, leading to improved connections and more fulfilling relationships. It is also important to note that *hādīths* provide guidance and direction in seeking divine assistance and recognising that healing ultimately comes from Allāh. This is reflected in the following: it was narrated from Abu Hurayrah that the Messenger of Allāh (ﷺ) said, "Allāh does not send down any disease but He also sends down the cure" (Ibn Majah).

Integrating classical scholars with psychospiritual challenges

Islāmic psychotherapy draws upon the profound writings of renowned Islāmic scholars who have delved into the *ilm-an-nafs* (psychology of the soul), offering valuable interpretations of Islāmic teachings in the context of psychospiritual health. Some of the prominent physicians and theologians include Ibn Miskawayh, Al-Rāzī, Ibn al-Qayyim al-Jawziyyah, Imam Ibn Hazm, Imam Al-Ghazālī, Al-Balkhī, Ibn Sīnā, Ibn Taymīyah Al-Ḥarrānī, Ar-Rāghib Al-Aṣbahānī, and Ibn Rajab Al-Ḥanbalī (Rassool & Luqman, 2023). Although their writings may not have explicitly focused on psychotherapy, they contain valuable psychological and spiritual insights that therapists can incorporate into their practices to promote mental and emotional well-being among Muslim clients. Islāmic psychotherapists benefit from engaging with these contributions, enriching their therapeutic methods by incorporating insights from the past.

Therapist integration of Qur'ânic verses and *hādīths* in psychotherapy

The integration of Qur'ânic verses in psychotherapy is a practice that many Muslim therapists may employ to provide spiritual and emotional support to their clients. One aspect of this approach is helping individuals identify Qur'ânic verses and *hādīths* that are relevant to their specific psychospiritual challenges. Through this approach, therapists can help clients discover profound spiritual guidance and solace within their faith. The therapist may also encourage individuals to reflect on the meaning of Qur'ânic verses or *hādīths* and explore how these teachings can be applied to their own life circumstances. This process of reflection allows clients to gain insights, find strength, and derive practical wisdom from the sacred texts.
Furthermore, the therapist may utilise Qur'ânic verses or *hādīths*, or both, to help individuals develop a more positive sense of the self by highlighting teachings that emphasise compassion, forgiveness, empathy, and kindness towards others. It is important to note that there is no one-size-fits-all approach to integrating Qur'ânic verses and *hādīths* into therapy. The best approach will vary depending on the individual's needs, the context and appropriateness during the therapeutic process. The following examples demonstrate how therapists can integrate specific Qur'ânic verses into therapy sessions to address various psychological and emotional challenges. However, it is essential to tailor one's approach to the client's unique needs

and ensure that the client finds value and meaning in these teachings as part of their therapeutic journey.

Therapists can integrate Qur'ānic verses in addressing anxiety through evidence-based techniques to help clients manage and alleviate their symptoms. The process typically begins with a thorough assessment to understand the nature and impact of the client's anxiety. The goal is to empower clients to effectively manage their anxiety, enhance their mental well-being, and develop strategies for preventing relapse. Throughout this process, therapists create a safe and empathetic environment for clients to express their feelings and concerns. Relaxation techniques, behavioural interventions, and exploration of underlying factors contributing to anxiety are also part of the therapist's toolkit.

Psychoeducation plays a vital role as well, where therapists provide clients with knowledge about anxiety, its causes, and its common symptoms. This helps clients gain insight into their condition and reduces uncertainty and fear. The core of anxiety treatment often involves evidence-based techniques such as Islām-modified CBT in which clients work with their therapists to identify and challenge irrational or negative thought patterns contributing to anxiety. Through Islām-oriented cognitive restructuring, clients learn to replace these thoughts with more balanced and realistic ones. Exposure therapy is another effective technique that involves gradual and controlled exposure to anxiety-inducing situations, helping clients reduce their anxiety over time.

The therapist may integrate Qur'ānic verses, such as "Verily, with every difficulty, there is relief" (Qur'ān 94:5), when addressing a client's anxiety and the belief that their challenges will never diminish. By exploring the meaning and application of this verse, the therapist helps the client find reassurance and comfort, reminding them that relief will eventually come after periods of hardship. The therapist can support the client in developing coping mechanisms such as reconnecting with Allāh, engaging in contemplation, or seeking solace through prayer, all rooted in these teachings. Integrating Qur'ānic verses into therapy sessions provides a spiritual perspective that aids individuals in finding strength, hope, and resilience through their faith while also addressing their anxiety. Regular progress monitoring ensures that the treatment plan remains effective, and clients receive homework assignments to practice and reinforce the skills they learn in therapy. By fostering a collaborative and trusting relationship, therapists enable clients regain control over their lives and build a foundation for lasting well-being.

In another example, therapists could address a client's anxiety by integrating the following Qur'ānic verse into therapy:

لِصَٰحِبِهِۦ لَا تَحْزَنْ إِنَّ ٱللَّهَ مَعَنَا

- *Do not grieve, for Allāh is with us.*

(At-Taubah 9:40, interpretation of the meaning)

The therapist might help the individual to reflect on the meaning of this verse and how it can be applied to their own life. For example, the therapist might ask the individual to think about the things that they are grieving about and how Allāh can help them through their difficulties. The therapist might also encourage the individual to recite this verse when they are feeling anxious or stressed. This could help to calm the individual down and remind them that Allāh is with them. During times of difficulty, Prophet Muhammad (ﷺ) has taught us a powerful supplication (*du'ah*) that we can recite. This *du'ah* can provide immense comfort and solace.

اللَّهُمَّ لاَ سَهْلَ إِلاَّ مَا جَعَلْتَهُ سَهْلاً، وَأَنْتَ تَجْعَلُ الْحَزْنَ إِذَا شِئْتَ سَهْلاً

- *Allāhumma lā sahla illā ma ja'altahu sahla wa anta taj'alu 'l-hazna idhā shi'ta sahla.*
- *Allāh, there is no ease other than what You make easy. If You please You ease sorrow.*
(Ibn Hibban et al.)

Another effective option for a therapist working with a Muslim client is to lead them in a guided contemplation of a Qur'ânic verse or passage. This approach can be particularly powerful in helping clients connect their faith with their emotional and psychological well-being. During this guided contemplation, the therapist selects a relevant Qur'ânic verse or passage based on the client's specific needs and challenges.

For example, if the client is grappling with feelings of anxiety, the therapist might choose this verse: "Allāh does not burden a soul beyond that it can bear" (Al-Baqarah 2:286). This verse offers reassurance that they have the inner strength to cope with their challenges. During guided contemplation, the therapist may invite the client to reflect on the verse's meaning, exploring how it applies to their anxiety, and how they can find solace and strength in their faith. Clients may share their thoughts and feelings during this contemplation, allowing them to verbalise their insights and emotions. Through this guided contemplation, clients may discover new perspectives, coping strategies, and a sense of spiritual connection and comfort. It can be a transformative experience that integrates their faith into their therapeutic journey, offering them a unique source of strength and guidance. Integrating Qur'ânic teachings into therapy provides profound spiritual guidance and support while addressing psychological well-being.

Another verse that could help a client grappling with anxiety and stress is the following:

ٱلَّذِينَ ءَامَنُواْ وَتَطْمَئِنُّ قُلُوبُهُم بِذِكْرِ ٱللَّهِ ۗ أَلَا بِذِكْرِ ٱللَّهِ تَطْمَئِنُّ ٱلْقُلُوبُ

- *Those who have believed, and whose hearts are assured by the remembrance of Allāh. Unquestionably, by the remembrance of Allāh hearts are assured.*
(Ar-Ra'd 13:28, interpretation of the meaning)

According to Ibn Kathir's exegesis (2000), this verse suggests that hearts find comfort in Allāh, becoming tranquil when remembering Him and feeling content to have Him as their Protector. It underscores the potency of remembering Allāh as a source of peace and reassurance during adversity. Therapists guide clients to reflect deeply on this verse, encouraging exploration of its relevance to their struggles with anxiety and stress.

The use of *hādīths* can also be used during the therapeutic process to illustrate, confirm, and support the therapist's narrative. A'isha reported God's messenger as saying, "When a servant acknowledges his sin and repents, God forgives him" (Bukhari & Muslim). Abdullah ibn 'Amr was heard to say, "Abu Bakr (may Allāh be pleased with him), said to the Prophet (ﷺ), 'Teach me a supplication which I can use in my prayer.' He said, 'Say, "O Allāh, I have wronged myself greatly. Only You forgive wrong actions. Forgive me with forgiveness directly from you. You are the Ever-Forgiving, Most Merciful"'" (Al-Adab Al-Mufrad 706).

Anas (may Allāh be pleased with him) reported that the Messenger of Allāh (ﷺ) said,

> "Allāh, the Exalted, has said, 'O son of Adam, I forgive you as long as you pray to Me and hope for My forgiveness, whatever sins you have committed. O son of Adam, I do not care if your sins reach the height of the heaven, then you ask for my forgiveness, I will forgive you. O son of Adam, if you come to Me with an earth load of sins, and meet Me associating nothing to Me, I would match it with an earthload of forgiveness.'"
>
> *(Tirmidhî)*

In another *hādīth*, the Messenger of Allāh (ﷺ) said, "There is not any slave of Allāh who commits a sin, then he perfects his purification and stands to pray two *rak'ahs* [unit] of prayer, then seeks Allāh's forgiveness, except that Allāh will forgive him" (Abu Dawud (a)).

In the wake of severe life losses, grief and loss can become deeply spiritual experiences, as people question their religion or grapple with feelings of anger and abandonment by God. Integrating *hādīths* about grief and loss into therapy offers a comprehensive approach to supporting clients through their emotional and psychospiritual struggles. It is narrated that the Messenger of Allāh (ﷺ) said, "What Allāh has been taken belongs to Him, what He has given (belongs to Him), and He has appointed time for everything" (Abu Dawud (b)).

In therapy, it is important for the therapist to provide a context for the *hādīth*, aiding clients in understanding its relevance to their grief and emphasising the temporary nature of worldly possessions. By providing contextualisation, therapists support clients in recognising that their grief is part of a larger divine plan and that solace can be found in the eternal rewards promised by Allāh. The therapeutic interventions combine psychological support with spiritual guidance, allowing clients to find comfort and hope in dealing with their loss and grief.

Surah Al-Inshirāḥ (Qur'ân 94) and *Adh-Dhuhā* (Qur'ân 93) are two beautiful and spiritually uplifting chapters from the Qur'ân. They contain profound messages of hope, comfort, and reassurance, making them especially relevant for individuals facing difficulties or seeking solace. For example, a therapist might suggest that the client recite *Surah Al-Inshirāḥ* every morning and evening, or that they take some time each day to reflect on a Qur'ânic verse or passage:

فَإِنَّ مَعَ ٱلْعُسْرِ يُسْرًا
إِنَّ مَعَ ٱلْعُسْرِ يُسْرًا

- *For indeed, with hardship* [will be] *comes ease* [i.e. relief].
- *Indeed, with hardship* [will be] *ease.*

(Al-Inshirāḥ 94:5–6, interpretation of the meaning)

Al-inshirah, meaning "solace" or "comfort," is also known as *Surah ash-Sharh*, literally, "The Opening-up of the Heart." *Surah al-inshirah* "thematically deals with comforting and offering solace to believers." Quranic Quotes (n.d.). It came as a word of encouragement from Allāh to the Prophet (ﷺ) and his *ummah*. This chapter repeats the verse "Verily, with hardship, comes ease" twice, effectively implying that for each difficulty we face, Allāh sends us twice the relief or reward and a reason to be grateful." *Surah Adh-Dhuhā* ("The Morning Hours") begins with the mention of the morning hours and the night, symbolising the cycles of life, including times of ease and hardship. It assures Prophet Muhammad (ﷺ) of Allāh's unwavering support and reminds him of the blessings bestowed upon him, such as guidance and protection. The *surah* then encourages gratitude and that even during challenging times, we should remain patient and trust in Allāh's plan. Allāh says in the Qur'ân,

وَٱلضُّحَىٰ
وَٱلَّيْلِ إِذَا سَجَىٰ
مَا وَدَّعَكَ رَبُّكَ وَمَا قَلَىٰ
وَلَلْءَاخِرَةُ خَيْرٌ لَّكَ مِنَ ٱلْأُولَىٰ
وَلَسَوْفَ يُعْطِيكَ رَبُّكَ فَتَرْضَىٰ
أَلَمْ يَجِدْكَ يَتِيمًا فَـَٔاوَىٰ
وَوَجَدَكَ ضَآلًّا فَهَدَىٰ
وَوَجَدَكَ عَآئِلًا فَأَغْنَىٰ
فَأَمَّا ٱلْيَتِيمَ فَلَا تَقْهَرْ
وَأَمَّا ٱلسَّآئِلَ فَلَا تَنْهَرْ
وَأَمَّا بِنِعْمَةِ رَبِّكَ فَحَدِّثْ

- *By the morning brightness*
- *And* [by] *the night when it covers with darkness,*
- *Your Lord has not taken leave of you,* [O Muḥammad], *nor has He detested* [you].

- *And the Hereafter is better for you than the first* [life].
- *And your Lord is going to give you, and you will be satisfied.*
- *Did He not find you an orphan and give* [you] *refuge?*
- *And He found you lost and guided* [you],
- *And He found you poor and made* [you] *self-sufficient.*
- *So as for the orphan, do not oppress* [him].
- *And as for the petitioner, do not repel* [him].
- *But as for the favour of your Lord, report* [it].

(Adh-Dhuhā 93: 1–11, interpretation of the meaning)

In the context of therapy, incorporating these *surah*s (chapters) can provide a spiritual framework for clients to find strength, hope, and a sense of purpose. Clients may explore the themes of patience, gratitude, and trust in their therapeutic processes, drawing upon the teachings of these chapters to navigate their challenges and find inner peace.

Conclusion

Incorporating the Qur'ân and *hādīths* into Islāmic psychotherapy recognises the interconnectedness of physical, emotional, psychological, and spiritual aspects of human beings. This holistic approach aims to empower individuals by providing a comprehensive path to healing, fostering solace, purpose, and resilience within their faith, thereby contributing to mental and emotional well-being. Therapists guide clients in developing spiritual practices such as Qur'ânic recitation, contemplation, supplication, and prayer, creating a structured framework for spiritual engagement. These practices enable clients to connect with God, seeking guidance and support in their daily lives. Therapists actively support clients in developing personalised spiritual routines, helping them draw strength from their faith and incorporate spiritual practices into their daily lives. By emphasising the practical implementation of Qur'ânic principles and *hādīths*, therapists facilitate a deeper connection to faith, offering a source of strength and support for individuals navigating the complexities of mental, emotional and spiritual well-being.

The integration of Qur'ânic verses and *hādīths* into psychotherapy involves a multifaceted approach aimed at enhancing clients' connection to their faith, fostering self-reflection, and providing a framework for navigating life's challenges. Encouraging clients to engage in writing reflections allows them to articulate their thoughts, emotions, and insights related to the teachings of the verses and their perception of remembrance of Allah in their lives. Discussions during therapy sessions provide opportunities for clients to explore the practical implementation of remembrance of Allāh in their daily lives.

Therapists assist clients in developing individualised practices aligned with their specific needs and beliefs, fostering a deeper connection to faith and drawing strength from spirituality as they navigate anxiety and stress. Integration should always be client-centred and voluntary, ensuring meaningful and beneficial support.

Therapists should be knowledgeable in both psychology and Islāmic teachings to provide effective and culturally sensitive assistance to their clients.

References

Abu Dawud (a) 2/86, At-Tirmidhi 2/257. Al-Albani graded it authentic in Sahih Abu Dawud 1/283. Hisn al-Muslim 140. https://sunnah.com/hisn:140

Abu Dawud (b). Sunan Abi Dawud 3125. In-book reference: Book 21, Hadith 37. English translation: Book 20, Hadith 3119. Sahih (Al-Albani). https://sunnah.com/abudawud:3125.

Abu-Raiya, H., Pargament, K. I., Krause, N., & Ironson, G. (2015). Robust links between religious/spiritual struggles, psychological distress, and well-being in a national sample of American adults. *American Journal of Orthopsychiatry, 85*(6), 565–575.

Al-Adab Al-Mufrad 706. In-book reference: Book 31, Hadith 103. English translation: Book 31, Hadith 706. Grade: Sahih (Al-Albani).

Ai, A. L., Tice, T. N., Huang, B., & Ishisaka, A. (2005). Wartime faith-based reactions among traumatized Kosovar and Bosnian refugees in the United States. *Mental Health, Religion, and Culture, 8*(4), 291–308.

Exline, J. J. (2013). Religious and spiritual struggles. In K. I. Pargament, J. Exline, & J. Jones (Eds.), *APA handbooks in psychology: APA handbook of psychology, religion, and spirituality: Vol. 1, Context, theory, and research* (pp. 459–476). American Psychological Association.

Gleig, A. (2010). Psychospiritual. In D. A. Leeming, K. Madden, & S. Marlan (Eds.), *Encyclopedia of psychology and religion*. Springer. https://doi.org/10.1007/978-0-387-71802-6_544

Ibn Hibban (no. 2427), and Ibn As-Sunni (no. 351). *Al-Hafidh* (Ibn Hajar) said that this Hadith is authentic. Declared authentic by 'Abdul-Qadir Al-Arna'ut -Nawawi's Kitabul-Athkarp. 106. Hisn al-Muslim 139. https://sunnah.com/hisn:139

Ibn Kathir. (2000). *Tafsir In Kathir* (J. Abualrub, N. Khitab, H. Khitab, A. Walker, M. Al-Jibali., & S. Ayoub, Trans.). Darussalam Publishers and Distributors.

Ibn Majah. *Sunan Ibn Majah 3439*. In-book reference: Book 31, Hadith 4. English translation: Vol. 4, Book 31, Hadith 3439. Sahih (Darussalam). https://sunnah.com/ibnmajah:3439

Owens, J., Rassool, G. Hussein, Bernstein, J., Latif, S., & Aboul-Enein, B. H. (2023). Interventions using the Qur'an to promote mental health: A systematic scoping review. *Journal of Mental Health, 32*(4), 842–862. https://doi.org/10.1080/09638237.2023.2232449

Pargament, K. I., & Exline, J. J. (2020). *Religious and spiritual struggles*. American Psychological Association. Retrieved September 20, 2023, from www.apa.org/topics/belief-systems-religion/spiritual-struggles

Pargament, K. I., Murray-Swank, N., Magyar, G., & Ano, G. (2005). Spiritual struggle: A phenomenon of interest to psychology and religion. In W. R. Miller & H. Delaney (Eds.), *Judeo-Christian perspectives on psychology: Human nature, motivation, and change* (pp. 245–268). APA Press.

Quranic Quotes. (n.d.). *Surah al-Inshirah: Peace and solace for troubled hearts*. Retrieved September 23, 2023, from https://quranicquotes.com/notes/surah-inshirah/

Rassool, G. Hussein, & Luqman, M. (2023). *Foundations of Islāmic psychology; From classical scholars to contemporary thinkers*. Routledge.

Sedlar, A. E., Stauner, N., Pargament, K. I., Exline, J. J., Grubbs, J. B., & Bradley, D. F. (2018). Spiritual struggles among atheists: Links to psychological distress and well-being. *Religions, 9*(8), 242.

Tirmidhî. *Reference: Riyad as-Salihin 442*. https://sunnah.com/riyadussalihin:442

Upenieks, L. (2022). Religious/spiritual struggles and well-being during the COVID-19 pandemic: Does "talking religion" help or hurt? *Review of Religious Research, 64*(2), 249–278. https://doi.org/10.1007/s13644-022-00487-0

Westgate, C. E. (1996). Spiritual wellness and depression. *Journal of Counseling & Development, 75*(1), 26–33.

16
JOURNEY THROUGH THE NIGHT
An Islāmic approach to dream interpretation

Introduction

Dream interpretation is a fascinating field within psychology that has seen the development of various approaches over the years. Dreams can be defined "as the images and thoughts that are experienced during sleep" (Blagrove, 2009). Throughout history, dream interpretation has intrigued people in various ancient societies, including Egypt, Greece, and Native American cultures as dreams were often perceived as a form of supernatural communication or divine intervention. Those believed to possess spiritual powers were thought to decipher the meanings of dreams. Furthermore, the Qur'ân features the story of Joseph (Yusuf), who gained renown for his ability to interpret dreams, highlighting the religious significance of dream interpretation in Islāmic tradition.

The significance and interpretation of dreams are subjects of debate among psychologists. Some believe that dreams hold deep significance, offering insights into unconscious desires and conflicts. Dream analysis aims to uncover symbolism and narratives, providing understanding of the individual's psyche. On the contrary, others view dreams as random brain processes during sleep, lacking psychological relevance. Despite these differences, dream interpretation offers valuable insights into psychological makeup by analysing symbols, themes, and emotions. This helps in constructing a psychological profile of the dreamer, aiding in deeper assessment of their condition (Pace-Schott et al., 2003).

The Qur'ân includes the story of Joseph (Yusuf), renowned for his skill in interpreting dreams, highlighting the religious importance of dream interpretation in Islāmic tradition. Islām has long acknowledged the value of dreams as a medium through which divine guidance and personal insights are communicated, as evidenced by narratives in the Qur'ân and the rich tapestry of *hādīths*. In the Islāmic worldview, dreams are a portal to the metaphysical realm, offering individuals the opportunity to receive divine messages, warnings, or glimpses into their own inner selves. The practice of dream interpretation, deeply rooted in Islāmic tradition, finds its origins in the Qur'ān and the teachings of Prophet Muhammad (ﷺ). Understanding the meaning of dreams in Islām involves exploring their functions as sources of inspiration, guidance, and spiritual illumination. With this chapter, the aim is to provide an overview of dream theories and approaches, including those of Freud, Jung, and Hall, while emphasising dream interpretation within the framework of Islāmic tradition.

Dreaming and the brain

Dreams and their interpretation are fascinating subjects intricately tied to the complex sleep stages of the human brain. Dreaming is associated with different sleep phases, including light sleep (stages 1 and 2), deep sleep (stages 3 and 4), and rapid eye movement (REM) sleep. Approximately 14% of individuals report dreaming every night, while 6% claim they never dream, with dream recall frequency declining with age. The sleep cycle encompasses these phases, each serving distinct functions: light sleep initiates the cycle, deep sleep aids immune system strengthening and cellular repair, and REM sleep exhibits brain activity resembling wakefulness despite low muscle tone.

REM sleep occurs roughly every 90 minutes, with durations increasing across cycles, and the final REM cycle near the morning can last up to 40 minutes, whereas the initial one may be as brief as 5 minutes. During stage 3 and REM (deep sleep), the immune system is strengthened, cell reparation and rebuilding take place, and hormones are secreted to promote bone and muscle growth (National Institutes of Neurological Disorders and Stroke, 2023). In addition, the brain consolidates declarative memories, such as general knowledge, facts or statistics, personal experiences, and new information (Feld & Diekelmann, 2015). Further memory consolidation occurs at stage 4. There is the suggestion that emotions and emotional memories are processed and stored (Glosemeyer et al., 2020). Solms (1997) and Hobson et al. (2000) examined the debates on whether dreaming is especially associated with REM sleep.

Significance of dreams

From a cognitive perspective, the scientific exploration of dreams suggests that they possess meaning and often reflect or depict recent waking experiences, particularly the emotions felt during wakefulness (Malinowski, 2012). Research indicates that in the majority of dreams (75%), distinct emotions or moods are observed, with joy being the most prevalent, followed by anger and fear (Strauch & Meier, 1996). Neuroscientific theories propose that bad dreams may prepare individuals to face real-life dangers (Sterpenich et al., 2020).

Lucid dreaming, where the dreamer is aware of being in a dream and can control its content, is a rare phenomenon explored through techniques like the "mnemonic induction of lucid dreams," involving repeating the phrase, "The next time I'm dreaming, I will remember that I'm dreaming" (Adventure-Heart et al., 2017). Additionally, research suggests that dream sharing can yield both personal and social benefits (Blagrove et al., 2019; Blagrove et al., 2021). Edwards et al. (2015) found that sharing dreams can lead to personal insight, with discussions enhancing insight gains. Blagrove et al. (2019) observed a correlation between trait empathy and dream-related behaviours, indicating that discussing dreams may increase empathy towards the dream sharer. Moreover, Blagrove et al. (2021) demonstrated that individuals with initially low empathy levels experienced a significant increase in empathy after engaging in dream discussions. This underlines the potential of dream conversations to foster empathy and deepen interpersonal connections over time.

The following is an abridged version of a quote from a 20-year-old self-diagnosed female student who was suffering from maladaptive daydreaming:

- *I have been lost in a daydream for as long as I can remember. . . . These daydreams tend to be stories . . . for which I feel real emotion, usually happiness or sadness, which have the ability to make me laugh and cry. . . . They're as important a part of my life as anything else; I can spend hours alone with my daydreams. . . . I am careful to control my actions in public, so it is not evident that my mind is constantly spinning these stories and I am constantly lost in them.*

(Soffer-Dudek & Somer, 2018)

This description portrays an individual's rich inner world, where daydreams induce both joy and grief. Despite the private nature of these experiences, the person acknowledges cultural norms by concealing them in public. Daydreams and mental narratives hold significant importance, and the person indulges in them frequently, experiencing genuine emotions like happiness and despair. These imaginative settings captivate individuals, leading them to lose track of time.

Psychological perspective on dreams

The study of dreams in modern psychology has been a diverse effort, with numerous schools of thought proposing interpretations on dreams. Freud (1900/1953) introduced the influential theory that dreams serve as a "royal road to the unconscious," offering insights into repressed desires and wishes. Freud posited that during sleep, thoughts encounter less censorship, allowing for the direct expression of repressed wishes.

Dreams, according to Freud, are not random but rather are "disguised fulfilments of repressed wishes." His dream analysis involves differentiating between manifest content (actual dream events) and latent content (hidden, symbolic meanings reflecting true desires). Symbols are crucial in Freud's interpretation, with elements like the human body, family relations, birth, and death bearing metaphorical significance. For example, a house may symbolise the individual, while parents may represent authoritative figures. Water often symbolises birth and regeneration, and embarking on a journey in a dream may symbolise death, reflecting life's transformative nature.

Freud's free-association technique is a cornerstone of psychoanalytic dream interpretation, involving the exploration of dream elements and encouraging uncensored expression of associated thoughts and ideas. This method aims to uncover the latent content of dreams, revealing hidden symbolic meanings, unconscious desires, or conflicts. Through free association, individuals establish connections between dream elements and personal experiences, childhood memories, or repressed desires, encompassing both narrative and emotional aspects of the dream. While Freud's work, notably *The Interpretation of Dreams*, was groundbreaking, it faced criticism for its subjectivity, contributing to a decline in Freud's influence in psychology and psychiatry over time (Grünbaum, 1984; Eagle, 1986; Yeung, 2021).

Carl Jung's approach to dream interpretation (Jung, 1977, 2016) shares some similarities with Freud's but also diverges in significant ways. Like Freud, Jung recognised that dreams hold latent meanings beneath manifest content. However, Jung proposed that dreams symbolise an individual's quest for balance in their personality rather than mere wish fulfilment as Freud suggested. Jung introduced the concept of the collective unconscious, positing that dreams express elements of a shared, universal unconscious beyond personal experiences.

In Jungian psychology, dreams reflect the current state of the psyche, including unconscious aspects, contrasting with Freud's belief that dreams distort unconscious meaning to protect sleep. Jung suggested that dreams can personify unintegrated or conflicted parts of the personality, such as complexes. This perspective stresses the notion that dreams provide insights into the dynamics of the psyche, aiding individuals in understanding and integrating unconscious elements (Roesler, 2020).

Jung also introduced the concept of "personification" in dreams, where psychological elements manifest as distinct persons or figures within the dream scenario. These personified elements engage in interactions, representing unresolved issues or aspects of the dreamer's psyche. Jung believed that dreams use this symbolic language to communicate with the conscious mind, allowing individuals to recognise and confront aspects of themselves that may be in conflict or not fully acknowledged. Through personification, dreams offer a pathway for integrating unconscious elements into conscious awareness, facilitating psychological growth and self-understanding.

Jungian dream analysis employs fundamental principles such as amplification, active imagination, and investigation of polarities to explore the deeper meanings of dreams. It explores the collective unconscious and the concept of individuation while examining mandala symbols (intricate geometric designs that hold significant spiritual and psychological meaning in various cultures, including Hinduism, Buddhism, and Jungian psychology) as representations of wholeness. This approach views dreams holistically, aiming to uncover both personal and universal meanings. Jungian therapy follows a three-stage process, considering the dreamer's personal context, cultural background, and archetypal content to elucidate connections between the dream and humanity as a whole.

Calvin S. Hall's cognitive theory of dreaming introduces a departure from Freud's and Jung's perspectives by focusing on how dreams represent personal lives through cognitive structures (Hall, 1966). In his theory, Hall suggests that dream images visually express invisible self-concepts, conceptions of others, and world conceptions. Self-concepts encompass how individuals perceive themselves, including their self-image and identity. Conceptions of others involve perceptions and relationships with significant individuals in one's life. World conceptions pertain to observations and understanding of the environment, society, culture, and the physical world.

Hall's theory of dreaming highlights that dream images serve as concrete embodiments of the dreamer's thoughts, giving visual expression to abstract concepts. Hall examines various cognitive concepts such as impulses, prohibitions, punishments, and perceptions of difficulties and conflicts within dreams. Impulses and prohibitions relate to our understanding of repressed wishes and desires, considering what is allowed or forbidden and the potential consequences. Issues and conflicts encompass the obstacles we encounter, including both external and internal factors such as hurdles, problems, and conflicts in our lives. Overall, Hall's theory highlights the cognitive aspects of dreams, exploring the complexities of suppressed desires, perceived norms, and internal and external challenges within the dream narrative.

Behavioural psychologists interpret dreams by examining the relationship between an individual's waking behaviours and the content of their dreams, emphasising how daily actions and experiences influence dream content. They analyse patterns in dream behaviour to understand a person's experiences and actions during wakefulness. In contrast, humanistic psychologists view dreams as reflections of the self and the dreamer's responses to their environment, considering them symbolic representations of inner thoughts, feelings, and desires. Humanistic psychologists value the personal interpretation of dreams as sources of insight into psychological well-being, self-understanding, and self-actualisation. While humanistic psychologists focus on self-concept and personal growth in dreams, behavioural psychologists emphasise behavioural and experiential aspects, offering distinct perspectives on dream interpretation and its connections to an individual's psychology and experiences.

Dreams in the Qur'ân and *hādīths*

Dreams hold a significant place in Islāmic tradition that is deeply rooted in the Qur'ân. The modes of revelation of the Qur'ân refer to the different ways in which Allāh communicated the divine message to Prophet Muhammad (ﷺ). The three main modes of revelation are *wahy* (inspiration or revelation); *ilham* (divine inspiration); and *ru'ya sadaqah* (dreams). The following is narrated by 'Aisha (the Mother of the faithful believers): "The commencement of the Divine Inspiration to Allāh 's Messenger was in the form of good dreams which came true like bright daylight, and then the love of seclusion was bestowed upon him" (Bukhârî (a)). The Noble Qur'ân was revealed to Prophet Muhammad (ﷺ), the last Messenger of Allāh, through a series of revelations over a period of 23 years. Many of these revelations were received by the Prophet during his sleep or in a visionary state. Allāh says in the Qur'ân,

وَكَذَٰلِكَ أَوْحَيْنَآ إِلَيْكَ رُوحًا مِّنْ أَمْرِنَا ۚ مَا كُنتَ تَدْرِى مَا ٱلْكِتَٰبُ وَلَا ٱلْإِيمَٰنُ وَلَٰكِن جَعَلْنَٰهُ نُورًا نَّهْدِى بِهِۦ مَن نَّشَآءُ مِنْ عِبَادِنَا ۚ وَإِنَّكَ لَتَهْدِىٓ إِلَىٰ صِرَٰطٍ مُّسْتَقِيمٍ

- *And it is not for any human being that Allāh should speak to him except by revelation or from behind a partition or that He sends a messenger* [i.e. the angel] *to reveal, by His permission, what He wills. Indeed, He is Most High and Wise.*
  (Ash-Shura 42:51, interpretation of the meaning)

The scholars of Qur'ânic sciences discuss this issue and have accordingly determined that "what comes in the true dreams of the Messengers and Prophets is also understood from the verse, except by revelation" (Abdul-Rasheed, 2023). This reinforces dreams as a means for Allāh to communicate with His chosen messengers as stated in Ash-Shura 42:51 of the Qur'ân and in *hadīths*. In the dream of Prophet Abraham – the patriarch of Judaism, Christianity, and Islām – Allāh commanded Abraham to sacrifice his son Ismail. Muslims regard Abraham's readiness to fulfil Allāh's order as a defining moment of total obedience to Allāh's will. Allāh says in the Qur'ân,

قَالَ يَٰبُنَىَّ إِنِّىٓ أَرَىٰ فِى ٱلْمَنَامِ أَنِّىٓ أَذْبَحُكَ فَٱنظُرْ مَاذَا تَرَىٰ ۚ قَالَ يَٰٓأَبَتِ ٱفْعَلْ مَا تُؤْمَرُ ۖ سَتَجِدُنِىٓ إِن شَآءَ ٱللَّهُ مِنَ ٱلصَّٰبِرِينَ

- *He said, "O my son, indeed I have seen in a dream that I [must] sacrifice you. So, see what you think." He replied, "O my father! Do as you are commanded. You will find me steadfast, if Allāh wills, of the steadfast."*
  (As Saffat 37: 102, interpretation of the meaning)

The dream of Prophet Yusuf (Joseph) is a significant example of the power and importance of dreams. According to the Qur'ânic account, Yusuf, as a young boy, had a dream that was highly symbolic and was interpreted as a sign of Yusuf's future authority and prominence. Allāh says in the Qur'ân,

إِذْ قَالَ يُوسُفُ لِأَبِيهِ يَٰٓأَبَتِ إِنِّى رَأَيْتُ أَحَدَ عَشَرَ كَوْكَبًا وَٱلشَّمْسَ وَٱلْقَمَرَ رَأَيْتُهُمْ لِى سَٰجِدِينَ

- [of the stories mentioned] *When Joseph said to his father, "O my father! Indeed, I have seen* [in a dream] *eleven stars, and the sun, and the moon; I saw them prostrating to me!"*
  (Yusuf 12:4. interpretation of the meaning)

The dream of Prophet Yusuf exemplifies the power and significance of dreams in Islām. It emphasises the concept that dreams can convey prophetic messages and heavenly guidance. Prophet Yusuf shared this dream with his father, Prophet Ya'qub (Jacob), and his brothers. However, due to jealousy and envy, his brothers plotted against him and threw him into a well, ultimately leading to Yusuf's separation from his family and his subsequent rise to power in Egypt. While imprisoned in Egypt, Prophet Yusuf gained a reputation as an interpreter of dreams. Allāh says in the Qur'ân,

وَكَذَٰلِكَ يَجْتَبِيكَ رَبُّكَ وَيُعَلِّمُكَ مِن تَأْوِيلِ ٱلْأَحَادِيثِ وَيُتِمُّ نِعْمَتَهُۥ عَلَيْكَ وَعَلَىٰٓ ءَالِ يَعْقُوبَ كَمَآ أَتَمَّهَا عَلَىٰٓ أَبَوَيْكَ مِن قَبْلُ إِبْرَٰهِيمَ وَإِسْحَٰقَ ۚ إِنَّ رَبَّكَ عَلِيمٌ حَكِيمٌ

- *And thus, will your Lord choose you and teach you the interpretation of narratives* [i.e. events or dreams] *and complete his favour upon you and the family of Jacob, as He completed it upon your fathers before, Abraham and Isaac. Indeed, your Lord is Knowing, and Wise.*

(Yusuf 12:6, interpretation of the meaning)

While Prophet Yusuf was in prison, the Pharaoh had a puzzling dream in which he sought guidance and interpretation. The Pharaoh learned of Yusuf's interpretative powers and invited him to interpret the dream, which predicted a period of wealth followed by a period of famine. The Pharaoh, impressed by Yusuf's wisdom and expertise, appointed him as his chief advisor, giving him authority and responsibility over Egypt's resources during the predicted famine. Prophet Yusuf's dream interpretation not only demonstrated his wisdom and knowledge but also led to his ascension to a position of authority and influence. The stories of the Prophets in the Qur'ân and the *hādīths* give emphasis to the belief that dreams can hold profound insights and significance, acting as a means for Allāh to convey messages and shape the destiny of individuals.

Significance of dreams in Islām (*hādīths*)

- True dreams are a part of prophethood. Anas bin Malik narrated that the Messenger of Allāh (ﷺ) said, "A good dream from a righteous man is one of the forty-six parts of prophecy" (Ibn Majah (a)).
- In one narration, the Messenger of Allāh (ﷺ) said, "The most truthful of you in their speech are those who see the truest visions" (Muslim (a)).
- Towards the end of time, hardly any dreams will be untrue. The Prophet (ﷺ) said,

That will be because the prophethood and its effects will be so far away in time, so the believers will be given some compensation in the form of dreams which will bring them some good news or will help them to be patient and steadfast in their faith.

(Bukhârî & Muslim (a))

These narrations highlight the significance of true dreams in Islām. True dreams, according to Prophet Muhammad's (ﷺ) teachings, are an element of prophethood. A pious person's good dream is believed to be equivalent to a small portion of prophethood itself; this emphasises the significance and spiritual relevance of such dreams. In addition, the Prophet (ﷺ) emphasised the sincerity of people who had authentic visions or dreams. This means that people who have realistic and significant dreams are thought to be truthful in their words and character. In relation to the future, it is believed that as the end of time approaches, there will be fewer untrue dreams.

Types of dreams

From an Islāmic perspective dreams are of three types: *rahmani* (those that come from Allāh); *nafsani* (psychological dreams that come from within a person); and *Shaytani* (those that come from Satan).

(Islām Q&A, 1999)

Abu Hurayrah (may Allāh be pleased with him) narrated that the Prophet (ﷺ) said,

> Dreams are of three types: glad tidings from Allāh, what is on a person's mind, and frightening dreams from Satan. If any of you sees a dream that he likes, let him tell others of it if he wishes, but if he sees something that he dislikes, he should not tell anyone about it, and he should get up and perform prayer.
>
> *(Ibn Majah (b))*

Al-Haafiz Ibn Hajar said that dreams are either of two types: true dreams or mixed-up false dreams. Ibn Hajar stated that true dreams are those experienced by Prophets and righteous individuals that come true in real life as they were seen in the dream; they may also occur to others, but that is rare. Mixed-up false dreams, which may warn of something, are of various types, such as those originating from the *shaytān* to distress a person or dreams that lack coherence. They may involve scenarios that the dreamer wishes for or experiences in real life, reflecting their current mood or situations. These dreams often relate to the future or the present but seldom to the past (Islām Q&A, 1999). There are different types of mixed-up false dreams:

- "Games of the *shaytān* to make a person distressed, such as when he sees his head cut off and he is following it, or he sees himself falling into a crisis and cannot find anyone to save him from it, and so on."
- "When he sees some of the angels telling him to do something forbidden, or other things that cannot possibly make sense."
- "When he sees something that happens to him in real life, or he wishes it would happen, and he sees it very realistically in his dream; or he sees what usually

happens to him when he is awake or what reflects his mood. These dreams usually speak of the future or the present, rarely of the past."

(Fath al-Bari (a))

In a narration by Abu Sa'id Al-Khudri (may Allāh be pleased with him), the Prophet (ﷺ) said,

If anyone of you sees a dream that he likes, then it is from Allāh, and he should thank Allāh for it and narrate it to others; but if he sees something else, i.e. a dream that he dislikes, then it is from *shaytān*, and he should seek refuge with Allāh from its evil, and he should not mention it to anybody, for it will not harm him.

(Bukhârî (b))

As narrated by Abu Qatada (may Allāh be pleased with him), the Prophet (ﷺ) said,

A good dream that comes true is from Allāh, and a bad dream is from Satan, so if anyone of you sees a bad dream, he should seek refuge with Allāh from Satan and should spit on the left, for the bad dream will not harm him.

(Bukhârî (c))

The "spitting" referred to here is a soft, dry spitting with no saliva ejected. Jabir bin 'Abdullah narrated that the Messenger of Allāh (ﷺ) said, "If anyone of you sees a dream that he dislikes, let him spit dryly to his left three times and seek refuge with Allāh from *shaytān* three times, and turn over onto his other side" (Ibn Majah (c)). Table 16.1 describes how to respond to dreams.

Muhammad B. Sirin said that in response to bad dreams, when one sees anything he dislikes he should not tell it to anyone but should get up and pray (Bukhârî & Muslim (b)). Jabir reported Allāh's Messenger (ﷺ) as saying, "If anyone sees a dream which he does not like . . . let him turn over from the side on which he was

TABLE 16.1 What you should do when you experience dreams

Good dreams	Bad dreams
• Praise Allāh for the good dream • Feel happy about it • Talk about it to those whom he loves but not to those whom he dislikes (Ibn Hajar)	• Seek refuge with Allāh from the evil of the dream • Seek refuge with Allāh from the evil of the *shaytan* • Spit to your left three times when you wake up • Do not mention it to anyone at all • Get up and pray (two *rak'ahs*) (Bukhârî & Muslim (b)) • Turn over from the side on which one was lying (Muslim)

Source: Adapted from Islām Q&A (1999).

sleeping" (Muslim (b)). For those with bad dreams, It was narrated from Abu Razin that he heard the Prophet (ﷺ) say, "[A person] should not tell them except to one whom he loves or one who is wise" (Ibn Majah (d)). According to another report, the individual should not talk about it except for a scholar or one who will give sincere advice. Al-Qaadi Abu Bakr Ibn al-'Arabi said,

> As for the scholar, he will interpret it in a good way for him as much as he can, and the one who will give him sincere advice will teach him something that will be of benefit to him and will help him to do that. The one who is wise is the one who knows how to interpret it and will tell him only that which will help him, otherwise he will keep quiet. The one who is dear, if he knows something good he will say it, and if he does not know or he is in doubt, he will keep quiet.
> *(Fath al-Bari (b), cited in Islām Q&A, 1999)*

However, it is also stated that,

> Whoever wants to have true dreams should strive to speak honestly, eat halal food, adhere to the commandments of *Shar'iah*, avoid that which Allāh and His Messenger (ﷺ) have forbidden, sleep in a state of complete purity facing the *qiblah* [direction of prayer towards Makkah], and remember Allāh until he feels his eyelids drooping. If he does all this, then his dreams can hardly be untrue.
> *(Islām Q&A, 1999)*

In addition,

> The most truthful of dreams are those that are seen at the time of *suhoor* [just before dawn], for this is the time when Allāh descends and when mercy and forgiveness are close. It is also the time when the devils are quiet, unlike the time of darkness just after sunset, when the devils and devilish souls spread out.
> *(Ibn Qayyim al-Jawziyyah-Madārij As Salikīn)*

Islāmic perspective on dream interpretation

The Qur'ân uses several terms to refer to dreams such as *ru'ya* (vision), *hulm* (dream), *manam* (sleep), and *bushra* (tidings). The Arabic terms *tabir* or *tafsir* describe dream interpretation, and Orientalists have used the term "oneiromancy" (Greek words *oneiros*, meaning "dream," and *manteia*, "divination") in the field of Islāmic dream interpretation. Dream interpretation, while valued in both Sunni and Shi'a communities, must be distinguished from oneiromancy, which entails predicting the future through dreams, a practice not universally accepted in Islāmic theology.

Dreams are considered significant across Muslim societies due to their potential for conveying divine insights and approval. Ozgen (2023) highlighted the historical and ongoing importance of dreams as indicators of divine favour and prophecy in Muslim societies. An illustrative example in contemporary Islāmic practice is the practice of *istikhara*, a dream incubation technique that translates to "seeking goodness" from Allāh. It is often undertaken when making important life decisions such as marriage, career choices, or business matters. Through *salat al-istikhara*, Muslims ask for Allāh's wisdom and insight to help them discern the best course of action. Following the prayer, individuals remain attentive to signs or feelings, including dreams, that may indicate divine guidance. Although results may not be immediate, *istikhara* reflects a deep faith in Allāh's wisdom and a commitment to making informed choices aligned with His will.

The Companions of Prophet Muhammad sought to share their dreams with only a select few individuals, primarily the Prophet himself and his close confidant Abu Bakr al-Siddiq. Both the Prophet (露) and Abu Bakr were recognised as proficient interpreters of dreams. In the subsequent generation of Muslims, Ibn Sirin, Ibn Qayyim al-Jawziyyah, Ibn Khaldūn, and Al-Baghawi emerged as prominent figures renowned for dream interpretation.

Ibn Sirin (653–728 C.E.) emphasised the importance of considering the dreamer's personal traits and life circumstances alongside the inherent meaning of dreams for accurate interpretation. His approach involved understanding the dreamer's unique context and experiences to provide contextually appropriate interpretations. Ibn Sirin aimed to offer representative interpretations by incorporating both the individual's characteristics and the content of the dream (Bulkeley, 2016).

While Ibn Sirin is revered as a great scholar, debates persist regarding the attribution of specific works to him, particularly on dream interpretation. Notably, renowned scholars like Imām al-Dhahabi (*Siyar A'lam al-Nubala*) and Ibn Kathir (*Al-Bidaya wa'l-Nihaya*) did not mention any dream interpretation book authored by Ibn Sirin (2007), casting doubt on its existence. Contemporary scholars such as Shaykh Bin Baz and Shaykh Saalih al-Fawzan have emphasised the lack of evidence for Ibn Sirin's authorship of such a book, with Shaykh Saalih al-Fawzan specifically denouncing its authenticity (Shaykh Abdullah ibn Jaru Allāh, 2020). It is reported that the book attributed to Ibn Sirin, *Tafsir al-Ahlam al-Kabir*, was actually compiled by Al-Dārī in the 15th century under a different title (Mavroudi, 2002). This consensus among scholars highlights the importance of critically evaluating historical attributions and relying on authenticated sources when assessing Ibn Sirin's works.

Ibn Khaldūn (1332–1402 C.E.), a renowned Muslim scholar, regarded dream interpretation as a science in his work *Muqaddimah (An Introduction to History)* (Al-Abid Zuhd, 2010). He categorised dreams into three distinct types. Firstly, dreams from God (Allāh) were considered explicit and clear, requiring no interpretation due to their unequivocal meaning. Secondly, angelic dreams were recognised as metaphorical, necessitating interpretation to unveil their intended significance. Lastly, dreams from *shaytān* were characterised as confusing and devoid of meaningful content, leading to futility (Al-Abid Zuhd, 2010; Pruett, 1985). Ibn Khaldūn's classification system reflects his meticulous examination of the diverse natures and sources of dreams, offering a framework for understanding their potential meanings based on their origin and qualities.

Ibn Qayyim al-Jawziyyah (1292–1350 CE), a prominent figure in medieval Islāmic jurisprudence and theology, stressed that the interpretation of dreams, considered a part of prophecy and revelation, is grounded in deductive reasoning and examples comprehensible through perception and intellect (Shaykh Abdullah ibn Jaru Allāh, 2020, p. 45). This perspective aligns with the notion that dream interpretation involves a rational and intellectual process wherein the interpreter employs their reasoning faculties to recognise the symbolic meanings embedded in dreams. The citation from Shaykh Abdullah ibn Jaru Allāh underscores Ibn Qayyim's emphasis on applying logical deduction and perceptible examples in analysing dreams, highlighting the intellectual dimension of this spiritual practice.

Imām al-Baghawi (1041 or 1044–1122 CE) was a renowned Islāmic scholar who is best known for his works in the field of *tafsir* (exegesis of the Qur'ân) and *hādīth* interpretation. Imām al-Baghawi said,

> Know that the interpretation of dreams falls into various categories. Dreams may be interpreted in the light of the Qur'ân or in the light of the *Sunnah*, or by means of the proverbs that are current among people, or by names and metaphors, or in terms of opposites.
> *(Sharh al-Sunnah 12/220, Shaykh Abdullah ibn Jaru Allāh, 2020)*

The declarations acknowledge various methods of dream interpretation, including those rooted in the Qur'ân, the *Sunnah*, cultural proverbs, and symbolic representations. It emphasises the significance of names and metaphors while also considering opposites as part of interpreting dreams. This holistic approach integrates religious, cultural, and symbolic perspectives to understand the meaning of dreams comprehensively.

Dream interpretation and analysis

Imām Malik's response to a question about dream interpretation underlines the gravity and profound significance attached to this practice in Islāmic tradition, rejecting the notion that it is a trivial matter. The imām asked the rhetorical question, "What! Is religion a plaything?" (Shaykh Gibril Haddad, 2009). Similarly, Ibn Qutaybah ad-Dinawari's statement emphasises the complexity and sacred nature of dream interpretation, likening it to a form of revelation and Prophethood. This further emphasised the complexity and importance of dream interpretation and this perspective reinforces the sacred and intricate nature of dreams within the Islāmic context.

In Islām, the interpretation of dreams is a practice reserved for scholars, a prohibition rooted in the acknowledgment of the profound impact dreams can have on emotions, actions, and decisions. By entrusting this task to scholars, Islām recognises the need for a cautious approach, as an incorrect interpretation or misjudgement of a dream can lead to significant consequences. The statement of Prophet Muhammad (ﷺ) that "dreams are one out of forty-six parts of Prophecy" illustrates the importance and potential significance attached to dreams. Ibn Sirin further emphasised the serious connection between dream interpretation and religion, cautioning against relying on amateurs and stating, "This matter is connected with religion, so look well from whom you take your religion!" (Shaykh Gibril Haddad, 2009). This highlights the careful consideration given to the interpretation of dreams within the Islāmīc tradition, linking it closely with matters of religious significance:

> A dream interpreter must have knowledge of the Qur'ânic references, interpretations, sayings of God's Prophet, A dream interpreter must have knowledge of the Qur'ânic references, Qur'ânic interpretations, sayings of God's Prophet, upon whom be peace, allegorical meanings and parables. He also must know the Prophetic traditions, tales of the Prophets, the wisdom they imparted to their followers through interpreting their dreams, and the conclusion they themselves have earned from that experience. A refined interpreter in this art also must cultivate the essence of social norms, history, fables, poetry, proverbs, languages, etymology of words, synonyms, homogeneity, contrariety, etcetera. He also must be an honest and respected person, and he must care for the way he earns his living, what he eats, and what he drinks, and he must be a sincere and a God-fearing person.
>
> *(Al-Akili, 1991, p. xxii)*

In the classical era, scholars adopted a comprehensive approach to dream analysis, as highlighted by Shaykh Yahya Ibrahim (2017): in the pursuit of dream analysis, "before delving into dream reflection, [the classical] scholars would perform ablution, seeking assistance and clarity through supplication to the Almighty. The comprehensive approach incorporated both scholarly wisdom and spiritual practices to provide insightful interpretations rooted in Islāmīc principles." This dual approach combined both scholarly wisdom and spiritual practices, emphasising a holistic understanding that goes beyond mere academic analysis, acknowledging the spiritual dimension in the pursuit of interpreting dream meanings.

The Islāmic methodology of dream interpretation

The Islāmic methodology of dream interpretation encompasses a multifaceted approach that incorporates teachings from the Qur'ân, practices of Prophet Muhammad (ﷺ), and insights from early Islāmic scholars. Imām al-Baghawi highlighted the diverse sources used in this interpretation, including the Qur'ân, the *Sunnah*, indigenous proverbs, linguistic analysis, and consideration of opposites. His comprehensive approach illustrates the richness and flexibility within the Islāmic tradition in understanding the profound messages conveyed in dreams. Scholars' methodologies present a broad spectrum, emphasising the holistic nature of dream interpretation in Islām. Here's a breakdown of the categories he mentions:

- Dream interpretation in the light of the Qur'ān: involves analysing and understanding dreams by correlating the dream content with relevant verses from the Qur'ān. This process requires seeking guidance from Qur'ānic texts to expose the meanings of symbols or events in the dream. For example, the word "rope" may symbolise a covenant or agreement, because Allāh says,

وَٱعْتَصِمُوا۟ بِحَبْلِ ٱللَّهِ جَمِيعًا

- *And hold firmly to the rope of Allāh.*
  (Ali 'Imran 3:103, interpretation of the meaning)

- Interpretation in the light of the *Sunnah*: the *Sunnah* serves as another source for interpreting dreams. Certain dreams or symbols may have been explained or alluded to by the Prophet (ﷺ) to provide a basis for interpretation, for example, the crow representing an immoral man (*fasiq*) because the Prophet (ﷺ) called it such.
- Dream interpretation through proverbs: involves using commonly known sayings and narratives within the community to interpret dreams. The collective wisdom embedded in these proverbs can provide insights into the meanings of dream symbols. For instance, the proverb "Whoever digs a hole will fall in it" may suggest that digging a hole in a dream symbolises plotting or creating trouble.
- Interpretation by means of names (and metaphor): dreams can be understood through the analysis of names and metaphors. This involves considering the symbolic or metaphorical significance of elements present in the dream. For example, seeing a man called Rashid meaning wisdom.
- Interpretation by means of opposites: Sometimes, the meaning of a dream may be understood by considering its opposite. For example, if a dream appears negative, its interpretation might be positive when viewed in terms of opposites. In the case of fear, it means safety, because Allāh says in the Qur'ān,

وَلَيُبَدِّلَنَّهُم مِّنۢ بَعْدِ خَوْفِهِمْ أَمْنًا

- *And He will surely substitute for them, after their fear, security.*
  (An-Nur 24:55, interpretation of the meaning)

Scholars in the field of Islāmic dream interpretation use a variety of subtle ways to deduce meaning from the symbolism revealed in dreams. Shaykh Yahya Ibrahim

TABLE 16.2 Methodologies of dream interpretation

Method	Interpretation	Explanation
Ta'wil al-asma	Etymology of names	Delve into the linguistic roots of names to extract deeper meanings, considering the etymology for nuanced interpretations
Ta'wil bil-ma'na	Via meaning	Consider the symbolic or literal meanings of the elements and events
Ta'wil bil Qur'ân	Using the Qur'ân	Analyse how the symbolism in a dream aligns with or relates to the teachings of the Qur'ân
Ta'wil bil-hādīths	Hādīths	Consult the *hādīths* to find insights into and explanations for symbols or events in dreams, based on the Prophet's own interpretations or comments
Ta'wil bil mathal wash-shi'r	Proverbs and poetry	Use cultural proverbs and poetic expressions to interpret the symbolism present in the dream
Ta'wil bil didd wal-maqloob	Via opposition and inversion	Explore interpretations by contemplating the reversed or opposing meanings of elements in the dream for interpretation
Ta'wil bil ziyaad wal-naqs	Increase	Consider elements that appear in abundance or are increased in the dream
Ta'wil bil naqs	Decrease	Consider elements that appear scarce or decreased in the dream, using this scarcity as a basis for interpretation
Ta'wil bil waqt	Consideration of time	The time at which the dream occurs or specific timelines within the dream may be significant for interpretation.

Source: Adapted from Shaykh Yahya Ibrahim (2017).

(2017) has proposed nine methods of dream interpretation (Table 16.2). Within this approach, dream interpretation frequently entails a deep engagement with the Qur'ân and *hādīths*, identifying parallels between dream content and the sacred texts via linguistic analysis, cultural wisdom, etymology of names, and religious teachings.

The methods of dream interpretation in Islām reflect a holistic approach, drawing from diverse tools such as Qur'ânic teachings, cultural proverbs, and spiritual insights. Each method offers a unique perspective for interpreting dream messages, considering language, culture, and spiritual guidance. To gain a thorough understanding of dream interpretation in Islām, consulting authentic literature is recommended. Noteworthy works include "Dream Interpretation" by Abu Ameena Bilal Philips (2003), "The Interpretation of Things Seen in Dreams" by Imām Al-Baghawi (Abdul-Wahid, 2023), "Interpretation of Dreams" by Ibn Rashid Al-Bakri Al-Qafsi (2010), and "Authentic Dream Interpretations from the Works of Ibn al-Qayyim & Al-Baghawi" by Shaykh Abdullah ibn Jaru Allāh (2020). These resources offer valuable insights into the principles and methods of Islāmic dream interpretation.

Conclusion

The significance of dreams in Islām is intricately tied to spirituality, guidance, and the believer's connection with the divine. The emphasis on dream interpretation becomes crucial given that humans spend approximately one-third of their lives sleeping. This focus emphasises the depth of Islāmic heritage, valuing the symbolic language of dreams as a pathway to divine communication and understanding. Dreams are seen as a conduit for spiritual insights, divine messages, and guidance, nurturing a deeper connection to one's faith. There is a call for further research into implementing authentic dream analysis and interpretation in Islāmīc psychotherapy, recognising the role that dreams play in shaping perceptions, beliefs, and connections to the spiritual realm. This acknowledgment contributes to a more comprehensive understanding of the human experience within the Islām context. And Allāh knows best.

References

Abdul-Rasheed. (2023). Ustadh Tariq Abdul-Rasheed. *How Was the Qur'ān Revealed?* Retrieved December 4, 2023, from https://Islamqa.org/?p=86620

Abdul-Wahid, A. K. (2023). *The interpretation of things seen in dreams by Imām Al-Baghawī.* A 15-page handwritten translation by Shaikh Abu Talhah Dawood Burbank (PDF). Retrieved December 5, 2023, from https://abukhadeejah.com/interpretation-of-things-seen-in-dreams-Imam-baghawi-pdf-dawood-burbank/

Adventure-Heart, D. J., Delfabbro, P., Proeve, M., & Mohr, P. (2017). Reality testing and the mnemonic induction of lucid dreams: Findings from the National Australian lucid dream induction study. *Dreaming, 27*(3), 206–231. https://doi.org/10.1037/drm0000059

Al-Abid Zuhd, E. (2010). The miracle verses and its impact about sleeping in Qur'ān. *Aljameah Alislamiah Journal, 18*, 50–215.

Al-Akili, M. M. (1991). *Ibn Seerin's dictionary of dreams according to Islāmic inner traditions.* Earl Publishing House.

Blagrove, M. (2009). Dreaming-motivated or meaningless? *The Psychologist.* Retrieved November 3, 2023, from www.bps.org.uk/node/10403

Blagrove, M., Hale, S., Lockheart, J., Carr, M., Jones, A., & Valli, K. (2019). Testing the empathy theory of dreaming: The relationships between dream sharing and trait and state empathy. *Frontiers in Psychology, 10*, 1351.

Blagrove, M., Lockheart, J., Carr, M., Basra, S., Graham, H., Lewis, H., Murphy, E., Sakalauskaite, A., Trotman, C., & Valli, K. (2021). Dream sharing and the enhancement of empathy: Theoretical and applied implications. *Dreaming, 31*(2), 128–139. https://doi.org/10.1037/drm0000165

Bukhârî (a). *Sahih al-Bukhârî 3.* In-book reference: Book 1, Hādīth 3. USC-MSA web (English) reference: Vol. 1, Book 1, Hādīth 3. https://sunnah.com/bukhari:3

Bukhârî (b). *Sahih al-Bukhârî 6985.* In-book reference: Book 91, Hādīth 4. USC-MSA web (English) reference: Vol. 9, Book 87, Hādīth 114. https://sunnah.com/bukhari:6985

Bukhârî (c). *Sahih al-Bukhârî 6986.* Book 91, Hādīth 5. USC-MSA web (English) reference: Vol. 9, Book 87, Hādīth 115. https://sunnah.com/bukhari:6986

Bukhârî & Muslim (a). *Bukhari, 6499; Muslim, 4200.* Cited in Islām Q&A. (1999). *6537 Dreams and Dream Interpretation.* Retrieved December 3, 2023, from https://Islamqa.info/en/answers/6537/dreams-and-dream-interpretation

Bukhârî & Muslim (b). *Mishkat al-Masabih 4614, 4615.* In-book reference: Book 24, Hādīth 8. https://sunnah.com/mishkat:4614

Bulkeley, K. (2016). *Big dreams: The science of dreaming and the origins of religion.* Oxford University Press.

Eagle, M. (1986). A. Grünbaum's *The Foundations of Psychoanalysis: A Philosophical Critique*. *Philosophy of Science*, *53*(1), 65–88. https://doi.org/10.1086/289292

Edwards, C. L., Malinowski, J. E., McGee, S. L., Bennett, P. D., Ruby, P. M., & Blagrove, M. T. (2015). Comparing personal insight gains due to consideration of a recent dream and consideration of a recent event using the Ullman and Schredl dream group methods. *Frontiers in Psychology*, *6*, 831.

Fath al-Bari (a). 12/352–354. Cited in Islām Q&A. (1999). *6537 Dreams and Dream Interpretation*. Retrieved December 3, 2023, from https://Islamqa.info/en/answers/6537/dreams-and-dream-interpretation

Fath al-Bari (b). 12/369. Cited in Islām Q&A. (1999). 6537 Dreams and Dream Interpretation. Retrieved December 3, 2023, from https://Islamqa.info/en/answers/6537/dreams-and-dream-interpretation

Feld, G. B., & Diekelmann, S. (2015). Sleep smart-optimizing sleep for declarative learning and memory. *Frontier Psychology*, *6*(1), 622. https://doi.org/10.3389/fpsyg.2015.00622.4

Freud, S. (1953). The interpretation of dreams. In J. Strachey (Ed. & Trans.), *Standard edition of the complete psychological works of Sigmund Freud* (Vols. 4–5). Hogarth Press. (Original work published 1900).

Glosemeyer, R. W., Diekelmann, S., Cassel, W., Kesper, K., Koehler, U., Westermann, S., Steffen, A., Borgwardt, S., Wilhelm, I., Müller-Pinzler, L., Paulus, F. M., Krach, S., & Stolz, D. S. (2020). Selective suppression of rapid eye movement sleep increases next-day negative affect and amygdala responses to social exclusion. *Scientific Reports*, *10*, 17325. https://doi.org/10.1038/s41598-020-74169-8

Grünbaum, A. (1984). *The foundations of psychoanalysis: A philosophical critique*. University of California Press.

Hall, C. S. (1966). *The meaning of dreams*. McGraw-Hill Education.

Hobson, J. A. Pace-Schott, E., & Stickgold., R. (2000). Dreaming and the brain: Towards a cognitive neuroscience of conscious states. *Behavioral and Brain Sciences*, *23*(6), 793–842.

Ibn Majah (a). *Sunan Ibn Majah 3893*. In-book reference: Book 35, Hādīth 1. English translation: Vol. 5, Book 35, Hādīth 3893. Sahih (Darussalam). https://sunnah.com/ibnmajah/35

Ibn Majah (b). *Sunan Ibn Majah 3906*. In-book reference: Book 35, Hādīth 14. English translation: Vol. 5, Book 35, Hādīth 3906. Sahih (Darussalam). https://sunnah.com/ibnmajah:3906

Ibn Majah (c). *Sunan Ibn Majah 3908*. In-book reference: Book 35, Hādīth 16. English translation: Vol. 5, Book 35, Hādīth 3908. Sahih (Darussalam). https://sunnah.com/ibnmajah:3908

Ibn Majah (d). *Sunan Ibn Majah 3914*. In-book reference: Book 35, Hādīth 22. English translation: Vol. 5, Book 35, Hādīth 3914. Hasan (Darussalam). https://sunnah.com/ibnmajah:3914

Ibn Qayyim al-Jawziyyah. *Madaarij al-Saalikeen*, 1/50–52. Cited in Islām Q&A. (1999). *6537 Dreams and dream interpretation*. Retrieved December 3, 2023, from https://Islamqa.info/en/answers/6537/dreams-and-dream-interpretation

Ibn Rashid Al-Bakri Al-Qafsi. (2010). *Interpretation of dreams*. Darussalam Publications.

Ibn Sirin. (2007). Muhammad Ibn Sirin Al-Basri. *Interpretation of Dreams*. Beirut Dar al-Kotob al-Ilmiyan.

Imām al-Baghawi. Sharh al-Sunnah [(Explanation of the Sunnah]12/220. Cited in Islām Q&A. (1999). *6537 Dreams and dream interpretation*. Retrieved December 5, 2023, from https://Islamqa.info/en/answers/6537/dreams-and-dream-interpretation

Imām Anwar al Awlaki. (2023). *Dreams and dream interpretations*. Islāmic Audio Lectures. Retrieved December 5, 2023, from www.Allahsword.com/Islamic_audio_lectures.html

Islām Q&A. (1999). *6537 Dreams and dream interpretation*. Retrieved December 3, 2023, from https://Islamqa.info/en/answers/6537/dreams-and-dream-interpretation

Jung, C. G. (1977). Symbols and the interpretation of dreams (1961). In *The symbolic life* Routledge.

Jung, C. G. (2016). *Dream interpretation ancient and modern: Notes from the seminar given in 1936–1941* – Updated edition. Bollingen Series. Princeton University Press.

Malinowski, J. (2012). *How and why we dream of waking life: An empirical investigation into the continuity hypothesis of dreaming* [PhD thesis, Leeds Metropolitan University]. Cited in Leeds, N., & Robinson, O. (2020). Dreams and their relationship to waking life. *The Psychologist*. Retrieved December 2, 2023, from www.bps.org.uk/psychologist/dreams-and-their-relationship-waking-life

Mavroudi, M. (2002). *A byzantine book on dream interpretation*. Koninklijke Brill NV.

Muslim (a). *An Nawawi's Riyad as-Salihin 838*. In-book reference: Book 4, Ḥadīth 26. https://sunnah.com/riyadussalihin:838

Muslim (b). *Sahih Muslim 2262*. In-book reference: Book 42, Ḥadīth 8. USC-MSA web (English) reference: Book 29, Ḥadīth 5620. https://sunnah.com/muslim:2262

National Institutes of Neurological Disorders and Stroke. (2023). *Brain basics: Understanding sleep*. National Institutes of Health (NIH). Retrieved December 3, 2023, from www.ninds.nih.gov/health-information/public-education/brain-basics/brain-basics-understanding-sleep

Ozgen, F. (2023). *Dreams and Islam*. Oxford biographies. Oxford University Press. https://doi.org/10.1093/obo/9780195390155-0296

Pace-Schott, E. F., Solms, M., Blagrove, M., & Harnad, S. (Eds.). (2003). *Sleep and dreaming: Scientific advances and reconsiderations*. Cambridge University Press. (Reprint of a special issue on dreaming in Behavioral and Brain Sciences, 2000.)

Philips, A. A. B. (2003). *Dream interpretation*. Islāmīc Book Service.

Pruett, G. E. (1985). Through a glass darkly: Knowledge of the self in dreams in Ibn Khaldūn's *Muqaddima*. *The Muslim World*, *75*(1), 29–44.

Roesler, C. (2020). Jungian theory of dreaming and contemporary dream research – findings from the research project 'Structural Dream Analysis.' *Analytical Psychology*, *65*(1), 44–62. https://doi.org/10.1111/1468-5922.12566

Shaykh Abdullah ibn Jaru Allāh. (2020). *Authentic dream interpretations. From the Works of Ibn al-Qayyim & Al-Baghawi*. Authentic Statements Publications.

Shaykh Gibril Haddad. (2009). *'True' dreams are 1/46 of prophecy*. Retrieved December 4, 2023, from https://seekersguidance.org/answers/general-counsel/true-dreams-146-of-prophecy-2/

Shaykh Yahya Ibrahim. (2017). *The art of dream interpretation - Part II*. Retrieved December 5, 2023, from https://muslimmatters.org/2017/07/19/the-art-of-dream-interpretation-part-ii/

Soffer-Dudek, N., & Somer, E. (2018). Trapped in a daydream: Daily elevations in maladaptive daydreaming are associated with daily psychopathological symptoms. *Frontiers in Psychiatry*, *9*, 194. https://doi.org/10.3389/fpsyt.2018.00194

Solms, M. (1997). *The neuropsychology of dreams: A clinico-anatomical study*. Lawrence Erlbaum Associates Publishers.

Sterpenich, V., Perogamvros, L., Tononi, G., & Schwartz, S. (2020) Fear in dreams and in wakefulness: Evidence for day/night affective homeostasis. *Human Brain Mapping*, *41*(3), 840–850. https://doi.org/10.1002/hbm.24843

Strauch, I., & Meier, B. (1996). *In search of dreams*. State University of New York Press.

Yeung, A. W. K. (2021). Is the influence of Freud declining in psychology and psychiatry? A bibliometric analysis. *Frontiers in Psychology*, *12*, 631516. https://doi.org/10.3389/fpsyg.2021.631516

17
CHALLENGING BOUNDARIES

Halāl/harām considerations in complementary therapies

Introduction and context

In the contemporary context, the increasing interest among Muslims in complementary therapies as remedies for various ailments highlights the importance of examining their permissibility in Islām, making a clear distinction between what is *halāl* (permissible) and *harām* (forbidden). Practices like herbal remedies, acupuncture, and cupping (*hijamah*) align with Islāmic principles and offer holistic approaches to health. However, the permissibility of complementary therapies becomes more intricate when considering therapies such as new age therapies, hypnotherapy, yoga, ayurveda, naturopathy, Unani medicine, Siddha, reflexology, herbal medicines, acupuncture, and manual therapies like chiropractic and osteopathy, as well as related techniques such as qigong, tai chi, yoga, thermal medicine, and other mind-body therapies. These treatments may conflict with Islāmic tenets, like the use of substances such as alcohol or associations with beliefs incompatible with Islām.

The World Health Organization (WHO) acknowledges the significance of traditional medicine in global health care systems and developed a strategy of traditional and complementary medicine (WHO, 2013) to optimise the benefits while ensuring safety, efficacy, and quality. The strategy aims to facilitate the appropriate integration, regulation, and supervision of traditional medicine, providing guidance for countries seeking to develop proactive policies in this area (WHO, 2013). Traditional medicine has a long history as the

> sum total of the knowledge, skill, and practices based on the theories, beliefs, and experiences indigenous to different cultures, whether explicable or not, used

in the maintenance of health as well as in the prevention, diagnosis, improvement or treatment of physical and mental illness.

(WHO, 2013, p. 15)

This chapter is an adaptation of Rassool and Morris's (2020) paper titled "Use of Complementary Therapies by Muslims: Halāl or Harām?" In this adaptation, the aim is to provide an overview of selected complementary and alternative therapies and assess their compatibility with the *halāl* and *harām* aspects of Islāmic beliefs and practices. The central question guiding this exploration is whether these therapies are permissible (*halāl*) or forbidden (*harām*). Evaluating their permissibility within an Islāmic framework involves analysing the practices, ingredients, and philosophical foundations of these therapies to determine their alignment with Islāmic principles. The answers to this fundamental question have implications not only for Islāmic psychotherapists and individuals seeking such therapies but also for the broader discourse on health choices within the Muslim community.

Seeking treatment and healing

The increasing interest among certain Muslims in complementary and alternative approaches to health and wellness reflects a growing curiosity about diverse methods of healing. However, this interest is not uniform across the Muslim community, as individuals make varied choices based on their unique interpretations and needs. For some, the perceived failure of orthodox therapy to effectively manage chronic illnesses or problems has prompted a search for what they see as the "ultimate" cure or respite. This shift often stems from dissatisfaction with conventional medicine and therapy, influenced by factors such as perceived limitations of conventional treatments, holistic and personalised approaches to health, and dealing with mental health conditions (Sharp et al., 2018); having pain, anxiety, depression, or a long-term condition (Hunt et al., 2010); the supportive nature and care of CAM (Rocha et al., 2017); and spirituality (Thomson et al., 2014).

Some Muslims are adopting health practices that may not align with standard Islāmic beliefs and practices, prompting debates among Islāmic psychotherapists and clinical psychologists. While some argue that elements conflicting with Islām can be removed to make therapeutic approaches *halāl*, caution is advised against relying on practices with incompatible origins. Alternative *halāl* practices compatible with Islām can provide similar benefits without such concerns (Rassool & Morris, 2020). Some researchers have proposed a conceptual model of traditional Arabic and Islāmic medicine that integrates Prophetic and Islāmic medicine with cultural practices, aiming to create an interconnected approach (Azaizeh et al., 2010; Alrawi & Fetters, 2012).

Certain complementary therapies, including herbal treatment, acupuncture, *ruqya* (incantation), and cupping, seem compatible with Islām due to similarities with practices like cupping (*hijamah*), which involves pressure points and a focus on spiritual and physical interaction. However, other practices such as homeopathy, yoga, reflexology, mind–body therapies, and hypnotherapy provoke controversy within clinicians and academics. The contentious nature arises from varying scholarly opinions on whether these practices are *halāl* or *harām* or if a middle ground can be found where a potentially *harām* practice is justifiable or can be adapted to align with Islāmic principles.

Complementary therapies can serve as valuable adjuncts to Islāmic psychotherapy, contributing to a holistic approach to mental and emotional well-being while adhering to Islāmic principles and values. Islāmic psychotherapy, which incorporates Islāmic principles, beliefs, and practices into the therapeutic process, can be complemented by these therapies, addressing various dimensions of an individual's holistic health. While traditional medicine remains a prevalent choice, there is an acknowledgment and utilisation of complementary therapies as supplementary means of promoting health and addressing chronic conditions.

In Islām, the pursuit of *halāl* treatment and cure is not only recommended but is considered a virtuous and encouraged practice. Seeking and obtaining treatment from sources aligned with Islāmic principles is seen as fulfilling this obligation. Prophet Muhammad (ﷺ) said, "There is no disease that Allāh has created except that He also has created its treatment" (Bukhāri (a)). Seeking *halāl* treatment and cure is recommended for Muslims. It was narrated that Usamah bin Sharik (may Allāh be pleased with him) said,

> I saw the Bedouins asking the Prophet (ﷺ) "Is there any harm in such and such, is there any harm in such and such?" He said to them, "O slaves of Allāh! Allāh has only made harm in that which transgresses the honour of one's brother. That is what is sinful." They said, "O Messenger of Allāh! Is there any sin if we do not seek treatment?" He said, "Seek treatment, O slaves of Allāh! For Allāh does not create any disease but He also creates with it the cure, except for old age."
>
> *(Ibn Majah (a))*

In another *hādīth*, the Prophet (ﷺ) said, "Seek healing, O slaves of Allāh, but do not seek it in that which is *harām*, for Allāh does not make the healing of my *ummah* in that which He has forbidden to it" (Islām Q&A, 2000). This *hādīth* emphasises the importance of utilising permissible and beneficial means, including medical treatments, to address health issues. It encourages Muslims to actively seek remedies and cures for illnesses, emphasising the importance of ensuring that the methods used align with *halāl* practices. This encouragement implies that Muslims should choose health care options that are not only effective but also ethically sound and in harmony with Islāmic values. To make informed decisions about treatment and health care, seeking the guidance of knowledgeable religious scholars or health care professionals who understand both medical and Islāmic perspectives is recommended. This approach ensures that individuals are mindful of both the effectiveness of the treatment and its alignment with Islāmic principles, fostering a holistic and conscientious approach to health and well-being.

However, the *hādīths* mentioned raise questions about what is considered *halāl* and *harām* in complementary therapies and whether seeking a cure through such methods contradicts trusting in Allāh's will. The *hādīth* "Allāh has sent down the disease and the cure and has made for every disease the cure. So, treat sickness, but do not use anything *harām*" (Abū Dāwūd) suggests a cautionary approach to ensure that the methods used do not involve anything forbidden. Upon closer examination of certain esoteric mind-body therapies, there is evidence of elements that may be deemed *harām*, including the use of forbidden substances and practices that imply seeking a cure from a source attributed to other than Allāh (*shirk*). This scrutiny highlights the need for therapists and individuals to carefully assess complementary therapies to ensure their alignment with Islāmic principles, avoiding any practices that may contradict or compromise the ethical and religious values prescribed by Islām. Some of the complementary therapies are discussed next.

Acupuncture

Acupuncture, a traditional Chinese medicine practice, involves inserting thin needles into specific points on the body to stimulate energy flow or *qi*. The term "acupuncture" is derived from the Latin words *acus*, meaning "needle," and *punctura*, meaning "to puncture," accurately describing the procedure. Similar to cupping or *hijamah*, acupuncture is believed to restore balance and unblock energy channels in the body, aiming to promote healing by addressing blood stagnation and improving blood flow to enhance the supply of vital nutrients to organs. Additionally, acupuncture stimulates the release of natural pain relievers, such as opioids (endorphins), within the body. There is no clear evidence suggesting that acupuncture is *harām*, as it does not involve the use of substances like alcohol, and it does not incorporate religious practices or incantations, making it distinct from some other complementary therapies that may have a basis in religious or spiritual beliefs.

While there is no clear evidence suggesting that acupuncture is inherently forbidden in Islām, several factors should be considered including the individual's intentions, the qualifications and competence of the practitioner, and adherence to ethical guidelines. It is advisable for Muslims to consult with knowledgeable Islāmic scholars or health care professionals who can provide guidance based on specific contexts and circumstances. According to Shaykh Ahmad Kutty (2016),

> There is nothing in Islām to forbid Muslims from resorting to alternative therapies or treatments so long as they do not involve beliefs or practices inimical to Islām. Acupuncture is one of such practices; it has been an integral part of traditional medicine in certain parts of the world like China, and it has been found to be effective and beneficial in some cases.

In addition, Shaykh 'Abd-Allaah ibn Jibreen said, with regard to the "Chinese needles" (i.e. acupuncture), if it is proven that this is beneficial, or if its benefit outweighs its harm – if it causes any harm – then there is nothing wrong with using this. And Allāh knows best (Islām Q&A, 2001). It is reported that if the practitioner

> who treats you does not practice any pagan rituals, then there is no harm in continuing. However, it is impermissible to be treated at the hands of those who practice acupuncture and connect it with any false beliefs, such as the Five Elements theory.
>
> *(Islāmweb.net, 2009)*

In addition, there are claims associating the changes and fluctuations of a certain power with the Five Elements theory, which in turn is said to be based on principles of astrology and ancient eastern philosophies (Islāmweb.net, 2009).

Aromatherapy

Aromatherapy, a complementary therapy that utilises natural plant extracts such as essential oils for therapeutic purposes, involves methods like inhalation, massage, or application to the skin surface (Ali et al., 2015; Shah et al., 2011). Aromatherapy primarily uses natural substances such as plant extracts, which are generally permissible in Islām, as Islām encourages the use of beneficial natural resources for healing purposes. The compatibility of aromatherapy with Islāmic beliefs is generally considered acceptable by many Muslims, depending on specific practices and ingredients. When assessing their congruence with Islāmic beliefs, several factors should be considered.

Muslims are encouraged to ensure that the ingredients comply with Islāmic dietary guidelines. In the context of aromatherapy, it is important to verify that the essential oils used are *halāl* (permissible) and free from any harmful or intoxicating elements. It is important to ensure that the essential oils used in aromatherapy do not contain alcohol or any other substance that may lead to intoxication. *Halāl* aromatherapy medicated oils, adhering to Islāmic guidelines and free from prohibited or *harām* ingredients, are available in the market. For example, *halāl* aromatherapy medicated oil has been successfully produced from "wintergreen oil, menthol, camphor and completed with essential oils that are widely found in Indonesia, namely rose, jasmine, frangipani, tangerine, and green tea" (Sardjono, 2018, p. 1531). Aromatherapy is often practiced in private spaces, aligning with the Islāmic value of modesty. It is important for Muslim clients to seek gender-specific options when receiving aromatherapy massages, and they may prefer treatments from therapists of the same gender to adhere to their religious principles and maintain a comfortable and respectful environment during the session.

While aromatherapy is generally compatible with Islāmic principles when focusing on the physical and psychological benefits of essential oils, caution is advised regarding practices that border on superstition or contradict Islāmic monotheism and principles. Some aromatherapy practices may claim mystical or supernatural powers beyond the physical benefits of essential oils, involving invoking spirits, reciting specific incantations, or attributing metaphysical properties to the oils, which goes against Islāmic beliefs in the oneness of Allāh and reliance on Him alone. Certain aromatherapy practices claim that essential oils have properties influenced by celestial bodies, corresponding to zodiac signs, which conflicts with Islāmic monotheism.

Additionally, using amulets or talismans containing essential oils for purported spiritual protection or warding off negative energies resembles superstitious practices and contradicts the Islāmic belief in seeking protection solely from Allāh. Muslims are advised to use aromatherapy with caution, avoiding superstitious beliefs or rituals that contradict Islāmic monotheism principles. Instead, they can use aromatherapy in a manner consistent with their faith by focusing on the physical and psychological benefits without attaching any supernatural abilities or engaging in practices that contravene Islāmic teachings.

Cupping

Cupping, known as *hijamah* in Arabic, has historical roots in Islāmic medicine and is mentioned in several *hādīths*. This practice involves placing cups on specific points on the skin to create suction, pulling the skin and superficial muscle layer into the cup and creating a vacuum. This may result in circular marks or bruises known as cupping marks. Cups can be made of various materials, such as glass, bamboo, or silicone.

Cupping therapy serves various purposes, including promoting blood flow, detoxifying the body, removing impurities from the blood, reducing muscle tension, and providing relief for conditions like pain and inflammation. It is also used for relaxation and overall well-being. In Islāmic medicine, cupping is employed to treat a range of complaints, including bronchitis, pneumonia, and back pain. Dry cupping, the most common form, works similarly to acupuncture by redirecting blockages to the lymphatic drainage system. On the other hand, wet cupping (*hijamah*) involves manually removing blood from the body through small incisions made to the skin surface under the cup.

There is little controversy in the use of cupping for Muslims as Prophet Mohammed (ﷺ) was an advocate of cupping and often used the method himself. This is documented numerous times in the *hādīths*. It is narrated by Abū Hurayrah (may Allāh be pleased with him) that the Prophet (ﷺ) said, "The best medical treatment you apply is cupping" (Abū Dāwūd (b)). In another *hādīth*, Abū Hurayrah (may Allāh be pleased with him) narrated that the Prophet (ﷺ) said, "If there is any good in any of the remedies you use, it is in cupping" (Ibn Majah (b)). Jabir bin 'Abdullah (may Allāh be pleased with him) narrated that I heard the Prophet (ﷺ) saying, "If there is any healing in your medicines, then it is in cupping, a gulp of honey or branding with fire (cauterisation) that suits the ailment, but I don't like to be (cauterised) branded with fire" (Bukhāri (b)). It is narrated by Ibn 'Abbas (may Allāh be pleased with him) that "The Prophet (ﷺ) was cupped on his head for an ailment he was suffering from while he was in a state of *ihrām* at a water place called Lahl Jamal" (Bukhāri (c)).

Some Muslims practice preventative *hijamah*, also known as Prophetic cupping. This involves undergoing cupping therapy as a preventive measure to maintain good health and prevent potential illnesses. Preventative *hijamah* is carried out regularly, typically on specific dates recommended in Islāmic teachings, such as the 17th, 19th, or 21st of the lunar month as prescribed by the Prophet (ﷺ). The Prophet (ﷺ) said, "If anyone has himself cupped on the 17th, 19th and 21st it will be a remedy for every disease" (Abū Dāwūd (c)). It is stated by Dr Magda Amir, an expert in the practice and study of *hijamah*, that, "Our body is affected by the moon, just as the tides are." She elaborates, "Because of the lunar magnetic field, when the moon is full [on the 15th day], all the toxins in our cells are accumulated beneath the surface of the skin. Applying *hijamah* in three even intervals after the full moon "detoxifies the body monthly" (Ibrahim, 2012). There is evidence to suggest that *hijamah* is highly effective in treating the severity and frequency of tension and migraine headaches, conditions that Western medicine has difficulty treating (Ahmadi et al., 2008). Some practitioners emphasise the importance of having the right intentions (*niyyah*) before undergoing cupping, linking the practice to seeking healing through the blessings of Allāh. However, like any medical or therapeutic procedure, it is advisable to consult a knowledgeable and qualified practitioner.

Herbal remedies and natural substances

More than a thousand years ago, Islāmic scientists and scholars utilised herbs as medicine, relying on recipes and formulas. *Tibb al-nabawi* refers to the medicine and remedies recommended by Prophet Muhammad (ﷺ). Many of these remedies involve the use of natural elements including herbs and plants. Islāmic medical texts typically

> included sections on herbs and other natural remedies, as well as instructions for compound remedies, providing details on geographical origin, physical properties, and methods of application. Some formularies were composed as independent collections of simples (single herbs with medicinal value) and compound recipes, some of which were specifically written for use in hospitals.
> *(Tschanz, 1998)*

Herbal remedies are considered *Shar'iah*-compliant as long as they adhere to Islāmic principles and do not involve ingredients or practices that are prohibited in Islām. Ensuring that these remedies are free from any *harām* elements is essential to maintain their compatibility with Islāmic teachings.

The uses of herbs for cures in the natural world stemmed directly from Prophet Mohammed (ﷺ). According to Sheikh 'Abd-Allaah ibn Jibreen, it is permissible to use herbal remedies because the Prophet (ﷺ) said, "Seek healing, O slaves of Allāh, but do not seek it in that which is *harām*, for Allāh does not make the healing of my Ummah in that which He has forbidden to it" (Islām Q&A, 2001). Sheikh ibn Jibreen added that "Seeking healing with herbs comes under the heading of permissible things. This does not contradict the idea of putting one's trust in Allāh (*tawakkul*)." It was narrated that a man said, "O Messenger of Allāh, what do you think of medicines with which we seek healing, and *ruqya* (incantations) which we use for healing? Do they change the decree of Allāh?" The Prophet (ﷺ) said, "

> They are part of the decree of Allāh . . . Allāh decrees that a person falls sick, then He decrees that this disease needs treatment, and that if it is treated with medicines or herbs, he may be healed by Allāh's leave. So, there is no reason why we should not use these medicines, including the use of needles and herbs.
> *(Islām Q&A, 2001)*

Black seed, also known as black cumin or *Nigella sativa*, holds a significant place in Islāmic culture and is highly regarded for its potential health benefits. It is mentioned in various Islāmic texts and has been used as a remedy by Muslims for centuries as part of *Tibb-e-Nabawi*, the Prophetic Medicine. This tradition is believed to have therapeutic properties and is used to treat various ailments.

Black seed is mentioned in a *hadith* narrated by Khalid bin Sa'd (may Allāh be pleased with him):

We went out and Ghalib bin Abjar was accompanying us. He fell ill on the way, and when we arrived at Medina, he was still sick. Ibn Abi 'Atiq came to visit him and said to us, "Treat him with black cumin. Take five or seven seeds and crush them (mix the powder with oil) and drop the resulting mixture into both nostrils, for 'Aisha has narrated to me that she heard the Prophet (ﷺ) saying, 'This black cumin is healing for all diseases except As-Sam.' Aisha said, 'What is As-Sam?' He said, 'Death'" (Bukhāri (c)).

This statement led to the recognition and appreciation of black seed for its potential health benefits among Muslims. Many Muslims consume black seed through various forms, such as oil, capsules, or directly as seeds, believing it may support the immune system, alleviate certain conditions, and provide overall nutritional benefits. It is important to note that scientific research on the specific health benefits of black seed is ongoing and may vary in terms of evidence. Some studies suggest black seed for illness and analgesia properties (Al-Ghamdi, 2001); potential anti-inflammatory, antioxidant, and antimicrobial properties (Ahmad et al., 2021; Ojueromi et al., 2022); and gastrointestinal effects (Shakeri et al., 2016). Further research is needed to fully understand its effectiveness.

Honey is not a traditional herbal medicine but a natural substance produced by bees from the nectar of flowers. However, honey has been used for its medicinal properties for centuries and is considered a natural remedy in many cultures, including Islāmic tradition. There is ample recommendation of the use of honey in managing disease conditions due to of its antibacterial, anti-inflammatory, apoptotic, and antioxidant properties (Abūelgasim et al., 2021; Palma-Morales et al., 2023; Samarghandian et al., 2017). Different types of honey have varying compositions and potential health benefits. For example, Manuka honey from New Zealand is well-known for its antibacterial properties.

In the context of Islāmic medicine, honey is highly regarded, and its benefits are mentioned in the Qur'ân and *hādīths*. In the Qur'ân, Allāh mentions the healing properties of honey:

ثُمَّ كُلِى مِن كُلِّ ٱلثَّمَرَٰتِ فَٱسْلُكِى سُبُلَ رَبِّكِ ذُلُلًا ۚ يَخْرُجُ مِنْ بُطُونِهَا شَرَابٌ مُّخْتَلِفٌ أَلْوَٰنُهُ فِيهِ شِفَآءٌ لِّلنَّاسِ ۗ إِنَّ فِى ذَٰلِكَ لَءَايَةً لِّقَوْمٍ يَتَفَكَّرُونَ

- *Then eat from all the fruits and follow the ways of your Lord laid down* [for you]. *There emerges from their bellies a drink, varying in colours, in which there is healing for people. Indeed, in that is a sign for a people who give thought.*

(An-Nahl 16:69)

The Prophetic tradition recommended honey for various ailments. There is a famous *hādīth* in which God's messenger (ﷺ) said, "Make use of the two remedies: honey and the Qur'ân" (Mishkat al-Masabih). Honey may also be used for abdominal pain. Abū Sa'id Al-Khudri narrates that a man came to the Prophet (ﷺ) and said,

"My brother has some abdominal trouble." The Prophet (ﷺ) said to him, "Let him drink honey." The man came for the second time and the Prophet (ﷺ) said to him, "Let him drink honey." He came for the third time, and the Prophet (ﷺ) said, "Let him drink honey." He returned again and said, "I have done that." The Prophet (ﷺ) then said, "Allāh has said the truth, but your brother's abdomen has told a lie. Let him drink honey." So, he made him drink honey and he was cured.

(Bukhāri (d))

Urwa (may Allāh be pleased with her) narrates that "Aisha used to recommend *at-talbinah*, a combination of barley, milk, and honey for grief, for the sick and for such a person as grieved over a dead person." She used to say, I heard Allāh's Messenger (ﷺ) saying, "'*At-talbinah* gives rest to the heart of the patient and makes it active and relieves some of his sorrow and grief.'"

(Bukhāri (e))

There is also the recommendation of the use of Indian incense for pleurisy. Umm Qais bint Mihsan (may Allāh be pleased with him) narrates, "I heard the

Prophet (ﷺ) saying, 'Treat with the Indian incense, for it has healing for seven diseases; it is to be sniffed by one having throat trouble, and to be put into one side of the mouth of one suffering from pleurisy.' Once I went to Allāh's Messenger (ﷺ) with a son of mine who would not eat any food, and the boy passed urine on him, whereupon he asked for some water and sprinkled it over the place of urine."

(Bukhārī (f))

Another *hadīth* regards the use of *kohl* (also known as *kajal or surma*) as a traditional eye cosmetic that has also been attributed with certain medicinal or protective qualities in traditional practices. Umm Salama (may Allāh be pleased with her) narrates the following: The husband of a lady died, and her eyes became sore, and the people mentioned her story to the Prophet (ﷺ). They asked him whether it was permissible for her to use *kohl* as her eyes were exposed to danger. He said,

Previously, when one of you was bereaved by a husband, she would stay in her dirty clothes in a bad unhealthy house (for one year), and when a dog passed by, she would throw a globe of dung. No, (she should observe the prescribed period '*iddah*) for four months and ten days.

(Bukhārī (g))

There is also the use of truffles (*manna*), a type of fungi that grow underground, primarily known as a culinary delicacy, may also be some medicinal properties for eye diseases. Sa'id bin Zaid narrates, "I heard the Prophet (ﷺ) saying, 'Truffles are like manna [i.e. they grow naturally without man's care], and their water heals eye diseases'" (Bukhārī (h)).

Homoeopathy

Homeopathy, a system of alternative medicine developed in the late 18th century by Samuel Hahnemann, operates on the principle of "like cures like." This means that a substance causing symptoms in a healthy person can be used to treat similar symptoms in a sick person. Homeopathy relies on small doses of natural remedies aiming to stimulate the immune system and assist the body in self-healing.

For instance, if a plant causes skin rashes, homeopathic treatment may involve using that plant to address a rash. Similarly, substances like onions, which induce tearing and a runny nose, may be used to treat cold-related nasal secretions (Islām Q&A, 2011a). However, there are debates among scholars about the use of potentially poisonous substances or alcohol in homeopathic medications. Some scholars strictly forbid the consumption of any poison, whether in large or small amounts, while others permit its use under strict criteria.

The scholars on the permissible side stated that

> the effect of this poison should be examined, and the extent to which it will benefit the patient's body; it is also essential that that be done in the light of numerous experiments so as to have peace of mind regarding the outcome; and these medicines should only be used to ward off a greater harm.
>
> *(Islām Q&A, 2011a)*

Ibn Qudâmah (may Allāh have mercy on him) said,

> With regard to medicines that contain poison, if it is thought most likely that drinking or using it will result in death or insanity, then it is not permissible to use it. If it is thought most likely that it is safe and there is the hope of benefit from it, then it is better to permit taking it, to ward off what is more dangerous, as is the case with other medicines.

That is, the principle of the greater evil is repelled by the lesser evil (*ad-darar al ashadd yuzaalu bi-darar al akhaff*).

The primary concern related to the use of homeopathy revolves around the inclusion of alcohol as a carrier and preservative in the medicine. Scholars hold divergent opinions regarding the permissibility of using medicines that contain alcohol, such as those in homeopathic treatments. Many scholars firmly assert that medicines containing alcohol are forbidden (*harām*), drawing on various *hādīths* as evidence and emphasising the general prohibition of alcohol in any form. This stance reflects a strict interpretation of Islāmic principles regarding the consumption of alcohol. Simak narrated that he heard 'Alqamah bin Wa'il narrate from his father that he witnessed the Prophet (ﷺ) being asked by Suwaid bin Tariq – or Tariq bin Suwaid – about *khamr*, and he forbade it. So, he said, "We use it as a treatment." The Messenger of Allāh said, "It is certainly not a treatment, rather, it is a disease" (Tirmidhî (b)).

Some scholars claimed that it is lawful to use homeopathic medicine that contains alcohol because the "quantity of alcohol is very less in homeopathic medicines, and now many alcohols are made of potato, vegetables and coals, etc. Hence you can use homeopathic medicines for treatment. It is lawful as per the *Shar'iah*" (Darul Ifta, Fatwa). According to Zaidi (2012),

> In homeopathy, remedies are made from mixing alcohol to extract the herb and to dilute the solution to the required potency. Once at the right potency a drop of the solution is placed on a sugar/lactose pill to be used as a carrier. In such a case, it would be permissible to consume. However, if the medicine is wetted in alcohol (with or without reason), meaning that after the medicine is made it is submerged, coated, or in any way mixed with alcohol, then it would not be permissible.

That is, when there is a mixture of the herbal plant and a very small amount of alcohol as an ingredient, and the alcohol has gone through change through this process (*istihala*), then it is permissible to consume the medications. Other scholars have the view that

> When alcohol is mixed with other medicines, it either has a clear, strong and obvious effect, or it does not. If its effect is clear, strong and obvious, the mixture is *harām* and using this medicine is *harām*. If the alcohol does not have that effect on this medicine, it is permissible to use it.
>
> *(Islām Q&A, 2011a)*

For a fatwa of the Scholars of the Standing Committee, Fataawa al-Lajnah al-Daa'imah (22/110) describes that,

> It is not permissible to mix medicines with intoxicants, but if it is mixed with alcohol, if drinking a lot of it will cause intoxication, it is *harām* to handle it and drink it, whether a small amount or a large amount. If drinking a lot of it will not cause intoxication, then it is permissible to handle it and drink it.
>
> *(Islām Q&A, 2005)*

Shaykh Ibn'Uthaymeen in *Liqaa'aat il-Baab il-Maftoohah, 3/231* said,

> With regard to some medicines that contain alcohol, if the effect of the alcohol in the medicine can be seen in the form of intoxication, then it is *harām*, but if no effect is seen, and the alcohol is only added to it as a preservative, then there is nothing wrong with it, because the alcoholic content does not have any effect.
>
> *(Islām Q&A, 2005)*

The effectiveness of homeopathy has generated mixed results from clinical studies, with clear trends indicating no positive impact (McKenzie, 2013). Meta-analyses have raised concerns that therapeutic claims of homeopathy lack scientific justification and may pose counter-therapeutic risks, including potential harm leading to fatalities (Freckelton, 2012).

A comprehensive assessment of evidence concluded that there is no reliable proof supporting the efficacy of homeopathy for any health condition (National Health and Medical Research Council, Australian Government, 2015). Furthermore, the presence of poisonous or dangerous substances in many homeopathic medicines, especially if doses are not controlled, raises concerns about potential harm outweighing benefits. In light of these uncertainties and controversies, individuals may prefer seeking treatments known to be *halāl* and beneficial according to the Qur'ān and *Sunnah* as a cautious approach to their health.

Hypnotherapy

Hypnotherapy involves guided hypnosis, inducing a trance-like state, and is utilised to address various psychological, emotional, and sometimes physical issues. However, its long-term efficacy has been questioned, with no substantial evidence supporting its effectiveness in certain disorders such as chronic anxiety (Pelissolo, 2016), pain of childbirth (Jones et al., 2012), or post-natal depression (Sado et al., 2012). While some studies suggest hypnotherapy as effective in reducing symptoms associated with irritable bowel syndrome, its overall impact remains debatable. Fuhr et al. (2021) found hypnotherapy to be comparably effective with CBT for treating mild to moderate depression. The diverse findings highlight the need for continued research to ascertain the specific applications and limitations of hypnotherapy in different contexts.

The acceptability of hypnotherapy remains controversial within the Muslim community due to its involvement of altered states of consciousness and suggestion. Some Islāmic scholars view hypnotherapy as impermissible as it may conflict with Islāmic beliefs and practices. Contemporary Islāmic scholars have raised concerns about the potential involvement of *jinn* in hypnotherapy, stating that seeking help from *jinn* or any other creatures to uncover matters of the unseen is not permissible. This highlights the importance of considering the compatibility of hypnotherapy with Islāmic principles and seeking guidance from knowledgeable scholars for individuals contemplating its use. Hypnotherapy is regarded as committing *shirk* because this is a kind of worship, and Allāh has taught His slaves to worship Him alone:

إِيَّاكَ نَعْبُدُ وَإِيَّاكَ نَسْتَعِينُ

- *It is You we worship, and You we ask for help.*
(Al-Fatihah 1:5) (Islām Q&A, 2002)

There is evidence from a *hādīth* that the Prophet (ﷺ) said to Ibn 'Abbaas, "If you ask, then ask Allāh [alone]; and if you seek help, then seek help from Allāh [alone]" (Tirmidhî (c)).

The scholars make a second point that hypnotism is a kind of fortune-telling or magic whereby the hypnotist uses the *jinn* to overpower the subject and then speak through his tongue and give him strength to do things by means of controlling his faculties; this is if the *jinn* is sincere towards the hypnotist and obeys him in return for the things by means of which the hypnotist draws close to him. So, the *jinn* makes the subject obey the wishes of the hypnotist to do things or tell him things, through the help of the *jinn*. Thus, using hypnotism as a means of finding out where stolen goods are hidden, or where a lost item is, or as a means of treating disease or of doing anything else is not permissible (Islām Q&A, 2002).

The Fatwas of the Permanent Committee stated that,

> Hypnosis [hypnotherapy] is a type of soothsaying in which a hypnotist seeks the help of a *jinn* and makes him overpower a hypnotised person and talk through him. The *jinn* gives the hypnotised person power to do certain actions if he agrees to obey the hypnotist and is truthful with him in return for mutual benefits. Accordingly, the *jinn* causes the hypnotised person to obey the hypnotist in any actions or to give any information asked from him if it is being honest with the hypnotist. It is therefore not permissible to utilise hypnosis or to use it to find a stolen or lost object, to cure a sick person, or to do anything through a hypnotised person. In fact, this is *shirk*, due to what was previously mentioned and because it entails resorting to other than Allāh in matters that are beyond those ordinarily permitted by Allāh for His Creation.
>
> *(Fatwa no. 1779)*

This is clear: hypnotherapy and all its forms are *harām*. However, it has been proposed that if hypnosis depends on any help from *jinn* and *shaytan*s through incantations and amulets, then it is prohibited. In addition, such an action will be a form of soothsaying, which is a kind of *shirk* (polytheism). But if hypnosis is performed without any form of prohibitions, then it comes under the rule of "means are subject to rulings of ends." In other words, if it is used for some legitimate goal, then it is *halāl*, and vice versa (Islāmweb.net, 2002). Allāh knows best.

Reflexology

Reflexology, a form of complementary therapy, involves applying pressure to specific points on the feet, hands, or ears to induce relaxation, reduce tension, and enhance overall well-being. This practice is based on the belief that the body has an invisible life force or *ch'i* and that clearing blockages in this energy field promotes healing. Rooted in Eastern mysticism and popular in the New Age movement, reflexology suggests that specific points correspond to various organs, glands, and body systems. Although it is used for relaxation and stress reduction, and believed by some to have health benefits, there is no conclusive medical evidence supporting its efficacy. The practice's alignment with Islāmic principles may raise concerns, and individuals should seek guidance from knowledgeable scholars when considering its use. It is stated that, "Reflexology works on three levels: the physical, the mental, the spiritual" (Berkson, 1992, p. 12).

The spiritual dimension of reflexology is based on "a healing force from the universe [which] is called upon and used, by both the client and the practitioner" (Berkson, 1992 p. 115). The basic philosophy behind reflexology has roots in the Taoist Chinese view of the life force *ch'i* and the concept of *chakras* in the Hindu practice of yoga. Furthermore, it is stated that "Amongst the shrines and temples of

Vishnu, there is a footprint painting. Ancient Sanskrit symbols are painted on the feet. These symbols correspond to modern day reflex points" (Google search). That means the reflex points in the foot are based on Hindu symbols.

According to Mookerjee (1971), the feet symbolise the unity of the entire universe, and he stated, "all the elements of the universe are represented by the signs, and they also indicate the many aspects of the Ultimate One" (p. 54). These symbols and concepts are totally incompatible with the belief of God as the only true God, Almighty, Creator, Healer and Source of Life. The considerations of the spiritual aspects associated with reflexology alone should nullify it as a choice for Muslims as believers.

Some Muslim clinicians who practice reflexology suggest that just because some people attach a spiritual meaning to reflexology, it does not nullify the acceptability of a Muslim practicing or receiving this type of treatment. There is the use of Sufi reflexology therapy (Islāmy et al., 2022) for patients with stroke; kidney, heart, liver, and gallbladder diseases; cysts; cancer; and other chronic illnesses. Sufi reflexology therapy is similar to general reflexology and focuses on the patient's hands and feet. The method "incorporates the spiritual values contained in the teachings of Islām. Akang [Akang Limbangan] believes that "success in curing a patient's illness depends on a treatment process that combines horizontal and vertical principles in the form of physical and spiritual elements" (Islāmy et al., 2022, p. 225). Currently, there is no known *fatwa* on the use of reflexology. The best action for a Muslim is to avoid this form of treatment even if it is claimed to be a mixture of reflexology with value-added Islāmic element, named Islāmic foot reflexology.

The following *hādīth* is relevant and appropriate in this context. An-Nu'man bin Bashir said,

> I heard the Messenger of Allāh (ﷺ) say, "That which is lawful is plain and that which is unlawful is plain, and between them are matters which are not as clear. I will strike a parable for you about that: indeed Allāh, the Mighty and Sublime, has established a sanctuary, and the sanctuary of Allāh is that which He has forbidden. Whoever approaches the sanctuary is bound to transgress upon it." Or he said, "Whoever grazes around the sanctuary will soon transgress upon it, and whoever indulges in matters that are not clear, he will soon transgress beyond the limits."
>
> *(An-Nasā'i (a))*

Furthermore, the following *hādīth* reflects the decision to be taken by practitioners and individual Muslims. It was narrated that Abu Al-Hawra' As-Sa'di said to Al-Hasan bin 'Ali (may Allāh be pleased with him), "What did you memorise from the Messenger of Allāh (ﷺ)?" He said, "I memorised from him, 'Leave that which makes you doubt for that which does not make you doubt.'"

(An-Nasā'i (b))

This *ḥadīth* lays down a very general principle that can be applied in all aspects of one's life. If a person truly applies the meaning of this *ḥadīth*, he should, Allah willing, find psychological well-being and inner peace. . . . If there is a conflict between something that is known for certain and something that is a matter of conjecture, then that which is known for certain take precedence over the conjecture.

(Zarabozo, 2008, pp. 468–475)

Yoga

The practice of yoga, with its physical, mental, and spiritual components, originated in ancient India and has become widespread for its health and well-being benefits. However, its acceptability within the Islāmic context has been a subject of discussion and of varying opinions among scholars and practitioners. Yoga's spiritual roots in Hinduism, including elements of meditation and mindfulness, have raised concerns among some Islāmic scholars. While some argue that yoga can be viewed as a means of attaining union with God and developing wisdom, others express reservations about its origins and potential conflicts with Islāmic beliefs.

Despite these debates, many Muslim women use yoga as a form of health exercise, and some Muslims, particularly in the Indian subcontinent, believe that it can be a permissible form of worship (*ibādah*) in Islām. The acceptability of yoga within Islām remains a nuanced and debated topic within the Muslim community. It is claimed that yoga is a desirable act for Muslims as evidenced in the second Yoga Sutra and should be undertaken as a spiritual pursuit (Rahman, 2012):

> *Yogas chitta vritti nirodhah* means 'yoga stops all the modulations of the mind.' Ceasing all the outward activities of the mind and reposing in Allāh is the ultimate goal of Islām. So, any act done to reach such a state cannot be un-Islāmic. In fact, it represents the highest form of *ibādah* (prayer).

Laa hawla wa laa quwwata illa Billaah (There is no power or might except with Allāh).

Yoga is both a spiritual and a physical exercise, so at first glance, one might assume that yoga is *halāl* and perhaps even beneficial since it is both physical exercise and a means to get close to God, Allāh. However, upon studying the practice further, there are other issues to consider. The Islāmic ruling on practicing yoga is that "it is not permissible for the Muslim to practice yoga at all, whether he does it on the basis of belief or imitating others, or because he is seeking a particular so-called benefit. That is due to a number of reasons" (Islām Q&A, 2011b). One summary is that yoga is contrary to *tawhīd* and involves associating other deities with Allāh (may He be exalted) and because it involves prostrating to the sun and repeating its names. Allāh says,

قُلْ إِنَّمَآ أُمِرْتُ أَنْ أَعْبُدَ ٱللَّهَ وَلَآ أُشْرِكَ بِهِۦ

- *Say, "I have only been commanded to worship Allāh and not associate [anything] with Him."*

(Ar-Ra'd 13:36, interpretation of the meaning)

لَئِنْ أَشْرَكْتَ لَيَحْبَطَنَّ عَمَلُكَ وَلَتَكُونَنَّ مِنَ ٱلْخَٰسِرِينَ

- *If you should associate [anything] with Allāh, your work would surely become worthless, and you would surely be among the losers.*

(Az-Zumar 39:65, interpretation of the meaning)

The whole essence of yoga involves the imitation of idol worshippers and resembling them. Ibn 'Umar (may Allāh be pleased with him) narrated that the Messenger of Allāh (ﷺ) said, "He who imitates any people (in their actions) is considered to be one of them" (Abū Dāwūd (d)). Ibn Taymiyyah said, "Imitating them in outward matters leads to imitating them in attitude and actions." Some of the yoga practices are harmful from a health and psychological point of view. According to Abū Saeed Saad ibn Maalik Ibn Sinaan al-Khudri, the Prophet (ﷺ) said, "There is not to be any causing of harm, nor is there to be any reciprocating of harm" (Ibn Majah (c)). Furthermore,

> It is a waste of time doing something that does not bring anything but harm and loss in this world, and calamity and despair in the Hereafter. It is a clear call to imitate animals and detracts from human dignity, such as: adopting nakedness, resting on all fours in most of the exercises and the special posture in the third and eighth exercises. Many of those who tried to practice what is called scientific yoga or behavioural therapy fell into the pit of drugs and addiction, and this remedy has been proven to be ineffective and of no benefit. This activity is based on lies and charlatanry; its promoters rely on deceit and twisting the facts in spreading it. A few of those who practice yoga, or some other esoteric or deviant trends may perform extraordinary feats, people are deceived by it. But in most cases, they are only using devils among the *jinn* as in the case of magic and so on, and this is *harām* according to Islām.
>
> (Islām Q&A, 2011c)

Despite the clear ruling on yoga, some Muslims would argue that just doing the exercise is not harmful or *harām*: It has been suggested that "while merely doing the physical movements of yoga without the worshipping and chanting might not be against religious beliefs, Muslims should avoid practising it altogether as "doing one part of yoga would lead to another" (The National Fatwa Council of Malaysia). Abū'd-Darda' (may Allāh be pleased with him) narrates that the Messenger of Allāh (露) said, "Allāh has created the sickness and the remedy, so treat sickness but do not treat sickness with anything that is *harām*" (At-Tabarāni). As with previous therapies addressed here, yoga falls in the grey area and therefore is best avoided. The same benefits experienced by the yoga practitioner can be achieved in *halāl* ways. The spiritual element can be attained through prayer and *dhikr* and the physical elements through exercise and stretching. It is important to also note here that if exercises that are normally done and accepted by sports scientists are Islāmically acceptable even if they may resemble that of those performed in yoga.

Conclusion

In determining the permissibility of complementary therapies in Islām, it is evident that the acceptability varies based on the specific therapy. Generally, herbal remedies, homeopathy, acupuncture, cupping, and aromatherapy are considered *halāl* as long as they adhere to Islāmic principles and do not involve prohibited substances or practices. However, more controversial therapies such as hypnotherapy, reflexology, and yoga have diverse opinions, with some scholars expressing concerns about their compatibility with Islāmic beliefs.

Muslims are advised to exercise caution when opting for complementary therapies, especially those that are less clear-cut or may contradict the concept of the Oneness of Lordship (*Tawhīd ar-Rubūbiyyah*). Seeking alternative therapies firmly grounded in Islāmic principles, such as those derived from Prophetic Medicine (*Tibb an-Nabawi*), is recommended. Additionally, adhering to Islāmic teachings involves consulting scholars and health care professionals to make well-informed decisions guided by the Qur'ân and *Sunnah*. It is worth reflecting on the following *hādīth*: Al-Hasan bin 'Ali said (may Allāh be pleased with him), "I remember that the Messenger of Allāh said, 'Leave what makes you in doubt for what does not make you in doubt. The truth brings tranquillity while falsehood sows doubt'" (Tirmidhî (d)). Allāh Knows Best (*Allāhu A'alam*).

References

Abū Dāwūd (a). Cited in Islām Q&A (2001). 2438: Ruling on medical treatment. Retrieved December 6, 2023, from https://Islamqa.info/en/2438

Abū Dāwūd (b). *Sunan Abū Dāwūd 3857*. In-book reference: Book 29, Hādīth 3. English translation: Book 28, Hādīth 3848. https://sunnah.com/Abūdawud:3857

Abū Dāwūd (c). *Sunan Abū Dāwūd 3861*. In-book reference: Book 29, Hadith 7. English translation: Book 28, Hadith 3852. Hasan (Al-Albani). https://sunnah.com/Abūdawud:3861

Abū Dāwūd (d). Book 16, Hadith 35. English translation: Book 16, Hadith 1514. Arabic reference: Book 16, Hadith 1471. https://sunnah.com/bulugh/16/35

Abūelgasim, H., Albury, C., & Lee, J. (2021). Effectiveness of honey for symptomatic relief in upper respiratory tract infections: A systematic review and meta-analysis. *BMJ Evidence-Based Medicine*, *26*(2), 57–64. https://doi.org/10.1136/bmjebm-2020-111336

Ahmad, M. F., Ahmad, F. A., Ashraf, S. A., Saad, H. H., Wahab, S., Khan, M. I., Ali, M., Mohan, S., Hakeem, K. R., & Athar, M. T. (2021). An updated knowledge of Black seed (*Nigella sativa* Linn.): Review of phytochemical constituents and pharmacological properties. *Journal of Herbal Medicine*, 25, 100404. https://doi.org/10.1016/j.hermed.2020.100404

Ahmadi, A., Schwebel, D. C., & Rezaei, M. (2008). The efficacy of wet-cupping in the treatment of tension and migraine headache. *The American Journal of Chinese Medicine*, 36(1), 37–44. https://doi.org/10.1142/S0192415X08005564

Al-Ghamdi, M. S. (2001). The anti-inflammatory, analgesic and antipyretic activity of Nigella sativa. *Journal of Ethnopharmacology*, 76(1), 45–48. https://doi.org/10.1016/S0378-8741(01)00216-1

Al-Haafiz Ibn Rajab. Jaami'al-'Uloom wa'l-Hukam, 1/280. Cited in Islām Q&A (2014) What is the meaning of the hadeeth *"Leave that which makes you doubt for that which does not make you doubt"*? Retrieved December 6, 2023, from https://Islamqa.info/en/answers/212227/what-is-the-meaning-of-the-hadeeth-leave-that-which-makes-you-doubt-for-that-which-does-not-make-you-doubt

Ali, B., Al-Wabel, N. A., Shams, S., Ahamad, A., Khan, S. A., & Anwar, F. (2015). Essential oils used in aromatherapy: A systemic review. *Asian Pacific Journal of Tropical Biomedicine*, 5(8), 601–611. https://doi.org/10.1016/j.apjtb.2015.05.007

Alrawi, S. N., & Fetters, M. D. (2012). Traditional Arabic & Islāmic medicine: A conceptual model for clinicians and researchers. *Global Journal of Health Science*, 4(3), 164–169. https://doi.org/10.5539/gjhs.v4n3p164

An-Nasā'i (a). *Sunan an-Nasa'i 4453*. Book 44, Hādīth 5. English translation: Vol. 5, Book 44, Hādīth 4458. Retrieved December 7, 2023, from https://sunnah.com/nasai/44

An-Nasā'i (b). Sunan An-Nasā'i 5711. In-book reference: Book 51, Hadith 173. English translation: Vol. 6, Book 51, Hādīth 5714. Sahih (Darussalam). https://sunnah.com/nasai:5711

At-Tabarāni. *al-Mu'jam al-Kabeer, 24/254*; Classed as Sahih by Sheikh Al-Albani in as-Silsilah as-Saheehah, 1633.

Azaizeh, H., Saad, B., Cooper, E., & Said, O. (2010). Traditional Arabic and Islāmic medicine, a re-emerging health aid. *Evidence Based Complementary and Alternative Medicine*, 7(4), 419–424. https://doi.org/10.1093/ecam/nen039

Berkson, D. (1992). *The foot book: Holistic guide to footcare using reflexology, massage, diet, exercise and visualization*. Harper Perennial.

Bukhāri (a). *Sahih al-Bukhāri 5678*. Book 76, Hādīth 1.USC-MSA web (English) reference: Vol.7, Book 71, Hādīth 582. https://sunnah.com/bukhari:5678

Bukhāri (b). *Sahih al-Bukhāri 5683*. In-book reference: Book 76, Hādīth 6. USC-MSA web (English) reference: Vol. 7, Book 71, Hādīth 587. https://sunnah.com/bukhari:5683

Bukhāri (c). *Sahih al-Bukhāri 5687*. In-book reference: Book 76, Hādīth 10.USC-MSA web (English) reference: Vol. 7, Book 71, Hādīth 591. https://sunnah.com/bukhari:5687

Bukhāri (d). *Sahih al-Bukhāri 5689*. In-book reference: Book 76, Hādīth 12.USC-MSA web (English) reference: Vol. 7, Book 71, Hādīth 593. https://sunnah.com/bukhari:5689

Bukhāri (e). *Sahih al-Bukhāri 5692*. 5693. In-book reference: Book 76, Hadith 15.USC-MSA web (English) reference: Vol. 7, Book 71, Hadith 596. https://sunnah.com/bukhari:5692

Bukhāri (f). *Sahih al-Bukhāri 5684*. Book 76, Hādīth. USC-MSA web (English) reference: Vol. 7, Book 71, Hādīth 588. https://sunnah.com/bukhari:5684

Bukhāri (g). *Sahih al-Bukhāri 5706*. In-book reference: Book 76, Hādīth 26.USC-MSA web (English) reference: Vol. 7, Book 71, Hādīth 607. https://sunnah.com/bukhari:5706

Bukhāri (h). *Sahih al-Bukhāri 5708*. In-book reference: Book 76, Hādīth 28. USC-MSA web (English) reference: Vol. 7, Book 71, Hādīth 609. https://sunnah.com/bukhari:5708

Darul Ifta. *Fatwa: It is lawful to use homeopathic medicine as it contains alcohol?* (Fatwa: 1111/1113/N=1433). Retrieved December 6, 2023, from https://Islamqa.org/hanafi/darulifta-deoband/78693

Freckelton I. (2012). Death by homeopathy: Issues for civil, criminal, and coronial law and for health service policy. *Journal of Law and Medicine*, *19*(3), 454–478.

Fuhr, K., Meisner, C., Broch, A., Cyrny, B., Hinkel, J., Jaberg, J., Petrasch, M., Schweizer, C., Stiegler, A., Zeep, C., & Batra, A. (2021). Efficacy of hypnotherapy compared to cognitive behavioral therapy for mild to moderate depression – Results of a randomized controlled rater-blind clinical trial. *Journal of Affective Disorders*, *286*, 166–173. https://doi.org/10.1016/j.jad.2021.02.069

Hunt, K. J., Coelho, H. F., Wider, B., Perry, R., Hung, S. K., Terry, R., & Erns, E. (2010). Complementary and alternative medicine use in England: Results from a national survey. *International Journal of Clinical Practice*, *64*(11), 1496–1502.

Ibn Majah (a). *Sunan Ibn Majah 3436*. In-book reference: Book 31, Hādīth 1 English translation: Vol. 4, Book 31, Hadith 3436. Sahih (Darussalam). https://sunnah.com/ibnmajah:3436

Ibn Majah (b). *Sunan Ibn Majah*. English reference: Vol. 4, Book 31, Hādīth 3476. Arabic reference: Book 31, Hādīth 3605. https://sunnah.com/ibnmajah:3476

Ibn Majah (c). *Hādīth No 32, Imâm an-Nawawî's 40 Hadîth*. The Forty Hādīth of Imam Nawawi. http://40hādīthnawawi.com/

Ibn Taymiyyah. *Iqtidaa' as-Siraat al-Mustaqeem Mukhaalafatu Ashaab'il-Jaheem* [In Pursuit of the Straight Path by Contradicting the People of the Hellfire].

Ibrahim, N. (2012). *Bad blood: A look at the controversial healing technique of blood-letting*. Retrieved December 7, 2023, from https://cloudflare.egyptindependent.com/bad-blood-look-controversial-healing-technique-blood-letting/

Islām Q&A. (2000). Cited in *Majmoo' Fataawa wa Maqaalaat Mutanawwi'ah li Samaahat al-Shaykh al-'Allaamah 'Abd al-'Azeez ibn 'Abd-Allaah ibn Baaz* [May Allāh have mercy on him], (Vol. 8, p. 112). Retrieved December 6, 2023, from https://Islamqa.info/en/11809

Islām Q&A. (2001). *11956. Medical treatment using herbs and needles (acupuncture)*. Retrieved December 6, 2023, from http://Islamqa.info/en/ref/11956

Islām Q&A. (2002). *12631: Ruling on hypnotherapy*. Al-Lajnah al-Daa'imah li'l-Iftaa', 1/74. Silsilat al-Fataawa al-Shar'iyyah. Retrieved December 7, 2023, from https://Islamqa.info/en/1263

Islām Q&A. (2005). 40530: *Ruling on medicines that are mixed with alcohol*. Retrieved December 7, 2023, from https://Islamqa.info/en/40530

Islām Q&A. (2011a). Cited in Ruling on homoeopathy111004: In al-Mawsoo'ah al-'Arabiyyah al'Aalamiyyah. Retrieved December 6, 2023, from https://Islamqa.info/en/111004

Islām Q&A. (2011b). *Fatwa 101591, Yoga, its origins and the ruling on practising it*. Retrieved December 7, 2023, from http://Islamqa.info/en/ref/101591

Islām Q&A. (2011c). *Fatwa 10159, Yoga, its origins and the ruling on practising it*. Cited in Al-Yoga fi Mizan al-Naqd al-'Ilmi (pp. 84–86). http://Islamqa.info/en/ref/101591

Islāmweb.net. (2002). *Untraditional treatments, Fatwa 83858*. Retrieved December 7, 2023, from https://Islamweb.net/en/fatwa/83858/untraditional-treatments

Islāmweb.net. (2009). U*sing the Five Elements theory in acupuncture treatment. Fatwa 127771*. Retrieved December 6, 2023, from https://Islamweb.net/en/fatwa/127771/using-the-five-elements-theory-in-acupuncturetreatment#:~:text=Acupuncture%20%E2%80%8Eis%20permissible%20as%20we%20mentioned%20in%20Fatwa,there%20is%20no%20reason%20for%20you%20to%20worry

Islāmy, M. R., Purwanto, Y., Romli, U., & Ramdani, A. H. (2022). Spiritual healing: A study of modern Sufi reflexology therapy in Indonesia. *Teosofi: Jurnal Tasawuf dan Pemikiran Islām*, *12*(2), 209–231. https://doi.org/10.15642/teosofi.2022.12.2.209-231

Jones, L., Othman, M., Dowswell, T., Alfirevic, Z., Gates, S., Newburn, M., Jordan, S., Lavender, T., & Neilson, J. P. (2012). Pain management for women in labour: An overview of systematic reviews. *The Cochrane Library*, *3*, CD009234.

McKenzie, B. (2013). Overview of homeopathy. *Science-Based Medicine*. Retrieved December 7, 2023, from https://sciencebasedmedicine.org/reference/homeopathy/

Mishkat al-Masabih. *Mishkat al-Masabih 4571*. In-book reference: Book 23, Hadith 56. https://sunnah.com/mishkat:4571.

Mookerjee, A. (1971). *Tantra asana: A way to self-realization*. Basilius Presse.

National Health and Medical Research Council (Australian Government). (2015). *NHMRC information paper: Evidence on the effectiveness of homeopathy for treating health conditions*. National Health and Medical Research Council website. Retrieved December 7, 2023, from www.nhmrc.gov.au/about-us/resources/homeopathy

Ojueromi, O. O., Oboh, G., & Ademosun, A. O. (2022). Black seed (Nigella sativa): A favourable alternative therapy for inflammatory and immune system disorders. *Inflammopharmacol, 30*, 1623–1643. https://doi.org/10.1007/s10787-022-01035-6

Palma-Morales, M., Huertas, J. R., & Rodríguez-Pérez, C. (2023). A comprehensive review of the effect of honey on human health. *Nutrients, 15*(13), 3056. https://doi.org/10.3390/nu15133056

Pelissolo, A. (2016). Hypnosis for anxiety and phobic disorders: A review of clinical studies. *Presse Medicale, 45*(3), 284–290. https://doi.org/10.1016/j.lpm.2015.12.002

Permanent Committee. ('Abdullah ibn Qa'ud, 'Abdullah ibn Ghudayyan, 'Abdul-Razzaq 'Afify,'Abdul-'Aziz ibn 'Abdullah ibn Baz). Fatwa no. (1779): Volume 1: 'Aqidah (1), Creeds, Swearing by other than Allāh, Jinn, hypnosis and swearing by people. (Part No. 1; p. 348). Retrieved December 7, 2023, from http://alifta.net/Fatawa/fatawaDetails.aspx?languagename=en&BookID=7&View=Page&PageNo=1&PageID=179

Rahman, R. (2012). *Yoga in Islām: A form of Ibaadat* (prayer). Retrieved September 7, 2023, from https://artoflivingsblog.wordpress.com/2012/07/19/yoga-the-highest-form-of-ibaadat-prayer-2/

Rassool, G. Hussein, & Morris, H. (2020). Use of complementary therapies by Muslims: Halāl or Harām? *Journal of Integrated Sciences, 1*(1), 11–26.

Rocha, V., Ladas, E. J., Lin, M., Cacciavillano, W., Ginn, E., Kelly, K. M., Chantada, G., & Castillo, L. (2017). Beliefs and determinants of use of traditional complementary/alternative medicine in pediatric patients who undergo treatment for cancer in South America. *Journal of global oncology, 3*(6), 701–710. https://doi.org/10.1200/JGO.2016.006809

Sado, M., Ota, E, Stickley, A., & Mori, R. (2012). Hypnosis during pregnancy, childbirth, and the postnatal period for preventing postnatal depression. *The Cochrane Library, 6*, CD009062. https://doi.org/10.1002/14651858.CD009062

Samarghandian, S., Farkhondeh, T., & Samini, F. (2017). Honey and health: A review of recent clinical research. *Pharmacognosy Research, 9*(2), 121–127. https://doi.org/10.4103/0974-8490.204647

Sardjono, R. E., Kadarohman, A., Musthapa, I., & Rachmawati, R. (2018). The development of halal aromatherapy products and identification of its chemical constituents. *World Journal of Pharmacy and Pharmaceutical Sciences, 7*(5), 1523–1534.

Shah, Y. R., Sen, D. J., Patel, R. N., Patel, J. S., Patel, A. D., & Prajapati, P. M. (2011). Aromatherapy: The doctor of natural harmony of body & mind. *International Journal of Drug Development and Research, 3*(1), 286–294.

Shakeri, F., Gholamnezhad, Z., Mégarbane, B., Rezaee, R., & Boskabady, M. H. (2016). Gastrointestinal effects of Nigella sativa and its main constituent, thymoquinone: A review. *Avicenna Journal of Phytomedicine, 6*(1), 9–20.

Sharp, D., Lorenc, A., Morris, R., Feder, G., Little, P., Hollinghurst, S., Mercer, S. W., & MacPherson, H. (2018). Complementary medicine use, views, and experiences: A national survey in England. *BJGP Open, 2*(4), bjgpopen18X101614. https://doi.org/10.3399/bjgpopen18X101614

Shaykh Ahmad Kutty (2016). *Cited in Is acupuncture permissible in Islām*. Retrieved January 6, 2024, from http://aboutIslam.net/counseling/ask-the-scholar/health-science/acupuncture-permissible-Islam-2/

The National Fatwa Council of Malaysia. *Malaysia Fatwa Council deems ancient form of exercise from India 'harām' for Muslims*. Retrieved December 7, 2023, from www.Islamicboard.com/general/134274720-malaysian-fatwa-yoga-haraam-muslims.html

Thomson, P., Jones, J., Browne, M., & Leslie, S. J. (2014). Psychosocial factors that predict why people use complementary and alternative medicine and continue with its use: A population based study. *Complementary Therapies in Clinical Practice, 20*(4), 302–310. https://doi.org/10.1016/j.ctcp.2014.09.004

Tirmidhî (b). *Jami' at-Tirmidhî* Vol. 4, Book 2, Hādīth 2046. Arabic reference: Book 28, Hādīth 2182. https://sunnah.com/urn/673490

Tirmidhî (c). Cited in Hādīth An-Nawawi 19. The Forty Hādīth of Imam Nawawi. Retrieved December 7, 2023, from http://40hadithnawawi.com/

Tirmidhî (d). *Jami' at-Tirmidhî 2518*. In-book reference: Book 37, Hadith 104. English translation: Vol. 4, Book 11, Hadith 2518. Sahih (Darussalam). https://sunnah.com/tirmidhi:2518

Tschanz, D. (1998). *History of Islāmic medicine and herbal remedies*. Retrieved December 7, 2023, from www.motherearthliving.com/health-and-wellness/history-of-Islamic-medicine-zm0z98ndzhou

World Health Organisation. (2013). *WHO traditional medicine strategy 2014–2023*. WHO.

Zaidi, R. (2012). *Alcohol in homeopathic medicine*. Approved by Dr Ashraf Muneeb of Qibla.com., according to the Hanafi School. Retrieved December 7, 2023, from www.mysticmedicine.com/natural-medicine/q-alcohol-in-homeopathic-medicine

Zarabozo, Jamaal al-Din M. (2008). *Commentary on the forty Hadith of al-Nawawi*. Vol 1, Hadith # 1 (pp. 468–475). Al-Basheer Company for Publication and Translation.

18
THE SIRAAT AL-ISLĀMIC PSYCHOTHERAPY PRACTICE MODEL

Introduction and context

In the field of psychotherapy, therapists often rely on theoretical models to understand human issues and guide clinical interventions aimed at helping clients achieve more fulfilling lives. Recognising the incongruity of certain aspects of conventional psychological therapeutic approaches with the values and beliefs of Muslim clients, scholars have undertaken a critical examination of theoretical foundations in the context of Islāmic psychotherapy and counselling (Al-Abdul-Jabbar & Al-Issa, 2000; Haque, 2010; Rassool, 2016). As Islāmic psychology advances and more literature on Islāmic psychotherapy and counselling emerges, there is a growing focus on developing Islāmic psychotherapy and counselling models that are each grounded in unique ideologies and methodologies.

Rassool (2018, 2020) redefines Islāmic psychotherapy as a practice that applies interpersonal skills for the development of the self (*nafs*), intellect (*'aql*), body (*jasad*), and heart (*qalb*) based on Islāmic spirituality. This therapeutic approach, deeply rooted in Islāmic tradition, recognises the interconnectedness of the human soul, mind, and body. Islāmic psychotherapy is versatile and applicable across diverse therapeutic settings, including individual psychotherapy and counselling, couples therapy, family interventions, and group therapy sessions. Diverse theoretical frameworks and approaches coexist, reflecting the diverse nature of Islāmic traditions and practices (Dharamsi, 2022; Keshavarzi & Haque, 2013; Keshavarzi et al., 2021; Rassool, 2016). Given the challenges and limitations of existing therapeutic models, there is a need to prioritise exploring and developing accessible, practical, and adaptable approaches that cater to diverse client populations and contexts. These models should address clients' readiness for change and a broad spectrum of mental health concerns, including complex mental health issues. The aim of this chapter is to examine the foundations, principles, and applications of the Siraat Al-Islāmic Psychotherapy Practice model (SIPPM), offering a comprehensive exploration of its key components and guiding principles.

Principles of the Islāmic psychotherapy practice model

The SIPPM is a holistic therapeutic approach that incorporates Islāmic principles and values to address the psychological, emotional, and spiritual well-being of individuals, aligning with the teachings of Islām. This practice model is grounded in Islāmic spirituality and psychology, offering individuals a structured framework for healing and personal growth. The principles of this model are outlined in Figure 18.1.

The SIPPM integrates Islāmic teachings with psychological methodologies guided by core principles such as *tawhīd,* emphasising the oneness of Allāh and the belief that true healing comes from a profound connection with Him. The Qur'ān

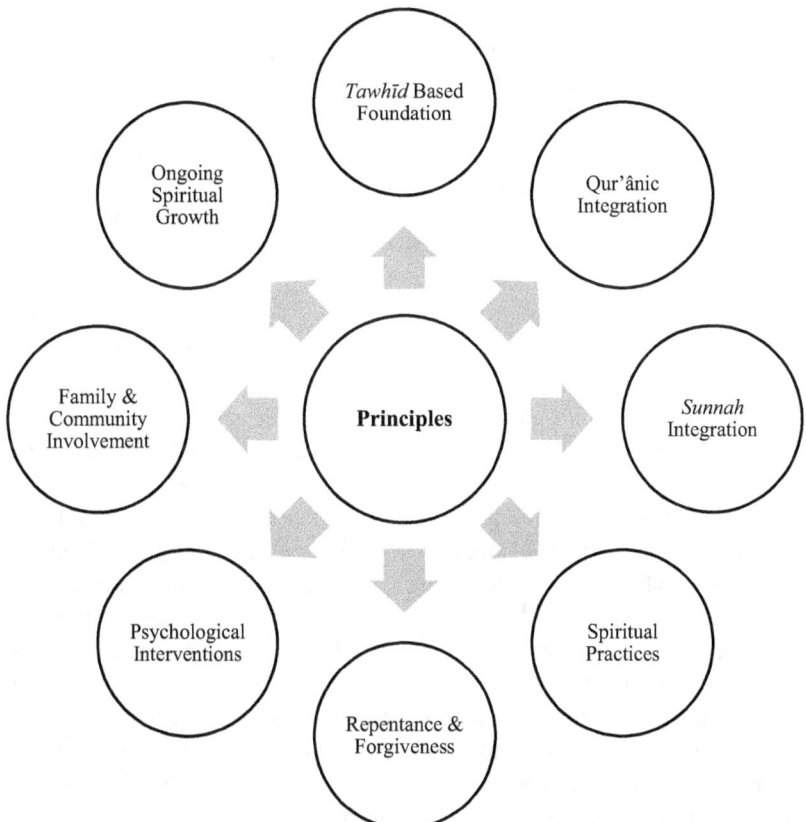

FIGURE 18.1 Principles of the Siraat Al-Islāmic psychotherapy practice model.

and *Sunnah* play a central role in this model, with therapists incorporating relevant verses and encouraging clients to emulate the character and teachings of Prophet Muhammad (ﷺ).

Spiritual practices like *dhikr*, supplications, and prayer are integrated with the concepts of repentance and forgiveness for emotional healing and growth. The model also incorporates evidence-based psychological techniques such as CBT, narrative therapy, and SFBT, tailored to align with Islāmic beliefs and practices to address psychospiritual struggles. The model stresses the importance of family and community (*ummah*) involvement, recognising their crucial role in Islāmic cultures for providing strong support in the recovery journey. Beyond symptom alleviation, the SIPPM promotes continuous spiritual growth, fostering a lifelong connection with Allāh and a deeper understanding of life purpose.

Towards an Islāmic psychotherapy practice model

A therapeutic practice model serves as a comprehensive framework guiding therapists and counsellors in their work with clients, encompassing ideas, knowledge, values, and practical applications related to the therapy process. The Islāmic Psychotherapy Practice Model (IIPM-12; Rassool, 2016) from Barise (2005) and Ibn Qayyim Al Jawziyyah. The stages include intention (*niyyah*), awakening (*Qawmah*), consultation (*istishara*), contemplation (*tafakkur*), guidance-seeking (*istikharah*), wilful decision (*'azm*), goal-and-route vision (*basirah*), absolute trust in God (*Al-tawakkul-Allāh*), action (*'amal*), help-seeking (*isti'aanah*), self-monitoring (*muraqabah*), and self-evaluation (*muhasabah*). A new model, the SIPPM, has been developed based on selected concepts and stages of the IIPM-12 (Rassool, 2016).

The SIPPM adopts a circular or spiral structure, departing from linear progression models. This design acknowledges that clients may undergo multiple cycles of certain stages, with progress not always straightforward. The circular format allows for flexibility, recognising the complex nature of therapeutic progress including potential relapses. Clients may revisit previous stages, gain further insights, or make adjustments before advancing, aligning with their unique circumstances and needs. This approach accommodates the individualised and fluid nature of therapy; for instance, setbacks or challenges may arise, necessitating revisits to previous stages or exploration of new perspectives, highlighting therapists' adaptability in providing ongoing support. While the model may be predominantly viewed as a cognitive and behavioural in its approach, it is through the cognitive processes that emotional and spiritual transformations are facilitated. By addressing cognitive distortions, promoting positive emotional experiences, and incorporating spiritual practices, the model can contribute to the holistic well-being of individuals within an Islāmic framework, ultimately fostering the transformation of the self.

In the SIPPM, the stages awakening (*qawnah*), contemplation (*tafakkur*), and goal and route vision (*basirah*), do not have clear cut-off points, suggesting that clients may revisit and readjust these stages as they progress through therapy before either reaching the action (*'amal*) or exiting the system without the attainment of the desired goals. The SIPPM distinguishes itself through remarkable flexibility, enabling therapists to effectively address the diversity of Muslim cultures. Tailored for clients assumed to be Muslim and aligned with Islāmic theological perspectives, the model respects client autonomy, making it suitable for individuals with different degrees of religiosity, including those with initially low motivation for change. The model's adaptability extends to family involvement and recognising the importance of understanding cultural and religious expectations within the broader family context.

The SIPPM: a process-drive model

The stages of the SIPPM encompass various concepts that are integral to the therapeutic process within an Islāmic framework. The model integrates awakening and intention with stages of contemplation, guidance seeking, goal-directed action, decision-making, maintenance of behaviour, self-monitoring, and evaluation. Here are some elaborations on these concepts.

Niyyah *(intention)*

The SIPPM incorporates the concept of behavioural intention (*niyyah*) as a fundamental component. It works in close collaboration with *Qawmah*. The meaning of *niyyah* and its derivatives are found in the Qur'ân: *al-iraada* (volition), *al-qasd* (purpose), and *al-azm* (determination). These terms all suggest "they want to do or not to do something specific and indicate both knowledge and action" (Zarabozo, 2008, p. 98). The initial step in any Islāmic undertaking typically involves setting *niyyah*. Allāh says in the Qur'ân,

فَأَقِمْ وَجْهَكَ لِلدِّينِ حَنِيفًا ۚ فِطْرَتَ

- *So, direct your face* [i.e. self] *towards the religion, inclining to the truth [adhere to] the fitrah.*

(Ar-Rum 30:30, interpretation of the meaning)

Umar bin Al-Khattab narrated, "I heard Allāh's Messenger (ﷺ) saying, 'The reward of deeds depends upon the intentions and every person will get the reward according to what he has intended'" (Bukhârî). Zarabozo (2008) explained this as follows – to complete an action successfully, three components are essential: knowledge of the act, the desire to perform the act, and the ability to carry out the act. This understanding suggests that without these three elements in place, the action cannot be accomplished effectively (pp. 106–107).

In Islām, *niyyah* is a fundamental concept that profoundly influences human deeds and actions. It is believed that the foundation of every action lies in one's intention. Muslims emphasise the significance of intention as it determines the sincerity and acceptance of deeds, both in this world and in the Hereafter. Ibn Qayyim al-Jawziyyah defined intention as the knowledge of a doer regarding what they are doing and the purpose behind their action. He emphasised that intelligent and voluntary actors always conceive and desire their actions before executing them, highlighting the intrinsic nature of intention to the individual's conceptualisation and purpose. Al-Suyooti described intention as the driving force in the heart that aligns with the individual's desires to bring about good or prevent harm, whether in the present or the future (cited in Zarabozo, 2008, p. 104).

Within the SIPPM, therapists and clients prioritise establishing clear and sincere intentions for engaging in therapy, recognising and articulating the purpose and objectives of the therapeutic process. By setting positive and sincere intentions, both therapist and client align their goals with seeking healing, personal growth, and spiritual well-being. *Niyyah* is not only important at the beginning of therapy but also continues to shape the therapeutic journey. Therapists consistently encourage clients to reflect on their intentions, assess their progress, and realign their actions accordingly.

Musharata *(contract)*

The SIPPM integrates the concept of a contract (*musharata*) as a key element in the therapeutic process (Al-Ghāzali, 1853/1986), encompassing both personal and professional agreements. The personal contract, established during the initial stage of contemplation (*tafakkur*), entails an agreement between the therapist and the client on therapy goals and targets. Through negotiation, both parties define the objectives, ensuring a shared understanding of expected outcomes. Additionally, a professional contract outlines responsibilities and expectations, including ethics, confidentiality, session logistics, fees, consent, record keeping, and termination. Endorsing this contract fosters transparency, accountability, and trust, upholding ethical standards and protecting client confidentiality. It serves as a guiding document for maintaining boundaries and facilitating effective communication in the therapeutic relationship. The consultation stages of the SIPPM are depicted in Figure 18.2.

Qawmah *(awakening)*

In the SIPPM, the stage of *Qawmah*, signifying awakening or becoming conscious, marks the initial phase of the therapeutic journey. It often serves as the catalyst prompting individuals to seek professional help. According to Ibn Qayyim al-Jawziyyah (1976), heightened sensitivity to the passage of time is a key sign of *Qawmah*, reflecting the realisation that time should not be wasted. Barise (2005)

FIGURE 18.2   The consultation stages of the SIPPM.

further defines *Qawmah* as the client's awareness of the need for change and recognition of the problem that must be addressed. *Qawmah* signifies the client's readiness for change and serves as the foundation for their active engagement in the therapeutic process, setting the stage for their transformation journey and reflecting a commitment to positive change.

In dealing with clients who lack readiness for change, therapists in the context of the SIPPM employ an empathetic approach to foster engagement and motivation. Assessing the client's readiness for change at the outset of therapy is vital, with the transtheoretical model (TTM) serving as an applicable framework (Prochaska et al., 1992; Prochaska & Velicer, 1997). The TTM outlines stages of change including pre-contemplation, contemplation, preparation, action, maintenance, and termination. The TTM maps stages of change: precontemplation (lack of awareness), contemplation (recognising the need for change with ambivalence), preparation (active planning for change), action (implementing strategies for change), and maintenance (sustaining behavioural change). For clients in the pre-contemplation stage, therapists prioritise building rapport, raising awareness about the need for change, and exploring the benefits of positive changes. Employing empathy, active listening, and collaborative goal setting are crucial strategies for enhancing clients' readiness for change.

The SIPPM integrates interventions from various therapeutic approaches to facilitate transitions between different stages of change. These interventions include support, psychotherapy, counselling, motivational interviewing (MI) (Miller & Rollnick, 2013), and CBT combined with MI (Naar & Safren, 2017). MI, particularly effective for clients in the contemplation stage, helps explore and resolve ambivalence, strengthen motivation, and create personalised change plans. This approach emphasises eliciting the client's motivations and goals, fostering intrinsic motivation for change. Research consistently demonstrates the effectiveness of MI in facilitating behavioural change and promoting healthier choices across diverse populations and settings, from reductions in sexual risk behaviours and substance use to improvements in diabetes management, medication adherence, and treatment compliance (Hall et al., 2012).

In the stages of change model, clients in the *Qawmah* stage typically reside in contemplation, preparation, and action phases, actively considering, planning, and implementing change strategies. On the contrary, those in the *pre-Qawmah* stage (pre-contemplation) may demonstrate denial, lack of problem recognition, inertia, or resistance to change, possibly due to a perceived inability to change. Therapists play a pivotal role in guiding clients from *pre-Qawmah* to *Qawmah* by employing techniques like gentle exploration, providing information, reflecting on experiences, and eliciting ambivalence (Prochaska et al., 1992; Prochaska & Velicer, 1997).

Istishara *(consultation)*

Istishara is the process of collecting relevant information about the client's past and presenting problems. The practice of consultation is highly esteemed in Islām and is encouraged as a means of seeking guidance and support. Allāh says in the Qur'ân,

وَشَاوِرْهُمْ فِى ٱلْأَمْرِ

- *Consult with them in the matter.*

(Ali 'Imrān 3:159)

وَأَمْرُهُمْ شُورَىٰ بَيْنَهُمْ

- *Whose affair is* [determined by] *consultation among themselves?*

(Ash-Shura 42:3)

In therapy, consultation serves as a key step in gathering information and assessing holistic needs. Therapists actively seek input from various sources, primarily the client and their family members or significant others, aligning with Islāmic teachings that emphasise considering multiple perspectives. Through consultation, therapists gain a comprehensive understanding of clients' bio-psychosocial and spiritual needs.

The assessment phase involves gathering information related to the presenting problem, exploring developmental and educational backgrounds, understanding family dynamics and history, conducting mental health assessments, and evaluating potential risks. In the assessment process, therapists focus on various cognitive, emotional, and behavioural factors, observing aspects like appearance, thoughts, feelings, and insight. Gathering information over time is crucial for a comprehensive understanding of the client's mental state. Therapists must establish a non-confrontational, empathetic, and respectful interaction style to create a safe and supportive environment. This ensures that clients feel heard, understood, and accepted. Consultation remains a dynamic and evolving process throughout therapy, emphasised by its central placement in therapeutic models. The placement of the consultation stage as a focal and central point in Figure 18.2 highlights its significance and continuous relevance throughout therapy. It signifies that consultation is not a standalone stage but an integral part of the entire therapeutic process.

Tafakkur *(contemplation)*

The stage of *tafakkur* in therapy involves creating a space for introspection and deep contemplation, rooted in Islāmic principles. *Tafakkur*, translated as contemplation or reflection, encompasses broader thinking processes aimed at deepening understanding and knowledge of Allāh as the Creator and Sustainer of the universe (Badri, 2000). Unlike Eastern meditative practices, Islāmic contemplation emphasises cognitive and intellectual aspects, with the depth of contemplation influenced by personal, social, cultural, and environmental factors (Badri, 2000). The depth of contemplation is also determined by one's level of faith, with a strong belief in God forming the foundation of Islāmic contemplation.

Through *tafakkur*, individuals seek to strengthen their connection with Allah and gain profound insights into His creation. The contemplation and reflection phase within the SIPPM is integral to the structured therapy process, persisting throughout the therapeutic journey. During this phase, therapists collaborate with clients to analyse issues, establish realistic goals, and identify intervention strategies. Active client engagement is crucial for the effectiveness of the plan, with emphasis on addressing underlying spiritual dimensions alongside psychological, cognitive, social, or biological issues. During *tafakkur*, clients engage in spiritual reflection, recognising God's wisdom and fostering a deeper connection with spirituality. Barise (2005) suggests integrating spiritual practices like gratitude and seeking spiritual strength using Qur'ānic verses and Prophetic traditions.

Istikharah *(seeking guidance)*

Following reflection and contemplation initiated by the therapist, the next stage is seeking guidance from the Almighty God: *istikharah*, according to Ibn Hijr, means to ask Allāh for help in making a choice, involving choosing the best option among alternatives (Islām Q&A, 1998). This Islāmic practice entails performing a specific prayer for guidance (*Salaat-l-Istikharah*) before making important decisions. Prior to this prayer, it is recommended that practitioners consult with trustworthy, caring, and knowledgeable individuals, such as a counsellor or an *imam*, emphasising the importance of seeking both divine and practical wisdom (Al-Nawawi, cited in Zarabozo, 2008). It was narrated that Jabir bin 'Abdullah said, "The Messenger of Allāh (ﷺ) used to teach his companions to perform *istikharah* in all matters, just as he used to teach them *surahs* [chapters] from the Qur'ân." He said, "If any one of you is deliberating about a decision he has to make, then let him pray two *rak'ahs* [unit of prayer] of non-obligatory prayer. Then say,

> *Allāhumma inni astakhiruka bi 'ilmika wa astaqdiruka bi qudratika wa as'aluka min fadlika, fa innaka taqdiru wa la aqdir, wa ta'lamu wa la a'lam, wa anta 'allam al-ghuyub. Allāhumma in kunta ta'lamu anna hadhal-amra khayrun li fi dini wa ma'ashi wa aqibati amri faqdurhu li wa yassirhu li thumma barik li fihi. Allāhumma, wa in kunta ta'lamu annahu sharrun li fi dini wa ma'ashi wa 'aqibati amri fasrifhu 'anni wasrifni 'anhu waqdur li al-khayr haythu kana, thumma radini bihi.*
>
> O Allāh, I seek Your guidance (in making a choice) by virtue of Your knowledge, and I seek ability by virtue of Your power, and I ask You of Your great bounty. You have power, I have none. And You know, I know not. You are the Knower of hidden things. O Allāh, if in Your knowledge, this matter (then it should be mentioned by name) is good for me in my religion, my livelihood and my affairs (or: both in this world and in the Hereafter), then ordain it for me, make it easy for me, and bless it for me. And if in Your knowledge it is bad for me and for my religion, my livelihood and my affairs (or: for me both in this world and the next), then turn it away from me and turn me away from it and ordain for me the good wherever it may be and make me pleased with it.
>
> (transliteration; cited in Islām Q&A, 1998)

Istikharah is confined to matters that are allowed, liked, or encouraged when there is a decision to be made as to which one should be given priority. The wisdom behind prescribing it is that it is a form of submission to the command of Allāh, signifying reliance on His guidance and acknowledging one's own limitations. It involves seeking to combine worldly and Hereafter goodness by turning to Allāh and expressing one's needs through prayer and supplication. *Istikharah* entails asking Allah for the best outcome and then taking action based on one's inclination after prayer (Islām Q&A, 2010). The scholars are unanimously agreed that for

Muslims, seeking guidance to the right decision from God is a *Sunnah*, and it is obligatory to believe in what the Prophet (ﷺ) has told us and to obey his instructions. In the Qur'ân, Allāh speaks of the importance of the *Sunnah*:

يَٰٓأَيُّهَا ٱلَّذِينَ ءَامَنُوٓا۟ أَطِيعُوا۟ ٱللَّهَ وَأَطِيعُوا۟ ٱلرَّسُولَ

- *You who believe! Obey Allāh and obey the Messenger.*
(An-Nisā' 4:59, interpretation of the meaning)

مَّن يُطِعِ ٱلرَّسُولَ فَقَدْ أَطَاعَ ٱللَّهَ

- *He who obeys the Messenger has indeed obeyed Allāh.*
(An-Nisā' 4:80, interpretation of the meaning)

The *istikharah* prayer is prescribed in all four schools of Islāmic jurisprudence for individuals facing uncertainty in decision-making. It is vital to approach *istikharah* with an open mind and without preconceived decisions. The purpose is to seek Allāh's guidance and wisdom for the best choice. Through this prayer, individuals express reliance on Allah's knowledge and seek His intervention. After *istikharah*, Allāh is believed to guide individuals towards the best decision, either through inclination or by removing doubts. It's advised to approach the decision with patience, trust, and sincerity, acknowledging Allāh's wisdom in guiding His creation.

Basirah *(goal-and-route vision)*

The guidance prayers emphasise maintaining commitment to clearly defined goals and action strategies. The concept of *basirah* represents a significant cognitive and spiritual transformation for the client, marked by the attainment of a goal-and-route vision. This shift not only brings clarity to the client's objectives but also deepens their understanding of the path to achieve them. It entails defining objectives, creating strategies, and devising action plans to attain the intended outcomes. *Tafakkur*, or contemplation, emerges as a crucial component in this process, allowing the individual to envision the spiritual rewards they will gain and the ensuing joys, both in this life and the hereafter (Barise, 2005). Through thoughtful reflection, the client envisions not only the tangible benefits and joys in their present life but also the spiritual merits extending into the afterlife.

'Azm *(wilful decisions)*

The stage of goal-and-route vision in the therapeutic process parallels the preparation stage in Prochaska et al.'s (1992) model of change. *'Azm* signifies the client's determination to change, and the therapist plays a pivotal role in supporting the client's readiness to change by assisting in plan creation, nurturing motivation, and enabling small experiments or trial changes to transition gradually into new behaviours. During the goal-and-route vision stage, clients exhibit strong determination to take action, requiring not just commitment but also appropriate skills and activities for a robust action plan. Therapists play a crucial role by providing concrete solutions, boosting self-esteem, and enhancing self-efficacy. Practical guidance and support help clients develop necessary skills and activities for successful plan implementation. In cases where clients feel compelled to change, therapists intervene to align behaviours with desired goals or societal norms, with resistance being less likely due to high motivation. Flexibility in goal setting and action strategies is essential to accommodate changing circumstances or developing needs, ensuring continued growth and progress.

Al-tawakkul-Allāh *(absolute trust in God)*

Tawakkul, a fundamental aspect of the Islāmic faith, entails absolute trust in and dependence on God, acknowledging His ultimate control over all aspects of life. It extends beyond decision-making to permeate various life situations, reflecting a belief in God's wisdom, divine intervention, and guidance. *Tawakkul* involves surrendering worries and anxieties to God, recognising Him as the best planner and caretaker of affairs. It is a spiritual act of reliance on God's support, protection, and guidance, emphasising the understanding that while individuals make careful choices, ultimate outcomes rest in God's hands. To make this point clear, Allāh says in the Qur'ân,

فَإِذَا عَزَمْتَ فَتَوَكَّلْ عَلَى ٱللَّهِ ۚ إِنَّ ٱللَّهَ يُحِبُّ ٱلْمُتَوَكِّلِينَ

- *And, when you have decided, then rely upon Allāh. Indeed, Allāh loves those who rely* [upon Him].

('Āli 'Imrān 3:159, interpretation of the meaning)

The psychospiritual benefits of *tawakkul* include a sense of relief and empowerment for the client, as they believe that whatever trials or tribulations they face are decreed by God. However, it is important to address a misconception that *tawakkul* does not require effort to change attitudes and behaviours. While trusting and relying on God are integral, it does not negate the need for active participation in personal growth and change. *Tawakkul* complements personal efforts rather than replacing them, emphasising a balanced approach to both spiritual trust and proactive engagement. The following illustrates this point: Anas ibn Malik reported that a man said, "O Messenger of Allāh, should I tie my camel and trust in Allāh, or should I leave her untied and trust in Allāh?" The Prophet (ﷺ) said, "Tie her and trust in Allāh" (Tirmidhī). There are other verses of the Qur'ân that explicitly enjoin Muslims to have reliance and trust in God in their lives (Qur'ân 65:3; 3:160;

9:51; 26:21). Having absolute trust in Allāh necessitates accepting that He alone controls the universe and that both good and bad events are within His will.

The stage of absolute confidence in God is not confined to the post-decision-making phase but is a continual and integral aspect throughout various therapy stages. The client is encouraged to maintain unwavering faith in God during all therapy stages, including assessment, goal setting, intervention, and evaluation, aligning intentions and actions with the principles of *tawakkul*. This practice ensures that the client remains grounded and connected to their spiritual convictions, extending from assessment and goal setting to intervention and evaluation. The therapist plays a vital role in nurturing and reinforcing the client's trust in God by providing guidance, support, and reminders about the significance of *tawakkul* in the therapeutic process.

'Amal *(action)*

During the transition from contemplation to action, clients actively pursue their desired goals by implementing the action plan. However, they must recognise that change encompasses not only external behaviours but also internal shifts in mindset, attitudes, and beliefs. Internal transformation is essential for achieving lasting and meaningful change. Success hinges on ensuring that actions align with intentions and understanding developed in earlier stages. Rushing into action without proper preparation can lead to failure.

'Amal emphasises the significance of an integrated approach to change, integrating external actions with internal transformations for comprehensive and sustainable progress. In the stage of direct action, clients transition from contemplation to actively pursuing their goals, ensuring that each action aligns with intended goals and incorporates lessons from earlier stages. Small goal attainment is rewarded to motivate further progress, with reinforcement and social support from family and the therapist being integral. Positive reinforcement boosts confidence and self-efficacy, while social support aids progress. However, clients are encouraged to develop self-reliance grounded in trust in God, recognising the importance of seeking divine guidance in the journey of change. Allāh says in the Qur'ân,

مَنْ عَمِلَ صَٰلِحًا فَلِنَفْسِهِۦ ۖ وَمَنْ أَسَآءَ فَعَلَيْهَا ۗ وَمَا رَبُّكَ بِظَلَّٰمٍ لِّلْعَبِيدِ

- *Whoever does righteousness-it is for his* [own] *benefit, and whoever does evil* [does so] *against it. And your Lord is not unjust to* [His] *servants.*
 (Fuṣṣilat 41:46, interpretation of the meaning)

According to the exegesis of Ibn Kathir (2000), Fuṣṣilat 41:46 means that everyone will be rewarded in accordance with his actions and the benefit and consequences which will come to him. This Qur'ânic verse highlights the importance of recognising our personal responsibility, and accountability for our actions, and acknowledging their impact on our spiritual dimension.

Isti'aanah *(seeking help)*

Help seeking, *isti'aanah*, is a fundamental aspect integrated consistently across all stages of the SIPPM. This process stresses the active pursuit of support, guidance, and assistance from both human and divine sources throughout the therapeutic journey. In moments of trials and tribulations, Muslims often turn to God as the ultimate source of assistance and support, finding solace and guidance in the teachings of the Qur'ân. The Qur'ân emphasises that believers will face trials and tests throughout their lives, and *isti'aanah* reminds individuals to exhibit patient perseverance and seek support through prayer during these challenges. Allāh says in the Qur'ân,

وَٱسْتَعِينُوا۟ بِٱلصَّبْرِ وَٱلصَّلَوٰةِ ۚ وَإِنَّهَا لَكَبِيرَةٌ إِلَّا عَلَى ٱلْخَٰشِعِينَ

- *And seek help through patience and prayer, and indeed, it is difficult except for the humbly submissive* [to Allāh].

(Al-Baqarah 2:45, interpretation of the meaning)

يَٰٓأَيُّهَا ٱلَّذِينَ ءَامَنُوا۟ ٱسْتَعِينُوا۟ بِٱلصَّبْرِ وَٱلصَّلَوٰةِ ۚ إِنَّ ٱللَّهَ مَعَ ٱلصَّٰبِرِينَ

- *You who have believed, seek help through patience and prayer. Indeed, Allāh is with the patient.*

(Al-Baqarah 2:153, interpretation of the meaning)

This highlights the importance of relying on God's guidance and seeking His assistance in overcoming difficult circumstances. Allāh calls upon Muslims to bear these trials with "patient perseverance and prayer."

From an Islāmic perspective, relying on God's guidance and seeking His assistance in overcoming trials is paramount, trusting in the Lord and avoiding despair. Seeking help from therapists or *imams* for family and personal issues is acceptable and even encouraged when necessary. However, it is essential to view helpers as intermediaries and recognise God as the ultimate provider of help and guidance. Consulting others is part of the Islāmic practice as emphasised in the *Sunnah* of the Prophet (ﷺ). God mentions consulting others in one's affairs as a positive trait of righteous believers in the Qur'ân:

وَٱلَّذِينَ ٱسْتَجَابُوا۟ لِرَبِّهِمْ وَأَقَامُوا۟ ٱلصَّلَوٰةَ وَأَمْرُهُمْ شُورَىٰ بَيْنَهُمْ وَمِمَّا رَزَقْنَٰهُمْ يُنفِقُونَ

- *And those who have responded to their Lord and established prayer and whose affair is [determined by] consultation among themselves, and from what We have provided them, they spend.*

(Ash-Shūraá 42:38, interpretation of the meaning)

Believers call on God and make supplications during prayers at least 17 times a day. They say,

إِيَّاكَ نَعْبُدُ وَإِيَّاكَ نَسْتَعِينُ

- *It is You we worship and You we ask for help.*
  (Al-Fātiḥah 1:5, interpretation of the meaning)

In the context of the SIPPM, *isti'aanah* highlights the significance of incorporating spiritual elements into the therapeutic process. Clients are encouraged to seek God's help and guidance in their healing journey, finding strength and solace in Islāmic practices. This includes incorporating prayers, supplication, and reflection on the words of Allāh as a means to navigate challenges and find inner resilience.

Muraqabah *(self-monitoring)* and muhasabah *(evaluation)*

The combined stage of *muraqabah*) and *muhasabah* is integral to the SIPPM. Self-monitoring serves as both an intervention strategy and a data collection method to assess therapy effectiveness. It enables clients to observe their behaviour, thoughts, and feelings, facilitating behaviour change through self-reflection and self-recording. In the Islāmic perspective, self-monitoring gains depth as it acknowledges God as the ultimate observer, adding spiritual accountability to the process of behaviour change (Mahoney, 2013). Clients recognise their accountability to a higher power, enriching the therapeutic journey with a sense of divine guidance and responsibility. Allāh says in the Qur'ân,

أَوَلَيْسَ ٱللَّهُ بِأَعْلَمَ بِمَا فِى صُدُورِ ٱلْعَٰلَمِينَ

- *Is not Allāh, most knowing of what is within the breasts of the worlds* [i.e. all creatures]*?*
  (Al-'Ankabūt 29:10, interpretation of the meaning)

وَٱللَّهُ يَعْلَمُ مَا تُسِرُّونَ وَمَا تُعْلِنُونَ

- *And Allāh knows what you conceal and what you declare.*
  (An-Naḥl 16:19, interpretation of the meaning)

يَعْلَمُ مَا فِى ٱلسَّمَٰوَٰتِ وَٱلْأَرْضِ وَيَعْلَمُ مَا تُسِرُّونَ وَمَا تُعْلِنُونَ ۚ وَٱللَّهُ عَلِيمٌۢ بِذَاتِ ٱلصُّدُورِ

- *He knows what is within the heavens and earth and knows what you conceal and what you declare. And Allāh is knowing of that within the breasts.*
  (At-Taghābun 64:4, interpretation of the meaning)

> وَرَبُّكَ يَعْلَمُ مَا تُكِنُّ صُدُورُهُمْ وَمَا يُعْلِنُونَ

- *And your Lord knows what their breasts conceal and what they declare.*
(Al-Qaṣaṣ 28:69, interpretation of the meaning)

The awareness of God leads clients to be honest and consistent in their internal and external processes (Barise, 2005). This concept, termed *muraqabah an-nafs*, involves self-observation to prevent undesirable actions and maintain behavioural changes. Serving as a protective mechanism, *muraqabah an-nafs* guides individuals to actively monitor their thoughts, words, and actions, ensuring alignment with their moral compass and facilitating sustained behavioural change.

Muhasabah, or evaluation, is the final process in the model. It involves assessing the outcomes of therapy to determine if it was helpful, looking at whether their symptoms improved, if they gained coping skills and achieved the desired changes. Evaluating the therapy process and outcomes is important for clients' ongoing psychosocial and spiritual development. Evaluation should be an ongoing process.

Siyanah at-taghyir as-suluki *(maintenance of behavioural change)*

Siyanah at-taghyir as-suluki encompasses the concept of preserving and sustaining desired behavioural changes over time. It emphasises not only initiating positive changes in behaviour but also ensuring their continuity and durability. This stage implies a commitment to long-term adherence to the newly adopted behaviours, fostering a sense of consistency and stability in one's conduct.

The emphasis on maintenance aligns with the understanding that behavioural changes should become ingrained habits, contributing to sustained personal growth and development. In the SIPPM, acknowledging both lapses and relapses in maintaining behavioural change is vital. A lapse involves a temporary deviation or slip into old habits, while a relapse entails a sustained return to previous behaviours. Preventing relapse is a primary goal, involving recognising and addressing contributing factors internally and externally. Seeking forgiveness from Allāh, recommitting to behavioural changes, seeking support, and employing strategies to maintain progress are integral. Learning from lapses, implementing strategies, and seeking support help prevent relapse in the journey of maintaining behavioural change.

From an Islāmic perspective, maintaining behavioural change involves continuous effort to uphold positive changes by implementing Islāmic principles and seeking God's guidance. Lapses and relapses are understood as natural occurrences, allowing for compassion, forgiveness, and repentance to regain focus. Islāmic psychotherapy may incorporate a relapse prevention programme rooted in Islāmic teachings, aiming to strengthen faith, enhance coping skills, promote self-reflection, offer ongoing support, and provide practical tools for managing triggers and stress. Islāmic psychotherapy integrates spiritual and psychological elements in its relapse prevention program, requiring commitment, self-awareness, and active participation from individuals.

Relapse prevention approaches vary across contexts and interventions, with Islāmic principles providing a spiritual framework for maintaining positive change. The relapse management plan within Islāmic psychotherapy is a critical aspect of relapse prevention, offering specific actions and strategies to address potential setbacks. It includes reaching out for support, reassessing goals, adjusting coping strategies, and seeking professional help if necessary. This plan encompasses identifying triggers, developing coping strategies, incorporating social support, making lifestyle changes, seeking forgiveness and renewal, integrating Islāmic principles, and engaging in self-reflection and contemplation. *Tazkiyah* therapy, as proposed by Riyono (2024), becomes a vital element in this plan, along with psycho-education, coping skills training, repentance, forgiveness, lifestyle changes, cognitive restructuring, spiritual guidance, contemplation, and building supportive networks. This comprehensive approach reflects the holistic nature of Islāmic psychotherapy, addressing both psychological and spiritual dimensions in the prevention and management of relapse. Key components of a relapse prevention programme in an Islāmic context, outlined in Table 18.1.

TABLE 18.1 Key components of a relapse prevention programme

Subject	Themes and contents
Psycho-education	Knowledge and understanding about the nature of relapse; identify common triggers; recognise potential risks and warning signs; prevention of relapse
Skills training	Practical skills and techniques to cope with stress, manage cravings, and handle challenging situations; relaxation techniques, problem-solving skills, assertiveness training, and improving emotional regulation
Repentance, forgiveness and renewal	Islāmic teachings; making *tawbah* (repentance), seeking forgiveness from Allāh, and seeking His guidance to renew commitment to positive change; these spiritual aspects helps individuals find strength, humility, and motivation to move forward
Lifestyle changes	Regular physical exercise, good nutrition, adequate sleep, and stress reduction techniques
Cognitive restructuring	Addressing negative thought patterns and irrational beliefs; challenging distorted thoughts and reframing negative self-talk
Spiritual guidance and practices	Incorporating Islāmic teachings and practices; regular prayer, recitation of Qur'ânic verses relevant to the specific challenges; seeking spiritual guidance from religious scholars; utilising supplications for strength and guidance; reflecting on Prophetic teachings, and engaging in acts of charity
Contemplation and *tazkiyah* therapy	Self-reflection, purification of the soul, and seeking to improve one's character in alignment with Islāmic values
Building supportive networks	Family units, *imams*, support groups, mentors

In Islām, the maintenance of behavioural change aligns with the concept of *tazkiyah an nafs*, or self-purification of the soul. *Tazkiyah* involves continuous efforts to purify oneself from negative traits, thoughts, and behaviours while aligning actions with Islāmic teachings and values. It emphasises self-reflection, self-discipline, and self-improvement, striving for spiritual growth and closeness to Allāh through righteous actions and intentions. *Tazkiyah* is viewed as a lifelong journey towards becoming a better Muslim and achieving spiritual excellence. In maintaining behavioural change, *tazkiyah* encourages individuals to seek forgiveness from Allāh for any lapses, promoting self-accountability, responsibility for actions, rectification of wrongdoings, and continuous improvement.

The SIPPM, with its emphasis on cognitive and behavioural processes, may indeed draw criticism from some who may perceive an explicit absence of interventions aimed at transforming the soul. However, it is essential to recognise that cognitive processes, as outlined in the model, can lead to changes at the affective or emotional level, which in turn can deeply impact the transformation of the soul. Drawing from the framework of Ibn Qayyim, a prominent Islāmic scholar, the model likely acknowledges the interconnectedness of cognitive processes, emotions, and spiritual well-being. According to Ibn Qayyim's framework, thoughts, beliefs, and cognitive patterns significantly influence emotional states and behavioural responses. He emphasised the importance of understanding and managing one's cognitive processes to achieve emotional and spiritual equilibrium.

For instance, negative or distorted thoughts can lead to negative emotions such as anxiety, sadness, or anger, while positive and rational thoughts can foster emotional well-being and spiritual growth. In the context of the SIPPM, interventions focusing on cognitive restructuring, reframing beliefs, and challenging negative thought patterns can lead to shifts in emotional experiences. Moreover, the model integrates spiritual practices such as *dhikr* (remembrance of God), *du'ahs* (supplication), and reflection on Qur'anic verses to evoke emotional responses and foster a deeper connection with one's spirituality. These practices can elicit profound emotional experiences and facilitate the process of inner transformation and growth at the soul level. This model offers a comprehensive approach that addresses both the psychological and spiritual aspects of the individual's journey towards maintaining positive behavioural changes and spiritual development.

Conclusion

The Siraat Al-Islāmic psychotherapy practice model offers a structure, process, and framework for Islāmic psychotherapists to apply in practice when working with Muslim clients. The proposed model presented in this chapter stands out from mainstream psychotherapy models by its emphasis on a psychosocial and spiritual orientation based on the creed of *Ahlus-Sunnah wa'l-Jamā'ah*. The proposed model integrates both non-directive and directive therapeutic techniques that are in harmony with Islāmic principles. It is important to recognise that the model is not exhaustive but serves as a basis for ongoing development and enhancement. As it evolves, specific techniques and illustrations pertinent to each stage can be integrated. The model is analogous to a preliminary exploration and agenda-setting, inviting collaboration and contribution from Muslim scholars, psychologists, and clinicians to further refine its efficacy and applicability.

References

Al-Abdul-Jabbar, J., & Al-Issa, I. (2000). Psychotherapy in Islāmic society. In I. al-Issa (Ed.) *Al-Junun: Mental illness in the Islāmic world* (pp. 277–293). International Universities Press.

Al-Ghāzali, A. H. M. (1986). *Revival of religious learning* (Trans. F. Karim). Kitab Bhavan. (Original work published 1853).

Badri, M. B. (2000). *Contemplation: An Islāmic psychospiritual study*. International Institute of Islāmic Thought.

Barise, A. (2005). Social work with Muslims: Insights from the teachings of Islām. *Critical Social Work, 6*(2). Retrieved December 11, 2023, from www1.uwindsor.ca/criticalsocialwork/social-work-with-muslims-insights-from-the-teachings-of-Islam

Bukhârî. *Sahih al-Bukhârî 1*. In-book reference: Book 1, Hadith 1 USC-MSA web (English) reference: Vol. 1, Book 1, Hadith 1. https://sunnah.com/bukhari:1

Dharamsi, S. (2022). How do Muslims survive and thrive within secular and prejudicial spaces? The authentic voice as an act of resistance in Islāmic Counselling training. *Psychotherapy Section Review, 67*. Retrieved December 10, 2023, from https://drive.google.com/file/d/1ri37LComzznBa267-ZXce0AG6YkODH_0/view

Hall, K., Gibbie, T., & Lubman, D. I. (2012). Motivational interviewing techniques: Facilitating behaviour change in the general practice setting. *Australian Family Physician, 41*(9), 660–667.

Haque, A. (2010). Mental health concepts in Southeast Asia: Diagnostic considerations and treatment implications. *Psychology, Health and Medicine, 15*(2), 127–134.

Ibn Qayyim al-Jawziyyah. (1976). *Madarij al-salikin [The Stages of the Travellers]*. A. M. al-Salih (Ed.). Wizarat al-Awqaf.

Islām Q&A. (1998). 2217: *How to pray Istikharah*. Retrieved December 12, 2023, from http://Islamqa.info/en/2217

Islām Q&A. (2010). 11981: *Istikharah prayer*. Retrieved December 12, 2023, from http://Islamqa.info/en/11981

Keshavarzi, H., & Ali, B. (2021). Foundations of traditional islāmically integrated psychotherapy. In H. Keshavarzi, F. Khan, B. Ali, & R. Awaad (Eds.), *Applying Islāmic principles to clinical mental health care: Introducing traditional Islāmically integrated psychotherapy*. Routledge.

Keshavarzi, H., & Haque, A. (2013). Outlining a psychotherapy model for enhancing Muslim mental health within an Islāmic context. *International Journal for the Psychology of Religion, 23*(3), 230–249. https://doi.org/10.1080/10508619.2012.712000

Mahoney, C. (2013). *Self-monitoring to enhance the effectiveness of a treatment for anxiety* [Counselling Psychology Dissertations, Paper 41, Northeastern University]. Retrieved December 12, 2023, from https://repository.library.northeastern.edu/files/neu:978/fulltext.pdf

Miller, W. R., & Rollnick, S. (2013). *Motivational interviewing: Preparing people for change*. (3rd ed.). Guilford Press.

Naar, S., & Safren, S. A. (2017). *Motivational interviewing and CBT: Combining strategies for maximum effectiveness (applications of motivational interviewing)*. Guilford Press.

Prochaska, J. O., DiClemente, C. C., & Norcross, J. C. (1992). In search of how people change. *American Psychologist, 47*(9), 1102–1114.

Prochaska, J. O., & Velicer, W. K. (1997). The trans-theoretical model of health behaviour change. *American Journal of Health Promotion*, *12(1)*, 38–48.

Rassool, G. Hussein (2016). *Islāmic counselling: An introduction to theory and practice*. Routledge.

Rassool, G. Hussein (2018). *Towards the development of a theoretical framework and model of Islāmic Psychotherapy and Counselling: Challenges and opportunities* (Unpublished paper).

Rassool, G. Hussein (2020). *Towards a redefinition of Islāmic psychotherapy and counselling.* Lecture at Al-Balagh Academy. Islāmic Counselling and Psychology-Level 2, July.

Riyono, B. (2024). *Tazkiyah therapy*. **Focus series on Islāmic psychology and psychotherapy. Routledge.**

Tirmidhī. *Sunan al-Tirmidhī 2517*. Hasan (fair) according to Al-Albani. Retrieved December 12, 2023, from www.abuaminaelias.com/dailyhadithonline/2012/11/17/trust-Allah-tie-your-camel/

Zarabozo, J. M. (2008). *Commentary on the Forty Hadith of al-Nawawi* (Vol. 1). Al-Basheer Company for Publications & Translation.

19
PSYCHOTHERAPY AND HARM REDUCTION IN ADDICTION

An Islāmic perspective

Introduction

Addiction poses a significant public health concern globally that goes beyond cultural boundaries to affect diverse populations. Rassool (2011, 2022) highlights the widespread nature of addictive behaviours, encompassing both pharmacological substances and non-substance-related activities like gambling, internet use, and sexuality. The sequelae of addiction extend beyond individual users to impact families, communities, and society at large. Muslims, like any other group, are susceptible to various forms of addiction, including alcohol and substance use disorder, gambling, and sex addiction. These challenges affect Muslims from diverse cultural backgrounds and geographic locations, highlighting the universal impact of addictive behaviours.

Psychotherapy and counselling are integral components in addressing addiction, offering individuals a supportive environment to explore underlying psychological factors. Various therapeutic approaches including pharmacological, psychosocial and spiritual interventions are utilised to manage addictive behaviours. Harm reduction strategies, crucial in mitigating risks associated with HIV/AIDS and hepatitis, are aligned with Islāmic teachings, aiming to minimise harm while promoting overall health within the Muslim community. Addressing addiction necessitates a comprehensive approach encompassing preventive education, harm reduction, psychosocial interventions, and spiritual support. For further insight, readers are directed to Rassool (2011, 2021), as this chapter's scope limits an exhaustive examination of the topic. The focus of the chapter will be to examine the Islāmic rulings on drugs, alcoholic intoxicants, and gambling. This chapter will explore the psychotherapeutic interventions, Islāmic perspectives on dealing with addiction, harm-reduction approaches, and the principles of Islāmic interventions.

Islāmic rulings on drugs, alcohol, and gambling

From an Islāmic perspective, the prohibition against drugs and other addictive substances/behaviours is rooted in teachings dating back 14 centuries. The Qur'ān and *hādīths* explicitly forbid intoxicants – substances that alter one's state of mind – and gambling, deeming them detrimental to spiritual, physical, and mental health. These prohibitions are conveyed through various verses in the Qur'ān revealed over several years. The earliest Qur'ânic verse addressing intoxicants was revealed in Makkah, emphasising the avoidance of alcohol and gambling for spiritual success. Allāh says in the Qur'ān,

وَمِن ثَمَرَٰتِ ٱلنَّخِيلِ وَٱلْأَعْنَٰبِ تَتَّخِذُونَ مِنْهُ سَكَرًا وَرِزْقًا حَسَنًا ۗ إِنَّ فِى ذَٰلِكَ لَءَايَةً لِّقَوْمٍ يَعْقِلُونَ

- *And from the fruits of palm trees and grapevines, you take intoxicant and good provision. Indeed, in that is a sign for a people who reason.*

(An-Naĥl 16:67, interpretation of the meaning)

This verse is made in reference to the drinks that people make from the fruits of the date palm and the grapevine. This also alludes to the fact that there are both evil and good possibilities in certain drinks. The next step in turning people away from consumption of alcohol is shown in the next verse:

يَسْـَٔلُونَكَ عَنِ ٱلْخَمْرِ وَٱلْمَيْسِرِ ۖ قُلْ فِيهِمَآ إِثْمٌ كَبِيرٌ وَمَنَٰفِعُ لِلنَّاسِ وَإِثْمُهُمَآ أَكْبَرُ مِن نَّفْعِهِمَا ۗ وَيَسْـَٔلُونَكَ مَاذَا يُنفِقُونَ قُلِ ٱلْعَفْوَ ۗ كَذَٰلِكَ يُبَيِّنُ ٱللَّهُ لَكُمُ ٱلْءَايَٰتِ لَعَلَّكُمْ تَتَفَكَّرُونَ

- *They ask you about wine and gambling. Say, "In them is great sin and [yet, some](some) benefit for people.*

(Al Baqarah 2:219, interpretation of the meaning)

The third mention of alcohol in the Qur'ān appeared as follows:

يَٰٓأَيُّهَا ٱلَّذِينَ ءَامَنُوا۟ لَا تَقْرَبُوا۟ ٱلصَّلَوٰةَ وَأَنتُمْ سُكَٰرَىٰ حَتَّىٰ تَعْلَمُوا۟ مَا تَقُولُونَ

- *You who have believe, do not approach prayer when you are intoxicated until you know what you are saying.*

(An-Nisā' 4:43, interpretation of the meaning)

This was one of the stages in turning people away from the consumption of alcoholic beverages. Finally, the focus of the rulings was on total abstinence from intoxicants and gambling. However, before this last Commandment was given, the Messenger of Allāh (ﷺ) addressed the people in order to prepare them for its absolute prohibition, warning, "Allāh does not like at all that people should drink wine. Probably absolute prohibition will soon be prescribed: therefore, those who possess wine are advised to sell it'" (Abū al-Aʿlā al-Mawdūdī). Allāh says in the Qurʾân,

$$\text{يَـٰٓأَيُّهَا ٱلَّذِينَ ءَامَنُوٓا۟ إِنَّمَا ٱلْخَمْرُ وَٱلْمَيْسِرُ وَٱلْأَنصَابُ وَٱلْأَزْلَـٰمُ رِجْسٌ مِّنْ عَمَلِ ٱلشَّيْطَـٰنِ فَٱجْتَنِبُوهُ لَعَلَّكُمْ تُفْلِحُونَ}$$
$$\text{إِنَّمَا يُرِيدُ ٱلشَّيْطَـٰنُ أَن يُوقِعَ بَيْنَكُمُ ٱلْعَدَاوَةَ وَٱلْبَغْضَآءَ فِى ٱلْخَمْرِ وَٱلْمَيْسِرِ وَيَصُدَّكُمْ عَن ذِكْرِ ٱللَّهِ وَعَنِ ٱلصَّلَوٰةِ ۖ فَهَلْ أَنتُم مُّنتَهُونَ}$$

- *You who have believed, indeed, intoxicants, gambling,* [sacrificing on] *stone altars* [to other than Allāh], *and divining arrows are but defilement from the work of Satan, so avoid it that you may be successful. Satan only wants to cause between you animosity and hatred through intoxicants and gambling and to avert you from the remembrance of Allāh and from prayer. So, will you not desist?*
  (Al-Māʾidah 5:90–91, interpretation of the meaning)

Abū al-Aʿlā al-Mawdūdī in his *tafsir* (exegesis) posited that in these verses,

Four things have been made absolutely unlawful. They are wine, gambling, ungodly shrines (which are dedicated to the worship of others than Allāh and in which sacrifices are made and offerings given in the name of others than Allāh), and divining devices. Within the Islāmic context, the term "intoxicant" encompasses narcotics, hashish, cannabis, cocaine, morphine, alcohol, and tobacco. Islām forbids both drugs and gambling. There is no doubt that taking drugs is forbidden (*haram*) because of their effects on mood and behaviour.

The first declaration made by the Prophet (ﷺ) was that not only is *khamr* (wine or alcohol) prohibited but that the definition of *khamr* extends to any substance that intoxicates, in whatever form or under whatever name it may appear. Thus, beer and similar drinks are *harām* (Al-Qaradawi, 1999). It was narrated that Ibn ʿUmar said, "Every intoxicant is *khamr* and every intoxicant is unlawful" (An-Nasaʾi (a)). The Prophet (ﷺ) said, "Every intoxicant is liquor (*khamr*), and every intoxicant is *harām*. Whoever drinks *khamr* in this world and dies persisting in that and without having repented, will not drink it in the Hereafter" (Muslim). Abu Bakr bin ʿAbdur-Rahman bin Al-Harith narrated that his father said, "Who came before you who was a devoted worshipper and used to stay away from people" and "avoid *khamr* for, by Allāh, it can never coexist with faith, but soon one of them will expel the other" (An-Nasaʾi (b)).

Prophet Muhammad (ﷺ) instructed people to avoid any intoxicating substances, whether in large amounts or even when taking in a small amount: "Whatever causes intoxication in large amounts, a small amount of it is (also) unlawful" (Ibn Majah (a)). For this reason, most observant Muslims avoid alcohol in any form, even small amounts that are sometimes used in cooking. Anas said that God's Messenger cursed ten people in connection with wine: the wine-presser, the one who has it pressed, the one who drinks it, the one who conveys it, the one to whom it is conveyed, the one who serves it, the one who sells it, the one who benefits from the price paid for it, the one who buys it, and the one for whom it is bought (Tirmidhî & Ibn Majah).

Prophet Muhammad (ﷺ) issued a warning of the punishment in Islām for alcohol drinkers. The Messenger of Allāh (ﷺ) said, "Every intoxicant is unlawful. Allāh, the Mighty and Sublime, has promised the one who drinks intoxicants that He will give him to drink from the mud of *Khibal*." They said, "O Messenger of Allāh, what is the mud of *Khibal*?" He said, "the sweat of the people of Hell" and "the juice of the people of Hell" (An-Nasa'i (c)). Allāh promised that whoever drinks *khamr* and becomes intoxicated, his prayers will not be accepted for 40 days. It was narrated that Ibn 'Umar said, "Whoever drinks *khamr* and does not get intoxicated, his *salah* [prayer] will not be accepted so long as any trace of it remains in his belly or his veins, and if he dies, he will die a *kafir*. If he becomes intoxicated, his Salah will not be accepted for 40 nights, and if he dies during them, he will die a *kafir*" (An-Nasa'i (d).

From an Islāmic perspective, the underlying principles and prohibitions regarding intoxicants apply to all mind-altering substances, including hashish. Birt (2001) suggested that there is a misconception among Muslim users that although drugs are unlawful, smoking hashish is not so serious (they say, "At least we don't drink!"). They seem to divide drugs into hard versus soft, a division that is baseless according to divine law: all drugs are Class A according to our religion.

Islāmic scholars unanimously agree on the prohibition of intoxicating substances, including contemporary drugs. This prohibition is grounded in Islāmic jurisprudence (*fiqh*), and scholars have applied principles derived from the Qur'ân and *hādīths* to make judgments on substances that were unknown at the time of the revelation of the Qur'ân. According to Philips (2007), the categorisation of drugs alongside activities such as games of chance, idolatry, and fortune telling, all of which have been unambiguously declared illegal, indicates that all intoxicants including plants with intoxicating properties fall into the category of prohibited substances. This alignment of drugs with forbidden behaviours and practices enhances Islāmic jurisprudence's stance against their intake. The legal schools' uniform agreement emphasises the seriousness of the prohibition: any chemical that causes intoxication is illegal. The prohibition is not confined to currently known substances but extends to include any intoxicating agent, emphasising the comprehensive nature of the Islāmic stance against mind-altering substances.

Gambling and games of chance are strongly discouraged and considered a great evil in Islām. Similar to the Qur'ânic verses, the teachings of Prophet Muhammad (ﷺ) emphasise the prohibition of gambling due to its detrimental effects on individuals and society as a whole. Even the mere consideration of participating in gambling is considered blameworthy in Islām. The Hanafi scholar Imam Abu Bakr al-Jassas observed that, "there is no difference of opinion between the scholars regarding the prohibition of gambling" (Ahkam al-Qur'ân, 1/329). The Messenger of Allāh (ﷺ) said, "Whoever says to his friend, 'Come, let me gamble with you' should give something in charity" (Bukhârî). This highlights the seriousness with which Islām views the issue and the necessity for individuals to refrain from engaging in such activities.

Problems and issues

The religious prohibition on addictive behaviours, particularly in Muslim communities, can lead individuals to hide their struggles due to fear of judgment and condemnation. Social stigma, especially regarding alcohol consumption, may result in individuals avoiding seeking help to prevent social exclusion and damage to their reputation. The fear of guilt, shame, and stigmatisation often prevents Muslims with addiction issues from seeking assistance. This delay in seeking help can lead to severe physical and social problems by the time individuals reach treatment centres.

Addiction not only affects the individual but also has significant impacts on the extended family, including parents, spouses, and children. However, the strong sense of shame and fear of judgment in many Muslim families can prevent them from seeking professional help. Instead, families may engage in a cycle of denial, hiding the addict's behaviours and enabling destructive actions. This co-dependence leads to chronic stress among family members, deteriorating family dynamics and relationships over time.

To address these challenges, it is important for family members to modify their behaviours and actively engage in the recovery process. Muslim families need to recognise that seeking help for addiction is not a sign of weakness but a courageous step towards healing. Breaking the cycle of hiding and denial is essential for creating an environment that supports recovery, open communication, and empathy. Seeking professional help, participating in family therapy, and engaging in comprehensive recovery programmes can contribute to the well-being of both the family and the individual struggling with addiction.

Psychotherapeutic approaches for addictive behaviours

Psychotherapy plays a crucial role in addressing addictive behaviours by providing individuals struggling with addiction a supportive and therapeutic environment to explore and overcome underlying psychological issues contributing to their alcohol and drug misuse. It is an evidence-based intervention that effectively aids in reducing addictive behaviours and promoting positive behavioural change. Alongside pharmacological interventions, various psychotherapeutic approaches have been employed to address addiction, including brief interventions, counselling, cognitive behavioural therapy, family therapy, motivational interviewing, dialectical behaviour therapy, mindfulness-based therapies, 12-step facilitation therapy, contingency management, family therapy, interpersonal therapy, social skills training, supportive work and complementary therapy. Each approach focuses on different aspects of addiction and targets specific cognitive, emotional, and behavioural patterns associated with addictive behaviours.

Cognitive–behavioral therapy (CBT) is a widely recognised and evidence-based therapeutic approach for addressing addiction. It focuses on identifying and modifying dysfunctional thoughts and behaviours, building coping skills, managing cravings and triggers, enhancing self-efficacy, and addressing underlying issues contributing to addiction. Studies such as those by McHugh et al. (2010) suggest that CBT interventions have demonstrated efficacy in controlled trials and can be combined with pharmacotherapy for more robust outcomes.

Motivational interviewing (MI), a person-centred therapeutic approach developed by Miller and Rollnick (2013), aims to enhance intrinsic motivation for changing addictive behaviours. MI helps individuals explore ambivalence toward change and set goals aligned with their values and emphasises empathy, collaboration, and evoking self-motivational statements. Meta-analytic reviews, including by Burke et al. (2003), indicate that MI has been moderately effective in reducing alcohol and drug use, comparable with other active treatment comparisons.

Contingency management is a behavioural therapy method that facilitates positive behaviour change and discourages alcohol and drug use by employing the principles of rewards and consequences. The central concept of contingency management involves providing substantial incentives or rewards to promote adherence to treatment plans and encourage abstinence from substance use. In practice, contingency management establishes specific treatment-related goals and behaviours, such as attending therapy sessions, passing drug tests, or engaging in healthful activities. Individuals who achieve these objectives are rewarded with increasingly incentives such as vouchers, privileges, or significant prizes. These incentives serve as positive reinforcement, motivating individuals to continue participating in positive behaviours and adhere to their treatment regimens. The approach leverages the power of positive reinforcement to strengthen the commitment to treatment and promote lasting behavioural change.

Dialectical behaviour therapy (DBT), as described by Axelrod (2019), combines cognitive–behavioural techniques with mindfulness and acceptance strategies. Effective in addressing emotional regulation, interpersonal effectiveness, and distress tolerance, DBT has shown promise in reducing addiction in patients with borderline personality disorder (Dimeff & Linehan, 2008). While conclusive evidence for standalone addiction disorders is lacking, supportive contextual evidence exists for both DBT and 12-step programmes in treating substance use disorders (Giannelli et al., 2019).

Mindfulness-based therapies, including relapse prevention and cognitive therapy, integrate mindfulness practices with cognitive–behavioural strategies. These therapies are designed to prevent relapse and address underlying issues by enhancing self-awareness, developing coping mechanisms, and fostering a non-judgmental mindset. The incorporation of mindfulness in these therapies allows individuals to cultivate present-moment awareness. By staying attuned to their thoughts, emotions, and sensations without judgment, individuals can better manage urges and triggers associated with addiction. Mindfulness practices promote a heightened awareness of these internal and external cues, providing individuals with the tools to respond skilfully rather than react impulsively.

Family therapy is a significant psychotherapeutic approach that incorporates the active participation of family members in the treatment for addiction. The primary goal of family therapy is to examine and address the dynamics within the family system that contribute to addiction while fostering a supportive and healing environment for all individuals involved. By addressing dysfunctional patterns and promoting healthier interactions, family therapy can enhance the overall functioning of the family unit. It provides a supportive foundation for the individual in recovery by involving family members in the process. Family therapy is instrumental in educating family members about addiction, enabling them to better understand the challenges their loved one is facing. Furthermore, family therapy plays a crucial role in the development of strategies for relapse prevention. It engages family members in creating a relapse management plan, turning it into a collective effort. The collaborative nature of family therapy not only supports the individual in recovery but also contributes to the overall well-being and resilience of the entire family system.

Twelve-Step programmes such as Alcoholics Anonymous (AA) and Gambling Anonymous (GA) are effective therapies that emphasise the acceptance of powerlessness over addiction and encourages individuals to actively engage in a spiritual path of recovery. These programmes provide a structured framework for individuals to navigate their journey towards recovery. Participation in 12-step programmes offers individuals a sense of belonging, accountability, and guidance. By acknowledging their powerlessness over addiction and working through the steps, individuals in recovery can cultivate strong support networks, adopt healthier coping strategies, and find meaning and purpose in their lives beyond addiction.

Complementary therapies in addiction treatment encompass holistic approaches that complement traditional therapeutic interventions, addressing the physical, mental, and emotional aspects of addiction (refer to Chapter 17). Interpersonal therapy is one such therapeutic approach that specifically targets interpersonal issues and relationships contributing to or resulting from addiction. This form of therapy acknowledges the substantial impact of social factors on addictive behaviours and seeks to enhance individuals' abilities to improve their relationships. Interpersonal therapy recognises that the quality of relationships can significantly influence addictive behaviours and aims to address underlying interpersonal issues as part of the comprehensive treatment plan. By focusing on improving communication, resolving conflicts, and fostering healthier connections, interpersonal therapy contributes to a more holistic and integrated approach to addiction treatment.

In summary, the psychotherapeutic approaches discussed offer valuable tools and techniques for individuals struggling with addictive behaviours. These approaches are typically integrated into individualised treatment plans, taking into account the unique needs and challenges of each person. It is worth noting that the effectiveness of psychotherapy for addiction can be enhanced when combined with other evidence-based interventions, creating a comprehensive and tailored approach to support individuals on their journey to recovery.

Motivational interviewing with addiction

Motivational interviewing, described by Miller and Rollnick (2013), is a directive yet client-centred counselling style aimed at facilitating behaviour change by addressing and resolving ambivalence. The approach is characterised as more focused and goal directed than non-directive counselling, with the therapist taking a directive stance to examine and resolve ambivalence, which is its central purpose. In the context of addiction, individuals often experience ambivalence about making changes in their behaviour. For example, a client may contemplate attending an addiction service or engaging with a therapist but simultaneously come up with various excuses to avoid it. The internal conflict may manifest in thoughts like, "It would be a missed opportunity if I don't attend the appointment, and I'll be bored if I stay here. I genuinely want to address my drug problem. However, I have observed others attending the treatment centre for months without achieving drug-free status." This ambivalence reflects the client's simultaneous desire to attend the appointment and doubts about the efficacy of seeking therapy.

MI is an approach that recognises and collaboratively works with ambivalence, allowing clients to explore and resolve conflicting feelings. One effective method to assist individuals in articulating their ambivalence is through the use of a "decisional balance" matrix (Table 19.1). This involves evaluating the pros and cons or costs and benefits, shedding light on the client's perspective regarding the addiction or problem at hand. The matrix considers two angles: one related to the current behaviour and the other related to change. The therapist engages in a discussion with the client, exploring factors that would fill each box and assessing the importance of each item.

For example, the therapist might inquire about the positive aspects of becoming drug-free, using a pro question like, "What are some of the benefits of achieving a drug-free lifestyle?" Conversely, a con question might be, "What are the potential drawbacks of giving up cannabis or gambling?" By visualising and mapping out

TABLE 19.1 A decisional balance matrix: pros/cons of current behaviour and pros/cons of change

Pros of current behaviour	*Cons of current behaviour*
Pros of change	*Cons of change*

this ambivalence, the client gains clarity on their priorities, facilitating a focus on potential solutions and supporting the process of behaviour change.

MI operates on four fundamental principles: expressing empathy, developing discrepancy, rolling with resistance, and supporting self-efficacy. To effectively apply these principles, various tools and strategies, such as pencil-and-paper exercises, structured questions, and focused reflections, have been developed (Mason, 2006). Among these principles, empathy stands out as a cornerstone in the MI approach.

Empathy involves comprehending another person's meaning through reflective listening, demanding keen attention to each client statement, and the continuous generation of hypotheses regarding underlying meanings (Miller & Rollnick, 2013). The therapist aims to grasp the client's experience at a profound level, recognising and valuing their perspective while conveying this understanding. Through empathy, clients become more open to exploring lifestyle issues and beliefs about substance use. Key components of expressing empathy include the use of open-ended questions and reflective listening. Examples of empathetic expressions include "It sounds like you genuinely want to change your gambling habits, but the process feels overwhelming because you're uncertain about where to start" and "in a situation like that, most clients I've worked with would likely feel anxious."

The principle of developing discrepancy in MI is closely tied to the concept of cognitive dissonance. According to Miller et al. (1992, p. 8), motivation for change arises when individuals perceive a gap between their current state and their desired state. Therapists aim to prompt clients to examine the inconsistencies between their beliefs and behaviours. This discrepancy is highlighted by making clients aware of the negative personal, familial, or community consequences associated with problematic behaviour and guiding them to confront the substance use contributing to those consequences (Substance Abuse and Mental Health Services Administration [SAMHSA], 2019). As clients recognise and acknowledge that their current behaviours are not leading to positive outcomes, they become more inclined to consider significant life changes. The therapist plays a crucial role in facilitating the client's awareness of this discrepancy.

The "Columbo approach" (Kanfer & Schefft, 1988) is one method used to help clients perceive this inconsistency. In this approach, the therapist invites the client to assist in making sense of conflicting information. The rationale is that a state of uncertainty or confusion can motivate the client to take control of the situation by offering a solution to the clinician (Van Bilsen, 1991). The Columbo approach is designed to be non-judgmental and non-blaming, allowing for the non-confrontational exploration of contradictory information (Sobell & Sobell, 2011, 2013). An illustration of developing discrepancy could be, "Help me understand – on one hand, you express the desire to return to your religious practices, yet on the other hand, you mention using heroin occasionally with your workmate. I'm curious about how using heroin might impact your ability to practice your religion."

In MI, the therapist adopts a non-confrontational approach to client resistance, opting to "roll with it." This metaphorical approach involves "dancing" with the client rather than "wrestling" with them (The Free Library, 2014). In the context of psychotherapy or counselling, resistance occurs when the client experiences a conflict between their perspective on the problem or the solution and that of the clinician. It may also emerge when the client perceives a threat to their freedom or autonomy. These experiences of resistance are often rooted in the client's ambivalence about change.

Resistance behaviours in therapy can manifest as excuses, blaming others, downplaying significance, presenting challenges, using hostile language, or displaying indifference. Clients who exhibit resistance may not be ready for change, and therapists should interpret it as a signal to alter the course of the conversation. When faced with resistance, therapists should maintain a non-judgmental stance, express empathy, and redirect communication without confrontation. Dealing with resistance involves using core skills like simple reflection, amplified reflection, double-sided reflection, shifting focus, agreement with a twist, reframing, and siding with the negative (SAMHSA, 2019).

MI operates on the belief that clients inherently possess the potential for change and is a strength-based approach. However, clients may conceal doubts about their ability to achieve behavioural change and question the potential benefits of such change. To enhance efficacy, therapists should actively elicit and support hope, optimism, and the feasibility of accomplishing change (SAMHSA, 2019). The therapist's role is to identify and emphasise the client's strengths, encouraging discussions about their skills, their past successes, and the support they can seek, for instance, "Can you recall the longest period you've been drug-free recently? What coping strategies did you find helpful during those times when you refrained from using the drug?" or "you've mentioned coping better in the past. What were you like during that time? What self-help strategies did you employ then? Are there any of those strategies you could apply now if you were to give up gambling?"

One approach to helping individuals understand their self-efficacy or confidence level is to use scaling questions, similar to those employed in solution-focused therapy (De Shazer et al., 1986) (refer to Chapter 10). Readiness for change is often indicated when both the perceived importance and confidence levels are high. Prochaska and DiClemente (1986) devised a model that elucidates readiness for change in terms of stages individuals traverse. This progression starts from pre-contemplation, where the person is not considering change, and moves through contemplation, determination (or preparation), action, and maintenance. MI gently guides the client through these stages of change. The enhancement of self-efficacy occurs when clients believe in the possibility of change and experience positive outcomes based on small, realistic goals. Therapists may employ various strategies in MI:

- *Asking open-ended questions*: Open-ended questions invite elaboration and thinking more deeply about an issue or problem.

- *Reflective listening*: The most crucial skills are expressing empathy and making reflective responses, supporting the goal-directed aspect of motivational interviewing.
- *Summarising*: Summaries communicate interest and understanding and call attention to important elements of the discussion.
- *Affirmation*: This includes statements that recognise client strengths, assist in building rapport, and help clients feel that change is possible.
- *Eliciting self-motivational statements*: This is a critical skill for clients who are not committed to change. There are four areas of questioning that can help elicit these concerns: problem recognition; expression of concerns; intention to change; and optimism about change.

The process of lapse and relapse is inherent in the addiction treatment journey. Clients benefit from assistance in recognising indicators of relapse, having these brought to their attention, and reinforcing their coping mechanisms. Relapse prevention, grounded in a cognitive–behavioural framework, aids individuals in maintaining their achieved goals related to substance use change.

Teaching coping skills involves pinpointing specific situations where coping challenges arise and employing techniques such as instruction, modelling, role plays, and behavioural rehearsal. Exposure to stressful situations is gradually increased as adaptive mastery occurs. To construct a relapse prevention plan, clients require support in identifying risks associated with their addictive behaviours. Such a plan is built on the identified risk factors and should encompass assertiveness work and social inclusion. Relapse prevention skills training covers exploring the consequences of continued use, self-monitoring for drug cravings, developing strategies to cope with cravings, identifying high-risk usage situations, and creating strategies to manage and avoid those situations. The inclusion of family, partners, caregivers, or significant others in the relapse prevention program strengthens its impact. Family engagement is particularly vital in the treatment of individuals with dual-diagnosis disorders (Clark, 2001). There is compelling evidence supporting the effectiveness of specific relapse prevention approaches in addressing drug problems and enhancing psychosocial functioning (Raistrick et al., 2006).

In summary, MI is adaptable and can be used in a variety of addiction treatment settings, including individual psychotherapy and counselling, group therapy, and even as part of a larger treatment program. Because of its person-centred and collaborative nature, it is especially helpful in addressing the complex and varied nature of addiction. MI is also congruent with Islāmic beliefs and practices. However, mindfulness-based therapies, including relapse prevention and cognitive therapy, may raise concerns within some Islāmic psychologists due to potential conflicts with Islāmic beliefs and practices for a number of reasons.

Mindfulness often involves non-judgmental awareness of present-moment experiences, including thoughts, emotions, and bodily sensations. However, Islāmic teachings emphasise the importance of directing one's focus primarily towards remembrance of God (*dhikr*) and religious practices rather than the self-focused awareness advocated in mindfulness practices. In addition, mindfulness practices have deep roots in Buddhist meditation traditions. While mindfulness has been secularised and adapted for therapeutic purposes, its historical association with Buddhism may raise theological concerns for Islāmic psychologists who prioritise adherence to Islāmic principles and teachings. In addition, there is also the perception that the adoption of mindfulness practices is a form of syncretism, where elements of non-Islāmic spiritual traditions are integrated into Islāmic practices. This can lead to apprehension about compromising the purity of Islāmic beliefs and rituals.

Motivational interviewing: an Islāmic perspective

When applying MI from an Islāmic perspective, several considerations emerge; respecting individual autonomy, which is consistent with the Islāmic belief in free choice and personal responsibility, is one of them. Empathy and compassion are expressed, which aligns with the Islāmic concept of offering kindness and understanding to those confronting hardships such as addiction. MI's non-confrontational attitude is consistent with Islāmic norms of peaceful and courteous communication, in which harshness is avoided. MI recognises the internal challenges that individuals may encounter as they balance desires and adherence to moral norms by acknowledging ambivalence, mirroring the Islāmic concept of the human condition. MI can also incorporate Islāmic beliefs and aims into the process of change.

MI involves establishing goals that are consistent with Islāmic teachings on temperance and well-being, allowing individuals to incorporate their faith into their recovery path. Individuals can draw on Islāmic principles of repentance, forgiveness, and requesting Allāh's support in their attempts for positive transformation by developing hope and optimism through MI. The involvement of the Islāmic community can supplement MI by offering support, cultivating a feeling of belonging, and supporting individuals on their path to recovery. To summarise, implementing MI from an Islāmic standpoint entails respecting autonomy, exhibiting empathy, avoiding conflict, accepting ambivalence, incorporating Islāmic values, creating optimism, and involving the Islāmic community. Blending these approaches can provide a holistic and culturally sensitive framework for supporting individuals in their quest for recovery within an Islāmic context.

Harm reduction: an Islāmic perspective

Despite the prohibition of addictive behaviours in Islām, such behaviours are prevalent in many Islāmic countries. While some nations have actively addressed addiction through harm reduction programmes, others have been slower to respond. Harm reduction aims to minimise the negative consequences associated with addiction, including HIV/AIDS and other infections. These programmes involve various measures like distributing disposable syringes, needle exchange, safe injection sites, opioid substitution therapy, education on safer practices, support services for individuals with addiction, and policy modifications. Additionally, harm reduction initiatives address social consequences by providing basic necessities like shelter to street-based individuals with drug or alcohol use disorders.

In Islām, there is a strong emphasis on abstaining from any psychoactive substances that can lead to addiction or harm. This zero-tolerance policy towards addictions can be traced to the time of the first Islāmic Caliphate, beginning in the seventh century to address addiction and promote public health. Allāh says in the Qur'ān,

وَلْتَكُن مِّنكُمْ أُمَّةٌ يَدْعُونَ إِلَى ٱلْخَيْرِ وَيَأْمُرُونَ بِٱلْمَعْرُوفِ وَيَنْهَوْنَ عَنِ ٱلْمُنكَرِ ۚ وَأُو۟لَٰٓئِكَ هُمُ ٱلْمُفْلِحُونَ

- *And let there be [arising] from you a nation inviting to [all that is] good, enjoining what is right and forbidding what is wrong, and those will be the successful.*
('Ali 'Imran 3 104, interpretation of the meaning)

Islām encourages the pursuit of practical solutions that prioritise the welfare of the community and the preservation of life. Embracing harm reduction programmes aligns with these principles, as they aim to minimise harm and promote the overall well-being of individuals and society. Thus, harm reduction programmes are considered permissible and even encouraged when they serve as a practical solution to preventing greater harm to society (Kamarulzaman & Saifuddeen, 2010).

One of the principles of Islāmic jurisprudence, known as "blocking means" (*sadd adh-dharā'i*), is also in line with prohibiting pending harm. "Blocking the means must necessarily be understood to imply blocking the means to evil, not to something good" (Kamali, 2003, p. 269). The concept of *darar* can be described as any form of harm or injury that is caused to a person, encompassing physical harm, financial loss, or psychological distress (Ibn Fāris, 1991, 3: 360). The principle of *sadd adh-dhara'i* provides a good example of the importance of prevention in Islām. Kamali (2003) stated that, "

> The whole concept of *sadd al-dhara'i* is founded in the idea of preventing an evil before it actually materialises. It is therefore not always necessary that the result should actually take place. It is rather the objective expectation that a means is likely to lead to an evil result that renders the means in question unlawful even without the realisation of the expected result.
>
> (p. 268)

In several Islāmic nations, the endorsement and application of harm reduction policies and practices face resistance, even in the face of widespread drug misuse and HIV epidemics linked to intravenous drug use. The challenges arise from a complex interplay of political, social, cultural, and religious factors within the Islāmic world, complicating the implementation of harm reduction strategies

(Rassool, 2024). It has been argued that "the implementation of harm reduction in the MENA [Middle East and North Africa] region will depend on finding ways to communicate its ideas in theologically and culturally sensitive ways" (Flemin, 2020).

A primary point of disagreement arises from the historical opposition of religious and political leaders to harm reduction approaches. Their contention rests on the belief that initiatives such as distributing needles and condoms might be seen as endorsing and accepting drug use and illegal sexual relations. Additionally, there is a concern that opioid substitution therapy could undermine the national objective of achieving a drug-free status (Reid et al., 2007; Todd et al., 2007). This means that harm reduction approaches are alien to Islāmic beliefs and practices and therefore cannot be applied as acceptable strategies. Madani et al. (2004) suggested that the strategies to prevent HIV infection in Islāmic countries should include the "strengthening of both Islāmic and health education; encouraging people to follow and implement the Islāmic rules and values that prohibit adultery, homosexuality, and intravenous drug use; and to practice safe sex only through legal marriage."

In Islāmic countries, advocates of harm reduction approaches to control the drug-driven HIV epidemics based their arguments on the *Maqâsid Ash-Shari'ah'* (Higher Objectives of Islām). These principles are the preservation and protection of faith, life, intellect, progeny, and wealth. According to Kamarulzaman and Saifuddeen (2010), "Harm reduction programmes are permissible and in fact provide a practical solution to a problem that could result in far greater damage to the society at large if left unaddressed" (p. 115). Moreover, the authors find that the principle of injury in Islām asserts that "no one should be hurt or cause hurt to others" (p. 116). That is applying the "lesser of two evils" principle that is used to justify the permissibility of harm reduction approaches to treating drug use and HIV, which pertain to matters of life and death. Another principle is "the necessity to overrule the prohibition in situations where there is great need, thereby rendering something that is originally prohibited to become permissible" (p. 116). Verse 173 of Al-Baqarah asserts this principle (Qur'ân 2: 173):

إِنَّمَا حَرَّمَ عَلَيْكُمُ ٱلْمَيْتَةَ وَٱلدَّمَ وَلَحْمَ ٱلْخِنزِيرِ وَمَآ أُهِلَّ بِهِۦ لِغَيْرِ ٱللَّهِ ۖ فَمَنِ ٱضْطُرَّ غَيْرَ بَاغٍ وَلَا عَادٍ فَلَآ إِثْمَ عَلَيْهِ ۚ إِنَّ ٱللَّهَ غَفُورٌ رَّحِيمٌ

- *He has only forbidden to you dead animals, blood, the flesh of swine, and that which has been dedicated to other than God. But whoever is forced [by necessity], neither desiring [it] nor transgressing [its limit], there is no sin upon him. Indeed, God is Forgiving and Merciful.*

(Al-Baqarah 2: 173, interpretation of the meaning)

Other principles include "harm must be treated and benefits must be brought forth" and "public interest should be given priority over personal interest" (Kamarulzaman & Saifuddeen, 2010, p. 117).

The model that Islām adopts in tacking addiction is based on prohibition leading to the total abstinence model, the 12-step faith-based model. The Islāmic model of 12-step recovery programmes is provided, for example, by the Millati Islāmi. Millati Islāmi is a "Fellowship of man and women look to Allāh (God) to guide us on Millati Islāmi (the Path of Peace). While recovering, we strive to become rightly guided Muslims, submitted our will and services to Allāh." These principles have been used to implement harm reduction approaches in a few Islāmic countries. The dominant approach to public health is based on a unified standard approach to abstinence. However,

> the typical policies that address only one dimension or one level of harm, such as public health or social security, have limited success. Therefore, to reduce the burden of addiction, we need a package of comprehensive, continuous, and integrated interventions that include all the harms of substance abuse and addiction. The variety of harms makes multi/inter-sectoral cooperation inevitable. This cooperation requires a mutual understanding of sectors with different characteristics from the considerations of others.
>
> *(Shafiee et al., 2023, p. 7)*

Islāmic perspective in dealing with addiction

The Islāmic approach towards addiction involves a holistic view, addressing spiritual, psychological, and physical aspects. Islām encourages a supportive and non-shaming environment for individuals seeking treatment for addiction. The process begins with addressing the soul, followed by the mind and body. Sincerity in the desire to give up addictive behaviours is emphasised, along with repentance (*tawbah*), which involves immediate cessation of the sinful behaviour, remorse, and a firm resolution not to repeat the sins. Reflection on Allāh's favours, gratitude, humbleness, and placing trust in Allāh are integral. Individuals are encouraged to maintain hope in the treatment process while accepting Allāh's predestination (*qadr*).

The Islāmic approach towards addicted individuals emphasises treating them with gentleness and compassion. While acknowledging that making mistakes and committing sins are inherent aspects of human nature, Islām encourages believers to approach those struggling with addiction with empathy and understanding. Recognising the vulnerabilities and struggles of individuals, the focus should be on guiding and supporting them to acknowledge their mistakes, seek forgiveness from Allāh, and actively work towards positive change. Islām encourages believers to have a balanced understanding of human nature, recognising the propensity for errors and temptations. Despite these challenges, addicted individuals are urged not to give up hope, as Allāh's mercy and forgiveness are boundless. The path to recovery involves taking responsibility, seeking Allāh's forgiveness through sincere repentance, and actively working towards self-improvement.

It was narrated from Abu Hurayrah (may Allāh be pleased with him) that the Prophet (ﷺ) said, "If you were to commit sin until your sins reach the heaven, then you were to repent, your repentance would be accepted" (Ibn Majah (b)). This *ḥādīth* clearly states that making *tawbah* or repenting sincerely to make up for mistakes and sins is important, since humans are not perfect. Through repentance, addicted Muslims are empowered to take ownership of their actions, learn from their mistakes, and strive for personal growth while relying on Allāh's guidance and mercy.

The Islāmic therapist has a responsibility to "enjoin what is good and forbid what is evil." According to Shaykh 'Abd al-'Azeez ibn Baz, the duty of believing men and women is to promote goodness and discourage evil within their community. Believers are urged not to remain silent when they witness wrongdoing but to address it with kindness, wisdom, and good manners. This includes advising fellow believers against harmful actions like smoking or drinking, doing so gently and respectfully. The goal is to guide others towards righteousness and adherence to Islāmic principles through compassionate counsel and positive communication (Cited in Islām Q&A, 2007). This statement highlights the importance of believers in Islām enjoining what is good and forbidding what is evil. It emphasises the responsibility of Muslims to speak out against wrongdoing, including addictive behaviours like smoking or drinking alcohol, when they witness it in their fellow believers. The approach advised in Islām is to bring to awareness such actions in a kind and gentle manner, using good manners and wisdom. The intention behind this approach is not to shame or humiliate but rather to guide and advise one another towards what is right and pleasing to Allāh. It is important to approach these conversations with empathy and compassion, showing genuine concern for the well-being of one's fellow believer.

In Islāmic psychotherapy, the therapist's role is to provide spiritual guidance and counselling, aiming to revive faith, facilitate repentance, and help individuals integrate cognitive beliefs and behavioural practices into disciplined lifestyles. Prophetic teachings emphasise constant engagement in prayer, meditation, remembrance of God, and other spiritual activities to transform the heart and draw closer to God. Spiritual interventions in Islāmic psychotherapy include supplications, prayers, remembrance of Allah, giving to charity, fasting, and reading the Qur'ân.

The psychospiritual programme at Al-Amal Hospital in Saudi Arabia serves as an exemplary model, integrating religion and psychiatric practices. This programme combines individual and group interventions, offering spiritual guidance, religious bibliotherapy, meditation and prayer, journal writing, scripture memorisation, acupuncture, relaxation techniques, eclectic psychotherapy, and group activities such as community meetings and recovery groups. Night prayer has also been found to be helpful, particularly for individuals experiencing insomnia during the residual withdrawal syndrome (Salem & Ali, 2008). Research on the effects of religious spirituality and biofeedback devices in drug addiction treatment among teenagers has shown that religious spirituality is associated with positive mental health outcomes. These outcomes include better coping abilities, reduced stress levels, a positive life orientation, and lower levels of anxiety (Salam & Wahab, 2014).

AA is a 12-step recovery programme that has helped many people stop the use of alcohol. The original programme focused on spirituality, religion, and God having an impact on changing a person's life. A modified 12-step programme related to drugs and conforming to Islāmic teachings is presented below (adapted from Salem & Ali, 2008):

1. We admit that we are powerless over drugs and that our lives have become unmanageable.
2. We have come to believe that Allāh can restore us to sanity.
3. We have made a decision to turn our wills and our lives over to the care of Allāh.
4. We have made a searching and fearless moral inventory of ourselves in the light of the Islāmic doctrines (*Shar'iah*).
5. We admit to Allāh and to ourselves the exact nature of our wrongs.
6. We are entirely ready to pray to Allāh to remove all these defects of character.
7. We have humbly asked Him to remove our shortcomings.
8. We have made a list of all persons we have harmed, and we have become willing to make amends to all.
9. We have made direct amends to such people wherever possible, except when to do so would injure them or others.
10. We continue to take personal inventory and, when we do wrong, we promptly admit it.
11. We seek through prayer and other religious commitments and activities to improve our conscious contact with Allāh, praying only for knowledge of His will for us and the power to carry that out.
12. We have had a spiritual awakening as the result of these steps. We try to carry this message to problem drug users and practise these principles in all our affairs.

Conclusion

Muslim individuals facing addiction may hesitate to seek help from non-Muslim agencies due to concerns about confidentiality, cultural competence, and the compatibility of services with Islāmic practices (Al-Ghafri et al., 2023). Barriers to accessing addiction treatment and harm reduction services in Muslim communities include lack of trust in the treatment system, fear of confidentiality breaches, and the perceived inadequacy of mainstream services in addressing cultural and religious needs (Fountain, 2014).

Muslims with substance use disorder often rate mainstream drug treatment services poorly due to unmet expectations and perceived lack of cultural and religious competence. In the recovery process, families play a crucial role and should be supported by Muslim doctors, *imams*, Islāmic therapists, or Islāmic organisations. Tailored treatment plans, including motivational interviewing, can effectively address addiction while preserving spiritual and cultural identities. Encouraging open dialogue, education, and awareness within Muslim communities about addiction and available treatment options is essential for breaking down stigmas and increasing understanding.

However, it is important to note that attitudes towards addictive behaviours use in the Muslim community can vary, although general religious guidance discourages consumption and the avoidance of gambling and other addictive behaviours. Creating an environment of open communication and support is crucial for individuals struggling with addiction to seek help without fear of condemnation. Encouraging dialogue, education, and empathy is vital to addressing challenges faced by addicted Muslims who may feel compelled to hide their actions. Providing access to appropriate support networks and therapeutic services helps individuals overcome addictive behaviours while finding understanding within their religious community. Prevention efforts and holistic treatment approaches are essential to addressing addictive behaviours effectively. Addiction is the responsibility not solely of the health care provider but of the *ummah* as a whole.

References

Abū al-Aʿlā al-Mawdūdī. *Mawdūdī Al-Qur'an Tafsir*. Retrieved December 8, 2023, from www.alim.org/quran/tafsir/maududi/surah/5/90/

Al-Ghafri, Q., Radcliffe, P., & Gilchrist, G. (2023). Barriers and facilitators to accessing inpatient and community substance use treatment and harm reduction services for people who use drugs in the Muslim communities: A systematic narrative review of studies on the experiences of people who receive services and service providers. *Drug and Alcohol Dependence*, 244, 109790. https://doi.org/10.1016/j.drugalcdep.2023.109790

Al-Qaradawi, Y. (1999). *The lawful and the prohibited in Islām (Al-Halal Wal Haram Fil Islām)*. American Trust Publications.

An-Nasa'i (a). *Sunan an-Nasa'i 5699*. In-book reference: Book 51, Hādīth 161. English translation: Vol. 6, Book 51, Hādīth 5702. Sahih (Darussalam). https://sunnah.com/nasai:5699

An-Nasa'i (b). *Sunan an-Nasa'i 5667*. In-book reference: Book 51, Hādīth 129. English translation: Vol. 6, Book 51, Hādīth 5670. Sahih (Darussalam). https://sunnah.com/nasai:5667

An-Nasa'i (c). *Sunan an-Nasa'i 5709*. In-book reference: Book 51, Hādīth 171. English translation: Vol. 6, Book 51, Hādīth 5712. Sahih (Darussalam). https://sunnah.com/nasai:5709

An-Nasa'i (d). *Sunan an-Nasa'i 5668*. In-book reference: Book 51, Hādīth 130. English translation: Vol. 6, Book 51, Hādīth 5671. (Sahih Mawquf). https://sunnah.com/nasai:5668

Axelrod, S. R. (2019). Dialectical behaviour therapy for substance use disorders. In M. A. Swales (Ed.), *The Oxford handbook of dialectical behaviour therapy* (pp. 595–614). Oxford University Press.

Birt, Y. (2001). *Being a real man in Islām: Drugs, criminality and the problem of masculinity*. Retrieved December 8, 2023, from http://masud.co.uk/ISLAM/misc/drugs.htm

Bukhârî. *Sahih al-Bukhârî 6650*. In-book reference: Book 83, Hādīth 29.USC-MSA web (English) reference: Vol. 8, Book 78, Hādīth 645. https://sunnah.com/bukhari:6650

Burke, B. L., Arkowitz, H., & Menchola, M. (2003). The efficacy of motivational interviewing: A meta-analysis of controlled clinical trials. *Journal of Consulting and Clinical Psychology, 71*(5), 843–861. https://doi.org/10.1037/0022-006X.71.5.843

Clark, R. E. (2001). Family support and substance use outcomes for persons with mental illness and substance use disorders. *Schizophrenia Bulletin, 27*(1), 93–101.

De Shazer, S., Berg, I. K., Lipchik, E., Nunnally, E., Molnar, A., Gingerich, W., & Weiner-Davis, M. (1986). Brief therapy: Focused solution development. *Family Process, 25*(2), 207–221. https://doi.org/10.1111/j.1545-5300.1986.00207.x

Dimeff, L. A., & Linehan, M. M. (2008). Dialectical behavior therapy for substance abusers. *Addiction Science & Clinical Practice, 4*(2), 39–47. https://doi.org/10.1151/ascp084239

Flemin, R. (2020). *Major report assesses the global state of harm reduction; 2020*. Retrieved December 9, 2023, from https://filtermag.org/harm-reduction-worldwide

Fountain, J. (2014). *Issues surrounding drug use and drug services among the South Asian communities in England*. Retrieved December 8, 2023, from https://core.ac.uk/download/pdf/24066655.pdf

Giannelli, E., Gold, S., Bieleninik, L., Ghetti, C., & Gelo O. C. G. (2019). Dialectical behaviour therapy and 12-step programmes for substance use disorder: A systematic review and meta-analysis. *Therapists and Knowledge, 19*(3), 274–285 https://doi.org/10.1002/capr.12228

Ibn Fāris, A. al-Ḥ. A. (1991). *Mu'jam Maqāyīs al-Lughah*. Ed: ʿAbd al-Salām Muḥammad Hārūn. Dār al-Jīl.

Ibn Majah (a). *Sunan Ibn Majah 339*. In-book reference: Book 30, Ḥadīth 23. English translation: Vol. 4, Book 30, Ḥadīth 3393. Hasan (Darussalam). https://sunnah.com/ibnmajah:3393

Ibn Majah (b). *Sunan Ibn Majah 4248*. In-book reference: Book 37, Ḥadīth 149. English translation: Vol. 5, Book 37, Ḥadīth 4248. Hasan (Darussalam). https://sunnah.com/ibnmajah:4248

Imam Abu Bakr al-Jassas. Cited in Clarke J. A. (2023). *The Fiqh of Gambling, Betting and Competitions in Islām*. Retrieved December 9, 2023, from https://thehalallife.co.uk/the-fiqh-of-gambling-betting-and-competitions-in-Islam/

Islām Q&A. (2007). 96662: Is he sinning if he sees an evil action and does not denounce it? Retrieved December 10, 2023, from http://Islamqa.info/en/ref/96662

Kamali, H. (2003). *Principles of Islāmic jurisprudence*. The Islāmic Texts Society.

Kamarulzaman, A., & Saifuddeen, S. M. (2010). Islām and harm reduction. *International Journal of Drug Policy, 21*(2), 115–118.

Kanfer, F. H., & Schefft, B. K. (1988). *Guiding the process of therapeutic change*. Research Press.

Madani, T. A., Al-Mazrou, Y. Y., Al-Jeffri, M. H., & Al Huzaim, N. S. (2004). Epidemiology of the human immunodeficiency virus in Saudi Arabia; 18-year surveillance results and prevention from an Islāmic perspective. *BMC Infectious Diseases, 4*, 25. https://doi.org/10.1186/1471-2334-4-25

Mason, P. (2006). Motivational interviewing. In G. Hussein Rassool (Ed.) *Dual diagnosis nursing*. Blackwell. https://doi.org/10.1002/9780470774953.ch25

McHugh, R. K., Hearon, B. A., & Otto, M. W. (2010). Cognitive behavioral therapy for substance use disorders. *The Psychiatric Clinics of North America, 33*(3), 511–525. https://doi.org/10.1016/j.psc.2010.04.012

Millati Islāmi. Retrieved December 9, 2023, from www.millatiIslami.org/

Miller, W. R., & Rollnick, S. (2013). *Motivational interviewing: Helping people change* (3rd ed.). Guilford Press.

Miller, W. R., Zweben, A., DiClemente, C. C., & Rychtarik, R. G. (1992). *Motivational enhancement therapy manual: A clinical research guide for therapists treating individuals with alcohol abuse and dependence*. National Institute on Alcohol Abuse and Alcoholism.

Muslim. Cited in Islām Q&A. (2005). 66227: Ruling on taking drugs, and do they come under the same heading as *khamr* (intoxicants)? Retrieved December 8, 2023, from http://Islamqa.info/en/66227

Philips, A. A. B. (2007). *The clash of civilizations: An Islāmic view.* Al-Hidaayah Publishing & Distributions.

Prochaska, J. O., & DiClemente, C. C. (1986). Towards a comprehensive model of change. In W. R. Miller & N. Heather (Eds.), *Treating addictive behaviors: Processes of change.* Plenum.

Raistrick, D., Heather, N., & Godfrey, C. (2006). *The National Treatment Agency for substance misuse review of the effectiveness of treatment for alcohol problems.* NTA. Retrieved December 9, 2023, from https://core.ac.uk/download/pdf/34711278.pdf

Rassool, G. Hussein (2011). *Understanding addiction behaviours: Theoretical and clinical practice in health and social care.* Palgrave Macmillan.

Rassool, G. Hussein (2021). *Mother of all evils: Addictive behaviours from an Islāmic perspective.* Islāmic Psychology Publication (IIP) & Institute of Islāmic Psychology Research (RIIPR). Amazon/Kindle.

Rassool, G. Hussein (2022). *Alcohol-the forbidden nectar: An Islāmic perspective.* Islāmic Psychology Publication (IIP) & Institute of Islāmic Psychology Research (RIIPR). Amazon/Kindle.

Rassool, G. Hussein (2024). Addictive behaviours and public health. In B. H. Aboul Enein, G. Hussein Rassool, N. Benajiba, J. Bernstein, & M. A. E. Faris (Eds.), *Contemporary Islāmic perspectives in public health.* Cambridge University Press.

Reid, G., Kamarulzaman, A., & Sran, S. K. (2007). Malaysia and harm reduction: The challenges and responses. *The International Journal on Drug Policy, 18*(2), 136–140. https://doi.org/10.1016/j.drugpo.2006.12.015

Salam, U. B., & Wahab, N. A. (2014). *Drug addiction intervention for adolescents with religious spirituality and biofeedback.* Retrieved December 10, 2023, from http://umpir.ump.edu.my/id/eprint/5067/3/pbmsk-nubli-2014-DrugAddictionIntervention.pdf

Salem, M. O., & Ali, M. M. (2008) Psycho-spiritual strategies in treating addiction patients: Experience at Al-Amal Hospital, Saudi Arabia. *Journal of the Islāmic Medical Association of North America, 40*(4). https://doi.org/10.5915/40-4-4434

Shafiee, S. A., Vedadhir, A., & Razaghi, E. (2023). Ups and downs of addiction harm reduction in Iran: Key insights and implications for harm reduction policy and policing. *Harm Reduction Journal, 20*(1), 8. https://doi.org/10.1186/s12954-022-00719-0

Sobell, L. C., & Sobell, M. B. (2011). *Group therapy with substance use disorders: A motivational cognitive behavioral approach.* Guilford Press.

Sobell, L. C., & Sobell, M. B. (2013). *Motivational techniques and skills for health and mental health coaching/counseling.* Retrieved December 9, 2023, from www.nova.edu/gsc/online_files.htm

Substance Abuse and Mental Health Services Administration (US). (2019). *Enhancing motivation for change in substance use disorder treatment.* Substance Abuse and Mental Health Services Administration (US). (Treatment Improvement Protocol (TIP) Series, No. 35.) *Chapter 3-Motivational Interviewing as a Counseling Style.* Retrieved December 9, 2023, from www.ncbi.nlm.nih.gov/books/NBK571068/

The Free Library. (2014). *Motivational Interviewing: An evidence-based approach to overcoming ambivalence; Envision the change process as dancing with another, rather than wrestling.* Retrieved December 9, 2023, from www.thefreelibrary.com/Motivational+Interviewing%3a+an+evidence-based+approach+to+overcoming...-a0132528146

Tirmidhî & Ibn Majah. *Mishkat al-Masabih 2776.* In-book reference: Book 11, Ḥadīth 18. https://sunnah.com/mishkat:2776

Todd, C. S., Nassiramanesh, B., Stanekzai, M. R., & Kamarulzaman, A. (2007). Emerging HIV epidemics in Muslim countries: Assessment of different cultural responses to harm reduction and implications for HIV control. *Current HIV/AIDS Reports, 4*(4), 151–157. https://doi.org/10.1007/s11904-007-0022-9

Van Bilsen, H. P. (1991). Motivational interviewing: Perspectives from the Netherlands with particular emphasis on heroin-dependent clients. In W. R. Miller & S. Rollnick (Eds.), *Motivational interviewing: Preparing people to change addictive behavior* (pp. 214–235). Guilford Press.

20
CLINICAL APPLICATIONS OF THE SIRAAT AL-ISLĀMIC PSYCHOTHERAPY PRACTICE MODEL

Introduction

This chapter explores in depth the application of the Siraat Al-Islāmic psychotherapy practice model (SIPPM; see Chapter 18), aiming to equip Islāmic psychotherapists, clinicians, and mental health practitioners, with the clinical application in addressing addictive behaviours in Muslim clients. The SIPPM serves as a framework for Islāmic psychotherapists to implement when working with Muslim clients. It comprises several stages, including consultation (*istisharah*), awakening (*Qawmah*), contemplation (*tafakkur*), goal-and-route vision (*basirah*), wilful decision (*'azm*), action (*'amal*), and maintenance of behavioural change (*siyanah at-taghyir as-suluki*). These stages are supported by pervasive processes such as absolute trust in God (*al-tawakkul-Allāh*); help-seeking (*isti'aanah*); guidance-seeking (*istikharah*); self-evaluation (*muhasabah*) and self-monitoring (*muraqabah*); and maintenance of behavioural change (*siyanah at-taghyir as-suluki*). Through the integration of these processes and stages, the SIPPM provides a structured approach that takes into account the unique perspectives and needs of Muslim clients.

Case study

Ahmed, a 32-year-old Muslim man, married with two children, sought therapeutic intervention for his struggle with alcohol use disorder. His supervisory role at a prominent fast-food restaurant added stress to his already demanding life. The weight of his responsibilities as a husband and father of two children heightened the impact of his addiction, leading to strained family relationships. Ahmed's realisation of the profound strain his addiction placed on his family became a turning point. The deterioration of relationships within his family, coupled with the

DOI: 10.4324/9781003453413-23

demands of his professional life, prompted him to acknowledge the urgent need for intervention. Ahmed's journey toward healing began with a community detoxification programme for alcohol, which proved to be a successful initial step (Nadkarni et al., 2017). This community-based approach addressed the physiological aspects of his addiction, setting the stage for a more comprehensive therapeutic intervention. Following this successful detoxification, Ahmed was referred to psychological services to undergo Islāmic psychotherapy and counselling, recognising the need for a holistic approach that would encompass his cultural and spiritual identity.

Clinical applications

For Muslims, the ultimate salvation from addiction is to turn to Allāh, read the Qur'ān, and seek Allāh's forgiveness and help. Muslims are required to seek such treatment, and the method of treatment is clearly prescribed. Alias and Majid (2015) stated that,

> Practices such as *wudu'* (ablution), *salat* (prayer), *dhikr* (utterance and remembrance of Allāh), *tilawah* (reading the Qur'ān), and *sawm* (fasting) provide positive potential to prepare for abstinence from alcohol. Besides that, some healthy practices such as proper diet (semi-vegetarian), eating supplements (honey and *habbat al-sawda'* or black seeds), and exercises may also have provided positive potentials to change behaviour.
>
> *(p. 11)*

Incorporating *niyyah* (intention) into Ahmed's treatment journey is a necessary aspect of an Islāmic psychotherapeutic approach, using the SIPPM. For Ahmed, *niyyah* serves as the foundational intention and commitment to seek therapy and positive transformation. Expressing *niyyah* allows Ahmed to make a sincere and personal commitment to overcome his addiction and his intention becomes a source of motivation, reminding him of his purpose whenever faced with challenges during the recovery process. In addition, *niyyah* includes the intention to seek Allāh's pleasure in every step of the journey by framing his recovery as an act of worship.

In the awakening stage (*Qawmah*), it is important for the therapist to assess Ahmed's readiness for change. In this case, Ahmed's readiness to address and change his alcohol addiction is a positive factor that can facilitate the therapeutic process and accelerate progress to the next stage. The therapist recognises Ahmed's motivation for seeking help and his willingness to make changes in his life. This readiness to change provides a strong foundation for effective therapy and increases the likelihood of successful outcomes. Ahmed's acknowledgment of the severity and consequences of his alcohol addiction demonstrates his commitment to addressing the issue and regaining control over his life.

To support Ahmed's understanding of the impact of alcohol addiction, the therapist utilises psychoeducation techniques. Through psychoeducation, Ahmed gains knowledge about the physical and mental health consequences of prolonged alcohol use. He becomes aware of the negative effects that alcohol addiction has had on his family relationships, emotional well-being, and overall quality of life.

Building a strong therapeutic alliance is key. Establishing trust and rapport with Ahmed allow him to feel understood and supported, creating a foundation for future exploration and change. Therapists can incorporate components of Islāmic beliefs and principles that resonate with the client's cultural and spiritual environment, potentially improving their sense of connection and participation. *Istisharah* (consultation) is the process of collecting relevant information about the client's past and presenting problems.

This is similar to undertaking a full assessment of the addict. The assessment should include a statement of the presenting problem, development and educational history, family history, a mental health assessment, and a risk assessment (if appropriate). The mental or psychological examination focused on the cognitive, affective, and behavioural factors (appearance, thoughts, feelings, insights, etc.) and observation over a period of time. The process of assessment can be enhanced by the style of interaction, which should be non-confrontational, empathic, and respectful of the client's subjective experiences. A confrontational and judgmental approach may increase the potential for client to disengage with the assessment and consultation process.

A collaborative approach was adopted involving Ahmed, his spouse, the psychotherapist, and an Islāmic scholar or *imam*. This consultation laid the foundation for a holistic treatment plan, incorporating psychological strategies and Islāmic principles. On assessment, it was identified that the turning point for Ahmed came when he recognised the profound strain his addiction placed on his familial bonds. The demands of his managerial role, coupled with the fast-paced nature of the industry, contributed to the complexity of his struggle with addiction on both professional and personal aspects of his life. His addiction to alcohol had had severe consequences, as his alcohol intoxication and constant lies had caused his wife to consider separation and divorce. He was facing the fear of losing both his wife and children due to the harm caused by his addiction. Additionally, Ahmed's parents and other family members were angered by his behaviour and had issued a final warning regarding his intoxication with alcohol.

One of the first tasks that Ahmed needed to do after the consultation process in his journey of recovery from addiction is making *tawbah* (repentance). This concept signifies sincere and faithful repentance to God due to the performance of sins and misdeeds. *Tawbah* is an integral part of the practice within the Islāmic psychotherapy paradigm. *Tawbah*, according to Al-Makki,

> is not an optional act of religious devotion meant primarily for those who have committed themselves completely to God, but a requirement for the generality of believers. Unlike other expressions of religious piety, *Tawbah* is an essential and inescapable requirement for anyone who surrenders to God. Nor is

repentance meant only for individual sins but must, instead, be an all-embracing process of self-purification.

(cited in Khalil, 2012, p. 8)

After repentance, the client must now resolve to remain upright and not to return to the bad deeds (see the process of change in *tawbah in* Rassool, 2021). Basiony (2017) suggested the following steps:

- Regret the sin.
- Stop the sin.
- Make a sincere intention to not go back to the sin.
- Seek forgiveness of Allāh and repent.
- Suffocate the sin with good deeds and do not let it suffocate you.

There is also the possibility that the Muslim addict may be encouraged through motivational interviewing to make ablution and praying two *rak'aa* (unit of prayers). That is performing the *salaat al-tawbah* (the prayer of repentance). It is reported that the prayer of repentance is two *rak'aa*, as it says in the statement of Abu Bakr al-Siddeeq (may Allāh. be pleased with him). It is prescribed for the one who is repenting to pray alone, because it is one of the optional prayers that it is not prescribed to offer in congregation.

After that, it is prescribed to ask Allāh for forgiveness. This prayer may be offered at any time, including times when prayer is disallowed. It is recommended that the repentant do some good deeds along with this prayer, such as charity. There is no report from the Prophet (ﷺ) to say that it is recommended to recite any particular *surah* [chapter of the Qur'ân] in these two *rak'aa*, so the worshipper may recite whatever he wants" (Islām Q&A, 2007).

The next stage of engagement with the client is in stage of *tafakkur* (contemplation). In this stage, both Ahmed and the therapist operate on a cycle of reflection in analysing the issues or problems, contemplating the impact of addiction on his spiritual, emotional, and familial well-being. Incorporating *tafakkur* facilitated a deeper understanding of the root causes and consequences of his behaviour, contemplation goals for behavioural change, and tentatively identify appropriate intervention strategies. Following reflection and contemplation initiated by the therapist, the next stage is guidance seeking from the Almighty God by undertaking *istikharah.* That is, whenever a Muslim wish to make an important decision, he or she should seek Allāh's guidance and wisdom and perform a specific prayer for guidance (*salat-l-istikharah*).

During the goal-and-route vision stage (*basirah*), the therapist works with Ahmed to help him develop a vision for a sober life that reflects his Islāmic values. Through guidance and support, Ahmed envisions a future where he can fulfil his roles as a responsible husband, father, and devout Muslim. In the goal-setting and decision-making stages, Ahmed and the therapist work together to set specific, achievable goals for his recovery. Breaking down larger objectives into smaller, more manageable steps helps build a sense of accomplishment and can contribute to a gradual shift in motivation. Ultimately, therapists need to be patient and attuned to the client's pace.

The set goals of Ahmed included identifying the steps he needed to take to overcome his addiction and the strategies he would employ to maintain abstinence. Ahmed's goals included attending support groups, participating in therapy sessions, abstaining from alcohol, rebuilding trust with his wife and family, seeking forgiveness and making amends for past mistakes, actively practicing his faith, and implementing healthy coping mechanisms. The therapist emphasised the importance of aligning Ahmed's goals with Islāmic teachings, as this will not only support his recovery from addiction but also nurture his spiritual growth. They explored how Ahmed can integrate Islāmic practices, such as prayer, supplication, recitation of the Qur'ân, and seeking knowledge, into his daily life as a means of support and guidance on his journey.

Additionally, the therapist encouraged Ahmed to explore ways to strengthen his family relationships and demonstrate his commitment to change, such as by engaging in open communication, participating in couples or family therapy, and actively finding ways to rebuild trust and repair the harm caused by his addiction. By envisioning a future that aligned with his Islāmic values, Ahmed gained a sense of purpose and direction on his road to recovery. The therapist supported Ahmed in creating a clear roadmap to navigate the challenges and obstacles that may arise along the way.

The next stage of wilful decision (*'azm*) was where the therapist nudged Ahmed to make a decision for action (*'amal*). Ahmed demonstrated a firm commitment to change. Driven by *'Azm*, he expressed a strong determination to overcome his addiction and actively participate in the therapeutic process. This corresponds with the preparation stage (intention to change the behaviour) of the model of change (Prochaska et al., 1992). The therapist engaged in open and respectful discussions with Ahmed, exploring how his choices and actions could align with Islāmic faith. During this stage, Ahmed could have attempted to make small changes in behaviour. The therapist could also have assisted Ahmed in understanding any conflicts or tension that arose during the decision-making process. This stage combines intention and determination in clients who appear to be ready and committed to action. As Ahmed was highly motivated and ready to change, resistance is less likely to occur.

However, Ahmed still needs to reflect on the long-term impacts of his decisions on his family and work and his relationships with Allāh. Once the final decision-making has taken place, Ahmed needs to have absolute trust in God. *Tawakkul* is a fundamental part of the Islāmic creed, and putting our trust in God is a matter of belief and can happened in all the stages, not necessarily at a particular stage in the practice model. During this stage of change (*'amal*), Ahmed begins taking direct action in order to accomplish his desired goals. This process involves intention and execution of the action plan. Ahmed's therapeutic roadmap encompassed a comprehensive plan integrating Islāmically modified cognitive–behavioural strategies, participation in support groups, and the infusion of Islāmic rituals. The attainment of small goals should be rewarded or reinforced, and they are part of the process in the maintenance of positive steps towards change.

Islāmically modified cognitive–behavioural approaches may be used to challenge and change negative thought patterns and behaviours associated with his addiction. In the Islāmically modified cognitive–behavioural approach, cognitive structuring is a focal component aimed at addressing addiction through the lens of Islāmic teachings and values. This adaptation recognises that addiction often stems from negative thought patterns that contradict Islāmic principles. By acknowledging these negative thought patterns, individuals begin to understand how they conflict with their Islāmic beliefs and values. This recognition serves as a foundation for change, prompting individuals to embark on a journey of introspection and self-awareness.

Through cognitive structuring, individuals are encouraged to critically examine the accuracy of their negative beliefs, especially as they relate to addiction. This process involves questioning the validity of these beliefs and examining them in light of Qur'ânic verses and *hadīths*. Islāmic scriptures offer profound insights into repentance, forgiveness, patience, and trust in Allāh's divine plan, which individuals can draw upon to challenge and reframe their negative thought patterns. By aligning their thoughts with Islāmic teachings, individuals develop a mindset rooted in hope, resilience, and spiritual fortitude.

Furthermore, cognitive structuring within an Islāmically modified approach emphasises the importance of continuous reflection and practice. Individuals are encouraged to contemplate and reflect, journal their thoughts and experiences, and seek guidance from knowledgeable mentors or counsellors within their religious community. Through ongoing reflection and practice, individuals deepen their connection to their faith, strengthen their resolve to overcome addiction, and foster spiritual growth and resilience in the face of adversity. In essence, cognitive structuring serves as a transformative process that enables individuals to confront addiction, align their thoughts and behaviours with Islāmic teachings, and embark on a path of holistic healing and recovery.

Support would be provided by the family and the therapist. Understanding the impact of addiction on family relationships, the therapist involves Ahmed's family in therapy sessions. Family therapy is used to educate and support the family, helping them understand addiction as a disease and learn how to actively contribute to Ahmed's recovery. It addresses issues of communication, trust, and strengthening family dynamics. Furthermore, the therapist can actively involve Ahmed's family in therapy sessions, providing education and support to help them understand addiction as a disease and how they can contribute to his recovery. Family therapy sessions can assist in rebuilding trust, improving communication, and strengthening family dynamics.

Spiritual interventions mainly comprise prayers, supplications, recitation of the Qur'ân, remembrance of Allāh, fasting, charity, Qur'ânic narratives, and Prophetic medicine. It is stated that religion may inhibit alcohol use through at least three possible mechanisms: positive peer groups, moral values, and increased coping skills (Rassool, 2016). At this stage, the client must be self-reliant after putting his trust in God. Help seeking or *isti'aanah* is one of the main processes that are employed throughout all of the stages of the SIPPM. *Du'ah* (supplication) is always the weapon of the believer.

Supplications are usually performed by Muslim clients for wishing the blessing of God and have enormous potential to help us ask. Prophet Muhammad (露) said, "*Du'ah* is worship" (Abū Dāwūd). The concept of remembrance of Allāh (*dhikr*) is central to Islāmic practices and Allāh, and His Prophet have praised the blessings of *dhikr* in numerous verses and sayings. The remembrance of Allāh, in the form of glorifying, exalting, and praising, is a powerful remedy related to feeling better and coping with difficulties.

Muraqabah or self-monitoring is another main all-encompassing process used throughout all of the stages of the Siraat Al-Islāmic Psychotherapy Practice Model. It consists of self-observation (for example, self-reflect and assess one's behaviour) and self-recording (for example, record assessment on paper) (Moore et al., 2001). *Muhasabah* or evaluation is the last process in the practice work model. However, one may observe decreasing symptoms in clients, whether they have improved or gained coping skills and realised the desired changes. Regular self-evaluation and monitoring enhanced Ahmed's awareness and accountability.

In the last stage of the model, maintenance of behavioural change (*siyanah at-taghyir as-suluki*), the therapist and Ahmed work together to develop a relapse prevention plan. This includes identifying potential triggers, developing coping strategies, and creating a support network. The therapist emphasises the importance of ongoing self-monitoring, self-evaluation, and seeking help and guidance from Allāh to maintain behavioural changes. Table 20.1 depicts a summary of the stages and intervention strategies of the SIPPM.

Outcome

Ahmed's journey, guided by the SIPPM, resulted in significant positive outcomes. The integrated approach of this model, which combined psychological techniques with Islāmic principles, provided Ahmed with the necessary support to achieve abstinence, changes in lifestyle, and behaviour; maintain the behaviour change; repair his family relationships; and deepen his spiritual connection. The combined pharmacological, psychological, and spiritual interventions addressed Ahmed's addiction from a holistic perspective accommodating his complex needs and Islāmic worldview.

Through following the stages of the model, Ahmed gained awareness of the severity and consequences of his addiction (awakening stage), engaged in contemplation

TABLE 20.1 Stages of the SIPPM

Stages	Process	Intervention strategy
Awakening (*Qawmah*) Intention (*niyyat*)	*Qawmah* is often what brings the client to seek professional help; includes assessment of the patient's readiness to change.	Support, counselling, motivational interviewing, and CBT
Consultation (*istisharah*)	Entails collecting relevant information about the client's past and presenting problems	Assessment
Contemplation (*tafakkur*)	Entails analysing the issues or problems	Contemplation or reflection; client engagement in the process
Guidance-seeking (*istikhaarah*)	Refers to seeking guidance from Allah, the Almighty before decision-making	Perform a specific prayer for guidance (*salat-l-istikharah*)
Goal-and-route vision (*basirah*)	Compliant with the goals and action strategies.	Clarify the goals and actions of the road map
Willful decision (*'azm*)	Preparation stage; readiness to change period	Facilitate decision-making for action; enhance self-esteem and self-efficacy
Absolute trust in God (*al-tawakkul – Allāh*)	Putting our trust in God is a matter of belief and contributes to our view regarding this life.	Contemplation or reflection; continuously used throughout the different stages of the therapeutic process
Action (*'amal*)	The process involves intention and execution of the action plan.	Reinforcement and support
Help-seeking (*isti'aanah*)	Seek help through patience and prayer.	Prayers and supplications
Self-monitoring (*muraqabah*)	Evaluation of self	Observing and recording one's behaviours, thoughts, and feelings may lead to behaviour change.
Evaluation (*muhasabah*)	Effectiveness of goals set	Evaluation
Maintenance of behavioural change (*siyanah at-taghyir as-suluki*)	Relapse prevention	Relapse prevention programme

Source: Adapted from Rassool (2016).

to explore underlying factors contributing to his addiction, and developed a vision for total abstinence rooted in Islāmic values (goal-and-route vision stage). With the support of the therapist, Ahmed made wilful decisions aligned with his Islāmic beliefs and took decisive actions towards his recovery (decision-making and action stages). This model also emphasised the importance of trust in Allāh (God), self-evaluation and self-monitoring, seeking help and guidance (*isti'aanah* and *istikharah*), and the maintenance of behavioural change. These processes and practices integrated into the therapeutic journey helped Ahmed cultivate a stronger spiritual connection and resilience, fostering long-term psychological resilience and spiritual development.

The positive outcomes achieved by Ahmed demonstrate the efficacy of culturally sensitive and spiritually informed psychotherapy within an Islāmic context. The Siraat Al-Islāmic psychotherapy practice model provided Ahmed with a structured framework, allowing the therapist to address his addiction and its impacts on his psychological, social, and spiritual health. It is important to note that the effectiveness of any psychotherapeutic model depends on various factors including the individual's readiness for change, the therapeutic relationship, and the client's active participation and engagement in the therapeutic process. In Ahmed's case, his motivation for change and his willingness to actively participate in therapy played significant roles in his positive outcomes. The therapist's understanding and appreciation of Ahmed's cultural and religious background fostered a safe and supportive therapeutic environment that supported his beliefs and values. This approach allowed Ahmed to feel validated in his experiences and facilitated his healing journey. The SIPPM serves as a valuable framework for Islāmic psychotherapists, providing a structured and culturally sensitive approach to addressing the complex needs of Muslim clients.

Reflections

Muslim clients often exhibit a lack of trust and engagement with addiction services, primarily because mainstream services do not adequately address their holistic needs. Current therapeutic addiction services often adopt a one-size-fits-all approach, lacking an understanding of the individual's Islāmic worldview, cultural and religious influences, and family pressures. This results in barriers such as a lack of confidentiality, inaccessible systems, and a dearth of cultural competence among service providers. To overcome these barriers, it is important to provide health information that accurately informs Muslim clients about alcohol and drug use and its effects so that they can make informed decisions.

In the initial session, offering health information or employing brief interventions can serve as catalysts for Muslims to seek long-term treatment. By providing accurate information and addressing their concerns, individuals may become more receptive to seeking further support and engaging in the recovery process. Addiction services can bridge the gap and establish trust with Muslim clients, ensuring that the services provided are responsive to their needs and preferences. Cultivating a culturally competent environment that acknowledges and respects Islāmic values and traditions can significantly enhance engagement and trust, increasing the likelihood of positive treatment outcomes for Muslim individuals struggling with addiction.

It is worth noting that an important principle within the Islāmic faith regarding addiction treatment and support promotes a compassionate and non-judgmental approach towards individuals seeking treatment, recognising the inherent worth and potential for change in every believer. Muhammad (2011) stated that, "Islām does not shame its believers when they come for treatment, based on the understanding that Alláh. forgives and we have the responsibility to support and assist in the rehabilitation of the individual whenever possible." By emphasising the forgiveness and support offered by Alláh, Islām encourages a supportive and empathetic attitude towards those struggling with addiction. This perspective aligns with the belief that individuals have the responsibility to assist and rehabilitate others when possible, fostering a sense of community and collective responsibility. This understanding can have a significant impact on the attitudes of Muslims towards seeking and receiving addiction treatment. It helps create an environment where there is no shame or stigma attached to seeking help, allowing individuals to openly access the support they need without fear of judgment or rejection. This can contribute to increased engagement with addiction services and facilitate the journey towards recovery.

One recommended remedy for addictive behaviours is to return to "the therapeutic village and the mosque" (Suliman, 1983). This integration involves actively engaging in the community, seeking support from fellow Muslims, and participating in religious and cultural activities within the mosque. The therapeutic village refers to the Muslim community as a whole, where one can find connection, guidance, and support from individuals who share similar values and beliefs. This integration can serve as a preventive measure for addiction (or other psychological or spiritual problems) and aid in the recovery process. Arguably, the deeper integration of Muslims into their communities can both prevent and cure alcoholism; at the same time, there may be non-religious therapies for alcoholism which could be combined with Islāmic therapies (Michalak & Trocki, 2006). One of the most important responsibilities we all have as Muslims is to put into action the following *hādīth*. It was narrated that Tariq bin Shihab said,

> Abu Sa'eed Al-Khudri (may Allāh be pleased with him) said, "I heard the Messenger of Allah (ﷺ) say, 'Whoever among you sees an evil and changes it with his hand, then he has done his duty. Whoever is unable to do that, but changes it with his tongue, then he has done his duty. Whoever is unable to do that, but changes it with his heart, then he has done his duty, and that is the weakest of Faith.'"
>
> *(An-Nasa'i)*

This is the challenge for all Islāmic psychotherapists.

References

Abū Dāwūd. Riyad as-Salihin 1465. In-book reference: Book 16, Hādīth 1. https://sunnah.com/riyadussalihin:1465

Alias, A., & Majid, H. S. A. (2015). Psychology of learning: An Islāmic theory. *International Journal of Islāmic Thoughts, 4* (1), 63–80.

An-Nasa'i. *Sunan an-Nasa'i 5009*. In-book reference: Book 47, Hādīth 25. English translation: Vol. 6, Book 47, Hādīth 5012. https://sunnah.com/nasai:5009

Basiony, D. M. (2017). *Your Tawbah (Repentance) to-do list: Action points for a fresh start. Repentance . . . for us!* Retrieved December 13, 2023, from https://productivemuslim.com/tawbah-to-do-list/

Islām Q&A. (2007). *Salaat al-tawbah* (the prayer of repentance). Retrieved December 13, 2023, from https://Islamqa.info/en/answers/98030/salaat-al-tawbah-the-prayer-of-repentance

Khalil, A. (2012). Tawba in the Sufi psychology of Abu Tâlib Al-Makki¯(d. 996). *Journal of Islāmic Studies*, 1–31. https://doi.org/10.1093/jis/ets053

Michalak, L., & Trocki, K. (2006). Alcohol and Islām: An overview. *Contemporary Drug Problems*, *33*(4), 523–562.

Moore, D. W., Prebble, S., Robertson, J., Waetford, R., & Anderson, A. (2001). Self-recording with goal setting; A self-management program for the classroom. *Educational Psychology*, *21*(3), 254–265.

Muhammad, J. K. (2011). *Islām and addiction*. Retrieved December 13, 2023, from http://pktaleem.blogspot.com/2011/03/Islam-and-addiction.html

Nadkarni, A., Endsley, P., Bhatia, U., Fuhr, D. C., Noorani, A., Naik, A., Murthy, P., & Velleman, R. (2017). Community detoxification for alcohol dependence: A systematic review. *Drug and Alcohol Review*, *36*(3), 389–399. https://doi.org/10.1111/dar.12440

Prochaska, J. O., DiClemente, C. C., & Norcross, J. C. (1992). In search of how people change. Applications to addictive behaviors. *American Psychologists*, *47*(9), 1102–1114.

Rassool, G. Hussein (2016). *Islāmic counselling: From theory to practice*. Routledge.

Rassool, G. Hussein (2021). Sins, Tawbah and the process of change. *International Journal of Islāmic Psychology*, *4*(1), 26–33.

Suliman, H. (1983). Alcohol and Islāmic faith. *Drug and Alcohol Dependence*, *11*(1), 63–65. https://doi.org/10.1016/0376-8716(83)90097-2.

21
BEYOND THE COUCH

Islāmic approaches to research in psychotherapy

Introduction and context

The term "research," or *bahth* in Arabic, conveys a sense of seeking or investigating a matter. It is also called *al-Tahqiq*, which means investigation inquiry or probing. In English, the word research originates from the French term *recherche*, indicating the act of searching closely for a specific person or thing. Presently, contemporary research in psychology tends to adopt a monocultural approach influenced by an orientalist orientation. This approach falls short in acknowledging the narrow focus that neglects the broader contextual influences shaping the experiences and well-being of individuals from different cultural backgrounds. This chapter aims to offer insight into the Muslim researcher, examining key aspects of Islāmic approaches to research in psychotherapy. It provides an overview of the *maqasid* methodology, exploring the challenges and opportunities inherent in researching Islāmic psychotherapy. Additionally, the chapter emphasises the significance of integrating qualitative and quantitative research methods to comprehensively capture holistic outcomes.

Overview of research

Contemporary research, shaped by a monocultural approach and an Orientalist orientation in psychology, tends to overlook the broader political, sociocultural, and religious influences on the psychosocial and mental health challenges faced by diverse ethno-cultural groups. Shaikh (2023), in relation to the research undertaken on British Muslims in general and Muslim women, points to "how Western literature reproduces certain dynamics of repressiveness and orientalisation, and the lack of meaningful growth and development in research" (p. 74). This underlines the necessity for a more inclusive research perspective that considers the multifaceted aspects of diversity, recognising various sociopolitical and religious dimensions contributing to mental health concerns within distinct ethno-cultural communities. Addressing the dominance of Eurocentric and Orientalist psychology epistemologies in research requires a paradigm shift, leading to the development of Islāmic research scholarship that integrates revealed and created knowledge. This scholarship, guided by the *maqasid* methodology in Islāmic psychology research (Auda, 2021a, 2021b), emphasises a holistic and interconnected understanding of reality and truth in knowledge production. In contrast to the individual-centric view of knowledge, the Islāmic research paradigm is based on "the fundamental belief that knowledge is integrated, connected with the Creator and wholistic rather than 'an individual entity . . . may be owed by an individual'" (Wilson, 2001, p. 176).

In Islāmic psychotherapy research, integrating Islāmic moral and epistemological values into methodologies serves multiple purposes:

(1) *refinement* of the Islāmic methodology; (2) discovering new sound knowledge within Islāmic psychology; (3) verifying existing knowledge in the context of health and social, political and cultural conditions; (4) providing evidence for the efficacy of therapeutic techniques and spiritual interventions; (5) problem-solving of psychosocial issues faced by the *ummah*.

(Rassool, 2023a, p. 7)

Research from an Islāmic perspective "is broader than the notion of the acquisition of knowledge as it is an all-encompassing term focusing on theory, action and education embedded with moral and sociopolitical implications" (Rassool, 2023a, p. 1). This approach emphasises the ethical application of knowledge, aiming for positive change and considering the broader impacts on individuals and society. Research from an Islāmic perspective seeks to address societal needs, contribute to social justice, and enhance overall well-being. It acknowledges the interconnectedness of knowledge, ethics, and societal context, emphasising the researcher's responsibility to engage in research aligned with Islāmic values and fostering positive societal outcomes.

Islāmic psychotherapist research's orientation

Research's nature and process usually operate within a specific theoretical framework often referred to as the research paradigm based on a philosophical perspective. The scientific research paradigm can be defined "as a wide structure encompassing perception, beliefs, and awareness of different theories and practices used to carry out scientific research" (Cohen et al., 2017, p. 657). The research paradigm is based on particular sets of theoretical assumptions: epistemology, ontology, methodology (Guba & Lincoln, 1994), and axiology (Heron & Reason, 1997).

The assumptions we make, according to Saunders et al. (2015), are about "human knowledge (epistemological assumptions), about the realities you encounter in your research (ontological assumptions) and the extent and ways your own values influence your research process (axiological assumptions)" (p. 124). This statement provides a comprehensive lens for understanding the foundational aspects shaping research.

Epistemological considerations involve examining how knowledge is perceived and acquired. These considerations influence the selection of research methods and reliance on various sources of information. Ontological assumptions pertain to the nature of reality and entities under investigation, shaping the researcher's worldview and guiding research strategies. Axiological assumptions address the ethical values of the researcher and their potential impact on the research process, underscoring the importance of transparency and reflexivity.

The term paradigm may also be used to describe a researcher's worldview, or "how the researcher views the world and go about conducting research" (Creswell & Plano Clark, 2007, p. 21). The Muslim researcher's philosophical position is based on the Islāmic worldview (*tasawur or ru'yah al-islām li al-wujud*), which is based on a system of values and principles derived from the Qur'ān and *Sunnah* and from Islāmic civilisation. The Islāmic and Qur'ānic worldviews are identical. Abu Sulayman (2011) provides an explanation:

> The Qur'ānic worldview is the Islāmic worldview, which determines and governs this [Islāmic] way of thinking with its related principles, concepts, and values – as well as the goals and higher aims which they seek to fulfil. This worldview should be reflected in a cogent, coherent, scientific manner in the structure of an Islāmic society's way of thinking, as well as in the ways in which this way of thinking is applied and the outcomes to which it leads.
>
> *(p. 2)*

The claim that the Qur'ānic worldview forms the basis for the Islāmic way of thinking, guiding its principles, concepts, values, and overarching goals, highlights the significance of integrating Islāmic principles with practical and scientific approaches. This alignment demonstrates a comprehensive integration of Islāmic principles into the fabric of society thought and behaviour.

It is from the rich philosophy and worldview of the Muslim researcher that we can extract the many research concepts, processes, and methodologies that form part of the Islāmic traditions based on the Qur'ānic or Islāmic paradigm: "[t]he methodologies of the Islāmic tradition are crucial as a paradigm by which to understand the way in which the Muslim scholars proceeded in a variety of sciences and fields" (Dar al-Ifta Al-Missriyyah, 2022). In Islāmic tradition, the essential ethical and moral values act as integrating principles, creating a cohesive framework that directs behaviours and values, forming a linked and united Islāmic worldview. Because it is based on the ethical and monotheistic paradigm of *tawhīd*, this worldview shapes how Muslims perceive and interact with the world (Rassool, 2023a). This perspective covers a thorough grasp of the world's reality, affecting Muslim interactions and guiding moral choices, thus leading to the characteristics of the worldview among Muslims. Abu Sulayman (2011) argues that,

> a genuinely Islāmic worldview is down-to-earth, comprehensive, law governed, positive, and disciplined. Unfortunately, however, the predominant worldview among Muslims, which purports falsely to be "Islāmic," is theoretical, atomistic, passive, and selective – its purpose being to justify or conceal a quasi-sacerdotal distortion of knowledge and the facts and the inability to master a comprehensive, objective scientific approach to research and analysis.
>
> *(p. 3)*

Abu Sulayman (2011) suggests that a truly Islāmic worldview is practical, wide-ranging, governed by principles, optimistic, and disciplined. However, the prevalent worldview among Muslims frequently incorrectly pretends to be Islāmic but is really fragmented and cannot allow for conducting extensive and objective scientific investigation and analysis. This viewpoint emphasises the need for Muslims to approach knowledge and analysis with a genuine Islāmic worldview that is rooted in practicality, consistency, and the pursuit of objective truth. It highlights the importance of adopting a holistic view of Islām that is compatible with modern scientific methodologies and encourages critical thinking.

The criticism implies that divergence from these principles can lead to a deviation from real Islāmic teachings, hence impeding research scholarship. However, for Muslim researchers in the field of Islāmic psychotherapy, it is crucial to gain the necessary knowledge, tools, and skills from the existing Islāmic research traditions. It is incumbent upon us to understand and adopt what can be referred to as the Islāmic paradigm. This goes beyond acquiring knowledge (*'ilm*) and research methodologies; it also entails examining the Muslim scholar's worldview and philosophical stance to ensure congruence with Islāmic beliefs and practices. It is essential for Muslim scholars to align their worldview and philosophical stance with Islāmic principles. This alignment ensures that their approach to research is rooted in the Islāmic tradition, reflecting an understanding and appreciation of the unique Islāmic epistemology. When Muslim scholars have integrated the Islāmic paradigm into their philosophy and worldview, they become resilient against the challenges posed by secular philosophical research paradigms.

The need to understand the epistemology, ontology, and source of Islāmic knowledge is of paramount importance. The sources of knowledge in Islām are from the Qur'ān and *Sunnah (ilm 'naqli)* and from rational knowledge based on human intellect (*'aql*), observation, and empiricism (*ilm 'aqli*). It has been suggested that "the systematic integration of the sources and means of knowledge into a synthesised approach is known as epistemological [relating to theory of knowledge] integration (*al-takamul alma'arifi*)" (Rassool, 2023a, p. 62). The foundation of knowledge is the Qur'ān and *ḥadīth*. Malkawi (2014) suggests that the Qur'ān

> is viewed as the springhead of all knowledge and all sciences, not because it contains the knowledge itself but, rather, because it inspires the Muslim to develop a distinctive vision of the unity among the various spheres of knowledge. The notion of this unity arises out of an awareness of the unity of the Divine and its applications to the various spheres of human knowledge.
>
> *(p. 20)*

This statement implies that the Qur'ān is considered the origin from which all knowledge and sciences derive. However, it does not suggest that the Qur'ān contains all knowledge; rather, it serves as an inspiration for Muslims to develop a comprehensive and integrated understanding of the unity among different fields of knowledge. This unity is rooted in recognising the oneness of the divine and applying this awareness to various domains of human knowledge.

This perspective highlights the interconnectedness of knowledge and stresses the importance of integrating Islāmic principles and teachings into different disciplines. It encourages Muslims to seek knowledge from diverse sources while approaching it with an understanding of the unity and coherence of creation. By recognising this unity and integrating Islāmic beliefs and principles, Muslims can foster a holistic perspective that goes beyond compartmentalised areas of study. Utz (2011) emphasises that understanding the true nature of the soul and the unseen world, as well as how to purify and develop the soul to its fullest potential, comes only through divine revelation. Speculation or guessing about this realm is discouraged, and seeking knowledge from Allāh is emphasised.

Knowledge can be obtained through various means, such as sense perception, intuition, and logical reasoning. It is important not to disregard these sources. However, there is no conflict between knowledge from religious texts like the Qur'ān and empirical, rational knowledge because both originate from God. Malkawi (2014) suggested that the classical Muslim scholars, despite their different school of thought, agreed that

> knowledge should be interconnected, complementary, and organically linked to the knowledge of God. In the view of these scholars, the fact that all sciences originate from a single divine source is the foundation for the ultimate integration and unity of knowledge.
>
> *(p. 12)*

The perspective that knowledge should be interconnected, complementary, and organically linked to the knowledge of God underscores a holistic understanding of knowledge and knowledge integration. Scholars advocating for the interconnectedness of all sciences and their origin from a single divine source emphasise the ultimate integration and unity of knowledge.

This viewpoint aligns with the idea that various branches of knowledge, whether religious or secular, can be harmoniously interconnected, contributing to a comprehensive and unified understanding of the world. This interconnectedness fosters a more holistic worldview, where the pursuit of knowledge is seen as a unified undertaking aimed at understanding the divine order inherent in all aspects of life. For Islāmic researchers, empirical evidence should be assessed based on the criteria of divine revelation. They are encouraged to prioritise Islāmic ethical values over rationality and empirical evidence, considering the latter as secondary to the primary sources of divine guidance.

Considering the significance of the Arabic language and linguistics is important due to the emphasis classical Muslims scholars placed on understanding the meanings of words in Islāmic traditions. According to Sradar (n.d., cited in the Foundation for Science, Technology and Civilisation, 2006), scientists bear accountability to God for their actions. They are obliged not only to serve the community but also to safeguard and advance its ethical and moral institutions. The application of science by Muslims should align with the values of the society they aim to benefit in the pursuit of truth within the ethical and values framework of Islām. Historically, Muslim scholars initiated their activities with this invocation:

بِسْمِ ٱللَّهِ ٱلرَّحْمَٰنِ ٱلرَّحِيمِ

- *In the name of God, the Merciful, the Compassionate.*

The scholars also expressed respect for Prophet Muhammad (ﷺ). Those scholars developed their ideas, theories, and methodologies from an interaction of the divine texts and empirical evidence and quoted from the Qur'ān and *Sunnah* if relevant and appropriate. Bucaille (2000) provides us a reminder of the Islāmic traditions: "Where in the Islāmic world, this did not prevent them from being both believers and scientists. Science was the twin of religion, and it should never have ceased to be so" (p. 85).

Table 21.1 presents the distinctions between a secular researcher and a Muslim researcher across various aspects, including orientation, reality, research philosophy, worldview, focus, religious relationship, sources of knowledge, values, ethics, process, and the relationship between mind and body. The table highlights the contrasting perspectives and approaches between these two types of researchers in terms of their underlying beliefs, methodologies, and guiding principles. It serves as a useful reference for understanding the divergent viewpoints and considerations that shape the research conducted by each group.

TABLE 21.1 Differences between secular and Muslim researchers

	Secular researcher	Muslim researcher
Orientation	Approaches research without a specific religious orientation; secular or Judaeo-Christian	Approaches research with an Islāmic worldview and perspective
Language	Primarily uses neutral, non-religious language	May incorporate Islāmic terminology and references in language
Purpose	Aims for general understanding and advancement of knowledge	Aims for general understanding and advancement of knowledge, wisdom, truth, meaning of life; ecological validity; research findings benefit for the *ummah*
Focus	Focuses on topics irrespective of religious considerations; limited focus on the physical world	Regard for spiritual aspects of human beings; seen and unseen worlds
Religious relationship	Oppositional, secular	Integrated; grounds research within the framework of Islāmic beliefs and principles
Sources of knowledge	Draws from various academic and empirical sources; man-made theories, empirical, parochial	Divine revelation Qur'ân and *Sunnah*; empirical
Values	Values are shaped by professional ethics and societal norms (value laden and dependent).	Values are influenced by Islāmic ethics and principles.
Process	Follows conventional research methodologies	Integrates Islāmic research methodologies (*maqasid* methodology, ethics)
Relationship between mind/body	Mind–body interaction; explores psychological and physiological connections	Mind–body–soul interaction; considers the holistic relationship, including spiritual dimensions
Study responses to illness	Examines illness from medical and psychological perspectives	Considers spiritual, psychological, and physical aspects in responses to illness

Source: Adapted from Rassool (2023a).

Key aspects of Islāmic approaches to research in psychotherapy

Islāmic approaches to research in psychotherapy involve integrating Islāmic principles, values, and perspectives into the research process. These approaches aim to align research methodologies with the ethical and spiritual foundations of Islām. Some of the key aspects of Islāmic approaches to research in psychotherapy include adherence to the Islāmic worldview and Islāmic ethics, incorporation of the spiritual dimension, interdisciplinary perspectives, engagement with Islāmic scholars, community-based research, validation of Islāmic interventions, and longitudinal studies. Research conducted in psychotherapy within an Islāmic framework places a strong emphasis on upholding ethical standards grounded in Islāmic principles. This commitment extends to ensuring participants' well-being through practices such as obtaining informed consent and maintaining confidentiality, all in configuration with the teachings found in the Qur'ān and the Prophetic traditions. For instance, informed consent is approached with a deep respect for the participant's autonomy, and confidentiality is regarded as a sacred trust, reflecting the Islāmic value of protecting individuals' privacy. This approach stresses the integration of ethical considerations derived from Islāmic teachings into the research practices of psychotherapy, fostering a matching alignment between the principles of the faith and the ethical conduct of research. This approach not only promotes the integrity of the research but also resonates with the broader goals of enhancing the psychological well-being of individuals within an Islāmic context.

Research in Islāmic psychotherapy recognises the fundamental significance of spirituality in mental well-being; researchers explore the influence of religious practices, including prayer, contemplation, and Qur'ānic recitation, on psychological outcomes. For instance, an investigator might examine how regular prayer routines contribute to stress reduction or assess the impact of Islāmic contemplative techniques rooted in Islāmic traditions on overall mental health. The recitation of the Qur'ān (Qur'ānic therapy) is another area of interest. Researchers may explore the psychological effects of regularly reciting and reflecting upon Qur'ānic verses, investigating how the engagement with sacred texts can provide solace, guidance, and emotional healing.

Additionally, therapeutic practices rooted in Islāmic teachings, such as contemplation and self-reflection, may be examined for their impacts on stress reduction, emotional regulation, and enhancing self-awareness. These studies aim to understand how spirituality can enhance emotional resilience, alleviate distress, and contribute to overall mental health. This approach highlights the acknowledgment of spiritual dimensions as integral components in understanding and enhancing psychological well-being within the context of Islāmic psychotherapy research. This holistic approach recognises the interconnectedness of the spiritual, psychological, and emotional dimensions and highlights the significance of spirituality in facilitating therapeutic outcomes within an Islāmic context.

Researchers within the field of Islāmic psychotherapy attempt to validate the efficacy of therapeutic interventions that are grounded in Islāmic principles. To achieve this, they employ rigorous research methodologies to gather empirical evidence on the impacts of these interventions on mental health outcomes. These studies aim to evaluate the effectiveness of specific psychotherapeutic techniques that incorporate Islāmic values and principles. Researchers applying the *maqasid* methodology (Auda, 2021a) conduct randomised controlled trials, observational studies, systematic or scoping reviews, mixed methodologies to gather evidence on the outcomes of interventions such as Islāmic-modified cognitive-behavioural therapy, Islāmic contemplation-based therapies, or Islāmic psychotherapy to address specific mental health issues. In addition to quantitative methodologies, qualitative research methods like phenomenological interviews, focus groups, and case studies may be employed to gain a deeper understanding of individuals' experiences with Islāmic therapies and their impacts on their psychosocial and psychospiritual health. This commitment to empirical validation reflects a dedication to integrating Islāmic therapies into mainstream mental health practices based on scientifically rigorous assessments, contributing to the evolving landscape of evidence-based approaches in the field of Islāmic psychotherapy.

The exploration of Islāmic psychotherapy research embraces a multidisciplinary approach, integrating insights from the social sciences and Islāmic studies. This approach seeks to combine empirical research methods from the social sciences with the principles and teachings derived from Islāmic sources to develop a comprehensive understanding of therapeutic interventions. One example of this multidisciplinary approach is in the field of Islāmic psychotherapy, in which researchers may draw on concepts and methodologies from disciplines such as psychology, sociology, psychotherapy, and counselling psychology while also incorporating Islāmic teachings and values.

They may explore how Islāmic principles and practices can enhance the therapeutic process and promote positive mental health outcomes. For instance, a researcher may examine the effectiveness of Islāmic psychotherapy interventions for addressing marital issues. Researchers may integrate principles from fields like couple and family therapy, psychology, and sociology while considering the Islāmic teachings on marriage, communication, and conflict resolution. By combining methodologies from the social sciences with Islāmic insights, researchers can provide more culturally relevant and effective interventions for Muslim couples facing marital and relationship challenges.

Researchers have the opportunity to engage in collaborative efforts with Islāmic scholars to ensure that their research aligns with Islāmic teachings. This partnership proves invaluable in gaining insights into effectively integrating Islāmic principles into psychotherapeutic interventions. For example, in a study investigating the effectiveness of an intervention based on Islāmic contemplation, researchers may engage with Islāmic scholars to ensure that therapeutic practices align with Islāmic teachings and do not contradict any religious principles. The scholars can provide guidance on selecting appropriate contemplative techniques that are congruent with Islāmic beliefs and values. The collaboration between researchers and Islāmic scholars serves to bridge the gap between academic research and religious guidance, ensuring that the interventions and research outcomes are in alignment with Islāmic teachings. This collaborative effort can enhance the credibility and cultural validity of the research, contributing to the development of effective and ethically sound psychotherapeutic interventions within an Islāmic framework.

Research in Islāmic psychotherapy should adopt a community-based or *ummah*-based approach, emphasising active participation from the community. Researchers actively collaborate with local Muslim communities to tailor research activities to address the distinctive needs and challenges encountered by the community. For instance, a study focusing on the mental health of Muslim youth might involve collaborating with local mosques, *imams* or faith leaders, or Islāmic centres, actively seeking the perspectives of community leaders, transformative agents, parents, and young individuals to shape the research questions and methodologies. This collaborative process not only enhances the relevance of the research but also fosters a sense of ownership and empowerment within the community.

Within the context of Islāmic psychotherapy, researchers actively engage with the diverse cultural aspects present among Muslims. This involves recognising variations in cultural practices, beliefs, and traditions that may impact individuals' mental health experiences. For example, a researcher may explore how cultural differences in expressions of distress or coping mechanisms among diverse Muslim communities influence the effectiveness of psychotherapeutic interventions. The commitment to recognising and respecting the diversity within the Muslim community emphasises the effort to develop psychotherapeutic interventions that are sensitive to the heterogeneity of Muslim communities.

Islāmic psychotherapy research should incorporate longitudinal studies to investigate the long-term impact of interventions on individuals' mental health and spiritual well-being over an extended period. Longitudinal studies enable the assessment of changes, growth, and the maintenance of mental health beyond the immediate post-intervention period. For example, a research project might follow individuals who have undergone Islām-based psychotherapy for anxiety over several years. By doing so, researchers can assess not only the immediate effectiveness of the intervention but also its sustained influence on mental health and spiritual health outcomes. Longitudinal studies offer valuable insights into the sustained benefits of interventions, facilitating the development of more effective and enduring mental health support within an Islāmic framework.

Integrated research methodologies

Research in Islāmic psychotherapy can greatly benefit from using mixed-methods approaches rather than a single methodology. A combination of qualitative and quantitative research methods allows for a more comprehensive understanding of the effectiveness and cultural appropriateness of therapies (for a comprehensive account of the aims and focus of qualitative, quantitative, or both, see Rassool, 2023a, p. 179). Qualitative research methods such as interviews, focus groups, and narrative analysis provide deep insights into individuals' lived experiences, cultural beliefs, and the impact of Islāmic interventions on their mental health. They focus on concepts, subjective experiences, themes, wordings, and ideas.

In contrast, quantitative research methods such as randomised controlled trials and surveys complement qualitative research by providing statistical data on the outcomes of Islāmic psychotherapeutic interventions. The integration of qualitative and quantitative research methods in Islāmic psychotherapy research enables researchers to triangulate data, validate findings, and gain a more holistic understanding of the complex nature of the phenomenon being studied. This combined methodological approach enhances the comprehensiveness of research design, capturing diverse dimensions within the study. There are two types of design: sequential exploratory and concurrent triangulation.

The sequential exploratory design in Islāmic psychotherapy research requires an initial phase of qualitative inquiry to explore lived experiences and generate hypotheses. Subsequently, a quantitative phase is employed to validate and test these hypotheses within a larger sample. This methodological approach enables researchers to leverage qualitative insights to inform and refine subsequent quantitative research, ending in a more robust and culturally sensitive study.

For instance, in the context of Islāmic psychotherapy, a researcher may initially conduct qualitative interviews with individuals seeking mental health support within an Islāmic framework. These interviews could explore the impacts of religious practices on well-being, offering rich narratives. The emergent themes and patterns identified through qualitative analysis then inform the development of hypotheses. The subsequent quantitative phase involves designing a survey to measure the prevalence and statistical significance of identified themes in a larger sample of participants. For instance, if the qualitative phase revealed themes related to the positive impact of prayer on mental well-being, the quantitative phase could involve assessing the prevalence of such experiences in a broader population.

In concurrent triangulation, both qualitative and quantitative data are collected concurrently. This design allows researchers to analyse and compare qualitative and quantitative findings, aiming to establish convergence or divergence between the two and providing a comprehensive understanding of the research topic. This approach is particularly effective when examining the impact of Islāmic psychotherapy across different populations, as it enables cross-cultural comparisons. For example, a researcher could study the effectiveness of an Islāmic psychotherapy intervention for individuals experiencing grief and loss.

In concurrent triangulation, qualitative interviews may be conducted to explore the subjective experiences, coping mechanisms, and spiritual perspectives of participants. These interviews can provide rich insights into the unique cultural and Islāmic aspects of dealing with grief. Simultaneously, quantitative measures can be administered to assess the participants' levels of grief, coping strategies, and psychological well-being. Validated scales or questionnaires can be used to gather numerical data. These quantitative measures allow for statistical analyses that can provide an overall picture of the effectiveness of the intervention in reducing grief symptoms and improving individuals' well-being.

By analysing and comparing both qualitative and quantitative findings, researchers can identify areas of convergence, such as qualitative narratives supporting quantitative results or vice versa. Furthermore, areas of divergence can highlight incongruities that need further exploration. The concurrent triangulation design enables researchers to gather a comprehensive understanding of the effectiveness of the intervention by combining qualitative depth with quantitative breadth. By utilising mixed-methods approaches and integrating qualitative and quantitative research methods, the limitations associated with each approach can be surmounted. Mixed-methods research enables researchers to capture the depth and breadth of experiences and outcomes, leading to more comprehensive evaluations and evidence-based practices in the field of Islāmic psychotherapy.

I proposed that the task of developing an integrated methodology of research in Islāmic psychology should have a fourfold aim (see Figure 21.1):

First, the new methodology should include Qur'ān and *Sunnah* as the primary source of knowledge. Secondly, the methodologies of the Islāmic traditions should also be used as a paradigm by Muslim psychologists and scholars should proceeded to develop research methodologies in Islāmic psychology. The use of historical works from Islāmic classical scholars and work from contemporary scholars are also sources of psychology knowledge. Thirdly, we need to use both qualitative and quantitative methodologies of research which provide a holistic and multidisciplinary approach. Fourthly, the desired methodology

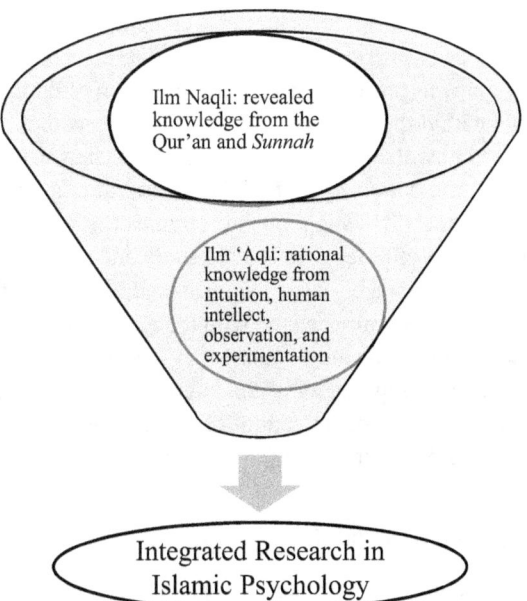

FIGURE 21.1 The integrated research methodology in Islāmic psychotherapy.

Note: For a framework for undertaking research in Islāmic psychology, see Rassool (2023a, p. 63).

must allow the integration of both revealed knowledge and knowledge from quantitative and qualitative research methodologies.

(Rassool, 2023b, p. 196)

An overview of the *maqasid* methodology

Auda (2021a) introduced a new method of research in Islāmic scholarship based on the Islāmic or Qur'ānic worldview. The primary goal of this intellectual Islāmic discourse is to bring back to life the original ideas of the Islāmic methodology, structure, and worldview in the modern era. This is reflected in the broad definition of the *maqasid* methodology "as a systematic approach in which connectivity, wholism and emergence are focal points" (Najimudeen, 2022). Auda (2021a) cautioned the researchers that this new *maqasid* methodology in itself

> will not address the researcher's specific inquiry. Instead, it will direct the scholar to the most suitable steps, content, meanings, emphases, connections and references that must be considered given their purpose or question. The methodology guides the researcher's analysis of particulars and generalities, and how the Revelation shifts seamlessly between the two.
>
> (p. 102)

The statement highlights that the *maqasid* methodology does not provide a direct answer or solution to the researcher's specific inquiry. Instead, it acts as a guide, directing the researcher to the appropriate steps, content, meanings, emphases, connections, and references necessary to address their research purpose or question. The methodology helps in the analysis and interpretation of both general concepts and precise details within the framework. It highlights how these two dimensions interact naturally and how the Divine Revelation moves between them.

This implies that the *maqasid* methodology provides a framework for the researcher to conduct their investigation and outlines the values and factors they need to take into account in order to produce significant and pertinent findings. In order to apply the different stages of the *maqasid* methodology in the research process, the researcher need to be re-oriented with the three most fundamental aspects of this re-orientation: (1) knowledge (*'ilm*), (2) reality (*waqi*), and (3) scholarship (*ijtihad*). There are five overlapping and interconnected *maqasid* methodology steps: (1) purpose, (2) cycles of reflection, (3) framework, (4) critical studies of literature and reality, and (5) formative theories and principles (Figure 21.2).

Stages of the *maqasid* methodology

The *maqasid* methodology's five stages are cyclical but do not form a rigid process that needs to be followed in order. The study subject, the researcher's competence, and the available resources will all influence how the stages are

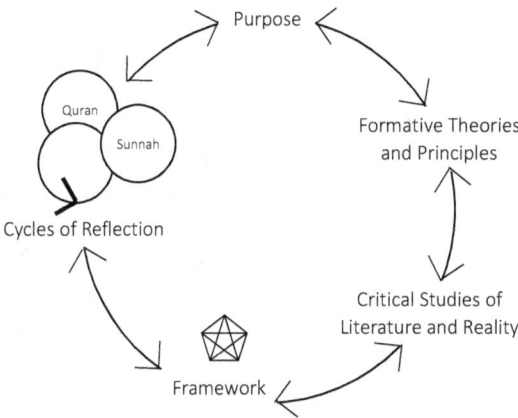

FIGURE 21.2 The five stages of the *maqasid* methodology.

used and where they start. The Higher Objectives of Islāmic Law (*Maqasid Ash-Shar'iah*) should be considered when considering the application of the *maqasid* methodology in Islāmic psychotherapy. These Higher Objectives include the preservation of the religion; the preservation of the self/soul; the preservation of lineage/offspring, progeny, and honour; the preservation of the mind/intellect ('*aql*'); and the preservation of wealth. At this point, "One could potentially assess how different psychological theories and perspectives are aligned or are incongruent from these Higher Objectives, or how the purpose of research is aligned with the dimensions of the Higher Objectives" (Rassool, 2023a, p. 76). There is potential to assess how different psychological theories and perspectives align or diverge in relation to the Higher Objectives (*maqasid*) within an Islāmic framework. Researchers can evaluate whether their research aims to enhance individual well-being, promote social justice and equity, nurture positive ethical values, and foster spiritual growth-all of which are in line with the *maqasid* methodology.

Intent (*niyyah*) is a fundamental concept in Islāmic practices. *Niyyah* refers to the sincere and conscious intention that a person holds in their heart before engaging in any act of worship or other Islāmic activities. The rationale for *niyyah* is reflected in the following: in a *hādīth*, 'Umar bin Al Khattab reported that the Apostle of Allāh as saying, "Surely, all actions are but driven by intentions" (Abu Dâwud). According to Zarabozo (2008), Imam Abu Dâwud affirmed that a particular *hādīth* represents one half of Islām. In this context, Islām encompasses both the outward expression of faith through actions and the inward intention behind those actions. Similarly, Al-Shafi'ee suggested that this concept also encompasses half of knowledge, emphasising that religion encompasses both the external aspects (deeds) and the internal aspects (intention) of one's faith (p. 98).

Purpose

In the *maqasid* methodology, once an intention is established, the next step is to define the purpose of the research. Unlike conventional research that identifies and examines a problem statement, the *maqasid* methodology focuses on defining the purpose of the research. This purpose is aligned with the with the Higher Objectives of Islām and aims to produce beneficial knowledge and contribute valuable insights from an Islāmic perspective. It seeks to address a research question or explore a topic in a way that aligns with the Higher Objectives (*maqasid*), emphasising the significance of producing knowledge that is beneficial and applicable in thought and action. This approach ensures that the research serves a higher purpose, not only addressing the identified problem but also contributing to the broader goals of promoting well-being, justice, and spiritual growth in society as guided by Islāmic traditions. Auda (2021a) clearly distinguishes between these problem definition and purpose definition:

> the *Maqasid* Methodology in conformance with revelation is purpose-, not problem-oriented. And while a certain perception of problems could be redefined through purposes, purposes should not be redefined through a certain perception of problems.
>
> *(p. 111)*

This suggests that the methodology emphasises a purpose-oriented approach rather than a problem-oriented one, aligning with the principles of revelation. In this methodology, the focus is on defining and understanding the purpose of the research rather than merely redefining it through a specific perception of problems. For instance, instead of limiting the definition of a research problem with preconceived ideas, the focus is on thoroughly looking at the bigger picture and goals of the research. This means considering different viewpoints, possible outcomes, and the overall importance of the study in its specific context.

The researcher aims to grasp the many aspects of the research purpose before getting into specific problem definitions. This method ensures a broader and more open-minded exploration of the research topic. The goals of the *maqasid* methodology can change how we perceive the problems, but it is important to keep them true to their purpose. This should not be altered based on a narrow or biased understanding of situations. By adhering to a purpose-oriented approach, the *maqasid* methodology ensures that the research is guided by the Higher Objectives of Islām. Another important question that requires careful consideration is, "Why am I conducting this research?" By reflecting on this question, the research process becomes purpose-driven, determined by the objectives identified or inferred from Revelation. This approach allows the researcher to align their work with the broader divine objectives and work towards achieving a purpose that is in accordance with Islāmic principles.

Cycles of reflection

The cycles of reflection of the Qur'ān-linking with the *Sunnah* is the second stage in the *maqasid* methodology. It is dynamic in nature, a continuous process throughout the enquiry or research:

> The one indispensable feature of the methodology that cannot be replaced or compromised is the Cycles of Reflection (*dawraat al-tadabbur*) upon the Qur'ān and *Sunnah*. This is the *Maqasid* Methodology's very core step that no scholar or researcher in Islāmic Studies [or in other disciplines] can do without.
>
> *(Auda, 2021a, p. 102)*

Figure 21.3 illustrates the repetitive nature of the reflection process within the *maqasid* methodology. After defining the research purpose, the researcher engages in a series of reflective activities to gain clarity and guidance. This involves contemplating and analysing relevant verses of the Qur'ān and *hādīths* that are applicable and aligned with the research purpose. These cycles of reflections are an integral part of the methodology and serve to deepen the researcher's understanding and provide specific positioning within an Islāmic framework. Through reflection, the researcher seeks to uncover insights, draw connections, and gain wisdom from the divine sources. This process of reflection helps align the research purpose with the teachings and principles of Islām, ensuring that the research is guided by Islāmic values and objectives. By engaging in multiple cycles of reflection, the researcher refines their understanding, allowing for continual clarification and fine-tuning of the research purpose.

Auda (2021a) highlighted that, "At this stage of the research, the researcher is not at liberty to be selective in their study of certain verses, *hādīth*, dimensions, themes

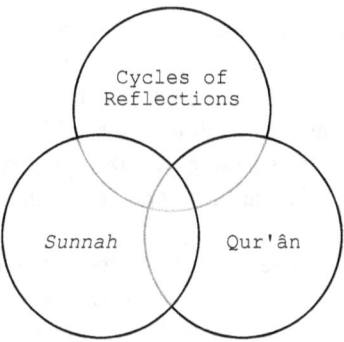

FIGURE 21.3 Cycles of reflections.

and techniques, but must instead perform full Cycles of Reflections" (p. 114). Allāh says in the Qur'ân,

$$\text{أَفَلَا يَتَدَبَّرُونَ ٱلْقُرْءَانَ أَمْ عَلَىٰ قُلُوبٍ أَقْفَالُهَآ}$$

- Then do they not reflect upon the Qur'ān [*yatadabbarun*], or are there locks upon [their] hearts?

(Muhammad 47:24, interpretation of the meaning)

Ibn Kathir (2000) provides an exegesis of the verse: in his interpretation, he suggests that there are indeed locks upon some hearts that prevent them from understanding and receiving the profound meanings contained in the Qur'an. Thus, the individuals remain closed off to the Qur'ān's spiritual and intellectual benefits.

Reflecting on the Qur'ān is not only a means of seeking guidance but also acts as a cure for the spiritual diseases of the heart (*qalb*). This process involves regular introspection using the cycles of reflections on both the Qur'ân and the *Sunnah*. In addition to personal introspection, reflection on the Qur'ân also guide the methodological objectives of research. The focus is on seeking out fundamental meanings, elements, and themes based on the Qur'ānic worldview. These reflections lead to the development of a composite *maqasid* framework that aligns the research with the Higher Objectives of Islām. To assist in this process, a mind map can be a useful tool for researchers. It allows for the identification and organisation of the interconnected web of meanings related to the research.

Framework

There are seven elements in the framework that conceptualise an Islāmic worldview: concepts (*mafahim*), objectives (*maqasid*), values (*qiyam*), commands (*awamir*), universal laws (*sunan*), groups (*fi'at*), and proofs (*hujaj*). This framework is presented in Figure 21.4.

However, as Auda (2021a) pointed out, "While definitive in their presence and meaning, each of the Seven Elements is open to further refinement, exploration and additions. Each element presents webs of meanings with cores and clusters that intersect" (p. 151). This statement highlights that while the seven elements within the *maqasid* methodology in Islāmic psychotherapy research are significant and carry definitive meanings, they are also open to further refinement, exploration, and additions.

Each element within the framework offers a network of entangled meanings with intersecting cores and groupings. This acknowledgment highlights the dynamic nature of the methodology and its potential for continuous development and expansion. As researchers explores each element, they may uncover additional layers of meaning and connections that enhance their understanding and application. Each element's basic meanings function as underlying concepts, and its clusters are

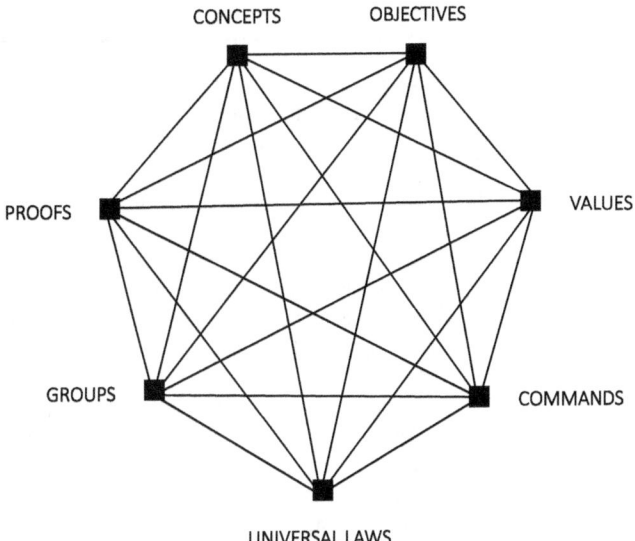

FIGURE 21.4   The seven elements of the *maqasid* framework.

associated ideas or subtopics that connect and enhance our comprehension of that particular element.

The interconnections in the *maqasid* methodology facilitate the exploration of its many features and implications by researchers in various study situations. By remaining open to further refinement, exploration, and additions, researchers can adapt the seven elements to specific research objectives, contexts, and emerging knowledge in the field of Islāmic psychotherapy research. Table 21.2 provides an overview of the seven-element conceptualisation of the framework. It is important to note that the basic guideline for contemplating all these seven elements is that, "they are to be understood through their textual expressions (*nass*) and through inference (*istinbat*) from their linguistic and webbed manifestations in the revelation" (Auda, 2021a, p. 152).

Critical studies of literature and reality

The fourth stage of the *maqasid* methodology involves critical dialogues and studies that serve as sources of inquiry and consolidation of knowledge (*'ilm*). This stage involves conducting a critical review of the literature, drawing from both classical and modern sources of Islāmic and non-Islāmic origins. Through critical discourses, researchers analyse and evaluate various perspectives, theories, and findings. This process allows for a broader understanding of the research topic, incorporating diverse viewpoints and insights. The use of non-Islāmic sources helps researchers incorporate different perspectives and insights derived from alternative

TABLE 21.2 The seven elements of the *maqasid* framework

Elements	Arabic	Characteristics
Concepts	*Mafahim*	Key words with authority and meaning
		Focus on core issues on Qur'ân and *Sunnah*
		Correct deviations in understanding the web of meanings
Objectives	*Maqasid*	Intention and purposes understood from the Qur'ân and *Sunnah*
		Based on realised in the lived reality
Values	*Qiyam*	Positive and negative
		Denote the importance that humans must place on thoughts, actions, and all created matter.
Commands	*Awamir*	Positive and negative
		Govern human behaviour in the Qur'ân and *Sunnah*
		Clarify what is beneficial and reprehensible
Universal laws	*Sunan*	Laws of creation, natural and social, based on the Qur'ân and *Sunnah*
		Govern human actions
		Promote awareness in human thought and action.
Groups	*Fi'at*	Parties, human and otherwise identified in the Qur'ân and *Sunnah*.
		Members and characteristics are detailed
		Special reference to human categories, both positive and negative, in order to increase awareness
Proofs	*Hujaj*	Aim is to establish truths in the minds and hearts of the believer
		Signs (*ayat*) and guideposts (*alamat*)
		Reinforcing the truth of arguments (*burhan*) or the soundness of logic (*mantiq*)

Source: Adapted from Auda (2021a).

methodologies and worldviews. This inclusive approach enriches the research by bringing together a wide range of perspectives, leading to a more comprehensive and nuanced understanding of the subject matter. Auda (2021a) argued that

> the Islāmic perspective (*manzur/muntalaq*) represented by the fundamental premises of the *Maqasid* Methodology differ in fundamental ways from other philosophies and ideologies, despite an acknowledgement of possible overlaps and similarities in many values, ideas and applications.
>
> (p. 127)

A challenging aspect is to avoid categorising knowledge as either Islāmic or non-Islāmic. Instead, all knowledge is acknowledged as coming from Allāh, The Almighty. It is essential to recognise that when utilising non-Islāmic sources of knowledge, they should align with Islāmic beliefs and practices and not contradict the fundamental principles of Islām and core teachings of Revelation. This perspective encourages researchers to approach knowledge with an open mind, recognising that beneficial insights can be found in a variety of sources. However, it also emphasises the importance of critically evaluating non-Islāmic knowledge to ensure its compatibility with Islāmic principles. The objective is to integrate knowledge that is congruent with Islāmic beliefs and does not compromise Islāmic beliefs and practices.

Performing a critical analysis of the literature allows researchers to broaden their perspective on the research theme, facilitating the refinement of a topic and the framing of research questions. This practice involves summarising and analysing previous research and theories, identifying areas of controversy and contested claims, and highlighting any research gaps that exist. Additionally, critical engagement with lived realities is an important aspect of the research process. It involves critically assessing the experiences and realities of individuals based on an Islāmic or Qur'ānic worldview. By examining lived realities through an Islāmic lens, researchers can gain insights into the intersection of Islāmic principles, personal experiences, and societal contexts. Auda (2021a) suggested that

> to perform this critical assessment of the reality, a comparison should be carried out between two frameworks, fully or partially. One is the Islāmic framework that the mujtahid [scholar] developed based on the purposes and Cycles of Reflection, and the other is a similar framework that contains the main elements that describe the lived reality. Describing the reality involves describing communities, organisations, professions, states, laws, technologies, natural environment, animals, organisms, etc.
>
> *(p. 133)*

This means that to conduct a critical assessment of the reality, it is important to compare two frameworks, either fully or partially. One framework is the Islāmic framework developed by scholars (*mujtahids*), which is based on the purposes and cycles of reflection within the *maqasid* methodology. The other framework is comparable and describes the main elements of the lived reality. The critical assessment of the reality involves examining and analysing various aspects such as communities, organisations, professions, laws, technologies, and the natural environment. Through this comparison between the Islāmic framework and the lived reality, researchers can gain a comprehensive understanding of the similarities, differences, challenges, and opportunities that arise, facilitating a deeper exploration of the subject matter. Through this critical assessment, researchers can identify areas of alignment or incongruence between the Islāmic framework and the lived reality.

Formative theories and principles

The last stage of the *maqasid* methodology involves developing formative theories and principles based on the wealth of information generated by the composite frameworks, encompassing concepts, objectives, values, commands, universal laws, groups, and proofs. This stage is complex and requires specific skills and Islāmic scholarship to synthesise the comprehensive information effectively. The intellectual discourse operated during this process is not based on inductive method of reasoning but on the Quranic expression of emergence as the concepts of *tawallud* or *nushu* (Qur'ān 2:333, 3:47, 11:72, 71:27, 112:3 and 6:98, 13:12, 23:14, 24:55, 6:73, respectively)'(Auda, 2021a, p. 138). Auda (2021a) suggested that

> the conclusion of theories and principles from the webs of meaning and critical studies of the literature and lived reality, also differ from the traditional – and typical – process of induction. Induction involves the search for instances in the texts where a certain meaning manifests.
>
> *(pp. 137–138)*

Thus, the process of concluding theories and principles from the webs of meaning and critical studies of the literature and lived reality differs from the conventional process of induction. Induction typically involves searching for specific instances in texts where a particular meaning is evident. However, in the *maqasid* methodology, the conclusion of theories and principles goes beyond a simple induction process. The methodology adopts a more holistic and comprehensive approach. It considers a wide range of sources, including texts, critical studies of literature, and analysis of lived reality, to derive meaningful conclusions. This approach goes beyond the simple search for isolated instances of meaning, acknowledging the complex interconnections and multidimensional nature of knowledge.

However, the seven elements of the *maqasid* framework are essential for understanding the *maqasid* methodology. These elements include the objectives, concepts, values, commands, universal laws, groups, and proofs. They serve as the foundation for conducting research within an Islāmic framework, aligning it with the Higher Objectives of Islām and guiding the research process with ethical principles. By comprehending these elements, researchers can ensure their work is rooted in Islāmic beliefs and practices.

Conclusion

This chapter presented the basic steps of the *maqasid* methodology, namely, purpose, cycles of reflections, critical studies of literature and reality, framework, and formative theories and principles. Auda (2021a) suggested that "[all] of the proposed five methodological steps, from defining a purpose to concluding theories and principles, would benefit from the above methods of reading the Qur'ân and integrating its meanings" (p. 137). It would be necessary to improve the *maqasid* methodology by adding cycles of reflection in order to adapt it to research in Islāmic psychotherapy. In the context of research in Islāmic psychotherapy, "All sciences are based on frameworks of concepts, objectives, values, commands, universal laws, groups and proofs, and thinking that any of these elements 'has nothing to do with faith' is not sanctioned by Revelation" (Auda, 2021a, pp. 128–129).

However, Islāmic psychotherapists are assigned with the responsibility of aligning psychology with the Islāmic or Qur'ānic worldview, utilising a composite framework that involves cycles of reflection on divine revelation. This methodology offers a comprehensive approach to comprehending and applying Islāmic sources of knowledge within an interdisciplinary context. However, a significant obstacle faced by Islāmic psychology is the integration of Islāmic ethics and studies with the principles and theories of secular psychology. The current challenge lies in the absence of a shared methodology or conceptual framework that can effectively integrate Islāmic epistemologies, ontologies, and secular knowledge sources. The *maqasid* methodology aims to address this gap and provide a solution. Above all, the researchers in Islāmic psychology and psychotherapy needs to develop familiarity with the *maqasid* methodology and identify those dimensions that relate most closely to purpose of the research.

Researching Islāmic psychotherapy presents both challenges and opportunities. Researchers must exhibit cultural competence by respecting Islāmic principles and collaborating with scholars for suitable interventions. Overcoming language barriers, especially in translating ancient texts, necessitates joint efforts between scholars and mental health researchers. The building of research capacity and establishing dedicated centres become a necessity. Overcoming these challenges can lead to meaningful advancements in Islāmic psychotherapy research and better mental health support within Islāmic communities.

References

Abu Dâwud. *Sunan Abi Dâwud Dawud 2201*. In-book reference: Book 13, Hādīth 27. English translation: Book 12, Hādīth 2195. Sahih (Al-Albani). https://sunnah.com/abudawud:2201

Abu Sulayman, A. H. (2011). *The Qur'ānic worldview: A springboard for cultural reform*. International Institute of Islāmic Thought (IIIT).

Auda, J. (2021a). *Re-envisioning Islāmic Scholarship: Maqasid Methodology as a New Approach*. Claritas Publishing House.

Auda, J. (2021b). The Maqasid methodology: A guide for the researcher in the research network. *Journal of Contemporary Maqasid Studies*, *1*(1), 1–30. https://doi.org/10.52100/jcms.v1i1.5

Bucaille, M. (2000). *The Bible, The Qur'ân and science the holy scriptures examined in the light of modern knowledge*. CreateSpace Independent Publishing Platform.

Cohen, L., Manion, L., & Morrison, K. (2017). *Research methods in education* (8th ed.). Routledge.

Creswell, J., & Plano Clark, V. (2007). *Designing and conducting mixed methods research*. Sage.

Dar al-Ifta Al-Missriyyah (2022). *The research methodology in traditional Islāmic scholarship*. Retrieved June 3, 2024, from https://www.dar-alifta.org/foreign/ViewArticle.aspx?ID=113

Foundation for Science, Technology and Civilisation. (2006) *Islāmic science, the scholar and ethics*. Retrieved December 19, 2023, from https://muslimheritage.com/Islamic-sciencescholar-ethics/

Guba, E. G., & Lincoln, Y. S. (1994). Competing paradigms in qualitative research. In N. K. Denzin, & Y. S. Lincoln (Eds.), *Handbook of qualitative research* (pp. 105–117). Sage.

Heron, J., & Reason, P. (1997). A participatory inquiry paradigm. *Qualitative Inquiry*, *3*(3), 274–294. https://doi.org/10.1177/107780049700300302

Ibn Kathir. (2000). *Tafsir Ibn Kathir* (J. Abualrub, N. Khitab, H. Khitab, A. Walker, M. Al-Jibali, & S. Ayoub, Trans.). Darussalam Publishers and Distributors.

Malkawi, F. H. (2014). *Epistemological integration: Essentials of an Islāmic methodology*. The International Institute of Islāmic Thought.

Najimudeen, M. R. (2022). Re-envisioning Islāmic scholarship: Maqasid methodology as a new approach. *ICR Journal*, *13*(1), 168–171. https://doi.org/10.52282/icr.v13i1.906

Rassool, G. Hussein (2023a). *Integrated research methodologies in Islāmic psychology*. Focus Series on Islāmic Psychology and Psychotherapy. Routledge.

Rassool, G. Hussein (2023b). Research methodology in Islāmic psychology. In G. Hussein Rassool (Ed.), *Islāmic psychology: The basics* (pp. 174–199). Routledge.

Saunders, M., Lewis, P., & Thornhill, A. (2015). *Research methods for business students* (7th ed.). Pearson.

Shaikh, A. (2023). Relevance of research methodologies used in health psychology for British Muslims: An epistemological critique on the colonisation of knowledge production. In S. Dogra (Ed.), *British Muslims, ethnicity and health inequalities*. Edinburgh University Press.

Utz, A. (2011). *Psychology from an Islāmic perspective*. International Islāmic Publishing House.

Wilson, S. (2001). What is an indigenous research methodology? *Canadian Journal of Native Education*, *25*(2), 175–179.

Zarabozo, J. M. (2008). *Commentary on the forty Ḥādīth of al-Nawawi*. Al-Basheer Company for Publication and Translation.

22
ISLĀMIC PSYCHOTHERAPY
Tackling challenges, employing strategies, cultivating competence

Introduction

The formalisation of Islāmic psychotherapy as a distinct field, addressing mental health concerns within Islāmic principles, has seen significant growth in interest and exploration during the late 20th and early 21st centuries. This has led to the emergence of specialised therapeutic approaches and institutions dedicated to promoting Islāmic therapeutic practices for mental health. Nevertheless, the field of Islāmic psychotherapy continues to face various challenges, and it is imperative to address these obstacles for the ongoing growth and widespread acceptance of this discipline and its therapeutic approach.

These hurdles encompass the integration of Islāmic psychotherapy with Western models, the establishment of a robust evidence base through research, the standardisation of practices and ethical guidelines, the necessity for cultural competence to address diverse perspectives within the Muslim population, the development of comprehensive education and training programmes, combating societal stigma surrounding mental health, the absence of clinical supervision, and fostering collaboration among Islāmic psychologists and psychotherapists with mainstream mental health professionals. Overcoming these challenges requires concerted efforts from practitioners, researchers, educators, and policymakers and will contribute to the further development and acceptance of Islāmic psychotherapy within the broader context of mental health services. This chapter aims to explore the challenges faced in the field of Islāmic psychotherapy and counselling and propose strategies to overcome these challenges.

Challenges

One key challenge is the limited research in the field, which impedes the establishment of evidence-based practices and limits its recognition within the broader mental health community. The lack of empirical support makes it challenging for practitioners to validate the effectiveness of Islāmic-oriented interventions, delaying integration into mainstream mental health practices. Concerns regarding the feasibility of international cooperation in the field of Islāmic psychology research arise from potential issues such as blind imitation, partialism, apologism, contradiction, epistemological biases, and deconstructionism within contemporary Islāmic psychology scholarship (Rassool, 2023b). These factors may pose challenges and obstacles that impede effective collaboration and knowledge exchange among clinicians, academics, and researchers.

The shortage of skilled Islāmic psychotherapists and counsellors, particularly in integrating Islāmic principles with psychotherapy, is a significant challenge due to limited specialised training and educational resources. A crucial aspect of this shortage is the lack of formal academic programmes or training courses specifically addressing the intersection of Islāmic principles and psychotherapeutic practice. Conventional psychotherapy training often overlooks diverse cultural and religious perspectives, including those rooted in Islām. Consequently, professionals aiming to incorporate Islāmic principles into their practice may struggle to acquire the necessary knowledge and skills.

To illustrate, imagine a scenario where a Muslim individual seeks therapy and wishes to integrate their Islāmic beliefs and values into the process. Without access to therapists with specialised training in Islāmic psychotherapy, Muslim clients may face difficulties finding a practitioner who can effectively address their holistic needs. This lack of specialised training can lead to a disconnect or misunderstanding between the therapist and the client, potentially compromising the therapeutic effectiveness and the client's overall psychological and psychospiritual health.

The integration of secular psychotherapy with Islāmic principles is complicated because it involves balancing different ways of thinking while still following Islāmic ethics. This balance needs careful planning and execution. Most of the chapters in this book specifically evaluate how different therapy methods are congruent with Islāmic beliefs and practices. However, combining these techniques with Islāmic principles can create ethical challenges that therapists need to navigate carefully. Therapists must make sure that the therapy follows the ethical rules of both regular psychotherapy and Islāmic teachings. This includes keeping things private, respecting the person's choices, and following the principles of doing no harm and acting in the client's best interest. Ethical issues may come up when regular therapy methods clash with Islāmic principles. Therefore, therapists need to make careful decisions to keep things ethical.

Islāmic psychotherapists, similar to their mainstream counterparts, are expected to work independently with the necessary professional skills to provide effective psychotherapy and counselling. They are accountable to their clients and their profession, adhering to ethical standards and guidelines. This requires delivering high-quality care, ensuring client confidentiality, and continuously improving their skills and knowledge through ongoing professional development. Their competence and accountability are important for offering therapy and counselling services that meet client needs while upholding professional ethical standards.

However, the lack of clinical supervision poses a challenge to the development of clinical competence in Islāmic psychotherapy. Clinical supervision plays a vital role in providing a structured space where therapists can reflect on their practice, receive feedback, and enhance their skills. In the context of Islāmic psychotherapy, supervision becomes even more critical as therapists steer through the process of integrating religious principles into their therapeutic approaches. Additionally, therapists may encounter ethical dilemmas specific to the intersection of mental health and Islāmic principles. Clinical supervision serves as a platform for discussing these dilemmas, obtaining ethical guidance, and deepening understanding of how to address complex issues within the framework of both psychological and religious perspectives.

While professional associations in Islāmic psychology are vital for fostering a sense of community among practitioners and promoting the field, their role in initiating and developing a research culture has been somewhat limited or hesitant. Instead of prioritising research activities, these associations have often directed their focus towards limited publications and networking among a selective group who shared the same school of thought. Additionally, there has been a trend for some Islāmic psychology associations to prioritise promoting its leadership accomplishments and presentations instead of actively encouraging and facilitating research initiatives within the field. These may overshadow the collective effort needed to advance the field through research and scholarship. This limited emphasis on research within professional associations can impact the overall growth and advancement of Islāmic psychology as an acceptable and valid discipline. When associations primarily concentrate on their own publications and exclusive networking, the potential for collaborative research efforts, knowledge exchange, and the development of a robust research culture may be hindered.

The diverse nature of the Muslim community, comprising individuals from various cultural, ethnic, and linguistic backgrounds with differing interpretations and practices of Islām, poses challenges for Islāmic psychotherapists. The problems are how to understand and address the complexities arising from different cultural backgrounds. Without this understanding, therapists risk unintentionally imposing assumptions or biases, leading to potential miscommunication. The challenge extends to tailoring therapy approaches to meet the unique needs of individual clients, considering factors such as level of religiosity, cultural practices, worldview, and expectations.

Strategies and solutions

Several strategies can be employed to overcome the challenges in the evolution and development of Islāmic psychotherapy.

Strategies for addressing the research gap in Islāmic psychotherapy involve various approaches. One key strategy is to invest in research infrastructure, including establishing dedicated research centres. Providing scholarships for students and researchers in Islāmic psychotherapy, supporting research-oriented programmes like the *maqasid* methodology, and funding projects focusing on clinical interventions contribute to building a strong foundation for empirical studies and evidence-based practices. Promoting a research culture within the Islāmic psychotherapy community is crucial. This involves encouraging clinicians, academics, and researchers from different schools of thought in Islāmic psychotherapy to engage in collaborative research activities. Fostering collaborations between academia and clinicians and creating an environment that supports research and knowledge exchange are essential steps.

To further elevate the status of Islāmic psychotherapy and psychology, it is important for professional associations to shift towards more proactive roles in supporting and promoting research initiatives. This may involve actively encouraging and facilitating research collaborations, providing resources for research projects, and fostering an environment that values and promotes rigorous scientific inquiry within the field. By doing so, professional associations can contribute significantly to the advancement and recognition of Islāmic psychotherapy as a legitimate and effective domain within the broader mental health community. International collaboration with professionals and researchers from different countries, each bringing diverse clinical and academic experiences, can provide a broader perspective and a more comprehensive understanding of the effectiveness of Islāmic psychotherapy across various populations. Sharing insights, data, and research findings through such collaborations strengthens the research foundation of Islāmic psychotherapy and contributes to its global acceptance.

Advocacy efforts aimed at raising awareness about the importance of research in Islāmic psychotherapy are also crucial. Educational initiatives can empower practitioners to actively contribute to the research agenda, fostering a sense of responsibility and commitment to advancing the field through rigorous scientific inquiry. By emphasising the significance of research, these initiatives can potentially inspire a more robust and research-focused culture within the realm of Islāmic psychotherapy.

Integrating secular psychotherapy with Islāmic principles is a meticulous process that demands a thoughtful evaluation of various therapeutic approaches. This involves analysing each approach and assessing its alignment with fundamental Islāmic principles and values. To achieve successful integration, therapists need to possess a profound understanding of Islāmic principles, including teachings from the Qur'ân and *hādīths*, while critically evaluating secular therapeutic methods. The examination and assessment process involves several key considerations.

Firstly, therapists must evaluate the conceptual frameworks of various therapeutic approaches and assess their alignment with Islāmic principles. This involves analysing the underlying theories and principles on which these approaches are built. By considering the foundational beliefs of Islām, therapists can determine if a particular therapeutic approach is in harmony with Islāmic values and principles. Secondly, therapists need to examine the methodologies used in different therapeutic approaches. This includes critically examining the techniques and strategies employed in each approach and assessing their compatibility with Islāmic teachings. It is important to ensure that these methodologies do not contradict or compromise Islāmic values and ethics. For example, Islāmic principles emphasise the importance of preserving the dignity and privacy of individuals, so therapists must ensure that the chosen methodologies respect these principles.

Thirdly, therapists should explore the underlying assumptions of secular therapeutic approaches. By examining the theoretical assumptions and beliefs that form the basis of these approaches, therapists can assess their alignment with Islāmic principles. This requires an understanding of both Islāmic teachings and the principles that underlie secular psychotherapy. Through a critical analysis of these foundational assumptions, therapists can determine if a particular approach complements Islāmic values. Lastly, therapists need to cultivate a comprehensive understanding of Islāmic principles by studying Qur'ânic teachings and *hādīths*. This involves gaining insights into concepts such as mental health, coping mechanisms, interpersonal relationships, and personal development as discussed within Islāmic teachings.

Deepening their knowledge of Islām enables therapists to navigate the integration process more effectively and make well-informed decisions in aligning therapy with Islāmic principles. For instance, CBT is commonly used in secular psychotherapy. To integrate CBT with Islāmic principles, clinicians should evaluate how the approach aligns with notions of the nature of man, its philosophical orientation, and its methodology. They may adapt CBT techniques and interventions to incorporate Islāmic values, such as cognitive reframing, using the cognitive restructuring model (Hamdan, 2008), from an Islāmic perspective, and employing spiritually modified CBT (Cucchi, 2022; Hodge & Nadir, 2008; Husain & Hodge, 2016).

Integrating secular therapeutic techniques with Islāmic principles can give rise to ethical dilemmas when conflicts emerge. A comprehensive understanding of both secular therapeutic approaches and Islāmic principles is crucial for identifying and addressing potential conflicts. Therapists must prioritise open communication, respecting client autonomy, and obtaining informed consent to uphold ethical standards. To mitigate dilemmas (see Chapter 5), collaboration with religious scholars is valuable, enabling the modification of therapeutic techniques in alignment with Islāmic values while adhering to professional guidelines. Continuous self-reflection and critical analysis of practice are essential for therapists to navigate these challenges effectively, ensuring the well-being and autonomy of clients while maintaining fidelity to Islāmic principles.

Addressing cultural competence in Islāmic psychotherapy requires clinicians to actively participate in ongoing education and training, aiming to enhance their knowledge and skills in cultural competence. This can involve attending workshops, seminars, and conferences that specifically focus on cultural diversity within the Muslim community, offering insights into the intersection of culture and psychology. Cultural competence is often developed through education, formal training, and clinical supervision, which makes it vital that "these training opportunities accurately reflect the proposed competencies that are being taught." (Constantine & Ladany, 2001, p. 494).

Research findings have indicated the effectiveness of training and workshops in developing culturally specific knowledge and cultural intervention skills (Majda et al., 2021). Authors recommend the necessity of designing and arranging cultural education initiatives with the goal of enhancing the formation of culturally sensitive attitudes. Through these educational opportunities, practitioners can deepen their understanding of the diverse cultural expressions, interpretations of Islām, and the cultural factors influencing mental health within the Muslim community.

Clinicians must also engage in self-reflection to become aware of their own biases, assumptions, and stereotypes. Reflective practices enable them to critically examine their cultural backgrounds and beliefs, challenging and expanding their understanding of diverse cultural perspectives. Approaching therapeutic interactions with an open mind is essential, acknowledging that clinicians' cultural background may influence their perceptions and interpretations of clients' experiences. While it may be unrealistic for clinicians to fully "master" the cultural diversity of Muslim communities, given the wide range of backgrounds and practices within these communities, they can focus on learning about the specific Muslim community they work with on a local basis. This local-level cultural knowledge allows clinicians to provide more effective, culturally sensitive care that respects the unique needs and perspectives of the Muslim clients they serve.

Seeking consultation and collaboration with experts who have expertise in specific cultural contexts or populations within the Muslim community is beneficial for enhancing cultural competence. Engaging in community dialogues is essential for practitioners to gain a deeper understanding of the cultural dynamics and specific needs within the Muslim community. Seeking supervision and consultation from experienced professionals who possess expertise in both Islāmic principles and psychotherapy is invaluable. Regular supervision allows practitioners to receive guidance and feedback on cultural considerations, ensuring that therapy remains culturally competent and aligned with Islāmic values. There is evidence that certain training variables (for example, completing academic coursework, attending workshops, receiving multicultural supervision) are significantly related to counsellors' perceived competence in working with diverse populations (Olfert, 2006; Pope-Davis et al., 1995; Sodowsky et al., 1998).

Clinical supervision plays a crucial role in providing a space for practitioners to explore and discuss challenges or dilemmas that may arise in their therapeutic work with Muslim clients, ultimately enhancing their efficacy and effectiveness in clinical practice. The lack of formal clinical supervision for practicing Islāmic psychotherapists and students is delaying the development of clinical competence. To address this challenge, it is essential to establish formal structures for clinical supervision within the field of Islāmic psychotherapy. This involves creating supervision programmes, mentorship initiatives, and collaborative platforms where experienced practitioners can guide and support those newer to the field.

Integrating supervision into training programmes and professional development opportunities ensures that therapists have the necessary support to navigate the complexities of applying Islāmic principles in their practice. By acknowledging the importance of clinical supervision, the field can better cultivate competent and ethically sound practitioners, ultimately enhancing the quality of care provided in the domain of Islāmic psychotherapy. This formalised support structure is critical for the ongoing development and proficiency of therapists working within the context of Islāmic principles.

Investing in specialised training programmes and educational resources focusing on Islāmic psychotherapy can help develop a skilled workforce capable of addressing the unique needs of Muslim clients. This involves providing therapists with a comprehensive understanding of Islāmic principles, teachings, and values, enabling them to integrate these into their therapeutic approaches. To overcome the challenge of a shortage of skilled Islāmic psychotherapists and counsellors, a multifaceted approach is proposed (Rassool, 2023a).

Firstly, collaboration between institutions and professional organisations is essential for the development of specialised training programmes. These programmes should cover both psychological theories and Islāmic values, offering practitioners a broad understanding of the intersection between mental health and religious principles. Secondly, the use of online resources, webinars, and workshops can bridge geographical gaps, ensuring accessibility for practitioners in regions where specialized programs are limited. This virtual approach enhances knowledge dissemination, particularly benefiting individuals facing logistical challenges in pursuing traditional training, as observed in limited instances in Australia, Indonesia, the United Kingdom, and the United States, Additionally, strategies involve incorporating cultural competence modules into existing Islāmic psychotherapy and counselling training programmes, focusing on the understanding of culturally and linguistically diverse communities.

Finally, but not exhaustively, Islāmic psychotherapists and counsellors have a responsibility to engage in social justice and advocacy. This involves both case advocacy, where therapists empower individuals and families to advocate for their own needs, and cause advocacy, where therapists advocate on behalf of individuals and communities for more just and equitable positions within society. In the context of Islāmic psychotherapy and counselling, case advocacy involves empowering clients to take action on their own behalf (Lee et al., 2013). This may include assisting them in accessing resources, building their skills and self-advocacy abilities, and supporting them in addressing personal challenges. Islāmic psychotherapists and counsellors aim to enable clients to navigate their sociocultural environments effectively, promoting their well-being and empowerment.

On the other hand, cause advocacy requires Islāmic psychotherapists and counsellors to advocate for social justice on behalf of their clients and communities (Crethar & Winterowd, 2012; McNutt, 2011). They stand with marginalised Muslims, working to challenge systemic barriers, inequalities, and injustices. This may involve raising awareness, engaging in community organizing, and lobbying for policy changes to create a more equitable society. This advocacy work aligns with the principles of justice and equity inherent in Islāmic teachings.

Conclusion: the way forward

Islāmic psychotherapy and counselling should be perceived from a comprehensive standpoint, encompassing health information, therapy, advice, guidance, advocacy, and spiritual interventions. It extends beyond conventional therapeutic approaches by integrating spiritual and cultural dimensions, providing clients with a holistic support system. Islāmic psychotherapists and counsellors address psychological, spiritual, and systemic factors, offering a holistic approach to promoting well-being and facilitating healing.

In the arena of psychotherapy and counselling, Inayat (2007) highlights four key aspects affected: the therapeutic alliance, the sociopolitical context in which therapy occurs, the awareness of personal characteristics and competencies facilitating multicultural psychotherapy and counselling, and the training requirements of multicultural therapists and counsellors. These aspects underline the importance of establishing a strong therapeutic relationship, recognising the impact of sociopolitical factors, developing self-awareness of biases, and obtaining appropriate training to effectively work with diverse populations. Addressing these challenges faced by Islāmic psychotherapists and counsellors involves the development of education and training programmes in Islāmically informed psychotherapy and counselling. Collaborative efforts between the academic and clinical communities are necessary to equip scholars and clinicians with the knowledge and skills needed to provide culturally sensitive care.

Furthermore, integrating Islāmic principles and practices into therapy is crucial. By incorporating Islāmic spirituality, values, and ethics, therapists can establish a stronger rapport with Muslim clients and tailor treatment approaches to meet their specific needs. Ongoing dialogue, research, and a steadfast commitment to cultural competence are essential in effectively supporting the well-being of Muslim individuals within a multicultural context. Tackling challenges, employing strategic initiatives, and cultivating competence in Islāmic psychotherapy represent a dynamic journey for all involved. This is the challenge!

References

Constantine, M. G., & Ladany, N. (2001). New vision for defining and assessing multicultural counseling competence. In J. G. Ponterotto, J. M. Casas, L. A. Suzuki., & C. M. Alexander (Eds.), *Handbook of multicultural counseling* (pp. 482–498). Sage Publications.

Crethar, H. C., & Winterowd, C. L. (2012). Values and social justice in counseling. *Counseling and Values, 57*(1), 3–9.

Cucchi, A. (2022). Integrating cognitive behavioural and Islāmic principles in psychology and psychotherapy: A narrative review. *Journal of Religion and Health, 61*(6), 4849–4870. https://doi.org/10.1007/s10943-022-01576-8

Hamdan, A. 92008). Cognitive restructuring: An Islāmic perspective. *Journal of Muslim Mental Health, 3*(1), 99–116.

Hodge, D. R., & Nadir, A. (2008). Moving toward culturally competent practice with Muslims: Modifying cognitive therapy with Islāmic tenets. *Social Work, 53*(1), 31–41. https://doi.org/10.1093/sw/53.1.31

Husain, A., & Hodge, D. R. (2016). Islāmically modified cognitive behavioral therapy: Enhancing outcomes by increasing the cultural congruence of cognitive behavioral therapy self-statements. *International Social Work, 59*(3), 393–405. https://doi.org/10.1177/0020872816629193

Inayat, Q. (2007). Islāmophobia and the therapeutic dialogue: Some reflections. *Psychotherapy and Counselling Psychology Quarterly, 20*(3), 287–293. https://doi.org/10.1080/09515070701567804

Lee, M. A., Smith, T. J., & Henry, R. G. (2013). Power politics: Advocacy to activism in social justice counseling. *Journal for Social Action in Counseling and Psychology, 5*(3), 70–94.

Majda, A., Zalewska-Puchała, J., Bodys-Cupak, I., Kurowska, A., & Barzykowski, K. (2021). Evaluating the effectiveness of cultural education training: Cultural competence and cultural intelligence development among nursing students. *International Journal of Environmental Research and Public Health, 18*(8), 4002. https://doi.org/10.3390/ijerph18084002

McNutt, J. (2011). Is social work advocacy worth the cost? Issues and barriers to an economic analysis of social work political practice. *Research on Social Work Practice, 21*(4), 397–403.

Olfert, P. K. (2006). *A critique of multicultural psychotherapy and counselling competencies and implications for counsellor education* [MA project, Campus Alberta Applied Psychology Psychotherapy and Counselling Initiative, Calgary University]. Retrieved December 20, 2023, from http://dtpr.lib.athabascau.ca/action/download.php?filename=caap/pamelaknelsenolfertProject.pdf

Pope-Davis, D. B., Reynolds, A. L., Dings, J. G., & Nielson, D. (1995). Examining multicultural counseling competencies of graduate students in psychology. *Professional Psychology: Research and Practice, 26*(3), 322–329. https://doi.org/10.1037/0735-7028.26.3.322

Rassool, G. Hussein (2023a). *Advancing Islāmic psychology education. Knowledge integration, model and application.* Focus Series on Islāmic Psychology and Psychotherapy. Routledge.

Rassool, G. Hussein (2023b). Critical reflections on current status of scholarship in Islāmic psychology: Challenges and solutions. *Australian Journal of Islāmic Studies, 8*(3), 37–54.

Sodowsky, G. R., Kuo-Jackson, P. Y., Richardson, M. F., & Corey, A. T. (1998). Correlates of self-reported multicultural competencies: Counselor multicultural social desirability, race, social inadequacy, locus of control racial ideology, and multicultural training. *Journal of Counseling Psychology, 45*, 256–264. https://doi.org/10.10370022-0167.45.3.256

INDEX

ablution 55, 258, 326, 328
abstinence 306, 310, 319, 326, 329, 331, 332
abuse 125, 216, 217, 313, 319, 323, 324
academic 20, 22, 23, 45, 53, 82, 127, 146, 198, 204, 214, 258, 342, 344, 360, 362, 364, 366
accountability 6, 11, 53, 54, 60, 61, 73, 86, 88, 119, 139, 159, 160, 162, 219, 290, 297, 299, 311, 331, 341, 361
acculturation 37, 223
action-oriented 128
activation 50, 128, 143, 144
actualisation 122
actualising 114, 121
acupuncture 264, 265, 267–269, 281, 283, 284, 320
adaptations 123, 143, 148, 159, 218, 220
addicted 319, 320, 322
addictions 150, 317
adolescents 222, 231, 324
adoption 17, 136, 316
advocacy 44, 46, 165, 362, 365–367
affiliation 59, 84, 216
agency 130, 162, 172, 177, 179, 186–190, 324
agenda-setting 303
aggression 99, 143
ailments 31, 32, 264, 271, 272
akhirah 12, 178
akhlāq 11

al-Albani 49, 63, 167, 231, 245, 281, 282, 304, 357
Al-Attas 11, 54, 63, 179, 183
al-azm 289
Al-Balkhi 24, 25, 141
al-Bukhârî 18, 63, 90, 108, 197, 229, 261, 303, 322
alchemy 108
alcohol 35, 68, 141, 264, 267, 268, 273–275, 282, 283, 285, 305–310, 317, 320–327, 329, 331, 333, 335
alcoholic 275, 305, 306
alcoholism 146, 323, 334
Al-Fatihah 276
Al-Ghazālī 13, 14, 18, 130, 132, 133, 142, 145, 239
Al-Haytham 136
Al-Hujurāt 59
alienation 21, 217
Al-Ikhlas 83
al-Inshirah 243, 245
Al-Jawzi 130, 145
al-Jawziyyah 14, 18, 24, 25, 31, 34, 142, 147, 198, 239, 256, 257, 262, 290, 303
Al-Junūn 90
al-lawwāma 12
Al-Mā'idah 3, 4, 58, 202, 307
Al-Missriyyah 338, 357
al-munkar 47
al-muṭma'innah 88
al-Qayyim 14, 18, 31, 53, 131, 132, 141, 142, 147, 239, 260, 263

Al-Talaq 193
Al-Thani 39, 49, 117, 118, 122–125
altruism 29
ambivalence 291, 292, 310, 312–314, 316, 324
amphetamine 185
amplification 101, 102, 249
amygdala 262
analgesic 282
anesthetic 157
angels 11, 13, 132, 178, 236, 253
anger-control 144
Ankabūt 299
an-nafs 10, 22, 61, 104, 119, 131, 237, 300
An-Nasā'i 278, 282
An-Nawawi 34, 199, 285
An-Nisā 122, 137, 227, 228, 295, 306
An-Nur 259
anthropology 17, 103, 106
anti-inflammatory 271, 272, 282
antimicrobial 271
antioxidant 271, 272
anxiety 6, 21, 25, 31, 38, 40–42, 48, 78, 81, 128–130, 143, 144, 146–149, 152, 157, 169, 173, 175, 176, 185, 196, 236, 240–242, 244, 265, 276, 284, 302, 303, 321, 345
apologism 360
archetypal 97, 98, 106, 107, 250
aromatherapy 268, 269, 281, 282, 284
Ar-Rūm 86, 209, 229
Ash-Shūraá 228, 298
Atheism 83
Attachment 15, 26, 82, 87, 88, 173, 184, 215, 217, 229, 230
Aṭ-Talāq 159
At-Tawbah 8, 122, 123, 137, 140, 180
at-Tirmidhî 34, 285
authenticity 100, 112, 113, 256
authoritative 37, 53, 249
autism 183
autonomy 41, 52, 58, 60, 61, 65–68, 78, 99, 108, 110–112, 114, 117, 119, 122, 136, 139, 142, 152, 179, 180, 201, 202, 204, 226, 289, 314, 316, 343, 363
awakening 20, 288–291, 321, 325, 326, 331, 332
axiological 338
axiology 4, 7, 10, 337
ayurveda 264
Az-Zumar 122, 164, 193, 280

Badri 83, 84, 88, 90, 117, 119, 120, 125, 129, 131, 141, 142, 146, 182–184, 293, 303
Basirah 288, 295, 325, 328, 332
Bedouins 266
beggars 11
behavioural 17, 25, 26, 40, 49, 50, 78, 109, 128, 129, 133–136, 139, 143–146, 151, 152, 155, 189, 204, 216, 218, 240, 250, 280, 288, 289, 291–293, 300, 302, 309, 310, 314, 315, 320, 325, 327, 328, 331–333, 367
behaviourism 110
behaviours 4, 11, 15, 17, 21, 28, 30, 40, 52, 60 68, 78, 86, 89, 93, 100, 104, 105, 111, 113, 117, 119, 120, 128, 130, 131, 133–136, 138, 139, 141, 143, 151, 155, 162, 172, 175, 181, 182, 203, 217, 219, 224, 248, 250, 292, 296, 297, 300, 302, 305, 306, 308–316, 319, 320, 322, 324, 325, 330, 332, 334, 338
belief 4, 6, 7, 9, 11–13, 15–17, 30–32, 45, 53, 57, 59, 82, 83, 89, 90, 94, 97, 106, 133, 137, 142, 146, 154, 161–163, 178–180, 186, 190–192, 194, 197, 236, 240, 249, 252, 269, 277–279, 287, 293, 296, 314, 316, 318, 329, 332, 334, 337
beneficence 52, 60, 61, 66
benevolence 190, 191
bereavement 144, 146
bibliometric 263
bibliotherapy 320
bioethics 52, 53, 63, 64
biofeedback 320, 324
biological 17, 29, 52, 78, 99, 293
bio-psychosocial 29, 293
bipolar 143
blood-letting 283
borderline 130, 310
boundaries 58, 61, 66, 67, 69–71, 113, 142, 220, 224–226, 231, 264, 290, 305
breasts 299, 300
brotherhood 140, 196
Buddhism 90, 92, 249, 316
Bukhârî 7, 15, 18, 56, 63, 87, 90, 96, 108, 121, 125, 194, 197, 228, 229, 251, 252, 254, 261, 289, 303, 309, 322
bulimia 144
burdens 196, 203, 237, 238

Caliphate 53, 317
cancer 198, 278, 284
cannabis 307, 312

care 4, 27, 34, 37, 44, 46, 49, 50, 52–54, 56–59, 61, 65–68, 72, 73, 90, 91, 119, 126, 223, 236, 242, 258, 264–267, 273, 281, 303, 321, 322, 324, 361, 364–366
caregivers 315
caring 64, 126, 127, 139, 148, 173, 294
catalysts 117, 333
categories 60, 209, 235, 257, 259, 354
Catholic 208
cauterisation 270
cave 95–97
celestial 269
cellular 247
censors 248
centred 65, 103, 134
cessation 319
characteristics 17, 96, 111, 115, 119, 120, 142, 207, 256, 319, 339, 354, 366
charity 11, 55, 59, 166, 301, 309, 320, 328, 331
chastity 88
chemical 284, 308
childbirth 276, 284
childcare 201
childhood 77–79, 82, 87, 88, 112, 133, 173, 219, 249
child-rearing 203, 210, 224
chiropractic 264
Christianity 7, 87, 94, 251
church-based 206
church-oriented 206
civilisation 338, 341, 357
classification 14, 15, 25, 257
client–counsellor 152
client–family 73
client-focused 40
clinical 22, 27, 34, 43, 44, 49, 50, 63, 70, 72, 74, 82, 90–92, 102, 103, 126, 127, 144, 146, 147, 149, 152, 163, 185, 198, 213, 230, 265, 275, 283–286, 303, 323–326, 359, 361, 362, 364–366
clinicians 38, 49, 141, 218, 266, 278, 282, 303, 325, 360, 362–364, 366
coaching 207, 324
cocaine 307
cognitive–behavioural 29, 35, 82, 128, 129, 134, 136, 145, 189, 196, 215, 217, 310, 315, 330
co-habiting 207
collaborations 362
collateral 180
collectivism 29, 140

communal 47, 60, 82, 121, 204
communities 16, 20, 21, 32, 39, 46, 56, 57, 60, 62, 63, 68, 84, 93, 120, 148, 173, 200, 201, 203, 204, 209, 213, 214, 216, 223, 224, 226, 229, 255, 305, 309, 321–323, 334, 337, 345, 355, 357, 364–366
community-based 326, 343, 345
compassionate 100, 119, 151, 236, 238, 320, 333, 341
competence 16, 17, 43, 44, 46, 50, 51, 54, 64–67, 73, 127, 139, 144, 153, 159, 173, 181, 267, 321, 333, 348, 357, 359, 361, 364–367
complementary 9, 21, 83, 137, 180, 264–268, 277, 281–285, 310, 311, 340
compliance 204, 205, 221, 292
conceptualisation 135, 139, 290, 353
condoms 318
confession 82
confidentiality 27, 44, 46, 58, 60, 61, 65–67, 70, 72, 74, 79, 104, 225, 226, 290, 321, 333, 343, 361
conflict 21, 66–70, 83, 84, 89, 117, 132, 136, 137, 139, 164, 179, 205–207, 209–212, 215, 217, 218, 220, 221, 227, 249, 264, 276, 279, 312, 314, 316, 330, 340, 344
conflict-resolution 206
confrontation 314
congruence 77, 84, 89, 107, 110–113, 115, 119, 120, 123, 145, 147, 152, 159, 160, 171, 177, 178, 181, 182, 215, 220, 268, 339, 367
consciousness 13, 24, 25, 29, 32, 60, 96, 119, 236, 276
construct 135, 151, 173, 176, 181, 218, 315
constructivism 133, 136, 149, 150
consumption 68, 273, 274, 306, 309, 322
contemplation 25, 36, 37, 115, 124, 142, 145, 146, 166, 181–184, 197, 238, 240, 241, 244, 288–295, 297, 301, 303, 314, 325, 328, 331, 332, 343, 344
contingency 310
convergence 103, 132, 346
conversion 78, 88
coping 16, 36, 40, 41, 78, 82, 129, 134, 135, 143, 144, 149, 156, 157, 166, 171, 196–198, 201, 211, 236, 240, 241, 300, 301, 310, 311, 314, 315, 321, 329, 331, 345, 346, 363
coronary 198
cost-effectiveness 151, 169

counselling 20–24, 27, 28, 33, 34, 39, 48–52, 74, 77, 78, 80, 84, 89, 92, 112, 115, 117–120, 122, 124–127, 165, 168, 169, 179, 182–184, 205–214, 216, 221, 286, 292, 303–305, 309, 312, 314, 315, 320, 326, 332, 335, 344, 359, 361, 365–367
counsellors 27, 51, 124, 185, 207, 209, 288, 330, 360, 364–366
countertransference 79, 101, 102, 104
cravings 301, 310, 315
creation 5–7, 9, 13, 42, 85–87, 138, 140, 142, 147, 174, 209, 210, 237, 277, 293, 295, 296, 340, 354
cross-cultural 50, 108, 126, 149, 346
cultural 16–18, 20, 21, 23, 24, 26, 30, 32, 33, 35, 37–40, 44–47, 51, 52, 61, 63–65, 67, 68, 73, 78, 97, 99, 100, 102, 103, 106, 107, 111, 119, 120, 123, 124, 127, 129 139, 141, 144, 147, 148, 159, 164, 165, 169, 172–174, 178, 179, 181, 184, 200–203, 205, 210, 211, 213, 215, 218–220, 223, 224, 226, 227, 248, 250, 257, 260, 265, 289, 293, 305, 317, 321, 322, 324, 326, 327, 333, 334, 336, 337, 344–346, 357, 359–361, 364–367
culture-infused 165, 168
cupping 264–267, 269, 270, 281
curriculum 210
customs 57, 203
cyclical 188, 348

Dāwūd 53, 267, 269, 270, 280, 281, 331, 334
daydream 248, 263
death 14, 78, 96, 191, 249, 271, 274, 283, 318
decision-making 11, 32, 38, 51, 57, 60, 65, 66, 68–74, 88, 115, 117, 119, 139, 151, 162, 173, 201, 202, 212, 289, 291, 295, 296, 328, 329, 332
deconstructionism 360
decrees 31, 138, 271
de-escalation 217
definition 24, 27, 134, 171, 185, 307, 348, 350
demographics 235
denial 78, 83, 113, 224, 292, 309
dependence 32, 237, 296, 322, 323, 335
depression 21, 25, 38, 40, 48, 50, 67, 81, 91, 128, 143, 144, 146–149, 152, 157, 173, 185, 198, 217, 236, 245, 265, 276, 283, 284

depressive 81, 144, 145, 147, 169
desensitisation 141
detoxification 326, 335
deviance 87
deviant 15, 280
devils 255, 280
devotion 27, 56, 63, 104, 106, 236, 327
diabetes 292
diagnosis 32, 44, 45, 173, 265, 323
dialectical 13, 128, 130, 147, 309, 310, 322, 323
dietary 203, 268
dilemma 51, 65–74, 90
directive 35, 37–41, 122–124, 142, 145, 152, 189, 219, 302, 312
disaster 55
discipline 167, 182, 359, 361
diseases 18, 19, 32, 271, 273, 278, 323, 352
disorders 20, 21, 25, 31, 35, 50, 81, 92, 128, 134, 136, 139, 141, 143, 144, 146–149, 152, 169, 182, 185, 223, 235, 247, 263, 276, 283, 284, 310, 315, 317, 322–324
disorientation 15
disparities 20, 140, 202
dissemination 22, 365
divergence 46, 103, 105, 117, 171, 177, 179, 339, 346, 347
diversity 11, 16, 20, 39, 65, 68, 126, 203, 209, 210, 219, 289, 337, 345, 364
dream 29, 80, 101, 102, 104–107, 246–263
dreams-and-dream-interpretation 261, 262
drug 284, 309, 310, 312, 314, 315, 317, 318, 320–324, 333, 335
drug-free 312, 314, 318
du'ahs 141, 302
dualistic 10
dysfunctional 113, 133, 136, 141, 142, 144, 147, 216, 310, 311
dysphoria 146
dysthymic 144, 147

ecological 342
economic 57, 204, 367
education 22, 34, 43, 44, 46, 64, 73, 87, 100, 126, 135, 169, 184, 200, 203–205, 207–214, 230, 231, 262, 305, 317, 318, 322, 330, 337, 357–359, 364, 366, 367
effectiveness 41, 46, 49, 73, 81, 89–91, 102, 109, 117, 129, 143, 144, 150–152, 168, 169, 173, 183–185, 208, 213, 217, 220, 229, 267, 271, 275, 276, 281, 284, 292, 293, 299, 303, 310, 312, 315, 324,

332, 333, 343–347, 360, 362, 364, 365, 367
ego 78, 81, 85, 87, 88, 90, 93, 95, 98, 99
emotion-focused 230
emotions 13, 14, 20, 24–26, 32, 38, 39, 41, 44, 77–79, 93, 98, 101, 102, 111, 113–116, 128–131, 135, 138, 140, 141, 148, 162, 172, 173, 176, 188, 217–219, 237, 241, 244, 246–248, 258, 302, 311, 315
empathy 4, 23, 38, 47, 80, 99–101, 111–114, 117, 119, 123, 127, 173, 179, 189, 215, 217–220, 225, 239, 248, 261, 291, 309, 310, 313–316, 319, 320, 322
empiricism 9, 133, 136, 230, 339
empowerment 43, 45, 111, 114, 138, 159, 162, 207, 237, 296, 345, 366
endorphins 267
enjoins 59
environment 20, 38, 46, 54, 79, 87, 101, 111–113, 115–118, 135, 153, 215, 217, 219, 220, 225, 226, 240, 250, 268, 293, 305, 309, 311, 319, 322, 327, 333, 334, 355, 362
envision 151, 152, 154, 163, 295, 324
epidemiology 323
epistemological 8–10, 12, 18, 125, 133, 178, 337–339, 358, 360
epistemology 4, 7–9, 19, 133, 179, 337, 339
equality 11, 52, 59, 61, 140, 202, 204
equity 58, 59, 61–63, 201, 349, 366
ethical 4–6, 8–13, 15, 17, 18, 21, 22, 26, 28, 30, 33, 38, 44, 49, 51–54, 56–58, 60–74, 103, 104, 106, 117, 119, 122, 130, 136, 139, 162, 165, 196, 221, 222, 226, 227, 267, 290, 337, 338, 341–343, 349, 356, 359–361, 363
ethics 8, 11, 17, 20, 22, 43–45, 51–58, 60, 63–66, 68, 69, 71, 73, 74, 82, 87, 104, 159, 212, 221, 227, 290, 337, 341, 342, 357, 360, 363, 366
ethnic 16, 84, 89, 179, 183, 203, 361
ethnicity 32, 62, 216, 358
ethnocentric 21
ethno-cultural 223, 336, 337
ethnopharmacology 282
etiquette 50, 53, 56, 147
etymology 258, 260
eurocentric 21, 33, 179, 181, 337
evaluation 69, 72, 117, 134, 147, 154, 168, 169, 206, 213, 215, 289, 297, 299, 300, 331, 332, 362
evidence-based 17, 28, 32, 33, 35, 44, 129, 130, 133, 136, 145, 151, 169, 170, 195, 219, 236, 240, 281, 288, 309, 310, 312, 324, 344, 347, 360, 362
evolution 21, 23, 54, 92, 115, 125, 127, 130, 362
excellence 54, 59, 60, 204, 302
exegesis 6, 45, 83, 97, 191, 237, 242, 257, 297, 307, 352
existential 5, 6, 30, 45, 48, 82, 94, 110, 111, 125, 177, 182–184, 235, 236
existentialism 174, 177
experiential 49, 101, 110, 112, 130, 179, 217, 250
externalisation 172, 174, 175
extramarital 216
eye 34, 214, 224, 231, 247, 262, 273

fabric 204, 338
face-saving 166
facilitating 4, 10, 23, 32, 46, 79, 80, 95, 102, 107, 113–115, 118, 120, 128, 133, 152–154, 174, 181, 206, 212, 214, 219, 249, 290, 292, 299, 300, 303, 312, 313, 343, 345, 355, 361, 362, 366
facilitators 152, 322
faith 4–7, 11, 12, 17, 18, 20, 23, 24, 27, 28, 30, 31, 33, 34, 39, 41–44, 46, 48, 49, 54, 56, 61, 62, 65, 67, 72, 82, 84, 87, 90, 91, 97, 103, 106, 120–122, 130, 132, 137–142, 150, 160, 161, 165–167, 181, 186, 191, 194, 196, 197, 201, 203, 207, 209, 210, 218, 220, 226, 229, 236–241, 244, 252, 256, 261, 269, 293, 296, 297, 300, 307, 316, 318, 320, 329, 330, 333–335, 343, 345, 349, 357
faith-based 12, 21, 22, 27, 69, 245, 319
faith-centred 73
families 22, 56, 57, 78, 122, 140, 168–171, 173, 180, 200, 202–204, 209, 210, 213, 214, 217, 224, 225, 229, 305, 309, 321, 365
family-based 144, 145
fantasies 14
fasting 95, 122, 320, 326, 331
fatigue 143
fatwa 68, 74, 168, 274, 275, 277, 278, 281–285
feedback 111, 135, 154, 158, 206, 207, 361, 364
feelings 38, 78, 79, 94, 98, 112, 113, 115, 116, 124, 128, 132–134, 142, 157, 158, 161, 162, 186, 202–204, 211, 217, 236, 240–242, 250, 256, 293, 299, 312, 327, 332
fertility 203

fidelity 52, 60, 61, 207, 209, 363
financial 201–207, 210–212, 216, 227, 228, 317
fitrah 6–8, 10, 15, 17, 30, 34, 86, 87, 89, 121, 164, 289
fixation 78, 84, 86
forgiveness 11, 33, 42–44, 48, 54, 55, 61, 122, 124, 143, 163, 166, 190, 191, 194, 195, 197, 198, 207, 209, 211, 212, 220, 221, 236, 237, 239, 242, 255, 287, 288, 300–302, 316, 319, 326, 328–330, 334
forgiving 121, 122, 164, 193, 318
fornication 120
fortune-telling 276
frameworks 38, 40, 51, 84, 85, 89, 105, 107, 204, 286, 355, 356, 363
free-association 249
Freudian 29, 77, 81, 82, 84, 85, 88, 92, 93
Fungi 273
Fuşşilat 297
future-oriented 154, 163–165

gambling 305–309, 311–314, 322, 323
games 253, 308
gastrointestinal 271, 284
gender 58, 59, 67, 68, 200, 201, 204, 210, 212, 221, 268
genetic 63, 111
genocide 20
genuine 15, 47, 100, 101, 112, 113, 119, 120, 132, 248, 320, 339
geographical 270, 365
geometric 249
gestalt 37, 177, 217
Ghazâlî 12, 18
glands 277
globalisation 20, 204
goal-directed 154, 186, 187, 289, 315
God-consciousness 62, 200
gratification 78
gratitude 10, 25, 26, 38, 40, 43, 55, 125, 143, 166, 190, 197, 237, 238, 243, 244, 293, 319
gratitude-focused 238
grief 35, 47, 235, 236, 242, 248, 272, 346
grievances 191
group 18, 26, 35, 36, 50, 68, 92, 119, 125, 146, 148, 162, 169, 179, 183–185, 196, 205–207, 230, 262, 286, 305, 315, 320, 324, 341, 361
guidance-seeking 288, 325, 332
guidelines 33, 38, 46, 53, 60, 65, 69, 70, 72, 216, 221, 222, 230, 231, 267, 268, 359, 361, 363
gynaecologist 210

habitat 326
habits 26, 27, 78, 123, 300, 313
hādīths 8, 9, 42, 45, 190, 194–197, 235, 236, 238, 239, 242, 244, 246, 250–252, 260, 267, 269, 272, 274, 306, 308, 351, 362, 363
halāl 264–268, 275, 277, 279, 281, 284
hallucinations 149
harām 264–268, 270, 271, 274, 275, 277, 280, 281, 284, 285, 307
hardship 48, 55, 57, 137, 141, 161, 166, 192, 193, 238, 240, 243
harm 23, 47, 51, 52, 56, 57, 60, 61, 66, 67, 72, 137, 191, 192, 254, 266, 268, 274, 275, 280, 290, 305, 316–319, 321–324, 327, 329, 360
harm-reduction 305
harms 171, 184, 319
hashish 307, 308
headache 282
healer 53, 278
healing 4, 6, 10, 12, 18, 20, 23, 25, 30, 32, 33, 37, 39, 44, 49, 50, 53, 61, 89, 100, 101, 105, 107, 118, 126, 128, 129, 146, 148, 166, 168, 174, 182, 184, 186, 219–221, 233, 235, 237, 239, 244, 265–273, 277, 283, 287, 288, 290, 299, 309, 311, 326, 330, 333, 343, 366
health 7, 8, 10, 12, 16–18, 20–30, 33–35, 37, 39, 41, 44, 46, 49, 50, 53, 56–59, 61, 64, 65, 67, 68, 74, 81, 90–92, 108, 114, 125, 126, 128, 129, 133, 136, 139, 140, 144–150, 169, 171, 184, 188, 196, 198, 211, 213, 214, 216, 219, 221, 223, 229–231, 236, 239, 245, 263–267, 270–272, 275, 277, 279–286, 293, 303–306, 313, 317–320, 322, 324, 325, 327, 333, 336, 337, 343–346, 357–367
health-information 263
healthy 15, 26, 29, 36, 87, 89, 102, 111, 112, 124, 140, 142, 200, 202, 205, 208, 210–213, 218, 219, 221, 230, 237, 273, 326, 329
hearts 15, 18, 19, 31, 62, 120, 235, 241, 242, 245, 352, 354
heavens 62, 209, 299
help-seeking 288, 325, 332
hepatitis 305
herbs 270, 271, 283
heroin 337, 358
heterogeneity 345
hierarchy 114, 127, 163
high-risk 315
hijamah 264, 266, 267, 269, 270

historical 20, 23, 24, 26, 82, 84, 97, 107, 141, 146, 167, 179, 255, 256, 269, 316, 318, 347
holistic 4, 8–10, 12, 16–18, 21, 22, 25–28, 30, 32, 33, 35, 37, 39, 40, 49, 57, 58, 73, 85, 89, 90, 94, 101, 103, 105, 106, 111, 114, 118, 130, 133, 146, 159, 165, 196, 197, 210, 219, 221, 235, 244, 257–260, 264–267, 282, 287, 288, 292, 301, 311, 316, 319, 322, 326, 327, 330, 331, 333, 336, 337, 339–343, 346, 347, 356, 360, 366
homeopathic 273–275, 282, 285
homeostasis 263
homoeopathy 273
homosexuality 318
honey 269, 271, 272, 281, 284, 326
hope-based 189
hope-building 196
hope-enhancing 190
hopelessness 94, 192, 236
hormones 247
humanistic 29, 35, 39, 45, 85, 107, 109–112, 114, 117, 119, 121, 124–127, 153, 250
humanistic-psychology 126
humanity 11, 56, 62, 98, 121, 159, 179, 238, 250
hyperactivity 173, 184
hypnosis 276, 277, 284
hypnotherapy 264, 266, 276, 277, 281, 283
hypocrisy 121
hypotheses 313, 346

iatrogenesis 64
ibâdah 24, 26, 27
Ibn-al-Qayyim 31
Ibn Majah 168, 198, 245, 262, 283, 323
Ibn-Sina 24, 25
identification 70, 154, 163, 175, 284, 352
ideologies 49, 286, 354
idiosyncratic 181
idolatry 14, 62, 308
Ihrām 270
ihsan 54, 59–61, 123
iIllness 28, 29, 49, 50, 90, 207, 265, 271, 278, 303, 323, 342
illegal 308, 318
illogical 134
illusions 82
imam 12, 13, 25, 26, 63, 67, 140, 167, 205, 208–210, 216, 224, 239, 283, 285, 294, 308, 323, 327, 349

Imams 27, 44, 208, 209, 216, 221, 230, 298, 301, 322, 345
imitation 88, 280, 360
immigrants 39
immoral 259
immorality 55, 58
immune 247, 271, 273, 284
immunodeficiency 323
impairment 63
Imrān 124, 162, 292, 296
incantation 37, 265
incisions 269
incongruence 84, 88, 107, 120, 165, 355
incubation 256
indigenous 33, 259, 264, 358
Individual-based 29
individual-centric 337
individual-differences 198
individual-focused 29
individualism 100, 104, 119, 216
individuation 93–95, 97–100, 102–104, 106, 107, 109, 249
induction 248, 261, 356
inductive 356
inequalities 61, 358, 366
inequities 141
inertia 292
infectious 323
inflammation 269
infrastructure 362
inhalation 268
inheritance 83, 227
inimical 267
injection 316
injustices 61, 366
innermost 13
insight 71, 78–80, 96, 98, 99, 101, 105, 106, 111, 113, 129, 160, 175, 181, 236, 240, 248, 250, 256, 262, 293, 305, 336
inspiration 13, 94, 166, 210, 236, 247, 250, 340
instillation 48, 123
instincts 12, 77, 78, 85, 98, 99, 111
integration 4, 8, 9, 14, 17, 18, 22, 23, 27–29, 34–37, 39, 40, 45, 61, 71, 84, 92, 95, 98–100, 102, 104, 106, 107, 111, 114, 115, 129, 132, 143, 165, 168, 178, 220, 221, 236, 239, 244, 264, 287, 325, 334, 338–341, 343, 346, 348, 357–360, 362, 363, 367
intellect 8, 10, 12, 13, 17, 24, 25, 27, 57, 62, 89, 130, 132, 136, 257, 286, 318, 339, 347, 349

intention 5, 60, 70, 130, 172, 216, 288–290, 315, 320, 326, 328–330, 332, 349, 350, 354
interconnectedness 4, 9, 10, 16, 20, 22, 24, 25, 28, 30, 32, 33, 58, 61, 105, 118, 180, 181, 244, 286, 302, 337, 340, 341, 343
intercultural 16, 18, 52, 201, 203, 209, 210, 213
interdisciplinary 53, 213, 343, 357
intergenerational 21
interpersonal 27, 46, 61, 62, 79–82, 91, 100, 102, 111, 114, 119, 124, 135, 152, 190, 205, 207, 208, 210, 217, 221, 235, 236, 248, 286, 310, 311, 363
inter-psychic 160
intoxicants 275, 305–308, 323
intoxication 268, 275, 307, 308, 327
intrapsychic 235
intra-psychically 84
intravenous 317, 318
introspection 10, 25, 26, 71, 84, 105–107, 293, 330, 352
intuition 8, 9, 14, 69, 100, 340, 347
invisible 17, 94, 250, 277
irrational 78, 94, 96, 133–136, 141, 240, 301
Islām-and-addiction 335
Islām-and-psychoanalysis 90
Islāmic-based 195–197
Islāmic-counseling 33
Islāmic-modified 344
Islāmophobia 21, 204, 367
isti'aanah 288, 298, 299, 325, 331, 332
Istikhaarah 332

jasad 27, 286
jealousy 252
Jewish 82, 83
Jinn 34, 86, 214, 231, 276, 277, 280, 284
joint 152, 211, 225, 357
journaling 40, 124, 143, 238
Judaeo-Christian 29, 51, 85, 103, 144, 342
judgment 57, 66, 71, 73, 79, 84, 96, 106, 113, 143, 219, 225, 236, 309, 311, 334
Jungian 29, 93–95, 97–109, 219, 249, 250, 263
Jungian-therapy 109
jurisdiction 228
jurisprudence 38, 44, 56, 57, 62, 71, 182, 224, 227, 257, 295, 308, 317, 323
justice 6, 10, 11, 52, 54, 55, 57–63, 68, 103, 104, 106, 201, 221, 238, 337, 349, 350, 365–367

khamr 274, 307, 308, 323
Khidr 95–97, 109
khilâfah 11
kifayah 47
kindness 4, 10, 47, 55, 59, 143, 190, 191, 194, 212, 237, 239, 316, 320

labelling 172
lactose 274
landscape 22, 344
language 16, 45, 121, 140, 153–155, 164, 174, 175, 203, 224, 249, 260, 261, 314, 341, 342, 357
lapses 158, 300, 302
latency 78
leaders 23, 26, 27, 44, 72, 205, 209, 212, 221, 318, 345
leadership 169, 361
learners 38
learning 38, 72, 74, 125–127, 146, 168, 197, 206, 209, 262, 300, 303, 334, 364
legal 54, 56, 57, 60, 63, 72, 204, 205, 216, 223, 224, 308, 318
legally 216, 228
legislated 31
legitimate 277, 362
leisure 206
lenses 52, 79
LGBTQ 68
liberation 61
life-saving 58
likeness 176
limitations 21, 73, 81, 95, 98, 117, 207, 238, 265, 276, 286, 294, 347
linear 115, 158, 288
linguistic 97, 224, 259, 260, 353, 361
listening 23, 27, 40, 113, 119, 122, 123, 153, 174, 175, 211, 218, 236, 238, 291, 313, 315
logical 145, 257, 340
loneliness 236
longevity 209
longitudinal 343, 345
lordship 281
loss 55, 191, 229, 235, 242, 280, 317, 346
loyalty 52, 60
lucid 248, 261
lunar 95, 270
luxuries 194
lying 120, 190, 254
lymphatic 269

376 Index

magic 276, 280
maintenance 28, 58, 115, 122, 265, 289, 291, 300, 302, 314, 325, 330–333, 345
maladaptive 128, 129, 133–135, 248
maladjusted 134
management 38, 92, 132, 135, 146, 148, 185, 204, 205, 207, 210–212, 219, 283, 292, 301, 310, 311
manifestations 32, 210, 353
manner 22, 48, 52, 59, 101, 147, 176, 202, 211, 269, 320, 338
manualization 92
mapping 155, 263, 312
maqasid 11, 17, 56, 64, 336, 337, 342, 343, 348–358, 362
marginalisation 201
marital 35, 36, 169, 173, 183, 184, 200–218, 220–229, 344
marriages 200–205, 209, 210, 212–214, 223, 228
masculinity 322
masjids 68
Maslow 110, 114, 126
massage 268, 282
materialistic 14, 29, 85
meaningful 95, 100, 133, 152–155, 160, 166, 201, 244, 257, 297, 336, 356, 357
measurable 135, 155
measurements 167
mechanisms 16, 41, 78, 79, 82, 129, 236, 240, 311, 315, 329, 331, 345, 346, 363
mediation 205, 226, 227, 229
mediator 226, 227
medical 19, 52, 53, 56, 58, 62–64, 89, 125, 143, 185, 210, 266, 269, 270, 275, 277, 281, 283, 284, 324, 342
medication 144, 147, 292
medicine 53, 56, 57, 64, 185, 198, 264–267, 269–275, 281–285, 303, 331
meditation 25, 33, 143, 279, 316, 320
memories 98, 178, 247, 249
menstruation 224
mental 7, 12, 16–18, 20–30, 33–35, 37, 41, 44, 46, 49, 50, 61, 65, 67, 68, 74, 81, 90–92, 125, 126, 128–133, 135, 136, 139, 145, 147, 149, 150, 166, 169, 184, 188, 196–198, 207, 209, 213, 214, 216, 219, 223, 229–231, 236, 239, 240, 244, 245, 248, 265, 266, 277, 279, 286, 293, 303, 306, 311, 313, 320, 323–325, 327, 336, 337, 343–346, 357, 359–365, 367
mentorship 365

mercy 31, 38, 42, 47, 48, 62, 63, 119, 122–124, 140, 161, 164, 166, 190–195, 197, 209, 212, 216, 220, 221, 229, 236–238, 255, 274, 283, 319, 320
metaphor 14, 95, 107, 126, 172, 174, 176, 178, 181, 185, 259
metaphysics 183
methodologies 23, 84, 137, 148, 200, 259, 260, 286, 287, 337–339, 341–345, 347, 348, 354, 358, 363
Microanalysis 168
middle-class 81
migraine 270, 282
Millati Islāmi 323
mindfulness 14, 279, 310, 311, 315, 316
mindfulness-based 128, 147, 148, 310, 315
miracle 156, 157, 159, 163–166, 261
mirror 15, 84, 113, 115, 154
mirroring 82, 218, 316
misguidance 15
misinterpretation 88
misuse 309, 317, 324
mixed-methods 345, 347
modelling 88, 315
modesty 54, 62, 67, 87, 88, 224, 268
modification 24, 125, 126, 135, 140, 178, 215, 363
modulations 279
monocultural 336
monotheism 4, 6, 7, 17, 18, 30, 56, 60, 89, 165, 221, 269
monotheistic 5, 9, 11, 59, 95, 103, 106, 163, 338
mood-related 152
moral 5, 6, 8, 10–15, 17, 27, 28, 31, 51–54, 56, 57, 60–62, 64, 66, 70, 71, 78, 84, 85, 87–89, 96, 104, 106, 117, 119, 120, 122, 123, 130–132, 136, 139, 140, 148, 163, 177, 181, 196, 211, 235, 236, 300, 316, 321, 331, 337–339, 341
morphine 307
mortality 82
mother 99, 250, 324
motivation 48, 102, 112, 126, 130, 131, 143, 157, 187, 189, 192, 196, 245, 289, 291, 292, 296, 301, 310, 313, 324, 326, 329, 333
motive 8, 57, 132
multicultural 51, 63, 65, 120, 126, 127, 204, 364, 366, 367
multidimensional 18, 22, 356
multidisciplinary 44, 67, 210, 344, 347
multi-ethnic 201

multi-professional 210
muraqabah 288, 299, 300, 325, 331, 332
Muslim-accommodative 144
Muslim-Arab-American 92
Muslim-contributions 183
Muslim heritage 357
mutual 3, 29, 90, 91, 140, 162, 196, 201, 202, 205, 212, 218, 220, 221, 224, 229, 277, 319
mystical 83, 269
mysticism 83, 277
mythology 103, 106

nafs 10, 12, 13, 17, 25, 27, 88, 89, 104, 105, 130, 133, 286, 302
narcissism 78
narcissistic 117
narrative-therapy 182–185
naseehah 23, 46, 47, 221
naturalistic 81
natural-medicine 285
naturopathy 264
nectar 271, 324
needles 267, 268, 271, 283, 318
networking 361
networks 166, 189, 301, 311, 322
neurological 247, 263
neuropsychology 263
neuroscience 262
neurosis 82, 86
neurotic 81, 82
newborns 87
nikah 200, 209, 214
niyyah 60, 70, 270, 288–290, 326, 349
non-blaming 313
non-confrontational 166, 293, 313, 314, 316, 327
non-congruent 75
non-directive 35, 37–41, 100, 101, 112, 117, 120, 122, 124, 219, 302, 312
non-disclosing 80
non-discriminatory 59
non-intervention 208
non-Islāmic 179, 229, 316, 353–355
non-judgmental 38, 41, 68, 104, 112, 113, 116, 120, 173, 225, 311, 313–315, 333
non-maleficence 52, 60, 61, 66
non-Muslim 179, 321
non-obligatory 294
non-pathological 45
non-religious 334
non-shaming 319
non-verbal 201, 224

nursing 63, 126, 146, 148, 183, 184, 198, 323, 367
nurturing 87, 91, 99, 114, 162, 196, 212, 218, 219, 237, 261, 296, 297
nutrients 267, 284
nutrition 301
nutritional 271

obedience 82, 117, 131, 142, 251
obligations 4, 52, 58, 60, 66, 67, 69, 71, 142
observation 8, 17, 32, 133, 182, 327, 339, 347
obsession 78
obsessive-compulsive 144, 145
Oedipus 82
oncology 284
oneiromancy 255
oneiros 255
one-size-fits-all 239, 333
ontological 10, 338
ontologically 10
ontologies 357
ontology-metaphysics 19
open-ended 136, 155, 175, 313, 314
openness 114, 115, 173, 207, 222
operational 22, 24
opioid 317, 318
oppositional 29, 342
oppressed 59
oppression 15, 20, 55, 58, 61
optimism 46, 151, 158, 161, 190, 191, 195, 196, 198, 236, 238, 314–316
optimistic 87, 186, 189, 195, 339
option 55, 66, 148, 152, 228, 241, 294
optional 327, 328
organ 13
organically 9, 340
organisations 21, 51, 209, 212, 223, 226, 322, 355, 365
organisms 114, 355
orientalisation 336
orientalists 255
orientation 29, 87, 150, 152, 158, 159, 163, 165, 215, 222, 302, 321, 336, 337, 341, 342, 363
original 87, 91, 262, 303, 321, 348
orphans 11, 59
orthodox 24, 265
orthopsychiatry 245
osteopathy 264
outcome 69, 81, 86, 164, 167–169, 198, 213, 274, 294, 331

outreach 2, 44
ownership 226, 320, 345

pagan 268
pandemic 235, 245
panic 128, 157
paradigm 4–6, 11, 16–18, 21, 29, 111, 125, 327, 337–339, 347, 358
paradise 120, 192–194
paraphrasing 174
paraverbal 158
parental 87, 142, 202, 205, 207
parent–child 87
parenthood 203, 204
parenting 150, 201, 203, 204, 211, 227
partialism 160
partners 194, 202–204, 207, 209, 210, 212, 216–218, 225, 315
partnership 207, 226, 344
Pastoral 168,169
pathology 110, 150, 153
patience 6, 25, 26, 29, 31, 55, 62, 123, 139, 143, 161, 163, 165, 166, 191, 194, 197, 211, 212, 220, 221, 237, 238, 244, 295, 298, 330, 332
pediatric 284
pencil-and-paper 313
perception 9, 12, 14, 24, 25, 32, 83, 96, 121, 130, 133, 244, 257, 316, 337, 340, 350
perfection 7, 123
performance 154, 155, 327
permanency 207
permissibility 264, 265, 274, 281, 318
perpetuation 84
perseverance 55, 140, 161, 166, 298
personal 10, 18, 25, 29, 30, 33, 36, 38, 41, 44, 45, 47, 54, 60, 61, 68, 70, 71, 73, 78–80, 82, 84, 88, 93, 94, 97, 98, 100, 102–107, 110–116, 118–121, 124, 126, 127, 131, 133, 142, 143, 152, 154, 159, 160, 162, 164, 165, 172, 173, 175, 179–181, 184, 187, 188, 190, 196, 200, 203, 204, 207, 208, 210, 211, 216, 217, 219, 235, 246–250, 256, 262, 287, 290, 293, 296–298, 300, 313, 316, 318, 320, 321, 326, 327, 352, 355, 363, 366
personalised 45, 143, 158, 206, 244, 265, 292
personality 8, 22, 26, 58, 77, 78, 80, 81, 87–92, 97–100, 102, 105, 107, 108, 117, 126, 127, 130, 143, 168, 198, 202, 206, 207, 217, 230, 231, 249, 310

person-centered-therapy 127
person-centred 38, 39, 113, 114, 116–118, 123, 125, 126, 177, 217, 310, 315
personification 249
persuasion 50
pessimism 161
pharmaceutical 284
pharmacognosy 284
pharmacotherapy 310
phenomenological 177, 183, 344
phenomenology 108
philosophical 7, 10, 22, 24, 53, 103, 104, 106, 107, 125, 133, 136, 138, 146, 167, 177, 179, 182, 262, 265, 337–339, 363
philosophy 7, 12, 51, 53, 63, 106, 128–130, 136, 262, 277, 338, 339, 341
phobic 284
physical 10, 13, 14, 16, 22, 24–26, 28, 29, 32, 58, 85, 188, 200, 201, 209, 211, 215, 221, 244, 250, 265, 266, 268–270, 276–281, 301, 306, 309, 311, 317, 319, 327, 342
phytochemical 282
pioneers 129, 130
planning 44, 49, 186, 210–212, 291, 292, 360
plant 268, 273, 275
pleasure-seeking 115
pleurisy 272, 273
pluralism 177
pneumonia 269
poetry 95, 258, 260
poisonous 273, 275
policymakers 359
political 20, 59, 172, 176, 179, 317, 318, 336, 337, 367
polygamy 78
polymath 24, 129
polytheism 14, 277
populations 21, 36, 144, 150, 286, 292, 305, 346, 362, 364, 366
positioning 351
positive psychology 182
possesses 98, 120, 151
post-colonial 20
post-decision-making 297
post-intervention 345
postmodernism 178, 184
post-natal 276
post-traumatic 173
poverty 193
powerlessness 202, 311

practitioners 49, 51, 53, 65, 77, 81, 133, 134, 153, 223, 238, 270, 278, 279, 294, 325, 359–362, 364, 365
pragmatic 41, 146, 151
pragmatism 133
prayers 29, 47, 106, 142, 164, 168, 182, 195, 295, 299, 308, 320, 328, 331, 332
praying 185, 211, 236, 321, 328
pre-contemplation 115, 291, 292, 314
predestination 42, 136–138, 146, 178, 236, 319
predisposition 6
prejudice 21
pre-marital 68, 200, 204–214
pre-marriage 209, 213
premature 39
pre-Qawmah 292
prescribed 59, 267, 270, 273, 295, 307, 326, 328
prescribing 94, 294
present-focused 159, 165
present-moment 311, 315
pre-therapy 155
prevalence 346
prevention 69, 135, 208, 213, 265, 300, 301, 310, 311, 315, 317, 322, 323, 331, 332
principle 4, 5, 9, 28, 30, 32, 47, 52, 54, 57–62, 67, 78, 91, 104, 112, 134, 150, 160, 162, 172, 177, 196, 219, 225, 273, 274, 279, 313, 317, 318, 333
prioritise 9, 41, 68, 70, 71, 87, 121, 139, 162, 180, 202, 203, 207, 219, 229, 286, 290, 291, 316, 317, 341, 361, 363
privileges 310
proactive 205, 209, 212, 264, 296, 362
problem-based 174
problem-free 156
problem-oriented 218, 350
problem-saturated 172, 175
problem-solving 37, 128, 134, 135, 150, 153, 155, 183, 195, 197, 200, 207, 211, 226, 227, 301, 337
process-drive 289
process-driven 73
process-oriented 155
Prochaska 115, 126, 291, 292, 295, 303, 304, 314, 324, 329, 335
procreation 203
profession 62, 71, 361
professionals 46, 49, 52, 54, 63, 66, 68, 178, 185, 206, 212, 223, 226, 266, 267, 281, 359, 360, 362, 364

proficiency 45, 53, 59, 365
programme 207, 210, 212, 300, 301, 320, 321, 326, 332
prohibitions 14, 31, 82, 250, 277, 306, 308
projection 78
proliferation 22
prophecy 252, 256–258, 263
prophethood 252, 253, 257
proverbs 257–260
pseudo-models 22
psyche's 101
psychiatric 81, 92, 183–185, 320, 323
psychiatrist 93, 168
psychoanalysis 29, 77–80, 82–85, 89–93, 103, 110, 112, 117, 177, 219, 262
psychodynamic 77–81, 83, 84, 89–92, 169, 218, 220
psychoeducation 135, 143, 145, 240, 326
psychoethics 52, 60
psychological 4, 6, 8, 10, 13, 16–18, 20–29, 32, 33, 35–37, 39–41, 43–45, 49, 52, 58, 63, 71, 74, 78, 79, 81–85, 92–95, 97, 98, 100, 103–108, 110–113, 118, 119, 123–128, 131, 133–135, 139, 141, 143, 145, 147, 149, 151, 152, 162, 167, 169, 171, 173, 182, 187, 188, 195–199, 219–223, 229, 230, 235, 236, 239, 241, 242, 244–246, 248–250, 253, 262, 268, 269, 276, 279, 280, 286–288, 293, 300–302, 305, 309, 317, 319, 326, 327, 331, 333, 334, 342, 343, 346, 349, 360, 361, 365, 366
psychologists 9, 32, 50, 52, 63, 66, 71, 74, 82, 89–91, 147, 246, 250, 265, 303, 315, 316, 335, 347, 359
psychopathological 263
psychopathology 91
psychosexual 78, 86, 88
psychosocial 10, 16, 21, 29, 36, 49, 81, 150, 285, 300, 302, 305, 315, 336, 337, 344
psychospiritual 4, 7, 10, 16, 24, 37, 94, 105, 108, 139, 141, 146, 148, 183, 184, 190, 219, 220, 235, 236, 238, 239, 242, 245, 288, 296, 303, 320, 324, 344, 360
psychotherapeutic 21, 22, 52, 75, 134, 171, 229, 305, 309, 311, 312, 326, 333, 343–346, 360
psychotherapists 16, 27, 35, 39, 43–46, 49, 51, 52, 54, 62, 65, 66, 68–70, 73, 74, 124, 167, 181, 182, 190, 205, 239, 265, 302, 325, 333, 334, 357, 359–361, 365, 366

psychotherapy 3–10, 12, 13, 16–18, 20–24, 26–38, 40, 41, 43–53, 59–63, 65–75, 77, 81, 89–94, 105, 107, 109, 112, 117, 119, 122, 123, 125–127, 144–148, 150, 152, 163, 167–169, 179–181, 183–186, 196, 198, 205, 216, 233, 235–239, 244, 261, 266, 286–288, 292, 300–305, 309, 312, 314, 315, 320, 325–327, 331, 333, 336, 337, 339, 342–347, 349, 352, 353, 356–367
puncture 267
punishments 139, 250
purification 25, 26, 61, 104, 105, 139, 242, 301
purpose-driven 350
purpose-oriented 350

qalb 10, 12–14, 17, 27, 89, 107, 130, 132, 133, 286, 352
Qawmah 289–292, 326, 332
qiblah 255
qiyam 352, 354
qiyamah 236
qualitative 102, 148, 168, 336, 344–348, 358
quantitative 137, 336, 344–348
quasi-sacerdotal 339
Qur'ân 3, 4, 8, 10, 18, 27–31, 36, 40, 42, 44, 53–55, 58, 59, 83, 85–87, 95, 97, 103, 104, 106, 107, 120–125, 136–138, 140–142, 159–162, 166, 167, 171, 179–182, 190–193, 196, 197, 200, 209, 220, 223, 227, 230, 235–238, 240, 243, 244, 246, 247, 250–252, 255, 257–261, 272, 281, 287, 289, 292, 294–299, 306–308, 317, 318, 320, 326, 328, 329, 331, 342, 351, 352, 354, 356, 357, 362
Qur'ānic 30, 36, 45, 107, 108, 160, 166, 338, 343, 348, 352, 355, 357

racial 367
radicalism 21
rahma 55, 56, 119
raja 190
rak'ahs 242, 254, 294
randomized 147, 169, 183, 185, 283
rapport-building 101
rapprochement 105, 107
Rassool 6, 8, 9, 12, 13, 18, 21–24, 26–31, 33, 34, 43, 45, 47, 48, 50, 51, 64, 84, 89, 92, 117, 118, 126, 127, 130, 137, 139, 141, 148, 152, 159, 161, 164, 169, 192, 196, 198, 203, 208, 214, 223, 231, 239, 245, 265, 284, 286, 288, 304, 305, 318, 323, 324, 328, 331, 332, 335, 337, 339, 340, 342, 345, 347–349, 358, 360, 365, 367
Rational 8, 9, 13, 33, 88, 96, 130, 136, 141, 182, 257, 302, 339, 340, 347
rationalisation 29
rationalism 9, 32, 136, 137, 149
reactions 29, 217, 245
realisation 99, 290, 317
realism 49
reality 10, 78, 98, 121, 136, 138, 141, 172, 178, 179, 182, 261, 337–339, 341, 348, 349, 353–356
real-world 73
reason 8, 9, 11, 12, 17, 96, 133, 137, 145, 147, 192, 243, 271, 274, 306, 307, 337, 358
re-authoring 174, 176, 177
reciprocal 129, 141, 196
reciprocating 60, 280
recitation 31–33, 36, 236, 244, 301, 329, 331, 343
reconciliation 59, 61, 212, 221, 227, 228
reconstruction 176
rectification 302
rediscover 10, 121, 183
reduction 128, 197, 277, 301, 305, 316–319, 321–324, 343
re-envisioning 20, 110, 357, 358
referral 44
refinement 26, 145, 337, 352, 353, 355
reflecting 23, 46, 49, 54, 62, 73, 82, 97, 113, 130, 161, 162, 181, 182, 190, 219, 221, 238, 248, 249, 253, 281, 286, 290–292, 296, 301, 339, 343, 350, 352
reflection 5, 27, 28, 31, 33, 63, 70–73, 80, 97, 99, 110, 113, 166, 175, 197, 210, 212, 236, 239, 258, 293–295, 299, 302, 314, 319, 328, 330, 332, 348, 351, 352, 355–357
reflections 155, 192, 197, 220, 244, 250, 313, 333, 351, 352, 356, 367
reflexology 264, 266, 277, 278, 281–283
reframing 43, 176, 301, 302, 314, 363
regeneration 249
regression 78, 86
rehabilitation 334
reinforce 174, 205, 240
reinforcement 158, 190, 197, 297, 310, 332
rejection 22, 83, 113, 122, 334
rejuvenating 97

relapse 135, 240, 300, 301, 310, 311, 315, 331, 332
relationship 14, 25, 27–29, 36, 39, 46, 53, 61, 67, 71, 77, 79, 80, 82, 83, 93, 95, 100–102, 104, 105, 112, 113, 116, 117, 119, 120, 123, 124, 128, 133, 135, 152–156, 158, 160, 171, 173, 174, 177, 188, 190, 202–208, 210–220, 222, 224, 225, 230, 236, 240, 250, 263, 290, 333, 341, 342, 344, 366
relatives 11, 55, 58, 209, 224
relativism 51, 63, 119, 177
relaxation 25, 141, 197, 240, 269, 277, 301, 320
religion 6, 7, 16, 20, 23, 32, 33, 46, 50, 56, 63, 69, 74, 77, 82–84, 87, 90–95, 103, 106, 108, 146, 147, 149, 165, 166, 180, 181, 209, 212–214, 221, 222, 228, 229, 231, 242, 245, 257, 258, 261, 289, 294, 303, 308, 313, 320, 321, 331, 341, 349, 367
religiosity 84, 117, 118, 144, 180, 220, 222, 223, 228–231, 289, 361
religiousness 222, 229
religious-oriented 145
remarriage 223
remarrying 207
remedies 264, 266, 269–274, 281, 285
remembrance 31, 32, 36, 37, 41, 61, 103, 166, 236, 238, 241, 244, 302, 307, 315, 320, 326, 331
re-orientation 348
repentance 26, 29, 44, 61, 122, 139, 143, 163, 195, 287, 288, 300, 301, 316, 319, 320, 327, 328, 330, 335
reproduction 203
research 17, 18, 22, 23, 32, 33, 38, 41, 43, 44, 49, 52, 53, 63, 74, 81, 92, 102, 117, 125, 127, 133, 143–148, 150, 152, 167–169, 179, 198, 208, 209, 213, 214, 217, 223, 231, 245, 247, 248, 261, 263, 271, 275, 276, 284, 292, 320, 323, 324, 336–339, 341–362, 364, 366, 367
research-oriented 362
resilience 6, 12, 36, 100, 125, 139, 143, 159, 161, 166, 171, 181, 188–191, 195, 196, 198, 205, 236, 237, 240, 244, 299, 311, 330, 333, 343
resistance 79, 80, 292, 296, 303, 313, 314, 317, 329
resolution 70, 72, 84, 163, 165, 205–207, 209–212, 215, 217, 219–221, 226–228, 319, 344

resources 22, 23, 44–46, 59, 69, 114, 136, 150, 151, 153–155, 157, 161, 166, 173, 184, 185, 189, 206, 209, 212, 214, 218, 221, 226, 229, 238, 252, 260, 268, 284, 348, 360, 362, 365
responsibilities 27, 44, 62, 65, 111, 121, 123, 134, 154, 201–203, 205, 208, 211, 212, 220–222, 228, 290, 325, 334
responsiveness 114
restoration 27, 28
re-storying 174, 176, 184
resurgence 24
resurrection 3, 195
revelation 8, 9, 13, 17, 29, 33, 103, 105, 106, 137, 178, 179, 250, 251, 257, 308, 340–342, 348, 350, 353, 354, 357
re-visions 185
revolution 20, 125
rewards 161, 192, 242, 295, 310
rhetorical 257
rituals 4, 16, 30, 56, 61, 82, 106, 178, 180, 203, 220, 268, 269, 316, 330
roadmap 188, 329, 330
rûh 10, 12, 13, 17, 18, 89, 107, 133
rule-bound 96
ruqya 36, 37, 265, 271

sacred 10, 62, 94, 178, 180, 182, 184, 200, 207, 215, 228, 235, 239, 257, 260, 343
sacrifice 251
sadness 31, 196, 248, 302
sakinah 31
salah 36, 166, 196, 221, 236, 308
saliva 254
salvation 83, 87, 118, 326
same-gender 67
same-sex 82
Satan 104, 132, 253, 254, 307
satanic 132
sativa 271, 282, 284
sawm 326
scaling 157, 159, 314
scepticism 59, 82, 103
schemas 64, 133, 134, 136, 146
scholarship 8, 9, 20, 23, 53, 97, 105, 106, 184, 337, 339, 348, 356–358, 360, 361, 367
scientific 9, 18, 21, 29, 32, 33, 82, 91, 117, 133, 137, 214, 247, 262, 263, 271, 275, 280, 337–339, 362
scriptural 103
seclusion 251

secular 9, 11, 17, 21, 29, 52, 61, 84, 85, 89, 103, 106–108, 118, 133, 163, 165, 177, 204, 205, 216, 218, 303, 339, 341, 342, 357, 360, 362, 363
secularism 83
seerah 45
self-acceptance 111, 113, 117, 141
self-accountability 302
self-actualisation 26, 110, 114, 116, 118, 119, 121, 122, 124, 250
self-advocacy 365
self-awareness 25, 26, 78, 80, 84, 95, 98, 100, 102, 105, 107, 115, 116, 118, 124, 139, 179, 300, 311, 330, 343, 366
self-belief 188
self-care 52, 63
self-change 151
self-compassion 40, 191
self-concept 111, 113, 121, 250
self-confidence 87, 121
self-congruence 116
self-control 136, 141
self-criticism 133
self-defeating 171
self-dependence 138
self-determination 112, 117
self-development 87, 111
self-diagnosed 248
self-direction 111, 141
self-disclosure 38, 80, 113, 151, 159, 164
self-discovery 84, 99, 100, 104, 106, 111–113, 117
self-efficacy 138, 296, 297, 310, 313, 314, 332
self-esteem 114, 121, 157, 209, 237, 296, 332
self-evaluation 288, 325, 331, 332
self-examination 25, 26
self-expression 38, 113
self-focused 180, 315
self-fulfilment 110
self-gratification 121
self-growth 110
self-harm 67, 81, 90
self-healing 273
self-help 196, 314
self-image 237, 250
self-improvement 12, 110, 162, 302, 319
self-knowledge 84, 102
self-management 335
self-monitoring 288, 289, 299, 303, 315, 325, 331, 332
self-motivational 310, 315
self-observation 300, 331

self-perception 184, 237
self-purification 119, 237, 302, 328
self-realisation 98, 107, 121
self-reflection 7, 10, 25, 26, 38, 41, 73, 105, 111, 131, 139, 143, 211, 244, 299–302, 343, 363, 364
self-regulation 84
self-reliance 138, 226, 297
self-sufficient 244
self-transformation 121
self-worth 42, 87, 104, 134, 141, 237
semantic 107
seminars 226, 364
sensations 311, 315
sensory-cognitive 130
separation 172, 216, 227, 252, 327
sexual 26, 66, 68, 78, 82, 85–88, 211, 216, 292, 318
sexualisation 78
shame 133, 309, 320, 334
Shar'iah-compliant 270
Shaykhul-Islām 15, 19
Shaytān 253, 254, 256
shrik 194
shukr 26, 38, 40, 43, 55, 143, 166, 237
sickness 182, 267, 281
sinful 3, 4, 25, 266, 319
Siraat 286, 287, 302, 325, 331, 333
Skills 27, 37, 43, 54, 73, 113, 133, 135, 142, 155, 171, 173–175, 181–184, 188, 189, 200, 204–206, 208, 210–213, 218, 220, 240, 286, 296, 300, 301, 310, 314, 315, 324, 331, 339, 356, 360, 361, 364–366
skills-oriented 210
skin 268–270, 273
slaves 96, 216, 266, 271, 276
smoking 78, 308, 320
society 8, 11, 18, 20, 39, 53, 54, 57, 58, 60, 74, 90, 94, 100, 108, 109, 118, 122, 125, 140, 163, 169, 179, 200, 201, 204, 229, 250, 303, 305, 308, 317, 318, 323, 337, 338, 341, 350, 365, 366
sociocultural 26, 85, 92, 148, 176, 336, 366
socioeconomic 20, 215, 235
socio-moral 29
sociopolitical 21, 124, 337, 366
solution 151, 153–155, 158, 159, 167–170, 226, 274, 313, 314, 317, 318, 323, 348, 357
solution-focused 35, 48, 150–155, 157, 159, 163, 166, 168–170, 186, 189, 196, 215, 218, 314
somatoform 143, 144

Index **383**

soothsaying 277
soul 6, 7, 10, 12, 13, 16–18, 20–22, 25, 26, 61, 83, 88–90, 92, 100, 104, 108, 128, 129, 146, 159, 182, 192, 237, 239, 241, 286, 301, 302, 319, 340, 349
soulless 21
spiritual 4–8, 10, 12–18, 20–37, 39–41, 43, 44, 47–49, 58, 60, 62, 65, 68, 83–85, 88, 89, 94, 95, 97, 99–101, 104–110, 118, 119, 122–127, 131–133, 139–145, 147, 148, 163, 166, 167, 178, 181, 182, 190, 191, 196, 197, 200, 208–212, 215, 219–222, 235–237, 239–242, 244–247, 249, 253, 257, 258, 260, 261, 266, 267, 269, 277–279, 281, 283, 287, 288, 290, 293, 295–297, 299–302, 305, 306, 311, 316, 319–322, 326–331, 333, 334, 337, 342, 343, 345, 346, 349, 350, 352, 366
Spiritual–divine 29
spiritual-infused 165
spirituality 4, 7, 10, 16–19, 21–23, 25, 27, 28, 30–35, 37, 39, 40, 44, 50, 69, 74, 77, 82, 83, 85, 91–95, 100, 102, 103, 105, 106, 109, 117, 118, 126, 129–131, 147, 149, 169, 178, 180, 181, 196–198, 206, 212, 218, 220, 231, 235, 236, 244, 245, 261, 265, 286, 287, 293, 302, 320, 321, 324, 343, 366
spiritual-struggles 245
statistics 231, 247
stereotypes 84, 204, 364
stigmatisation 309
storytelling 32, 174, 181, 190
stress 54, 58, 104, 115, 128, 135, 138, 139, 143, 144, 169, 173, 175–177, 184, 194, 195, 197, 203, 204, 211, 217, 223, 236, 238, 241, 242, 244, 277, 300, 301, 309, 321, 325, 343
subcontinent 279
submission 29, 104, 106, 228, 294
Sufi 49, 95, 97, 102, 103, 278, 283, 335
sufism 53, 83, 84, 92, 93, 95, 97, 102, 108, 109
sunnah 4, 9, 10, 17, 27–30, 33–38, 40, 43, 53, 54, 63, 64, 90, 103, 104, 106–108, 123, 125, 126, 142, 167, 168, 179, 181, 182, 197–200, 229, 245, 257, 259, 261–263, 275, 281–285, 287, 288, 295, 298, 303, 322–324, 334, 335, 338, 339, 341, 342, 347, 349, 351, 352, 354, 357
superego 78, 81, 85, 87, 88
supernatural 17, 100, 235, 246, 269
superstition 269

supervision 43, 44, 49, 65, 70, 72, 145, 264, 359, 361, 364, 365
supplication 5, 26, 36, 37, 42, 61, 141, 164, 191, 241, 242, 244, 258, 294, 299, 302, 329, 331
suppressed 114, 250
suspicion 83, 204
sustenance 129, 146
symbolic 100–103, 107, 109, 181, 248–251, 257, 259–262
sympathy 119
symptomatic 82, 281
symptomatology 81
symptoms 80, 81, 91, 102, 147, 152, 169, 173, 184, 240, 263, 273, 276, 300, 331, 346
syndrome 276, 320
syringes 316
system 12, 54, 56, 70, 71, 94, 104, 133, 140, 179, 236, 247, 257, 269, 271, 273, 284, 289, 311, 321, 338, 366

tadabbur 181
tafakkur 25, 166, 181, 182, 288, 290, 293, 295, 325, 328, 332
tafsir 18, 45, 50, 64, 91, 97, 126, 181, 198, 245, 255–257, 307, 322, 358
tajdīd 20
talaq 228
tapestry 246
taqwa 60, 62, 236
tasawur 10, 338
tawakkul 6, 42, 43, 53, 61, 62, 124, 141, 163, 165, 166, 180, 190, 191, 195, 196, 237, 271, 296, 297
tawbah 26, 61, 143, 148, 301, 319, 320, 327, 328, 335
tawhīd 4–9, 17, 60, 61, 104, 142, 236, 279, 281, 287
tawhīdic 5, 6, 11, 18
Taymiyyah 15, 19, 24, 25, 280, 283
tazkiyah 10, 25, 61, 104, 105, 119, 237, 301, 302, 304
technique 29, 97, 101, 141, 142, 156–158, 175, 177, 240, 249, 256, 283
temperance 316
temptations 14, 15, 68, 104, 132, 319
terminology 21, 107, 123, 133, 342
thanatos 78
theism 11
theists 236
theological 12, 53, 85, 88, 89, 97, 103, 105, 106, 125, 139, 165, 195, 289, 316

theology 5, 7, 12, 24, 45, 53, 63, 107, 130, 133, 137, 168, 255, 257
theories 17, 20, 29, 33, 37, 39, 40, 77, 85, 91, 98, 103, 110, 117, 125, 127, 172, 219, 247, 264, 337, 341, 342, 348, 349, 353, 355–357, 363, 365
therapies 24, 39, 45, 81, 84, 125, 136, 146–148, 180, 183, 216, 218, 220, 264–267, 281, 284, 285, 310, 311, 315, 334, 344, 345
therapist 37, 38, 40–42, 45, 46, 48–50, 67–69, 71, 72, 79, 80, 100–102, 112–114, 116, 117, 124, 125, 131, 134, 135, 145, 147, 148, 151–154, 156–158, 162, 165, 166, 173, 174, 176, 177, 179, 181, 184, 189, 190, 196, 206, 210, 218–220, 222, 225, 226, 239–243, 290, 294, 295, 297, 312–314, 320, 326, 328–333, 360
therapist-client 120
therapist-worldview 183
Tibb-e-Nabawi 271
Tirmidhî 32, 34, 54, 64, 229, 231, 242, 245, 274, 276, 281, 285, 308, 324
tobacco 307
tolerance 11, 62, 141, 310
toolkit 240
toxic 26
traditions 10, 16, 20, 22, 40, 49, 84, 97, 102, 103, 105–107, 110, 119, 123, 136, 142, 162, 177, 180, 181, 202, 203, 208, 229, 258, 261, 286, 293, 316, 333, 338, 339, 341, 343, 345, 347, 350
training 37, 41, 43, 49, 54, 117, 130, 135, 168, 215, 301, 303, 310, 315, 359, 360, 364–367
transcendence 84, 91, 118
transcultural 148
transference 79, 80, 91, 101, 102
transgenderism 74
transgression 3, 120, 202
transpersonal 101, 110
trans-theoretical 304
trauma 21, 35, 152, 217, 235
treatment 26, 32, 40, 45, 49, 50, 52, 54, 55, 59, 61, 66, 81, 84, 90, 112, 125, 134, 135, 139–142, 144, 147–149, 152, 158, 159, 167, 169, 170, 180, 184, 217, 240, 265–267, 269, 271, 273, 274, 278, 281–284, 292, 303, 309–312, 315, 319–322, 324, 326, 327, 333, 334, 366
treatments 25, 81, 147, 148, 264–268, 274, 275, 283

triangulation 346, 347
tribulations 8, 31, 48, 139, 163, 164, 188, 191, 229, 236, 296, 298
trilogy 88
trust 5, 6, 27, 40, 42, 43, 46, 48, 53, 61, 72, 79, 87, 97, 100, 101, 111, 123, 124, 146, 152, 161, 163, 165, 166, 180, 189–191, 195–197, 212, 218, 225, 237, 238, 243, 244, 271, 288, 290, 295–297, 319, 321, 322, 325, 327, 329–333, 343
truths 27, 82, 84, 95, 130, 173, 179, 181, 354
Twelve-Step 311

ummah 104, 121, 139, 140, 196, 197, 203, 209, 243, 266, 271, 288, 322, 337, 342
unconditional 38, 99, 112–115, 120, 123, 207
unconscious 77–80, 85, 88, 89, 93–95, 97–108, 110, 132, 218, 246, 248, 249
unhappiness 224
unicity 95, 163
unification 97
un-Islāmic 229, 279
universal 51, 52, 54, 60, 61, 64, 98, 114, 148, 177, 179, 202, 208, 219, 249, 305, 352–356
usul 45
Uthaymeen 275
Utz 121, 127, 340, 358

value-added 278
value-laden 29
values 4–6, 10–12, 15–17, 20–23, 26, 28, 29, 33, 35–45, 49, 51–54, 56, 58–63, 65–74, 84, 100, 103, 106, 107, 111, 113 119, 120, 122–124, 127, 129, 136, 139, 140, 142, 143, 145, 157, 159, 162, 163, 165–167, 171, 172, 175, 178–182, 198, 200–209, 211, 212, 218–223, 226, 227, 266, 267, 278, 286–288, 301, 302, 310, 316, 318, 328–334, 337, 338, 341–344, 348, 349, 351–356, 360, 362–367
verbal 147, 224
vicegerence 11, 160
vicegerents 121
victim 172, 192
viewpoints 51, 52, 85, 89, 110, 112, 135, 203, 341, 350, 353
violence 56, 150, 173, 217, 224
virtues 5, 26, 43, 89, 179, 211

vision 8, 140, 151, 153, 161, 179, 182, 230, 255, 288, 295, 296, 325, 328, 332, 340, 367
visualisation 101
volition 132, 289

wakefulness 247, 250, 263
wa'l-Jamaa'ah 103
weaknesses 151, 225, 238
wealth 11, 55, 57, 62, 191, 193, 194, 228, 252, 318, 349, 355
wedding 92, 169, 210, 229
welfare 47, 53, 56, 60, 65, 70, 226, 317
wellness 20, 28, 63, 105, 110, 119, 142, 197, 245, 265
Western-oriented 22, 119
wet-cupping 282
whirling 95
wholeness 95, 97–100, 111, 249
wholistic 337
women 54, 81, 140, 146, 169, 184, 201, 204, 207, 213, 224, 225, 229, 279, 283, 319, 320, 336
worldviews 11, 21, 39, 79, 106, 179, 181, 223, 338, 354

Yaqeen 145
yoga 264, 266, 277, 279–281, 283, 284
youth 97, 345
youthful 96
Yūnus 137
Yusuf 12, 25, 88, 166, 193, 246, 251, 252

zakat 140
Zarabozo 50, 140, 149, 279, 285, 289, 290, 294, 304, 349, 358
zodiac 269

For Product Safety Concerns and Information please contact our EU
representative GPSR@taylorandfrancis.com
Taylor & Francis Verlag GmbH, Kaufingerstraße 24, 80331 München, Germany

www.ingramcontent.com/pod-product-compliance
Lightning Source LLC
Chambersburg PA
CBHW050526300426
44113CB00012B/1966